Lecture Notes in Computer Science 15898

Founding Editors

Gerhard Goos
Juris Hartmanis

Editorial Board Members

Elisa Bertino, *Purdue University, West Lafayette, IN, USA*
Wen Gao, *Peking University, Beijing, China*
Bernhard Steffen⊙, *TU Dortmund University, Dortmund, Germany*
Moti Yung⊙, *Columbia University, New York, NY, USA*

The series Lecture Notes in Computer Science (LNCS), including its subseries Lecture Notes in Artificial Intelligence (LNAI) and Lecture Notes in Bioinformatics (LNBI), has established itself as a medium for the publication of new developments in computer science and information technology research, teaching, and education.

LNCS enjoys close cooperation with the computer science R & D community, the series counts many renowned academics among its volume editors and paper authors, and collaborates with prestigious societies. Its mission is to serve this international community by providing an invaluable service, mainly focused on the publication of conference and workshop proceedings and postproceedings. LNCS commenced publication in 1973.

Osvaldo Gervasi · Beniamino Murgante ·
Chiara Garau · Yeliz Karaca ·
Maria Noelia Faginas Lago · Francesco Scorza ·
Ana Cristina Braga
Editors

Computational Science and Its Applications – ICCSA 2025 Workshops

Istanbul, Turkey, June 30 – July 3, 2025
Proceedings, Part XIII

Editors
Osvaldo Gervasi
University of Perugia
Perugia, Italy

Chiara Garau
University of Cagliari
Cagliari, Italy

Maria Noelia Faginas Lago
University of Perugia
Perugia, Italy

Ana Cristina Braga
University of Minho
Braga, Portugal

Beniamino Murgante
University of Basilicata
Potenza, Italy

Yeliz Karaca
University of Massachusetts
Worcester, MA, USA

Francesco Scorza
University of Basilicata
Potenza, Italy

ISSN 0302-9743 ISSN 1611-3349 (electronic)
Lecture Notes in Computer Science
ISBN 978-3-031-97656-8 ISBN 978-3-031-97657-5 (eBook)
https://doi.org/10.1007/978-3-031-97657-5

© The Editor(s) (if applicable) and The Author(s), under exclusive license to Springer Nature Switzerland AG 2026

This work is subject to copyright. All rights are solely and exclusively licensed by the Publisher, whether the whole or part of the material is concerned, specifically the rights of translation, reprinting, reuse of illustrations, recitation, broadcasting, reproduction on microfilms or in any other physical way, and transmission or information storage and retrieval, electronic adaptation, computer software, or by similar or dissimilar methodology now known or hereafter developed.
The use of general descriptive names, registered names, trademarks, service marks, etc. in this publication does not imply, even in the absence of a specific statement, that such names are exempt from the relevant protective laws and regulations and therefore free for general use.
The publisher, the authors and the editors are safe to assume that the advice and information in this book are believed to be true and accurate at the date of publication. Neither the publisher nor the authors or the editors give a warranty, expressed or implied, with respect to the material contained herein or for any errors or omissions that may have been made. The publisher remains neutral with regard to jurisdictional claims in published maps and institutional affiliations.

This Springer imprint is published by the registered company Springer Nature Switzerland AG
The registered company address is: Gewerbestrasse 11, 6330 Cham, Switzerland

If disposing of this product, please recycle the paper.

Preface

The compiled 14 volumes (LNCS volumes 15886–15899) consist of the peer-reviewed papers from the 68 Workshops of the 2025 International Conference on Computational Science and Its Applications (ICCSA 2025), which was held between June 30 – July 3, 2025 in Istanbul (Türkiye). The peer-reviewed papers of the main conference tracks are published in a separate set made up of three volumes (LNCS 15648–15650).

The conference was held in a hybrid form, with the large majority of participants in presence, hosted by Galatasaray University, Istanbul, Türkiye. We enabled virtual participation for those who did not attend the event in person due to logistical, political and economic problems, by adopting a technological infrastructure via open-source software (jitsi + riot) and a commercial Cloud infrastructure.

With the 2025 edition, ICCSA celebrated its 25th anniversary, a quarter of a century as a memorable moment that is harmoniously aligned with Istanbul, an extraordinary city located at the crossroads and acting as a bridge connecting Asia and Europe, representing different cultures, beliefs as well as lifestyles, which highlights its intercultural fabric.

ICCSA 2025 marked another fruitful and thought-provoking academic event in the International Conferences on Computational Science and Its Applications (ICCSA) conference series, previously held in Hanoi, Vietnam (2024), Athens, Greece (2023), Málaga, Spain (2022), Cagliari, Italy (hybrid with a few participants in presence in 2021 and completely online in 2020), whilst earlier editions took place in Saint Petersburg, Russia (2019), Melbourne, Australia (2018), Trieste, Italy (2017), Beijing, China (2016), Banff, Canada (2015), Guimaraes, Portugal (2014), Ho Chi Minh City, Vietnam (2013), Salvador, Brazil (2012), Santander, Spain (2011), Fukuoka, Japan (2010), Suwon, South Korea (2009), Perugia, Italy (2008), Kuala Lumpur, Malaysia (2007), Glasgow, UK (2006), Singapore (2005), Assisi, Italy (2004), Montreal, Canada (2003), and (as ICCS) Amsterdam, the Netherlands (2002) and San Francisco, USA (2001).

Computational Science constitutes the main pillar of most present research, industrial and commercial applications, and plays a unique role in exploiting ICT innovative technologies, and the ICCSA conference series has, accordingly, provided ample opportunities to researchers and industry practitioners to discuss new ideas, to share complex problems and their solutions, and to shape new trends in Computational Science. As the conference mirrors society from a scientific point of view, this year's undoubtedly dominant theme was large language models, machine learning and Artificial Intelligence (AI) and their applications in the most diverse technological, economic and industrial fields, amongst the others.

The ICCSA 2025 conference was structured in six general tracks covering the fields of computational science and its applications: Computational Methods, Algorithms and Scientific Applications – High Performance Computing and Networks – Geometric Modeling, Graphics and Visualization – Advanced and Emerging Applications – Information Systems and Technologies – Urban and Regional Planning. In addition, the conference consisted of 68 workshops, focusing on topical issues of utmost importance to science, technology and society: from new computational approaches for earth science, to mathematical methods for image processing, new statistical and optimization methods, several Artificial Intelligence approaches, sustainability issues, smart cities and related technologies, to name some.

In the Workshops' proceedings, we accepted 362 full papers, 37 short papers and 2 Ph.D. Showcase papers from total of 1043 submissions (Acceptance rate 38.4%). In the Main Conference Proceedings, we accepted 71 full papers, 6 short papers and 1 Ph.D. Showcase paper from 269 submissions to the General Tracks of the Conference (with an acceptance rate of 29.9%). We would like to convey our sincere appreciation to the workshops' chairs and co-chairs and program committee members for their diligent work, commitment and dedication.

The success and consistent maintenance of the ICCSA conference series in general, and of ICCSA 2025 in particular, rely upon the support of many people: authors, presenters, participants, keynote speakers, workshop chairs, session chairs, organizing committee members, student volunteers, Program Committee members, Advisory Committee members, International Liaison chairs, reviewers and other individuals in various roles. Thus, we take this opportunity to wholehartedly thank each and everyone.

We additionally wish to thank publisher Springer for their agreement to publish the proceedings, besides sponsoring part of the best papers awards and for their kind assistance and cooperation during the editing process.

We would cordially like to invite you to refer to the ICCSA website https://iccsa.org, where you can find the relevant details regarding this academic endeavor and event of ours.

June 2025

Osvaldo Gervasi
Yeliz Karaca
Beniamino Murgante
Chiara Garau

A Welcome Message from the Organizers

The International Conference on Computational Science and Its Applications (ICCSA) reflects a culmination of meticulous and dedicated efforts and academic endeavors toward the progress of science and technology.

One of the most noteworthy aspects of ICCSA is its fostering of a collective spirit, bringing together a plethora of participants from all over the world. Correspondingly, this merging power manifests itself in the 25th anniversary of ICCSA, which is a quarter of a century, in Istanbul, Türkiye, which connects and acts as a bridge between two continents, namely Asia and Europe. This unique location in the world hosts the 25th year of ICCSA at Galatasaray University, located on Çırağan Avenue by Istanbul's Bosphorus, which is an established international university bestowed with a distinctive past of teaching tradition, research and education exceeding five centuries.

Istanbul, having served as the capital city of four empires, namely the Roman Empire (330–395), the Byzantine Empire (395–1204 and 1261–1453), the Latin Empire (1204–1261) and the Ottoman Empire (1453–1922), is an exceptional city of the Republic of Türkiye founded by Mustafa Kemal Atatürk.

Situated at a strategic location along the historic Silk Road, Istanbul is at the core of extending rail networks which span across Europe and West Asia along with the only sea route between the Black Sea and the Mediterranean.

The cultural, historical and economic pulses of the country are evident in Istanbul whose rooted origins have embraced varying beliefs, lifestyles and populace, which highlights the city's mosaic quality with blended fabric in a constant harmonious flow. This has enabled cultures to grow and be nurtured, which is profoundly rooted in its urban culture.

Computational Science constitutes the main pillar of most present research, industrial and commercial activities besides manifesting a unique role in exploiting and addressing innovative Information and Communication Technologies. Thus, the 25-year-old ICCSA conference series provides remarkable opportunities to get acquainted with leading researchers, scientists, scholars, practitioners and many more while exchanging innovative ideas and initiating new partnerships, associations and bonds.

With the hosting of Galatasaray University, I would personally and on behalf of the Local Organizing Committee, with the members Emre Alptekin, Gülfem Işıklar Alptekin, Cengiz Kahraman, Abdullah Çağrı Tolga and Ayberk Zeytin, like to convey our sincere gratitude and thanks to everyone who exerted their efforts in and contributed to the realization of ICCSA 2025. With these notes and remarks, welcome to Istanbul!

Cordially yours,
On behalf of the Local Organizing Committee.

June 2025   Yeliz Karaca

Organization

Honorary General Chairs

Bernady O. Apduhan — Kyushu Sangyo University, Japan
Kenneth C. J. Tan — Sardina Systems, UK

General Chairs

Yeliz Karaca — University of Massachusetts, USA
Osvaldo Gervasi — University of Perugia, Italy
David Taniar — Monash University, Australia

Program Committee Chairs

Beniamino Murgante — University of Basilicata, Italy
Chiara Garau — University of Cagliari, Italy
Ana Maria A. C. Rocha — University of Minho, Portugal
A. Çağrı Tolga — Galatasaray University, Turkey

International Advisory Committee

Jemal Abawajy — Deakin University, Australia
Dharma P. Agarwal — University of Cincinnati, USA
Rajkumar Buyya — Melbourne University, Australia
Claudia Bauzer Medeiros — University of Campinas, Brazil
Manfred M. Fisher — Vienna University of Economics and Business, Austria
Pierre Frankhauser — University of Franche-Comté/CNRS, France
Marina L. Gavrilova — University of Calgary, Canada
Sumi Helal — University of Florida, USA & Lancaster University, UK
Bin Jiang — University of Gävle, Sweden
Yee Leung — Chinese University of Hong Kong, China

International Liaison Chairs

Ivan Blečić	University of Cagliari, Italy
Giuseppe Borruso	University of Trieste, Italy
Elise De Donker	Western Michigan University, USA
Maria Noelia Faginas Lago	University of Perugia, Italy
Maria Irene Falcão	University of Minho, Portugal
Robert C. H. Hsu	Chung Hua University, Taiwan
Yeliz Karaca	University of Massachusetts Chan Medical School, USA
Tae-Hoon Kim	Zhejiang University of Science and Technology, China
Vladimir Korkhov	Saint Petersburg University, Russia
Takashi Naka	Kyushu Sangyo University, Japan
Rafael D. C. Santos	National Institute for Space Research, Brazil
Maribel Yasmina Santos	University of Minho, Portugal
Anastasia Stratigea	National Technical University of Athens, Greece

Workshop and Session Organizing Chairs

Beniamino Murgante	University of Basilicata, Italy
Chiara Garau	University of Cagliari, Italy

Award Chair

Wenny Rahayu	La Trobe University, Australia

Publicity Committee Chairs

Elmer Dadios	De La Salle University, Philippines
Nataliia Kulabukhova	Saint Petersburg University, Russia
Daisuke Takahashi	Tsukuba University, Japan
Shangwang Wang	Beijing University of Posts and Telecommunications, China

Local Organizing Committee Chairs

Emre Alptekin   Galatasaray University, Turkey
Gülfem Işıklar Alptekin   Galatasaray University, Turkey
Cengiz Kahraman   İstanbul Technical University, Turkey
A. Çağrı Tolga   Galatasaray University, Turkey
Ayberk Zeytin   Galatasaray University, Turkey

Technology Chair

Damiano Perri   University of Perugia, Italy

Program Committee

Vera Afreixo   University of Aveiro, Portugal
Vladimir Alarcon   Northern Gulf Institute, USA
Filipe Alvelos   University of Minho, Portugal
Debora Anelli   Polytechnic University of Bari, Italy
Hartmut Asche   Hasso-Plattner-Institut für Digital Engineering Ggmbh, Germany
Nizamettin Aydın   İstanbul Technical University, Turkey
Ginevra Balletto   University of Cagliari, Italy
Nadia Balucani   University of Perugia, Italy
Socrates Basbas   Aristotle University of Thessaloniki, Greece
David Berti   ART SpA, Italy
Michela Bertolotto   University College Dublin, Ireland
Sandro Bimonte   CEMAGREF, TSCF, France
Ana Cristina Braga   University of Minho, Portugal
Tiziana Campisi   Kore University of Enna, Italy
Yves Caniou   Université Claude Bernard Lyon 1, France
Alessandra Capolupo   Polytechnic University of Bari, Italy
José A. Cardoso e Cunha   Universidade Nova de Lisboa, Portugal
Rui Cardoso   University of Beira Interior, Portugal
Leocadio G. Casado   University of Almería, Spain
Mete Celik   Erciyes University, Turkey
Maria Cerreta   University of Naples Federico II, Italy
Ta Quang Chieu   Thuyloi University, Vietnam
Rachel Chien-Sing Lee   Sunway University, Malaysia
Birol Ciloglugil   Ege University, Turkey
Mauro Coni   University of Cagliari, Italy

xii   Organization

Florbela Maria da Cruz Domingues Correia	Polytechnic Institute of Viana do Castelo, Portugal
Alessandro Costantini	INFN, Italy
Roberto De Lotto	University of Pavia, Italy
Luiza De Macedo Mourelle	State University of Rio De Janeiro, Brazil
Marcelo De Paiva Guimaraes	Federal University of Sao Paulo, Brazil
Frank Devai	London South Bank University, UK
Joana Matos Dias	University of Coimbra, Portugal
Aziz Dursun	Virginia Tech University, USA
Laila El Ghandour	Heriot-Watt University, UK
Rafida M. Elobaid	Canadian University Dubai, United Arab Emirates
Maria Irene Falcao	University of Minho, Portugal
Florbela P. Fernandes	Polytechnic Institute of Bragança, Portugal
Paula Odete Fernandes	Polytechnic Institute of Bragança, Portugal
Adelaide de Fátima Baptista Valente Freitas	University of Aveiro, Portugal
Valentina Franzoni	University of Perugia, Italy
Andreas Fricke	University of Potsdam, Germany
Raffaele Garrisi	Centro Operativo per la Sicurezza Cibernetica, Italy
Ivan Gerace	University of Perugia, Italy
Maria Giaoutzi	National Technical University of Athens, Greece
Salvatore Giuffrida	University of Catania, Italy
Teresa Guarda	Universidad Estatal Peninsula de Santa Elena, Ecuador
Sevin Gümgüm	Izmir University of Economics, Turkey
Malgorzata Hanzl	Technical University of Lodz, Poland
Maulana Adhinugraha Kiki	Telkom University, Indonesia
Clement Ho Cheung Leung	Chinese University of Hong Kong, China
Andrea Lombardi	University of Perugia, Italy
Marcos Mandado Alonso	University of Vigo, Spain
Ernesto Marcheggiani	Katholieke Universiteit Leuven, Belgium
Antonino Marvuglia	Luxembourg Institute of Science and Technology, Luxembourg
Michele Mastroianni	University of Salerno, Italy
Hideo Matsufuru	High Energy Accelerator Research Organization, Japan
Fernando Miranda	Universidade do Minho, Portugal
Giuseppe Modica	University of Reggio Calabria, Italy
Majaz Moonis	University of Massachusetts, USA
Nadia Nedjah	State University of Rio de Janeiro, Brazil
Paolo Nesi	University of Florence, Italy

Suzan Obaiys	University of Malaya, Malaysia
Marcin Paprzycki	Polish Academy of Sciences, Poland
Eric Pardede	La Trobe University, Australia
Ana Isabel Pereira	Polytechnic Institute of Bragança, Portugal
Damiano Perri	University of Perugia, Italy
Massimiliano Petri	University of Pisa, Italy
Telmo Pinto	University of Coimbra, Portugal
Alessandro Plaisant	University of Sassari, Italy
Maurizio Pollino	ENEA, Italy
Alenka Poplin	Iowa State University, USA
Marcos Quiles	Federal University of São Paulo, Brazil
Nguyen Huu Quynh	Thuyloi University, Vietnam
Albert Rimola	Universitat Autònoma de Barcelona, Spain
Humberto Rocha	University of Coimbra, Portugal
Marzio Rosi	University of Perugia, Italy
Lucia Saganeiti	University of L'Aquila, Italy
Francesco Scorza	University of Basilicata, Italy
Marco Paulo Seabra dos Reis	University of Coimbra, Portugal
Jie Shen	University of Michigan, USA
Francesco Tajani	Sapienza University of Rome, Italy
Rodrigo Tapia Mcclung	Centro de Investigación en Ciencias de Información Geoespacial, Mexico
Eufemia Tarantino	Polytechnic University of Bari, Italy
Sergio Tasso	University of Perugia, Italy
Ana Paula Teixeira	Universidade do Minho, Portugal
Yiota Theodora	National Technical University of Athens, Greece
Giuseppe A. Trunfio	University of Sassari, Italy
Toshihiro Uchibayashi	Kyushu University, Japan
Marco Vizzari	University of Perugia, Italy
Frank Westad	Norwegian University of Science and Technology, Norway
Fukuko Yuasa	High Energy Accelerator Research Organization, Japan
Ljiljana Zivkovic	Republic Geodetic Authority, Serbia

Workshops

Workshop on Advancements in Applied Machine-Learning and Data Analytics (AAMDA 2025)

Workshop Organizers
Alessandro Costantini	INFN, Italy
Daniele Cesini	INFN, Italy
Elisabetta Ronchieri	INFN, Italy
Barbara Martelli	INFN, Italy

Workshop Program Committee Members
Alessandro Costantini	Istituto Nazionale di Fisica Nucleare (INFN), Italy
Daniele Cesini	Istituto Nazionale di Fisica Nucleare (INFN), Italy
Elisabetta Ronchieri	Istituto Nazionale di Fisica Nucleare (INFN), Italy
Barbara Martelli	Istituto Nazionale di Fisica Nucleare (INFN), Italy
Luca Dell'Agnello	Istituto Nazionale di Fisica Nucleare (INFN), Italy

Advanced and Innovative Web Apps 2025 (AIWA 2025)

Workshop Organizers
Damiano Perri	University of Perugia, Italy
Osvaldo Gervasi	University of Perugia, Italy
Stelios Kouzeleas	International Hellenic University, Greece
Sergio Tasso	University of Perugia, Italy

Workshop Program Committee Members
David Berti	ART SpA, Italy
JungYoon Kim	Gachon University, South Korea
TaiHoon Kim	Zhejiang University of Science and Technology, China

Advanced Processes of Mathematics and Computing Models in Complex Data-Intensive Computational Systems (AMCM 2025)

Workshop Organizers

Yeliz Karaca	University of Massachusetts Chan Medical School and Massachusetts Institute of Technology, USA
Dumitru Baleanu	Lebanese American University, Lebanon
Osvaldo Gervasi	University of Perugia, Italy
Yudong Zhang	University of Leicester, UK
Majaz Moonis	University of Massachusetts Chan Medical School and Massachusetts Institute of Technology, USA

Workshop Program Committee Members

TaeHoon Kim	Zhejiang University of Science and Technology, China
Martin Bohner	Missouri University of Science and Technology, USA
Shuihua Wang	University of Leicester, UK
Khan Muhammad	Sungkyunkwan University, South Korea
Mahmoud Abdel-Aty	Sohag University, Egypt
Aziz Dursun	Virginia Polytechnic Institute and State University, USA
Kemal Güven Gülen	Namık Kemal University, Turkey
Akif Akgül	Hitit Üniversitesi, Turkey

Advanced Numerical Approaches for Assessment and Design of No-Tension Masonry Structures (ANAMS 2025)

Workshop Organizers

Antonino Iannuzzo	Universitá degli studi del Sannio, Italy
Carlo Olivieri	Universitá Telematica Pegaso, Italy
Andrea Montanino	CIMNE, Spain
Elham Mousavian	University of Edinburgh, UK

Workshop Program Committee Members

Pietro Meriggi	Roma Tre University, Italy
Francesca Perelli	University of Naples Federico II, Italy
Marialuigia Sangirardi	University of Oxford, UK
Sam Cocking	University of Cambridge, UK

Matteo Salvalaggio	University of Minho, Portugal
Vittorio Paris	University of Bergamo, Italy
Luigi Sibille	Norwegian University of Science and Technology, Norway
Natalia Pingaro	Politecnico di Milano, Italy
Martina Buzzetti	Politecnico di Milano, Italy
Generoso Vaiano	Pegaso Telematic University, Italy
Alessandra Capolupo	Politecnico di Bari, Italy
Amal Gerges	Università degli Studi di Cagliari, Italy
Fabian Orozco	National Autonomous University of Mexico, Mexico
Nathanael Savalle	Polytech Clermont and Université Clermont Auvergne, France
Luca Umberto Argiento	University of Naples Federico II, Italy
Bartolomeo Pantó	Durham University, UK

Unveiling the Synergies Between Air Quality and Climate PlAnning (AQCliPA 2025)

Workshop Organizers

Angela Pilogallo	University of L'Aquila, Italy
Luigi Santopietro	University of Basilicata, Italy
Filomena Pietrapertosa	IMAA CNR, Italy
Monica Salvia	IMAA CNR, Italy
Carlo Trozzi	IMAA CNR, Italy
Valeria Scapini	Central University of Chile, Chile

Workshop Program Committee Members

Lucia Saganeiti	IMAA-CNR, Italy
Lorena Fiorini	University of L'Aquila, Italy
Antonio Mazza	IMAA-CNR, Italy
Gabriele Nolè	IMAA-CNR, Italy
Carmen Guida	University of Naples "Federico II", Italy
Floriana Zucaro	University of Naples "Federico II", Italy
Sabrina Lai	University of Cagliari, Italy
Chiara Garau	University of Cagliari, Italy

Advancements in Spatial assessment of Socio-Ecological SystemS (ASSESS 2025)

Workshop Organizers
Daniele Cannatella	TU Delft, The Netherlands
Giuliano Poli	University of Naples Federico II, Italy
Eugenio Muccio	TU Delft, The Netherlands
Claudiu Forgaci	TU Delft, The Netherlands

Workshop Program Committee Members
Daniele Cannatella	TU Delft, The Netherlands
Giuliano Poli	University of Naples Federico II, Italy
Eugenio Muccio	University of Naples Federico II, Italy
Claudiu Forgaci	TU Delft, The Netherlands
Maria Cerreta	University of Naples Federico II, Italy
Maria Somma	University of Naples Federico II, Italy
Laura Di Tommaso	University of Naples Federico II, Italy
Sabrina Sacco	Politecnico di Milano, Italy
Piero Zizzania	University of Naples Federico II, Italy
Gaia Daldanise	CNR IRISS, Italy
Benedetta Grieco	University of Naples Federico II, Italy
Giuseppe Ciciriello	University of Naples Federico II, Italy
Marta Dell'Ovo	Politecnico di Milano, Italy
Francesco Piras	University of Cagliari, Italy
Diana Rolando	Politecnico di Torino, Italy
Stefano Cuntò	University of Naples Federico II, Italy
Ludovica La Rocca	University of Naples Federico II, Italy

Blockchain and Distributed Ledgers: Technologies and Applications (BDLTA 2025)

Workshop Organizers
Vladimir Korkhov	Saint Petersburg State University, Russia
Elena Stankova	Saint Petersburg State University, Russia
Nataliia Kulabukhova	Saint Petersburg State University, Russia

Workshop Program Committee Members
Adam Belloum	University of Amsterdam, the Netherlands
Dmitrii Vasiunin	Deutsche Telekom Cloud Services E.P.E., Greece
Serob Balyan	Osensus Arm LLC, Armenia
Suren Abrahamyan	Osensus Arm LLC, Armenia
Ashot Sergey Gevorkyan	NAS of Armenia, Armenia

Michal Hnatic	Univerzita Pavla Jozefa Šafárika v Košiciach, Slovakia
Michail Panteleyev	Saint Petersburg Electrotecnical University, Russia
Martin Vala	Univerzita Pavla Jozefa Šafárika v Košiciach, Slovakia
Nodir Zaynalov	Tashkent University of Information Technologies named after Muhammad al Khwarizmi, Uzbekistan
Michail Panteleyev	Saint Petersburg Electrotecnical University, Russia
Alexander Degtyarev	Saint Petersburg University, Russia
Alexander Bogdanov	St. Petersburg State University, Russia

Bio and Neuro Inspired Computing and Applications (BIONCA 2025)

Workshop Organizers

Nadia Nedjah	State University of Rio de Janeiro, Brazil
Luiza de Macedo Mourelle	State University of Rio de Janeiro, Brazil

Workshop Program Committee Members

Nadia Nedjha	State University of Rio de Janeiro, Brazil
Luiza de Macedo Mourelle	State University of Rio de Janeiro, Brazil
Luigi Maciel Ribeiro	State University of Rio de Janeiro, Brazil
Joelmir Ramos	Federal University of Rio de Janeiro, Brazil
Rogério Moraes	Brazilian Navy, Brazil
Marcos Santana Farias	Institute of Nuclear Energy, Brazil
Luneque Silva Jr.	Federal University of ABC, Brazil
Alan Oliveira	University of Lisboa, Portugal
Brij Bhooshan Gupta	Asia University, Taiwan

Computational and Applied Mathematics (CAM 2025)

Workshop Organizers

Maria Irene Falcão	University of Minho, Portugal
Fernando Miranda	University of Minho, Portugal

Workshop Program Committee Members

Fernando Miranda	University of Minho, Portugal
Graça Tomaz	Polytechnic of Guarda, Portugal
Helmuth Malonek	University of Aveiro, Portugal

Isabel Cacao	University of Aveiro, Portugal
João Morais	Autonomous Technological Institute of Mexico, Mexico
Lidia Aceto	University of Eastern Piedmont, Italy
Luís Ferrás	University of Porto, Portugal
M. Irene Falcão	University of Minho, Portugal
Patrícia Beites	University of Beira Interior, Portugal
Paulo Amorim	FGV EMAp, Brazil
Regina de Almeida	University of Trás-os-Montes e Alto Douro, Portugal
Ricardo Severino	University of Minho, Portugal

Computational and Applied Statistics (CAS 2025)

Workshop Organizer

Ana Cristina Braga	ALGORITMI Research Centre, LASI, University of Minho, Portugal

Workshop Program Committee Members

Adelaide Freitas	University of Aveiro, Portugal
Andreas Futschik	Johannes Kepler University Linz, Austria
Ana Cristina Braga	University of Minho, Portugal
Ângela Silva	University of Minho, Portugal
Arminda Manuela Gonçalves	University of Minho, Portugal
Carina Silva	Polytechnic Intitute of Lisbon, Portugal
Elisete Correia	University of Trás-os-Montes e Alto Douro, Portugal
Frank Westad	Norwegian University of Science and Technology, Norway
Isabel Natario	New University of Lisbon, Portugal
Irene Oliveira	University of Trás-os-Montes e Alto Douro, Portugal
Ivan Rodriguez Conde	University of Vigo, Spain
Joaquim Gonçalves	Instituto Politécnico do Cávado e do Ave, Portugal
Lino Costa	University of Minho, Portugal
Marco Reis	University of Coimbra, Portugal
Maria Filipa Mourão	Polytechnic Institute of Viana do Castelo, Portugal
Maria João Polidoro	Polytechnic Institute of Porto, Portugal
Martin Perez Perez	University of Vigo, Spain
Michal Abrahamowicz	McGill University, Canada
Vera Afreixo	University of Aveiro, Portugal

Werner G. Müller	Johannes Kepler University Linz, Austria
Bruna Silva Ramos	University Lusiada de Famalicão, Portugal
Inês Sousa	University of Minho, Portugal
Luís Miguel Rocha Matos	University of Minho, Portugal
Manuel Carlos Figueiredo	University of Minho, Portugal

Cyber Intelligence and Applications (CIA 2025)

Workshop Organizer

Gianni D'Angelo	University of Salerno, Italy

Workshop Program Committee Members

Gianni D'Angelo	University of Salerno, Italy
Francesco Palmieri	University of Salerno, Italy
Massimo Ficco	University of Salerno, Italy
Arcangelo Castiglione	University of Salerno, Italy

Computational Methods for Business Analytics (CMBA 2025)

Workshop Organizers

Cláudio Alves	Universidade do Minho, Portugal
Telmo Pinto	Universidade do Minho, Portugal

Workshop Program Committee Members

Abdulrahim Shamayleh	American University of Sharjah, United Arab Emirates
Ana Rocha	University of Minho, Portugal
Angelo Sifaleras	University of Macedonia, Greece
Cristóvão Silva	University of Coimbra, Portugal
José Valério de Carvalho	University of Minho, Portugal
Miguel Vieira	Universidade Lusófona, Portugal
Rita Macedo	Université de Lille, France
Ana Moura	Universidade de Aveiro, Portugal
Cristina Lopes	ISCAP, Portugal
Eliana Costa e Silva	Instituto Politécnico do Porto, Portugal

Computational Methods, Statistics and Industrial Mathematics (CMSIM 2025)

Workshop Organizers

Maria Filomena Teodoro	IST ID, Instituto Superior Técnico, Portugal
Marina Alexandra Pedro Andrade	ISCTE – Lisbon University Institute, Portugal
Paula Simões	University of Lisbon, Portugal
Teresa A. Oliveira	IST ID, Instituto Superior Técnico, Portugal

Workshop Program Committee Members

Amilcar Oliveira	Universidade Aberta and Universidade de Lisboa, Portugal
Victor Lobo	Escola Naval and NOVA IMS Almada, Portugal
António Pacheco	IST Universidade de Lisboa, Portugal
Eliana Costa	Escola Superior de Tecnologia e Gestão IPPorto, Portugal
Aldina Correia	Escola Superior de Tecnologia e Gestão IPPorto, Portugal
Fernando Carapau	University of Évora, Portugal
Ricardo Moura	Portuguese Naval Academy, Portugal
Ana Borges	Escola Superior de Tecnologia e Gestão IPPorto, Portugal
Cristina Lopes	ISCAP IPPorto, Portugal
Fernanda Costa	University of Minho, Portugal
Cabrita Carlos	IPBeja, Portugal
Maria Luísa Morgado	University of Trás os Montes e Alto Douro and University of Lisboa, Portugal
Rosário Ramos	Universidade Aberta, Portugal
Sofia Rézio	Iscal, Instituto Politécnico de Lisboa, Portugal
Matteo Sacchet	University of Turin, Italy
Marina Marchisio Conte	University of Turin, Italy
António Seijas-Macias	University of Coruña, Spain
Luís F. A. Teodoro	University of Glasgow, UK and University of Oslo, Norway
Christos Kitsos	University of West Attica, Greece
M. Filomena Teodoro	Universidade de Lisboa, Portugal
Marina A. P. Andrade	Instituto Universitário de Lisboa, Portugal
Paula Simões	Military Academy and Universidade Nova de Lisboa, Portugal
Teresa Oliveira	Universidade Aberta and Universidade de Lisboa, Portugal

Computational Optimization and Applications (COA 2025)

Workshop Organizers

Ana Rocha	ALGORITMI Research Centre, LASI, University of Minho, Portugal, Portugal
Humberto Rocha	ALGORITMI Research Centre, LASI, University of Minho, Portugal, Portugal

Workshop Program Committee Members

Florbela Fernandes	Polytechnic Institute of Bragança, Portugal
Clara Vaz	Polytechnic Institute of Bragança, Portugal
Ana Pereira	Polytechnic Institute of Bragança, Portugal
Filipe Alvelos	University of Minho, Portugal
Joana Dias	University of Coimbra, Portugal
Eligius M. T. Hendrix	University of Málaga, Spain
Emerson José de Paiva	Federal University of Itajubá, Brazil
Ana Paula Teixeira	University of Trás-os-Montes and Alto Douro, Portugal
Lino Costa	Universidade do Minho, Portugal

Coastal Cities Versus Inland Areas. Hypotheses for Sustainable Regeneration Through Ecosystem Services of 'Hooking' and Rehabilitation of Brownfield Sites (CoastalCities_VS_InlandAreas 2025)

Workshop Organizers

Celestina Fazia	Università di Enna Kore, Italy
Angrilli Massimo	University of Chieti-Pescara, Italy
Valentina Ciuffreda	University of Chieti-Pescara, Italy
Maurizio Oddo	Università di Enna Kore, Italy
Marcello Sestito	Università di Enna Kore, Italy
Clara Stella Vicari Aversa	University of Reggio Calabria, Italy

Workshop Program Committee Members

Alessandro Camiz	Università d'Annunzio, Italy
Thowayeb Hassan	King Faisal University, Saudi Arabia
Alessandro Barracco	Università Kore di Enna, Italy
Mario Morrica	University of Urbino, Italy
Mariana Ratiu	University of Oradea, Romania
Alanda Akamana	Mohammed VI Polytechnic University, Morocco
Kaoutare Amini Alaoui	Mohammed VI Polytechnic University, Morocco

Computational Astrochemistry 2025 (CompAstro 2025)

Workshop Organizers
Marzio Rosi	University of Perugia, Italy
Daniela Ascenzi	University of Trento, Italy
Nadia Balucani	University of Perugia, Italy
Stefano Falcinelli	University of Perugia, Italy

Workshop Program Committee Members
Dario Campisi	Università degli Studi di Perugia, Italy
Giacomo Giorgi	Università degli Studi di Perugia, Italy
Andrea Giustini	Università degli Studi di Perugia, Italy
Luca Mancini	Università degli Studi di Perugia, Italy
Albert Rimola	Universitat Autònoma de Barcelona, Spain
Gianmarco Vanuzzo	Università degli Studi di Perugia, Italy
Dimitrios Skouteris	Master-Tec, Italy
Piero Ugliengo	Università degli Studi di Torino, Italy
Franco Vecchiocattivi	Università degli Sudi di Perugia, Italy
Giacomo Pannacci	Università degli Studi di Perugia, Italy
Costanza Borghesi	Università degli Studi di Perugia, Italy
Marco Parriani	Università degli Studi di Perugia, Italy
Marta Loletti	Università degli Studi di Perugia, Italy
Fernando Pirani	Università degli Studi di Perugia, Italy
Andrea Lombardi	Università degli Studi di Perugia, Italy
Noelia Faginas Lago	Università degli Studi di Perugia, Italy
Paolo Tosi	Università di Trento, Italy
Cecilia Coletti	Università degli Studi Chieti-Pescara, Italy
Nazzareno Re	Università degli Studi Chieti-Pescara, Italy
Linda Podio	Osservatorio Astrofisico di Arcetri INAF, Italy
Claudio Codella	Osservatorio Astrofisico di Arcetri INAF, Italy
Gabriella Di Genova	Università degli Studi di Perugia, Italy

Computational Methods for Porous Geomaterials (CompPor 2025)

Workshop Organizers
Vadim Lisitsa	IPGG SB RAS, Russia
Evgeniy Romenski	IPGG SB RAS, Russia

Workshop Program Committee Members

Vadim Lisitsa	Institute of Petroleum Geology and Geophysics SB RAS, Russia
Evgeniy Romenski	Sobolev Institute of Mathematics SB RAS, Russia
Vladimir Cheverda	Sobolev Institute of Mathematics SB RAS, Russia
Tatyana Khachkova	IPGG SB RAS, Russia
Dmitry Prokhorov	IPGG SB RAS, Russia
Mikhail Novikov	Sobolev Institute of Mathematics SB RAS, Russia
Sergey Solovyev	Sobolev Institute of Mathematics SB RAS, Russia
Kirill Gadylshin	LLC RNBashNIPIneft, Russia
Olga Stoyanovskaya	Lavrentev Institute of Hydrodynamics SB RAS, Russia
Yerlan Amanbek	Nazarbaev University, Kazakstan

Workshop on Computational Science and HPC (CSHPC 2025)

Workshop Organizers

Elise de Doncker	Western Michigan University, USA
Hideo Matsufuru	High Energy Accelerator Research Organization, Japan

Workshop Program Committee Members

Elise de Doncker	Western Michigan University, USA
Hideo Matsufuru	High Energy Accelerator Research Organization (KEK), Japan
Fukuko Yuasa	KEK, Japan
Issaku Kanamori	RIKEN, Japan
Hiroshi Daisaka	Hitotsubashi University, Japan
Norikazu Yamada	KEK, Japan
Naohito Nakasato	University of Aizu, Japan
Robert Makin	Western Michigan University, USA

Cities, Technologies and Planning 2025 (CTP 2025)

Workshop Organizers

Giuseppe Borruso	University of Trieste, Italy
Beniamino Murgante	University of Basilicata, Italy
Malgorzata Hanzl	Lodz University of Technology, Poland
Anastasia Stratigea	National Technical University of Athens, Greece
Ljiljana Zivkovic	Republic Geodetic Authority, Serbia
Ginevra Balletto	University of Trieste, Italy

Workshop Program Committee Members

Giuseppe Borruso	University of Trieste, Italy
Beniamino Murgante	University of Basilicata, Italy
Malgorzata Hanzl	Lodz University of Technology, Poland
Anastasia Stratigea	National Technical University of Athens, Greece
Ljiljiana Zivkovic	Republic Geodetic Authority of Serbia, Serbia
Ginevra Balletto	University of Cagliari, Italy
Silvia Battino	University of Sassari, Italy
Mara Ladu	University of Cagliari, Italy
Maria del Mar Munoz Leonisio	University of Cádiz, Spain
Ahinoa Amaro Garcia	University of Las Palmas of Gran Canaria, Spain
Maria Attard	University of Malta, Malta
Enrico D'agostini	World Maritime University, Sweden
Francesca Krasna	University of Trieste, Italy
Brisol Garcia Garcia	Polytechnic University of Quintana Roo, Mexico
Tu Anh Trinh	UEH University, Vietnam
Giovanni Mauro	Università degli Studi della Campania, Italy
Maria Ronza	University of Naples Federico II, Italy
Massimiliano Bencardino	University of Salerno, Italy
Tomasz Bradecki	Silesian University of Technology, Poland
Dorota Kamrowska-Załuska	Gdańsk University of Technology, Poland
Iwona Jażdżewska	University of Lodz, Poland
Yiota Theodora	National Technical University of Athens, Greece
Apostolos Lagarias	University of Thessaly, Greece
George Tsilimigkas	University of the Aegean, Greece
Akrivi Leka	National Technical University of Athens, Greece
Maria Panagiotopoulou	National Technical University of Athens, Greece
Andrea Gallo	Ca' Foscari University of Venice, Italy
Francesca Sinatra	University of Trieste, Italy

Digital Transition: Effects on Housing Mobility, Market, Land Governance (DIGITRANS 2025)

Workshop Organizers

Fabrizio Battisti	University of Florence, Italy
Fabiana Forte	University of Campania, Italy
Orazio Campo	Sapienza University of Rome, Italy
Alessio Pino	Kore University of Enna, Italy
Carlo Pisano	University of Florence, Italy
Mariolina Grasso	Kore University of Enna, Italy

Workshop Program Committee Members

Fabrizio Battisti	University of Florence, Italy
Fabiana Forte	Università della Campania Luigi Vanvitelli, Italy
Orazio Campo	University of Rome "La Sapienza", Italy
Alessio Pino	Kore University of Enna, Italy
Carlo Pisano	University of Florence, Italy
Mariolina Grasso	Università Kore di Enna, Italy

Evaluating Inner Areas Potentials (EIAP 2025)

Workshop Organizers

Diana Rolando	Politecnico di Torino, Italy
Alice Barreca	Politecnico di Torino, Italy
Manuela Rebaudengo	Politecnico di Torino, Italy
Giorgia Malavasi	Politecnico di Torino, Italy

Workshop Program Committee Members

John Accordino	Virginia Commonwealth University, USA
Francesco Bruzzone	Università Iuav di Venezia, Italy
Maria Cerreta	Università degli Studi di Napoli Federico II, Italy
Maddalena Chimisso	Università degli Studi del Molise, Italy
Chiara Chioni	Università degli Studi di Trento, Italy
Annalisa Contato	Università degli Studi di Palermo, Italy
Cristina Coscia	Politecnico di Torino, Italy
Marta Dell'Ovo	Politecnico di Milano, Italy
Benedetta Di Leo	Università Politecnica delle Marche, Italy
Sara Favargiotti	Università degli Studi di Trento, Italy
Maddalena Ferretti	Università Politecnica delle Marche, Italy
Salvo Giuffrida	Università degli Studi di Palermo, Italy
Barbara Lino	Università degli Studi di Palermo, Italy
Umberto Mecca	Politecnico di Torino, Italy
Beatrice Mecca	Politecnico di Torino, Italy
Giuliano Poli	Università degli Studi di Napoli Federico II, Italy
Marco Rossitti	Politecnico di Milano, Italy
Alexandra Stankulova	Politecnico di Torino, Italy
Elena Todella	Politecnico di Torino, Italy
Asja Aulisio	Politecnico di Torino, Italy
Giulia Datola	Politecnico di Milano, Italy

Francesco Calabrò Università degli Studi Mediterranea di Reggio Calabria, Italy
Valeria Saiu Università degli Studi di Cagliari, Italy
Maria Rosa Trovato Università di Catania, Italy

Econometric and Multidimensional Evaluation in Urban Environment (EMEUE 2025)

Workshop Organizers

Maria Cerreta University of Naples Federico II, Italy
Carmelo Maria Torre Polytechnic University of Bari, Italy
Pierluigi Morano Polytechnic University of Bari, Italy
Simona Panaro University of Naples Federico II, Italy
Felicia Di Liddo University of Naples Federico II, Italy
Debora Anelli University of Naples Federico II, Italy

Workshop Program Committee Members

Carmelo Maria Torre Polytechnic University of Bari, Italy
Maria Cerreta University of Naples Federico II, Italy
Pierluigi Morano Polytechnic University of Bari, Italy
Francesco Tajani Sapienza University of Rome, Italy
Simona Panaro University of Naples Federico II, Italy
Felicia di Liddo Polytechnic University of Bari, Italy
Debora Anelli Sapienza University of Rome, Italy
Giuliano Poli University of Naples Federico II, Italy
Maria Somma University of Naples Federico II, Italy
Simona Panaro University of Campania Luigi Vanvitelli, Italy
Laura Di Tommaso University of Naples Federico II, Italy
Caterina Loffredo University of Naples Federico II, Italy
Ludovica La Rocca University of Naples Federico II, Italy
Sabrina Sacco Politecnico di Milano, Italy
Piero Zizzania University of Naples Federico II, Italy
Gaia Daldanise CNR IRISS, Italy
Benedetta Grieco University of Naples Federico II, Italy
Giuseppe Ciciriello University of Naples Federico II, Italy
Marta Dell'Ovo Politecnico di Milano, Italy
Daniele Cannatella TU Delft University, The Netherlands
Eugenio Muccio University of Naples Federico II, Italy
Sveva Ventre University of Naples Federico II, Italy

Governance of Energy Transition: Environmental, Landscape, Social and Spatial Planning (ENERGY_PLANNING 2025)

Workshop Organizers

Mara Ladu	University of Cagliari, Italy
Ginevra Balletto	University of Cagliari, Italy
Emilio Ghiani	University of Cagliari, Italy
Alessandra Marra	University of Salerno, Italy
Roberto De Lotto	University of Pavia, Italy
Balázs Kulcsár	Chalmers University of Technology, Sweden

Workshop Program Committee Members

Riccardo Trevisan	University of Cagliari, Italy
Marco Naseddu	University of Cagliari, Italy
Giuseppe Borruso	University of Trieste, Italy
Andrea Gallo	University of Trieste, Italy
Francesca Sinatra	University of Trieste, Italy
Maria Attard	University of Malta, Malta
Tu Anh Trinh	UEH University Ho Chi Minh City, Vietnam
Marcello Tadini	University of Eastern Piedmont, Italy
Luigi Mundula	University for Foreigners of Perugia, Italy
Silvia Battino	University of Sassari, Italy
Maria del Mar Munoz Leonisio	University of Cádiz, Spain
Anna Richiedei	University of Brescia, Italy
Michele Pezzagno	University of Brescia, Italy
Federico Mertellozzo	University of Firenze, Italy
Marco Mazzarino	IUAV University Venice, Italy

Ecosystem Services in Spatial Planning for Climate Neutral Urban and Rural Areas (ESSP 2025)

Workshop Organizers

Sabrina Lai	University of Cagliari, Italy
Francesco Scorza	University of Basilicata, Italy
Corrado Zoppi	University of Cagliari, Italy
Beniamino Murgante	University of Basilicata, Italy
Carmela Gargiulo	University of Naples Federico II, Italy
Floriana Zucaro	University of Naples Federico II, Italy

Workshop Program Committee Members

Alfonso Annunziata	University of Basilicata, Italy
Ginevra Balletto	University of Cagliari, Italy
Ivan Blečić	University of Cagliari, Italy
Giuseppe Borruso	University of Trieste, Italy
Barbara Caselli	University of Parma, Italy
Maria Cerreta	University of Naples Federico II, Italy
Chiara Garau	University of Cagliari, Italy
Carmen Guida	University of Naples Federico II, Italy
Federica Isola	University of Cagliari, Italy
Francesca Leccis	University of Cagliari, Italy
Federica Leone	University of Cagliari, Italy
Silvia Rossetti	University of Parma, Italy
Luigi Santopietro	University of Basilicata, Italy
Carmelo Torre	Polytechnic of Bari, Italy

The 15th International Workshop on Future Information System Technologies and Applications (FiSTA 2025)

Workshop Organizers

Bernady O. Apduhan	Kyushu Sangyo University, Japan
Rafael Santos	Brazilian National Institute for Space Research, Brazil

Workshop Program Committee Members

Agustinus Borgy Waluyo	Monash University, Australia
Andre Ricardo Abed Grégio	Federal University of Paraná, Brazil
Eric Pardede	La Trobe University, Australia
Kai Cheng	Kyushu Sangyo University, Japan
Ching-Hsien Hsu	Asia University, Taiwan
Fenghui Yao	Tennessee State University, USA
Yusuke Gotoh	Okayama University, Japan
Alvaro Fazenda	Federal University of São Paulo, Brazil
Kazuaki Tanaka	Kyushu Institute of Technology, Japan
Tengku Adil	MARA Technological University, Malaysia
Toshihiro Yamauchi	Okayama University, Japan
Yasuaki Sumida	Kyushu Sangyo University, Japan
Earl Ryan Aleluya	MSU-Iligan Institute of Technology, Philippines
Cherry Mae G. Villame	MSU-Iligan Institute of Technology, Philippines
Anton Louise De Ocampo	Batangas State University, Philippines
Krishnamoorthy Ranganthan	Chennai Institute of Technology, India

Flow Management in Urban Contexts (FMUC 2025)

Workshop Organizers
Alessio Pino	Kore University of Enna, Italy
Giovanna Acampa	Kore University of Enna, Italy

Workshop Program Committee Members
Giovanna Acampa	University of Florence, Italy
Alessio Pino	Kore University of Enna, Italy
Mariolina Grasso	Università Kore di Enna, Italy
Fabrizio Battisti	University of Florence, Italy
Fabrizio Finucci	Roma Tre University, Italy
Antonella G. Masanotti	Roma Tre University, Italy
Daniele Mazzoni	Roma Tre University, Italy

Geographical Analysis, Urban Modeling, Spatial Statistics 2025 (Geog-And-Mod 2025)

Workshop Organizers
Beniamino Murgante	University of Basilicata, Italy
Giuseppe Borruso	University of Trieste, Italy
Hartmut Asche	University of Potsdam, Germany
Rodrigo Tapia McClung	CentroGeo, Mexico
Andreas Fricke	University of Potsdam, Germany

Workshop Program Committee Members
Giuseppe Borruso	University of Trieste, Italy
Beniamino Murgante	University of Basilicata, Italy
Hartmut Asche	University of Potsdam, Germany
Rodrigo Tapia-McClung	Centro de Investigación en Ciencias de Información Geoespacial (CentroGeo), Mexico
Andreas Fricke	University of Potsdam, Germany
Malgorzata Hanzl	Lodz University of Technology, Poland
Anastasia Stratigea	National Technical University of Athens, Greece
Ljiljiana Zivkovic	Republic Geodetic Authority of Serbia, Serbia
Ginevra Balletto	University of Cagliari, Italy
Silvia Battino	University of Sassari, Italy
Mara Ladu	University of Cagliari, Italy
Maria del Mar Munoz Leonisio	University of Cádiz, Spain
Ahinoa Amaro Garcia	University of Las Palmas of Gran Canaria, Spain
Maria Attard	University of Malta, Malta

Enrico D'agostini	World Maritime University, Sweden
Francesca Krasna	University of Trieste, Italy
Brisol García García	Polytechnic University of Quintana Roo, Mexico
Tu Anh Trinh	UEH University, Vietnam
Giovanni Mauro	Università degli Studi della Campania, Italy
Maria Ronza	University of Naples Federico II, Italy
Massimiliano Bencardino	University of Salerno, Italy
Andrea Gallo	Ca' Foscari University of Venice, Italy
Francesca Sinatra	University of Trieste, Italy
Salvatore Dore	University of Trieste, Italy

Geogames for Sustainable Development (Geogames 2025)

Workshop Organizer

Alenka Poplin	Iowa State University, USA

Workshop Program Committee Members

Alenka Poplin	Iowa State University, USA
Bruno Amaral de Andrade	Portucalense University, Portugal
Brian Tomaszewski	Rochester Institute of Technology, USA
Deepak Marhatta	Tribhuvan University, Nepal
Alessandro Plaisant	University of Sassari, Italy
David Schwartz	Rochester Institute of Technology, USA
Silvia Rossetti	University of Parma, Italy
Floriana Zucaro	University of Naples Federico II, Italy
Alfonso Annunziata	University of Basilicata, Italy
Reza Askarizad	University of Cagliari, Italy
Chiara Garau	University of Cagliari, Italy
Tanja Congiu	University of Sassari, Italy

Geomatics for Resource Monitoring and Management (GRMM 2025)

Workshop Organizers

Alberico Sonnessa	Politecnico di Bari, Italy
Eufemia Tarantino	Politecnico di Bari, Italy
Alessandra Capolupo	Politecnico di Bari, Italy

Workshop Program Committee Members

Umberto Fratino	Politecnico di Bari, Italy
Valeria Monno	Politecnico di Bari, Italy

Antonino Maltese	Università degli studi di Palermo, Italy
Athos Agapiou	Cyprus University of Technology, Cyprus
Michele Mangiameli	Università di Catania, Italy
Angela Gorgoglione	Universidad de la República de Uruguay, Uruguay
Roberta Ravanelli	University of Liège, Belgium
Ester Scotto di Perta	Università degli studi di Napoli Federico II, Italy
Giacomo Caporusso	CNR, Italy
Andrea Montanino	International Centre for Numerical Methods in Engineering of Barcelona, Spain
Antonino Iannuzzo	Università degli studi del Sannio, Italy
Alessandro Pagano	Politecnico di Bari, Italy
Francesco Di Capua	Università degli Studi della Basilicata, Italy
Albertini Cinzia	CNR-IREA, Italy
Alessandra Saponieri	Università degli studi del Salento, Italy
PierFrancesco Recchi	Università degli studi di Napoli Federico II, Italy
Vincenzo Totaro	Politecnico di Bari, Italy
Stefania Santoro	CNR Water Research Institute, Italy
Francesco Bimbo	University of Foggia, Italy
Cristina Proietti	Istituto Nazionale di Geofisica e Vulcanologia, Italy
Carla Cavallo	University of Salerno, Italy
Gaetano Falcone	Università degli Studi di Napoli Federico II, Italy
Valeria Belloni	Sapienza University of Rome, Italy
Alessandra Mascitelli	University of Chieti-Pescara, Italy

HERitage and CLIMAte neutrality. Resilient approach for nature centered/based sustainable cities (HERCLIMA 2025)

Workshop Organizers

Celestina Fazia	Università di Enna Kore, Italy
Angrilli Massimo	University of Chieti-Pescara, Italy
Clara Stella Vicari Aversa	University of Reggio Calabria, Italy
Dorina Camelia Ilies	University of Oradea, Romania
Mariana Ratiu	University of Oradea, Romania

Workshop Program Committee Members

Alessandro Camiz	Università d'Annunzio, Italy
Mario Morrica	University of Urbino, Italy
Thowayeb Hassan	King Faisal University, Saudi Arabia
Alessandro Barracco	Università Kore di Enna, Italy
Kaoutare Amini Alaoui	Mohammed VI Polytechnic University (UM6P), Morocco

Mariana Ratiu University of Oradea, Romania
Valentina Ciuffreda Università Chieti-Pescara, Italy

International Workshop on Information and Knowledge in the Internet of Things (IKIT 2025)

Workshop Organizers

Teresa Guarda Universidad Estatal Península de Santa Elena, Ecuador
Luis Enrique Chuquimarca Jimenez Universidad Estatal Península de Santa Elena, Ecuador
Gustavo Gatica Universidad Andrés Bello, Chile
Filipe Mota Pinto Polytechnic Institute of Leiria, Portugal
Arnulfo Alanis Instituto Tecnológico de Tijuana, Mexico
Luis Mazon Universidad Estatal Península de Santa Elena, Spain

Workshop Program Committee Members

Arnulfo Alanis Instituto Tecnológico de Tijuana, Mexico
Bruno Sousa University of Coimbra, Portugal
Carlos Balsa Instituto Politécnico de Bragança, Portugal
Filipe Mota Pinto Instituto Politécnico de Leiria, Portugal
Gustavo Gatica Universidad Andrés Bello, Chile
Isabel Lopes Instituto Politécnico de Bragança, Portugal
José-María Díaz-Nafría Universidad a Distancia, Spain
Maria Fernanda Augusto BiTrum Research Group, Spain
Maria Isabel Ribeiro Instituto Politécnico Bragança, Portugal
Modestos Stavrakis University of the Aegean, Greece
Simone Belli Universidad Complutense de Madrid, Spain
Walter Lopes Neto Instituto Federal de Educação, Brazil

International Workshop on territorial Planning to integrate Risk prevention and urban Ontologies (IWPRO 2025)

Workshop Organizers

Beniamino Murgante University of Basilicata, Italy
Roberto De Lotto University of Pavia, Italy
Elisabetta Maria Venco University of Pavia, Italy
Caterina Pietra University of Pavia, Italy

Workshop Program Committee Members

Stefano Borgo	Consiglio Nazionale delle Ricerche ISTC, Italy
Valentina Costa	Università di Genova, Italy
Hamid Danesh Pajouh	Middle East Technical University, Turkey
Ilaria Delponte	Università di Genova, Italy
Lorena Fiorini	Università de L'Aquila, Italy
Veronica Gazzola	Politecnico di Milano, Italy
Ghazaleh Goodarzi	Islamic Azad University, Iran
Michele Grimaldi	Università degli Studi di Salerno, Italy
Alessandra Marra	Università degli Studi di Salerno, Italy
Naghmeh Mohammadpourlima	Åbo Akademi University, Finland
Francesca Pirlone	Università di Genova, Italy
Silvia Rossetti	Università di Parma, Italy
Bahareh Shahsavari	University of Minnesota, USA
Ilenia Spadaro	Università di Genova, Italy
Maria Rosaria Stufano Melone	Politecnico di Bari, Italy

Regional Connectivity, Spatial Accessibility and MaaS for Social Inclusion (MaaS 2025)

Workshop Organizers

Mara Ladu	University of Cagliari, Italy
Ginevra Balletto	University of Cagliari, Italy
Gianfranco Fancello	University of Cagliari, Italy
Tanja Congiu	University of Sassari, Italy
Patrizia Serra	University of Cagliari, Italy
Francesco Piras	University of Cagliari, Italy

Workshop Program Committee Members

Marco Naseddu	University of Cagliari, Italy
Italo Meloni	University of Cagliari, Italy
Giuseppe Borruso	University of Trieste, Italy
Andrea Gallo	University of Trieste, Italy
Francesca Sinatra	University of Trieste, Italy
Maria Attard	University of Malta, Malta
Tu Anh Trinh	UEH University, Vietnam
Marcello Tadini	University of Eastern Piedmont, Italy
Luigi Mundula	University for Foreigners of Perugia, Italy
Silvia Battino	University of Sassari, Italy
Brunella Brundu	University of Sassari, Italy
Veronica Camerada	University of Sassari, Italy

Maria del Mar Munoz Leonisio University of Cádiz, Spain
Anna Richiedei University of Brescia, Italy
Michele Pezzagno University of Brescia, Italy
Marco Mazzarino IUAV University Venice, Italy

The Development of Urban Mobility Management, Road Safety and Risk Assessment (MANTAIN 2025)

Workshop Organizers
Antonio Russo Università degli Studi di Enna, Italy
Corrado Rindone University of Reggio Calabria, Italy
Antonio Polimeni University of Messina, Italy
Florin Rusca Politehnica University of Bucharest, Romania
Grigorios Fountas Aristotle University of Thessaloniki, Greece
Antonio Comi University of Rome Tor Vergata, Italy

Workshop Program Committee Members
Massimo Di Gangi University of Messina, Italy
Orlando Marco Belcore University of Messina, Italy
Antonio Polimeni University of Messina, Italy
Socrates Basbas Aristotle University of Thessaloniki, Greece
Claudia Caballini Polytechnic of Torino, Italy
Efstathios Bouhouras Aristotle University of Thessaloniki, Greece
Stefano Ricci Sapienza University of Rome, Italy
Marina Zanne University of Lubljana, Slovenia
Kh Md Nahiduzzaman Mohammed VI Polytechnic University, Morocco
Alexsandra Deluka Tibljaš University of Rijeka, Croatia
Guilhermina Torrao Aston University, UK

Multidimensional Evolutionary Evaluations for Transformative Approaches (MEETA 2025)

Workshop Organizers
Maria Cerreta University of Naples Federico II, Italy
Giuliano Poli University of Naples Federico II, Italy
Maria Somma University of Naples Federico II, Italy
Gaia Daldanise CNR IRISS, Italy
Ludovica La Rocca University of Naples Federico II, Italy

Workshop Program Committee Members

Maria Cerreta	University of Naples Federico II, Italy
Giuliano Poli	University of Naples Federico II, Italy
Maria Somma	University of Naples Federico II, Italy
Laura Di Tommaso	University of Naples Federico II, Italy
Sabrina Sacco	Politecnico di Milano, Italy
Piero Zizzania	University of Naples Federico II, Italy
Gaia Daldanise	CNR IRISS, Italy
Benedetta Grieco	University of Naples Federico II, Italy
Giuseppe Ciciriello	University of Naples Federico II, Italy
Marta Dell'Ovo	Politecnico di Milano, Italy
Daniele Cannatella	TU Delft, The Netherlands
Eugenio Muccio	University of Naples Federico II, Italy
Francesco Piras	University of Cagliari, Italy
Diana Rolando	Politecnico di Torino, Italy
Sveva Ventre	University of Naples Federico II, Italy
Caterina Loffredo	University of Naples Federico II, Italy
Ludovica La Rocca	University of Naples Federico II, Italy
Simona Panaro	University of Campania Luigi Vanvitelli, Italy

Building Multi-dimensional Models for Assessing Complex Environmental Systems (MES 2025)

Workshop Organizers

Vanessa Assumma	University of Bologna, Italy
Caterina Caprioli	Politecnico di Torino, Italy
Giulia Datola	Politecnico di Milano, Italy
Federico Dell'Anna	University of Bologna, Italy
Marta Dell'Ovo	Politecnico di Milano, Italy
Marco Rossitti	Politecnico di Milano, Italy

Workshop Program Committee Members

Vanessa Assumma	Università di Bologna, Bologna
Caterina Caprioli	Politecnico di Torino, Italy
Giulia Datola	DAStU Politecnico di Milano, Italy
Federico Dell'Anna	Politecnico di Torino, Italy
Marta Dell'Ovo	Politecnico di Milano, Italy
Marco Rossitti	Politecnico di Milano, Italy
Francesca Torrieri	Politecnico di Milano, Italy
Mariarosaria Angrisano	Università Telematica Pegaso, Italy
Maksims Feofilovs	Riga Technical University, Latvia

Danny Caprini	Politecnico di Milano, Italy
Giulio Cavana	Politecnico di Torino, Italy
Sebastiano Barbieri	Politecnico di Torino, Italy
Marta Bottero	Politecnico di Torino, Italy
Francesco Cosentino	Politecnico di Milano, Italy
Silvia Ronchi	Politecnico di Milano, Italy
Chiara Mazzarella	TU Delft, Netherlands
Marco Volpatti	Politecnico di Torino, Italy
Chiara D'Alpaos	Università degli Studi di Padova, Italy
Alessandra Oppio	Politecnico di Milano, Italy
Alessia Crisopulli	Politecnico di Milano, Italy
Domenico D'Uva	Politecnico di Milano, Italy
Giorgia Malavasi	Politecnico di Torino, Italy
Rubina Canesi	Università degli Studi di Padova, Italy
Elena Todella	Politecnico di Torino, Italy
Beatrice Mecca	Politecnico di Torino, Italy
Giulia Marzani	University of Bologna, Italy
Isabella Giovanetti	University of Bologna, Italy
Lucia Petronio	University of Bologna, Italy
Franco Corti	University of Padova, Italy
Salvatore De Pascalis	Politecnico di Milano, Italy
Valeria Vitulano	Politecnico di Torino, Italy
Lorenzo Diana	Università degli studi di Napoli Federico II, Italy
Maksims Feofilovs	Riga Technical University, Latvia
Marco De Luca	Politecnico di Torino, Italy
Ilaria Cazzola	Politecnico di Torino, Italy
Andrea De Toni	Politecnico di Milano, Italy
Eugenio Muccio	University of Naples Federico II, Italy
Giuliano Poli	University of Naples Federico II, Italy
Francesco Sica	University "La Sapienza" of Rome, Italy
Elena Di Pirro	Università degli Studi del Molise, Italy
Riccardo Alba	Università di Torino, Italy
Irene Regaiolo	Università di Torino, Italy
Francesca Cochis	Università di Torino, Italy

Modelling Liveable Cities: Techniques, Methods, Challenges, and Perspectives Behind the 'X-Minute' City (MLC 2025)

Workshop Organizers

Federico Mara	University of Pisa, Italy
Valerio Cutini	University of Pisa, Italy
Alessandro Araldi	Université Côte d'Azur, France

Flávia Lopes　　　　　　　　　Chalmers University of Technology, Sweden
Giovanni Fusco　　　　　　　　Université Côte d'Azur, France

Workshop Program Committee Members
Simone Rusci　　　　　　　　　University of Pisa, Italy
Lorena Fiorini　　　　　　　　　University of L'Aquila, Italy
Chiara Di Dato　　　　　　　　　University of L'Aquila, Italy
Francesco Zullo　　　　　　　　University of L'Aquila, Italy
Alfonso Annunziata　　　　　　University of Basilicata, Italy
Beniamino Murgante　　　　　　University of Basilicata, Italy
Alessandro Araldi　　　　　　　Université Côte d'Azur, France
Chiara Garau　　　　　　　　　University of Cagliari, Italy
Giampiero Lombardini　　　　　Università di Genova, Italy
Flavia Lopes　　　　　　　　　Chalmers University of Technology, Sweden
Giovanni Fusco　　　　　　　　Universitè Côte d'Azur, France

Mathematical Methods for Image Processing and Understanding 2025 (MMIPU 2025)

Workshop Organizers
Ivan Gerace　　　　　　　　　　Università degli Studi di Perugia, Italy
Gianluca Vinti　　　　　　　　　Università degli Studi di Perugia, Italy
Arianna Travaglini　　　　　　　Università degli Studi della Basilicata, Italy

Workshop Program Committee Members
Ivan Gerace　　　　　　　　　　University of Perugia, Italy
Gianluca Vinti　　　　　　　　　University of Perugia, Italy
Arianna Travaglini　　　　　　　University of Basilicata, Italy
Marco Baioletti　　　　　　　　University of Perugia, Italy
Marco Donatelli　　　　　　　　University of Insubria, Italy
Anna Tonazzini　　　　　　　　C.N.R. Pisa, Italy
Muhammad Hanif　　　　　　　Ghulam Ishaq Khan Institute of Engineering Sciences and Technology, Pakistan
Francesco Marchetti　　　　　　University of Padua, Italy
Wolfgang Erb　　　　　　　　　University of Padua, Italy
Danilo Costarelli　　　　　　　　University of Perugia, Italy
Francesco Santini　　　　　　　University of Perugia, Italy
Valentina Giorgetti　　　　　　　University of Perugia, Italy

Mobility Opportunities Bridging Inequalities: Social Inclusion and Gender Equity Initiatives Strategies Against Fragmentation and Complexity of Mobility (MOBIL-EGI 2025)

Workshop Organizers

Tiziana Campisi	University of Enna Kore, Italy
Guilhermina Torrao	Aston University, UK
Socrates Basbas	Aristotle University of Thessaloniki, Greece
Tanja Congiu	University of Sassari, Italy
Stefanos Tsigdinos	National Technical University of Athens, Greece
Florin Nemtanu	Politehnica University of Bucharest, Romania

Workshop Program Committee Members

Massimo Di Gangi	University of Messina, Italy
Orlando Marco Belcore	University of Messina, Italy
Francesco Russo	Mediterranean University of Reggio Calabria, Italy
Alexandros Nikitas	University of Huddersfield, UK
Marilisa Nigro	Rome Tre University, Italy
Kh Md Nahiduzzaman	Mohammed VI Polytechnic University, Morocco
Efstathios Bouhouras	Aristotle University of Thessaloniki, Greece
Antonio Comi	University of Rome Tor Vergata, Italy
Edouard Ivanjko	University of Zagreb, Slovenia
Osvaldo Gervasi	University of Perugia, Italy
Beniamino Murgante	University of Basilicata, Italy
Chiara Garau	University of Cagliari, Italy

MOdels and indicators for assessing and measuring the urban settlement deVElopment in the view of NET ZERO by 2050 (MOVEto0 2025)

Workshop Organizers

Lorena Fiorini	University of L'Aquila, Italy
Lucia Saganeiti	CNR-IMAA, Italy
Angela Pilogallo	CNR-IMAA, Italy
Alessandro Marucci	University of L'Aquila, Italy
Francesco Zullo	University of L'Aquila, Italy

Workshop Program Committee Members

Ginevra Balletto	University of Cagliari, Italy
Giuseppe Borruso	University of Trieste, Italy
Chiara Garau	University of Cagliari, Italy

Beniamino Murgante	University of Basilicata, Italy
Giulia Desogus	University of Cagliari, Italy
Ljiljana Zivkovic	Republic Geodetic Authority, Serbia
Luigi Santopietro	University of Basilicata, Italy
Ilaria Delponte	University of Genoa, Italy
Carmen Guida	University of Naples Federico II, Italy
Chiara Di Dato	University of L'Aquila, Italy

5th Workshop on Privacy in the Cloud/Edge/IoT World (PCEIoT 2025)

Workshop Organizers

Lelio Campanile	Università degli Studi della Campania Luigi Vanvitelli, Italy
Mauro Iacono	Università degli Studi della Campania Luigi Vanvitelli, Italy
Michele Mastroianni	Università degli Studi di Foggia, Italy

Workshop Program Committee Members

Arcangelo Castiglione	Università degli Studi di Salerno, Italy
Maria Ganzha	Warsaw University of Technology, Poland
Daniel Grzonka	Cracow University of Technology, Poland
Antonio Iannuzzi	Università degli Studi Roma Tre, Italy
Armando Tacchella	Università degli Studi di Genova, Italy
Biagio Boi	University of Salerno, Italy
Marco De Santis	University of Salerno, Italy
Fiammetta Marulli	Università degli Studi della Campania "L. Vanvitelli", Italy
Christian Riccio	Università degli Studi della Campania "L. Vanvitelli", Italy
Luigi Piero Di Bonito	Università degli Studi di Napoli Federico II, Italy

Preserving Our Past: Spatial and Remote Sensing Technologies for Cultural Heritage in a Changing Climate (POP 2025)

Workshop Organizers

Maria Danese	CNR-ISPC, Italy
Nicola Masini	CNR-ISPC, Italy
Rosa Lasaponara	CNR-IMAA, Italy

Workshop Program Committee Members

Maria Danese	CNR-ISPC, Italy
Nicola Masini	CNR-ISPC, Italy
Rosa Lasaponara	CNR-IMAA, Italy
Dario Gioia	CNR-ISPC, Italy
Giuseppe Corrado	Università degli Studi della Basilicata, Italy
Canio Sabia	CNR-ISPC, Italy

Processes, methods and tools towards RESilient cities and cultural and historic sites prone to SOD and ROD disasters (RES 2025)

Workshop Organizers

Elena Cantatore	Polytechnic University of Bari, Italy
Dario Esposito	Polytechnic University of Bari, Italy
Alberico Sonnessa	Polytechnic University of Bari, Italy

Workshop Program Committee Members

Elena Cantatore	Politecnico di Bari, Italy
Dario Esposito	Politecnico di Bari, Italy
Alberico Sonnessa	Politecnico di Bari, Italy
Valeria Belloni	Sapienza University of Rome, Italy
Michela Ravanelli	Sapienza University of Rome, Italy
Silvano Dal Sasso	University of Basilicata, Italy
Francesco Chiaravalloti	CNR - IRPI, Italy
Roberta Ravanelli	University of Liège, Belgium
Alessandra Mascitelli	University of Chieti-Pescara, Italy
Francesco Di Capua	University of Basilicata, Italy
Gabriele Bernardini	Università Politecnica delle Marche, Italy
Vito Domenico Porcari	University of Basilicata, Italy
Carmen Rosa Fattore	University of Basilicata, Italy
Stefania Santoro	Water Research Institute, Italy

Scientific Computing Infrastructure (SCI 2025)

Workshop Organizers

Vladimir Korkhov	Saint Petersburg State University, Russia
Elena Stankova	Saint Petersburg State University, Russia
Nataliia Kulabukhova	Saint Petersburg State University, Russia

Workshop Program Committee Members

Adam Belloum	University of Amsterdam, the Netherlands
Dmitrii Vasiunin	Deutsche Telekom Cloud Services E.P.E., Greece
Serob Balyan	Osensus Arm LLC, Armenia
Suren Abrahamyan	Osensus Arm LLC, Armenia
Ashot Sergey Gevorkyan	NAS of Armenia, Armenia
Michal Hnatic	Univerzita Pavla Jozefa Šafárika v Košiciach, Slovakia
Michail Panteleyev	Saint Petersburg Electrotecnical University, Russia
Martin Vala	Univerzita Pavla Jozefa Šafárika v Košiciach, Slovakia
Nodir Zaynalov	Tashkent University of Information Technologies named after Muhammad al Khwarizmi, Uzbekistan
Michail Panteleyev	Saint Petersburg Electrotecnical University, Russia
Alexander Degtyarev	Saint Petersburg University, Russia
Alexander Bogdanov	St. Petersburg State University, Russia

Ports and Logistics of the Future - Smartness and Sustainability (SmartPorts 2025)

Workshop Organizers

Andrea Gallo	Università degli Studi di Trieste, Italy
Gianfranco Fancello	University of Cagliari, Italy
Giuseppe Borruso	Università degli Studi di Trieste, Italy
Enrico D'agostini	World Maritime University, Sweden
Silvia Battino	Università degli Studi di Sassari, Italy
Veronica Camerada	Università degli Studi di Sassari, Italy

Workshop Program Committee Members

Giuseppe Borruso	University of Trieste, Italy
Beniamino Murgante	University of Basilicata, Italy
Ginevra Balletto	University of Cagliari, Italy
Silvia Battino	University of Sassari, Italy
Mara Ladu	University of Cagliari, Italy
Maria del Mar Munoz Leonisio	University of Cádiz, Spain
Ahinoa Amaro Garcia	University of Las Palmas of Gran Canaria, Spain
Maria Attard	University of Malta, Malta
Enrico D'agostini	World Maritime University, Sweden
Francesca Krasna	University of Trieste, Italy

Tu Anh Trinh	UEH University - Ho Chi Minh City, Vietnam
Giovanni Mauro	Università degli Studi della Campania, Italy
Maria Ronza	University of Naples Federico II, Italy
Massimiliano Bencardino	University of Salerno, Italy
Andrea Gallo	Ca' Foscari University of Venice, Italy
Francesca Sinatra	University of Trieste, Italy
Salvatore Dore	University of Trieste, Italy
Veronica Camerada	University of Sassari, Italy
Brunella Brundu	University of Sassari, Italy
Gianfranco Fancello	University of Cagliari, Italy
Marcello Tadini	University of Eastern Piedmont, Italy
Marco Mazzarino	IUAV University Venice
José Ángel Hernández Luis	University of Las Palmas de Gran Canaria, Spain
Marco Naseddu	University of Cagliari, Italy
Maurizio Cociancich	Adriafer, Italy
Giovanni Longo	University of Trieste, Italy
Luca Toneatti	University of Trieste, Italy
Martina Sinatra	University of Cagliari, Italy
Enrico Vanino	University of Sheffield, UK
Patrizia Serra	University of Cagliari, Italy
Agostino Bruzzone	University of Genoa, Italy
Marco Petrelli	University of Roma 3, Italy

Smart Transport and Logistics - Smart Supply Chains (SmarTransLog 2025)

Workshop Organizers

Francesca Sinatra	University of Trieste, Italy
Maria del Mar Munoz	Universidad de Cádiz, Spain
Brunella Brundu	University of Sassari, Italy
Patrizia Serra	University of Cagliari, Italy
Salvatore Dore	University of Trieste, Italy
Marco Naseddu	University of Cagliari, Italy

Workshop Program Committee Members

Giuseppe Borruso	University of Trieste, Italy
Beniamino Murgante	University of Basilicata, Italy
Ginevra Balletto	University of Cagliari, Italy
Silvia Battino	University of Sassari, Italy
Mara Ladu	University of Cagliari, Italy
Maria del Mar Munoz Leonisio	University of Cádiz, Spain
Ahinoa Amaro Garcia	University of Las Palmas of Gran Canaria, Spain

Maria Attard	University of Malta, Malta
Enrico D'agostini	World Maritime University, Sweden
Francesca Krasna	University of Trieste, Italy
Tu Anh Trinh	UEH University, Vietnam
Giovanni Mauro	Università degli Studi della Campania, Italy
Maria Ronza	University of Naples Federico II, Italy
Massimiliano Bencardino	University of Salerno, Italy
Andrea Gallo	Ca' Foscari University of Venice, Italy
Francesca Sinatra	University of Trieste, Italy
Salvatore Dore	University of Trieste, Italy
Veronica Camerada	University of Sassari, Italy
Brunella Brundu	University of Sassari, Italy
Gianfranco Fancello	University of Cagliari, Italy
Marcello Tadini	University of Eastern Piedmont, Italy
Marco Mazzarino	IUAV University Venice
José Ángel Hernández Luis	University of Las Palmas de Gran Canaria, Spain
Marco Naseddu	University of Cagliari, Italy
Maurizio Cociancich	Adriafer, Italy
Giovanni Longo	University of Trieste, Italy
Luca Toneatti	University of Trieste, Italy
Martina Sinatra	University of Cagliari, Italy
Enrico Vanino	University of Sheffield, UK
Patrizia Serra	University of Cagliari, Italy
Agostino Bruzzone	University of Genoa, Italy
Marco Petrelli	University of Roma 3, Italy

Smart Tourism (SmartTourism 2025)

Workshop Organizers

Silvia Battino	University of Sassari, Italy
Francesca Krasna	University of Trieste, Italy
Ainhoa Amaro	University of Las Palmas de Gran Canaria, Spain
Maria del Mar Munoz	University of Cádiz, Spain
Brisol García García	Polytechnic University of Quintana Roo, Mexico
Marta Meleddu	University of Sassari, Italy

Workshop Program Committee Members

Giuseppe Borruso	University of Trieste, Italy
Beniamino Murgante	University of Basilicata, Italy
Gianfranco Fancello	University of Cagliari, Italy
Mara Ladu	University of Cagliari, Italy

Martina Sinatra	University of Cagliari, Italy
Salvatore Dore	University of Trieste, Italy
Marco Mazzarino	IUAV University Venice, Italy
Veronica Camerada	University of Sassari, Italy
Brunella Brundu	University of Sassari, Italy
Maria Attard	University of Malta, Malta
Ginevra Balletto	University of Cagliari, Italy
Giovanni Mauro	University degli Studi della Campania, Italy
Salvatore Lampreu	University of Sassari, Italy
Maria Ronza	University of Naples, Italy
Massimiliano Bencardino	University of Salerno, Italy

Sustainable evolution of long-Distance frEight and paSsenger Transport (SOLIDEST 2025)

Workshop Organizers

Francesco Russo	University of Reggio Calabria, Italy
Andreas Nikiforiadis	Democritus University of Thrace, Greece
Orlando Marco Belcore	University of Messina, Italy
Antonio Comi	University of Rome Tor Vergata, Italy
Tiziana Campisi	Kore University of Enna, Italy
Aura Rusca	Politehnica University of Bucharest, Romania

Workshop Program Committee Members

Massimo Di Gangi	University of Messina, Italy
Orlando Marco Belcore	University of Messina, Italy
Antonio Polimeni	University of Messina, Italy
Socrates Basbas	Aristotle University of Thessaloniki, Greece
Efstathios Bouhouras	Aristotle University of Thessaloniki, Greece
Marina Zanne	University of Lubljana, Slovenia
Marilisa Nigro	Rome Tre University, Italy
Edoardo Marcucci	Molde University College, Norway
Eugen Rosca	Polytechnic University of Bucharest, Romania
Kh Md Nahiduzzaman	Mohammed VI Polytechnic University, Morocco
Beniamino Murgante	University of Basilicata, Italy
Chiara Garau	University of Cagliari, Italy

Sustainability Performance Assessment: Models, Approaches, and Applications Toward Interdisciplinary and Integrated Solutions (SPA 2025)

Workshop Organizers

Francesco Scorza	University of Basilicata, Italy
Sabrina Lai	University of Cagliari, Italy
Francesco Rotondo	Università Politecnica delle Marche, Italy
Jolanta Dvarioniene	Kaunas University of Technology, Lithuania
Michele Campagna	University of Cagliari, Italy
Corrado Zoppi	University of Cagliari, Italy

Workshop Program Committee Members

Federico Amato	University of Lausanne, Switzerland
Ferdinando Di Carlo	University of Basilicata, Italy
Maddalena Floris	University of Cagliari, Italy
Federica Isola	University of Cagliari, Italy
Giuseppe Las Casas	University of Basilicata, Italy
Federica Leone	University of Cagliari, Italy
Giampiero Lombardini	University of Genoa, Italy
Federico Martellozzo	University of Florence, Italy
Alessandro Marucci	University of L'Aquila, Italy
Ana Clara Moura	Universidade Federal de Minas Gerais, Brazil
Beniamino Murgante	University of Basilicata, Italy
Silviu Nate	Lucian Blaga University of Sibiu, Romania
Anastasia Stratigea	National Technical University of Athens, Greece
Francesco Zullo	University of L'Aquila, Italy
Luigi Santopietro	University of Basilicata, Italy
Benedetto Manganelli	University of Basilicata, Italy

Specifics of Smart Cities Development in Europe (SPEED 2025)

Workshop Organizers

Chiara Garau	University of Cagliari, Italy
Katarína Vitálišová	Matej Bel University, Slovak Republic
Marco Fanfani	University of Florence, Italy
Anna Vaňová	Matej Bel University, Slovak Republic
Kamila Borsekova	Matej Bel University, Slovak Republic
Paola Zamperlin	University of Florence, Italy

Workshop Program Committee Members

Claudia Loggia	University of KwaZulu-Natal, South Africa
Francesca Maltinti	University of Cagliari, Italy
Alessandro Plaisant	University of Sassari, Italy
Alenka Poplin	Iowa State University, USA
Silvia Rossetti	University of Parma, Italy
Gerardo Carpentieri	University of Naples Federico II, Italy
Carmen Guida	University of Naples Federico II, Italy
Floriana Zucaro	University of Naples Federico II, Italy
Anastasia Stratigea	National Technical University of Athens, Greece
Yiota Theodora	National Technical University of Athens, Greece
Giovanna Concu	University of Cagliari, Italy
Paolo Nesi	University of Florence, Italy
Emanuele Bellini	University of Roma Tre, Italy
Mana Dastoum	Polytechnic University of Madrid, Spain
Barbara Caselli	University of Parma, Italy
Martina Carra	University of Brescia, Italy
Alfonso Annunziata	University of Basilicata, Italy
Elisabetta Venco	University of Pavia, Italy
Caterina Pietra	University of Pavia, Italy
Enrico Collini	University of Florence, Italy
Luciano Alessandro Ipsaro Palesi	University of Florence, Italy

Smart, Safe, and Healthy Cities (SSHC 2025)

Workshop Organizers

Chiara Garau	University of Cagliari, Italy
Gerardo Carpentieri	University of Naples Federico II, Italy
Carmen Guida	University of Naples Federico II, Italy
Tanja Congiu	University of Sassari, Italy
Martina Carra	University of Brescia, Italy
Alenka Poplin	Iowa State University, USA

Workshop Program Committee Members

Rosaria Battarra	Istituto di Studi sul Mediterraneo, Italy
Barbara Caselli	University of Parma, Italy
Francesca Maltinti	University of Cagliari, Italy
Romano Fistola	Università degli Studi di Napoli Federico II, Italy
Alessandro Plaisant	University of Sassari, Italy
Silvia Rossetti	University of Parma, Italy
Marco Fanfani	University of Florence, Italy
Reza Askarizad	University of Cagliari, Italy

Floriana Zucaro University of Naples Federico II, Italy
Anastasia Stratigea National Technical University of Athens, Greece
Yiota Theodora National Technical University of Athens, Greece
Giovanna Concu University of Cagliari, Italy
Francesco Zullo University of L'Aquila, Italy
Paola Zamperlin University of Florence, Italy
Vincenza Torrisi University of Catania, Italy
Tiziana Campisi University of Enna Kore, Italy
Katarína Vitálišová Matej Bel University, Slovakia
Tazyeen Alam University of Cagliari, Italy
Mana Dastoum Polytechnic University of Madrid, Spain
Martina Carra University of Brescia, Italy
Alfonso Annunziata University of Basilicata, Italy
Elisabetta Venco University of Pavia, Italy
Caterina Pietra University of Pavia, Italy

Smart and Sustainable Island Communities (SSIC 2025)

Workshop Organizers
Chiara Garau University of Cagliari, Italy
Anastasia Stratigea National Technical University of Athens, Greece
Yiota Theodora National Technical University of Athens, Greece
Giovanna Concu University of Cagliari, Italy

Workshop Program Committee Members
Milena Metalkova-Markova University of Portsmouth, UK
Tarek Teba University of Portsmouth, UK
Alenka Poplin Iowa State University, USA
Gerardo Carpentieri University of Naples Federico II, Italy
Carmen Guida University of Naples Federico II, Italy
Floriana Zucaro University of Naples Federico II, Italy
Silvia Rossetti University of Parma, Italy
Barbara Caselli University of Parma, Italy
Martina Carra University of Brescia, Italy
Alfonso Annunziata University of Basilicata, Italy
Maria Panagiotopoulou National Technical University of Athens, Greece
Apostolos Lagarias University of Thessaly, Greece
Paola Zamperlin University of Florence, Italy
Vincenza Torrisi University of Catania, Italy
Giuseppina Vacca University of Cagliari, Italy
Roberto Minunno Curtin University, Australia
Marco Zucca University of Cagliari, Italy

Elisabetta Venco   University of Pavia, Italy
Caterina Pietra   University of Pavia, Italy
Pietro Crespi   Politecnico di Milano, Italy

From STreet Experiments to Planned Solutions (STEPS 2025)

Workshop Organizers
Silvia Rossetti   Università degli Studi di Parma, Italy
Angela Ricciardello   Kore University of Enna, Italy
Francesco Pinna   Università degli Studi di Cagliari, Italy
Chiara Garau   Università degli Studi di Cagliari, Italy
Tiziana Campisi   Kore University of Enna, Italy
Vincenza Torrisi   University of Catania, Italy

Workshop Program Committee Members
Martina Carra   University of Brescia, Italy
Barbara Caselli   University of Parma, Italy
Tanja Congiu   University of Sassari, Italy
Gabriele D'Orso   University of Palermo, Italy
Matteo Ignaccolo   University of Catania, Italy
Md Kh Nahiduzzaman   Mohammed VI Polytechnic University, Morocco
Muhammad Ahmad Al-Rashid   University of Malaya, Malaysia
Alessandro Plaisant   University of Sassari, Italy
Marianna Ruggieri   University of Enna Kore, Italy
Michele Zazzi   University of Parma, Italy

Sustainable Tourism Evaluations: approaches, methods and indicators (STEva 2025)

Workshop Organizers
Mariolina Grasso   Università Kore di Enna, Italy
Fabrizio Finucci   Roma Tre University, Italy
Daniele Mazzoni   Roma Tre University, Italy
Antonella G. Masanotti   Roma Tre University, Italy
Giovanna Acampa   University of Florence, Italy

Workshop Program Committee Members
Giovanna Acampa   University of Florence, Italy
Fabrizio Finucci   Roma Tre University, Italy
Mariolina Grasso   "Kore" University of Enna, Italy

Alberto Marzo	Ministero della Cultura, Italy
Antonella G. Masanotti	Roma Tre University, Italy
Daniele Mazzoni	Roma Tre University, Italy
Rocco Murro	Sapienza University of Rome, Italy
Claudio Piferi	University of Florence, Italy
Alessio Pino	"Kore" University of Enna, Italy
Nicoletta Setola	University of Florence, Italy
Laura Calcagnini	Roma Tre University, Italy
Antonio Magarò	Roma Tre University, Italy
Janos Ghyerghyak	University of Pécs, Hungary
Ágnes Borsos	University of Pécs, Hungary
Fabrizio Battisti	University of Florence, Italy

Sustainable Development of Ports (SUSTAINABLEPORTS 2025)

Workshop Organizers

Tiziana Campisi	University of Enna KORE, Italy
Giuseppe Musolino	University of Reggio Calabria, Italy
Efstathios Bouhouras	Aristotle University of Thessaloniki, Greece
Elen Twrdy	University of Ljubljana, Slovenia
Elena Cocuzza	University of Catania, Italy
Aura Rusca	Politehnica University of Bucharest, Romania

Workshop Program Committee Members

Massimo Di Gangi	University of Messina, Italy
Orlando Marco Belcore	University of Messina, Italy
Antonio Polimeni	University of Messina, Italy
Claudia Caballini	Polytechnic of Torino, Italy
Gianfranco Fancello	University of Cagliari, Italy
Marina Zanne	University of Lubljana, Slovenia
Stefano Ricci	Sapienza University of Rome, Italy
Beniamino Murgante	University of Basilicata, Italy
Chiara Garau	University of Cagliari, Italy

Theoretical and Computational Chemistry and Its Applications (TCCMA 2025)

Workshop Organizers

Noelia Faginas Lago	Università di Perugia, Italy
Andrea Lombardi	Università di Perugia, Italy
Marcos Mandado Alonso	University of Vigo, Spain

Workshop Program Committee Members

Noelia Faginas-Lago	University of Perugia, Italy
Andrea Lombardi	University of Perugia, Italy
Marcos Mandado	University of Vigo, Spain
Angeles Peña	University of Vigo, Spain
Luca Mancini	Universiy of Perugia, Italy
Massimiliano Bartolomei	CSIC, Spain
Cecilia Coletti	University of Chieti-Pescara, Italy
Iñaki Tuñón	Universidad de Valencia, Spain
Albert Rimola Gilbert	Universitat Autònoma de Barcelona, Spain
Stefano Falcinelli	University of Perugia, Italy
Dario Campisi	University of Perugia, Italy
Ernesto García Para	University of the Basque Country, Spain
Giacomo Giorgi	University of Perugia, Italy
Tomás González Lezana	IFF CSIC, Spain
Enrique M. Cabaleiro Lago	Universidade de Santiago de Compostela, Spain
Aurora Costales	Universidad de Oviedo, Spain
Angel Martin	Universidad de Oviedo, Spain
Jose Manuel	University of Vigo, Spain
Annarita Laricchiuta	CNR ISTP Bari, Italy
Fernando Pirani	University of Perugia, Italy

Transport Infrastructures for Smart Cities (TISC 2025)

Workshop Organizers

Francesca Maltinti	University of Cagliari, Italy
Mauro Coni	University of Cagliari, Italy
Benedetto Barabino	University of Brescia, Italy
Nicoletta Rassu	University of Cagliari, Italy
James Rombi	University of Cagliari, Italy

Workshop Program Committee Members

Francesco Pinna	University of Cagliari, Italy
Chiara Garau	University of Cagliari, Italy
Mauro D'Apuzzo	University of Cassino, Italy
Roberto Minunno	Curtin University, Australia
Tiziana Campisi	University of Enna Kore, Italy
Roberto Ventura	University of Brescia, Italy
Alessandro Plaisant	University of Sassari, Italy
Massimo Di Francesco	University of Cagliari, Italy

Vincenza Torrisi University of Catania, Italy
Paola Zamperlin University of Florence, Italy

Transforming Urban Analytics: The Impact of Crowdsourced Mapping and Advanced AI Techniques on Future Cities (Tr-UrbAna 2025)

Workshop Organizers
Ayse Giz Gulnerman Gengec Ankara Hacı Bayram Veli University, Turkey
Müslüm Hacar Tildiz Technical University, Turkey
Himmet Karaman Istanbul Technical University, Turkey

Workshop Program Committee Members
Beniamino Murgante University of Basilicata, Italy
Abdulkadir Memduhoğlu Harran University, Turkey
Zeynel Abidin Polat İzmir Katip Çelebi University, Turkey
Güzide Miray Perihanoğlu Van Yüzüncü Yıl University, Turkey
Tugba Memisoglu Baykal Ankara Hacı Bayram Veli University, Turkey

From structural to TRAnsformative-change of City Environment: challenges and solutions and perspectives (TRACE 2025)

Workshop Organizers
Pierluigi Morano Polytechnic University of Bari, Italy
Maria Rosaria Guarini Sapienza University of Rome, Italy
Francesco Sica Sapienza University of Rome, Italy
Francesco Tajani Sapienza University of Rome, Italy
Marco Locurcio Polytechnic University of Bari, Italy
Debora Anelli Polytechnic University of Bari, Italy

Workshop Program Committee Members
Felicia di Liddo Politecnico di Bari, Italia
Valeria Saiu Università di Cagliari, Italia
Emma Sabatelli Sapienza Università di Roma, Italia
Antonella Roma Sapienza Università di Roma, Italia
Giuseppe Cerullo Sapienza Università di Roma, Italia
Lucia della Spina Università di Reggio Calabria, Italia
Alejandro Segura de la Cal Politecnico di Madrid, Spain
Yilsy Nuñez Politecnico di Madrid, Spain
Gabriella Maselli Università di Salerno, Italy
Maria Rosa Trovato Università di Catania, Italy

Manuela Rebaudengo	Politecnico di Torino, Italy
Pierfrancesco De Paola	Università di Napoli Federico II, Italy
Daniela Tavano	Università della Calabria, Italy
Maria Saez	University of Granada, Spain
Paola Amoruso	LUM "Giuseppe Degennaro" University, Italy

Temporary Real Estate management: Approaches and methods for Time-integrated impact assessments and evaluations (TREAT 2025)

Workshop Organizers

Chiara Mazzarella	TUDelft, The Netherlands
Hilde Remoy	TUDelft, The Netherlands
Maria Cerreta	University of Naples Federico II, Italy

Workshop Program Committee Members

Chiara Mazzarella	TU Delft, The Netherlands
Hilde Remoy	TU Delft, The Netherlands
Maria Cerreta	University of Naples Federico II, Italy
Maria Somma	University of Naples Federico II, Italy
Simona Panaro	University of Campania Luigi Vanvitelli, Italy
Laura Di Tommaso	University of Naples Federico II, Italy
Caterina Loffredo	University of Naples Federico II, Italy
Ludovica La Rocca	University of Naples Federico II, Italy
Sabrina Sacco	Politecnico di Milano, Italy
Piero Zizzania	University of Naples Federico II, Italy
Gaia Daldanise	CNR IRISS, Italy
Benedetta Grieco	University of Naples Federico II, Italy
Giuseppe Ciciriello	University of Naples Federico II, Italy
Marta Dell'Ovo	Politecnico di Milano, Italy
Daniele Cannatella	TU Delft, The Netherlands
Eugenio Muccio	University of Naples Federico II, Italy
Sveva Ventre	University of Naples Federico II, Italy

Supporting the Transition to Ecological Economy in Cities Regeneration: Circular Model Tools for Reusing Architecture and Infrastructures (TReE 2025)

Workshop Organizers

Mariarosaria Angrisano	Pegaso University, Italy
Giulio Cavana	Politecnico di Torino, Italy
Francesca Buglione	CNR-ISPC, Italy

Antonia Gravagnuolo   CNR-ISPC, Italy
Piera Della Morte   Pegaso University, Italy

Workshop Program Committee Members
Giulia Datola   Politecnico di Milano, Italy
Vanessa Assumma   University of Bologna, Italy
Marco Volpatti   Politecnico di Torino, Italy
Sebastiano Barbieri   Politecnico di Torino, Italy
Caterina Caprioli   Politecnico di Torino, Italy
Marta Dell'Ovo   Politecnico di Milano, Italy
Federico Dell'Anna   Politecnico di Torino, Italy
Elena Todella   Politecnico di Torino, Italy
Danny Casprini   Politecnico di Milano, Italy
Grazia Neglia   Università Telematica Pegaso, Italy
Francesca Nocca   Università degli Studi di Napoli Federico II, Italy
Giulio Cavana   Politecnico di Torino, Italy
Francesca Buglione   CNR-IPSC, Italy
Marco Rossitti   Politecnico di Milano, Italy
Jhon Escorcia   Politecnico di Torino, Italy
Beatrice Mecca   Politecnico di Torino, Italy
Sara Biancifiori   Politecnico di Torino, Italy

Urban Digital Twins and Data Spaces: Shaping the Future of Sustainable Cities (TwinAbleCities 2025)

Workshop Organizers
Dessislava Petrova Antonova   Sofia University, GATE Institute, Bulgaria
Beniamino Murgante   University of Basilicata, Italy
Senthil Rajendran   RMSI, Bahrain
Tiziana Campisi   Kore University of Enna, Italy
Mila Koeva   University of Twente, The Netherlands

Workshop Program Committee Members
Dessislava Petrova-Antonova   Sofia University, Bulgaria
Mila Koeva   The University of Twente, The Netherlands
Beniamino Murgante   University of Basilicata, Italy
Senthil Rajendran   RMSI, Bahrain
Tiziana Campisi   Kore University of Enna, Italy

Urban Regeneration: Innovative Tools and Evaluation Model (URITEM 2025)

Workshop Organizers

Fabrizio Battisti	University of Florence, Italy
Giovanna Acampa	University of Florence, Italy
Orazio Campo	Sapienza University of Rome, Italy
Melania Perdonò	University of Florence, Italy

Workshop Program Committee Members

Fabrizio Battisti	University of Florence, Italy
Giovanna Acampa	University of Florence, Italy
Orazio Campo	University of Rome "La Sapienza", Italy
Melania Perdonò	Università degli Studi di Firenze, Italy

Urban Space Accessibility and Mobilities (USAM 2025)

Workshop Organizers

Chiara Garau	DICAAR, University of Cagliari, Italy
Alessandro Plaisant	University of Sassari, Italy
Barbara Caselli	University of Parma, Italy
Mauro D'Apuzzo	University of Cassino and Southern Lazio, Italy
Gabriele D'Orso	University of Palermo, Italy
Matteo Ignaccolo	University of Catania, Italy

Workshop Program Committee Members

Mauro Coni	University of Cagliari, Italy
Martina Carra	University of Brescia, Italy
Tiziana Campisi	University of Enna Kore, Italy
Tanja Congiu	University of Sassari, Italy
Francesca Maltinti	University of Cagliari, Italy
Silvia Rossetti	University of Parma, Italy
Barbara Caselli	University of Parma, Italy
Angela Pilogallo	University of L'Aquila, Italy
Lorena Fiorini	University of L'Aquila, Italy
Reza Askarizad	University of Cagliari, Italy
Francesco Pinna	University of Cagliari, Italy
Aime Tsinda	University of Rwanda, Rwanda
Youssef El Ganadi	International University of Rabat, Morocco
Marco Migliore	University of Palermo, Italy
Alessio Salvatore	Italian National Research Council, Italy
Giuseppe Stecca	Italian National Research Council, Italy

Paola Zamperlin	University of Florence, Italy
Vincenza Torrisi	University of Catania, Italy
Gerardo Carpentieri	University of Naples Federico II, Italy
Carmen Guida	University of Naples Federico II, Italy
Floriana Zucaro	University of Naples Federico II, Italy
Alfonso Annunziata	University of Basilicata, Italy
Elisabetta Venco	University of Pavia, Italy
Caterina Pietra	University of Pavia, Italy
Tazyeen Alam	University of Cagliari, Italy
Valerio Cutini	University of Pisa, Italy

UX Mobility 2025: Placing User Experience at the Center of Urban Mobility: Methods and Frameworks (UXM 2025)

Workshop Organizers

Carmen Guida	Università degli Studi di Napoli Federico II, Italy
Gerardo Carpentieri	Università degli Studi di Napoli Federico II, Italy
Federico Messa	Systematica srl, Italy
Lamia Abdelfattah	Systematica srl, Italy

Workshop Program Committee Members

Rosaria Battarra	Istituto di Studi sul Mediterraneo CNR, Italy
Romano Fistola	Università degli Studi di Napoli Federico II, Italy
Lucia Saganeiti	IMAA-CNR, Italy

Virtual Reality and Augmented reality and applications (VRA 2025)

Workshop Organizers

Damiano Perri	University of Perugia, Italy
Osvaldo Gervasi	University of Perugia, Italy
Chau Ma Thi	University of Engineering and Technology, Vietnam National University, Hanoi, Vietnam
Paolo Nesi	University of Florence, Italy
Pierfrancesco Bellini	University of Florence, Italy

Workshop Program Committee Members

David Berti	ART SpA, Italy
JungYoon Kim	Gachon University, South Korea

TaiHoon Kim	Zhejiang University of Science and Technology, China
Marcelo de Paiva Guimares	Federal University of São Paulo, Brazil
Sergio Tasso	University of Perugia, Italy

Workshop on Advanced and Computational Methods for Earth Science Applications (WACM4ES 2025)

Workshop Organizers

Luca Piroddi	University of Cagliari, Italy
Patrizia Capizzi	University of Palermo, Italy
Marilena Cozzolino	University of Molise, Italy
Sebastiano D'Amico	University of Malta, Malta
Chiara Garau	University of Cagliari, Italy
Giuseppina Vacca	University of Cagliari, Italy

Workshop Program Committee Members

Andrea Angelini	CNR ISPC, Italy
Ilaria Barone	Università degli Studi di Padova, Italy
Patrizia Capizzi	University of Palermo, Italy
Luigi Capozzoli	CNR, Italy
Alberto Carletti	University of Cagliari, Italy
Emanuele Colica	University of Malta, Malta
Marilena Cozzolino	Università del Molise, Italy
Sebastiano D'Amico	University of Malta, Malta
Chiara Garau	University of Cagliari, Italy
Luciano Galone	University of Malta, Malta
Peter Iregbeyen	University of Malta, Malta
Mariano Lisi	Basilicata Aerospace Cluster CLAS, Italy
Raffaele Martorana	Università di Palermo, Italy
Paolo Mauriello	Università del Molise, Italy
Veronica Pazzi	University of Florence, Italy
Raffaele Persico	Università della Calabria, Italy
Luca Piroddi	University of Cagliari, Italy
Sina Saneiyan	Binghamton University, USA
Mercedes Solla	Universidade de Vigo, Spain
Deodato Tapete	ASI, Italy
Giuseppina Vacca	University of Cagliari, Italy
Enrica Vecchi	University of Cagliari, Italy

Sponsoring Organizations

ICCSA 2025 would not have been possible without the tremendous support of many organizations and institutions, for which all organizers and participants of ICCSA 2025 express their sincere gratitude:

Galatasaray University, Istanbul, Türkiye
(https://gsu.edu.tr/en)

African Mathematical Union
(https://www.africanmathunion.org/)

Springer Nature Switzerland AG, Switzerland
(https://www.springer.com)

The University of Massachusetts, USA
(https://www.umass.edu/)

University of Perugia, Italy
(https://www.unipg.it)

University of Basilicata, Italy
(http://www.unibas.it)

Monash University, Australia
(https://www.monash.edu/)

Kyushu Sangyo University, Japan
(https://www.kyusan-u.ac.jp/)

Organization

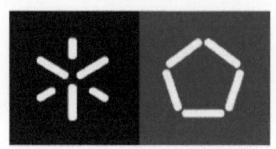

Universidade do Minho
Escola de Engenharia

University of Minho, Portugal
(https://www.uminho.pt/)
Venue
ICCSA 2025 took place in: **Galatasaray University, Istanbul, Türkiye**

Additional Reviewers

Reviewers
The review tasks for each workshop have been carried out by the workshop Organizers and the members of the workshop Program Committee.

Plenary Lectures

Sky Safe with GAI and Post-quantum Computing

Elizabeth Chang

Professor of Cyber Security and Head of Discipline, University of the Sunshine Coast, Australia

Abstract. Professor Chang's talk in this presentation has two distinct parts. To start, she will introduce the landscape of cybersecurity development, attacks, threats, and vulnerabilities, as well as state-of-the-art cyber protection, cyber defence, and cyber incident prevention. This is followed by a discussion of the impact of Generative AI (GAI) and quantum-safe cryptographic computing, highlighting the major issues and challenges in research, education, and training. In conclusion, she will present a vision for Sky Safe solutions, aiming to achieve cyber resilience that supports business and economic stability, enhances human capabilities, and promotes environmental sustainability.

Disaster Preparedness and Risk Profiling in the Digital Era from Earth Observation Lens

Jagannath Aryal

Department of Infrastructure Engineering, University of Melbourne, Australia

Abstract. Natural hazards which turn into disasters result in severe losses of lives, infrastructure, and property. Disasters such as earthquakes and landslides and their impacts on transportation safety, infrastructure resilience, and displacement of people to new places are challenges. To address such challenges, earth observation data and intelligent methods can provide potential solutions in developing decision support systems. This talk will present the state of the art in Earth observation for disaster resilience using intelligent methods. In the Earth observation space, digitalisation has revolutionised the way we map, monitor, and develop decision support systems. Global case study examples covering earthquake-induced landslides from the Himalayan region will cover the digital capabilities. The digital capabilities will embrace object recognition, interpretation, and their accurate and precise capture to integrate into digital models. The developed digital models from representative case studies can be leveraged in other jurisdictions in profiling risks to protect lives and infrastructure and creating disaster preparedness in the era of digital age and digital economy.

Intelligent Image Enhancement for Real-World Applications in Adverse Atmospheric Conditions

Khan Muhammad

Department of Global Convergence, Sungkyunkwan University, South Korea

Abstract. The adverse impacts of atmospheric conditions such as haze, fog, and low-light environments pose significant challenges for real-world applications reliant on computer vision, including autonomous driving, surveillance, and remote sensing. This keynote explores cutting-edge advancements in intelligent image enhancement, drawing insights from two pivotal studies. The first introduces HazeSpace2M, a comprehensive dataset and novel classification-guided dehazing framework that improves image clarity across diverse atmospheric conditions, addressing the gap between synthetic and real-world dehazing performance. The second focuses on LoLI-Street, a benchmark for low-light image enhancement tailored to urban environments, extending beyond enhancement to enable robust object detection and scene understanding. Taken together, these contributions demonstrate how integrating domain-specific datasets, advanced algorithms, and performance benchmarks can significantly elevate the reliability of computer vision systems under challenging weather and lighting conditions. Attendees will gain valuable insights into the methodologies, datasets, and practical applications driving innovation in this field, with implications for research and industry alike.

In Memory of Carmelo Torre

Unfortunately, Professor Carmelo Torre, one of the cornerstones of the ICCSA Conference, passed away last December, leaving everyone stunned and deeply saddened. His loss has created a profound void within our academic community. Carmelo was not only a respected scholar and dedicated contributor to the success and growth of ICCSA, but also a generous colleague, mentor, and friend to many. His intellectual rigor, warm personality, and unwavering commitment to advancing research will be remembered with great admiration. As we continue the work he helped shape, we honor his legacy and the indelible mark he left on all of us. Carmelo Torre graduated in engineering at the Polytechnic of Bari with a thesis on urban planning under Dino Borri's guidance. He began his research career by collaborating with Franco Selicato. During his PhD at the University of Naples Federico II under Luigi Fusco Girard, he specialized in real estate market analysis and multi-criteria evaluation methods. He explored the social impacts of urban transformations with his lifelong friend Maria Cerreta. His first ICCSA participation was in Perugia in 2008, in the session Geographical Analysis, Urban Modeling, Spatial Statistics. Instantly captivated by the conference, his charisma enabled him to involve various Italian scientific communities, including those in real estate and statistics. ICCSA became a yearly commitment for him, where he valued the high editorial quality of the proceedings and the dynamic post-presentation discussions and debates he passionately and expertly enriched. In 2012, alongside Maria Cerreta and Paola Perchinunno, he organized the workshop Econometrics and Multidimensional Evaluation in the Urban Environment (EMEUE), fostering dialogue on critical topics. His influence steadily grew, drawing numerous research groups to ICCSA and establishing real estate and assessment as one of the conference's leading fields. A pillar of ICCSA, he was involved across all facets of the event. Torre's contributions to academic discourse were marked by intellectual rigor and innovative thinking. His conference interventions consistently challenged conventional wisdom, offering insights transcending disciplinary boundaries. Beyond the conference, he passionately advocated for equity and social justice. His left-leaning ideology, though firm, earned respect from those with differing views, thanks to his sincerity and loyalty. He was creative, generous, and always willing to help, even at a personal cost. Despite battling illness, he maintained his characteristic optimism, warmth, cheerfulness, and commitment, supported by his partner, Caterina Rinaldo. His legacy lives on in his ideas, dedication, and unmatched generosity.

Contents – Part XIII

Urban Space Accessibility and Mobilities (USAM 2025)

Pedestrian Crash Severity Prediction and Contributory Factors Analysis by Using Machine Learning Methods 3
   Giuseppe Cappelli, Sofia Nardoianni, Mauro D'Apuzzo, and Vittorio Nicolosi

A Brief Overview of Pedestrian Accident Modelling 15
   Giuseppe Cappelli, Sofia Nardoianni, Mauro D'Apuzzo, and Vittorio Nicolosi

A New Methodology for Using Hybrid Configurational Tools for Local Analysis of Pedestrian Flows in Large Areas 32
   Sofia Nardoianni, Giuseppe Cappelli, Mauro D'Apuzzo, Martina Furioso, and Vittorio Nicolosi

Managing Sustainable Tourist Flows and Heritage Preservation in the Medina of Sousse: A Space Syntax and GIS-Based Approach 49
   Khelil Cherfi Khadidja, Merzelkad Rym, Benacer Hamza, Boudjema Sara, Mara Federico, and Esposito Dario

The Role of Environmental Awareness in Transport Mobility Behaviour: Evidence from Survey-Based Approach in Catania (Italy) 67
   Vincenza Torrisi, Luisa Sturiale, Matteo Ignaccolo, Giuseppe Inturri, Marco Migliore, and Gabriele D'Orso

Mapping Risk Factors to Build Inclusive Roads: A Systematic Diagnosis for Enhancing Vulnerable Users and Persons with Reduced Mobility Safety 87
   Davide Maestroni, Giuseppe Cappelli, Valerio Gagliardi, Sofia Nardoianni, Pooyan Hejazi Mahabadi, Trigaluh Prastyana Tika, Neritan Caushaj, Francesco Bella, Mauro D'Apuzzo, and Francesco Edoardo Misso

Functional Organisational Strategies and Practices in Sparsely Populated Areas (SPA). A Place-Based Proximity-Oriented Approach 105
   Alessandro Plaisant, Chiara Garau, and Tanja Congiu

Beyond Traffic Congestion: Developing Digital Twin to Enhance
Accessibility to Points of Interest 123
*Torrisi Vincenza, Pierfrancesco Leonardi, Matteo Ignaccolo,
and Sheila Bellia*

Smart and Happy Cities: Towards a Definition and a Methodology
for Evaluating the Emotional Perception of Happiness 141
Chiara Pinna, Alessia Torlini, Alenka Poplin, and Chiara Garau

GIS-Based Accessibility and Safety Assessment in Small Historic
Centres in Inner Areas. Pilot Application in Stigliano and Interoperability
with a Digital Twin 160
Barbara Caselli, Altea Panebianco, Silvia La Placa, and Rossella Laera

UX Mobility 2025: Placing User Experience at the Center of Urban Mobility: Methods and Frameworks (UXM 2025)

WizRD: A Personalized Wayfinding Platform for Enhanced Urban
Navigation 181
Jacopo Maltagliati, Alberto Leporati, and Daniela Micucci

Development of a Walkability Index in Support of Urban Planning
Decision-Making 197
Gerardo Carpentieri, Carmen Guida, and Andrés David Maglione

Virtual Reality and Augmented reality and applications (VRA 2025)

Real-Time Rigging and Secondary Motion for Sketch-Based 3D Characters 213
Chau Thi Ma and Tam Minh Le

Digital Heritage to Improve Accessibility and Break Down Architectural
Barriers 229
*Damiano Perri, Sara Martinelli, Osvaldo Gervasi, David Berti,
and Gilberto Zinourov Roncalli di Montorio*

Hierarchical Sort-Based Parallel Interest-Matching Algorithm
for Distributed Simulations 242
Ma Thị Châu and Lê Thái Thịnh

Fast Agent-Based Solution to Evaluate the Matching of Public Transport
Offer vs Citizen Mobility Demand 255
*Marco Fanfani, Alberto Giovannoni, Luciano Alessandro Ipsaro Palesi,
Ammarah Irum, and Paolo Nesi*

A Strategy Utilizing an LLM and Augmented Reality for Handling
the Missing Data: A Case Study Using Unity, Vuforia and ChatGPT 273
  *Enio Vicente de Limas, Rita de Fátima Rodrigues Guimarães,
  Bianchi Serique Meiguins, Leonardo Chaves Dutra da Rocha,
  Diego Roberto Colombo Dias, and Marcelo de Paiva Guimarães*

Workshop on Advanced and Computational Methods for Earth Science Applications (WACM4ES 2025)

A Bridge Between Soil Science and Photonics: A Novel Framework
for Urban Green Space Assessment 291
  *Francesca Sanfilippo, Lorenza Tuccio, Lucia Cavigli, Francesca Rossi,
  Giorgio Querzoli, Ivan Blecic, Andrea Vacca, and Paolo Matteini*

A Multiparametric Investigation of an Earthquake by a Jupyter Notebook:
The Case Study of the Amatrice-Norcia Italian Seismic Sequence
2016-2017 309
  *Dedalo Marchetti, Daniele Bailo, Jan Michalek, Rossana Paciello,
  Giuseppe Falcone, and Alessandro Piscini*

Mapping of the Multi-risk Analysis for the Cultural Heritage of Sardinia
from the Pre-Nuragic and Nuragic Periods: Initial Results of the RETURN
Project 327
  *Enrica Vecchi, Marco Cigagna, Donatella Rita Fiorino,
  Battista Grosso, Elisa Pilia, Francesco Pinna, and Giuseppina Vacca*

PHD Showcase Papers

Effects of Different Attention Mechanisms Applied on 3D Models
in Video Classification 347
  Mohammad Rasras, Iuliana Marin, Șerban Radu, and Irina Mocanu

The Real-Time IoT Data Security 364
  Evelyne Hakizimana and Gennady Dik

Short Papers

Machine Learning Models for Intelligent Test Case Selection 377
  Yousof Darwish, Mohammed Al-Refai, and Ahmed Alzubi

Continuous Sky View Factor Calculations Using a Parallel GPU Workflow ... 388
  Max van der Waal and Daniela Maiullari

Building the Transition to Clean Energy in Small and Rural Communities:
Lessons from the LIFE LOCAL GoGREEN Project 399
    Luigi Santopietro, Monica Salvia, Filomena Pietrapertosa,
    Benjamin Hueber, Michael Strobel, Uli Jakob, Cveta Dimitrova,
    and Roman Kekec

Air Quality and Climate Planning: Paving the Way for Better Integration 408
    Angela Pilogallo, Luigi Santopietro, Filomena Pietrapertosa,
    and Monica Salvia

Ensemble Machine Learning Model to Analyse the Correlation Between
Environmental Features and Respiratory Admissions in the Emergency
Room 417
    Vito Telesca and Maríca Rondinone

Author Index 431

Urban Space Accessibility and Mobilities (USAM 2025)

Pedestrian Crash Severity Prediction and Contributory Factors Analysis by Using Machine Learning Methods

Giuseppe Cappelli[1,2](✉) ⓘ, Sofia Nardoianni[1] ⓘ, Mauro D'Apuzzo[1] ⓘ, and Vittorio Nicolosi[2] ⓘ

[1] University of Cassino and Southern Lazio, Via G. Di Biasio 43, 03043 Cassino, Italy
{giuseppe.cappelli1,sofia.nardoianni,dapuzzo}@unicas.it,
cppgpp01@uniroma2.it
[2] University of Rome "Tor Vergata", Via del Politecnico, 1, 00133 Rome, Italy
nicolosi@uniroma2.it

Abstract. Pedestrians occupy a leading position among the most vulnerable road users. Each year about 270,000 pedestrians die due to road accidents, so this study aims to highlight the most influencing contributory factors and the most promising models to predict pedestrian crash severity. ISTAT data for the City of Rome (2013–2020) are used and different Machine Learning Methods are trained and tested, after balancing the data with oversampling techniques. In addition, analysis of the most influencing contributory factor is carried out, by using the ROC curve method, Variable Importance Analysis (VIP), and Support Vector Machine with a Linear Kernel. The findings suggest that the model with the best prediction performance is the Random Forest, followed by the Decision Tree and k-nearest neighbour algorithm. Regarding the analysis of contributory factors, the methods implemented highlight that the hour in which the accident occurs, pedestrian gender, and age seem to be the most critical factors that increase the severity of a pedestrian crash. There are also some limitations in this study: the first is connected to the black-box nature of these models; the second regards how these variables could influence positively or negatively the outcome.

Keywords: Sustainable Mobility · Road Safety · Pedestrian accidents · pedestrian safety · Random Forest · Support Vector Machines (SVM) · Machine Learning

1 Introduction

Road accidents are among the top ten causes of death worldwide, ranking seventh overall. On the other hand, they occupy the first place as regards deaths between the ages of 15 and 29 [1]. More than 1.2 million people in a single year lose their lives and most of them incur not-fatal injuries that lead often to injury [2].

Although the damages to the human body are unfortunately well known, thanks also to the current scientific literature review [3–7], accidents may cause a large economic toll [8], and knowing and understanding this macroeconomic burden could give a strong direction in an effective policy-making decision process.

Among the most vulnerable road users, pedestrians occupy a leading position. Pedestrian accidents are a serious public health issue that can cause injuries, disabilities, and even death. According to the World Health Organization, more than 1.3 million people die each year as a result of road traffic crashes, and about 20% (270,000) of them are pedestrians [9, 10].

Pedestrian accidents can be caused by various factors, such as human error, vehicle design, road environment, weather conditions, and enforcement of traffic rules. Some of the common causes of pedestrian accidents are speeding, lack of visibility, alcohol, distractions, and road design.

Higher vehicle speeds increase both the likelihood of a pedestrian being struck by a car and the injury severity [11]. Most pedestrian deaths (60% in 2020) occur on high-capacity urban roads that typically have posted speed limits of 45–55 miles per hour [12].

Poor lighting, especially at night or in bad weather, can make it difficult for pedestrians to see approaching vehicles or hazards. Some authors suggest that pedestrians should wear reflective clothing or use flashlights when walking in low-light conditions [13].

Driving under the influence of alcohol or other psychoactive substances impairs a driver's ability to react to changing situations and increases the risk of crashing into pedestrians. Alcohol is involved in about 30% of all road traffic fatalities worldwide [13].

Using a mobile phone or other devices while walking can divert a pedestrian's attention from the road and increase the chance of collision, so the authors suggest that pedestrians should avoid using their phones or other devices while walking and keep them out of sight [14].

Streets designed to be narrower and for slower speeds experience the lowest rates of vehicle-pedestrian crashes, and those with wide lanes and higher operating speeds experience the highest rates [15]. Effective countermeasures include sidewalks, pedestrian-only signal phasing, and optimal roadway lighting [16].

According to the literature [9, 17], changes to the road environment and legislation and a higher focus on education effectively reduce pedestrian accidents.

In this paper, several Machine Learning Methods are used to classify pedestrian accidents. The dependent variable is the outcome of the crash and so the severity, i.e., if the road accident led to an injury or death. The study aims also to discover the role of the main variables in pedestrian accidents, by using Machine Learning Methods.

2 Crash Data

To choose the most adequate dataset, it was necessary to review a series of data collections over several years, focusing more attention on accidents involving vulnerable users (namely, cyclists and pedestrians). The area in which this analysis is performed is the City of Rome. The main data that could be used are those provided by ISTAT (National Institute of Statistics) [18] and by the City of Rome through "Rome mobility" which, despite being similar in content, have some differences [19]. Finally, the ISTAT dataset was chosen because it covers more years than the other one.

ISTAT is a public body that carries out numerous researches, surveys, and censuses in Italy, providing essential information for statistical research and for numerous fields of study. ISTAT records, using checks and police reports, incidents in which at least one person involved is injured or dead, with a maximum viewing time of 30 days, further classifying the dead as deceased within 24 h or 30 days.

At the national level, the data are recorded thanks to the collaboration of the police in charge of intervening at the site of the accident. ISTAT sets the annual dataset by recording some key features:

- Date
- Time
- Accident Location
- Road type
- Road surface
- Signposting information
- Weather conditions
- Nature of the accident
- Type of vehicles involved
- Consequences of the accident
- Personal data of drivers, passengers and pedestrians
- Circumstances of the accident

3 Method

Machine Learning (ML) is an Artificial Intelligence (AI) branch. It is renewed as an important tool to analyse large amounts of data and use models to forecast the dependent variable, in the context of regression or classification tasks [20]. With Machine Learning it is possible to develop algorithms that can analyse the data provided and their properties and characteristics. Another important feature of such types of models is that they can learn and become more and more stable and reliable by putting inside more and more data [20, 21].

In Fig. 1, the flow chart of the common methodology that is used with Machine Learning Methods is here proposed. The first step is the data collection, that is needed to train and test the several models. Different data sources could be used and this depends on the type of field or task that needs to be undertaken. After this collection phase, datasets were cleaned, pre-processed, and transformed or standardized properly to complete the classification task. Then, several models proposed according to the most used models in the scientific literature are trained on the training set (usually 70% of data in the data set are used) and finally, the performance metrics for each model are evaluated on the test set. The best model is selected according to the best prediction performances. The reason why focusing on Machine Learning Methods is that they show better performances according to the current literature review.

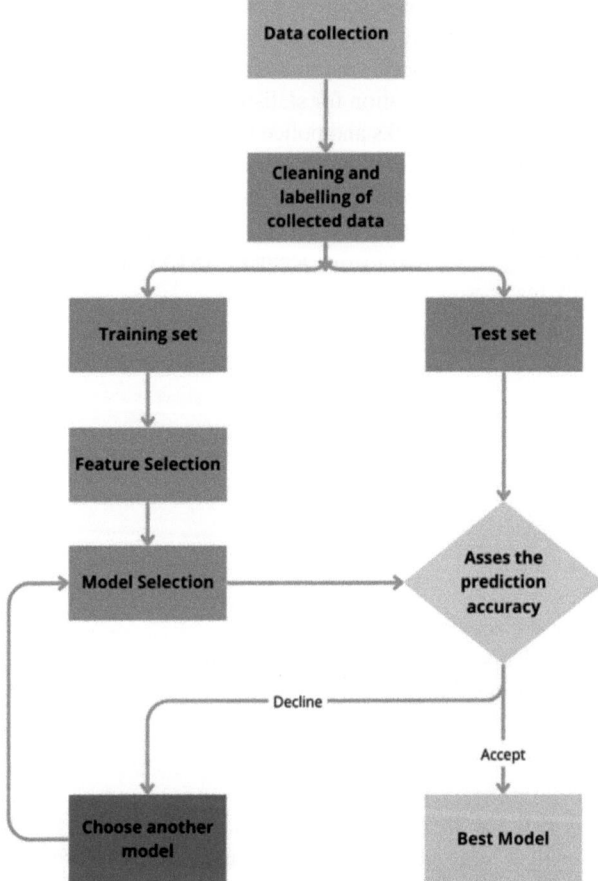

Fig. 1. Flow chart of a common Machine Learning Process

3.1 Linear Discriminant Analysis (LDA) and Quadratic Discriminant Analysis (QDA)

Linear Discriminant Analysis (LDA) and Quadratic Discriminant Analysis (QDA) are two common classifiers, among the Discriminant Analysis (DA) methods [22]. As the names suggest, the decision boundary in LDA is a linear plan [23], while in QDA is a non-linear one. The models aim to find the best hyperplane that maximizes the distance between the several observations. The two methods are often used as a classifier but sometimes also as a feature selection method [24].

3.2 K-Nearest Neighbour (KNN)

K-Nearest Neighbour (KNN) is a classifier first introduced by Fix and Hodges [25]. The method is based on the assumption that similar and related features create a different cluster in the whole space of features [26]. That means that an object in this space is classified under a class or another based on the characteristics of the nearest neighbours. The number of neighbour is represented by the parameter k: if the magnitude of k increases, the complexity of the model increases, while the errors could decrease. For this reason, the number of neighbours is always an even number, to avoid uncertainties in the classification.

3.3 Decision Tree (DT) and Random Forest (RF)

Decision Tree (DT) and Random Forest (RF) are two Machine Learning methods used for both classification and regression. A DT works by creating some partition within the original data in sub-groups [27]. These regions are also called leaves that are connected with branches to internal nodes that define a hierarchical structure. The structure of a tree is made hierarchically, by splitting the feature space according to some measure of homogeneity [28]. To avoid a high number of splits, the tree is pruned. Decision Tree Models are characterized by high variance and to avoid this problem some other algorithms, such as Random Forest, are introduced. The main idea behind RF is to collect information from several Decision Trees and then combine them to improve prediction accuracy [29–31].

3.4 Support Vector Machine (SVM)

The development of Support Vector Machines (SVM) dates back to the 1990s. SVM aims to find a hyperplane that separates observations to make classifications [32]. To find the best hyperplane, it is possible to maximize the margin (the distance between the plane and the closest observation). An important parameter used for the optimization phase is the tuning parameter cost (c): when the value of this parameter is higher, the wider the margin and the more stable will be the hyperplane [33]. The feature space could be also enlarged and so transformed into a higher-dimensional feature space with a kernel function, to handle the non-linear relationship between dependent and independent variables. In this new transformation of the space, the decision boundary is a linear function, but in the original feature space could be, for instance, a radial or a polynomial boundary [26].

3.5 Variable Importance Analysis (VIP)

To complete an analysis of the most influencing factor, a Variable Importance Analysis (VIP) could be implemented. VIP is a built-in algorithm in the Random Forest method: the importance of a variable is evaluated as a mean decrease in accuracy by using out-of-bag observations (OOB) ($L_{b,oob}$), because the tree grows from a bootstrapped sample (L_b) from the original training sample (L) [34].

Another method to select classifiers is the Receiver Operating Characteristic Curve (ROC) graph tool [35, 36], usually used instead of an accuracy performance measure that in some cases could not be an adequate metric [37, 38].

4 Results

In this section, the main results of the analysis carried out are shown. First, comparisons between the Machine Learning Algorithms are proposed, by evaluating the F1 score of the different models. The F1 score is a common metric that is often used for these purposes [21]. In addition to that, an analysis of contributory factors is performed to cover the gap between the lack of interpretability that is often attributed to Machine Learning Methods.

4.1 Model Performances

F measures, such as the F1-score, represent a common way to assess Machine Learning Method performances. These metrics give information on how the model is reliable and accurate. To define these metrics, it is essential to introduce the confusion matrix concept. A confusion matrix is a sort of way to visualize the results of classification methods and how many observations have been classified in the correct or wrong way by the Machine Learning Algorithm. In the confusion matrix, the number of True Positive (TP), False Positive (FP), False Negative (FN), and True Negative (TN) are organized as it is possible to see in Fig. 2.

	Actual Values	
Predicted Values	True Positive (TP)	False Positive (FP)
	False Negative (FN)	True Negative (TN)

Fig. 2. Example of a confusion matrix.

The four elements of the matrix, on the diagonal and the anti-diagonal, describe the relationships between the actual values (that represent the real observation in the dataset) and the model's forecast. It is so possible to summarize:

- The True Positives (TP) are the observation that the forecasting model has correctly classified as a positive class and that in reality, they belong to the positive class (for instance, the model predicts some accidents with an injury, and in fact, the accident led to an injury);
- The True Negatives (TN) are the observation that the forecasting model has correctly classified as a negative class and that in reality, they belong to the negative class (for instance, the model predicts some accidents with a death, and in fact, the accident led to a death);
- The False Positives (FP) are the observation that the forecasting model has correctly classified as a positive class and that in reality, they belong to the negative class (for

instance, the model predicts some accidents with an injury, and in fact, the accident led to a death). The error related to this misclassification is usually known as Type I error;
- The False Negatives (FN) are the observation that the forecasting model has correctly classified as a negative class and that in reality, they belong to the positive class (for instance, the model predicts some accidents with death, and in fact, the accident led to an injury). The error related to this misclassification is usually known as Type II error.

The F1 score in Eq. 1 (that is used as the main metric to assess performances and compare them) could be considered as the harmonic mean of recall (Eq. 2) and precision (Eq. 3):

$$F1 - score = \frac{2 * \text{Precision} * \text{Recall}}{\text{Precision} + \text{Recall}} \quad (1)$$

$$\text{Recall} = \frac{TP}{TP + FN} \quad (2)$$

$$\text{Precision} = \frac{TP}{TP + FP} \quad (3)$$

In Table 1, the performances in terms of F1 score are listed for each model analyzed in this paper, and they are compared with a prior study [21]. As highlighted, in this paper the performances of QDA and kNN are lower than the previous models, Support vector machines with different kernels remain quite the same, but there is a huge improvement with decision tree and random forest, compared to previous models.

Table 1. Performance metrics of the analyzed models.

Method	Current study F1-score	Prior study [21] F1-score
Linear Discriminant Analysis (LDA)	0.6582	0.6741
Quadratic Discriminant Analysis (QDA)	0.7909	0.7594
K-Nearest Neighbor (KNN, k = 3)	0.9007	0.9370
K-Nearest Neighbor (KNN, k = 5)	0.9011	–
K-Nearest Neighbor (KNN, k = 7)	0.8976	–
Decision Tree (DT)	0.9821	0.9639
Random Forest (RF)	0.9824	0.9678
Support Vector Machine with Linear Kernel (SVM-L)	0.6922	0.6367
Support Vector Machine with Radial Kernel (SVM-P)	0.7674	0.7687
Support Vector Machine with Polynomial Kernel (SVM-R)	0.8771	0.8764

4.2 Variable Importance Analysis

As further results of this analysis, a variable importance analysis is carried out to highlight the main contributory factors in pedestrian road crashes. As it is possible to see in Fig. 3, there are some Machine Learning Methods that could be used to perform such a type of analysis. For the ROC curve method, the algorithm evaluates and calculates the area

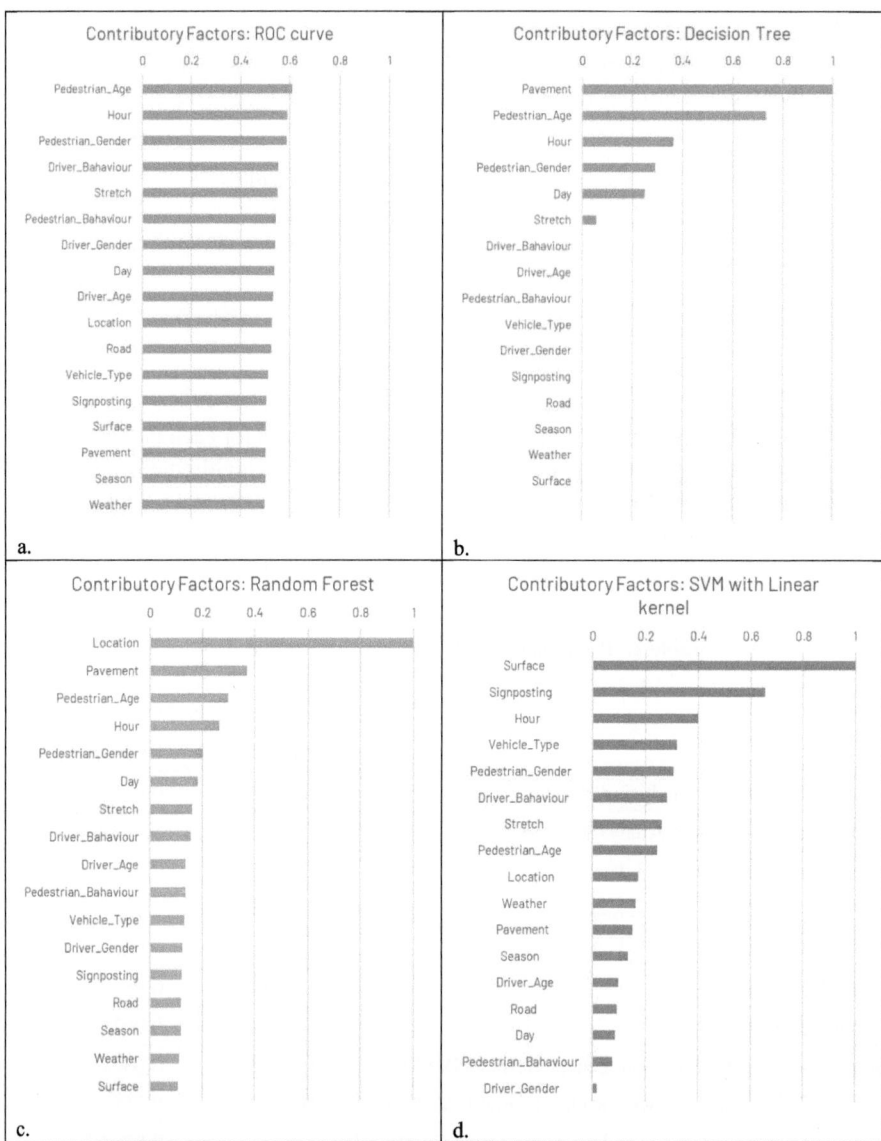

Fig. 3. Comparison of the selected feature Selection algorithm and contributing factors in pedestrian road crashes.

under the ROC curve when a single independent variable is compared with the dependent variable: the higher this area, the higher the correlation between the dependent and the independent variable. Random Forest and Decision Tree have a built-in algorithm to evaluate the most influential features (as is possible to read in the section "Methods"). SVM with linear kernel does not have such a type of feature importance built-in the algorithm: for this reason, to perform an analysis on contributing factors, it is possible to have an idea of which variable is highly related to the outcome by comparing the estimate of the coefficients of the hyperplane that divides observations.

Among the top selected features, pedestrian-related features are the most important ones. Pedestrian age is one of the most influential factors according to the ROC curve method, Random Forest, and Decision Tree. Only in the SVM model is it in 8th place. Pedestrian Gender occupies the top five in all selected methods, highlighting that males and females, in addition to their age, resist crashes based on their different vulnerability. Another variable is the hour of the day, and this is due mainly to the different traffic road conditions in terms of vehicular flows and speeds. Other selected variables are Pedestrian Behaviours and Stretch (intersection or road, in the ROC curve Method), Pavement (Decision Tree and Random Forest), Day (Decision Tree), Location (Random Forest), Surface, Vehicle Type and Signposting (SVM).

5 Conclusions

A review of current scientific and technical literature highlights the need to identify the main contributory factors that contribute to accidents. Determining effective measures to mitigate the severity of injuries among vulnerable road users is a leading priority. Given the complexity of this issue, Machine Learning Models are often used. In this study, an initial attempt was made to predict accident outcomes using ISTAT data from Rome's metropolitan area. The research began with the training and testing of multiple Machine Learning Models. Model performance was evaluated on the test set to ensure validity. Several models were assessed based on their complexity, with no bias toward any particular approach. The Random Forest model demonstrated the highest F1 score, and so the highest capabilities to predict the outcome of a pedestrian crash.

The results of the analysis of contributory factors (see Fig. 3) show that a main role is played by the hour, pedestrian age, and pedestrian gender: all four proposed methods (in particular the ROC curve Method, Decision Tree, Random Forest, and Support Vector Machine with Linear kernel) select these three variables among the first five positions of the ranking (exception made for SVM, where pedestrian age is on the 7th place). The hour, such as the pavement and the location (as selected from Decision Tree and Random Forest) could give an idea for which reason they are so important: the hour is something related to traffic flows, while pavement and location to vehicle speeds.

Despite these results, the study presents some limitations. The first is connected to the black-box nature of these models because there is some lack on the interpretability side. The second regards the methods of variable importance analysis. As it is possible to see in Fig. 3, the output of these analyses is only a ranking of the most influential features that contribute to predicting pedestrian accident severity, and not how these could positively or negatively affect the outcome. For instance, if the variable "Hour" is selected, it is difficult to understand how daylight or nighttime hours increase or decrease the probability of fatal crashes. Another limitation is that the analysis is carried out only in the city of Rome, so the model is well trained and tested for this context. From this last sentence, as further steps, it could be interesting if the same variables selected with the aforementioned methods are the most influential also in other cities in Italy. Another future development aims to combine models and different methodologies to improve the interpretability of the models and understand how a single variable quantitatively affects the pedestrian severity. A point in favour of this methodology and models is that they could be replicated in different contexts and also on different scales, from the city level to the national level. This is also a first step in pedestrian accident analysis, but the findings could be useful to be a reference point to improve safety conditions for pedestrians in cities. The analysis carried out shows that pedestrian-related variables are the most influential factors, alongside variables that could be related to traffic conditions.

Acknowledgments. The research reported in this paper was developed in the EMOTIVEs Research Project, supported by the "FESR Lazio 2021–2027 Program - RSI Competitive Repositioning Notice".

Author Contributions. **Conceptualization**, C.G. and N.S.; **methodology**, C.G. and N.S.; **software**, C.G. and N.S.; **validation**, C.G. and N.S.; **formal analysis**, C.G. and N.S.; **investigation**, C.G. and N.S.; **resources**, C.G. and N.S.; **data curation**, C.G. and N.S.; **writing—original draft preparation**, C.G. and N.S.; **writing—review and editing**, C.G. and N.S.; **visualization**, C.G. and N.S..; **supervision**, D.A.M. and N.V.; **project administration**, D.A.M. and N.V.; **funding acquisition**, D.A.M. and N.V. All authors have read and agreed to the published version of the manuscript.

References

1. WHO: Global status report on road safety 2015. World Health Organization, Geneva (2015)
2. World Health Organization (WHO): Road traffic injuries
3. Shang, S., et al.: The predictive capacity of the MADYMO ellipsoid pedestrian model for pedestrian ground contact kinematics and injury evaluation. Accid. Anal. Prev. **149**, 105803 (2021)
4. McNally, D.S., Rosenberg, N.M.: MADYMO simulation of children in cycle accidents: a novel approach in risk assessment. Accid. Anal. Prev. **59**, 469–478 (2013)
5. Guo, R., Yuan, Q., Sturgess, C.E.N., Hassan, A.M., Li, Y., Hu, Y.: A study of an Asian anthropometric pedestrian in vehicle–pedestrian accidents using real-world accident data. Int. J. Crashworth. **11**(6), 541–551 (2006)
6. Mizuno, K., et al.: Analysis of fall kinematics and injury risks in ground impact in car-pedestrian collisions using impulse. Accid. Anal. Prev. **176**, 106793 (2022)
7. Nie, J., Li, G., Yang, J.: A study of fatality risk and head dynamic response of cyclist and pedestrian based on passenger car accident data analysis and simulations. Traffic Inj. Prev. **16**(1), 76–83 (2015)
8. Chen, S., Kuhn, M., Prettner, K., Bloom, D.E.: The global macroeconomic burden of road injuries: estimates and projections for 166 countries. Lancet Planet. Health **3**(9), e390–e398 (2019)

9. Namatovu, S., et al.: Interventions to reduce pedestrian road traffic injuries: a systematic review of randomized controlled trials, cluster randomized controlled trials, interrupted time-series, and controlled before-after studies. PLoS ONE **17**(1), e0262681 (2022)
10. World Health Organization: Pedestrian safety: a road safety manual for decision-makers and practitioners. World Health Organization (2023)
11. Road Safety (WHO). https://www.who.int/health-topics/road-safety#tab=tab_2
12. Kendi, S., Johnston, B.D.: Epidemiology and prevention of child pedestrian injury. Pediatrics **152**(1), e2023062508 (2023)
13. Pedestrian Safety: Prevent Pedestrian Crashes. https://www.nhtsa.gov/road-safety/pedestrian-safety
14. European Road Safety Observatory. https://road-safety.transport.ec.europa.eu/system/files/2021-07/facts_figures_pedestrians_final_20210323.pdf
15. Road Safety Statistics. https://transport.ec.europa.eu/background/2021-road-safety-statistics-what-behind-figures_en
16. Road Traffic Injuries. https://www.who.int/news-room/fact-sheets/detail/road-traffic-injuries
17. Fisa, R., Musukuma, M., Sampa, M., Musonda, P., Young, T.: Effects of interventions for preventing road traffic crashes: an overview of systematic reviews. BMC Public Health **22**(1), 513 (2022)
18. Istat. https://www.istat.it/. Accessed July 2024
19. Roma Mobilità. https://romamobilita.it/it. Accessed Oct 2024
20. Pugliese, R., Regondi, S., Marini, R.: Machine learning-based approach: global trends, research directions, and regulatory standpoints. Data Sci. Manag. **4**, 19–29 (2021)
21. D'Apuzzo, M., Cappelli, G., Naranni, S., De Guidi, M., Nicolosi, V.: Machine learning tools for predicting the outcome of pedestrian crashes: preliminary findings in the Metropolitan city of Rome. In: Gervasi, O., Murgante, B., Garau, C., Taniar, D., C. Rocha, A.M.A., Faginas Lago, M.N. (eds.) ICCSA 2024. LNCS, vol. 14824, pp. 116–132. Springer, Cham (2024). https://doi.org/10.1007/978-3-031-65332-2_8
22. Mika, S., Ratsch, G., Weston, J., Scholkopf, B., Mullers, K.R.: Fisher discriminant analysis with kernels. In: Neural Networks for Signal Processing IX: Proceedings of the 1999 IEEE Signal Processing Society Workshop (Cat. No. 98TH8468), pp. 41–48. IEEE, August 1999
23. Tharwat, A.: Linear vs. quadratic discriminant analysis classifier: a tutorial. Int. J. Appl. Pattern Recogn. **3**(2), 145–180 (2016)
24. Makaba, T., Doorsamy, W., Paul, B.S.: Exploratory framework for analysing road traffic accident data with validation on Gauteng province data. Cogent Eng. **7**(1), 1834659 (2020)
25. Fix, E., Hodges, J.: Discriminatory analysis. Nonparametric discrimination: Consistency properties. Technical Report 4, US AF School of Aviation Medicine, Randolph Field, Texas (1951)
26. Sarraf, J., Pattnaik, P.K.: Brain-computer interfaces and their applications. In: An Industrial IoT Approach for Pharmaceutical Industry Growth, pp. 31–54. Academic Press (2020)
27. James, G., Witten, D., Hastie, T., Tibshirani, R.: An Introduction to Statistical Learning, vol. 112, p. 138. Springer, New York (2013)
28. Chen, M.M., Chen, M.C.: Modeling road accident severity with comparisons of logistic regression, decision tree and random forest. Information **11**(5), 270 (2020)
29. Elyassami, S., Hamid, Y., Habuza, T.: Road crashes analysis and prediction using gradient boosted and random forest trees. In: 2020 6th IEEE Congress on Information Science and Technology (CiSt), pp. 520–525. IEEE, June 2021
30. Rella Riccardi, M., Galante, F., Scarano, A., Montella, A.: Econometric and machine learning methods to identify pedestrian crash patterns. Sustainability **14**(22), 15471 (2022)
31. Scarano, A., Riccardi, M.R., Mauriello, F., D'Agostino, C., Pasquino, N., Montella, A.: Injury severity prediction of cyclist crashes using random forests and random parameters logit models. Accid. Anal. Prev. **192**, 107275 (2023)

32. Cesarini, L., Figueiredo, R., Monteleone, B., Martina, M.L.: The potential of machine learning for weather index insurance. Nat. Hazards Earth Syst. Sci. **21**(8), 2379–2405 (2021)
33. Mas, J.F., Flores, J.J.: The application of artificial neural networks to the analysis of remotely sensed data. Int. J. Remote Sens. **29**, 617–663 (2008). https://doi.org/10.1080/01431160701352154
34. Archer, K.J., Kimes, R.V.: Empirical characterization of random forest variable importance measures. Comput. Stat. Data Anal. **52**(4), 2249–2260 (2008)
35. Fawcett, T.: An introduction to ROC analysis. Pattern Recogn. Lett. **27**, 861–874 (2006)
36. Güvenir, H.A., Kurtcephe, M.: Ranking instances by maximizing the area under ROC curve. IEEE Trans. Knowl. Data Eng. **25**(10), 2356–2366 (2012)
37. Provost, F., Fawcett, T.: Analysis and visualization of classifier performance: comparison under imprecise class and cost distributions. In: Proceedings of the Third International Conference on Knowledge Discovery and Data Mining, pp. 43–48 (1997)
38. Provost, F., Fawcett, T., Kohavi, R.: The case against accuracy estimation for comparing induction algorithms. In: Proceedings of the 15th International Conference on Machine Learning, pp. 445–453 (1998)

A Brief Overview of Pedestrian Accident Modelling

Giuseppe Cappelli[1,2] 🆔, Sofia Nardoianni[1] 🆔, Mauro D'Apuzzo[1](✉) 🆔, and Vittorio Nicolosi[2] 🆔

[1] University of Cassino and Southern Lazio, Via G. Di Biasio 43, 03043 Cassino, Italy
{giuseppe.cappelli1,sofia.nardoianni,dapuzzo}@unicas.it,
cppgpp01@uniroma2.it
[2] University of Rome "Tor Vergata", Via del Politecnico, 1, 00133 Rome, Italy
nicolosi@uniroma2.it

Abstract. Thanks to the advancement of models and methodologies to handle large amounts of data in conjunction with the increased attention of national and international governments toward safety issues, this paper aims to provide a brief overview of the main models that are used to study pedestrian crashes. The reason why this type of analysis is conducted starts from three main research questions: What are the main datasets needed to study pedestrian accidents, what are the main models utilized, and what are the main gaps that emerge in the pedestrian safety field? This proposed state-of-the-art overview starts from the analysis of statistical approaches in the context of risk factor analysis to the most recent machine learning methods to evaluate pedestrian crash severity by emphasizing the purposes for which the models are used, why they are used, and the data needed to achieve the task. The results of the analysis show how the models could be classified and the main research gaps in this field that could be useful for researchers as starting points in their studies.

Keywords: Pedestrian crashes · Pedestrian accident modeling · Empirical Bayes Approach · Statistical Frequency Models · Econometric Models · Machine Learning

1 Introduction

As a leading plan for improving safety conditions for all road users, Agenda 30, promoted by the United Nations (UN) [1], is one of the first plans to address environmental and safety issues. The shared models, approved back in 2015, define 17 goals (Sustainable Development Goals, SDGs); the problem of road users' safety falls under objective 3.6 (under the SDG "Good Health and Well-being") and objective 11.2 (under the SDG "Sustainable Cities and Communities"). With objective 3.6, the UN plan aims to halve, by 2020, the number of injuries and deaths in road accidents, and, with objective 11.2, by 2030, ensure access to a safe, sustainable, and affordable road transportation system.

In 2010, the UN General Assembly proclaimed the 2011–2020 Decade of Action for Road Safety to reduce road accidents with the resolution A/RES/64/255 [2, 3]. A year later, there was the launch of "The Decade of Actions for Road Safety 2011–2020", to "help all countries drive along the path to a more secure future" and "save millions of lives", according to the UN Secretary-General Ban Ki-moon [2]. Some years later, in 2017, the WHO, in collaboration with the UN, the Global Road Safety Partnership (GRSP), and the VIAS Institute, known until recently as BRSI (Belgian Road Safety Institute), provided a document on safety issues and measures to reduce the number of accidents, all resumed in 12 voluntary global targets for road safety [4].

In August 2020, the resolution A/RES/74/299 "Improving Global Road Safety" was approved by the United Nations General Assembly, and the second "Decade of Action for Road Safety 2021–2030" was launched [2, 5]. This second decade of actions aims to reduce at least 50% of road traffic deaths by 2030. The UN General Assembly, with the WHO (World Health Organization), and the UN Regional Commission, prepared the plan for this second decade [6].

In February 2020, "The Ten Step Plan for Safer Road Infrastructure", produced by the Project Group "Safer Roads and Mobility" of the United Nations Road Safety Collaboration Group (UNRSC), was published [7]. As the name of the plan suggests, the action to promote was resumed in ten steps. Still, they could be resumed in three main priority actions: the first is to make a gap analysis, the second regards the development of National standards and training, and the third is the Infrastructure Safety Management, to enhance a National Road Assessment Programme and make Road Safety Audits.

In the European context, the European Commission launched the EU Road Safety Policy Framework 2021–2030, a comprehensive document outlining the EU's objectives and actions to reduce road deaths and serious injuries by 50% by 2030 and ultimately achieve "Vision Zero" by 2050 [8]. Adopted by the European Parliament on October 6, 2021, this framework builds upon a resolution from April 27, 2021, welcoming the implementation report on the road safety aspects of the Roadworthiness Package [9].

The framework is rooted in a staff working document published in June 2019, introducing a new EU road safety policy approach and a medium-term strategic action plan [8]. The novel approach emphasizes fostering a culture of zero fatalities and serious injuries by addressing the root causes of road crashes, enhancing enforcement and compliance, improving data collection and analysis, promoting innovation and research, and strengthening international cooperation. This framework is part of the "Europe on the Move" package [10], which also encompasses documents related to sustainable and smart mobility, such as the Sustainable and Smart Mobility Strategy [11].

The objectives of the plan are organized in a three-time period. Between intermediate outcome targets (based on Key Performance Indicators) and long-term goals (zero deaths by 2050), there is an interim target of reducing half-serious injuries and deaths by 2030. An interesting point is the definition of action areas and their relative Key Performance Indicators (KPIs), highlighting which variables are related to road accidents. As action areas is it possible to find safe infrastructure, vehicles, speed, driving, use of the road, use of seat belts and helmets, post-care services. The KPIs are so related to evaluating the percentage of users that have safe behaviours, according to the areas described.

Regarding the Management of Road Infrastructures in the field of Safety Issues, the European Parliament, in 2008, enacted the "Directive 2008/96/EC of the European

Parliament and of the Council of 19 November 2008 on road infrastructure safety management" [12], aimed to create and promote "the establishment and implementation of procedures relating to road safety impact assessments, road safety audits, the management of road network safety and safety inspections by the Member States". As it is possible to read in this Directive, it is crucial to assess safety in the initial planning stages and after the project's approval. All safety design solutions need to be justified with proper analysis to assess the impact in terms of safety advantages. The Directive also stresses the importance of Safety Audits (Article 4) as an important step in the design phase, as well as controls on existing infrastructure that have a high ranking in terms of accident concentration, at least every three years, and safety inspections during operational phases.

On 16 January 2023, the European Commission released guidelines containing also methodologies for conducting network-wide road safety assessments [13]. These guidelines are designed to assist public authorities in EU Member States in fulfilling the requirements of the Road Infrastructure Safety Management Directive [14].

The guidance encompasses a comprehensive framework that addresses both reactive (accident-based) and proactive (feature-based) safety assessments. It covers various factors such as lane width, road curvature, junction design, roadside layout, and potential conflicts between motorized vehicles and vulnerable road users. Additionally, it proposes a methodology for establishing a common safety rating system to classify the existing road network, allowing each road section to be rated on a 5-level scale. This approach aims to help authorities identify priorities for future actions and investments to improve road safety.

At the bottom of this methodology, there are two approaches: the Reactive and the Proactive Approach. The main difference is that in the reactive approach, safety problems are studied after a crash happens, while in the Proactive Approach, the aim is to improve the safety of the road before an accident happens. In other terms, with the Reactive Approach, it is possible to evaluate the frequency of accidents, while with the Proactive Approach, how the risk could be reduced.

The proposed paper aims to give researchers a brief guide and comprehensive framework of the most used models in the pedestrian accident field. To conduct this brief analysis of the state-of-the-art, seventy-seven (77) studies are analysed. In Sect. 2, the main research questions and the selection criteria are shown, while in Sect. 3, a classification of the main models used is proposed, to answer the research questions. Lastly, a brief discussion of the results obtained is proposed in Sect. 4, alongside the conclusions.

2 Research Questions and Selection Criteria

National and International Safety Plans emphasize the need to guarantee safety for vulnerable road users and achieve sustainable development goals at the same time. Several researches' studies have been conducted in the past and nowadays on this topic. This proposed overview of the current state of the art aims to give a clear framework of the data required and the models needed to model pedestrian accidents, as well as the new challenges in this field for the future. For these reasons, the research questions that have emerged and led to the writing of this paper are:

1. What are the main datasets needed to study pedestrian accidents?
2. What models are used to study pedestrian accidents?
3. What are the main gaps that emerge in this field?

To try to answer these research questions, a collection of papers is made to create an exhaustive database. Seventy-seven (77) studies are selected according to several inclusion and exclusion criteria. For the inclusion criteria, the papers that respond to the following requirements are selected:

1. Papers that dealt with pedestrian crashes without any time-period restriction;
2. Studies that use national or available datasets collected by agents or agencies;
3. Studies that implement models or descriptive analysis.

The exclusion criteria adopted are listed below:

1. Vulnerability-based studies are not included because they focus on what happens in particular crash scenarios after the crash happens.
2. Studies that rely on the use of Floating Car Data (FCD) and video cameras or that focus on pedestrian behaviours.
3. Studies in which pedestrian crashes are combined with other vulnerable user accidents to make a common class of analysis.

The reasons related to these selection and exclusion criteria are that the main idea behind them is not to exclude too many papers, but at the same time, to focus on the papers that present studies that could be replicated by other researchers.

3 Classification of Pedestrian Crash Models

Starting from the analysis of the selected papers, it emerges that mainly three subsets could be drawn according to the outcomes and purposes to achieve (see Fig. 1). A first class includes Risk Factor Analysis, which could be seen as a preliminary and explanatory type of analysis of pedestrian crash data, that aim to identify contributory factors and crash scenarios.

The second subset includes pedestrian crash frequency models that aim to evaluate and estimate the number of pedestrian crashes at road segments, intersections, traffic analysis zones (TAZ), and census tracts. The two main classes of methods that emerge from the analysis of the literature are Statistical Frequency Models and the Empirical Bayes Approach.

Lastly, Pedestrian Crash severity Models are identified as a third subset of methods for analysing pedestrian accidents. This category of methods (from the Econometric and Machine Learning fields) is implemented to evaluate the probability of the severity of accidents, which are the features that lead to a fatal outcome, for instance.

The following three subsections are proposed with the aim to give a deeper dive into these three classes of approaches, while, in Fig. 1, a graphic and conceptual framework is shown to guide readers and have a clear vision of the classification performed.

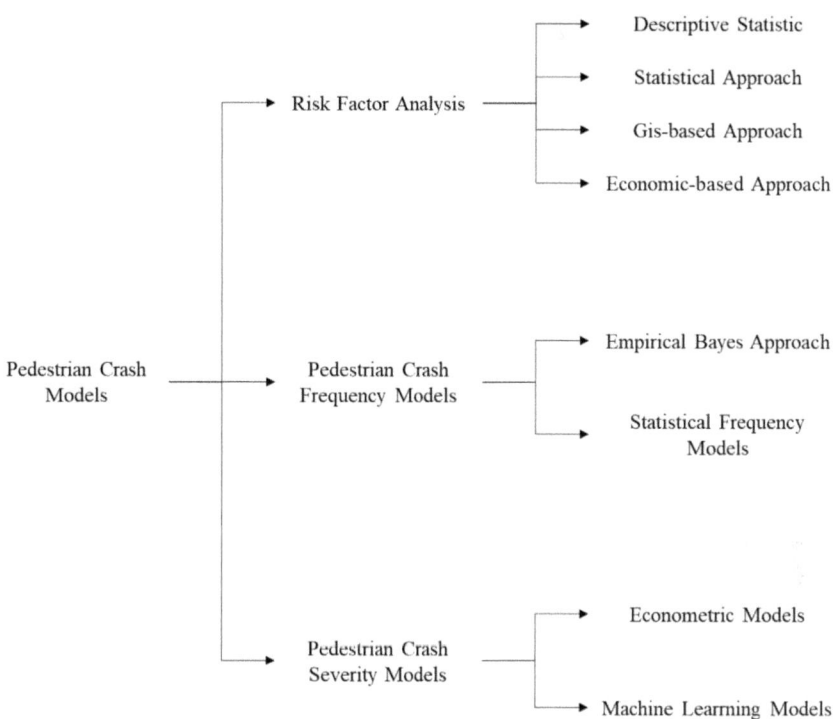

Fig. 1. Proposed classification of implemented models and approaches in the pedestrian safety field.

3.1 Risk Factor Analysis

This model category aims to identify contributory risk factors when pedestrian crashes occur. As it emerges in Table 1 below, four different categories to study the contributory risk factor in pedestrian accidents are reported. Descriptive statistics [15] are often used to measure the frequency and how often that particular scenario or that particular variable occurs. The higher the frequency, the higher the contribution of the variable [16–29].

The other class, defined as Statistical Approach, contains mainly three methods, as it emerges from this review of the state of the art. Double Pair comparisons Approach focuses [28, 30–45] on the comparisons of different scenarios or conditions. Usually, as the name suggests, only two pair conditions are compared to identify some effects and some factors that play a key role. Two pairs of comparisons need to be illustrated to clarify the method. For instance, it is possible to imagine a city manager installing a pedestrian crossing table (CPT) to decrease speeds and reduce pedestrian accidents. The big question is whether this measure can effectively decrease crashes. For this reason, two pairs are created: the first pair include roads where CPT are installed (threaded locations); the second pair include roads (control locations) on which no CPT are installed. For both pairs, accident data before and after the installation are collected. By evaluating the predicted reduction, compared with the actual reduction, the method is able to evaluate the reduction in terms of accidents and also to quantify the contribution of a factor.

Quasi-induce Exposure Models (QIE) are one of the most common responsibility-based methods [37–39]. As suggested, the model selects only crashes in which it is possible to attribute two different roles: one user is responsible, the other one not. The non-responsible user is passively involved in the crash. The ratio between responsible and non-responsible users defines the relative accident involvement ratio, which is similar to the odd ratio. This coefficient substitutes the crash rate.

The third method is called the Two-step clustering algorithm [40–42]. The technique aims to group observations in some clusters based on similarities or differences. The method involves two steps during the clustering task to reduce the total amount of computational requirements.

A third category is represented by the Gis-based Approach [28, 43]. These methods are often used in the context of supporting plans, making comparisons among municipalities, or ranking high pedestrian crash zones on several territory or city levels. For example, Lam et al. [45] explore the spatiotemporal relationships of individual travel patterns and crash locations. In addition, this study demonstrates that the travel diary data can generate a uniquely useful exposure measure because of its highly disaggregated nature. From the analysis, one can see that both crash frequency and risk varied by space and time. The results show that the district's town centre during the afternoon rush hours was the most hazardous location and time for elderly pedestrians.

Lastly, economic-based studies implemented to highlight contributory factors in pedestrian crashes are classified. The study of this category [44] applies two methods to make an analysis: Willingness to pay and Contingent Evaluation Method alongside Descriptive Statistic Analysis. The study finds that the estimated value of statistical life (VOSL) for Sudanese people is between US$0.019 to US$0.101 million. The willingness to pay to reduce fatalities increases with age, income, education level, safety perception, and time spent on social activities. The willingness to pay method is widely applied in road accidents, but as it emerges from this review, exclusively for road crashes in general [45–50], to evaluate the maximum amount of money to avoid a risk. As far as the contingent valuation (CV) method [51], it is a widely applied approach for non-market valuation, particularly in environmental cost-benefit analysis and environmental impact assessments. In environmental economics, it is used to estimate non-use values, nonmarket use values, or a combination of both for environmental resources.

3.2 Pedestrian Crash Frequency Models

Crash-frequency models represent the second modelling category. Common applications of these models regard the understanding of relationships between dependent and independent variables, screening variables to understand if a variable has a significant effect on the outcome (by using technique to rank the importance of variables) and sensitivity of variables, which is an in-depth analysis of the coefficients of the model in greater detail than the screening variable (by evaluating the marginal effects of a variable and so how dependent variable changes when an independent variable changes), and finally to make prediction, and in this case, to forecast the number of the accident on a road or at intersections [52].

Following this classification according to the application of the models, the collected and analysed papers fall into two classes: understanding relationships, and modelling.

Table 1. Risk Factor Analysis Categories.

Categories	Methods	Datasets	Results	References
Descriptive Statistics	Frequency Distribution	Accident data	Recurrent patterns and scenarios Risk reduction assessment	[16–29]
Statistical Approach	Double Pair Comparisons Approach, Quasi-induce Exposure Models, Two-step cluster analysis,	Accident data Census data	Risk reduction assessment Crash rate	[36, 39, 42]
GIS-based Approach	Spatial Statistical Analysis, Kernel-based Methods	Accident data Census data	Ranking High pedestrian crash zone	[28, 43]
Economic-based Approach	Willingness to pat methods Contingent evaluation methods	Survey	Willingness to pay	[44]

In all cases analysed, relationships among variables and the need to forecast accident frequency were bounded, which were also the main objectives of the collected papers. For this reason, it was not possible to follow this classification.

From the analysed literature, it emerges that the distinctive feature regards the spatial unit, namely the unit on which the analysis is carried out. In the context of determining the pedestrian crash frequency, the forecasting number of accidents could be evaluated on pedestrian crossings [53], road segments [54–59], intersections [60–64], Traffic Analysis Zone (TAZ) [65–70], or Census Tracts level [56, 57]. As it is possible to observe in Table 2, in comparison also with Table 1 in the previous section, the need to create accident prediction models requires a larger amount of data than the data required for risk factor studies: the higher the complexity of the spatial unit, the higher the number of datasets required to describe in an adequate way the unit. A common characteristic regards the employment of traffic data and, in particular cases, also pedestrian exposures [53, 55–57, 70, 72].

It emerges also that by increasing the complexity of the spatial unit, different models could be employed. For pedestrian crossings, road segments, and intersections, both the Empirical Bayes Approach and Statistical models are often used [53–64]; while the complexity of the spatial unit increases (TAZ and Census Tracts), Statistical Distributions are exclusively implemented [65–72].

Statistical Frequency Models can predict a crash that happens at a constant average rate (such as Poisson Models) or with a higher variability (i.e., Negative Binomial Models, which are more able than Poisson Models to describe this phenomenon when the

Table 2. Classification of the pedestrian crash frequency studies according to the spatial unit.

Spatial Unit	Datasets	Models	References
Pedestrian Crossings	Pedestrian crashes, Geometric Characteristics, Pedestrian and Traffic data	Empirical Bayes Approach	[53]
Road Segment	Pedestrian crashes, built environment, Pedestrian and traffic data, survey	Empirical Bayes Approach, Statistical Frequency Models	[54–59]
Intersection	Pedestrian crashes, built environment, Pedestrian and traffic data, socio-demographic data	Empirical Bayes Approach, Statistical Frequency Models	[60–64]
Traffic Analysis Zone (TAZ)	Pedestrian crashes, built environment, Pedestrian and traffic data, socio-demographic data	Statistical Frequency Models	[65–70]
Census Tracts	Pedestrian crashes, built environment, Pedestrian and traffic data, socio-demographic data	Statistical Frequency Models	[71, 72]

variance is greater than the mean) [52, 73, 74]. The vast majority of analysed papers heavily rely on Negative Binomial Models. As highlighted by some authors [75, 76], it is common that such type of models are characterized by the regression to the mean frequency, a statistical phenomenon that occurs in forecasting future crashes in locations in which the number of accidents is very high or very low. Future values are more likely to assume the average value. The Empirical Bayes Approach can mitigate this issue.

The Empirical Bayes Approach is often implemented to evaluate Safety Performance Functions (SPFs), which are regression models that can predict the number of road accidents, based on several factors such as traffic volumes, geometry, and so on [77, 78]. The Empirical Bayes Approach tends to combine observed crash data with prior historical crash data or with data from similar sites to account for variations in crash frequency [76]. The Approach relies on the definition of prior and posterior distribution. The prior distribution is based on historical crash data to evaluate crash count at a specific site level [79, 80]. When data for a specific location are unavailable, similar sites could also be considered. The posterior distribution is obtained through Bayes' Theorem by combining the prior distribution (that gives the number of crash that happens) and the likelihood that accidents could happen on observed crash data [79, 80]. The expected crash frequency, evaluated as the mean of the posterior distribution, provides a more accurate estimate.

3.3 Pedestrian Crash Severity Models

Crash severity refers to the damages a pedestrian or road user may have when a crash occurs [81]. It could be classified into levels according to the degree of lesions [82, 83]. Pedestrian crash severity models can predict the outcome of a crash and evaluate the probability of the accident itself. From the analysed literature, the idea of classification performed is shown in Table 3. Pedestrian crash severity models are often used to perform pattern recognition tasks [84–86], Variable importance Analysis [87–103], and model development [85, 86, 104–111]. For each of the tasks described in Table 3, econometric and Machine Learning Approaches could be implemented to achieve the purposes of the task.

Regarding the pattern recognition task, Latent Class Analysis (LCA) [84], Association Rules, and Classification Tree [85, 86] are often used to solve the proposed model: the first technique belongs to the Econometric field, the other to the Machine Learning Approach. LCA is an econometric technique that aims to find subgroups that share features in the dataset [112], while association rules is a data mining technique that aims to find relationships among variables [113]. The Decision Tree algorithm split the observation into several leaves, with the aim (similar to LCA) to find groups as homogeneous as possible [85].

The decision tree method is not only used for pattern recognition tasks but also for performing variable importance analysis and model development. The reason why it is divided into Variable Importance and Model Development Tasks is that some models (especially some machine learning algorithms) cannot be implemented to find relationships between dependent and independent variables. Logistic Regression Models and their evolutions and tree-based models, such as Decision Tree and Random Forest, can be used to achieve both tasks. Other models among the Machine learning algorithms (Neural Network, Support Vector Machine, k-nearest neighbour, Bagging, Boosting, XGBoost, Naïve Bayes) are only used to model development.

Table 3. Classification of the pedestrian crash severity studies according to the spatial unit.

Task	Approach	Models	References
Pattern Recognition	Econometric	Latent Class Analysis	[84]
	Machine Learning	Association Rules	[85, 86]
		Classification Tree	[85, 86]
Variable Importance Analysis	Econometric	Logistic Regression	[84, 87–90, 93–95, 100, 101]

(*continued*)

Table 3. (*continued*)

Task	Approach	Models	References
		Mixed/Random Parameter Logit	[85, 86, 102, 103]
		Multivariate Logit	[91]
		Ordered Logit	[86, 95]
		Partial Proportional Odds	[95, 96]
		Ordered Probit	[99]
	Machine Learning	Decision Tree	[85, 86, 104–106]
		Random Forest	[85, 86, 107, 108]
Model Development	Econometric	Logistic Regression	[84, 87–90, 93–95, 100, 101]
		Mixed/ Random Parameter Logit	[85, 86, 102, 103]
		Multivariate Logit	[91]
		Ordered Logit	[86, 95]
		Partial Proportional Odds	[95, 96]
		Ordered Probit	[99]
		Linear Discriminant Analysis	[104]
		Quadratic Discriminant Analysis	[104]
	Machine Learning	Decision Tree	[85, 86, 105–107]
		Random Forest	[85, 86, 108, 109]
		Bagging	[106]
		Boosting	[106]
		Support Vector Machine	[86, 110]
		XGBoost	[109, 111]
		Naïve Bayes	[109]
		K-nearest Neighbour	[108]
		Neural Network	[98, 100, 108]

4 Discussion and Conclusions

The classification proposed here aims to answer the research questions shown in Sect. 2. As it emerges from the previous sections, by analysing the studies collected, the discriminant on which the classification is based is the output of the model. Studies based on identifying the contributory factors with the implementation of statistical techniques identify the first category, which is named Risk Factor Analysis. Studies that aim to predict the number of pedestrian accidents use models from the statistical field and are classified as Pedestrian Crash Frequency Models, while the last category aims to predict the severity of crashes involving pedestrians by using econometric and Machine Learning Models, and these models are classified as Pedestrian Crash Severity Models.

As it is shown in the analysis, the main dataset needed to study pedestrian accidents (Research Question 1) depends on the output of the model. If the purpose is to study with statistical techniques the contributory factor, the pedestrian crash dataset is enough to perform such type of analysis and evaluate the severity of accidents with Pedestrian Crash Severity Models. If the objective of the analysis is frequency forecasting, more datasets are needed.

The availability of some datasets over others also regulates the typology of methods that could be implemented (Research Question 2). Regarding Risk Factor Analysis, Descriptive Statistics, Statistical Approach, GIS-based Approach, and Economic-based Approach could be implemented (see Table 1); for Pedestrian Crash Frequency Models, mainly Empirical Bayes Approach and Statistical Models are the predominant methods used (see Table 2); while for Pedestrian Crash Severity Models, Econometric and Machine Learning Methods are the most used approaches (see Table 3).

But which are the main research gaps? From the analysis of the selected studies, the datasets used to create crash frequency models are very detailed and take into account, for instance, traffic and pedestrian flows, which are some data difficult to retrieve. This highly detailed framework is not present when the objective is to evaluate the severity of pedestrian accidents. When Pedestrian Crash Severity Models are applied, national datasets provided by agencies that collect such types of data are used. Despite the high number of features that are collected, some information regarding some variables that are related to the severity of the involved pedestrians (such as pedestrian and vehicular flows and speeds) is not available.

Alongside this aspect, Machine Learning Models that are strongly utilized in predicting the severity of pedestrian crashes are not implemented as regression methods to evaluate and forecast the pedestrian crash frequency. In addition to that, among the Pedestrian Crash Frequency studies, there is a limited number of studies that focus on predicting crash frequency for pedestrian crossings.

In conclusion, this paper aims to give a brief overview of methods and models that could be implemented in pedestrian safety. Based on the availability of some datasets or others and the study's objective, several models could be used to perform the analysis. In a complex field of analysis in which every day new methods and technologies are applied, this paper aims to give a guide and also a tutorial for the first steps in pedestrian accident modelling. A deep dive with selecting only a few papers and highlighting their limitation and innovative elements is a future development of this paper.

Acknowledgments. The research leading to these results has received funding from Project "Ecosistema dell'innovazione Rome Technopole" financed by the EU in the NextGenerationEU plan through MUR Decree n. 1051 23.06.2022 - CUP H33C22000420001. This manuscript reflects only the authors' views and opinions, neither the European Union nor the European Commission can be considered responsible for them.

Author Contributions. Conceptualization, C.G. and N.S.; **methodology**, C.G. and N.S.; **software**, C.G. and N.S.; **validation**, C.G. and N.S.; **formal analysis**, C.G. and N.S.; **investigation**, C.G. and N.S.; **resources**, C.G. and N.S.; **data curation**, C.G. and N.S.; **writing—original draft preparation**, C.G. and N.S.; **writing—review and editing**, C.G. and N.S.; **visualization**, C.G. and N.S..; **supervision**, D.A.M. and N.V.; **project administration**, D.A.M. and N.V.; **funding acquisition**, D.A.M. and N.V. All authors have read and agreed to the published version of the manuscript.

References

1. United Nations, Department of Economic and Social Affairs. https://sdgs.un.org/goals. Accessed July 2024
2. UNECE, United Nations Economic Commission for Europe. https://unece.org/second-decade-action#:~:text=Second%20Decade%20of%20Action%20%7C%20UNECE%20Second%20Decade,of%20road%20traffic%20deaths%20and%20injuries%20by%202030. Accessed July 2024
3. Decade of Action for Road Safety 2011–2020. https://www.who.int/groups/united-nations-road-safety-collaboration/decade-of-action-for-road-safety-2011-2020. Accessed July 2024
4. Van den Berghe, W., Fleiter, J.J., Cliff, D.: Towards the 12 voluntary global targets for road safety. Guidance for countries on activities and measures to achieve the voluntary global road safety performance targets. Vias Institute, Brussels and Global Road Safety Partnership, Geneva (2020)
5. United Nations, UN, Department of Safety and Security. https://www.un.org/en/safety-and-security/road-safety. Accessed July 2024
6. WHO, World Health Organization. Decade of Action for Road Safety 2011–2020. https://www.who.int/teams/social-determinants-of-health/safety-and-mobility/decade-of-action-for-road-safety-2021-2030. Accessed July 2024
7. The Ten Step Plan for Safer Road Infrastructure. https://unece.org/DAM/Road_Safety_Trust_Fund/Projects/20200219-202801-4216-UNRSF_10_STEPS_INFRASTRUCTURE_FINAL.pdf. Accessed July 2024
8. European Commission, Directorate-General for Mobility and Transport, Next steps towards 'Vision Zero' – EU road safety policy framework 2021–2030, Publications Office (2020). https://data.europa.eu/doi/10.2832/391271
9. EU Road Safety Policy Framework 2021–2030 – Recommendations on next steps towards "Vision Zero". https://www.europarl.europa.eu/doceo/document/TA-9-2021-0407_EN.html
10. Sustainable and Smart Mobility Strategy, EU. https://road-safety.transport.ec.europa.eu/eu-road-safety-policy/what-we-do/key-policy-documents_en
11. Multimedia Centre, European Parliament. https://multimedia.europarl.europa.eu/en/topic/road-safety_20303
12. Directive 2008/96/EC of the European Parliament and of the Council of 19 November 2008 on road infrastructure safety management. https://eur-lex.europa.eu/legal-content/EN/TXT/?uri=CELEX%3A32008L0096. Accessed Sept 2024

13. New guidelines to assess safety of road infrastructure. https://road-safety.transport.ec. europa.eu/news-events/news/new-guidelines-assess-safety-road-infrastructure-2023-01-16_en. Accessed Sept 2024
14. Directive (EU) 2019/1936 of the European Parliament and of the Council of 23 October 2019 amending Directive 2008/96/EC on road infrastructure safety management. https://eur-lex.europa.eu/eli/dir/2019/1936/oj?eliuri=eli%3Adir%3A2019%3A1 936%3Aoj&locale=en. Accessed Sept 2024
15. Kaur, P., Stoltzfus, J., Yellapu, V.: Descriptive statistics. Int. J. Acad. Med. **4**(1), 60–63 (2018). https://doi.org/10.4103/IJAM.IJAM_7_18
16. Nicaj, L., Wilt, S., Henning, K.: Motor vehicle crash pedestrian deaths in New York City: the plight of the older pedestrian. Inj. Prev. **12**(6), 414–416 (2006)
17. Sullivan, J.M., Flannagan, M.J.: Determining the potential safety benefit of improved lighting in three pedestrian crash scenarios. Accid. Anal. Prev. **39**(3), 638–647 (2007)
18. Huang, S., Yang, J., Eklund, F.: Evaluation of remote pedestrian sensor system based on the analysis of car-pedestrian accident scenarios. Saf. Sci. **46**(9), 1345–1355 (2008)
19. Sherony, R., Zhang, C.: Pedestrian and bicyclist crash scenarios in the US. In: 2015 IEEE 18th International Conference on Intelligent Transportation Systems, pp. 1533–1538. IEEE, September 2015
20. Stutts, J.C., Hunter, W.W., Pein, W.E.: Pedestrian crash types: 1990s update. Transp. Res. Rec. **1538**(1), 68–74 (1996)
21. Williams, J.S., Graff, J.A., Uku, J.M.: Pedestrian intoxication and fatal traffic accident injury patterns. Prehosp. Disaster Med. **10**(1), 30–35 (1995)
22. Holm, A., Jaani, J., Eensoo, D., Piksööt, J.: Pedestrian behaviour of 6th grade Estonian students: implications of social factors and accident-prevention education at school. Transp. Res. F: Traffic Psychol. Behav. **52**, 112–119 (2018)
23. Vasudevan, V., Pulugurtha, S.S., Nambisan, S.S.: Methods to prioritize pedestrian high-crash locations and statistical analysis of their relationships. Transp. Res. Rec. **2002**(1), 39–54 (2007)
24. Miao, M., Yang, Y., Liang, Y.: Pedestrian crash risk assessment and intervention. Adv. Mech. Eng. **8**(7), 1687814016653296 (2016)
25. Kushchenko, L.E., Kushchenko, S.V., Kravchenko, A.A., Shatova, J.S.: Improving traffic safety and accident prediction at pedestrian crossings. In: IOP Conference Series: Materials Science and Engineering, vol. 913, no. 4, p. 042060. IOP Publishing, August 2020
26. Martínez-Ruiz, V., Valenzuela-Martínez, M., Lardelli-Claret, P., Molina-Soberanes, D., Moreno-Roldán, E., Jiménez-Mejías, E.: Factors related to the risk of pedestrian fatality after a crash in Spain, 1993–2013. J. Transp. Health **12**, 279–289 (2019)
27. Pulugurtha, S.S., Penkey, E.N.: Assessing use of pedestrian crash data to identify unsafe transit service segments for safety improvements. Transp. Res. Rec. **2198**(1), 93–102 (2010)
28. Santos, B., Carvalheira, C.: Pedestrian road accident index for municipalities: the Portuguese case. In: IOP Conference Series: Materials Science and Engineering, vol. 603, no. 4, p. 042084. IOP Publishing, September 2019
29. Wootton, I.A., Spainhour, L.K.: Examining deficiencies in Florida pedestrian crash data. Transp. Res. Rec. **2002**(1), 31–38 (2007)
30. Evans, L.: Double pair comparison—A new method to determine how occupant characteristics affect fatality risk in traffic crashes. Accid. Anal. Prev. **18**(3), 217–227 (1986)
31. Evans, L.: Factors influencing pedestrian and motocyclist fatality risk. J. Traffic Med. **19**(2), 69–73 (1991)
32. Evans, L.: Traffic Safety and the Driver, vol. 20. Van Nostrand Reinhold (1991)
33. Abrams, M.Z., Cameron, R.: Female vs. Male Relative Fatality Risk in Fatal Crashes: 1975–2018

34. Evans, L.: Rear seat restraint system effectiveness in preventing fatalities. Accid. Anal. Prev. **20**(2), 129–136 (1988)
35. Islam, S., Mannering, F.: Estimation of seat belt effectiveness values using double pair comparison method based on state highway crash data (2015)
36. Keall, M.D.: Pedestrian exposure to risk of road accident in New Zealand. Accid. Anal. Prev. **27**(5), 729–740 (1995)
37. Lenguerrand, E., Martin, J.L., Moskal, A., Gadegbeku, B., Laumon, B.: Limits of the quasi-induced exposure method when compared with the standard case–control design: application to the estimation of risks associated with driving under the influence of cannabis or alcohol. Accid. Anal. Prev. **40**(3), 861–868 (2008)
38. Jiang, X., Lyles, R.W., Guo, R.: A comprehensive review on the quasi-induced exposure technique. Accid. Anal. Prev. **65**, 36–46 (2014)
39. Onieva-García, M.Á., et al.: Gender and age differences in components of traffic-related pedestrian death rates: exposure, risk of crash and fatality rate. Inj. Epidemiol. **3**, 1–10 (2016)
40. Chiu, T., Fang, D., Chen, J., Wang, Y., Jeris, C.: A robust and scalable clustering algorithm for mixed type attributes in large database environment. Paper Presented at the Proceedings of the Seventh ACM SIGKDD International Conference on Knowledge Discovery and Data Mining, San Francisco, CA (2001)
41. Zhang, T., Ramakrishnan, R., Livny, M.: BIRCH: an efficient data clustering method for very large databases. Paper Presented at the ACM SIGMOD Record, Montreal, PQ, Canada (1996)
42. Kashani, A.T., Besharati, M.M.: Fatality rate of pedestrians and fatal crash involvement rate of drivers in pedestrian crashes: a case study of Iran. Int. J. Inj. Control Saf. Promot. **24**(2), 222–231 (2017). https://doi.org/10.1080/17457300.2016.1166139
43. Lam, W.W., Loo, B.P., Yao, S.: Towards exposure-based time-space pedestrian crash analysis in facing the challenges of ageing societies in Asia. Asian Geogr. **30**(2), 105–125 (2013)
44. Mofadal, A.I., Kanitpong, K., Jiwattanakulpaisarn, P.: Analysis of pedestrian accident costs in Sudan using the willingness-to-pay method. Accid. Anal. Prev. **78**, 201–211 (2015)
45. Andersson Järnberg, L., Andrén, D., Hultkrantz, L., Rutström, E.E., Vimefall, E.: Willingness to pay for private and public traffic safety improvements: the importance of the underlying good. Appl. Econ. 1–14 (2024)
46. Jomnonkwao, S., Wisutwattanasak, P., Ratanavaraha, V.: Factors influencing willingness to pay for accident risk reduction among personal car drivers in Thailand. PLoS ONE **16**(11), e0260666 (2021)
47. Haddak, M.M., Lefèvre, M., Havet, N.: Willingness-to-pay for road safety improvement. Transp. Res. Part A: Policy Pract. **87**, 1–10 (2016)
48. Sakashita, C., Jan, S., Ivers, R.: The application of contingent valuation surveys to obtain willingness to pay data in road safety research: methodological review and recommendations. In: Australian Road Safety Research, Policing and Education Conference, October 2012
49. Puttawong, C., Chaturabong, P.: Willingness-to-pay for estimation the risk pedestrian group accident cost. Civ. Eng. J. **6**(6), 1064–1073 (2020)
50. Hosseini, H., Golestani, M., Bazargani, H.S., Saadati, M.: Estimating willingness to pay for motorcycle helmet and its determinants through contingent valuation method. J. Inj. Violence Res. **16**(02), 101–108 (2024)
51. Venkatachalam, L.: The contingent valuation method: a review. Environ. Impact Assess. Rev. **24**(1), 89–124 (2004)
52. Lord, D., Qin, X., Geedipally, S.R.: Highway Safety Analytics and Modeling. Elsevier (2021)
53. Olszewski, P., Osińska, B., Szagała, P., Włodarek, P.: Development of accident prediction models for pedestrian crossings. In: MATEC Web of Conferences, vol. 231, p. 03002. EDP Sciences (2018)

54. Bowman, B.L., Vecellio, R.L., Miao, J.: Vehicle and pedestrian accident models for median locations. J. Transp. Eng. **121**(6), 531–537 (1995)
55. Omer, I., Gitelman, V., Rofe, Y., Lerman, Y., Kaplan, N., Doveh, E.: Evaluating crash risk in urban areas based on vehicle and pedestrian modeling. Geogr. Anal. **49**(4), 387–408 (2017)
56. Nabavi Niaki, M.S., Fu, T., Saunier, N., Miranda-Moreno, L.F., Amador, L., Bruneau, J.F.: Road lighting effects on bicycle and pedestrian accident frequency: case study in Montreal, Quebec, Canada. Transp. Res. Rec. **2555**(1), 86–94 (2016)
57. Kröyer, H.R.: Pedestrian and bicyclist flows in accident modelling at intersections. Influence of the length of observational period. Saf. Sci. **82**, 315–324 (2016)
58. Rankavat, S., Tiwari, G.: Association between built environment and pedestrian fatal crash risk in Delhi, India. Transp. Res. Rec. **2519**(1), 61–66 (2015)
59. Schneider, R.J., Ryznar, R.M., Khattak, A.J.: An accident waiting to happen: a spatial approach to proactive pedestrian planning. Accid. Anal. Prev. **36**(2), 193–211 (2004)
60. Kitali, A.E., Sando, T., Castro, A., Kobelo, D., Mwakalonge, J.: Using crash modification factors to appraise the safety effects of pedestrian countdown signals for drivers. J. Transp. Eng. Part A-Syst. 4018011 (2018)
61. Lee, J., Abdel-Aty, M., Shah, I.: Evaluation of surrogate measures for pedestrian trips at intersections and crash modeling. Accid. Anal. Prev. **130**, 91–98 (2019)
62. Sacchi, E., Sayed, T., Osama, A.: Developing crash modification functions for pedestrian signal improvement. Accid. Anal. Prev. **83**, 47–56 (2015)
63. Pulugurtha, S.S., Sambhara, V.R.: Pedestrian crash estimation models for signalized intersections. Accid. Anal. Prev. **43**(1), 439–446 (2011)
64. Schneider, R.J., Diogenes, M.C., Arnold, L.S., Attaset, V., Griswold, J., Ragland, D.R.: Association between roadway intersection characteristics and pedestrian crash risk in Alameda County, California. Transp. Res. Rec. **2198**(1), 41–51 (2010)
65. Cai, Q., Lee, J., Eluru, N., Abdel-Aty, M.: Macro-level pedestrian and bicycle crash analysis: incorporating spatial spillover effects in dual state count models. Accid. Anal. Prev. **93**, 14–22 (2016)
66. Chen, P., Zhou, J.: Effects of the built environment on automobile-involved pedestrian crash frequency and risk. J. Transp. Health **3**(4), 448–456 (2016)
67. Ukkusuri, S., Miranda-Moreno, L.F., Ramadurai, G., Isa-Tavarez, J.: The role of built environment on pedestrian crash frequency. Saf. Sci. **50**(4), 1141–1151 (2012)
68. Wang, Y., Kockelman, K.M.: A Poisson-lognormal conditional-autoregressive model for multivariate spatial analysis of pedestrian crash counts across neighborhoods. Accid. Anal. Prev. **60**, 71–84 (2013)
69. Wang, J., Huang, H., Zeng, Q.: The effect of zonal factors in estimating crash risks by transportation modes: motor vehicle, bicycle and pedestrian. Accid. Anal. Prev. **98**, 223–231 (2017)
70. Ding, C., Chen, P., Jiao, J.: Non-linear effects of the built environment on automobile-involved pedestrian crash frequency: a machine learning approach. Accid. Anal. Prev. **112**, 116–126 (2018)
71. Ukkusuri, S., Hasan, S., Aziz, H.A.: Random parameter model used to explain effects of built-environment characteristics on pedestrian crash frequency. Transp. Res. Rec. **2237**(1), 98–106 (2011)
72. Mansfield, T.J., Peck, D., Morgan, D., McCann, B., Teicher, P.: The effects of roadway and built environment characteristics on pedestrian fatality risk: a national assessment at the neighborhood scale. Accid. Anal. Prev. **121**, 166–176 (2018)
73. Lord, D., Mannering, F.: The statistical analysis of crash-frequency data: a review and assessment of methodological alternatives. Transp. Res. Part A: Policy and Pract. **44**(5), 291–305 (2010)

74. Washington, S.P., Karlaftis, M.G., Mannering, F.L.: Statistical Methods for Transportation Engineers. Wiley (2010)
75. Persaud, B., El-Basyuni, S.: Safety performance functions for different types of crashes and their application to the safety evaluation of roadway projects. Transp. Res. Rec. **2430**, 41–49 (2014)
76. Hauer, E., Briere, M.: Empirical Bayes methods for estimating safety performance functions. Accid. Anal. Prev. **46**, 61–69 (2012)
77. Miaou, S.P., Lum, H.: Modeling vehicle accident frequency as a function of highway geometric design and traffic volume. Accid. Anal. Prev. **25**(6), 689–709 (1993)
78. Hauer, E., Harwood, D., Council, F., Griffith, M.: Estimating safety at intersections. Transp. Res. Rec.: J. Transp. Res. Board **1897**, 1–12 (2004)
79. Eby, D.W., Vivoda, J.M.: Empirical Bayes method for estimating the expected number of crashes at a location. J. Saf. Res. **42**(4), 257–265 (2011)
80. Milton, J.C., Mannering, F.L.: The relationship between highway geometric design and traffic safety: a review and analysis. Accid. Anal. Prev. **30**(4), 607–616 (1998)
81. Ivan, J.N., Konduri, K.C.: Crash severity methods. In: Safe Mobility: Challenges, Methodology and Solutions, vol. 11, pp. 325–350. Emerald Publishing Limited (2018)
82. Bhuiyan, H., et al.: Crash severity analysis and risk factors identification based on an alternate data source: a case study of developing country. Sci. Rep. **12**(1), 21243 (2022)
83. Nowakowska, M.: Logistic models in crash severity classification based on road characteristics. Transp. Res. Rec. **2148**(1), 16–26 (2010)
84. Sasidharan, L., Wu, K.F., Menendez, M.: Exploring the application of latent class cluster analysis for investigating pedestrian crash injury severities in Switzerland. Accid. Anal. Prev. **85**, 219–228 (2015)
85. Rella Riccardi, M., Galante, F., Scarano, A., Montella, A.: Econometric and machine learning methods to identify pedestrian crash patterns. Sustainability **14**(22), 15471 (2022)
86. Rella Riccardi, M., Mauriello, F., Sarkar, S., Galante, F., Scarano, A., Montella, A.: Parametric and non-parametric analyses for pedestrian crash severity prediction in Great Britain. Sustainability **14**(6), 3188 (2022)
87. Amoh-Gyimah, R., Aidoo, E.N., Akaateba, M.A., Appiah, S.K.: The effect of natural and built environmental characteristics on pedestrian-vehicle crash severity in Ghana. Int. J. Inj. Control Saf. Promot. **24**(4), 459–468 (2017)
88. Olszewski, P., Szagała, P., Wolański, M., Zielińska, A.: Pedestrian fatality risk in accidents at unsignalized zebra crosswalks in Poland. Accid. Anal. Prev. **84**, 83–91 (2015)
89. Moudon, A.V., Lin, L., Jiao, J., Hurvitz, P., Reeves, P.: The risk of pedestrian injury and fatality in collisions with motor vehicles, a social ecological study of state routes and city streets in King County, Washington. Accid. Anal. Prev. **43**(1), 11–24 (2011)
90. Mukherjee, D., Mitra, S.: Impact of road infrastructure land use and traffic operational characteristics on pedestrian fatality risk: a case study of Kolkata, India. Transp. Dev. Econ. **5**(2), 6 (2019)
91. Koopmans, J.M., Friedman, L., Kwon, S., Sheehan, K.: Urban crash-related child pedestrian injury incidence and characteristics associated with injury severity. Accid. Anal. Prev. **77**, 127–136 (2015)
92. Park, S., Ko, D.: A multilevel model approach for investigating individual accident characteristics and neighborhood environment characteristics affecting pedestrian-vehicle crashes. Int. J. Environ. Res. Public Health **17**(9), 3107 (2020)
93. Salon, D., McIntyre, A.: Determinants of pedestrian and bicyclist crash severity by party at fault in San Francisco, CA. Accid. Anal. Prev. **110**, 149–160 (2018)
94. Sarkar, S., Tay, R., Hunt, J.D.: Logistic regression model of risk of fatality in vehicle–pedestrian crashes on national highways in Bangladesh. Transp. Res. Rec. **2264**(1), 128–137 (2011)

95. Sasidharan, L., Menéndez, M.: Partial proportional odds model—An alternate choice for analyzing pedestrian crash injury severities. Accid. Anal. Prev. **72**, 330–340 (2014)
96. Sasidharan, L., Menéndez, M.: Application of partial proportional odds model for analyzing pedestrian crash injury severities in Switzerland. J. Transp. Saf. Secur. **11**(1), 58–78 (2019)
97. Tay, R., Choi, J., Kattan, L., Khan, A.: A multinomial logit model of pedestrian–vehicle crash severity. Int. J. Sustain. Transp. **5**(4), 233–249 (2011)
98. Kopsacheilis, A., Politis, I.: Exploring factors influencing pedestrian accident severity: a multi-source study in the city of Berlin. Eur. Transp. Res. Rev. **16**(1), 63 (2024)
99. Rifaat, S.M., Chin, H.C.: Accident severity analysis using ordered probit model. J. Adv. Transp. **41**(1), 91–114 (2007)
100. Hosseinian, S.M., Najafi Moghaddam Gilani, V., Mirbaha, B., Abdi Kordani, A.: Statistical analysis for study of the effect of dark clothing color of female pedestrians on the severity of accident using machine learning methods. Math. Probl. Eng. **2021**(1), 5567638 (2021)
101. Gálvez-Pérez, D., Guirao, B., Ortuño, A.: Analysis of the elderly pedestrian injury severity in urban traffic accidents in Spain using machine learning techniques. Transp. Res. Proc. **71**, 6–13 (2023)
102. Aziz, H.A., Ukkusuri, S.V., Hasan, S.: Exploring the determinants of pedestrian–vehicle crash severity in New York City. Accid. Anal. Prev. **50**, 1298–1309 (2013)
103. Haleem, K., Alluri, P., Gan, A.: Analyzing pedestrian crash injury severity at signalized and non-signalized locations. Accid. Anal. Prev. **81**, 14–23 (2015)
104. D'Apuzzo, M., Cappelli, G., Naranni, S., De Guidi, M., Nicolosi, V.: Machine learning tools for predicting the outcome of pedestrian crashes: preliminary findings in the Metropolitan City of Rome. In: Gervasi, O., Murgante, B., Garau, C., Taniar, D., Rocha, A.M.A.C., Faginas Lago, M.N. (eds.) ICCSA 2024. LNCS, vol. 14824, pp. 116–132. Springer, Cham (2024). https://doi.org/10.1007/978-3-031-65332-2_8
105. Li, D., Ranjitkar, P., Zhao, Y., Yi, H., Rashidi, S.: Analyzing pedestrian crash injury severity under different weather conditions. Traffic Inj. Prev. **18**(4), 427–430 (2017)
106. Toran Pour, A., Moridpour, S., Tay, R., Rajabifard, A.: Modelling pedestrian crash severity at mid-blocks. Transp. A: Transp. Sci. **13**(3), 273–297 (2017)
107. Toran Pour, A., Moridpour, S., Tay, R., Rajabifard, A.: Neighborhood influences on vehicle-pedestrian crash severity. J. Urban Health **94**, 855–868 (2017)
108. Arifeen, S.U., Ali, M., Macioszek, E.: Analysis of vehicle pedestrian crash severity using advanced machine learning techniques. Arch. Transp. **68**(4), 91–116 (2023)
109. Santos, D., Saias, J., Quaresma, P., Nogueira, V.B.: Machine learning approaches to traffic accident analysis and hotspot prediction. Computers **10**(12), 157 (2021)
110. Das, S., Le, M., Dai, B.: Application of machine learning tools in classifying pedestrian crash types: a case study. Transp. Saf. Environ. **2**(2), 106–119 (2020)
111. Guo, M., Yuan, Z., Janson, B., Peng, Y., Yang, Y., Wang, W.: Older pedestrian traffic crashes severity analysis based on an emerging machine learning XGBoost. Sustainability **13**(2), 926 (2021)
112. Weller, B.E., Bowen, N.K., Faubert, S.J.: Latent class analysis: a guide to best practice. J. Black Psychol. **46**(4), 287–311 (2020)
113. Kumbhare, T.A., Chobe, S.V.: An overview of association rule mining algorithms. Int. J. Comput. Sci. Inf. Technol. **5**(1), 927–930 (2014)

A New Methodology for Using Hybrid Configurational Tools for Local Analysis of Pedestrian Flows in Large Areas

Sofia Nardoianni[1](✉)[ID], Giuseppe Cappelli[1,2][ID], Mauro D'Apuzzo[1][ID], Martina Furioso[1], and Vittorio Nicolosi[2][ID]

[1] University of Cassino and Southern Lazio, Via G. Di Biasio 43, 03043 Cassino, Italy
{sofia.nardoianni,giuseppe.cappelli1,dapuzzo}@unicas.it,
martina.furioso@studentmail.unicas.it
[2] University of Rome "Tor Vergata", Via del Politecnico, 1, 00133 Rome, Italy
nicolosi@uniroma2.it

Abstract. In recent years, the concept of sustainable mobility has been increasingly pursued; as a result, the need for effective planning of pedestrian infrastructure is highlighted. This research employs configurational analysis, specifically the spatial syntax methodology, to examine pedestrian flows in urban environments. Spatial analysis was integrated with demographic data to assess pedestrian movement patterns and network accessibility. The area in question falls within a district of the city of Rome, such as the Nomentano-Tiburtina. To improve predictive accuracy, an approach is proposed that studies the influence of neighboring municipalities on the estimation of pedestrian crowding. The results reveal that this consideration significantly influences the integration and estimates of pedestrian flow. This study offers valuable insights for urban planners seeking to optimize pedestrian networks and promote sustainable urban mobility.

Keywords: Sustainable mobility · Pedestrian · Space Syntax · Configurational approach

1 Introduction

Sustainable mobility refers to a mode of transport and movement that is responsible and has minimal environmental impact. It includes a set of virtuous mobility practices that can bring environmental, social, and economic benefits. Thus, not only does the environment benefit from this alternative mobility, but also the entire population experiencing it.

The issue of managing sustainable transport modes has become one of the most debated issues in recent years within local, national, and international environmental policies aimed at reducing the environmental impact from the movement of people and goods. Improving the environmental aspects of mobility demand, particularly in urban areas, is a priority to promote a better quality of life for citizens. This includes social and cultural relationships, as well as the health benefits of increased physical activity and the creation of new economic and development opportunities. Furthermore, if walking or cycling becomes an alternative to motorized transport, it improves the urban environment by reducing emissions, whether in terms of noise and air pollutants or fine particulates in the atmosphere, congestion of vehicles (measured by the time spent by motorists in traffic to cover the same distances), and allows greater usability of public spaces within the urban fabric.

In recent years, also due to the pandemic emergency, especially in urban areas, citizens' habits have changed. They preferred alternative methods for their trips to keep the distance and move safely, with walking or cycling among the most interesting options. This has led administrations to reorganize urban areas to make them attractive but also safe for users.

However, this increase in pedestrian mobility has led to increased exposure to the risk of accidents [1], whose exposure can be defined as the annual number of vehicle-pedestrian collisions divided by the estimated annual volume of pedestrians at a given intersection [2, 3]. It is therefore necessary to assess the pedestrian congestion and its routes and understand what the main risks are that these vulnerable users face in order to be able to address them. The study of pedestrian congestion involves first going to investigating the pedestrian network and its shape.

In the literature, this is often investigated by means of "proximity" models implemented with a specific algorithm in a QGIS plugin called Space Syntax [4–9]. Among the descriptive parameters of the model, the one investigated in this research is the Integration, which describes the probability that each section could be chosen or not by the pedestrian to carry out the movement from a point of origin to a point of destination.

However, previous studies have shown a weak correlation between Integration and real pedestrian flows [10–12], obtaining low correlation coefficients ranging from 0.2 to 0.4. It is in this context that numerous studies have shown how network connectivity affects pedestrian activity, but not only, other variables such as population, land use, purpose of travel, and means of connection also affect the behaviour of pedestrians [13–15]. A recent literature review [16] has shown that most studies focus on high-density urban areas and limit themselves to the pedestrian network configuration analysis, without integrating socio-demographic or contextual factors.

In addition, there is little detail on issues such as pedestrian congestion, flow volume management, and the influence of surrounding areas on pedestrian behaviour.

So, the possibility of introducing population weight to identify the right configuration parameters could be an approach that leads to an improvement of the model [17–20]. This research therefore proposes to use a hybrid approach, developed on a real case study, combining configurational analysis with a proximity model based on population density, evaluated by means of concentric buffers with increasing radius.

Not only, among the parameters that influence the assessment of pedestrian crowding, especially in large-scale areas, was investigated the influence of the areas surrounding the case study area [21, 22].

A methodology has been developed that allows not only the assessment of pedestrian crowding through proximity methods with the use of Open-Source GIS software but also a methodology to identify the portion of area bordering the area of the case study to be considered in the development of the hybrid approach described, to achieve results that are as close to reality as possible.

2 Vulnerable Users of the Road

In the panorama of urban mobility, the pedestrian component is certainly fundamental, but at the same time is considered weak.

Even if sustainable mobility is a widespread and consolidated concept, the pedestrian's aspect remains marginal compared to other transport policies, because, to walk, little space is needed, no infrastructure, no organization, and no means. It is also well known that walking is always possible within a generic urban environment, and therefore, it is not necessary to deal with the studies associated with it in depth.

In the organization of public services, people have mistakenly become accustomed to thinking in terms of supply, so that pedestrian mobility does not seem to need anything to be developed, being perceived as a sort of "natural" endowment deriving from urbanization, which does not necessarily imply accurate planning, projects or specific resources.

The lack of disciplinary and political attention to pedestrian mobility greatly undermines its proper development. Outside the historic centers and in the suburbs, the space reserved for pedestrians, or in any case intended for means of transport other than vehicles, tends to reduce to a minimum, inevitably losing quality and in some cases reaching to be physically not feasible or difficult to use for part or the totality of potential users.

According to ISTAT in Europe [23], 30% of journeys by car cover distances less than 3 km and 50% less than 5 km; such movements could be easily completed in 15–20 min with cycles or 30–50 min on foot. It is clear, therefore, that the conversion of a significant proportion of car journeys to walking or other means an alternative to motor vehicles is not only desirable, but also possible, to benefit also from the increasing rates of sedentariness and for the reduction of accidents concerning the pedestrian fraction of road users, equal to 485 deaths only during 2022, increasing compared to previous years.

3 Methodology

To obtain a model of pedestrian flows, the methodology shown in the following flow chart has been implemented (see Fig. 1).

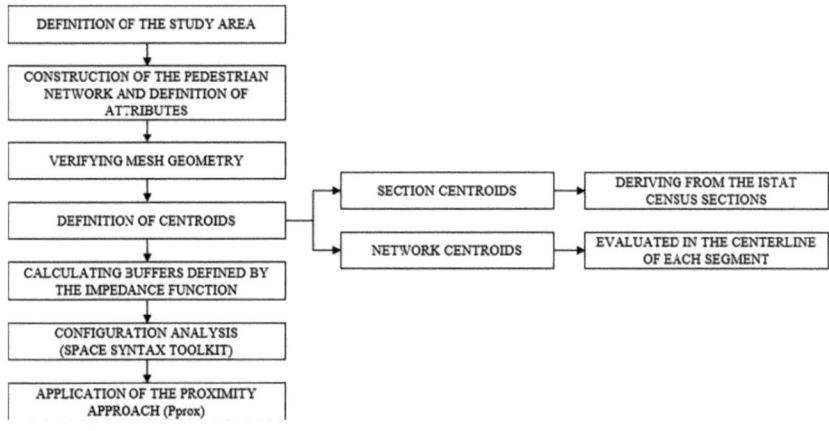

Fig. 1. Flow chart of methodology.

The study of pedestrian crowding using Spatial Syntax includes a configurational analysis that is independent of factors such as emissions or modal choice, focusing solely on the shape of the network. This approach is influenced by the historical development of urban areas, where city centers typically consist of dense and interconnected road networks.

Between key indicators used in this analysis includes the *connectivity* that is a local measure indicating the number of elements directly linked to a space; the *choice* that reflects the flow of movement through a space, with higher values associated with shorter pathways connecting multiple areas; the *integration* that is a global measure of accessibility, representing the minimum number of steps required to reach a point from another within a graph.

Integration thus makes it possible to assess the probability that a place will be chosen as a destination by users [10]. This is particularly relevant in urban contexts where pedestrian flows are strongly influenced by the distribution of destinations, services, and housing densities. Several studies see the use of the integration variable to run it on pedestrian flows in different contexts [10–12, 19, 24].

Various mathematical formulations exist to calculate integration, with the method proposed by Raford and Regland [1] being commonly used (see Eq. 1).

$$INT = \frac{2(MD - 1)}{K - 2} \qquad (1)$$

where:

- MD is the Mean Depth of the entire system; it is the measure that indicates, starting from a specific point, how many road segments on average are needed to reach all other points of the network [4].
- K is the number of nodes in the network.

Since a purely configurational approach does not seem to reflect the complexity of urban pedestrian behaviour, this study proposes a hybrid methodology combining spatial syntax analysis with land use data. This integration aims to improve the accuracy of pedestrian flow forecasts by incorporating both spatial and functional aspects of the urban environment.

The analysis in this study comprises two main phases. Initially, it was established road and pedestrian networks by establishing spatial connections between census sections and road segments. To attribute population values to network segments, obtained from the Italian National Institute of Statistics (ISTAT) databases [25], a proximity approach is used. This method links the attributes of each network centroid (i.e., the midpoint of each road segment) with surrounding centroids using a series of buffers with increasing radii. The radii of these buffers range from 100 to 1600 m, determined by an impedance function [26] that describes pedestrians' likelihood to travel as travel distance varies (see Eq. 2).

$$P_{prox,i} = \sum_{j=100\ m}^{1600\ m} k_{Mj}\ M_{ij} \qquad (2)$$

where:

- k_{Mj} is the propensity to perform a trip;
- M_{ij} is the average population value.

In the initial phase, it was determined a weight, denoted as P_{prox}, was determined for each network centroid. This weight was calculated at increasing distances from the individual centroid, considering the actual propensity of users to move as their distance from it increases. The objective was to establish a weight factor representing the attractiveness of pedestrian flows, based on the average population residing in the specific circular crown area for each road segment.

Subsequently, in the second phase, configurational analysis was conducted within the Space Syntax framework. It was conducted that both "weighted" and "unweighted" analyses were conducted to evaluate the effectiveness of the new "hybrid" approach in comparison to a conventional configurational analysis in predicting pedestrian flows in a real urban setting. In the weighted analysis, the respective P_{prox} values are associated as attributes to the network segments, it will be possible to use them as weights in the predictive analysis with Space Syntax.

4 Case Study

The study area on which this research focuses is located in central Italy, in particular in an area of the metropolitan city of Rome (see Fig. 3) that includes Municipality 2 (see Fig. 2).

The study area (see Fig. 3) includes the zones of Nomentano–Tiburtino located within Municipality 2 of the metropolitan city of Rome.

Fig. 2. Municipalities of the metropolitan city of Rome (in red the Municipality 2 under study).

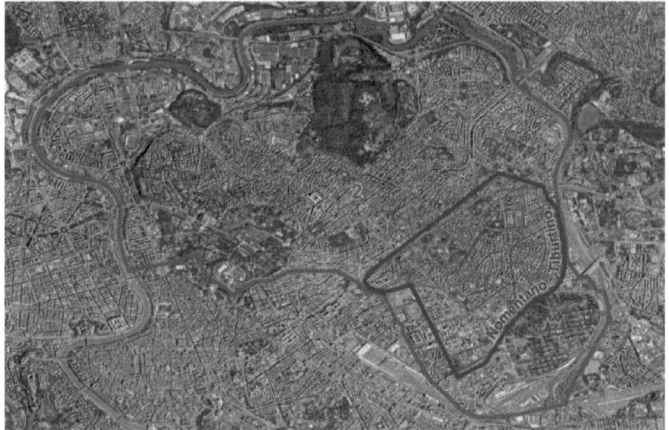

Fig. 3. Case study area (in blue) located in Municipality 2 (in red).

This area sees the presence of metro stations, the proximity to the Roma Tiburtina station, the presence of the University of Rome "La Sapienza", and the Polyclinic "Umberto I". This makes it an area of strong pedestrian attraction, where it becomes crucial to analyze pedestrian flows and the related pedestrian network in order to highlight any disconnections present and provide for their resolution.

4.1 Analysis of the Results

The study area was divided into census sections, each having a centroid as its representation. Following the transfer of population information from section centroids to network centroids, proximity weights (P_{prox}) were assigned to network segments. Subsequently, the hybrid forecasting analysis was initiated. This approach was adopted due to the observation that the pure configurational approach failed to fully capture urban pedestrian activities. Hence, a hybrid method integrating Space Syntax-based configurational analysis with land use and pedestrian travel behavior was proposed.

The results, categorized based on the type of weight used, are displayed on the screen along with corresponding chromatic representations of the network (see Fig. 4 and Fig. 5).

Fig. 4. Configurational analysis (unweighted) of the pedestrian network.

Fig. 5. Configurational analysis (Proximity weight) of the pedestrian network.

Both analyses lead to almost similar results, the substantial difference is that in the unweighted analysis (see Fig. 4), the most loaded sections of the pedestrian network are the most interconnected and belong to the Central Business District (CBD). In the analysis weighted with the weight of proximity (see Fig. 5), interacting the geometric component with that relating to the population and the willingness of pedestrians to move, it can be seen that the central area still has high integration values, in particular the area where there is the metro station and in the vicinity of the Roma Tiburtina station.

In this case, the peripheral area at the top also has high Integration values, probably because this area has a high resident population that generates more trips.

In order to determine the configuration of the pedestrian paths, the areas with and without the presence of sidewalks (see Fig. 6) and the uneven areas in the network due to missed pedestrian crossings (see Fig. 7) were detected. Because of these areas, pedestrians tend to cross in an "abusive" and therefore unsafe way, increasing the risk of accidents, and this could lead the pedestrian to give up following this path and perhaps prefer the car and/or other modes of transport to travel it.

Fig. 6. In red, the sections of the pedestrian network where there are no sidewalks.

Fig. 7. Disconnected areas (in red) in pedestrian paths due to missed crossings.

4.2 Configurational Analysis of the Case Study in Relation to Neighboring Areas

In order to study the behavior of pedestrian flows influenced by the areas bordering the area of the case study, the construction of the pedestrian network was extended to Municipalities 3 and 4 (see Fig. 8).

Fig. 8. New study area conveying the case study area and Municipality 3 and 4.

A configurational analysis was carried out of the new pedestrian network, comparing it to the one in the case study, described above, and those of Municipalities 3 and 4.

In Fig. 9 is possible to see the configurational analysis result expressed by the Integration indicator.

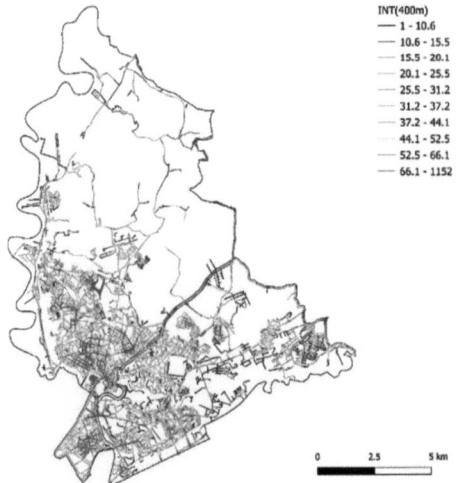

Fig. 9. Values of Integration that combined the Nomentano-Tiburtina pedestrian network between the neighboring Municipalities.

In Fig. 10 is possible to see the configurational analysis result expressed by the P_{prox} weight indicator.

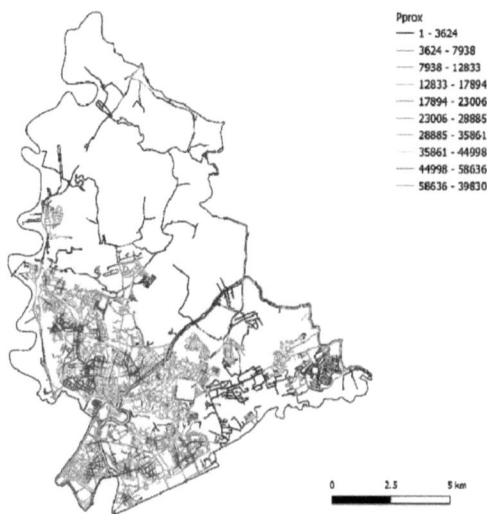

Fig. 10. Values of P_{prox} that combined the Nomentano-Tiburtina pedestrian network between the neighboring Municipalities.

In order to be able to evaluate any differences between the indicators obtained from the configurational approach applied only to the Nomentano-Tiburtina area and those

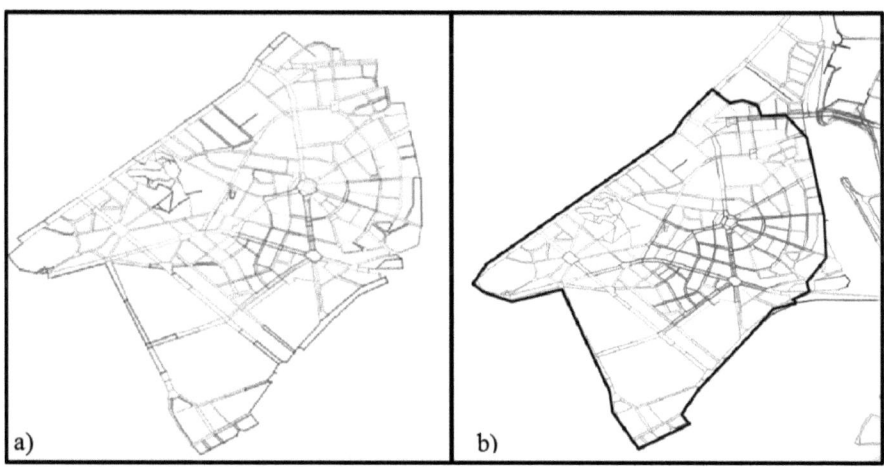

Fig. 11. a) Values of Integration Indicator without the influences of the neighboring Municipalities. **b)** Values of Integration Indicator that combined the Nomentano-Tiburtina pedestrian network between the neighboring Municipalities.

obtained also considering the neighboring municipalities, a focus is carried out on the study area (see Fig. 11 and Fig. 12).

In Fig. 11 and b, it is possible to see the comparison, in terms of Integration Indicator, of the two cases analyzed.

What can be seen is that the presence of the neighboring municipalities greatly influences the values of Integration because, as can be seen in Fig. 11a, they are much stricter than those obtained for the Nomentano-Tiburtina area alone, not considering this influence. In particular, in the vicinity of the border between the Nomentano-Tiburtina area and the Municipalities III and IV of Rome, the values of Integration are strict. This is probably due to the influence of these neighboring municipalities, which have an estimated high pedestrian turnout in these areas. The same comparison was made in terms of P_{prox} (see Fig. 12a and b). Also in this case, the influence of the neighboring municipalities leads to an increase in the aforementioned indicator, but in a more modest way.

Fig. 12. a) Values of Pprox weight Indicator without the influences of the neighboring Municipalities. **b)** Values of Pprox weight Indicator that combined the Nomentano-Tiburtina pedestrian network between the neighboring Municipalities.

In order to define how much the presence of neighboring municipalities influences, in terms of results, the correct Integration values were related to the weight of proximity, considering only the Nomentano-Tiburtina area, and also considering the neighboring municipalities.

As can be seen from Fig. 13, there is a differentiation of the Integration values in the two configurations, reaching a Pearson of 0.8.

By virtue of this, an in-depth study was carried out, considering only the portion of the pedestrian network within the study area, leaving out the external cordon that connects the Nomentano-Tiburtina with the neighboring municipalities. To determine the extension of the pedestrian network of the Nomentano-Tiburtina district that is not affected by the influence of neighboring municipalities, progressive buffers of 20 m

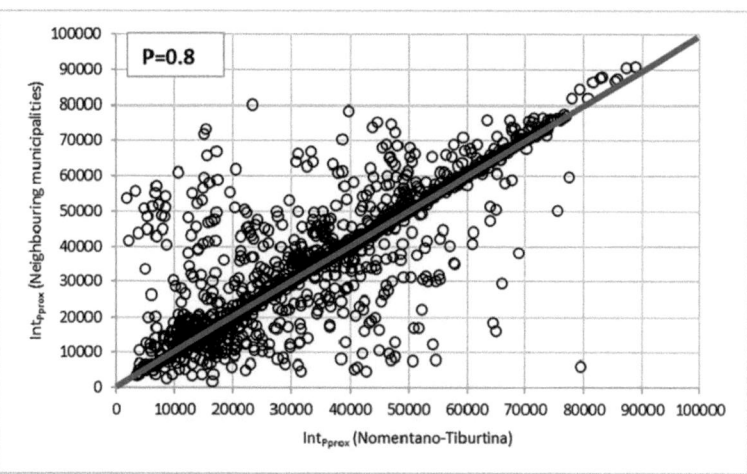

Fig. 13. Relationship between Int_{Pprox} considering only the Nomentano-Tiburtina area and on the other hand, also considering the neighboring municipalities.

were generated towards the interior of the area. With each iteration, the portion of the pedestrian network outside the buffer is subtracted, progressively redefining the study area. To assess the consistency of the process, Pearson's correlation coefficient was calculated at each step. The iteration was interrupted when the Pearson value reached about 0.9, indicating that the external influence is negligible and the portion of the network considered is statistically representative of the study area.

Figure 14 shows the relationship between the value of the Pearson correlation coefficient, calculated at each iteration of the process described above, and a dimensionless term introduced to quantify the effect of the progressive reduction of the area considered. This term has been defined as the ratio between the radius representing the area of the portion subtracted through the application of buffers (r) and the original radius of the study area (R). The trend of the relationship illustrated in the figure allows us to highlight how the variation of the spatial extension affects the correlation, providing a quantitative criterion to determine the threshold beyond which the influence of neighboring municipalities becomes negligible.

What can be deduced from the trend in Fig. 14 is that in the initial phase, there is a strong reduction in the Pearson value, indicating that the pedestrian network near the boundary of the study area is influenced by the presence of neighboring municipalities.

However, for values of the r/R ratio less than about 0.5–0.6, the variation of the Pearson coefficient becomes less pronounced, suggesting that the effect of neighboring municipalities is progressively reduced until it becomes negligible. The iterative process was interrupted when the Pearson coefficient reached the value of 0.91, as this threshold represents a good compromise between the elimination of external influence and the preservation of a statistically significant study area.

The analysis, therefore, confirms that the progressive reduction of the study area makes it possible to mitigate the effect of external conditions, stabilizing the correlation

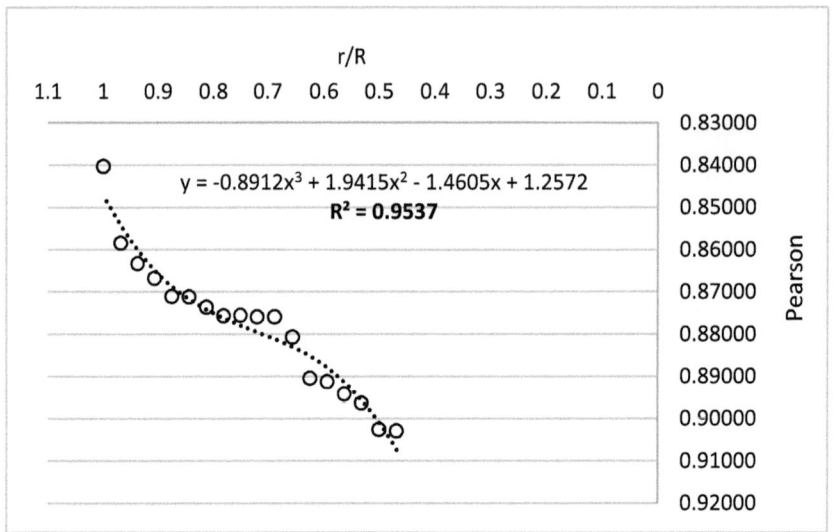

Fig. 14. Pearson's trend concerning the progressive reduction of the area considered

and making the analysis of the pedestrian network in the Nomentano-Tiburtina district more robust.

The portion of the area that identifies the best Pearson is represented in Fig. 15.

Fig. 15. Area of the Nomentano-Tiburtina pedestrian network that is not affected by the presence of neighboring municipalities.

Therefore, the correlation between the Integration values corrected with the proximity weight considering the presence of neighboring municipalities and the Integration values corrected with the proximity weight considering the Nomentano-Tiburtina pedestrian network subtracted from the portion of the area defined above is shown in Fig. 16.

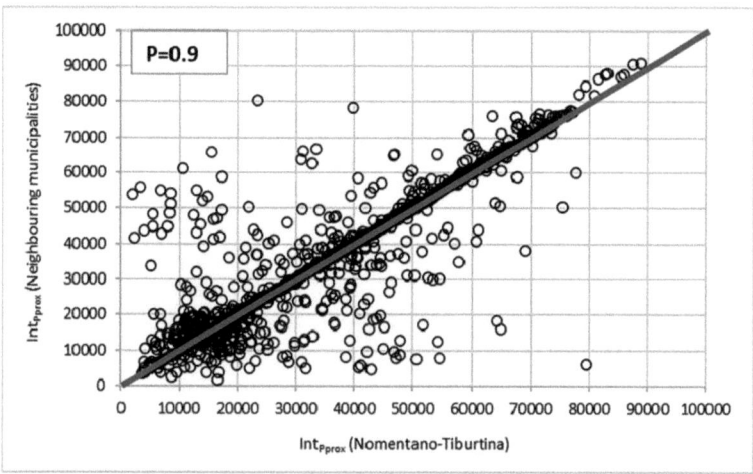

Fig. 16. Relationship between Int_{Pprox} considering only the Nomentano-Tiburtina inner area, and on the other hand, also considering the neighboring municipalities.

This implies that the presence of neighboring municipalities influences the external cordon of the study area, i.e., the one soon to communicate with them.

5 Conclusion

To encourage the adoption of soft mobility, it is necessary to integrate cycle and pedestrian paths into urban projects, ensuring that they are well-designed and convenient for users. It is important to understand the needs of the population and to create a network of connections that is efficient and accessible. To adequately size these routes, it is essential to analyze the flows of people and their movements in the urban context. An innovative approach to estimating pedestrian displacements was developed. However, further experimental validation is needed to refine this model. This approach could be invaluable for city administrators, allowing them to assess and mitigate risks related to road safety and pedestrian traffic by integrating data on pedestrian activities with information on vehicular traffic.

The analyses carried out showed that the presence of neighboring municipalities has a significant impact on the values of Integration and P_{prox} in the Nomentano-Tiburtina area. When considering these neighboring areas, the integration values become considerably stricter, probably due to the higher pedestrian influx influenced by neighboring municipalities. Similarly, P_{prox} values also increase, although to a lesser extent, indicating a modest influence of neighboring areas on this indicator. These findings underscore the importance of considering broader geographical contexts in urban planning and analysis to accurately assess and address various urban parameters and dynamics.

In particular, it has been demonstrated that the presence of these areas influences the results obtained in terms of Integration in a particular area of influence or the area immediately bordering the adjacent areas. As far as the "internal" part of the study area is concerned, it presents a strong agreement between the configurational analysis conducted without the presence of the neighboring municipalities and with the presence of the latter. This leads to say that, as far as the development of configurational analyses of large areas is concerned, it is necessary to consider an "internal" area that is not affected by the influence of confined areas, which, on the contrary, have a strong impact on the cordon area near the latter.

A potential limitation of this study concerns the use of topological buffers as reference areas for pedestrian density estimation.

Although this approach is effective for general modelling of proximity, it does not take into account travel speeds influenced by various factors such as land use or infrastructure quality [27]. The literature also shows that informal links are often used by pedestrians and significantly influence real movement patterns [28].

In the future, it is planned to extend the modelled pedestrian network by integrating it with other informal links and to consider speed of travel and quality of pedestrian infrastructure as additional variables influencing the results on pedestrian congestion.

What is more, this research aims to be able to assess whether and how the presence of shops can influence the assessment of pedestrian traffic, and it is also planned to calibrate the model with a collection of pedestrian flow data.

Acknowledgments. The research leading to these results has received funding from Project "Ecosistema dell'innovazione Rome Technopole" financed by the EU in the NextGenerationEU plan through MUR Decree n. 1051 23.06.2022 – CUP H33C22000420001. This manuscript reflects only the authors' views and opinions, neither the European Union nor the European Commission can be considered responsible for them.

Author Contributions. Conceptualization, N.S and C.G.; **methodology**, N.S and C.G.; **software**, N.S, C.G. and F.M.; **validation**, N.S and C.G.; **formal analysis**, N.S, C.G. and F.M.; **investigation**, N.S and C.G.; **resources**, N.S and C.G; **data curation**, N.S and C.G.; **writing—original draft preparation**, N.S and C.G; **writing—review and editing**, N.S and C.G; **visualization**, N.S and C.G.; **supervision**, D.A.M. and N.V.; **project administration**, D.A.M. and N.V.; **funding acquisition**, D.A.M. and N.V. All authors have read and agreed to the published version of the manuscript.

Disclosure of Interests. The authors have no competing interests to declare that are relevant to the content of this article.

References

1. Raford, N., Ragland, D.: Space syntax: innovative pedestrian volume modeling tool for pedestrian safety. Transp. Res. Rec. **1878**(1), 66–74 (2004)
2. Jacobsen, P.: Safety in numbers: more walkers and bicyclists, safer walking and bicycling. Inj. Prev. **9**(3), 205–209 (2003)

3. Leden, L.: Pedestrian risk decrease with pedestrian flow. A case study based on data from signalized intersections in Hamilton, Ontario. Accid. Anal. Prev. **34**(4), 457–464 (2002)
4. Al Sayed, K.: Space Syntax Methodology. Bartlett School of Architecture. UCL, London, UK (2018)
5. D'Apuzzo, M., Santilli, D., Evangelisti, A., Pelagalli, V., Montanaro, O., Nicolosi, V.: An exploratory step to evaluate the pedestrian exposure in urban environment. In: Gervasi, O., et al. (eds.) ICCSA 2020. LNTCS, vol. 12255, pp. 645–657. Springer, Cham (2020). https://doi.org/10.1007/978-3-030-58820-5_47
6. D'Apuzzo, M., Santilli, D., Evangelisti, A., Nicolosi, V.: Some remarks on soft mobility: a new engineered approach to the cycling infrastructure design. In: Gervasi O., et al. (eds.) ICCSA 2021. LNTCS, vol. 12958, pp. 441–456. Springer, Cham (2021). https://doi.org/10.1007/978-3-030-87016-4_33
7. Cutini, V., Di Pinto, V., Rinaldi, A.M., Rossini, F.: Informal settlements spatial analysis using space syntax and geographic information systems. In: Misra, S., et al. (eds.) ICCSA 2019. LNTCS, vol. 11621, pp. 343–356. Springer, Cham (2019). https://doi.org/10.1007/978-3-030-24302-9_25
8. Santilli, D., D'Apuzzo, M., Evangelisti, A., Nicolosi, V.: Towards sustainability: new tools for planning urban pedestrian mobility. Sustainability **13**(16), 9371 (2021)
9. D'Apuzzo, M., Santilli, D., Evangelisti, A., Nicolosi, V., Cappelli, G.: Estimation of pedestrian flows in urban context: a comparison between the pre and post pandemic period. In: Gervasi, O., Murgante, B., Misra, S., Rocha, A.M.A.C., Garau, C. (eds.) ICCSA 2022. LNCS, vol. 13380, pp. 484–495. Springer, Cham (2022). https://doi.org/10.1007/978-3-031-10542-5_33
10. Hiller, B.P.A.: Natural movement: or configuration and attraction in urban pedestrian movement. Environ. Plan. B: Plan. Des. **20**(1), 29–66 (1993)
11. Lerman, Y., Rofè, Y.: Using space syntax to model pedestrian movement in urban transportation planning. Geogr. Anal. **46**(4), 392–410 (2014)
12. Dai, W.: A configurational exploration of pedestrian and cyclist movements: using Hangzhou as a case study. In: Kim, Y.O., Park, H.T., Seo, K.W. (eds.) The Ninth International Space Syntax Symposium 2013, vol. 31. Urban Morphology, Seoul, Korea (2013)
13. Cervero, R.A.: Travel Choices in Pedestrian versus Automobile Oriented Neighborhoods. Working Paper 644, University of California at Berkeley, Berkeley, CA (1995)
14. Fan, M., Hedayati Marzbali, M., Abdullah, A., Maghsoodi Tilaki, M.J.: Using a space syntax approach to enhance pedestrians' accessibility and safety in the Historic City of George Town, Penang. Urban Sci. **8**(1), 6 (2024)
15. Sirjani, A.H., Szabó, Á.: Evaluating walkability in Budapest through space syntax analysis: a case study of Egyetem square and Corvin promenade. Period. Polytech. Archit. **54**(3), 238–246 (2023)
16. Mehrinejad Khotbehsara, E., Yu, R., Somasundaraswaran, K., Askarizad, R., Kolbe-Alexander, T.: The walkable environment: a systematic review through the lens of Space Syntax as an integrated approach. Smart Sustain. Built Environ. (2025)
17. Cutini, V.: Spazio urbano e movimento pedonale Uno studio sull'ipotesi configurazionale [Urban space and pedestrian movement–a study on the configurational hypothesis]. CYBERGEO **111**(111), 1–9 (1999)
18. Hillier, B., Hanson, J.: Ideas are in things: an application of the space syntax method to discovering house genotypes. Environ. Plan. B: Plan. Des. **14**, 363–385 (1987)
19. Hillier, B.: Network effects and psychological effects: a theory of urban movement. In: van Nes, A. (eds.) International Conference on Spatial Information Theory 2005, pp. 475–490. Techne Press, Delft (2005)
20. Hoogendoorn, S.P.: Pedestrian route-choice and activity scheduling theory and models. Transp. Res. Part B **38**(2), 169–190 (2004)

21. Kitamura, R.M.: A micro-analysis of land use and travel in five neighborhoods in the San Francisco Bay Area. Transportation **24**(2), 125–158 (1997)
22. Southworth, M.: The evolving metropolis: studies of community, neighborhood, and street form at the urban edge. J. Am. Plan. Assoc. **59**(3), 271–287 (1993)
23. ISTAT Homepage. https://www.istat.it/it/files/2023/10/Incidenti-stradali-in-Italia_aggiornamento-dati-provinciali_anno-2022.pdf. Accessed 20 Mar 2024
24. Helbing, D.P.: Self-organizing pedestrian movement. Environ. Plan. B: Plan. Des. **28**(3), 361–383 (2001)
25. ISTAT: Atti del 9° Censimento generale dell'industria e dei servizi e Censimento delle istituzioni non profit, 5 - Le sezioni di censimento, vol. 5, pp. 162–168 (2015)
26. Kuzmyak, J.R., Walters, J.: NCHRP REPORT 770 - Estimating Bicycling and Walking for Planning and Project Development: A Guidebook, TRB, Washington, D.C. (2014)
27. Gaglione, F., Gargiulo, C., Zucaro, F., Cottrill, C.: Urban accessibility in a 15-minute city: a measure in the city of Naples, Italy. Transp. Res. Proc. **60**, 378–385 (2022)
28. Carra, M., Rossetti, S., Tiboni, M., Vetturi, D.: Urban regeneration effects on walkability scenarios. TeMA-J. Land Use Mob. Environ. 101–114 (2022)

Managing Sustainable Tourist Flows and Heritage Preservation in the Medina of Sousse: A Space Syntax and GIS-Based Approach

Khelil Cherfi Khadidja[1], Merzelkad Rym[1], Benacer Hamza[2], Boudjema Sara[1], Mara Federico[3], and Esposito Dario[4](✉)

[1] University of Blida 1, Blida, Algeria
[2] University of Larbi Ben M'hidi, Oum El Bouaghi, Algeria
[3] University of Pisa, Pisa, Italy
[4] Polytechnic University of Bari, Bari, Italy
dario.esposito@poliba.it

Abstract. The Mediterranean's historic urban centres are often facing rising challenges due to overtourism, threatening both cultural heritage and local urban balance. This paper investigates the interplay between spatial configuration and tourist mobility in the historic Medina of Sousse, a UNESCO World Heritage Site facing rising tourism pressure. Despite the growing body of research on over tourism and heritage management, there remains a lack of spatially grounded analytical tools that diagnose tourist flow imbalances within historic urban fabrics. By combining Space Syntax and GIS-based spatial analysis, the study develops a diagnostic framework to assess connectivity, accessibility, and spatial vulnerability. The methodology identifies patterns of tourist concentration in highly integrated areas and highlights underutilized peripheral zones. These imbalances pose threats to both heritage conservation and social equity. The results support a spatial zoning strategy that redirects flows through alternative routes, promoting a more balanced and sustainable tourism model. The study provides practical insights for urban planners and heritage managers seeking to harmonize tourist experience with the protection of historic urban landscapes.

Keywords: Medina of Sousse · Tourism Management · Heritage Preservation · Spatial Vulnerability · Space Syntax · GIS

1 Introduction

Overtourism poses a significant challenge for historic cities, particularly for globally recognized sites that attract a massive influx of tourists from around the world. A series of spatial initiatives and regulatory measures have arisen to manage the impacts caused by overtourism. The Historic Urban Landscape (HUL) approach initiated by UNESCO, for example, serves as a useful tool for the protection of the cultural heritage in the cities and also facilitates their sustainable urban development [2]. In the case of Venice, the new regulations aim at controlling and managing the massive flow of tourists and short-term rentals [21]; in Dubrovnik, through the use of smart technologies, the tourist numbers in the old town have been tracked in real time, and therefore, the city has been able to devise flexible strategies [23]. Obtained results have also been the inspiration for cities like Barcelona to introduce an upper limit on tourism and shift the tourists from the historical city centre to the lesser-known neighbourhoods for a more even distribution of the population in the area.

However, despite these advancements, there is a notable methodological research gap. Current studies largely focus on policy frameworks and technological applications for managing overtourism, yet lack a systematic spatial method to assess patterns of tourist concentration in highly integrated areas and to identify underutilized peripheral zones. Moreover, there is a need for a practical analytical tool to support spatial zoning strategies that redirect flows through alternative routes, thereby promoting a more balanced and sustainable tourism model.

In this vein, the ground for this research is represented by the Medina of Sousse, a UNESCO World Heritage Site, where unequal distribution of tourists causes congested and underused areas. The high concentration of visitors in specific zones disrupts the balance of urban activity and increases the risk of structural degradation of historic buildings and streets. This Medina, known for its strategic coastal position, has evolved a hierarchical street system of main roads, which are connected to the main gates and are the ones that serve as commercial focal points and so accommodate the largest group of visitors and secondary alleys, which are mostly footpaths; hence, they are used by residents for walking, and the local businesses are located there. This differentiation creates socio-spatial imbalances since traffic flow led to the visit of some locations and imbalance in areas utilization, where only some of the main POIs Ribat, Great Mosque, and Kasbah are crowded along the most vibrant corridors. The research looks at how GIS and space syntax analysis can help find areas that are either underperforming or very crowded with tourists, which helps identify risks to heritage and the Medina management? based on the use of spatial analysis techniques to assess the impact of accessibility, integration values, and land utilization on the flow of tourists.

The current situation of the Medina seems to indicate that it is viable to change visitor flows and reach the sustainable goals of the community by using Space Syntax indexes in conjunction with POI location on GIS to make the analysis for movement patterns and area functionality redistribution. it provides indications about general logics of movement, highlighting underdeveloped areas through the examination of values, such as AGI and ACI, and placement of POIs, etc., which disaggregates Medina into zones based on the intensity of tourism impact and the urgency of conservation needs, thus enabling targeted vulnerability zoning and the redirection of visitor flows to promote balanced urban use.

Thus, the paper aim is to answer to the following question:

How can spatial configuration analysis, through Space Syntax and GIS tools, support sustainable tourist flow management while preserving the heritage integrity of historic urban areas like the Medina of Sousse?

To do that, the paper is organized according to the following structure: an introduction and background of the Medina's heritage followed by a section on methods describes the integration of space syntactic models, GIS spatial analysis, underlining important inequities in accessibility and congestion, a Results section showcasing spatial indicators (AGI, ACI, network density, POI, accessibility, etc.). A discussion Focusing on their consequences for Medina's planning, cultural heritage preservation, and sustainable tourism management, reinforcing it with a comparison to another case study, concluding with notes on key findings, identifying constraints, and advice for future research and intervention projects, particularly with similar historical sites like Casbahs and Ksours cities. Which highlights a historical preservation in line with local socioeconomic needs.

2 Background

2.1 The Medina of Sousse History and Urban Configuration

Medina of Sousse, declared in the list of World Cultural Heritage of UNESCO in 1988, originates from a coastal town in the central part of Tunisia, which was historically a strategic place for the power's dynamic control on the central coast of North Africa, it remains one of the few places in the world where urban life has eluded the otherwise settling process over more than 3000 years [25].

Sousse was rebuilt as a remarkable harbour city by the Aghlabid dynasty; its assured location on the seashore was the main factor in creating a tight trade network and defence system [23].

Foremost among the city's fortified installations the medina includes contour walls, ribat, and the grand mosque, the city of Sousse first existed as a military fortress and then became a spiritual centre [3].

Sousse, during the urbanization process, reconstructed urban layout, and went beyond the architectural development thus the city gradually took one of a kind urban fabric [4] especially after the arrival of the Maltese and Sicilians at the end of the 19th century to the 20th.

This, in turn, was the socio-cultural basis of Medina's economic and cultural transformation [13]. Management of tourist traffic flow and congestion in the medina mostly takes place with the road system and POI as the core elements into consideration.

2.2 Urban Morphology and Road Hierarchy

Medina of Sousse represents an example of urban planning during early Islamic times. It was a setting where the defensive strategy, the social organization, and the commercial vitality were all harmoniously combined to a coherent design. The scientific studies and the conservation work, e.g., carried out by the UNESCO, have proved that its layout reveals a decided hierarchical structuring.

Enclosure, Road and Gate System
The medina is enclosed by a wall, originally pierced by several gates. The actual number of gateways is not explicitly confirmed, but only eight are historically reported, yet of

these, two are the main access for a vehicle and pedestrian—Bab Kairouan (south) and Bab El Gharbi (west), aside from the fact that they form the network spaces they control the entry and exit organized the internal traffic.

Studies have found that a medina road is planned as an axis system. One of them goes through a key gate in a meridian direction to the ribat (a fortified religious structure) and the former interior port, while the other connects Bab El Jadid to Bab El Gharbi. This double-axis system was a platform for defence and commerce: the main roads were used for trade, public processions, and government functions and the in-between network composed of narrow, winding alleys was used for local residential life and pedestrian movement [23].

Moreover, scholarly case studies on the urban fabric of Sousse confirm that these primary hierarchies had been intentionally planned to make a spatial disposition that regularized the urban functions and later this system controlled the growth of the urban expansions patterns. The road network of the medina is designed with a two-level hierarchy:

- Primary Roads: These wide, straight streets begin from the main gates and go deep into the medina's heart which is one of the historical sites. They were the most important commercial roads containing large commercial activities and connected to the main public and religious buildings.
- Secondary Alleys: On the other hand, the smaller, interconnecting roads designed to meet local needs. Curvy paths that indicate the historical city fabric where pedestrian movements are the first priority while cars have access in the minimum way.

Principal Points of Interest (POIs)

The key monuments and landmarks within the medina are arranged along these historical axes. Below is a sequential guide to the most significant POIs, each of which contributes to the medina's multifunctional character (Table 1):

2.3 The Importance of Sustainable Multidisciplinary Approach

The UNESCO World Heritage site's recognition of the medina emphasized the international collaboration in heritage conservation [31]. The role of the medina extends to more than just a cultural object; it is also recognized as a place of social and economic change [16]. Nowadays, we need to focus even more on urban pressure. But one of the modern-day challenges is the growing gap between the city's social and environmental needs, which could potentially negatively influence the urban landscape and the cultural reality of the city [12].

In this context, the challenge needs to be addressed with a multidisciplinary approach to urban planning that combines the revitalization of the medina with the acknowledgment of the socio-economic needs of the present time [12]. Space syntax and GIS (Geographic Information Systems) are the primary tools for achieving this aim. They represent a complete approach to analysing the urban layout, especially as they provide insights on the predictive movement patterns, which opens new opportunities in an integrated urban environment that is economically productive. Space syntax-based models

Table 1. Historical POIs of the Medina

No	Site Name	Date	Description	Source
1	Ribat of Sousse	821 AD	Fortified religious retreat with watchtowers; essential to coastal defence and served as city landmark	[24]
2	Great Mosque of Sousse	9th century	Fortified prayer hall with minaret and walled courtyard; included defensive positioning	[32]
3	Bou Ftata Mosque	838–841 AD	Early Islamic architecture in Ifriqiya; features one of the earliest examples of Kufic script in North Africa	[11]
4	Medersa Zakkak	Ottoman period	Religious and educational building; reflects how the Medina integrated worship, trade, and education	[9]
5	Zaouïa Zakkak	Late Islamic era	Mausoleum-mosque-Medersa complex; aligned with a major urban axis; represents late Islamic decorative styles	[1]
6	Kasbah & Archaeological Museum	Various/Modern	Formerly public offices; now a museum hosting Roman mosaics and historical artifacts	[31]
7	Dar Echaraa	Modern use	Originally a courthouse; transformed into a cultural centre	[31]
8	Citterns de la Sofra	Byzantine period	Urban water management system in arid climate; demonstrates Byzantine engineering excellence	[15]
9	Tour de Khalef	Historical/Present	Former Kasbah tower; now a lighthouse; symbolizes the city's defensive and maritime heritage	[33]

have shown they can help understand how people think about space and how they move around in complicated city areas [8].

Recent studies have looked into detailed ways to map and evaluate the multiple vulnerabilities of outdoor spaces, showing that older urban areas are especially at risk from combined dangers [5]. This view matches earlier research that emphasized the need to combine geomatics data, agent-based simulation, and building performance assessment to enhance resilience in historic urban areas facing various risks [22]. These tools can help measure how different areas in Medina are connected and how people move around, which helps create plans that balance tourist access with protecting historical sites [6, 7, 29, 30]. On the other hand, GIS is capable of providing information on spatial charts and also giving the ability to organize data, which is essential for the purpose of identifying and managing tourism, the number of visitors in every area, and the infrastructure. All support the creation of flexible and sustainable tourism strategies [14, 27].

In addition, the GIS-based methodologies of designing can be deployed to build the tourist routes that divert the tourists away from the main sites and facilitate them to explore the unknown architectural elements and structures constructed in the rest of the city. This will balance tourist traffic and reduce pressure on popular sites.

3 Methodology

3.1 Research Approach

The approach is a mixed method approach (quantitative/qualitative) based on the development of a research framework that integrates the use of space syntax analysis and geographic information systems to evaluate accessibility, congestion, and the impacts of tourism on heritage preservation (Fig. 1).

3.2 Data Collection

- Primary and secondary data are the basis of the research.
- Geospatial Data: These include roads, land use, and historical landmarks that were obtained through GIS databases and historical maps.
- Tourist Flow Data: The data was collected through GPS tracking.
- Urban Morphology: This information is obtained from satellite imagery and land surveys (Table 2).

3.3 Analytical Framework

The methodology outlines a triple process:

- **Step 1:** Spatial Network Analysis (Space Syntax)
  Objective: Identify the main places in which tourists move and their accessibility.
  Tools Used: Depthmapx, Space Syntax Software.
- **Step 2:** GIS-Based Spatial Analysis
  Objective: To distinguish the places characterized by high tourist density and the ones underutilized.
  Tools Used: ArcGIS, QGIS.

In the following section we have explained in a detail the indicators related to the study:

1. **AGI (Average Global Integration):** Measures global accessibility of streets in the axial map. It is computed as the mean value of global integration (Rn) across all segments using the formula: $\mathbf{AGI = (1/n) \times \Sigma\, Rn_i}$

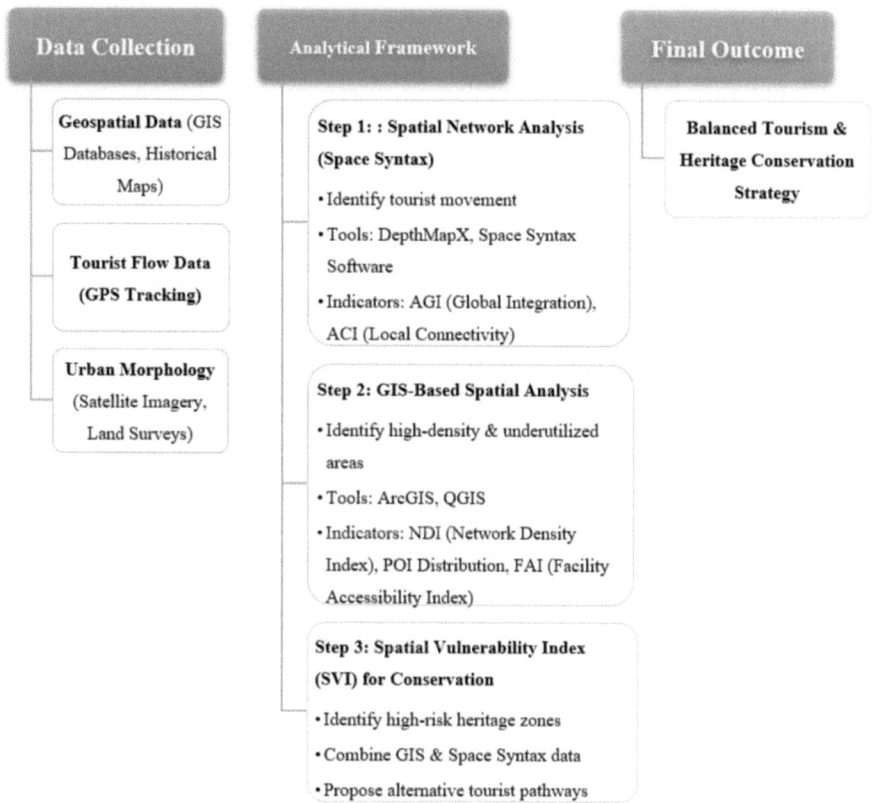

Fig. 1. Tourism Impact Assessment Framework

Table 2. Data Sources and Collection Methods.

Data Type	Source	Collection Method
Road Networks	OpenStreetMap, Municipal Maps	GIS Mapping
POI (Points of Interest)	Historical archives, Fieldwork	Spatial Analysis
Pedestrian Flow	GPS Tracking	Movement Analysis
Land Use	Satellite Images, City Records	GIS Classification

2. **ACI (Average Connectivity Index):** Reflects the average number of direct connections per street segment. It is calculated as the total number of connections divided by the total number of segments: **ACI = Σ k_i/n**
3. **NDI (Network Density Index):** Indicates the density of the street network in relation to the study area. It is computed by dividing the total street length by the area: **NDI = L_total/A**

4. **NDI$_n$ (Normalized Network Density Index):** A scaled version of NDI used in the SVI formula, calculated with min-max normalization: **NDI_normalized = (NDI − NDI_min)/(NDI_max − NDI_min)**
5. **POI Concentration:** Refers to the percentage of Points of Interest (POIs) located along highly integrated streets. This is measured by computing the proportion of POIs within a buffer of top quartile integration lines: **POI% = (POIs on integrated streets/Total POIs) × 100**
6. **FAI (Fabric Aging Index):** Measures the aging and degradation of the built environment. It is calculated as the sum of weighted degradation scores inversely proportional to their distance from the segment: **FAI$_i$ = Σ (W$_j$/d$_{ij}$)**
7. **SAS (Spatial Attractor Score):** Indicates how strongly a segment is influenced by nearby heritage and tourist attractors. It is computed by summing the attraction weights of nearby nodes, inversely weighted by distance: **SAS$_i$ = Σ (A$_k$ × 1/(d$_{ik}$ + 1))**
8. **LUII (Land Use Interaction Index):** Captures the intensity and diversity of land-use pressure on a segment. It is calculated as the sum of the product of land use diversity and conflict weights: **LUII$_i$ = Σ (D$_1$ × C$_1$)**
9. **PRCR (Pedestrian-Road Conflict Ratio):** Measures spatial conflict between pedestrian pathways and vehicular roads. Computed as the ratio of pedestrian segments intersecting traffic to the total pedestrian network length: **PRCR = L_conflict/L_pedestrian**
10. **SVI (Spatial Vulnerability Index):** A composite index assessing spatial stress and congestion risk, calculated as a weighted sum of five sub-indicators: **SVI = 0.3 × FAI + 0.3 × SAS + 0.2 × LUII + 0.1 × NDI_normalized + 0.1 × PRCR**

3.4 Expected Outcomes

This particular methodology would identify areas with higher traffic flow known as congestion hotspots. Such congested points impact on the environment and heritage structures. This will then lead to the identification of strategies that will be utilized within this study and similar contexts for effective conservation and sustainable development of tourism:

- **Identification of Tourist Congestion Hotspots:** The research will map, analyse, and evaluate the tourism density of the areas involved, quantitatively revealing congestion hotspots that could negatively impact both their visitors' experience and the physical integrity of heritage structures. Enhance the visitors experience through enriching tourist itinerary planning
- **Detection of Underutilized and Peripheral Urban Areas:** Through sophisticated spatial analysis and mapping techniques, which will guarantee equal opportunities for all the parts of the Medina
- **A proposal for a spatial zoning strategy:** To control tourist flows effectively so that the experience is better balanced, more resolute, and inclusively satisfying, it will be necessary to develop a framework that could distribute them by promoting the use of less urbanized.
- **Formulation of a Heritage Preservation Plan:** That uses computational science, which can serve to map and archive the geographical and syntactical information of the Medina.

4 Results

(See Figs. 2, 3 and 5, Table 3).

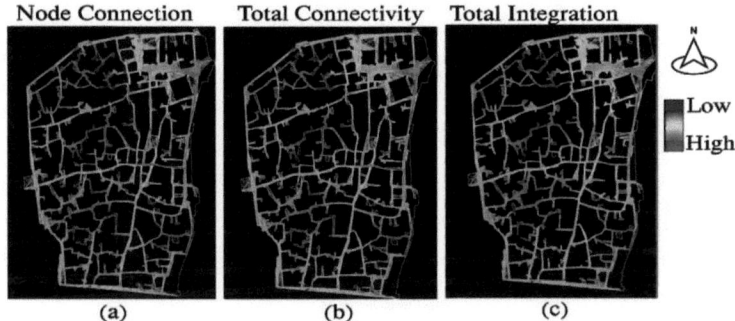

Fig. 2. Axial Analysis of the Medina (KHELIL CHERFI, 2023)

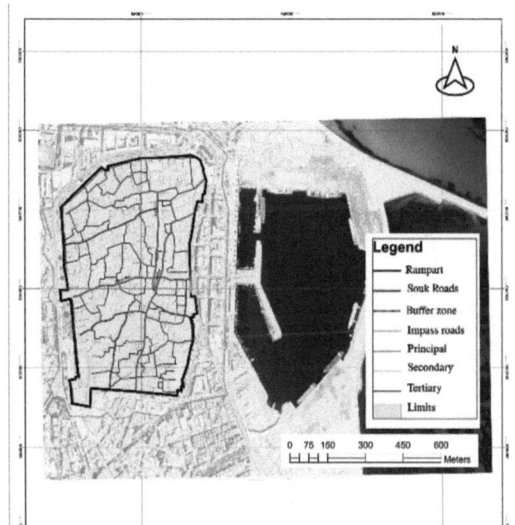

Fig. 3. Spatial Network of Roads and the Mechanics of Tourist Flow (GIS course by BEN-HAMOUCH, BOUALAM, 2023).

Then for each part of this Medina we calculated the SVI Formula

$$\mathbf{SVI = 0.3 \times FAI + 0.3 \times SAS + 0.2 \times LUII + 0.1 \times NDI\_normalized + (1)\, 0.1 \times PRCR} \tag{1}$$

The SVI Formula results highlight a moderate level of spatial vulnerability, particularly in peripheral neighbourhoods. Notably, historical landmarks such as the Kasbah, the Ribat, and the main gates appear more exposed to spatial and infrastructural limitations.

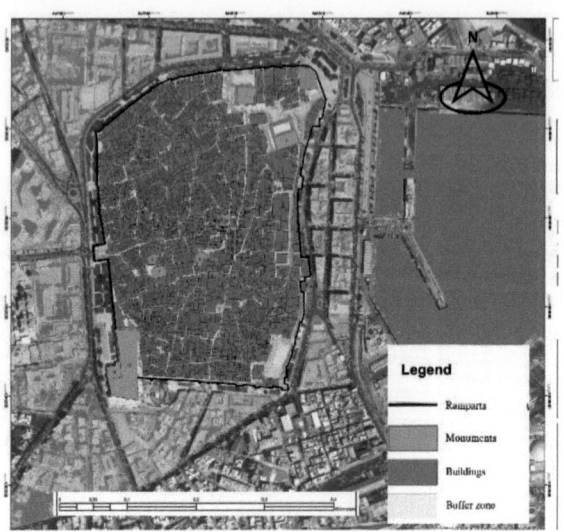

Fig. 4. Monuments of the Medina (GIS course by BENHAMOUCH, CHOUIAL 2024).

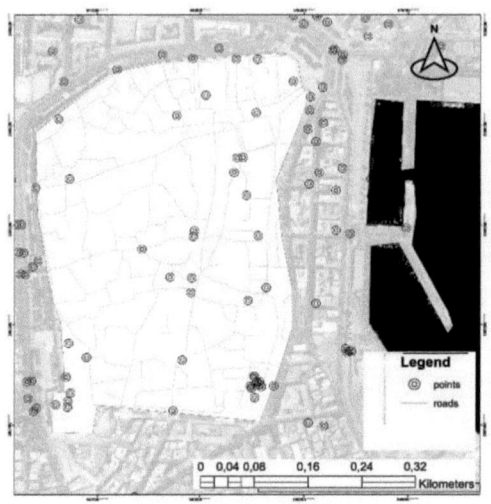

Fig. 5. Commercial and Historical Points of Interest of the Medina (GIS course by BENHAMOUCH, KHELIL CHERFI, 2024). (Map data: © OpenStreetMap contributors, available under the Open Database License (ODbL)).

These areas exhibit higher aging in the built fabric, reduced accessibility due to narrow alleyways, and lower infrastructure provision, as well as increased pedestrian-vehicular conflict—all contributing to their elevated vulnerability. This pattern is clearly illustrated in Fig. 4, where these peripheral zones stand out in contrast to the better-integrated and more accessible core of the Medina.

Table 3. Urban Spatial Structure Assessment: Key Metrics and Insights.

Category	Indicator	Highest value	Interpretation
Spatial Configuration	Average Global Integration (AGI)	0.75	High accessibility and movement potential in the northern sector of the Medina
	Average Connectivity Index (ACI)	12	Core streets are well-connected; peripheral areas (ACI < 5) are less integrated
Road Infrastructure	Network Density Index (NDI)	6.5 km/km^2	Moderately dense network with discontinuities in the southwest quadrant
Functional Distribution	POI Concentration	70%	Most commercial and service activities align with the most integrated axial lines
Structural Scheme	Spatial Vulnerability Index (SVI)	0.65	Indicates moderate vulnerability; peripheral areas show low accessibility and infrastructure deficits
	FAI: Fabric Aging Index	0.72	Represents structural aging; high values indicate deteriorated traditional buildings
	SAS: Spatial Accessibility Score	0.65	Measures accessibility from major entrances; low in narrow interior alleys
	LUII: Land Use Infrastructure Index	0.60	Evaluates infrastructure provision; lower in residential-dominant or informal zones
	PRCR: Pedestrian-Road Conflict Ratio	0.55	Captures the level of overlap between pedestrian paths and vehicular traffic areas

4.1 Spatial Configuration and Connectivity

Space syntax analysis demonstrates that the northern portion has the highest integration scores, with an average global integration (AGI) score of 0.75, which is the best place to look for strong accessibility and directions first. Along with the Average Connectivity Index (ACI) being 12, it is revealed that streets in the core area are well connected, but streets toward the edge are not (ACI < 5), letting down spatial integration.

4.2 Road Infrastructure and Accessibility

The road network analysis gives the Network Density Index (NDI) the value of 6.5 km/km^2, which means it is a moderately dense road system. However, some sections, particularly in the southwestern periphery, lack connectivity, making it challenging for people to have fair and equal access.

4.3 Functional Distribution and Points of Interest (POI)

The POI results reveal that the most integrated streets, particularly in the central and northern sectors, host 70% of commercial and service, suggesting potential for densification or functional reinforcement.

4.4 Pertinence Area Analysis

The Spatial Vulnerability Index (SVI) = 0.65, indicating a moderate level of spatial vulnerability. This suggests that while core areas exhibit relatively stable accessibility and infrastructure, peripheral zones remain underserved, requiring targeted interventions to enhance connectivity and service distribution.

5 Discussion

5.1 Critical Reflection on Results in Relation to the Research Question and Hypothesis

The current research topic is the study that examined how spatial analysis techniques such as the space syntax and GIS-based modelling can assist in optimizing the tourist flow and consequently, help in the preservation of the heritage in the Medina of Sousse. The outcomes are scientifically supported that a high spatial integration and connectivity in the particular infrastructure of the Medina of Sousse creates concentrated tourist movements, whereas the peripheral areas are not properly utilized, which in turn is the cause of spatial and also economic imbalances.

The spatial configuration analysis is another reason that this assessment is valid; the north sector actually has the highest Average Global Integration (AGI) score of 0.75, highlighting its central role in attracting movement and activity. But, the lower the Average Connectivity Index (ACI) value which is (<5) in the peripheral streets the congested it becomes, and it also implies a lack of alternative paths, thus, there will be more traffic of cars in the central zones. The road network analysis further confirms by the fact that the Network Density Index (NDI) is 6.5 km/km^2, which means that there is a moderately dense network but it is still not continuous in the southwest sectors, hence there are unequal movements.

This distribution is functional from points of interest (POI) is another proof to the hypothesis. Unfortunately, 70% of commercial and service activities are found among the most integrated streets. Thus, there is under development in the other parts and balanced spatial planning is required as the most satisfied with the services. Therefore, the need for more balanced spatial planning is still essential.

The spatial analysis clearly confirms that high integration scores are directly correlated with tourist concentration. However, this condition, while useful for economic clustering, also exacerbates congestion, wear on infrastructure, and tourism dependency in a few streets, while neglecting peripheral heritage assets. These findings suggest that urban morphology itself is an active agent shaping tourism impact.

Therefore, sustainable tourism strategies should not only rely on branding and promotion, but on evidence-based spatial redistribution, supported by syntactic and GIS-based metrics.

Moreover, the presence of commercial and service activities (70% located along high-integration axes) reveals a reinforcing loop between functional centrality and spatial accessibility. This supports the need for planning policies that incentivize functional diversification and decentralization. Ultimately, these insights call for integrated planning approaches that treat heritage spaces as living urban systems, rather than static artifacts (Fig. 6).

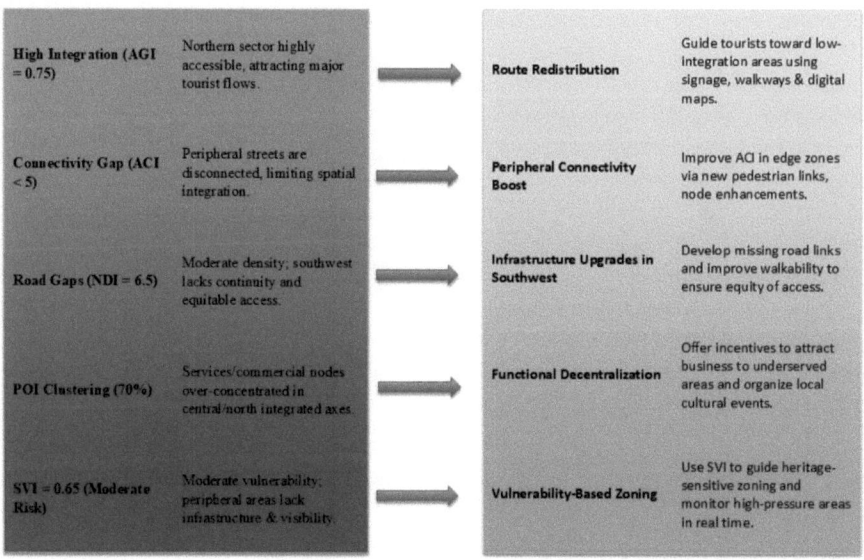

Fig. 6. Outcomes of the Study

5.2 The Implications of the Findings for Heritage Site Management, Urban Planning, and Tourism Regulation

Rebalancing Visitor Flow Through Secondary Networks

The fact that both the AGI and ACI values are high in the core areas confirms that the accessibility factor is the main reason for congestion. One way to address this issue is to steer the guests to the streets that are not crowded and are in-between. It can be made through the use of route descriptions, restricted access to saturating areas, and ameliorated paths to the pedestrians in the scarcely visited places.

Zoning and Commercial Redistribution for Sustainable Tourism

The concentration of the POIs and business activities (70% in the central areas) is a clear message for the management of the decentralized economy. The local government can award fiscal incentives to the local business units in the underutilized zones and create cultural events in the underestimated areas, thus both reducing the economic and tourism dependency on the northern corridors.

Urban Requalification to Enhance Peripheral Areas

The development of the infrastructure, the increase of walkability, and the reinforced connectivity is the main part of the issue, which has been neglected. Directing the resources into these areas can boost the social justice issues and thus the sustainability of tourism.

Integration of Vulnerability Zoning for Heritage Protection

This problem with the strong correlation between accessibility and congestion should be solved by the application of a Localized Spatial Vulnerability Indicator, which would serve to indicate the risk-prone areas allows for the quantification of vulnerability based on tourist pressure, accessibility, and historical fragility, ensuring targeted conservation efforts.

Smart Tourism and Real-Time Monitoring

The SVI results suggest that digital guidance tools, interactive maps, and real-time monitoring could optimize visitor experience while redistributing traffic. Implementing geofencing technologies and augmented reality navigation could encourage tourists to explore underutilized areas, balancing visitor distribution.

5.3 Consideration of Possible Limitations and the Applicability Boundaries of the Method

Comparative Case Study

A similar approach was applied in Beirut, combined with HBIM where vulnerability zoning and controlled access measures successfully redistributed tourist flows and minimized congestion. By integrating predictive modelling and smart tourism solutions, planners were able to mitigate risks to fragile heritage sites while maintaining economic viability. This example highlights the adaptability of GIS-based spatial analysis in different urban heritage contexts, though variations in local infrastructure and governance structures may affect outcomes [17].

While the methodology effectively diagnoses spatial imbalances, several limitations must be acknowledged:

Dependence on Spatial Configuration Metrics

The study relies on space syntax and GIS indicators, which capture structural accessibility but do not account for visitor motivations, behavioural patterns, or seasonal fluctuations. To expand our current understanding of the theme, forthcoming studies might focus perception surveys or movement tracking of visitor or local residents with the data processing of visitor density, occupancy rates, and user company's data.

Limited Socioeconomic and Stakeholder Engagement.

The methodology that focused on analysis of roads in computer models only seems to overlook the local businesses, and residents' perspectives as well. The utilization of participatory planning procedures could vastly improve the realization of set-forth methods.

Scalability to Other Heritage Sites. Moreover, the NDI, and AGI, etc. Are a good way to get things started, but the extent to which they may be used in other heritage cities is still unclear and will depend on the differences in morphology and governance among the cities.

A cross-sectional research design across different cities can provide a platform from which to measure these indicators across the various settings and spread the use of this methodology.

Challenges in Implementing Vulnerability Zoning

The formula of which (the SVI) is a useful framework, is fully a model of a good and innovative application. But it still needs a comprehensive examination period based on the collection of field data for visitor mobility, accessibility values, and different building types. In some heritage sites, the availability of data may not be the same as in others and the prescriptive zoning of permitted uses might not always be precise.

Future studies should also consider integrating real-time movement flow data or tourist attractor analysis to more accurately model dynamic visitor behaviour and better inform spatial interventions.

6 Conclusions

The spatial distribution of tourist flows in the Medina of Sousse reflects deep-rooted asymmetries in urban connectivity, infrastructure typology, and the location of attractions. Without proactive planning, tourism can aggravate congestion in core areas while marginalizing peripheral spaces. The study demonstrates that Space Syntax and GIS are powerful tools to visualize, quantify, and address such imbalances.

To preserve the integrity of Medina and promote equitable urban development, it is essential to diversify visitor routes, redistribute commercial functions, and invest in underserved areas. Additionally, introducing vulnerability-based zoning and smart monitoring systems can guide decision-makers in implementing adaptive and sustainable tourism strategies.

Future research should integrate behavioural, economic, and participatory data to enrich the spatial analysis and better capture the complexities of human interaction with heritage environments. Only through a multidimensional, flexible, and community-cantered approach can historic cities like Sousse thrive in the face of urban and tourism pressures.

It is now clear that the differences in the passage of tourists in the Medina of Sousse are the outcomes of the spatial differentiation of the space integration models, the typologies of the road infrastructure, and also the presence of the mobility of attractions located close to the main accessibility lanes.

If not well planned, the excessive traffic in certain areas could lead to potential threats to the preservation of the heritage and also to the neglect of other valuable sites far located from main roads.

The conclusion drawn from the study is in line with the hypothesis that means of space GIS and syntax can provide comprehensive details to heritage protection. Such a method provides a valuable insight into the spatial and geographical specificity of the Medina weakness and potential zones.

Urban Governance and Policy Implications

From a policy perspective, the findings of this study provide actionable insights for urban decision-makers. Planners and heritage managers should not rely solely on static preservation principles, but adopt spatially-informed governance tools that monitor movement dynamics and anticipate pressure zones. Urban authorities should:

- Reconfigure signage and pedestrian routing systems to encourage alternative tourist paths and relieve congested core areas;
- Invest in infrastructure and services in low-integration, high-potential areas to balance visibility and access;
- Integrate spatial indicators (e.g., axial integration, visibility fields) into heritage protection guidelines and tourism zoning plans;
- Engage local communities through participatory mapping and co-design processes, reinforcing cultural identity and stewardship.

Ultimately, this evidence-based approach supports a transition from reactive to proactive heritage management, aligning daily urban operations with long-term sustainability goals. However, the study needs integrating other methods, especially behavioural, economic, and participatory views in subsequent research.

This study demonstrates that spatial configuration is not a neutral backdrop, but a powerful lever for shaping tourist behaviours and managing heritage sustainability. Integrating spatial analytics into urban policy is no longer optional—it is essential for the future of historic cities under pressure.

Acknowledgments. I would like to express my sincere gratitude to **Prof. Benhamouch** for his invaluable guidance and for delivering the **GIS course**, which laid the foundation for the spatial analysis presented in this study.

I also extend my appreciation to **LabEtap** and **Arch.** Chouial Lamia and **Arch** Boualem Imane:for providing technical support throughout this research.

The authors would like to acknowledge the use of QuillBot for grammar and language enhancements during manuscript preparation.

References

1. Athoillah, S.: Model sistem institusi madrasah nidzamiyah di era dinasti saljuk. JSPI **3**(2), 33–42 (2020). https://doi.org/10.30659/JSPI.V3I2.15533
2. Bandarin, F., van Oers, R.: The Historic Urban Landscape: Managing Heritage in an Urban Century. Wiley-Blackwell (2012). https://doi.org/10.1002/9781119968115
3. Bigio, A.G., Licciardi, G.: The Urban Rehabilitation of Medinas: The World Bank Experience in the Middle East and North Africa. World Bank, Washington, D.C. (2010). https://documents.worldbank.org/curated/en/479461468152969198/pdf/549350NWP0UDS910Box349431B01PUBLIC1.pdf
4. Bousemma, A., et al.: A case study of an urban landscape in Sousse city. Int. J. Environ. Geoinf. **5**(1), 36–50 (2018). https://doi.org/10.3390/ijeg5010036
5. Cantatore, E., Esposito, D., Sonnessa, A.: Mapping the multi-vulnerabilities of outdoor places to enhance the resilience of historic urban districts: the case of the Apulian region exposed to slow and rapid-onset disasters. Sustainability **15**(19), 14248 (2023)
6. Chakraborty, S., Ji, S.: A review of integrating space syntax analysis into heritage impact assessment: a comprehensive framework for sustainable historic urban development. Int. J. Urban Sci. 1–28 (2024). https://doi.org/10.1080/12265934.2024.2438190
7. Christiansen, J.: Les phares antiques, entre défense et aide à la navigation. Exemples en Méditerranée Occidentale 65–70 (2015). https://doi.org/10.4995/FORTMED2015.2015.1723
8. Esposito, D., Santoro, S., Camarda, D.: Agent-based analysis of urban spaces using space syntax and spatial cognition approaches: a case study in Bari, Italy. Sustainability **12**(11), 4625 (2020)
9. Fein, A.: Kufic epigraphy between Norman Sicily and Ifriqiya. Muqarnas **40**(1), 43–67 (2024). https://doi.org/10.1163/22118993_0040_004
10. Vicente-Gilabert, C., López-Sánchez, M., del Pulgar, M.L.G.: GIS-based design for urban heritage routes. In: Ródenas-López, M.A., Calvo-López, J., Salcedo-Galera, M. (eds.) EGA 2022. SSDI, vol. 21, pp. 117–127. Springer, Cham (2022). https://doi.org/10.1007/978-3-031-04632-2_13
11. Harrison, P.: Castles of God: Fortified Religious Buildings of the World (2004). https://www.amazon.com/Castles-God-Fortified-Religious-Buildings/dp/1843833387
12. Jlassi, A., Essouaid, D.E., Rejeb, H.: The socio-environmental impacts of the urbanization of Sousse city. TIJ's Res. J. Commer. Behav. Sci. - RJCBS (2019)
13. Kamel, J.: Siciliens et Maltais en Tunisie aux XIXe et XXe siècles: Le cas de la ville de Sousse (2013)
14. Knaap, W.G.M.: GIS oriented analysis of tourist time-space patterns to support sustainable tourism development. Tour. Geogr. **1**(1), 56–69 (1999). https://doi.org/10.1080/14616689908721294
15. Lamare, N.: Thirsty cities? The supply, management, and perception of water in Byzantine North Africa. J. Rom. Archaeol. **35**, 247–279 (2022). https://doi.org/10.1017/S1047759421000714
16. Majdoub, W.: Médina de Sousse: les enjeux de la gestion touristique d'une ville historique inscrite au patrimoine mondial (2012). https://doi.org/10.7202/1012241AR
17. Misilmani, A.H., El-Bastawissi, I., Ayad, H., El Sayary, S.: BIM-GIS integration: an innovative tool to enhance urban heritage management in the digital era. Archit. Plan. J. (2024). https://doi.org/10.1016/j.autcon.2019.03.005
18. Othman, F., Yusoff, Z., Salleh, S.A.: Assessing the visualization of space and traffic volume using GIS-based processing and visibility parameters of space syntax. Geo-Spat. Inf. Sci. **23**(3), 209–221 (2020). https://doi.org/10.1080/10095020.2020.1811781

19. Ruiz, R.A.: El ribat califal. Excavaciones y estudios (1984–1992) (2004). https://dialnet.uni rioja.es/servlet/libro?codigo=429519
20. Santelli, S.: Atlas des médinas tunisiennes (1992)
21. Seraphin, H., Zaman, M., Olver, S., Dosquet, F.: Destination branding and overtourism. J. Hosp. Tour. Manag. **38**, 1–4 (2018). https://doi.org/10.1016/j.jhtm.2018.11.003
22. Sonnessa, A., Cantatore, E., Esposito, D., Fiorito, F.: A multidisciplinary approach for multi-risk analysis and monitoring of influence of SODs and RODs on historic centres: the ResCUDE project. In: Gervasi, O., et al. (eds.) ICCSA 2020. LNTCS, vol. 12252, pp. 752–766. Springer, Cham (2020). https://doi.org/10.1007/978-3-030-58811-3_54
23. UNESCO World Heritage Centre: Medina of Sousse (2009). https://whc.unesco.org/en/list/498/. Accessed 07 Mar 2025
24. Van Staëvel, J.-P.: Ribât in early Islamic Ifrîqiya: another Islam from the edge. Religions **14**(8) (2023). https://doi.org/10.3390/rel14081051
25. Vergara-Muñoz, J., Martínez-Monedero, M.: Las murallas de Tetuán en la literatura de 1860 a 1956 (2015). https://doi.org/10.4995/FORTMED2015.2015.1695
26. Wang, M.: Extending geographic information systems to urban morphological analysis with a space syntax approach (2012). http://www.diva-portal.org/smash/get/diva2:567667/FULLTEXT03
27. Wei, X.: Leveraging GIS for sustainable tourism development: a comprehensive spatial approach. Appl. Comput. Eng. **106**(1), 13–18 (2024). https://doi.org/10.54254/2755-2721/106/20240911
28. Xing, Z., Guo, W.: A new urban space analysis method based on space syntax and geographic information system using multisource data. ISPRS Int. J. Geo-Inf. **11**(5), 297 (2022). https://doi.org/10.3390/ijgi11050297
29. Yan, Y.: Space optimization methods of great site surrounding areas based on space syntax and GIS. In: Proceedings of the International Conference on Mechanic Automation and Control Engineering (MACE), pp. 1393–1396. IEEE (2010). https://doi.org/10.1109/MACE.2010.5536215
30. Yang, C.S., Qian, Z.: Street network or functional attractors? Capturing pedestrian movement patterns and urban form with the integration of space syntax and MCDA. Urban Des. Int. **28**(1), 1–16 (2022). https://doi.org/10.1057/s41289-022-00178-w
31. Yousse, Z., Kharrat, F.: The conservation of the Roman mosaics in the Museum of Sousse, Tunisia: between doctrines and practices. Int. J. Humanit. Soc. Sci. **2**(1) (2015). http://ijcs.uaic.ro/public/IJCS-15-41_Youssef.pdf

Books:

32. Brebbia, C.A., Martínez Boquera, A. (eds.): Islamic Heritage Architecture and Art. WIT Press, Southampton (2016)
33. Hayajneh, H. (ed.): Cultural Heritage: At the Intersection of the Humanities and the Sciences. Proceedings of the International Humboldt-Kolleg (Jordan, 16–18 April 2019). LIT Verlag, Münster (2023)

The Role of Environmental Awareness in Transport Mobility Behaviour: Evidence from Survey-Based Approach in Catania (Italy)

Vincenza Torrisi[1](✉) ⓘ, Luisa Sturiale[2](✉), Matteo Ignaccolo[2] ⓘ, Giuseppe Inturri[1], Marco Migliore[3], and Gabriele D'Orso[3]

[1] Department of Electric, Electronic and Computer Engineering, University of Catania, Catania, Italy
vincenza.torrisi@dica.unict.it
[2] Department of Civil Engineering and Architecture, University of Catania, Catania, Italy
luisa.sturiale@unict.it
[3] Department of Engineering, University of Palermo, Palermo, Italy

Abstract. According to the European Environment Agency (EEA) estimates, road transport represents one of the main contributors to greenhouse gas emissions in Europe. Reducing its environmental impact is a key challenge in achieving sustainable mobility systems. While policies are increasingly oriented toward low-carbon fuels, zero-emission technologies, and modal shifts to public transport, recent research has highlighted the growing importance of users' perceptions and attitudes in influencing mobility behaviors. Environmental awareness has emerged as a key factor in shaping transport choices. Based on this premise, this study investigates the role of environmental awareness in the transport mode choices of citizens in Catania (Italy), a context characterized by high motorization rates and traffic congestion. Based on a structured questionnaire administered to a sample of 1,373 respondents via both CAWI (Computer-Assisted Web Interviewing) and CATI (Computer-Assisted Telephone Interviewing) techniques, the analysis explores the association between environmental awareness and variables such as frequency of public transport use, gender, age, and occupational status. Respondents' awareness was assessed with reference to air quality, traffic congestion, and noise pollution through a 5-point Likert scale. Descriptive and non-parametric statistical analyses (i.e. Mann–Whitney U test, Kruskal–Wallis and Dunn's post-hoc) were applied to examine correlations between awareness and socio-demographic variables, as well as travel behaviour. Effect size was also computed to assess the practical relevance of the results. The findings provide valuable insights for designing more targeted and effective sustainable mobility policies, especially in contexts with high car dependency. Further research will examine how the willingness to adopt alternative transport varies according to personal motivation and perceived convenience.

Keywords: Public perception · Environmental externalities · Sustainable transport · Demand Responsive Transit (DRT) · Urban mobility

1 Introduction

The notion of *'sustainable development'* [1] combines the requirements of economic growth with those of human and social development, quality of life and protection of the planet from a long-term welfare perspective.

Since the concept of *"sustainable development"* was enunciated, numerous initiatives, protocols and regulations have been established for its implementation, across the different aspects involving the life of the community. Over the past decades, moreover, the emergence of climate change is becoming increasingly pressing, and adaptation and mitigation measures are becoming necessary to prevent the related problems that are already ongoing (floods, urban heat islands, loss of biodiversity, air pollution, increase in greenhouse gases, etc.).

The United Nations (UN) has developed 17 Sustainable Development Goals (SDGs) in the 2030 Agenda [2], among which Goal 11*"Sustainable Cities and Communities"* aims to *"make cities and human settlements inclusive, safe, resilient and sustainable"*. Among the different targets it aims to promote a participatory and integrated transport-land planning; to reduce the environmental impact of the cities; to ensure access to safe and economic living spaces and transport systems.

The European strategy [3] has as its aim to make the European Union (EU) economy sustainable through a set of initiatives geared toward making the economy achieve climate neutrality Union by 2050. The Green Deal is the EU's new growth strategy that aims to transform the EU into a modern, efficient and competitive economy, with the goal of zero net greenhouse gas emissions by 2050. It also intends to protect, conserve and enhance the EU's natural capital and protect the health and well-being of citizens from environmental hazards and their consequences. The Green Deal intends, therefore, to guide the EU toward a socially just transition and a sustainable economic system so that no person and no place is excluded. It will contribute to the goal of creating an economy that serves citizens by strengthening the EU's social market economy, generating stability, jobs, growth, and sustainable investment [3]. The principal actions are the efficient use of resources through the transition to a clean, circular economy, the curbing of biodiversity loss, the reduction of pollution, sustainable transport and actions against climate change.

Cities play a key role in combating climate change and implementing actions aimed at reducing greenhouse gases, especially through sustainable transportation planning. Promoting sustainable transport is crucial to reducing greenhouse gas emissions and improving public health. Measures such as increasing bicycle lanes, enhancing public transportation, and adopting electric vehicles can reduce pollution and encourage a more active lifestyle.

Programs such as the Recovery and Resilience Plan (RRP) and the European Green New Deal aim to integrate sustainability into urban policies, promoting a circular economy and greater social cohesion.

The transport sector is one of the largest sources of greenhouse gas emissions in the EU. Since 2005, however, transport emissions have not decreased significantly, despite the implementation of some measures aimed at reducing them (such as increasing the diffusion of electric vehicles). The EU expects domestic transport emissions to decrease below 1990 levels only in 2032 and, among the various transport modes, emissions from international aviation and maritime transport will continue to increase. The reduction of emissions is one of the biggest challenges for achieving the sustainable transformation of EU mobility systems [4]. The analysis of domestic greenhouse gas emissions in the EU transport sector shows a weak downward trend since 2005. Obviously, the most significant decrease occurred in 2020 because of the Covid-19 pandemic. Since 2021, as expected, emissions have recovered, although showing a weak decline of 0.8% in 2023 (Fig. 1). Based on European data projections, Member States expect transport emissions to decrease overall in the coming decades. This scenario is projected based on both emission reductions due to current policies and measures and additional reductions that the planned measures may generate (Fig. 2).

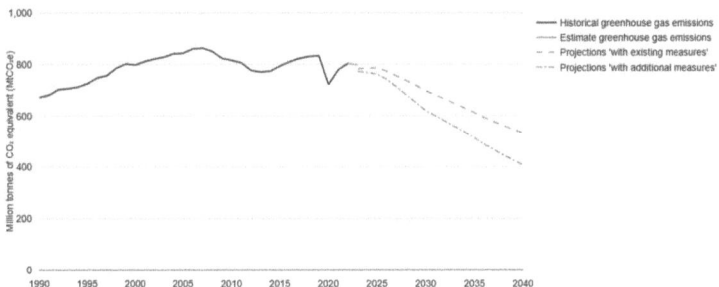

Fig. 1. Historical, estimate and projections greenhouse gas evolution [4].

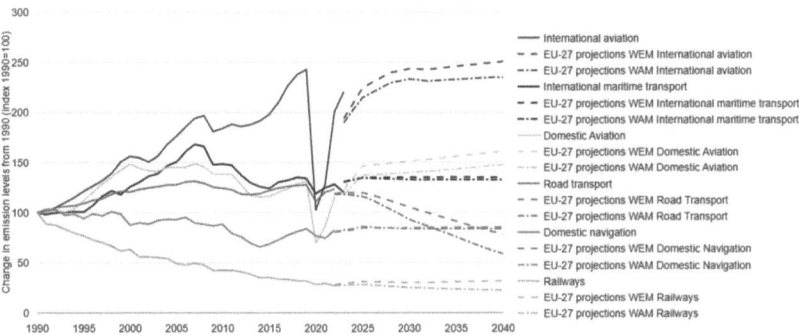

Fig. 2. Trends in greenhouse gas emissions by transport type and their projections [4]

Greenhouse gas emissions from transport are projected to be 4% higher than 1990 levels by 2030 with current policies and measures. In contrast, if additional measures are taken, these emissions would be 8% below 1990 levels. Most of the planned policies and measures in the transport sector involve promoting low-carbon fuels or zero-emission technologies, as well as encouraging modal shift to public transport [4].

According to EEA estimates, by 2022, the mode of transportation with the greatest impact on greenhouse gas emissions is road transportation (71.7%), in which cars account for 60.6% and heavy-duty trucks for 27.1%, followed by water navigation (14.0%) and civil aviation (13.4%) (Fig. 3).

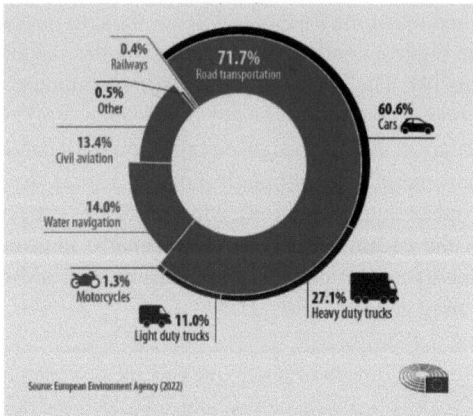

Fig. 3. Transport greenhouse emissions in the EU breakdown by transport mode (2022)

In Italy, the transport sector is directly responsible for 25.2% of greenhouse gas emissions and 30.7% of CO2 emissions, in addition to emissions from international aviation and maritime transport. 92.6% of national emissions in the entire sector are attributable to road passenger and freight transport, a sector for which there was a 3.2% increase in emissions between 1990 and 2019, in contrast to the 19% drop in total emissions during the same period. To help achieve the European objectives of the "Fit for 55" package, which envisage a 55% reduction in climate-changing emissions by 2030 and their zeroing by 2050, it is necessary to accelerate the decarbonisation process, starting with the mobility sector (Mims, 2022) [5].

In recent decades, economically advanced countries have activated various actions in order to reduce their level of emissions and, consequently, the environmental and social impacts caused on the lives of their citizens. Many of these impacts are concentrated on urban ecosystems, which, at present, represent about 3.0% of the earth's surface, but are responsible for 75.0% of carbon emissions due to human activities [6].

Considering the three dimensions of sustainable development, the externalities mainly considered associated with the transport sector are: air pollution (environmental), fuel consumption (economic), traffic congestion and road accidents (social) [7, 8]. The literature has shown in various research that the transport sector determines the generation of positive and negative externalities, which affect the quality of life, especially in urban areas [9–11].

Literature offers the results of numerous studies that have analysed the variables influencing the choice of mode of transport and intermodality (cost [12], distance, [13], comfort [13], time [14], connectivity [15]), but few studies examined the motivations linked to the aspects of environmental sustainability in the choice of mode of transport.

In recent years, the literature on urban transport has been enriched by applications analyzing perceptions and attitudes of transport users [16], which have examined the convenience of using certain modes [17], greater or lesser risk aversion or perceived safety [18], perceptions of the level of service [19]. Recently, increased attention has been paid to the study of environmental variables in the choice of modes of transport, and environmental awareness has been identified as a significant variable in studies on the choice of mode of transport among the general population [7, 8, 20–23] or targeted user groups, such as university students [7, 8, 24, 25].

This work examines the role of environmental awareness on transport mode choice among the citizens of Catania (Italy), through a sample of 1,373 respondents, with the use of a structured questionnaire, carried out by telephone and online. Knowing the degree of awareness of environmental issues, in general, and those related to urban transport, in particular, are of fundamental importance for developing effective sustainable mobility actions, in a co-governance approach with citizenship in the transition towards a model of sustainable and resilient cities, especially in cities with high rates of motorisation and traffic congestion. The results presented are part of a more extended survey that was carried out with the general objective of assessing the propensity of users towards innovative shared transport systems (Demand Responsive Transit – DRT) and also the willingness to pay for the service [7, 8].

Section 2, after briefly illustrating the territorial framework, describes the survey data collection and the statistical methods; Sect. 3 reports the main results obtained and discussion, finally, Sect. 4 concludes the paper. The empirical analysis in this research focused on the degree of environmental awareness present among citizens, especially with reference to urban transport. The results could provide valuable insights for policymakers seeking to promote sustainable urban transport and improve the quality of life in urban areas, pursuing what is envisioned by SDG 11"*Sustainable Cities and Communities*" of the UN 2030 Agenda [2].

2 Materials and Methods

This section presents the analytical framework adopted for the study, starting with the description of the case study context. Then, it outlines the main aspects investigated through a structured survey, which served as the basis for data collection. Finally, the analysis statistical and methodological approaches applied for data processing and interpretation are described.

2.1 Territorial Framework

The selected case study coincides with the metropolitan city of Catania, located in the southeast coast of Sicily (Italy). Only the city of Catania has a territorial extension of 180,000 m^2 and a population of about 300,000 inhabitants [26].

The city of Catania is densely populated in its northern part, while the southern part (corresponding to the VI municipality) is mainly an industrial, airport and commercial area. However, it is necessary to highlight that some populous suburban neighborhoods administratively belong to neighboring municipalities as fractions. There are ten first-crown municipalities which, through urban sprawl processes, have been characterized by a strong increase in population to the detriment of the municipality of Catania, which has gone from over 400,000 residents in the early seventies to around 300,000 nowadays. The total population of these municipalities is about 400,000.

Catania is a city facing significant mobility challenges, primarily due to a functional imbalance in its urban structure, a scattered and disordered population distribution over a wide and heterogeneous territory, and the inefficiency of adequate transport systems. These critical issues contribute to a general decline in the quality of life for its residents, particularly in terms of health and well-being. According to the national *Quality of Life* ranking published by *Il Sole 24 Ore*, Catania ranks 83rd out of 107 Italian cities. Among the evaluated dimensions, the city shows its worst performance in the *urban ecosystem* index, which includes the assessment of urban transport, where it has dropped five positions compared to 2023 [27].

In such urban contexts, it becomes essential to foster environmental awareness among citizens. Raising consciousness about the negative impacts of traffic-related pollution, while simultaneously demonstrating that concrete and accessible actions can be taken to mitigate these effects, plays a crucial role. Encouraging individuals to recognize both the consequences of their mobility choices and the opportunities for more sustainable behaviors represents a necessary step towards improving urban livability and promoting collective responsibility.

To this end, the study proposes an analysis of a complex real-world context, focusing on the urban area of Catania and its surrounding municipalities. Particular attention is given to assessing users' environmental awareness through an extensive survey, as detailed in the following subsection.

2.2 Survey Data Collection

The data for this study were collected through a structured questionnaire, designed to assess the environmental awareness of users regarding mobility patterns. The questionnaire was distributed using both CAWI (Computer-Assisted Web Interviewing) and CATI (Computer-Assisted Telephone Interviewing) techniques, which were employed to maximize respondent diversity and reduce selection bias [7, 8]. The use of both methods allows for a more representative sample, as it reaches individuals with varying access to technology and communication preferences, thus enhancing the robustness and generalizability of the results.

The first section of the questionnaire focused on socio-demographic variables to create a comprehensive profile of the respondents. These variables included gender, age, level of education, employment status, income, household structure, presence of people with disabilities in the household, and residential location. The second section gathered information on transport-related variables, primarily addressing respondents' mobility patterns and access to various transport modes. Variables such as possession of a driving license, the number of household cars, motorcycles, bicycles, and e-scooters were examined. Additionally, the frequency of public transport use and possession of a public transport season ticket were also considered. In the third section, respondents were asked to evaluate statements related to environmental awareness. They were specifically asked to assess the impact of habitual car use and the potential change in mobility habits (i.e. replacing cars with public transport) could have an impact on air quality, traffic congestion, and noise pollution. To capture these judgments, a 5-point Likert scale was employed, ranging from "not at all" to "very much.", as it is a well-established tool for measuring attitudes and perceptions on an ordinal scale. In this way, it is possible to effectively quantify subjective assessments, enabling reliable analysis for further descriptive and inferential statistics.

2.3 Statistical Methods

Following the data collection, a pre-processing phase was conducted to ensure the quality of the dataset. During this phase, incomplete interviews were excluded, and the response times were checked to ensure that only those interviews with reasonable completion times were considered, in line with the expected time necessary for respondents to answer thoughtfully. Once the data had been cleaned and organized into a final dataset, an initial descriptive statistical analysis was performed to examine the profile of the respondents and explore their mobility habits. This preliminary analysis served as the foundation for the subsequent correlation analyses.

Based on the judgments provided via the Likert scale, the respondents' environmental awareness was assessed in relation to air quality, traffic congestion, and noise pollution. Then, correlation analyses were conducted to investigate the relationship between environmental awareness and the following variables:

- frequency of public transport use, distinguishing non-users, occasional users, and frequent users;
- gender, i.e., male and female;
- age, divided into four groups, 18–25, 26–40, 41–55, and 56 and over;
- occupation, considering the following categories: Full-time/part-time employed, Self-employed, Unemployed, Housewife/Househusband, Student, and Retired.

To examine differences in environmental awareness across these categorical variables, non-parametric statistical methods were employed. Specifically, the Kruskal-Wallis test was employed, as it is suitable for comparing more than two independent groups when the dependent variable is measured on an ordinal scale. Following, Dunn's post-hoc test with Bonferroni adjustment was performed to identify which pairs of groups differed from each other. The Mann–Whitney U test was used as the non-parametric alternative to assess whether significant differences existed between two independent groups [28], as in the case of gender. Additionally, the effect size [28] was computed to quantify the magnitude of the observed differences, providing an indication of their practical relevance beyond statistical significance.

3 Results and Discussion

This section presents the main findings of the study. First, a descriptive statistical analysis is provided to outline the profile of the respondents and offer an overview of their mobility habits and socio-demographic characteristics. Then, the outcomes of the correlation analysis are discussed, with a focus on the relationship between respondents' environmental awareness and several categorical variables related to their socio-demographic status and transport behavior.

3.1 Descriptive Statistical Analysis

After conducting data cleaning and excluding inconsistent answers, a total of 1,373 valid responses were obtained. Table 1 provides a summary of the socio-economic and demographic characteristics of the sample. The survey was administered to a heterogeneous sample approximately evenly distributed between urban and suburban residents, living either within the city of Catania and within the surrounding municipalities. The composition of the sample was almost evenly balanced between male and female respondents. To ensure age diversity, participants were classified into four age groups; however, given the focus of the study on mobility habits and the willingness to adopt innovative transport alternatives, a slight predominance was observed among respondents aged 26–40 and 41–55.

The survey also investigated participants' level of education and employment status. Over 85% of the sample had achieved an education level of at least upper secondary school. In terms of occupation, more than 50% of respondents declared being employed, either full-time, part-time, or self-employed. Nevertheless, other categories such as students, unemployed individuals, housewives/househusbands and retirees were also meaningfully represented. From an economic standpoint, just over half of the respondents declared to have a lower-middle income, while approximately 30% identified themselves as earning an upper-middle income. The average household size was three to four members, with more than 10% of respondents reporting the presence of at least one person with a disability in their household.

Regarding transport-related variables (see Table 2), the data reveals a strong reliance on private vehicles, as more than 80% of the respondents reported owning one or two cars per household. Additionally, nearly half of the sample identified as non-users of public transport, further confirming a predominant preference for private mobility solutions.

3.2 Correlation Analysis

To investigate respondents' environmental awareness, they were asked to rate on a 5-point Likert scale from "not at all" to "very much" how much habitual car use and changing mobility habits by replacing cars with public transport could impact air quality, traffic congestion, and noise pollution. Table 3 shows the frequency distribution of the respondents' scores in percentile. Respondents' general perceptions reveal a clear awareness of the environmental impacts associated with habitual private car use. Among the assessed dimensions, traffic congestion is perceived as the most significant consequence (mean = 3.517), followed by effects on air quality (mean = 3.434) and noise pollution (mean = 3.386). These findings suggest that the negative consequences of car use are widely acknowledged, particularly in relation to urban traffic and environmental health. In contrast, the perceived benefits of replacing cars with public transport appear slightly less pronounced, with average scores ranging from 3.253 (for air quality) to 3.306 (for congestion). While respondents recognize the potential environmental advantages of public transport, they seem to attribute more weight to the harms caused by private cars than to the improvements brought by sustainable alternatives. Overall, the data suggest a stronger consensus on the negative environmental effects of car dependency than on the positive impact of increased public transport use.

Table 1. Profile of the respondents (n = 1373).

Sociodemographics	Subgroup	Respondents	% sample
Gender	Male	646	47.1
	Female	720	52.4
	Prefer not to say	7	0.5
Age	18–25	201	14.6
	26–40	417	30.4
	41–55	474	34.5
	56 and over	281	20.5
Level of education	Primary education	29	2.1
	Lower secondary education	145	10.6
	Upper secondary education	720	52.4
	Bachelor's degree/Master's degree	396	28.8
	P.h.D or postdoctoral	83	6.0
Employment status	Full-time/part-time employed	609	44.4
	Self-employed	188	13.7
	Housewife/Househusband	183	13.3
	Student	126	9.2
	Unemployed	183	13.3
	Retired	78	5.7
	Other	6	0.4
Income	Low	133	9.7
	Lower middle	778	56.7
	Upper middle	436	31.8
	High	26	1.9
Household structure	I live alone	136	9.9
	Two people	293	21.3
	Three people	414	30.2
	Four people	415	30.2
	Five people	115	8.4
Presence of people with disability in household	Yes	155	11.3
	No	1218	88.7
Residential location	Catania	754	54.9
	Outside Catania	619	45.1

The distribution of response frequencies for groups defined by the frequency of use of the TPL is reported in Table 4.

Following the Kruskal-Wallis test, which indicated significant differences (p = 0.006) in the perceptions of the impacts of private cars on air quality (ENVC1) across the groups defined by the frequency of public transport (PT) usage, a Dunn's post-hoc test with Bonferroni adjustment was performed to identify specific differences between the groups (Table 5).

Table 2. Transport-related variables.

Variable		Respondents	% sample
Public transport season ticket	Yes	346	25.2
	No	1027	74.8
Frequency of use of public transport	Non-users	675	49.1
	Occasional	474	34.5
	Frequent	224	16.3
Number of household cars	0	91	6.6
	1	618	45.0
	2	521	37.9
	3 or more	143	10.4
Driving license	Yes	1212	88.3
	No	161	11.7
Number of household motorcycles	0	823	59.9
	1	435	31.7
	2	89	6.5
	3 or more	26	1,9
Number of household bicycles	0	639	46.5
	1	435	31.7
	2	220	16.0
	3 or more	79	5.8
Number of household e-scooters	0	1181	86.0
	1	121	8,8
	2	38	2.8
	3 or more	33	2.4

The results showed that group 0 (non-users) gave significantly higher scores on the impact of private cars on air quality ($z = 2.93$, $p = 0.005$) compared to group 1 (occasional users). Group 2 (frequent users) had significantly higher scores compared to group 1 ($z = -2.47$, $p = 0.020$). No significant difference was found between non-users and frequent users ($p = 1.000$).

Thus, perceptions of the impact of private cars on air quality (ENVC1) vary significantly with the frequency of public transport usage, especially between occasional users and both frequent users and non-users. This finding suggests that environmental concern may not be limited to those who frequently use PT: non-users may also be aware of the environmental consequences of habitual car use, possibly due to their daily exposure to traffic-related air pollution. Conversely, frequent PT users may hold stronger pro-environmental values or experience the comparative benefits of PT, reinforcing their perception of the car's negative impacts. Occasional users, who engage with both modes, may lack a consistent evaluative framework, leading to more neutral or attenuated perceptions.

Table 3. Perceptions about impacts of private cars and PT on environmental issues.

Statements	1	2	3	4	5	mean
ENVC1: How much does habitual car use affect air quality?	6.1%	14.3%	34.1%	21.1%	24.4%	3.434
ENVC2: How much does habitual car use affect traffic congestion?	6.1%	11.3%	34.8%	20.2%	27.5%	3.517
ENVC3: How much does habitual car use affect noise pollution?	7.0%	13.8%	35.6%	20.7%	22.9%	3.386
ENVPT1: How much does replacing cars with public transport affect air quality?	7.4%	17.3%	37.3%	18.4%	19.5%	3.253
ENVPT2: How much does replacing cars with public transport affect traffic congestion?	6.9%	16.5%	36.4%	19.3%	20.8%	3.306
ENVPT3: How much does replacing cars with public transport affect noise pollution?	6.8%	17.3%	38.4%	18.7%	18.9%	3.256

In addition to ENVC1, the Kruskal-Wallis tests revealed significant differences between PT usage frequency groups for ENVC2 ($p = 0.003$), ENVPT1 ($p = 0.028$), and ENVPT3 ($p = 0.004$).

Post-hoc Dunn tests showed that for ENVC2 (perceived impact of car use on traffic congestion), significant differences emerged between non-users and occasional users ($z = 3.38$, $p = 0.001$), with non-users assigning higher impact scores. Using mainly private cars, non-users experience more congestion and perceive higher impacts.

Regarding ENVPT1 (perceived effect of replacing cars with public transport on air quality), a significant difference was found between occasional users and frequent users ($z = -2.66$, $p = 0.011$). Finally, for ENVPT3 (perceived effect of public transport on noise pollution), frequent users perceived significantly greater benefits compared to both non-users ($z = -2.72$, $p = 0.010$) and occasional users ($z = -3.27$, $p = 0.002$). Thus, frequent users reported significantly stronger beliefs in the positive effects of the use of PT on air quality and noise reduction. No significant group differences were observed in perceptions of car-related noise (ENVC3; $p = 0.144$) and PT's effect on congestion (ENVPT2; $p = 0.109$), suggesting that these impacts may be viewed as either less salient or more uniformly distributed among users regardless of their mobility habits.

Moreover, calculating effect sizes, we found that the comparison between occasional and frequent users regarding the perception of the positive environmental impact of public transport on noise pollution (ENVPT3) yielded the highest effect size ($r = 0.124$), which can be interpreted as small to medium. A small to medium effect size ($r = 0.101$) was also observed for ENVPT1, again between occasional and frequent users. The other pairwise comparisons with significant differences reported smaller effects.

The impact of gender on the response frequency distribution was further investigated (Table 6). The Mann-Whitney U test revealed significant gender differences in perception of the impacts of car use and the efficacy of PT in addressing environmental issues, although the effect sizes were found small (<0.1). Women were significantly more

Table 4. Perceptions about the impacts of private cars and public transport on environmental issues by frequency of use of PT (0: non-users, 1: occasional users, 2: frequent users).

Statements		1	2	3	4	5	mean
ENVC1: How much does habitual car use affect air quality?	0	5.6%	13.9%	31.3%	23.7%	25.5%	3.495
	1	6.1%	15.4%	39.5%	19.6%	19.4%	3.308
	2	7.6%	12.9%	31.3%	16.5%	31.7%	3.518
ENVC2: How much does habitual car use affect traffic congestion?	0	5.9%	11.0%	30.2%	22.2%	30.7%	3.607
	1	5.7%	11.2%	43.0%	17.7%	22.4%	3.399
	2	7.6%	12.5%	31.3%	19.6%	29.0%	3.5
ENVC3: How much does habitual car use affect noise pollution?	0	6.5%	13.8%	33.5%	24.7%	21.5%	3.409
	1	7.2%	13.8%	42.0%	15.8%	21.7%	3.316
	2	8.0%	15.2%	28.6%	18.8%	29.5%	3.464
ENVPT1: How much does replacing cars with public transport affect air quality?	0	8.1%	17.5%	35.6%	18.1%	20.7%	3.258
	1	6.8%	17.9%	42.0%	18.6%	14.8%	3.167
	2	6.7%	15.6%	32.6%	19.2%	25.9%	3.420
ENVPT2: How much does replacing cars with public transport affect traffic congestion?	0	7.7%	15.4%	35.1%	19.9%	21.9%	3.329
	1	6.5%	16.2%	42.2%	18.4%	16.7%	3.224
	2	5.4%	20.5%	28.1%	19.6%	26.3%	3.411
ENVPT3: How much does replacing cars with public transport affect noise pollution?	0	7.3%	18.4%	36.0%	20.0%	18.4%	3.239
	1	6.8%	16.9%	44.1%	16.7%	15.6%	3.175
	2	5.4%	14.7%	33.5%	19.2%	27.2%	3.482

likely than men to perceive habitual car use as detrimental to air quality (mean score = 3.519, p = 0.005) and noise pollution (mean score = 3.457, p = 0.033), and to believe that replacing cars with public transport would improve air quality (mean score = 3.332, p = 0.007) and reduce noise (mean score = 3.317, p = 0.047). These findings are consistent with previous research suggesting that women often report higher levels of environmental concern and greater sensitivity to environmental risks [20, 25]. However, small effect sizes suggest that these differences in perceptions are subtle and probably not relevant from a practical point of view. The absence of significant gender differences

Table 5. Dunn's test results for the differences in perceptions by PT usage frequency.

Comparison	ENVC1		ENVC2		ENVPT1		ENVPT3	
	z	p-value	z	p-value	z	p-value	z	p-value
0–1	2.932	0.005	3.376	0.001	1.347	0.267	0.932	0.527
0–2	−0.318	1.000	1.178	0.358	−1.752	0.120	−2.716	0.010
1–2	−2.474	0.020	−1.381	0.251	−2.663	0.011	−3.271	0.002

in the perception of car-related traffic congestion (ENVC2) and the impact of PT on congestion (ENVPT2) ($p > 0.1$) may reflect a shared experience of traffic-related issues across genders, or a more pragmatic view of congestion as a functional, rather than environmental, problem.

Table 6. Perceptions about impacts of private cars and PT on environmental issues by gender.

Statements		1	2	3	4	5	mean
ENVC1: How much does habitual car use affect air quality?	Male	7.9%	16.6%	33.6%	18.1%	23.8%	3.334
	Female	4.6%	12.4%	34.4%	23.8%	24.9%	3.519
ENVC2: How much does habitual car use affect traffic congestion?	Male	7.3%	12.7%	33.4%	19.5%	27.1%	3.464
	Female	5.0%	10.0%	36.1%	21.0%	27.9%	3.568
ENVC3: How much does habitual car use affect noise pollution?	Male	8.5%	15.0%	34.7%	20.6%	21.2%	3.310
	Female	5.4%	12.9%	36.5%	20.8%	24.3%	3.457
ENVPT1: How much does replacing cars with public transport affect air quality?	Male	9.0%	20.0%	36.1%	15.2%	19.8%	3.169
	Female	5.8%	15.1%	38.3%	21.4%	19.3%	3.332
ENVPT2: How much does replacing cars with public transport affect traffic congestion?	Male	8.4%	18.1%	34.7%	17.6%	21.2%	3.352
	Female	5.7%	15.3%	37.8%	20.8%	20.4%	3.35
ENVPT3: How much does replacing cars with public transport affect noise pollution?	Male	8.4%	18.6%	36.8%	18.6%	17.6%	3.186
	Female	5.4%	16.1%	39.7%	18.9%	19.9%	3.317

The relationship between age and environmental awareness was also analysed (Table 7). Overall, the mean scores across all age groups generally hover around 3 on the 5-point Likert scale, suggesting a moderate level of awareness regarding the environmental impacts of private car use and the potential benefits of public transport. However, in some cases - particularly among younger respondents - mean scores fall below 3, indicating a skeptical stance. For instance, individuals aged 18–25 report a mean score below 3 for the belief that replacing cars with public transport would reduce air quality and traffic congestion, reflecting limited conviction about this specific benefit. These lower scores may indicate a lack of awareness or concern about some environmental issues among younger participants.

Table 7. Perceptions about impacts of private cars and PT on environmental issues by age

Statements		1	2	3	4	5	mean
ENVC1: How much does habitual car use affect air quality?	18–25	5.8%	13.2%	36.2%	21.1%	23.7%	3.229
	26–40	7.6%	15.4%	33.3%	21.9%	21.7%	3.439
	41–55	3.2%	11.4%	28.5%	24.2%	32.7%	3.348
	56 and over	5.8%	13.2%	36.2%	21.1%	23.7%	3.719
ENVC2: How much does habitual car use affect traffic congestion?	18–25	10.4%	11.9%	42.8%	14.9%	19.9%	3.219
	26–40	5.5%	10.8%	40.3%	17.0%	26.4%	3.480
	41–55	7.4%	12.7%	34.0%	20.7%	25.3%	3.439
	56 and over	1.8%	9.3%	22.4%	28.1%	38.4%	3.922
ENVC3: How much does habitual car use affect noise pollution?	18–25	11.9%	17.4%	33.8%	16.4%	20.4%	3.159
	26–40	7.4%	12.9%	39.1%	16.8%	23.7%	3.365
	41–55	7.2%	16.5%	34.4%	22.2%	19.8%	3.310
	56 and over	2.5%	8.2%	33.8%	27.0%	28.5%	3.708
ENVPT1: How much does replacing cars with public transport affect air quality?	18–25	11.9%	17.4%	33.8%	16.4%	20.4%	2.950
	26–40	7.4%	12.9%	39.1%	16.8%	23.7%	3.336
	41–55	7.2%	16.5%	34.4%	22.2%	19.8%	3.177
	56 and over	2.5%	8.2%	33.8%	27.0%	28.5%	3.473
ENVPT2: How much does replacing cars with public transport affect traffic congestion?	18–25	9.0%	27.4%	34.3%	16.4%	12.9%	2.970
	26–40	7.0%	14.6%	39.3%	16.3%	22.8%	3.333
	41–55	7.4%	13.9%	38.8%	21.7%	18.1%	3.293
	56 and over	4.6%	16.0%	29.5%	21.7%	28.1%	3.527
ENVPT3: How much does replacing cars with public transport affect noise pollution?	18–25	10.0%	20.9%	40.8%	15.4%	12.9%	3.005
	26–40	7.2%	13.9%	41.2%	16.5%	21.1%	3.305
	41–55	6.8%	18.1%	40.7%	18.1%	16.2%	3.190
	56 and over	3.9%	18.1%	28.5%	25.3%	24.2%	3.477

Significant generational differences in perceptions were found for all the items according to the Kruskal-Wallis tests ($p = 0.000$). Post-hoc Dunn tests (Table 8) revealed that older respondents (aged 56 and over) consistently report higher perceptions of the negative impacts of private car use (ENVC1–3) and of the positive environmental effects of shifting to public transport (ENVPT1–3), compared to younger age groups. These differences are statistically significant across most comparisons, particularly with the youngest group (18–25), for whom the z-values are strongly negative and p-values below 0.001 in all cases. Also, the effect sizes for this comparison (56 and over vs. 18–25) are all over 0.2 and almost 0.3 in the case of ENVC2. These findings suggest that perceived negative environmental impacts of the use of private cars and benefits of public transportation appear to increase with age. One possible explanation is that older adults, due to their greater exposure to urban environmental problems, may be more aware of the consequences of car dependence. Meanwhile, younger individuals, who may rely less on private cars or have less direct exposure to their effects, might perceive these issues as less pressing or less tangible in everyday life.

Table 8. Dunn's test results for the differences in perceptions by age

Comparison	ENVC1		ENVC2		ENVC3		ENVPT1		ENVPT2		ENVPT3	
	z	p-value	z	p-value	z	p-value	z	p-value	z	p-value	z	p-value
[18–25]–[26–40]	−2.264	0.071	−2.361	0.055	−1.795	0.218	−3.772	0.001	−3.883	0.000	−3.166	0.005
[18–25]–[41–55]	−1.408	0.478	−2.093	0.109	−1.239	0.646	−2.324	0.061	−3.640	0.001	−1.987	0.141
[18–25]–[56 and over]	−4.670	0.000	−6.358	0.000	−4.812	0.000	−4.667	0.000	−5.369	0.000	−4.516	0.000
[26–40]–[41–55]	1.134	0.770	0.397	1.000	0.744	1.000	1.919	0.165	0.404	1.000	1.564	0.354
[26–40]–[56 and over]	−3.078	0.006	−4.997	0.000	−3.773	0.001	−1.387	0.496	−2.107	0.105	−1.885	0.178
[41–55]–[56 and over]	−4.168	0.000	−5.478	0.000	−4.533	0.000	−3.136	0.005	−2.521	0.0351	−3.329	0.003

Finally, the distribution of responses' frequency in percentile based on employment status is reported in Table 9.

The Kruskal-Wallis tests revealed significant differences between occupation groups for ENVC1 ($p = 0.010$), ENVC2 ($p = 0.046$) and ENVC3 ($p = 0.025$). No significant differences were found for all the items related to the perception of the impacts of replacing cars with public transport (ENVPT1: $p = 0.150$; ENVPT2: $p = 0.615$; ENVPT3: $p = 0.051$). Post-hoc Dunn tests (Table 10) with Bonferroni correction revealed a limited number of significant differences in environmental perceptions across occupational groups. Notably, retired individuals perceive significantly higher impacts of car use on air quality, congestion and noise pollution compared to other occupation groups. This is also confirmed by the mean scores reported for ENVC1–3: retired people gave higher scores on average than other occupation groups. Considering the effect sizes, small to medium effects were found for the comparisons between unemployed and retired people ($r = 0.238$) for ENVC1, and between students and retired people for ENVC1 ($r = 0.218$) and ENVC3 ($r = 0.202$).

These findings provide relevant insights for the development of DRT services, particularly in urban contexts, which seek to reduce car dependency through flexible and user-centred solutions. Widespread awareness of the environmental impacts of private car use, particularly in terms of congestion and air pollution, suggests a receptive ground for promoting alternative mobility services. DRT systems could take advantage of these perceptions by framing their offer not only in terms of convenience and flexibility, but also as a concrete response to environmental quality concerns.

Moreover, the perceptions observed across segmented user profiles - such as the heightened environmental concerns of frequent public transport users, women and older

Table 9. Perceptions about the impacts of private cars and public transport on environmental issues by occupation (1: Full-time/part-time employed; 2: Self-employed, 3: Unemployed, 4: Housewife/Househusband, 5: Student, 6: Retired).

Statements		1	2	3	4	5	mean
ENVC1: How much does habitual car use affect air quality?	1	7.9%	13.3%	34.0%	22.0%	22.8%	3.386
	2	4.8%	16.5%	35.6%	13.3%	29.8%	3.468
	3	6.0%	16.9%	35.0%	23.5%	18.6%	3.317
	4	4.9%	13.7%	35.5%	20.2%	25.7%	3.481
	5	4.8%	15.1%	38.1%	19.0%	23.0%	3.405
	6	1.3%	11.5%	17.9%	34.6%	34.6%	3.897
ENVC2: How much does habitual car use affect traffic congestion?	1	7.6%	9.7%	37.1%	18.7%	26.9%	3.478
	2	6.9%	12.8%	35.6%	16.0%	28.7%	3.468
	3	5.5%	12.6%	36.6%	20.8%	24.6%	3.464
	4	3.8%	10.9%	31.7%	21.9%	31.7%	3.667
	5	5.6%	15.1%	34.9%	19.8%	24.6%	3.429
	6	1.3%	12.8%	16.7%	38.5%	30.8%	3.846
ENVC3: How much does habitual car use affect noise pollution?	1	8.2%	14.3%	36.0%	21.2%	20.4%	3.312
	2	4.8%	16.5%	35.1%	15.4%	28.2%	3.457
	3	8.2%	10.4%	39.3%	21.9%	20.2%	3.355
	4	4.9%	10.4%	39.9%	21.3%	23.5%	3.481
	5	9.5%	19.0%	30.2%	15.1%	26.2%	3.294
	6	1.3%	12.8%	23.1%	33.3%	29.5%	3.769
ENVPT1: How much does replacing cars with public transport affect air quality?	1	8.9%	15.1%	35.6%	18.2%	22.2%	3.297
	2	5.3%	17.0%	39.4%	16.0%	22.3%	3.330
	3	6.6%	20.2%	43.7%	15.8%	13.7%	3.098
	4	5.5%	17.5%	38.3%	21.3%	17.5%	3.279
	5	7.9%	22.2%	36.5%	20.6%	12.7%	3.079
	6	7.7%	21.8%	25.6%	23.1%	21.8%	3.295
ENVPT2: How much does replacing cars with public transport affect traffic congestion?	1	8.2%	14.1%	36.5%	18.4%	22.8%	3.335
	2	4.8%	19.7%	37.8%	13.8%	23.9%	3.324
	3	5.5%	16.4%	41.5%	21.9%	14.8%	3.240
	4	6.0%	15.3%	35.0%	24.6%	19.1%	3.355

(continued)

Table 9. (*continued*)

Statements		1	2	3	4	5	mean
	5	7.9%	21.4%	31.7%	20.6%	18.3%	3.198
	6	6.4%	24.4%	29.5%	19.2%	20.5%	3.231
ENVPT3: How much does replacing cars with public transport affect noise pollution?	1	8.2%	14.8%	36.8%	20.2%	20.0%	3.291
	2	3.7%	14.9%	44.1%	16.5%	20.7%	3.356
	3	7.1%	20.2%	41.0%	17.5%	14.2%	3.115
	4	6.0%	15.3%	37.7%	21.3%	19.7%	3.333
	5	7.9%	21.4%	42.1%	13.5%	15.1%	3.063
	6	2.6%	34.6%	23.1%	17.9%	21.8%	3.218

Table 10. Dunn's test results for the differences in perceptions by occupation.

Comparison	ENVC1		ENVC2		ENVC3	
	z	p-value	z	p-value	z	p-value
1–2	−0.591	1.000	0.159	1.000	−1.260	1.000
1–3	0.991	1.000	0.208	1.000	−0.538	1.000
1–4	−0.791	1.000	−1.787	0.554	−1.580	0.855
1–5	0.147	1.000	0.670	1.000	0.290	1.000
1–6	−3.604	0.002	−2.590	0.072	−3.211	0.010
2–3	1.279	1.000	0.042	1.000	0.569	1.000
2–4	−0.167	1.000	−1.579	0.857	−0.271	1.000
2–5	0.552	1.000	0.455	1.000	1.158	1.000
2–6	−2.852	0.033	−2.411	0.119	−2.087	0.277
3–4	−1.436	1.000	−1.602	0.819	−0.833	1.000
3–5	−0.599	1.000	0.412	1.000	0.637	1.000
3–6	−3.816	0.001	−2.426	0.114	−2.509	0.091
4–5	0.699	1.000	1.865	0.466	1.394	1.000
4–6	−2.712	0.050	−1.189	1.000	−1.871	0.461
5–6	−3.103	0.014	−2.614	0.067	−2.874	0.030

individuals - highlight the importance of tailoring DRT communication and service design to specific demographic segments.

4 Conclusions and Further Research

Concerns about climate change and pollution from greenhouse gas emissions, especially from car transport, are particularly evident in cities. Therefore, sustainable mobility policies and actions that aim to increase citizens' environmental awareness are crucial for building sustainable and resilient cities. Deliberate action in the planning of cities and territories can contribute directly or indirectly to improve overall health and wellbeing [29]. To this end, knowing the degree of environmental awareness and the resulting transport mode choices become important to identify the best possible policy actions. The results presented in this paper, although representing only a part of the more complete survey carried out, concerning the degree of environmental awareness in relation to urban transport, could become important elements for implementing effective urban planning actions. The general perception of the respondents reveals a good level of awareness of the environmental impacts associated with the habitual use of private cars and trust in public transport as a possible solution with average scores above 3. The results of the statistical tests showed that there is a slight difference between men and women in the perception of the impacts on air and noise pollution of habitual car use and in the perception of the benefits deriving from the shift towards public transport. This slight difference, although significant, does not suggest the application of differentiated strategies between men and women.

Frequent PT users and non-users do not seem to have given statistically very different scores, highlighting how the use of public transport may not be linked to greater environmental awareness in this context. Significant differences between frequent users and non-users can be observed only when considering the perceived effect of the switch to public transport on noise pollution. Moreover, occasional users seemed to assign significantly lower scores than frequent users, showing a lower environmental concern. Finally, retired people and people over 56 seemed to be more environmentally conscious. Thus, campaigns targeting students can be promoted to increase environmental awareness among younger people.

By incorporating user perception into the planning and promotion of DRT systems, it becomes possible to design more effective and inclusive strategies that are aligned with both behavioral trends and broader sustainability goals. As suggested by the UN Habitat and WHO (2020) International Guidelines (IG-UTP) [30], these results would be a valid support to develop the Urban and Territorial Planning for improved environments and wellbeing. The IG-UTP advocates for urban and territorial planning as an integrated and participatory decision-making process to plan and manage our cities and territories in a holistic manner.

Acknowledgements. The present work has been supported under the PIA.CE.RI. Research program of the University of Catania, 2020-2022, Project ADDRESS "Advanced Design for Demand Responsive transport and Services of general interest in inner areas for the Sustainable territorial re-equilibrium". The work of Vincenza Torrisi related to the model conceptualization and development is funded by the European Union (NextGenerationEU), through the MUR-PNRR project SAMOTHRACE (ECS00000022).

References

1. UN: Our Common Future. The World Commission on Environment and Development, Oxford University Press (1987)
2. UN: Transforming Our World: The 2030 Agenda For Sustainable Development. United Nations. Department of Economic and Social Affairs: New York, NY, USA (2015)
3. EC: The European Green Deal. 2019. Available online: EUR-Lex - 52019DC0640 - EN - EUR-Lex (2019). Accessed 16 Dec 2024
4. EEA: Greenhouse gas emissions from transport in Europe, 31 October 2024. https://www.eea.europa.eu/en/analysis/indicators/greenhouse-gas-emissions-from-transport?activeAccordion=ecdb3bcf-bbe9-4978-b5cf-0b136399d9f8
5. Mims: Rapporto STEM. Decarbonizzare i trasporti (2022)
6. U.N. Habitat: Urbanization and development: emerging futures. Professionale case management (2016). https://doi.org/10.1097/NCM.0000000000000166
7. Sturiale, L., Ignaccolo, M., Torrisi, V., Scuderi, A.: An integrated approach for the co-governance of sustainable and resilient cities: a focus on Green Infrastructures and Transport Mobility in Catania (Italy). In: Gervasi, O., et al. (eds.) Computational Science and Its Applications – ICCSA 2023 Workshops: Athens, Greece, July 3–6, 2023, Proceedings, Part II, pp. 213–230. Springer, Cham (2023). https://doi.org/10.1007/978-3-031-37108-0_14
8. Sturiale, L., Torrisi, V., Cocuzza, E., Ignaccolo, M.: A possible model of resilient and environment-friendly transport: assessment of users' propensity towards demand responsive transit (DRT) service. In: Calabrò, F., Madureira, L., Morabito, F.C., Piñeira Mantiñán, M.J. (eds.) Networks, Markets & People. Lecture Notes in Networks and Systems, vol. 1187, pp. 365–375. Springer, Cham (2024). https://doi.org/10.1007/978-3-031-74704-5_36
9. Santos, G., Behrendt, H., Maconi, L., Shirvani, T., Teytelboym, A.: Part I: externalities and economic policies in road transport. Res. Transp. Econ. **28**(1), 2–45 (2010)
10. Sovacool, B.K., Kim, J., Yang, M.: The hidden costs of energy and mobility: a global meta-analysis and research synthesis of electricity and transport externalities. Energy Res. Soc. Sci. **72**, 101885 (2021)
11. Chatziioannou, I., Alvarez-Icaza, L., Bakogiannis, E., Kyriakidis, C., Chias-Becerril, L.: A structural analysis for the categorization of the negative externalities of transport and the hierarchical organization of sustainable mobility's strategies. Sustainability **12**(15), 6011 (2020)
12. Rotaris, L., Danielis, R.: The impact of transportation demand management policies on commuting to college facilities: a case study at the University of Trieste, Italy. Transp. Res. Part A Policy Pract. **67**, 127–140 (2014)
13. Cattaneo, M., Malighetti, P., Morlotti, C., Paleari, S.: Students' mobility attitudes and sustainable transport mode choice. Int. J. Sustain. High. Educ. **19**, 942–962 (2018)
14. Collins, C.M., Chambers, S.M.: Psychological and situational influences on commuter-transport-mode choice. Environ. Behav. **37**, 640–661 (2005)
15. Crotti, D., Grechi, D., Maggi, E.: Proximity to public transportation and sustainable commuting to college. A case study of an Italian suburban campus. Case Stud. Transp. Policy **10**, 218–226 (2022)
16. Ramos, E.M.S., Bergstad, C.J., Nassen, J.: Understanding daily car use: driving habits, motives, attitudes, and norms across trip purposes. Transp. Res. Part F Traff. Psychol. Behav. **68**, 306–315 (2020)
17. Nordfjærn, T., Egset, K.S., Mehdizadeh, M.: "Winter is coming": psychological and situational factors affecting transportation mode use among university students. Transp. Policy (Oxf) **81**, 45–53 (2019)

18. Kamargianni, M., Polydoropoulou, A.: Hybrid choice model to investigate effects of teenagers' attitudes toward walking and cycling on mode choice behavior. Transp. Res. Rec. **2382**, 151–161 (2013)
19. Ingvardson, J.B., Thorhauge, M., Kaplan, S., Nielsen, O.A. Raveau, S.: Incorporating psychological needs in commute mode choice modelling: a hybrid choice framework. Transportation (Amst) 1–29 (2021)
20. Jia, N., Li, L., Ling, S., Ma, S., Yao, W.: Influence of attitudinal and low-carbon factors on behavioral intention of commuting mode choice– a cross-city study in China. Transp. Res. Part A Policy Pract. **111**, 108–118 (2018)
21. Sturiale, L., Scuderi, A., Timpanaro, G.: Citizens' perception of the role of urban nature-based solutions and green infrastructures towards climate change in Italy. Front. Environ. Sci. **11**, 1105446 (2023)
22. Scuderi, A., Sturiale, L.: Evaluations of social media strategy for green urban planning in metropolitan cities. In: Calabrò, F., Spina, L.D., Bevilacqua, C. (eds.) ISHT 2018. SIST, vol. 100, pp. 76–84. Springer, Cham (2018). https://doi.org/10.1007/978-3-319-92099-3_10
23. Ming, Y., Deng, H., Wu, X.: The negative effect of air pollution on people's pro-environmental behavior. J. Bus. Res. **142**, 72–87 (2022)
24. Sottile, E., Tuveri, G., Piras, F., Meloni, I.: Modelling commuting tours versus non-commuting tours for university students. A panel data analysis from different contexts. Transp. Policy (Oxf) **118**, 56–67 (2022)
25. Vazquez-Paja, B., Feo-Valero, M., del Saz-Salazar, S.: Environmental awareness and transportation choices: a case study in Valencia, Spain. Transp. Res. Part D **137**, 104487 (2024)
26. National Institute of Statistics (ISTAT): Bilancio demografico mensile anno 2023 (dati provvisori), su demo.istat.it, ISTAT, 7 aprile 2023
27. 35rd Quality of Life Survey from Il Sole 24 ore (2024). https://lab24.ilsole24ore.com/qualita-della-vita/
28. Okoye, K., Hosseini, S.: Mann-Whitney U test and Kruskal Wallis H test statistics in R. In: Okoye, K., Hosseini, S. (eds.) R programming, pp. 225–246. Springer, Singapore (2024). https://doi.org/10.1007/978-981-97-3385-9_11
29. Cohen, J.: Statistical Power Analysis for the Behavioral Sciences, 2nd edn. Routledge, New York (1988)
30. UN Habitat and WHO: Integrating health in urban and territorial planning: a sourcebook. Geneva: UN-HABITAT and World Health Organization, 2020. 20002_Integrating Health in Urban and Territorial Planning A Sourcebook (2020)

Mapping Risk Factors to Build Inclusive Roads: A Systematic Diagnosis for Enhancing Vulnerable Users and Persons with Reduced Mobility Safety

Davide Maestroni[1(✉)], Giuseppe Cappelli[2], Valerio Gagliardi[3], Sofia Nardoianni[2], Pooyan Hejazi Mahabadi[1], Trigaluh Prastyana Tika[1], Neritan Caushaj[1], Francesco Bella[3], Mauro D'Apuzzo[2], and Francesco Edoardo Misso[1]

[1] BV Tech S.P.A, Via Delle Coppelle, 35, 00186 Rome, Italy
{Davide.Maestroni,Pooyan.HejaziMahabadi,trigaluhprastyana.tika, francesco.misso}@bvtech.com
[2] University of Cassino and Southern Lazio, Via G. Di Biasio 43, 03043 Cassino, Italy
{giuseppe.cappelli1,sofia.nardoianni,dapuzzo}@unicas.it
[3] Department of Civil, Computer Science and Aeronautical Technologies Engineering, Roma Tre University, Via Vito Volterra 62, 00146 Rome, Italy
{valerio.gagliardi,francesco.bella}@uniroma3.it

Abstract. Sustainable transport has been a growing focus for several decades, particularly following the Paris Agreement in 2015 and the Glasgow Climate Pact in 2021. The United Nations Sustainable Development Goal (SDG) 11 promotes accessibility, safety, energy, efficiency and use of sustainable public transport. Access to safe, reliable, and affordable transportation is fundamental for social inclusion, education, healthcare, and employment. Building on these global initiatives, this research aims to identify critical road safety risks and proposes targeted interventions to improve mobility for vulnerable road users (VRUs) and persons with reduced mobility (PRMs) in Italy. It applies principles of social sustainability in transportation to assess road safety in Rome's Nomentano-Tiburtina area through three interrelated studies. First, the accident analysis identifies high-risk "black points" by mapping accidents involving VRUs through Geographic Information System (GIS) and Kernel Density Estimation (KDE). Then, the vehicle-infrastructure interaction analysis evaluates road infrastructure risks using floating car data (FCD) to analyze driver behavior and correlates it with road accident data. Finally, the accident potential analysis assesses pedestrian accident risk by examining pedestrian flows and urban network structures, integrating configurational analysis with SpaceSyntax tools. Using FCD, multi-year accident data and pedestrian flow analysis, this research provides a comprehensive assessment of road safety risks in Nomentano-Tiburtina. The integration of the three quantitative information, allows the identification of critical areas and the development of targeted interventions. Findings offer actionable insights for policymakers and urban planners to enhance pedestrian, cyclist and vulnerable users' safety and promote sustainable mobility in urban environments.

Keywords: Road Safety · Kernel Density Analysis · Pedestrian Crowding

1 Introduction

In 2021, the Federal Highway Administration (FHWA) launched the Safe System Strategic Plan [1], as an approach toward zero traffic deaths. The main principle on which this plan is founded is the need to adopt a Safe System approach, aimed at ensuring no one is killed or injured on roads. It is worth mentioning that other initiatives, such as Vision Zero [2], Toward Zero Deaths: A National Strategy on Highway Safety [3], and Road to Zero [4], are all focused on reducing road accidents and are also implementing this Approach. Although there are several measures to improve safety, the Proven Safety Countermeasures promoted by FHWA aim to help ensure the five elements proposed in the Safe System Approach, with emphasis on safe road users, speeds, and roads [5–7]. The area in which these countermeasures are proposed regards speed management, roadway departure, intersections, pedestrian and cyclist infrastructures, and crosscutting.

The category of vulnerable users that is most at risk is people with reduced mobility. Among people with reduced mobility, it is possible to find old pedestrians. Jancey et al. [8] in their work highlight the importance of maintaining high levels of activity when physical and mental activity levels start to decline, and walking is one of the most common activities among the elderly. For these reasons, the authors assume that safety should be prioritized to promote safe walking activities in urban areas, thereby enhancing the safety of Vulnerable Road Users.

In a study conducted in the city of Itajubá, Brazil, Lima e Machado [9] evaluate the accessibility of individuals with reduced mobility with a quantitative and a qualitative methodology, by introducing an accessibility index, based on the judgements of participants. They found that the width, the ground surface, and the slope of the sidewalk have a strong impact on the accessibility of these users.

In agreement with these results, Gaglione et al. [10] found that factors that limit accessibility for the elderly are the slope of sidewalks (especially when this value exceeds 5%), poor street lighting, and the volume of vehicular traffic.

Kwon and Akar [11] study the interaction between the use of public transit and disabled people in California. They found that individuals with reduced mobility use transit services more frequently than not disabled persons, and this phenomenon is higher when individuals live in walkable and accessible neighborhoods. Non-worker disabled, on the contrary, are less prone to use transit. They also found that, in general, a high level of walkability is strongly related to a high level of transit usage by disabled individuals.

To make safer and more accessible roads for vulnerable users and individuals with reduced mobility, this paper presents an innovative and hybrid methodology (as described in Sect. 2) that integrates the analysis of floating car data (FCD), road users' accidents, and pedestrian crowding models. The methodology is applied to the Nomentano-Tiburtino area in Rome, with a brief description of the case-study area provided in Sect. 3. In Sect. 4, all the results with the different methodologies applied in Sect. 2 are reported and shown. In the same Section, by combining all the outputs from the three different analyses, critical areas are identified and ranked by using a Risk Indicator factor (Subsect. 4.4). After that, countermeasures (Subsect. 4.5) are proposed to reduce the probabilities of road accidents by modifying the crash modification factor (CMF).

2 Method

2.1 Data Description and Kernel Density Estimation (KDE)

To develop the methodology for identifying hazard levels across different sections of the road network, several types of datasets have been acquired:

- Road Accident Data (2011–2020) [12], to identify accident hotspots, which contains the main details on vulnerable user's road crashes
- FCD (2022–2023): Real-time data collected from devices installed inside vehicles, capturing valuable information such as GPS coordinates, date and time, speed, weather conditions, direction, and more. This data provides insights into driver behavior, including anomalous events like sharp braking and rapid acceleration, which we will use in our study.
- Road Accident Data (2017–2019): Extracted from the official site of 'Roma Capitale' [12], this dataset includes information on location, date and time, and type of incident. It serves as the ground truth to evaluate whether anomalous driving patterns from FCD correlate with actual crash events, helping to identify high-risk zones.

Kernel densities of these data have been estimated. KDE [13] is a non-parametric statistical technique used for smoothing data and estimating the probability density function (PDF) of a random variable (Eq. 6):

$$f(x) = \frac{1}{nh}\sum_{i=1}^{n} K\left(\frac{x - x_i}{h}\right) \tag{6}$$

where:

f(x) is the kernel density.
n represents the number of data points (e.g., FCD or accident data).
h denotes the bandwidth, beyond which any data point is disregarded.
K(.) represents the kernel function, which can take various forms (e.g., triangular, uniform, quartic, Gaussian, etc.). In this research, the Gaussian form was used.

2.2 Accident Analysis of Events Involving VRUs

This step of the research aims to map the spatial distribution of accidents involving VRUs in Rome, focusing on the Nomentano-Tiburtina area, selected as a case-study area. The goal is to identify accident hotspots to improve road safety measures. As part of a collaboration with Roma Servizi per la Mobilità, a dataset spanning 10 years (2011–2020) was collected, containing detailed information on accident locations (coordinates in WGS 84), dates, times, types, and VRU categories (pedestrians, motorcyclists, cyclists). A Geographic Information System (GIS) and a KDE approach were applied to identify high-risk areas, or "black points." The KDE with barriers enabled the identification of the most critical areas for VRU accidents, establishing a legend based on statistical values, such as the mean and standard deviations. An analysis of sensitivity was conducted by varying the parameter h among values of 50, 100, and 150 m, revealing that the measure of 100 m provides the most suitable results considering the characteristics of the study area. This outcome confirms findings from similar investigations conducted in urban areas in Italy, akin to the study area [14]. To develop density analysis while considering the urban nature of the study zones, surfaces were modeled using external software outside the GIS environment to create "barrier" entities for use in subsequent KDE approaches. Both building structures and barrier positions were considered to obtain an accurate and detailed representation of the road network graph of the study area (Fig. 1). The spatial distribution of incidents was analyzed using KDE, incorporating the presence of physical barriers. This approach facilitated the identification of areas with higher incident concentrations, accounting for the influence of barriers (buildings, green areas, etc.) in determining kernel density.

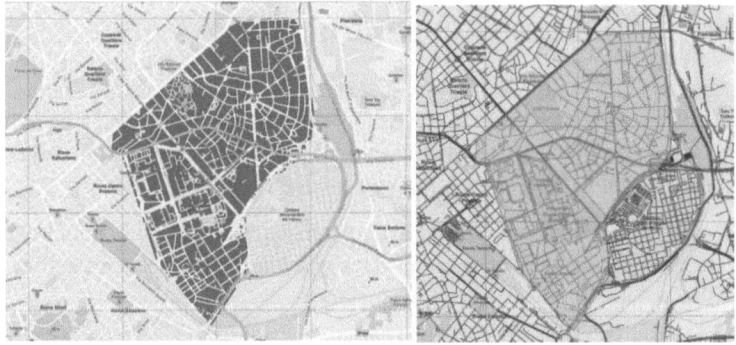

Fig. 1. Creation of a road network graph, consisting of edges and nodes within the study area and creation of barriers (in gray), corresponding to areas excluded from the KDE calculation.

In this study, given the complexity of statistical models and the absence of comprehensive data for model development, a statistical definition was chosen with some degree of arbitrariness in setting interval extremes, consistent with literature recommendations from similar studies conducted in urban environments of Italian cities [14]. Specifically, the risk classification was established as follows:

$$f(u, v) \leq \mu \tag{1}$$

$$\mu \leq f(u, v) \leq \mu + 2\sigma \tag{2}$$

$$\mu + 2\sigma \leq f(u, v) \leq \mu + 4\sigma \tag{3}$$

$$\mu + 4\sigma \leq f(u, v) \leq \mu + 6\sigma \tag{4}$$

$$f(u, v) \geq \mu + 6\sigma \tag{5}$$

where μ is the mean value of the density surface, σ is the standard deviation, and $f(u, v)$ represents the density value at a generic position (u, v). The final interval (class 5) was chosen/selected to identify hazardous road sites. The selection of the last interval highlights points with a very high concentration of collision events, characterized by kernel densities exceeding the mean value plus 6 standard deviations. In other words, selecting the last interval, which is highly restrictive from a statistical perspective, highlights points with significant concentrations of incidents, directing the analysis toward those sites that are highly critical in terms of VRU accidents.

2.3 KDE of Road Accidents and FCD

To identify the most dangerous intersections using FCD, KDE was applied to analyze the data. Several preprocessing steps were necessary to evaluate whether there is a correlation between anomalous FCD and incident data. These steps enabled the subsequent evaluation of the correlation between FCD and incident data.

First, KDE was applied to the data with a bandwidth (h) of 100 m to account for barriers in urban environments, on both FCD anomalies (acceleration values exceeding + 0.35g and falling below -0.45g) [15] and incident data. The final output is a georeferenced raster image, with each 10-m pixel representing road infrastructure and containing the Kernel Density value.

Next, a mask was created from the road network of the study area. This involved creating a 10-m buffer around the road network, resulting in a shapefile. The buffered shapefile was rasterized to produce a raster with a pixel size of 1 m by 1 m, assigning a value of 1 to all pixels within the buffered area to create a mask.

The mask was then applied to the KDE with barriers heatmap using the Raster Calculator, producing a refined heatmap that includes only the areas of interest within the buffered road network. Finally, the KDE of accidents was compared with FCD anomalies to assess correlation between the two datasets, using the Pearson Index.

2.4 Assessing Pedestrian Crowding Using Space Syntax

Pedestrian analysis was conducted through an integrated hybrid approach combining configurational spatial analysis techniques with predictive demand-driven models for spatial analysis techniques with predictive models of pedestrian mobility [16, 17].

The objective was to assess the accessibility of the pedestrian network, identify critical points in terms of accident risk exposure, and propose mitigation measures based on quantitative indicators.

To examine the structure of the pedestrian network, a new configurational approach was employed, combining Space Syntax analysis, a configurational method that quantifies the geometric and functional characteristics of pedestrian infrastructures, with a demand-driven pedestrian analysis.

In particular, Integration, the minimum number of steps required to reach a network node, has been taken into consideration as a key indicator.

3 Case Study

After monitoring several urban sectors of Rome, the Nomentano – Tiburtino area (see Fig. 2), which is part of Municipio II, was selected as the study area as it aligns with the future context of Pietralata for the following reasons: presence of hospitals, university buildings and of several metro stations in both areas, proximity to Roma Tiburtina Railway Station, usage for productive activities and service distribution rather than residential purposes. However, each area has its specific characteristics, such as: higher population density in Nomentana Tiburtina area compared to other areas [18], greater touristic attractiveness of Nomentana Tiburtina due to its central location. Analytical distortions arising from the presence of the Roma Termini railway station and the Verano cemetery in the Nomentana-Tiburtina area [19], as well as the forthcoming stadium in Pietralata, which is absent in the Nomentana-Tiburtina area [20].

In addition, a high incidence of accidents involving Vulnerable Road Users (VRUs), particularly pedestrians and motorcyclists, was observed, making this case study particularly suitable for testing the proposed analysis methodology.

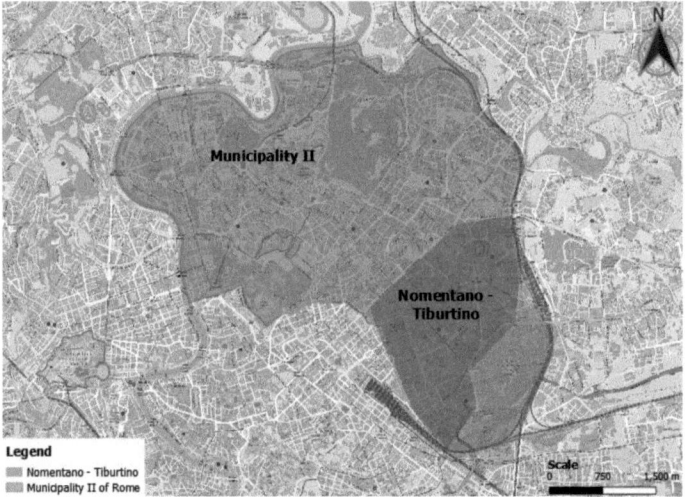

Fig. 2. Case study framework

4 Results

4.1 Road Accidents Involving VRUs - Identification of Black Points

The identification of black points, defined as critical areas with a high concentration of road accidents involving Vulnerable Road Users (VRUs), was carried out using a Kernel Density Estimation (KDE) analysis, following the methodology described in Sect. 2.2. This approach enabled the detection of spatial clusters where accident density is significantly elevated. In particular, accident classes 4 and 5, as detailed in Sect. 2.2, revealed an anomalous concentration of incidents involving VRUs. Based on this analysis, five black points were identified, characterized by heterogeneous features: two located in urban squares and three at road intersections.

More specifically, based on the analysis of the KDE with barriers, the following sites have emerged as high-risk points (Fig. 3):

- Piazzale del Verano.
- Piazza delle Provincie.
- Viale Regina Elena and Viale dell'Università.
- Via Giovanni B. Morgagni and Viale Regina Margherita.
- Viale Pretoriano and Viale Piero Gobetti

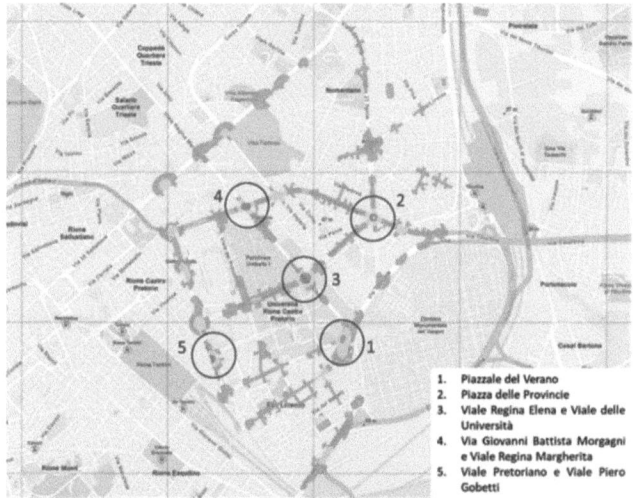

Fig. 3. Output of KDE with barriers - Identification of black-points (in orange).

4.2 Correlation Between FCD and Road Accidents to Identify Critical Areas

As the first step to individualize high-risk intersections, the KDE of accidents and FCD are correlated. In this case, KDE values from FCD can be used to identify streets or intersections with a higher risk of accidents, based on the assumption that FCD could be used as a surrogate safety measure.

Accordingly, the KDE was applied to analyze the spatial distribution of incidents and FCD data (acceleration and deceleration rates higher than threshold values), excluding, employing physical barriers, buildings and green spaces and therefore determining the values of densities relating to the road network (see Fig. 4).

This method enabled an accurate analysis and the identification of areas with elevated concentrations of anomalous/critical FCD by accounting for the influence of barriers on the kernel density (see Fig. 5).

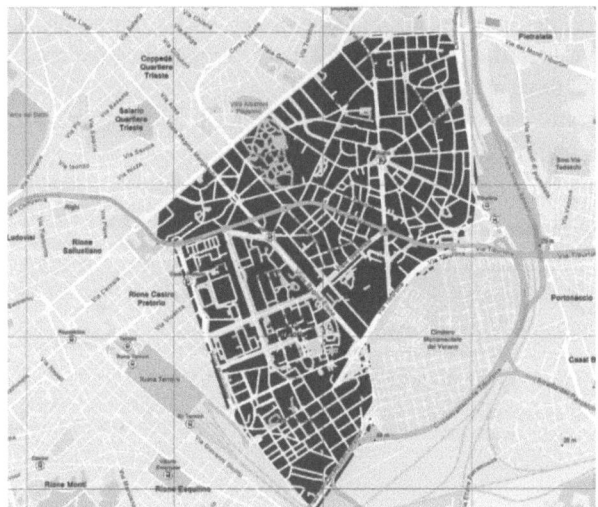

Fig. 4. Barriers (in grey), composed of building structures and vegetated areas.

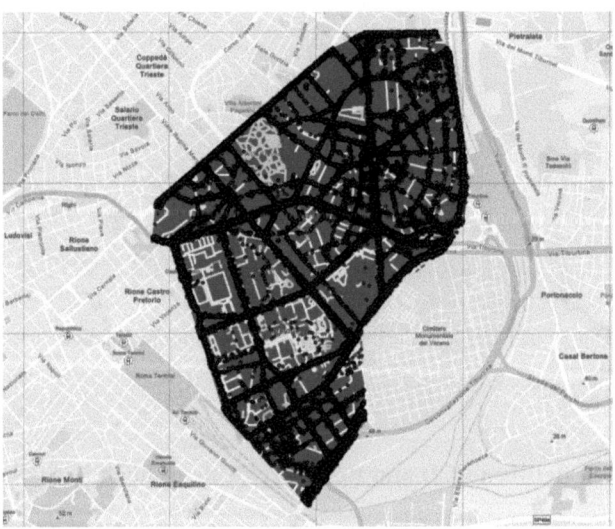

Fig. 5. Anomalies FCD values and barriers imported in GIS

The final output consisted of a georeferenced raster image, with each pixel representing a 10-m section of road infrastructure and containing the Kernel Density value (see Fig. 6), that is then compared and integrated with the other KDE for road accidents (see Fig. 7).

Kernel density values for both incident and FCD data are calculated and classified based on the mean and standard deviation of point values [14]. This classification helps identify areas that require more detailed investigation.

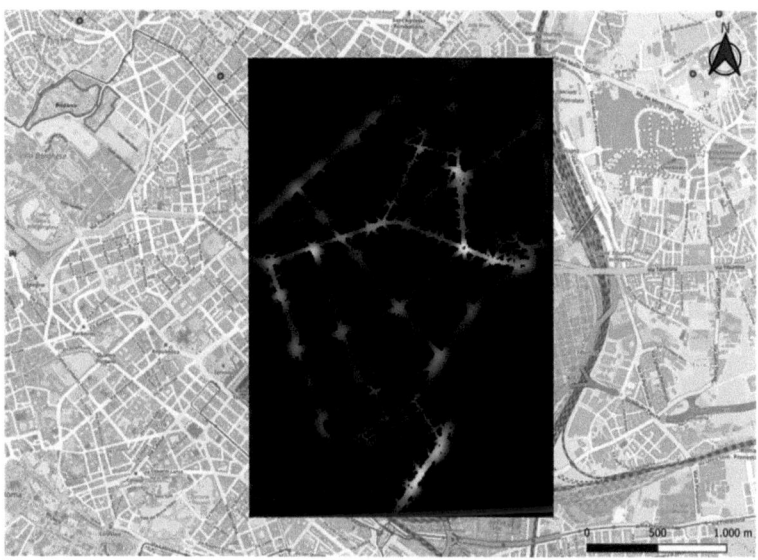

Fig. 6. KDE with barriers calculated for the FCD and visualization in GIS

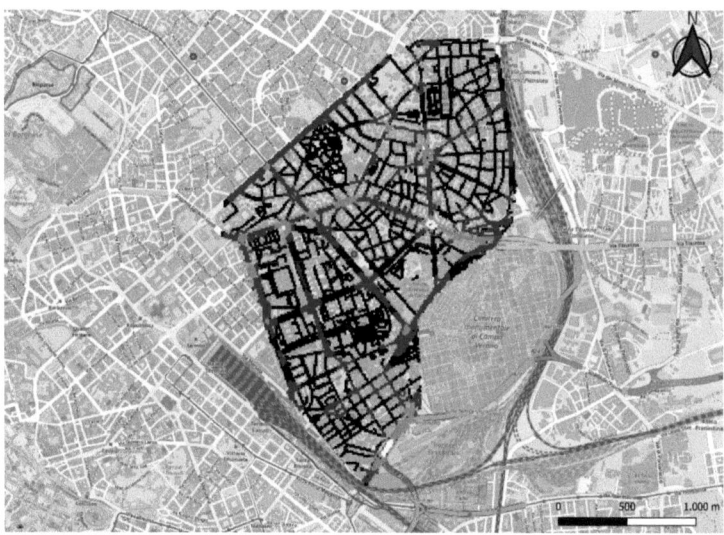

Fig. 7. KDE image with FCD values and barriers

A Python script classified data using the proposed threshold, while GIS software visualized risk levels to identify high-risk intersections or road sections.

In this study, the Pearson correlation coefficient was used to assess whether accident data hotspots aligned with those identified using FCD which was conducted for the entire study area. The coefficient was computed automatically using the 'r.covar' tool in QGIS, utilizing filtered raster data from accident records and FCD. Results were interpreted according to established literature [21].

After calculating the value of the Pearson correlation between FCD and accidents data, we have obtained the value of 0.61 and based on what we have mentioned in the previous section, this value indicates a moderate correlation. As a result, the use of FCD is a statistically significant method to outline the most relevant road critical points.

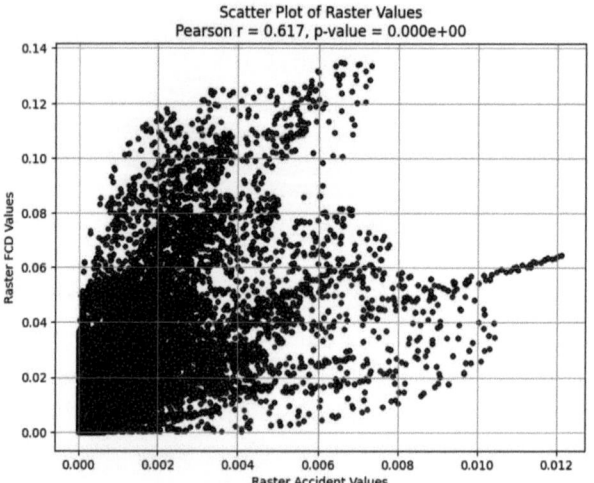

Fig. 8. Scatter Plot of Raster Values

According to the previously mentioned danger level classification (paragraph 2.2.), the percentage distribution of the FCD-based risk levels in the Nomentano Tiburtino district is as follows in Table 1.

Table 1. Percentage distribution of risk levels in the Nomentano Tiburtino area

Risk Level	Percentage [%]
Level 1	63.36
Level 2	30.86
Level 3	5.20
Level 4	0.59
Level 5	0.00

Observing the results, risk levels 1 and 2 together exceed 90% of the total, while no point in the Nomentano Tiburtino area reaches level 5. However, levels 3 and 4 are interesting enough to be selected for further detailed investigation.

4.3 Pedestrian Crowding Results

In addition to previous analyses pedestrian crowding analysis has been carried out to evaluate exposure to risk and critical areas: in Fig. 8 the graphic results are reported and in red the most critical areas are shown.

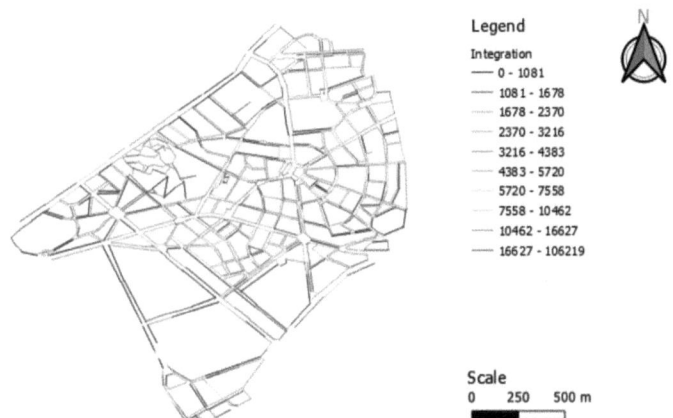

Fig. 9. Distribution of Integration on the Nomentano – Tiburtino in the context of pedestrian crowding analysis [22].

The analysis carried out is based on the evaluation of the Integration quantity which defines pedestrian crowding based on the geometric characteristics of the pedestrian network, in particular, an area with higher Integration will tend to attract pedestrians as it is well connected to the network.

However, for the present analysis, the value of Integration has been "corrected" with a weight that refers to the presence of shops along the pedestrian network, as it has been shown that this correction better represents the real situation [22].

The results obtained show that most of the areas with significant crowding (in red) are located in the central part of the study area.

4.4 Classification of Dangerous Road Intersections

With the analysis carried out on pedestrian crowding, it was possible to create a heatmap that could categorize areas from the least crowded to the most crowded.

The classification of the most hazardous sites is based on the results of three analyses aimed at identifying:

- A high concentration of accidents involving vulnerable road users;
- A high concentration of abnormal acceleration/deceleration events detected through FCD data;
- Pedestrian crowding.

The proposed aggregation is based on the following considerations:

- The significant weight assigned to findings related to the abnormal concentration of accidents involving vulnerable road users (pedestrians, cyclists, motorcyclists) recorded over the decade 2011–2020;
- The high relevance of the analysis results based on FCD data, considering that these data are regarded as potential predictors of accidents for the overall incident occurrence (moderate correlation between FCD data and accidents in the period 2018–2020);
- The lower relevance assigned to pedestrian crowding data, which is considered an additional potential factor contributing to accident occurrence.

Based on the above criteria, the weights for the Vulnerable User Accident Analysis with accident data, the FCD Analysis, and the Pedestrian Crowding Analysis (see Table 2) are reported and assigned to the different classes.

Table 2. Weights assigned to the Vulnerable User Accident Analysis carried out.

Class	Weight α	Weight β	Weight γ
<3	-	4	1
3–4	-	5	2
4–5	8	-	-

A comprehensive Risk Indicator (RI) is proposed as follows (Eq. 7):

$$RI = \alpha + \beta + \gamma \quad (7)$$

where:

- $\alpha = 8$ for sites classified as 4–5 in terms of high accident concentration.
- $\beta = 5$ for sites classified as 3–4, and $\beta = 4$ for sites classified as 3, based on the concentration of abnormal acceleration/deceleration events detected through FCD data.
- $\gamma = 2$ for sites classified as 4 and 3–4, and $\gamma = 1$ for sites classified as < 3, based on pedestrian crowding levels.

Based on the value obtained from the risk indicator, sites are aggregated into the following four groups in Table 3.

For the identified groups, the predominant causes of accidents (further detailed in the following sections) are primarily the following:

- Road Surface Conditions: The intersections consist of streets with pavements made of different materials, such as asphalt and stone, leading to inconsistent road friction for vehicles. Numerous potholes further increase the risk of accidents, particularly for two-wheeled vehicles such as motorcycles and bicycles, which are more susceptible to losing control on uneven surfaces.
- Horizontal Signage: The condition of horizontal road markings is poor, with pedestrian crossings partially erased. This lack of clear markings can create confusion

Table 3. Classification of sites based on the risk indicator value and main common characteristics.

Group	Risk Indicator	Number of sites	Characteristics
1	>13	1	High concentration of VRU accidents and FCD data; moderate to high levels of pedestrian crowding
2	9–13	4	High concentration of VRU accidents and significant concentration of FCD data; high pedestrian crowding during certain hours of the day
3	5–8	6	Sites characterized by the absence of high concentrations of VRU accidents, with high or moderate concentrations of FCD data and moderate to high pedestrian crowding
4	<5	8	Sites characterized by the absence of high concentrations of VRU accidents and the absence of high or moderate concentrations of FCD data; moderate to high pedestrian crowding

for both drivers and pedestrians, increasing the likelihood of accidents, especially in low-light conditions or during inclement weather.
- Illegal Parking: High presence of illegally parked vehicles, particularly near pedestrian crossings. These parked vehicles can obstruct drivers' visibility of pedestrians, increasing the risk of accidents as pedestrians attempt to cross the street.
- Pedestrian and Vehicle Interactions: Public transport stops and pedestrian crossings are located in positions that do not prevent illegal pedestrian behaviors (jaywalking). The increased pedestrian presence, combined with the aforementioned poor visibility and road conditions, further heightens the risk of pedestrian-vehicle collisions.

4.5 Intervention Effectiveness Matrix

Several key interventions are necessary to enhance road safety and mitigate accident risks. Improving road surface conditions by repairing potholes and ensuring uniform pavement materials can reduce hazards, particularly for two-wheeled vehicles. Enhancing horizontal signage, including repainting pedestrian crossings, will improve visibility and clarity for both drivers and pedestrians. Enforcing regulations against illegal parking near crossings is crucial to maintaining clear sightlines. Additionally, optimizing the placement of public transport stops and pedestrian crossings can help discourage unsafe pedestrian behavior, reducing the likelihood of collisions. These measures collectively address critical safety concerns and improve overall urban mobility.

Following the identification of critical sites in the Nomentano-Tiburtino Area an original methodology to evaluate the best safety improving measures was developed. The core of this methodology is based on an *"Intervention Effectiveness Matrix"*.

The matrix, which follows, represents an analysis of the causes and the related mitigation interventions, based on Crash Modification Factors (CMF).

The CMF values were obtained from the consultation of the "Highway Safety Manual" (HSM) [23], the CMF Clearinghouse database [24] and "The Handbook of Road Safety Measures" [25] using the following values as classification criteria:

- CMF ≥ 0.8: Moderate effectiveness of the intervention.
- CMF < 0.8: High efficacy of the intervention.

The CMF values reported represent average values calculated from the individual CMFs, which may vary for each intervention according to specific factors related to the context and the peculiar characteristics of the intervention itself; however, a filter has been applied to the type of area of interest by setting it as "Urban and Suburban" (see Fig. 9).

Subsequently, targeted interventions were identified for each site under investigation, based on the matrix shown above.

Based on the causes, through the analysis of road accidents, FCD data and finally pedestrian crowding, it was possible to assign priority to interventions.

The prioritization process has been divided into the following phases:

First of all, by consulting the interaction matrix, the most appropriate interventions were associated with the specific causes detected for each site.

The interventions were divided into two main categories:

- ***Priority***: interventions that see two or more interactions between the various causes;
- ***Secondary***: interventions act on a single cause without interaction with others.

In light of the above, therefore, the intervention strategy provides for priority to be given to interventions in the Priority category, postponing the implementation of those classified as Secondary.

In addition, within the respective "Priority" and "Secondary" categories, the interventions that, from the CMF study, were found to be the most effective (in green), while the least effective (in orange) will be carried out only after the former (Fig. 10).

While several studies have employed stand-alone approaches based on accident data, FCD, and pedestrian crowding, there remains a gap in the literature regarding the analysis of integrated methods, underscoring the novelty of the proposed approach. In this context, the proposed method and the obtained results are promising, paving the way for more advanced analyses to validate its effective application in additional intersections with varying configurations.

Causes / Interventions	Road surface repair	Reconstruction of road markings	Renovation of vertical signs	Installation of physical barriers	Strict controls illegal parking	Removing obstructions	Improving lighting	Marked pedestrian crossings	Dedicated pedestrian traffic lights	Lower speed limits	Physical bollards (speed bumps)
Poor paving condition	☑	☑	☑	X	X	X	☑	X	X	☑	X
Lack of visibility	X	☑	☑	X	☑	☑	☑	☑	X	X	X
Reckless user behavior	X	☑	☑	☑	☑	☑	☑	☑	☑	☑	☑
Inadequacy in signage	X	☑	☑	X	X	☑	☑	☑	☑	X	X
Excessive speed	X	X	X	☑	X	X	☑	☑	☑	☑	☑
Illegal parking and parked vehicles	X	☑	☑	☑	☑	X	X	X	X	X	X
Presence of pedestrians in unprotected areas*	X	☑	☑	☑	☑	☑	☑	☑	☑	☑	☑

* Effective intervention for people with DVA

Fig. 10. Description of Intervention Effectiveness Matrix. The matrix is read through the following visual scale: Green (Effective intervention), Orange (Moderate efficacy), Red (Not effective Intervention).

5 Conclusions

The proposed procedure and risk indicator provide a systematic approach to identifying high-risk areas for vulnerable road users by integrating accident data, FCD analysis, and pedestrian density. This method stands as a starting point for a more comprehensive methodology understanding of accident-prone locations, supporting data-driven decision-making for targeted safety interventions. Furthermore, the findings can guide urban planning and road maintenance strategies to enhance overall traffic safety.

These findings can serve as a foundation for future on-site analyses and to promote regular maintenance interventions, such as the restoration of signage or the improvement of road conditions. Addressing these issues could significantly enhance road safety in the areas under investigation.

The study focuses on identifying risks and critical road areas to assist decision-makers in developing solutions for safe and efficient mobility, particularly for vulnerable users (VRU) and individuals with reduced mobility (PMR). This process involves the use of GIS software and techniques and statistical analyses for data handling.

Accident data was enriched with details such as location, date, time, and accident dynamics. This data was then incorporated into GIS to examine its distribution to vehicular traffic patterns. Then Kernel density estimation was applied to further identify the most hazardous intersections and explore correlations between driver behavior and accident rates.

Comparing Kernel density data for accidents with FCD-based data revealed significant overlap in high-risk areas. The statistical analysis confirmed a moderate positive linear correlation between the two datasets, with a correlation coefficient of 0.61.

Alongside, pedestrian crowding analyses were carried out to identify the most crowded areas, characterized by a high level of exposures. In the risk evaluation field, vulnerability, hazard, and exposures are essential to evaluate risk values.

For each of the analyses made, a weight coefficient is applied to evaluate Risk Indicator (RI) for several areas: the higher the RI, the higher the risk levels. Once the most critical areas are identified, according to RI, several interventions are proposed and organized in an Intervention Effectiveness Matrix. The level of effectiveness is assessed by evaluating the Crash Modification Factors, associated with a single intervention: this factor indicates how the probability of road accident will decrease, so the lower the CMF, the lower the probability. The proposed approach and the obtained results are promising and pave the way for more advanced analyses to validate its effective application in additional intersections with varying configurations. This initial achievement lays the foundation for future studies that will refine and expand the methodology, ensuring its robustness and applicability across different types of road environments, VRU and traffic scenarios.

Acknowledgments. The research leading to these results has received funding from Project "Ecosistema dell'innovazione Rome Technopole" financed by the EU in the NextGenerationEU plan through MUR Decree n. 1051 23.06.2022 - CUP H33C22000420001. This manuscript reflects only the authors' views and opinions, neither the European Union nor the European Commission can be considered responsible for them.

Disclosure of Interests. The authors have no competing interests to declare that are relevant to the content of this article.

References

1. Federal Highway Administration (FHWA): Safe System Strategic Plan. https://highways.dot.gov/safety/zero-deaths/safe-system-approach-toward-zero-traffic-deaths. Accessed July 2024
2. Vision Zero. https://visionzeronetwork.org/. Accessed July 2024
3. Toward Zero Deaths. https://www.towardzerodeaths.org/. Accessed July 2024
4. Road to Zero. https://www.nsc.org/road/resources/road-to-zero/road-to-zero-home. Accessed July 2024
5. TIME, O. C. A. A. Making Our Roads Safer
6. U.S. Department of Transportation. Federal Highway Administration. Making our Roads Safer. One Countermeasure at a time. 28 Proven Safety Countermeasures that offer significant and measurable impacts to improving safety. https://safety.fhwa.dot.gov/provencountermeasures/pdf/FHWA-SA-21-071_PSC%20Booklet_508.pdf. Accessed July 2024
7. U.S. Department of Transportation, Federal Highway Administration. Proven Safety Countermeasures. https://highways.dot.gov/safety/proven-safety-countermeasures. Accessed July 2024
8. Jancey, J., Cooper, L., Howat, P., Meuleners, L., Sleet, D., Baldwin, G.: Pedestrian and motorized mobility scooter safety of older people. Traffic Inj. Prev. **14**(6), 647–653 (2013)
9. Lima, J.P., Machado, M.H.: Walking accessibility for individuals with reduced mobility: a Brazilian case study. Case Stud. Transp. Policy **7**(2), 269–279 (2019)
10. Gaglione, F., Cottrill, C., Gargiulo, C.: Urban services, pedestrian networks and behaviors to measure elderly accessibility. Transp. Res. Part D: Transp. Environ. **90**, 102687 (2021)
11. Kwon, K., Akar, G.: People with disabilities and use of public transit: the role of neighborhood walkability. J. Transp. Geogr. **100**, 103319 (2022)
12. Roma Capitale Road Accident data. https://www.comune.roma.it/web/it/home.page. Accessed 28 Feb 2025
13. Xie, Z., Yan, J.: Kernel density estimation of traffic accidents in a network space. Comput. Environ. Urban Syst. **32**(5), 396–406 (2008)
14. Bassani, M., Rossetti, L., Catani, L.: Spatial analysis of road crashes involving vulnerable road users in support of road safety management strategies. Transp. Res. Procedia **45**, 394–401 (2020)
15. Simons-Morton, B.G., Zhang, Z., Jackson, J.C., Albert, P.S.: Do elevated gravitational-force events while driving predict crashes and near crashes? Am. J. Epidemiol. **175**(10), 1075–1079 (2012). https://doi.org/10.1093/aje/kwr440
16. Santilli, D., D'apuzzo, M., Evangelisti, A., Nicolosi, V.: Towards sustainability: new tools for planning urban pedestrian mobility. Sustainability **13**(16), 9371 (2021)
17. D'Apuzzo, M., Santilli, D., Evangelisti, A., Nicolosi, V., Cappelli, G.: Estimation of pedestrian flows in urban context: a comparison between the pre and post pandemic period. In: Gervasi, O., Murgante, B., Misra, S., Ana, M.A., Rocha, C., Garau, C. (eds.) Computational Science and Its Applications – ICCSA 2022 Workshops: Malaga, Spain, July 4–7, 2022, Proceedings, Part IV, pp. 484–495. Springer, Cham (2022). https://doi.org/10.1007/978-3-031-10542-5_33
18. Comune di Roma: Roma Capitale - Annuario statistico 2022, CAP.1 Territorio e climatologia (2022). https://www.comune.roma.it/web-resources/cms/documents/01_Territorio_Annuario_2022.pdf
19. Grandi Stazioni: Roma Termini. https://www.grandistazioni.it/it/le-nostre-stazioni/roma-termini.html. Accessed Feb 2025
20. A.S. Roma S.p.A: Piano economico-finanziario nuovo stadio di Roma-Progetto di fattibilità tecnico ed economica (2022). http://www.urbanistica.comune.roma.it/images/stadio-roma/elab2022/03-00-piano-economico.pdf

21. Evans, J.D: Straightforward Statistics for the Behavioral Sciences. Brooks/Cole Publishing Company (1996)
22. Naranni S., Cappelli G., D'Apuzzo M., Nicolosi V.: Estimation of pedestrian flows with open-source crowding data: integrated model between configurational and physical approach in Nomentano-Tiburtina district, Rome. In: The 25th International Conference on Computational Science and Its Applications., Istanbul, Turkey. 30 June- 3 July 2025 (2025, in press)
23. National Research Council (US). Transportation Research Board. Task Force on Development of the Highway Safety Manual, & Transportation Officials. Joint Task Force on the Highway Safety Manual. Highway safety manual, vol. 1. Aashto (2010)
24. Clearinghouse Database. Crash Modification Factors (CMFs). https://cmfclearinghouse.fhwa.dot.gov/. Accessed Feb 2025
25. Elvik, R., Høye, A., Vaa, T., Sørensen, M.: The Handbook of Road Safety Measures. Emerald Group Publishing Limited (2009)

Functional Organisational Strategies and Practices in Sparsely Populated Areas (SPA). A Place-Based Proximity-Oriented Approach

Alessandro Plaisant[1(✉)], Chiara Garau[2], and Tanja Congiu[1]

[1] Department of Architecture, Design and Urban Planning, University of Sassari, Piazza Duomo 6, 07041 Alghero, Italy
plaisant@uniss.it

[2] Department of Civil, Environmental Engineering and Architecture, University of Cagliari, Via Marengo 2, 09123 Cagliari, Italy

Abstract. The proximity approach has typically been applied at the neighbourhood or district level as a model for increasing accessibility to opportunities and resources that ensure a better quality of life, while its potential in spatial planning has received less attention in both research and practice. The proximity approach used at regional scale presents challenges and issues. Reconsidering the concept of proximity at regional level means rethinking the conditions of accessibility. It requires considering the interrelations and interdependencies between different polarities and, consequently, the economic and social links and ties, according to a network of complementary communities. This paper contributes to the debate initiated by the Organisation for Economic Co-operation and Development (OECD) on peripheral regions. It focuses on the concept of functional urban area referring to sparsely populated peripheral areas (SPAs), whose institutional paucity calls for the need for multilevel governance to align programs and strategies. In an inter-service compensation perspective, including rebalancing between compact and less densely populated urban systems, the authors provide a comprehensive and interconnected place-based proximity-oriented approach aimed at 1. Identifying the parameters and factors to identify functional proximity areas (FPUAs) in SPAs and 2. Strategizing the organisational connectivity for different functional proximity areas. To accomplish this, the authors focus on a case study in SPA with latent tourism potential in Southwestern Sardinia (Italy).

Keywords: Proximity approach · FUAs · Sparsely populated areas (SPA) · Place-based organisational connectivity · regional development · Sardinia

1 Introduction

In 2020, the European institutions allocated a substantial part of the EU budget to the "transition to sustainability," in line with the European Green Deal, to foster and advance a common policy aimed at improving urban environments and social conditions, as cities will be crucial in addressing the effects of climate change and preventing emergencies in the forthcoming years [1, 2]. The proximity concept as an urban planning approach for enhancing the quality of urban life [3–5], aims to design cities so that all essential services, conveniences, and social activities are in physical relationship with each other, close in space in terms of distance to travel and in terms of time to arrive. This not only reduces the reliance on private car, but also promotes social cohesion, health, and well-being by enhancing the city's liveability and quality of life. Furthermore, this concept aligns perfectly with current sustainable urban mobility policies, which promote low impact means of transport that are accessible to all citizens, thereby contributing to climate change mitigation and the development of resilient cities [6–8].

However, the proximity approach is typically debated in terms of single neighbourhoods or districts, and its potential in regional planning has attracted less attention in both research and practice. Regional expansion of this concept requires to consider the interrelationships and interdependencies between various urban polarities and, consequently, a group of cities or urban centres linked by economic and social connections, thereby forming a network of interdependent and complementary communities. This approach on a regional scale generates "regional polarities" and effective regional planning, which could be a successful way of addressing contemporary sustainability challenges and enhancing the liveability and quality of life throughout the entire region.

According to the Organization for Economic Co-operation and Development (OECD) data, some 280 million people in Europe are organised in 110 large urban areas, where only 10 cities assume the role of "special" metropolitan governments with some distinctions: London, with a metropolitan government established by law; Hamburg, Amsterdam, Berlin, Madrid, Vienna, with the role of city-states, in which specific legal authorities exercise powers in specific fields in cooperation with local governments; Paris as a city-district; Barcelona, Lyon and Marseille with the role of unions of municipalities, in which the role of functional cooperation between local administrative entities for the management of common problems is evident [9].

These situations are far removed from those of the Italian regions, especially those dealing with demographic rarefaction [10, 11], with reference to peripheral areas with low population density [12]. Not to mention that the GDP generated in cities is a central issue in the economy of the EU and Italy, since urban areas contribute significantly to economic growth and value creation, compared to rural or less densely populated areas, thanks to their high population density, qualified human capital and access to advanced infrastructure and services. If, on the one hand, GDP growth is closely related to economic growth and employment, on the other hand, it is mainly linked to the consumption of material resources (above all, soil and energy) and competition between territories, not in line with the principles of sustainability, which lean towards reducing this consumption [13]. Therefore, is crucial a reorganisation that provides the rebalancing between compact urban systems and less densely populated ones, with a view to possible offsets between advanced services, present in urban areas, and other types of services, above all, dematerialised services [13] and ecosystem services.

From this point of view, this paper contributes to the debate initiated by the OECD on peripheral regions. It focuses on the concept of functional urban area referring to sparsely populated peripheral areas (SPAs), whose institutional paucity calls for the need for multilevel governance to align programs and strategies [14].

In an inter-service compensation perspective, including rebalancing between compact and less densely populated urban systems, the authors provide a comprehensive and interconnected approach proximity-oriented aimed at:

A) delineating the parameters and factors to identify functional proximity areas in SPAs, so that all the elements and limiting factors for the development of an efficient organisation of the territory are included, and thus it can be regenerated and innovated. B) Recognise the elements of stabilising travel times to plan spatial policies that aim to limit accessibility and infrastructure deficits and shape infrastructure and economic development [15].

To accomplish this, the authors focus on a sustainable alternative and smart mobility network in a peripheral sparsely populated area with latent tourism potential in Sardinia (Italy) is considered as a case study.

2 FUAs and SPAs. A Possible Organisational Correlation

Functional urban areas (FUAs) [16, 17] may more effectively address the needs and potentials of territories that may extend beyond a single administrative boundary.

The OECD's concept of FUA encompasses a "city and its surrounding, less densely populated local units that are part of the city's labour market ('commuting zone')" [16] emphasising their economic and functional interconnections beyond mere density and population size. The FUA definition expands urban boundaries to include areas economically connected through workplace commuting, by using population density and travel-to-work flows as key information. In brief, a FUA capture meaningful connections between cities and their surrounding areas. The degree of urbanisation provides an outlined urban area based on population density and cell contiguity. The FUA concept is used for urban planning policies and territorial cohesion policies to support disadvantaged areas to reduce their one-directional dependency from core areas.

The ESPON 2019 [18] program identifies several indicators to assess accessibility and spatial connectivity that are critical to understanding mobility dynamics within FUAs. Specifically, an interactive web tool - ESPON FUORE[1] (Functional Urban Areas and Regions in Europe) - presents a package of disaggregated indicators to compare FUAs (Fig. 1), offering a synchronised display of maps and graphs, useful for assessing accessibility and travel times in FUAs. The conclusions of ESPON FUORE final report (2020) highlights that "the FUAs are considered as the most common and stable definition of functional regions in the urban environment" (p. 8), although in some cases it is mentioned that delineations areas of geographical specificities originating from ESPON GEOSPECS [19] could be updated or improved[2].

---

[1] https://fuore.espon.eu/.

[2] GEOSPECS territories complement the selection of the functional regions as defined in the TERCET (Territorial typologies from Eurostat), namely: Islands (with no fixed link to continent); Mountain massifs; Sparsely populated areas; Borders (45 and 90 min) both will be included as the 45 min threshold stands as proxy for cross-border commuting functionality, whereas the 90 min one provides a larger perspective to border influence (Ibid. p. 9).

Key sources that analyse the definition of FUAs and their role in spatial organisation include, for example, the analysis of FUAs through the joint EU-OECD methodology based on commuting flows and travel times [20]. The relationship between commute times, planning, and mobility in relation to the impact on FUAs is the subject of numerous analyses and methods [21–23], including in relation to public transport service planning [24]. Others highlight growth trends in FUAs based on the relationship between population distribution and accessibility [25–27].

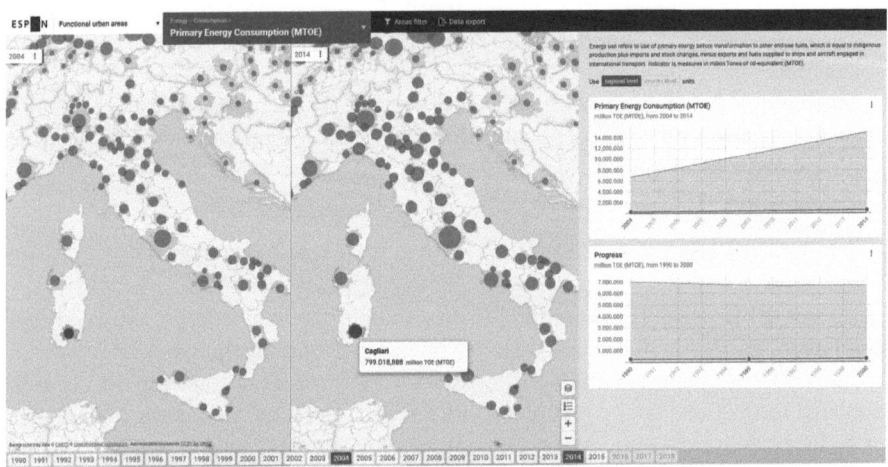

Fig. 1. Espon FUORE. Example of indicator: Primary energy consumption, Energy, FUA

Most definitions based on travel times include the following tripartition for FUAs: 1. *Central* FUAs (Core Functional Urban Areas), areas with a travel time within 30 min of the main city, usually covered by efficient public transport; 2. Intermediate FUAs, areas with travel times between 30 and 60 min, with greater reliance on the private car; Peripheral FUAs, areas beyond 60 min, often characterised by lower population density and less integrated transportation networks. Central FUAs are distinguished by high density of housing and services, high accessibility to public transportation and concentration of advanced economic functions (business, financial, administrative centres). *Intermediate* FUAs are characterised by moderate population density and functional mix (residential, manufacturing, tertiary), presence of satellite cities and secondary poles with partial economic autonomy. They strongly depend on the regional transportation (railways, highways). *Peripheral* FUAs are connected to the central city but with lower density and high dependence on private transportation. The higher incidence of urban sprawl and long-distance commuting is a symptom of a lower accessibility to services than centres and intermediate areas and shows a strong exposure to problems of economic and social marginalisation.

The proximity approach at different spatial scales points to go beyond the traditional core-periphery framework [28]: *the possibility of development of peripheral areas is connected to its potential influence on the changes taking place in the wider area.* Hence, the involvement of peripheral regions, rural areas, and SPAs in spatial organisation and development processes because of the opportunities arising from the wide availability and their proximity to ecosystem services [29–31], and the establishment of new criteria for defining functional areas in relation to these.

By contrast, Peripheral sparsely populated areas (SPAs) cope with structural limitations in terms of accessibility, depopulation, and rarefaction of services, which hinder their ability to align with EU 2021–2027 Programming. These difficulties often stem from weak cooperation among local and regional stakeholders and limited endowment [31–33] and institutional capacity [34–36]. The OECD stresses the need for multi-level governance frameworks aligned with business needs [37] and calls for multi-level governance to facilitate local cooperative efforts and coordinate strategies effectively [14]. Due to their small scale, these areas cannot act as traditional urban nodes, requiring a distinct spatial and economic development model tailored to their characteristics. Indeed, the small size of many towns and hamlets does not allow them to automatically become the nodes of a network to have supra-local comparability. Hence, a different spatial model is needed for sparsely populated suburban areas than for urban areas, highlighting the economic basis for their development [38]. For our purposes, the authors take into consideration various recent urban planning models centred on the proximity approach. Among them, the territorial model included in the Spanish and Basque urban agenda is considered for its methodological comprehensiveness. In this model urban and rural areas are considered as "entities" operating in a complementary and fractal way, according to the principles of *Ecosystem Urbanism* of Salvador Rueda. The territorial model proposes urban systems – and their functional areas –compact in their morphology, complex in their organisation, metabolically efficient and socially cohesive [38].

Putting this differently, the criteria for defining a functional area cannot be objective because very different variables come into play that depend on the characteristics of the territories in relation to water, waste, energy. etc. Consider, for example, situations where supply sources or treatment plants are outside the functional area of reference (Fig. 2).

Therefore, a functional area must also represent a model of territorial governance that aims for self-sufficiency in food, water, energy and waste cycle [38]. Hence, the delimitation of functional areas depends on very different variables, including metabolic ones, and various interrelated elements, including structural processes, flows of materials, capital and information, space for human living, production, recreation and business activities. These internal conditions are more conducive to development with respect to other areas, especially for their territorial capital [39], 2022). Thus, they require variable geometries for efficient management [38].

A functional proximity urban area (FPUA) is a polycentric organisation organised around urban cores of different nature, where "proximally located cities relate to each other in a synergetic way, making the whole network of cities more than the sum of its parts", particularly in terms of co-operation and complementarity [40]. Thus, the polycentric organisation is structured in a fractal way, developing from the neighbouring proximity unit, which involves a network of complementary communities aimed at promoting multi-level governance and facilitating local cooperative efforts, in accordance with the three micro, meso and macro levels [40, 41].

In conclusion, a FPUA must promote proximity first and foremost through accessibility, connecting the polycentric structure with urban cores within an acceptable time frame. According to this model, the traditional mobility system which generated suburbs is redefined to identify a network of nodes (cores) connected by public transport, sustainable modes of transport and smart infrastructures.

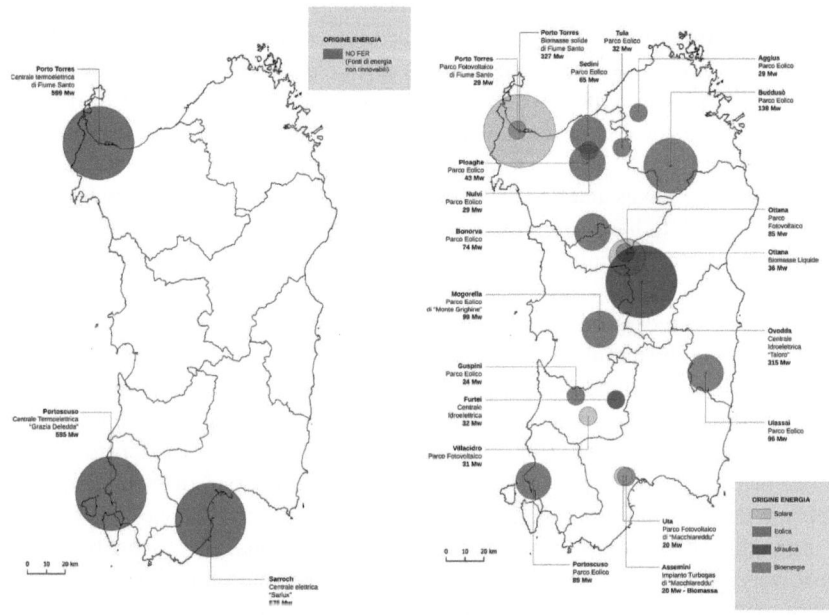

Fig. 2. Energy sources: no RES (left), RES (right), TERNA source. In 2023, production exceeds demand by 43% (consumption: 4.855 KWh per capita)

In other words, it is crucial to strategize the organisational connectivity for different functional proximity areas, by recognizing the elements of stabilizing travel times to plan spatial policies that aim to limit accessibility and infrastructure deficits and shape infrastructure and economic development [15]. Meanwhile, the perspectives of each proximity functional area will depend on its ability to offer different opportunities and forms of comparative advantage based on accessibility to resources, knowledge and, in general, ecosystem services.

3 Defining a Functional Proximity Organisation Model for a SPA. The Implementation of the TSulky Project in S-W Sardinia

Based on these assumptions, the authors attempt to make a theoretical contribution to the potential application of the functional proximity approach on a regional scale by identifying parameters and factors that can satisfy the needs of highly vulnerable regions that cannot achieve a high level of socioeconomic and environmental development due to geographical constraints. To accomplish this, the authors focus on a case study of Sardinia

(Italy). The proposal suggests the development of an interpretive tool for defining a FPUA in a SPA with weak connectivity, such as the Sulcis-Iglesiente (SI) region in S-W Sardinia, Italy. A spatial organisation through a network system of accessible nodes is planned. The aim is to promote interconnections and interdependencies among the network nodes, which are linked to the places of greatest strategic potential in terms of services and attractiveness. The results of the TSulki research project – Tourism and Sustainability in Sulcis (see Acknowledgements) are here considered [42].

The region of Sardinia[3], being an island, has precise boundaries and limits, within which two FUAs are identified, corresponding to its main hubs: Cagliari and Sassari. The island system is divided between coastal areas with high daily traffic and inland areas with low service centralisation [43]. Second, its morphological, geographical, political, and social characteristics determined significant geographical disparities between the coastal and inland organisation from the administrative and political point of view, since structural interdependencies have not been activated to include inland areas in a functional qualifying perspective determined by economic, social, and infrastructure concerns [44–46]. A considerable part of the population commutes every day mainly by private automobile for employment, study, or other purposes. Indeed, compared to inhabitants of the island's main centres, which are supplied with all necessary services, population out of the FUAs and, in general, residents of the smaller centres are obliged to travel every day, incurring extra travel time and financial resources [46].

The SI region in southwestern Sardinia, Italy, where a natural environment of considerable public interest coexists alongside abandoned areas severely degraded by mining and industrial activity, is the context of the research project. This decline is evidenced by demographic indicators, with a disappearing population, high average age, and employment below the regional average, concentrated mainly in the service and tourism sectors[4] [42].

3.1 The Methodological Path

The main objective of the T-Sulky project is to develop a systemic and interdisciplinary approach to enhance the natural, historical, cultural and tourism resources of the SI territorial context. The project aims to improve accessibility to information and services at a *functional proximity area scale*, by organising efficiently physical connections and information, by identifying and making accessible areas of greatest strategic potential in terms of attractiveness of the tangible and intangible resources, with a focus on the

---

[3] 1.587.413 inhabitants; 24.099,45km^2; Pop. Density 65,36 inhab/km^2 (Italy 195 inhab/km^2); Old-age index 241,8; Turnover index 177,2 (*Source ISTAT 2022*).

[4] The Analysis of the demographic structure divided by age group shows a strong demographic rarefaction, attributable to the decline in the 0–14 age group. The +65 age group accounts for 23%, while the population in the productive age group (15–64), although tending to increase (+1%), grows little compared to the unproductive age groups, which show an increase in average life span. The dependency index of municipalities in the area follows the trend of the regional one, while it is lower than the national index, insular Italy and N-E Italy. The educational level of the population is medium-low, leading to low competitiveness. Employment for the Province is currently among the lowest of the regional average and is concentrated in the service and tourism sectors (ISTAT data 2005–2015).

connections among archaeological-mineral, religious, blue and green landscapes and the system of services in this territory. The first phase of context analysis involved the retrieval and structured organisation of a significant amount of data from various sources, for which careful validation and compliance verification had to be carried out. The Open Data base of Sardegna Geoportale[i] was compared and integrated with cartography and content drawn from official documents and other informal but certified information sources. For example, the framework of physical connections is derived by integrating the existing trail base map taken from OpenStreetMap (OSM) with the trail network from the Regional Hiking Trail Network Plan and IGM tables.

Other analyses include a. the existing and potential spatial networks taken from the unstructured information base of the "S. Barbara Mining Trail Foundation", which includes 21 municipalities of the region; b. Web data and User Generated Contents (UGC) taken from specialised platforms and sites with the help of GIS tools, OpenStreetMap[ii] (OSM) and other applications. The result produced a usable and consultable dataset, as well as a good balance between quantity and quality of the data, fundamental characteristics in the creation of the geospatial database.

The second phase focuses on the interpretive device of spatial knowledge to co-plan accessibility links at different levels of knowledge and scales. This model of place-based organisation is planned through a networked system of accessibility nodes with relationships of mutual influence and conditioning. Each node refers to an inhabited location, as surveyed by National Institute of Statistics (ISTAT), and is characterised by several attributes. The following have been identified: *nodes with contextual attributes*, which have played a generative role in the definition and evolution of the mining landscape; *nodes with general attributes*, specified with respect to three typologies: *spatial, functional, and sociocultural accessibility*. Each node is defined by a description, attributes and indicators [42].

3.2 Context Analysis

The analysis of settlement patterns in terms of appearance, and uses, endowment and distribution of resources and services (Fig. 3), has been of crucial importance in defining organisational – functional proximity areas with which to describe the present and possible functioning of the spatial network and the interactions between nodes (Fig. 3). The analysis of Ecosystem Services [47] follows established procedures already tested in numerous studies [48]. In the first instance, it started with the management of the cartographic data (CLC Land Use 2008 – Areals) from RAS Geoportale. This datum was subdivided, by merging operations of the categories present in the attributes table, into the four ES reference categories .

Each land use class was assigned a value from a minimum of 0 and a maximum of 5. The score indicates the quality level of a parcel concerning each ES[5] (Fig. 4).

---

[5] For example, a plot of "arable land" might score a low score of 1 for the Cultural ES and simultaneously score a high score of 5 for the Supply ES.

Functional Organisational Strategies and Practices in Sparsely Populated Areas (SPA)   113

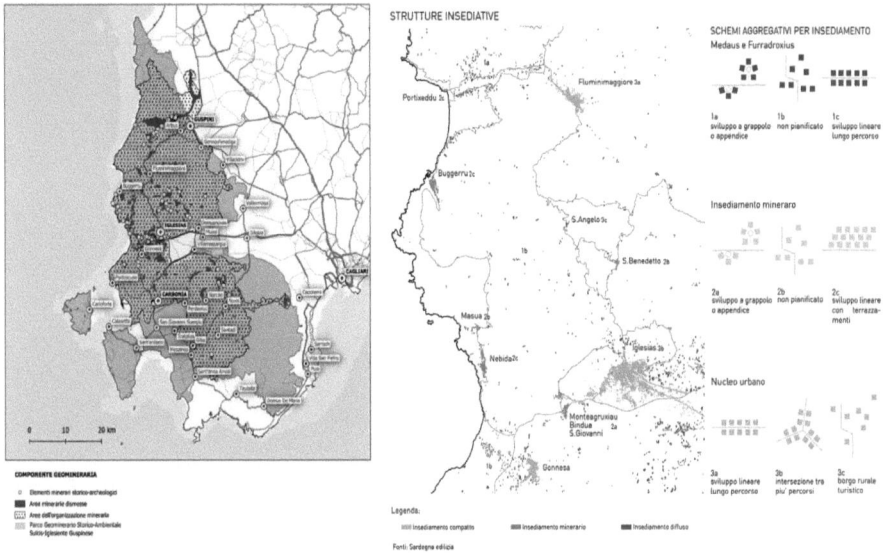

Fig. 3. Archaeological - mining heritage. Elements and areas (left); Settlement patterns (right)

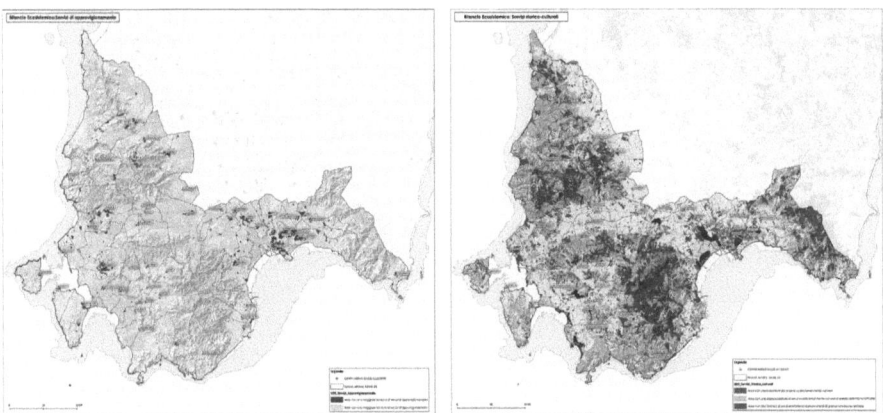

Fig. 4. Ecosystem services balance: provision services (left) and historical and cultural services (right)

Personal services activities were identified and represented through the different databases and classified according to OSM) categories. The final macro-categories of services include: Amenity (general services), Tourism (tourist services), Shop (commercial activities) and Historic (services with cultural-historical significance) (Fig. 5).

A heatmap-based approach was adopted, implemented in a GIS environment using the "density analysis" plugin. The parameters used were defined according to the type of service, for example: for Amenity, values between 0 and 40 services within a radius of 5 km were set, given their greater diffusion (Fig. 6); for Historic and Shop (Fig. 7),

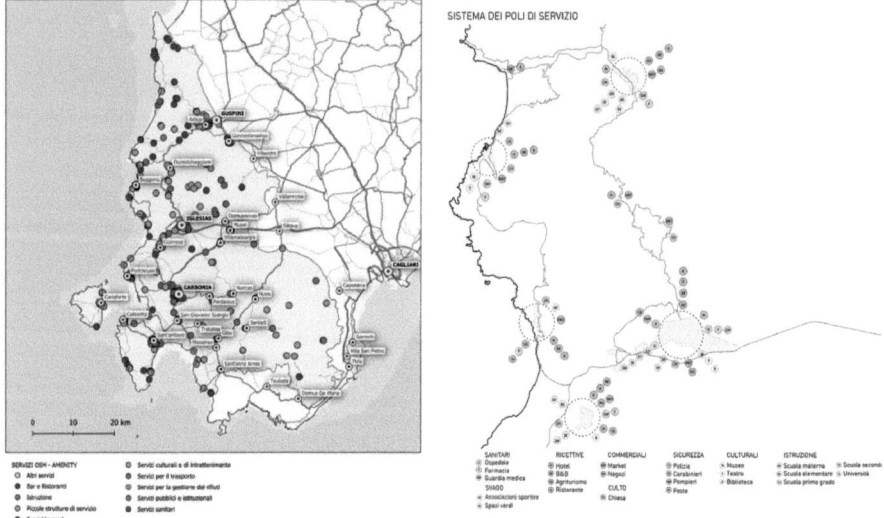

Fig. 5. OSM Services: Amenities, and service centre systems

present in lower numbers, values between 0 and 20 services in the same radius. The results show an uneven distribution of services, with significant concentrations in coastal areas and core centers (Iglesias, Carbonia, Guspini). Amenity services were particularly dense along the coastal belt (S. Antioco, Carloforte, Portoscuso and Buggerru). Tourism services show a more pronounced concentration in the coastal stretch between Gonnesa and Buggerru, as well as in Iglesias (Fig. 6). Shop services show an even distribution, with higher densities in the main centres.

Finally, Historic services show a predominantly coastal distribution and in the southern hinterland, with significant densities around S. Giovanni Suergiu and in S. Antioco. Hence, an overall heatmap was created (Fig. 8), which allowed to highlight the overall distribution of services, confirming the high density of services in the core centres of Iglesias and Carbonia, but pointing out a significant spread also along the coast, from Buggerru to Carbonia, with relevant concentrations in the islands of S. Antioco and S. Pietro. These results underscore the strong polarisation that core centres exert over the entire territory, and reflect the socioeconomic dynamics strongly seasonally affected by tourist flows to coastal areas (Fig. 9). This framework acknowledges the importance of stabilising travel times to plan spatial policies that aim to limit accessibility and infrastructure deficits while guiding infrastructure and economic development.

3.3 Organisation of Physical Connectivity

The infrastructural layout of the area is defined using OSM data, which allowed for an updated and hierarchically classified representation of the road network. The analysis of the road network shows a significant infrastructural deficiency throughout the SI area, with criticality found in the Iglesiente area. The latter, presents a limited road system, mainly characterised by the presence of the SS126 (state highway) and the

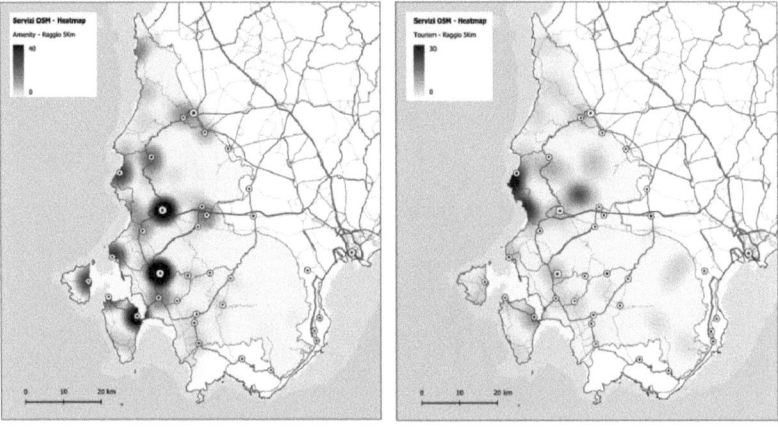

Fig. 6. OSM Services heatmaps: Amenities (left) and Tourism (right) services

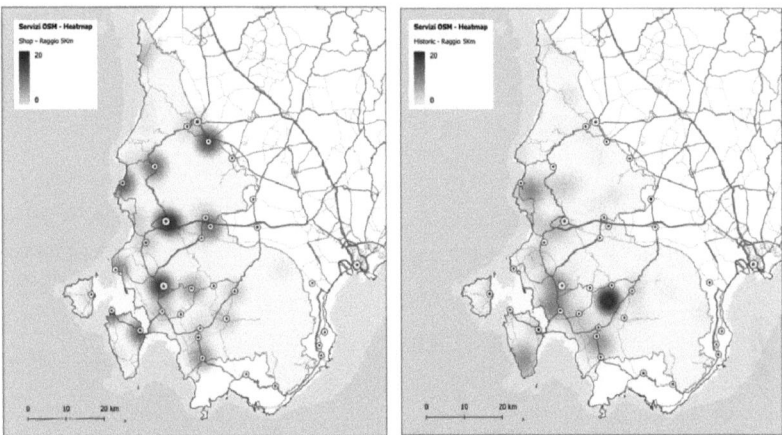

Fig. 7. OSM Services heatmaps: Shop (left) and Historic (right) services

SP83 (provincial road) as the only access routes, a condition strongly influenced by the complex morphology of the territory and the low population density. In contrast, the road network in the Sulcis area is more articulated and interconnected. This situation can be attributed both to a more favourable orographic context and to a greater settlement development, characterised by the presence of numerous towns with related hamlets, embedded in a specialised and organised agricultural fabric. A further factor contributing to the greater viability of the lower Sulcis area is the influence exerted by the industrial hub of Portovesme, which has historically conditioned the socioeconomic dynamics and territorial relations of the area, acting as an attractor and catalyst. The study of the traffic

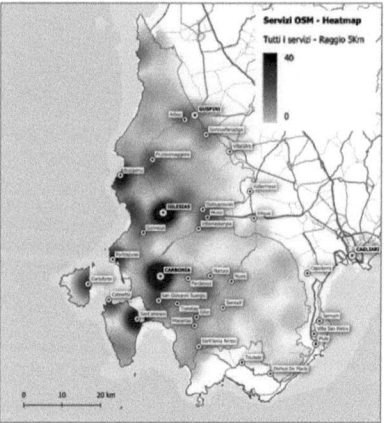

Fig. 8. Overall OSM Services heatmaps

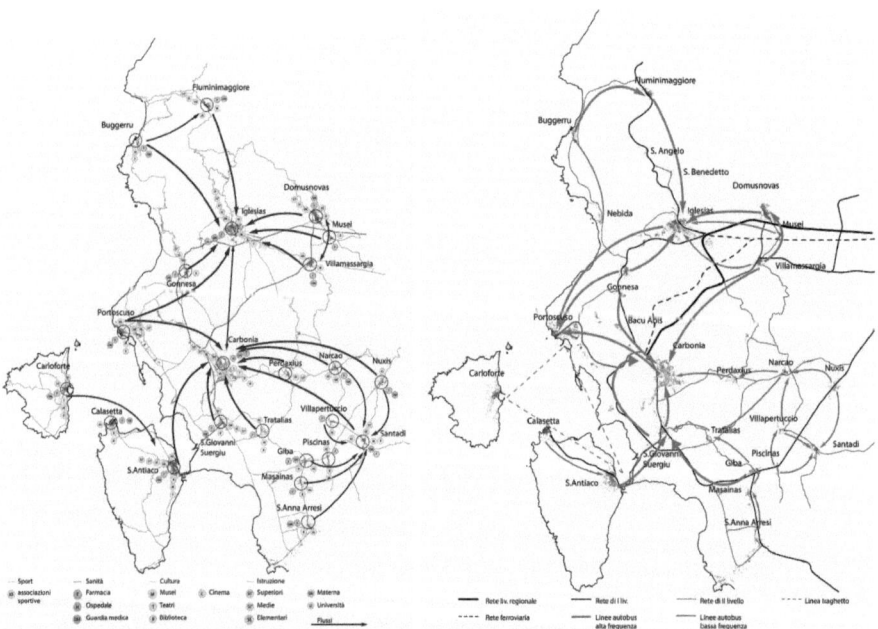

Fig. 9. The system of connections: the system of services and the system of mobility

circulation system in the area is conducted through the analysis of spatial accessibility using the isochrones[6].

The analysis is aimed at assessing accessibility by car, with isochrones of 5, 10 and 15 min (Fig. 10). The results show greater accessibility in the south of the area, between

---

[6] They are identified in the GIS environment using the ORS Tools Plugin, processed for each municipality considered, assuming the town halls as the point of origin.

the towns of the Sulcis area, with a high interposition of isochrones at 10 min and, in some cases, even at 5 min. On the contrary, in the northern part, the Iglesiente area is less accessible, characterised by a poor intersection of isochrones in the 5- and 10-min bands and showing effective coverage only in the 15-min band.

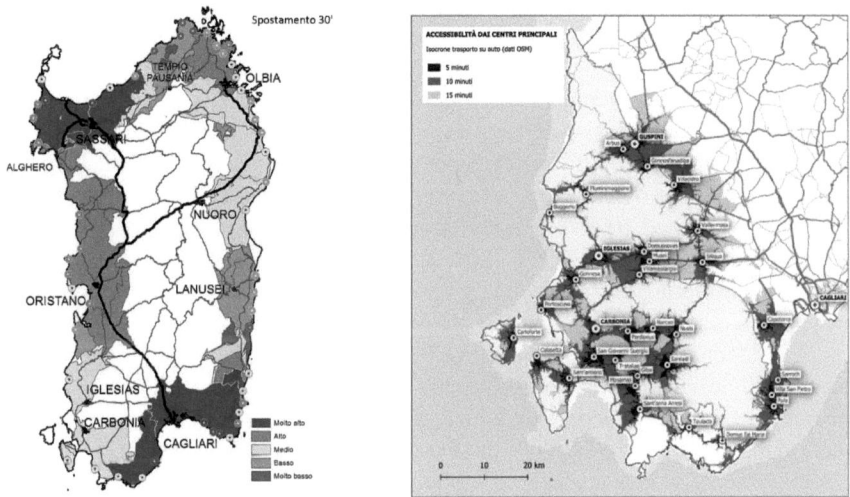

Fig. 10. Displacements in 30 min (left). Accessibility map of urban centres by car (right)

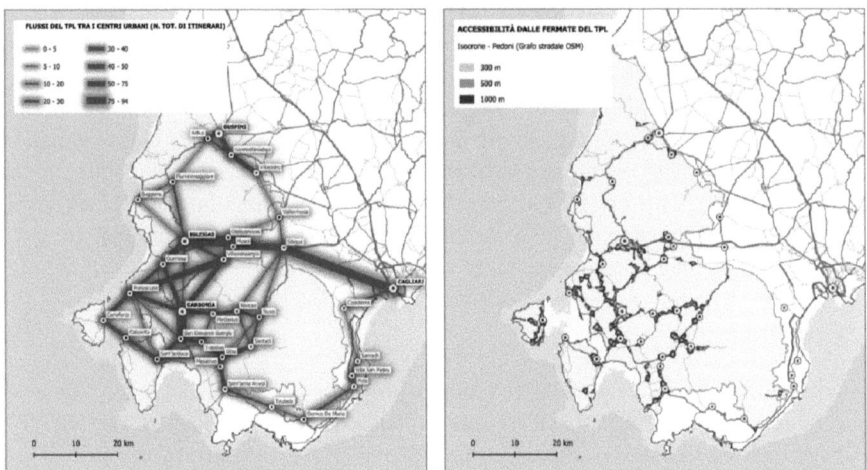

Fig. 11. Map of accessibility of urban centres showing the main PTS flows (left); Map of accessibility to PTS stops on foot (right)

Regarding mobility, data were acquired for local public transport service (PTS) by road and rail (Fig. 11). This phase proved particularly complex both because of the difficulty of retrieving the information and its inherent quality. In particular, the data for bus lines had some errors, and despite the support provided by the responsible entities, it was not possible to obtain a more accurate version of the information. In any case, the impact of incompleteness of some geometries on the expected results was marginal. As for the dataset related to bus stops, it was possible to conduct a detailed analysis, which allowed the extraction of significant information, useful for the formulation of subsequent conclusions.

Note that PTS analysis takes into consideration the assessment of the service efficiency in terms of the density of stops in urban and rural settings, the spatial distribution of lines across the territory, and their frequency. The latter was examined both in terms of the number of routes passing through a single stop and the number of trips each route makes on a typical weekday. Therefore, to assess the accessibility of local PTS from the pedestrian's point of view, the area was analysed by construction of the Service Areas[7] of 300, 500 and 1000 m (Fig. 11) from the centre of each bus stop (by the plugins "ORS Tools" and "QNEAT3"). These areas were not calculated as simple circular buffers, but considering the OSM street graph, which can be travelled by the pedestrian. This approach made it possible to generate polygons representing the sections of road, reachable by foot within the three specified distances. The results show that in the main urban cores (Iglesias, Carbonia and Guspini) the density of stops was optimal for most of the compact urbanised perimeter, with some small portions not covered. In contrast, sparsely populated areas, especially rural areas, show insufficient coverage, with less accessibility to PTS. The distance of 1,000 m was chosen because it corresponds to about a 15-min walk, which is considered the upper limit for defining a stop as nearby in an urban context[8]. This criterion is essential to ensure that the public transportation service is effectively accessible to pedestrians.

In conclusion, the data on accessibility, transportation and mobility in the area, starting with those made available on the Sardinia Region' Sardinia Mobility portal, do not offer alternatives or additional options for moving around the area to the information already available to residents and visitors. This weakness may represent an opportunity for multimodal integration models involving PTS and operators and associations offering accompanying or moving services (rental with driver, periodic shuttles, car-bike sharing, *etc.*). This collaborative activity deploys on three interconnected levels: expanding knowledge of available routes and services, sharing data, and implementing a communication plan, including from road signs.

4 Conclusions

In conclusion, an organisation of functional proximity urban area (FPUA) in terms of accessibility, co-operation and complementarity is recommended in peripheral or insulated regions, like the Sardinian context, characterised by structural disparities such

---

[7] A Service Area is a defined geographic area that represents the area that can be reached from a specific point (e.g., an infrastructure or service) within a given time or distance, considering the road or transportation network. It is used to analyse the accessibility and coverage of services such as hospitals, police stations, or public transportation.

[8] Proximity in urban mobility refers to the ease of access to a public transportation stop, which is considered accessible if it is within a 15-min walk. This limit is used to assess the efficiency and equity of transportation services.

as: (i) the demographic evolution, concentrated near the coast and in the main Sardinian municipality, Cagliari, causing serious dysfunctions in the local economy, particularly for inland areas [49, 50]; (ii) fragile territorial balances associated with the survival of the island's internal centres (National strategy for internal areas, 2019; Urban area strategy, 2018; Territorial Planning, 2020) and (iii) administrative governance related to weak cooperation among local and regional stakeholders and limited endowment.

Promoting stronger territorial cooperation (core-periphery, urban-rural), starting from main urban processes, can support identifying and provisioning environmental and cultural assets and ensuring better management of them in terms of: a) better management of natural resources; b) better services (public transport, health, education, etc.); c) more sustainable land use and planning; d) to reduce inequalities and social exclusion; e) to create competitive and sustainable economies; f) to enhance the capacity of participating in planning and finance investments and services for sustainable development.

In an inter-service compensation perspective, including rebalancing between compact and less densely populated urban systems, the authors provide a comprehensive and interconnected approach proximity-oriented aimed at: (1) represent and maximise the knowledge-based development potential of SPAs and rural areas and their existing networks, and, on the other hand, to outline possible ways to enhance accessibility to information and services, both for residents and visitors. (2) identifying the parameters and factors depending on different variables, including metabolic ones, and various interrelated elements to identify functional proximity areas in SPAs according to a permanent and replicable program, so that all the elements and limiting factors for the development of an efficient organisation of the territory are included, and thus it can be regenerated and innovated. (3) Recognise the elements of stabilizing travel times by identifying a network that optimizes the available resources to plan spatial policies that aim to limit accessibility and infrastructure deficits and shape infrastructure and economic development. The regionalisation of the functional proximity approach allows to facilitate the regional development process, by establishing and enhancing physical ties (infrastructure, shared services) that generate social and economic ties.

This paper faces several limitations, which deserve further work. First, regarding the funding tools, the survey of this study has investigated S3 strategy for the region of Sardinia, and the authors have not been able to fully assess the implications for specific peripheral SPA like the Sulcis – Iglesiente region. Second, the difficulties in identifying and verifying all the factors depending on different variables to identify functional proximity areas in SPAs especially the metabolic ones concerning self-sufficiency in production and exchange of material resources (food, water, energy and waste cycle).

Acknowledgements. This study implements the results of the Tsulky ("Tourism and Sustainability in Sulcis-Iglesiente area") research project final report – 3rd unit. Project funded by Autonomous Region of Sardinia - fundamental or basic research projects for the implementation of interventions under the research for the "Sulcis Plan", CIPE Resolution n. 31 20.02.2015, and resolution n. 52/36 28.10.2015, "Sulcis Strategic project" – public-private research project. It was supported by "DM 737/2021 risorse 2022–2023". It was also supported by the MUR through the project "SMART3R-FLITS: SMART Transport for Travellers and Freight Logistics Integration Towards Sustainability" (Project protocol: 2022J38SR9; CUP Code: F53D23005630006), financed with the PRIN 2022 (Research Projects of National Relevance) program. We authorise the MUR to reproduce and distribute reprints for Governmental purposes, notwithstanding any copyright notations thereon. This manuscript reflects only the authors' views and opinions, neither the European Union nor the European Commission can be considered responsible for them.

Authors' Contributions. This paper is the result of the joint work of the authors. 'Abstract', '1', '2' '4' were written jointly by the authors. CG: '3' and AP: '2.1', '2.2'; TC: '2.3'. Schemes and figures produced by Viola Fonnesu (DADU-UNISS): 5, 9, 15, 16. Schemes and figures produced by Adriano Benatti and Gabriele Congia (DADU-UNISS): 4, 6, 7, 8, 10, 11, 12, 13, 14, 18, 19, 20. AP coordinated and supervised the paper. All authors have read and agreed to the published version of the manuscript.

References

1. Pagano, G., Losco, S.: EU cohesion-policies and metropolitan areas. Procedia-Social Behav. Sci. **223**, 422–428 (2016)
2. Runkel, M., et al.: Climate Change and the EU Budget 2021–2027, Brussels (2019)
3. Zhang, S., Zhen, F., Kong, Y., Lobsang, T., Zou, S.: Towards a 15-minute city: a network-based evaluation framework. Environ. Plan. B: Urban Anal. City Sci. **50**(2), 500–514 (2023). https://doi.org/10.1177/23998083221118570
4. Ferrer-Ortiz, C., Marquet, O., Mojica, L., Vich, G.: Barcelona under the 15-Minute City Lens: mapping the accessibility and proximity potential based on pedestrian travel times. Smart Cities **5**, 146–161 (2022). https://doi.org/10.3390/smartcities5010010
5. Yamu, C., Garau, C.: The 15-min city: a configurational approach for understanding the spatial, economic, and cognitive context of walkability in Vienna. In: Gervasi, O., Murgante, B., Misra, S., Rocha, A.M.A.C., Garau, C. (eds.) Computational Science and Its Applications. Lecture Notes in Computer Science, vol. 13377, pp. 387–404. Springer, Cham (2022). https://doi.org/10.1007/978-3-031-10536-4_26
6. Pozoukidou, G., Chatziyiannaki, Z.: 15-minute city: decomposing the new urban planning eutopia. Sustainability **13**, 928 (2021). https://doi.org/10.3390/su13020928
7. Allam, Z., Bibri, S.E., Chabaud, D., et al.: The '15-Minute City' concept can shape a net-zero urban future. Humanit. Soc. Sci. Commun. **9**, 126 (2022). https://doi.org/10.1057/s41599-022-01145-0
8. Song, G., et al.: Improving the spatial accessibility of community-level healthcare service toward the '15-minute city' goal in China. ISPRS Int. J. Geo-Inf. **11**, 436 (2022). https://doi.org/10.3390/ijgi11080436
9. CENSIS: Rileggere i territori per dare identità e governo all'area vasta. Il governo delle aree metropolitane in Europa. Rapporto di ricerca-febbraio 2014, CENSIS, Roma (2014)
10. Moretti, L.: Geografia e storia. Territorio, insediamenti e comunità umane: un rapporto dialettico, in Caneva, G., Travaglini C.M. (a cura di), Atlante storico-ambientale. Anzio e Nettuno, Roma, De Luca, pp. 97–105 (2003)
11. Breschi, M.: Popolamento e transizione demografica in Sardegna. Editrice Universitaria Udinese, Udine (2017)

12. ESPON FUORE: Functional Urban Areas and Regions in Europe, final report, Version 10/07/2020, ESPON EGTC, Luxembourg (2020)
13. Rueda, S., de Càceres, R., Albert Cuchì, L.B.: El urbanismo ecosistémico: Su aplicación en el diseño de un ecobarrio en Figueres (Ebook). Icaria Editorial, Barcelona, pp.18–19 (2018)
14. Sörvik, J., Teräs, J., Dubois, A., Pertoldi, M.: Smart Specialisation in sparsely populated areas: challenges, opportunities and new openings. Reg. Stud. **53**(7), 1070–1080 (2019)
15. Copus, A.K.: Territorial cohesion in remote rural and sparsely populated areas. Eur. Plan. Stud. **26**(2), 281–301 (2018)
16. OECD, Dijkstra, L., Poelman, H., Veneri, P.: The EU-OECD definition of a functional urban area, OECD Regional Development Working Papers 2019/11, p. 5 (2019)
17. Castells-Quintana, D., Royuela, V., Veneri, P.: Inequality and city size: an analysis for OECD functional urban areas. Pap. Reg. Sci. **99**(4), 1045–1065 (2020)
18. ESPON: Policy Brief "Indicators for Integrated Territorial and Urban Development" (2019)
19. ESPON; GEOSPECS. European Perspective on Specific Types of Territories (2012). https://www.espon.eu/sites/default/files/attachments/GEOSPECS_Final_Report_v8_revised_version.pdf
20. Dijkstra, L., Poelman, H., Veneri, P.: The EU-OECD definition of a functional urban area. Reg. Stud. **53**(3), 441–453 (2019)
21. Gutiérrez, J., et al.: Using accessibility indicators and GIS to assess spatial spillovers of transport infrastructure investment. J. Transp. Geogr. **18**(1), 141–152 (2010)
22. Salonen, M., Toivonen, T.: Modelling travel time in urban networks: comparing Google Maps and transport surveys. Appl. Geogr. **63**, 23–31 (2013)
23. Batty, M.: The New Science of Cities. MIT Press, Cambridge (2013)
24. Horner, M.W., Murray, A.T.: Spatial representation and scale impacts in transit service assessment. Environ. Plann. B. Plann. Des. **31**(5), 785–797 (2004)
25. Veneri, P.: Urban spatial structure in OECD cities: Is urban population decentralising or clustering? OECD Regional Development Working Papers, 2018/02 (2018)
26. Christiansen, P., et al.: Parking facilities and the built environment: impacts on travel behaviour. Transp. Res. Part A: Policy Pract. **95**, 198–206 (2017)
27. Páez, A., Scott, D.M., Morency, C.: Measuring accessibility: positive and normative implementations of various accessibility indicators. J. Transp. Geogr. **25**, 141–153 (2012)
28. Glückler, J., Shearmur, R., Martinus, K.: Liability or opportunity? Reconceptualizing the periphery and its role in innovation. J. Econ. Geogr. **23**(1), 231–249 (2023)
29. ESPON: "ESPON PROFECY – Inner Peripheries: National territories facing challenges of access to basic services of general interest" (2017). https://www.espon.eu/inner-peripheries
30. OECD. A Territorial Approach to the Sustainable Development Goals: Synthesis Report; OECD: Paris, France (2020)
31. Rodríguez-Pose, A.: The revenge of the places that don't matter. Camb. J. Reg. Econ. Soc. **11**(1), 189–209 (2018)
32. Ghinoi, S., et al.: Smart specialisation strategies on the periphery: a data-triangulation approach to governance issues and practices. Reg. Stud. **55**(3), 402–413 (2021)
33. Huggins, R., Prokop, D.: Network structure and regional innovation: a study of university–industry ties. Urban Stud. **54**(4), 931–952 (2017)
34. Rodríguez-Pose, A., et al.: The role of government institutions for Smart Specialisation and regional development, (RIS3 Policy Brief Series, No. 04/2014). Retrieved from (2014)
35. Karo, E., Kattel, R.: Economic development and evolving state capacities in central and Eastern Europe: can 'smart specialisation' make a difference?". J. Econ. Policy Reform **18**(2), 172–187 (2015)
36. Wang, C., Madsen, J.B., Steiner, B.: Industry diversity, competition and firm relatedness: the impact on employment before and after the 2008 global financial crisis. Reg. Stud. **51**(12), 1801–1814 (2017)

37. Organisation for Economic Co-operation and Development (OECD). OECD territorial reviews, northern sparsely populated areas, policy highlights. Retrieved October 17, 2018 (2016)
38. Rueda-Palenzuela, S.: El urbanismo ecosistémico. "Estudios Territoriales" 51.202 (2019)
39. Blečić, I., Cecchini, A., Muroni, E., Saiu, V., Scanu, S., Trunfio, G.A.: Addressing peripherality in Italy: a critical comparison between inner areas and territorial capital-based evaluations. Land **12**(2), 312 (2023)
40. Meijers, E.: Polycentric urban regions and the quest for synergy: is a network of cities more than the sum of the parts? Urban Stud. **42**(4), 765–781 (2005)
41. Capello, R., Rietveld, P.: The concept of network synergies in economic theory: policy implications. In: Button, K., Nijkamp, P., Priemus, H. (eds.) Transport Networks in Europe, pp. 57–83. Edward Elgar, Cheltenham (1998)
42. Congiu, T., Fonnesu, V., Garau, C., Plaisant, A.: Planning strategies and practices for accessibility in peripheral sparsely populated areas (SPA). A spatial knowledge interpretation approach. In: Gervasi, O., Murgante, B., Garau, C., Taniar, D.C., Rocha, A.M.A., Faginas Lago, M.N. (eds.) Computational Science and Its Applications. Lecture Notes in Computer Science, vol. 14822, pp. 407–420. Springer, Cham (2024). https://doi.org/10.1007/978-3-031-65318-6_27
43. Garau, C., Desogus, G., Stratigea, A.: Territorial cohesion in insular contexts: assessing external attractiveness and internal strength of major Mediterranean Islands. Eur. Plan. Stud. (2020). https://doi.org/10.1080/09654313.2020.1840524
44. Regional Transport Plan: Strategic instrument for the integrated development of the maritime and land air transport policy in Sardinia (2022). http://www.regione.sardegna.it/speciali/pianotrasporti/
45. Sardinia mobility: Regional Transport Plan (2022). http://www.sardegnamobilita.it/index.php?xsl=1058&s=33&v=9&c=6684&na=1&n=10&nodesc=2
46. Garau, C., Desogus, G., Barabino, B., Coni, M.: Accessibility and public transport mobility for a smart (er) island. evidence from Sardinia (Italy). Sustain. Cities Soc. **87**, 104145 (2022)
47. M. E. Assessment: Synthesis report. Island, Washington, DC, 748 (2005)
48. Burkhard, B., Kroll, F., Nedkov, S., Müller, F.: Mapping ecosystem service supply, demand and budgets. Ecol. Ind. **21**, 17–29 (2012)
49. Crenos: Economy of Sardinia, 27th Report 2020 (2020). https://crenos.unica.it/crenosterritorio/sites/default/files/allegati-pubblicazioni-tes/CRENoS%20-%2027%C2%B0%20Rapporto%20sull%27Economia%20della%20Sardegna%20-%202020.pdf
50. Svimez Report (2019). http://lnx.svimez.info/svimez/il-rapporto/. Accessed 09 May 2023

Beyond Traffic Congestion: Developing Digital Twin to Enhance Accessibility to Points of Interest

Torrisi Vincenza[1], Pierfrancesco Leonardi[2], Matteo Ignaccolo[2], and Sheila Bellia[2]

[1] Department of Electrical, Electronic and Computer Engineering, University of Catania, Viale Andrea Doria, 6, 95125 Catania, Italy
vincenza.torrisi@unict.it
[2] Department of Civil Engineering and Architecture, University of Catania, Viale Andrea Doria, 6, 95125 Catania, Italy

Abstract. The growing phenomenon of traffic congestion in urban areas, due to increasing motorization rates, has significant social, economic and environmental impacts. High vehicle congestion results in longer travel times and reduced accessibility to Points of Interests (POIs), especially during peak hours. While traditional strategies have prioritized infrastructure development, recent policies targeting the reduction of avoidable car journeys have shown some success in decreasing vehicle flows. However, it is crucial that these policies also develop measures to improve the accessibility of those who are dependent on the private car for their mobility due to the lack of modal alternatives, still existing in many areas.

To address these issues, a comprehensive approach is proposed based on microsimulation of vehicle flows, developing a small-scale digital twin, to replicate daily operating conditions. The methodology consists of several steps: (i) supply reconstruction through microsimulation model, (ii) demand analysis driven by advanced surveys and sensor technologies, (iii) evaluation of intervention scenarios aimed at optimizing the use of resources and minimizing infrastructure interventions.

The application of this methodology, tested on a real case study, consists of a main road in the urban area of Catania, characterised by high traffic volumes due to its strategic position and the presence of two attractive poles. It shows how targeted interventions, such as the improvement of road signs and the optimized management of car park entrances, can be effective solutions for improving accessibility and vehicle movements. Future developments will extend the model to assess the impact on the surrounding road network and to evaluate long-term interventions.

Keywords: Traffic microsimulation · Digital twins · Urban mobility · Traffic management · Urban accessibility

1 Introduction

Mobility planning plays a key role in urban areas, as it makes it possible to limit vehicle congestion, an increasingly widespread phenomenon that has a negative impact on quality of life, the environment and transport efficiency [1, 2].

At national level, this phenomenon is very significant: in fact, Italy has one of the highest motorisation rates in Europe. According to Eurostat [3] there will be 694 cars per 1,000 inhabitants in 2023, which is higher than the EU average of 571 cars per 1,000 inhabitants. Moreover, the Italian car fleet is growing steadily, with an average annual increase of 1.3% since 2018, a higher rate than in other major European economies such as Germany (+0.7%), Spain (+0.4%) and France (+0.3%). At the urban level, some Italian cities are well above the national average, such as Catania, with 815 cars per 1,000 inhabitants. These data highlight the need for effective mobility planning strategies to mitigate the negative effects of high vehicle density [4, 5].

In recent years, despite policies to discourage car use, such as the introduction of Limited Traffic Zones (LTZs) and Low Emission Zones (LEZs) [6, 7], motorisation rates have not decreased significantly. At the same time, modal shift to public transport has not achieved satisfactory results, highlighting the need for more integrated strategies and complementary interventions to make mobility alternatives more attractive and efficient [7].

This modal imbalance in favour of private transport over public transport may be the result of a poor public transport supply, characterised by a limited territorial coverage, a low frequency of trips and an insufficient level of integration between the different modes of transport [8].

The lack of adequate public transport planning combined with insufficient dedicated infrastructure further limits the potential for effective modal shift. In order to stimulate a significant modal shift, an upgrading of the public transport system through investment in infrastructure improvements, favourable pricing policies and innovative solutions, such as the promotion of shared mobility and on-demand services, is essential [9, 10].

The result is imbalance between transport demand and supply, which forces users to rely on private cars, particularly to reach specific destinations such as hospitals, schools, universities and employment areas. These journeys, often linked to well-defined timetables and schedules, fuel the creation of real urban hotspots where the demand for mobility exceeds the response capacity of the public transport system, further exacerbating congestion and increasing the burden on road infrastructure.

To address and solve this problem, one possible solution to the modal imbalance lies in transport system optimisation, which can be supported by modelling and simulation of the urban transport system [11]. Such techniques allow a detailed assessment of the current state and critical issues related to mobility management, providing a precise view of traffic flows and nodes within the city. In addition, by simulating alternative management scenarios, both short and long term, it is possible to test the effectiveness of different strategies without the risk of implementing real interventions without prior evaluation. Different mobility management scenarios can be designed, distinguishing between long-term interventions, which involve significant changes to the transport system and the implementation of new infrastructure, with a time horizon of 10–15 years, and short-term interventions, which focus on targeted actions and rapid improvements to existing infrastructure, with an implementation period of around 2 years. These scenarios allow critical issues to be addressed in a differentiated manner, optimising available resources and responding to immediate needs in a timely manner, without compromising the long-term vision.

Modelling at different scales, both macro and micro-simulation, using advanced traffic flow analysis and mobility management software, provides an in-depth understanding of the transport system from both a qualitative and quantitative point of view. By measuring specific indicators such as vehicle saturation rates, travel times, time lost, queues, service levels and public transport efficiency, it is possible to identify optimal solutions to improve mobility management, reduce congestion and promote accessibility to strategic points in the city.

Within this framework, the concept of a Digital Twin is introduced as a core component of the analysis. A digital twin refers to a virtual representation of a physical system, in this case, a section of the urban road network, capable of replicating its dynamic behavior under different conditions [12–14]. Through the integration of simulation models and real-world data collected via sensors and surveys, the digital twin allows for continuous calibration and testing of various scenarios [15, 16]. This enhances decision-making by providing a flexible and data-driven environment for evaluating targeted interventions in terms of their impact on accessibility and overall network performance [17].

The main tools available to develop the base model of Digital Twin include VISSIM and VISUM, which allow microscopic simulation and macro-level planning respectively, but also AIMSUN [18, 19], a versatile traffic simulation software that integrates both microscopic and mesoscopic simulation, and TransModeler, which provides powerful simulation capabilities for detailed analysis of traffic behaviour. Other useful tools include MATSim, for multi-agent simulation of modal choice, and Synchro, for traffic light and intersection design and optimisation.

Microsimulation tools like VISSIM are widely used for assessing traffic flow quality and Level of Service (LOS) on complex freeway facilities and intersections [20, 21]. These models can evaluate various scenarios, such as signal control applications at roundabouts [21] and the impact of pedestrian numbers on intersection performance [22]. However, proper calibration and validation of microsimulation models are crucial for obtaining meaningful results.

The objective of the paper is to propose an integrated approach based on microsimulation of vehicle flows, developing a small-scale digital twin to replicate daily operating conditions. The methodology is structured into several phases: traffic supply reconstruction through a microsimulation model, demand analysis using advanced surveys and sensor technologies, and evaluation of intervention scenarios aimed at optimizing resource utilization while minimizing infrastructure modifications. The proposed approach has been tested on a real-world case study involving a main urban road in Catania, characterized by high traffic volumes due to its strategic location and the presence of two major attraction poles. The results demonstrate that targeted interventions, such as improved road signage and optimized car park entrance management, can effectively enhance accessibility and vehicle flow.

The paper consists of five sections: Sect. 1 introduces the research by identifying the problem and providing a literature review on its implications and potential solutions.

Section 2 outlines the methodological approach and describes the data sources used for the analysis. Section 3 presents the case study, detailing its context, characteristics, and relevance to the problem under investigation. Section 4 discusses the results, interpreting the findings in relation to the research objectives and comparing them with existing studies. Finally, Sect. 5 concludes the paper by summarizing the key insights, highlighting the study's contributions, and suggesting directions for future research.

2 Methodological Approach

The proposed methodological approach follows a multi-step process to implement a robust microsimulation model with a view toward developing a digital twin. First, traffic data collection integrates multiple sources, including sensors, cameras, and radar, ensuring a comprehensive dataset for model calibration and validation. The next step involves the reconstruction of travel demand by analysing the routes between the various O/D pairs to identify possible itineraries along the road network. In parallel, the supply-side reconstruction consists in defining network characteristics and operational conditions. Then, the interaction between demand and supply is modelled to capture system behaviours. Finally, scenario analysis is conducted to evaluate different interventions, technological innovations, or infrastructure management modifications, providing insights into enhancing system accessibility under varying conditions.

The procedural steps are listed below and schematized in Fig. 1:

- Data collection (i.e. demand data and supply data);
- Demand reconstruction;
- Reconstruction of the transport supply;
- Supply-demand interaction and scenario analysis.

2.1 Data Collection

This phase involves the collection of all the required data for the reconstruction of the transport simulation model. Specifically, data can be divided into two main categories: supply data and demand data.

The data required to reconstruct the supply model includes all the infrastructure characteristics of the road network, such as the number of lanes and width, the priority rules, the presence of impedance elements (i.e. obstacles, discontinuity, gradient) and other geometric and functional characteristics. The data required for demand modelling consists of vehicle flows measured at of on-site monitoring sections. The positioning of these sections must be carefully planned in accordance with the reconstruction of the routes used by vehicles because, after that, the observed flows must be assigned to the travel paths, following the information obtained during the survey campaign.

To conduct field surveys, the study area must be zoned, within which all possible permitted manoeuvres are identified, including any manoeuvres that are not permitted according to the Italian Highway Code (from Italian "Codice della Strada"). The choice of technology to perform the survey depends on the complexity of the section to be analysed. For sections characterized by a limited number of manoeuvres, manual counting can be employed, involving an operator recording the passage of vehicles on printed tables, organised in separate quadrants for each vehicle category. For more complex sections, it is advisable to use sensors based on radar technology, able to automatically detect the passage of vehicles, speeds and vehicle classification on a continuous 24/7 basis. However, these sensors could be subject to the phenomenon of obscuration in case of congestion or illegal parking. In this case, one solution may be the use of cameras for image acquisition and further processing. This second solution, using artificial intelligence algorithms [23], allows not only automatic counting of vehicles, but also their classification according to vehicle category, travel speeds and identification of illegal manoeuvres.

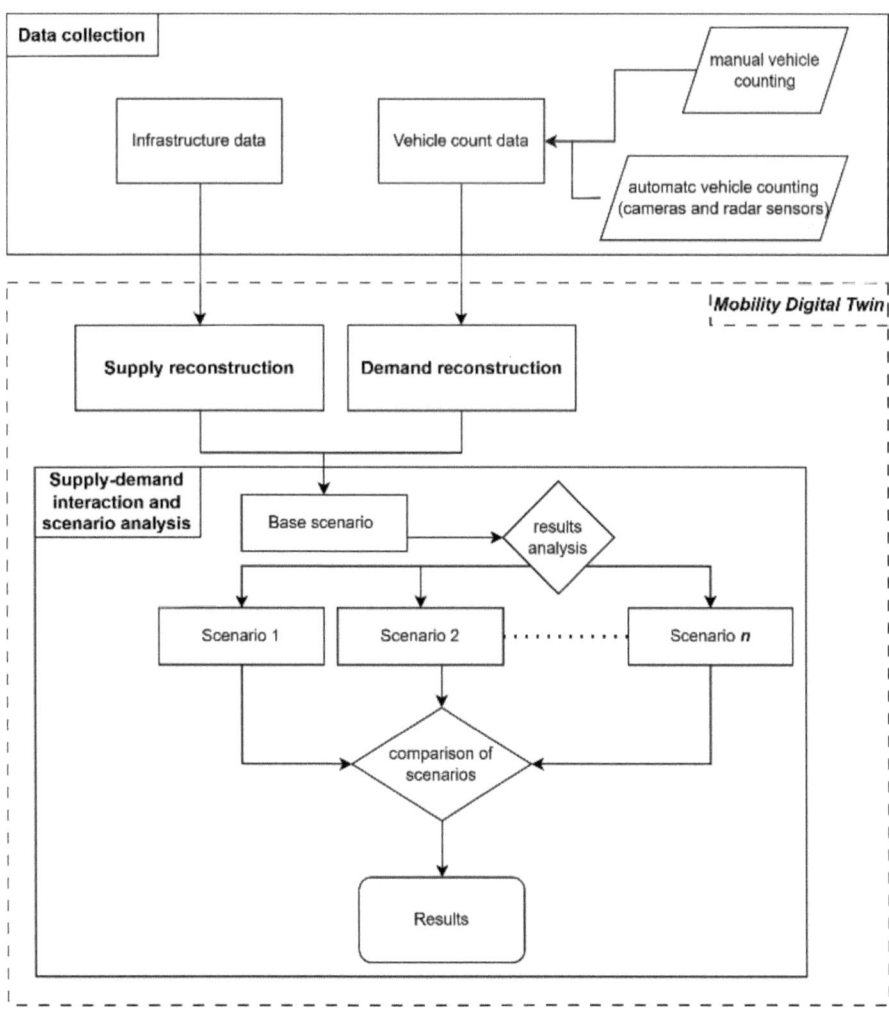

Fig. 1. Methodological framework for developing Digital Twin

2.2 Demand Reconstruction

This second phase involves processing and analysing the travel demand data. In this regard, it is necessary to examine the results from the survey campaign to identify the most critical time intervals and to define peak hours to be used as a reference for reconstructing of the demand matrix. Then, it is required to identify all possible routes between origins and destinations within the network and assign vehicle flows upon them considering the inputs derived from data collected within the counting sections. This allows to obtain a coherent representation of mobility demand within the analysed transport network.

2.3 Reconstruction of Transport Supply

The reconstruction of the transport supply involves the definition of the road network graph, which consists of links representing the lanes with their operational characteristics (i.e. number of lanes, width, travel directions, etc.) and connectors identifying turning manoeuvres. This operation must be closely integrated with the data collection phase, as the in-field survey can support an accurate characterisation of the road graph. At this stage, it is also necessary to identify and define and manage the conflict areas at junctions, generated by the interaction between traffic flows that intersect or overlap in space and time.

2.4 Supply-Demand Interaction and Scenario Analysis

After the reconstruction of both supply and demand, vehicle flows are simulated through the application of the Wiedemann 74 car-following model. Through traffic simulation we can reproduce traffic dynamics and evaluate the performance of the road network under different conditions. The main Key Performance Indicators (KPIs) used in the scenario analysis are level of service (LOS), travel time and queue length, evaluated on each analysed route. The level of service (LOS) assesses traffic quality on the simulated routes, considering speed, density, travel time and queue length. It follows the HCM classification, from LOS A (free flow) to LOS F (congestion). The analysis can be carried out at different level of details: focusing on junctions and evaluating single manoeuvres or at the network level, examining the formation of queues in specific road sections and the travel times within the study area. Based on critical points identified at this stage, it is possible to define scenario interventions and quantify the impact of the proposed solutions to improve network performances.

3 Case Study

Our methodological approach has been applied to a real case study consists of a main road in the urban area of Catania. Catania is one of the main metropolitan cities in Sicily, Italy, with an urban area of about 180 square kilometres and a population of about 300,000. However, its functional urban area extends well beyond the city boundaries and includes numerous neighbouring municipalities whose inhabitants daily commute to Catania for work, education and access to other essential services. This high influx of commuters constitutes a significant transport demand, resulting in heavy congestion, longer travel times and a general decline in network efficiency. One of the main challenges contributing to this issue is the limited effectiveness of the public transport system, which does not provide adequate coverage and frequency in different across the city. As a result, in some of these areas, particularly those where essential services such as health, education and administrative offices are concentrated, remain largely inaccessible without the use of private vehicles.

3.1 Territorial Framework

Due to the commuting phenomena, the main traffic routes coincide with those which serve the function of penetration into the city. Among these, Via Santa Sofia stands out, both for the high intensity of traffic flows and for the presence of many attractive Point of Interests (POIs). This urban roadway originates in the north of the district named Cibali and runs in a northerly direction crossing the ring road of the city (Fig. 2).

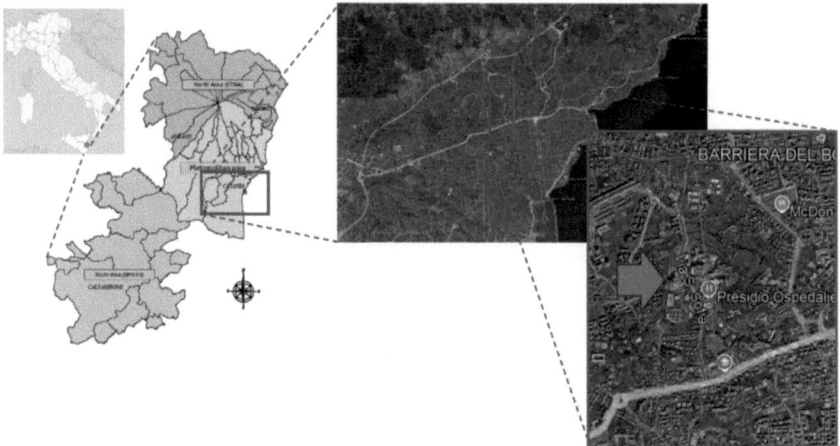

Fig. 2. Territorial framework

In recent years, the study area has seen a significant increase in the number of POIs, i.e. the University, the Polyclinic and the Biological Tower, resulting in a substantial increase in vehicle flows (Fig. 3).

In parallel, the road configuration has been changed several times (Fig. 4). The first, which was introduced in 2013, consisted in the implementation of a dedicated lane for the Bus Rapid Transit line BRT1. The more significant intervention, implemented between 2017 and 2018, involved the addition of two new turnarounds (Fig. 5).

3.2 Data Collection

The surveys have been carried out on nine monitoring sections along Via Santa Sofia. As shown in Fig. 6, these sections are classified according to their purpose: orange

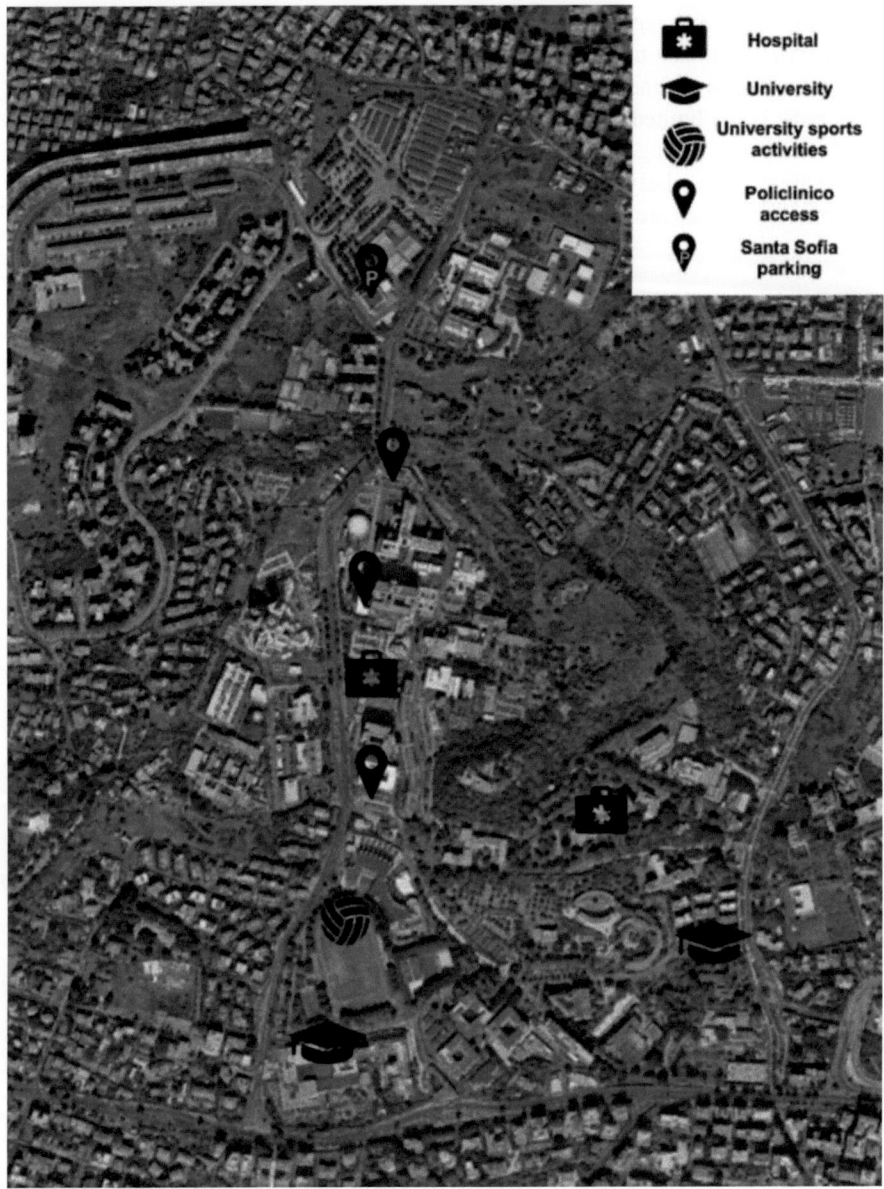

Fig. 3. Location of Point of Interests (POIs)

indicates segments monitoring through traffic on the road network, while blue refers to those monitoring vehicle movements access and egress from car parking facilities.

All sections have been monitored through manual counts carried out by operators using printed tables. In addition, surveys with sensor radar and cameras have been carried out at points 1, 2 and 3 (shown in green). In particular, the cameras have detected for

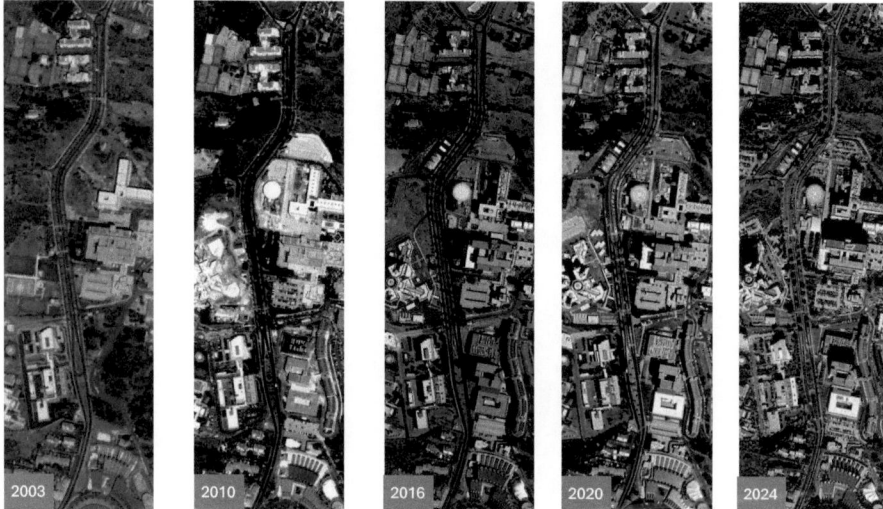

Fig. 4. Expansion of the urban area in Via S. Sofia

Fig. 5. Change Road configuration

the same duration as the manual surveys, while the radar sensor surveys started three days before the manual survey campaign and lasted a total of six days. The radar sensor surveys have been also used to analyse the traffic flow trends during the day within the area and to identify peak hours.

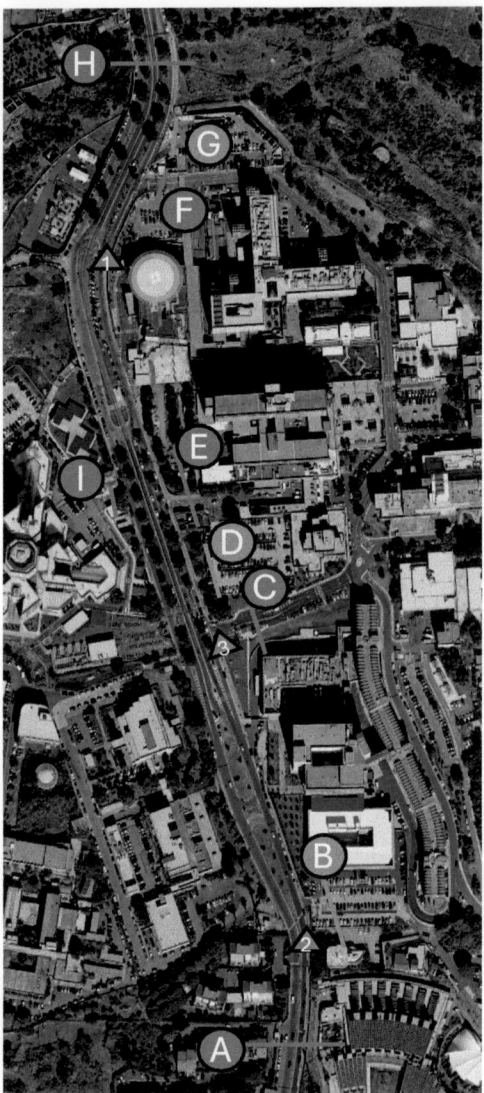

Fig. 6. Monitoring sections

3.3 Simulation Model Implementation

Then, the entire transport network has been reconstructed through a microsimulation model using VISSIM software (see state of affairs in Fig. 7). The model simulates all vehicle lanes and the two pedestrian crossings with traffic lights. The detected flows have been assigned as traffic flows to each identified path, based on the demand analysis. In addition, traffic signs and priority rules have been modelled, and a calibration of Wiedmann parameters has been carried out to better simulate user behaviour.

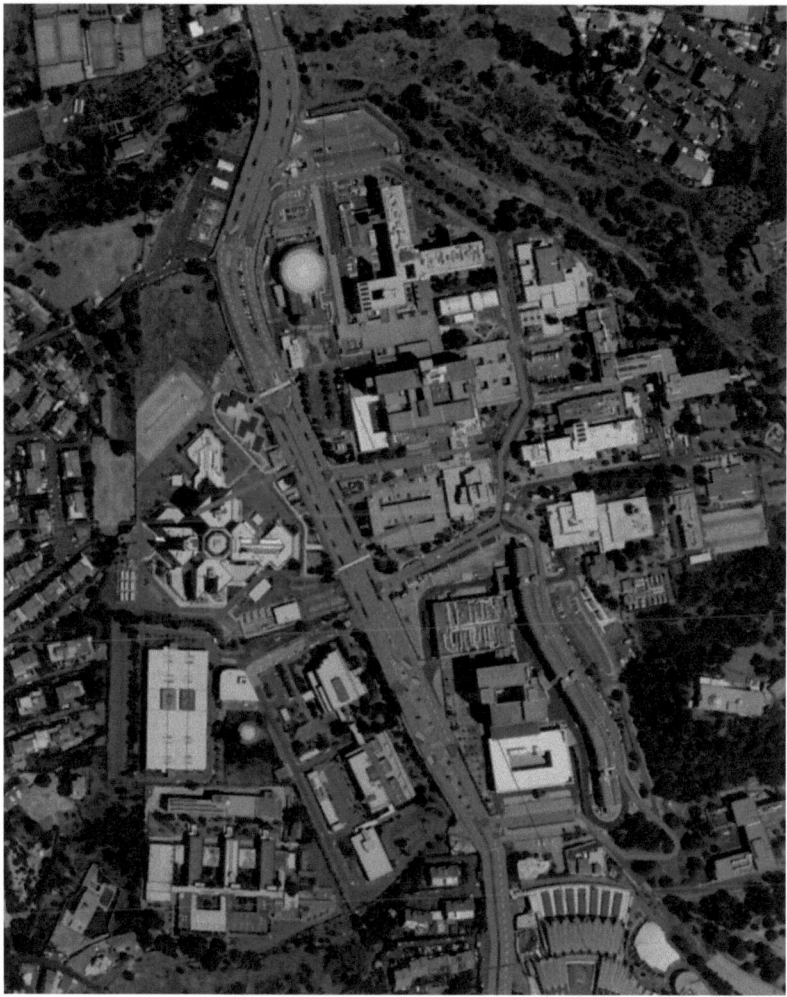

Fig. 7. Microsimulation model network in VISSIM

4 Results and Discussion

This section presents the results obtained through the simulation model. First, the current state is analysed to highlight emerging criticalities and guide the proposal of targeted intervention strategies. These strategies led to the definition of three different scenarios with incrementally applied solutions. Their outcomes are then compared with the baseline to evaluate overall effectiveness. The analysis focuses on key performance indicators such as travel time and queue length, which directly influence the perceived and actual quality of the driving experience. By reducing travel times and congestion, the proposed interventions improve users' ability to reach their destinations more efficiently, thereby contributing to greater accessibility at the network level.

4.1 Results of the State of Affairs

Once the state model had been reconstructed, initial analyses were carried out. As shown in Table 1, the obtained results highlight numerous criticalities in almost all the analysed manoeuvres, with a level of service at the lowest value. Furthermore, both travel times and queue lengths are particularly high, indicating a situation of generalized congestion along the section under study.

Table 1. Scenario 1 results, LOS, Travel time and Length of queue

Path	LOS
A-B	F
A-C	F
A-D	F
A-E	F
A-H (outer lane)	F
A-F	F
A-G	F
A-H (BRT1 lane)	F
A-H (inner lane)	F
B-H (outer lane)	F
C-A	F
C-H (outer lane)	F
H (outer lane)-A	C
H (outer lane)-C	F
H (outer lane)-D	F
H (outer lane)-E	F
H (outer lane)-F	F
H (inner lane)-A	D
H (inner lane)-G	F

Path	Travel time
A (from start of street) - H (inner lane)	7,36 min
A (from start of street) - H (outer lane)	9,07 min
A (from start of street) - H (outer lane)	2,70 min

Section	Length of queue
1	790 m
2	524 m
3	330 m

This confirmed what has already been observed during the survey phases, which revealed several critical issues, including illegal manoeuvres, significant slowing and stop-and-go of traffic flow due to the access to the car park facilities of the Polyclinic. We also observed unauthorised stops for passengers entering and exiting the polyclinic, illegal parking and a general lack of clear signage for road users.

Based on the findings, short-term interventions have been proposed, aimed at simulating tactical and immediate solutions to address the demanding problems on this area. These measures, characterised by relatively low costs and short-term implementation, aim to ensure definite benefits for improving accessibility to POIs with consequent benefits for users.

4.2 Project Scenarios Results

The analysed scenarios have been setup with an "incremental" configuration, with each scenario maintaining the measures adopted in the previous one while introducing new measures. In the following paragraphs, the three proposed scenarios are described, and the results are presented comparing them with the current state of affairs.

Scenario 1

The main objectives of the first intervention in Scenario 1 are to reduce waiting times needed to access parking facilities, to prevent long queues formation and consequently congestion phenomena in the whole area. In addition, the intervention aims to minimise interference between traffic flow entering and exiting the car parks. The first solution (intervention *a*) involves speeding up the entry procedure to the car parks. Currently, each vehicle entering car parks corresponding to manoeuvres 'B', 'D' and 'G' (Fig. 6) experiences a significant delay. The proposed measure reduces the entry time per individual vehicle from approximately 30 to 25 s, which can be achieved through the the implementation of simple and widely adopted parking management technologies, such as license plate recognition or automatic ticketing systems.

A second modification (intervention *b*) involves closing access to car park "B", resulting in the redistribution of outflows to the upstream entrance of car park "C". This measure stems from two main observations: the first, already identified during the infield survey phase, concerns the queues generated by the current access system to the car parks, which cause significant slowdowns in through traffic; the second, identified by the simulation, shows that the entrance to car park "B" is placed along a section with a reduced roadway, causing a significant slowdown in vehicle flows and hindering the proper use of the two available lanes.

In brief, the changes proposed in this scenario are as follows:

a. "Reduction in access time to car park facilities"
b. "Deactivated Exit from car park in B"

Scenario 2

The second scenario includes the interventions proposed in the first scenario and, in addition, it involves a change in the location of the entrance to the Policlinico (intervention *c*), aiming to reduce the volume of traffic on Via Santa Sofia. The aim of this measure is to prevent users from travelling along the entire road in order to access the hospital area.

Currently, a user coming from the south must enter on F and exit on C, driving along a long stretch of Via Santa Sofia. However, in most cases they are forced to re-enter the road network at C and look for parking elsewhere, effectively doubling the number of passages on this road. The proposed intervention is to eliminate the access from F by reversing the traffic flow and consolidating all access points at C. This solution aims to minimize unnecessary trips and reduce congestion on the main arterial road.

In summary, the changes proposed in this scenario are as follows:

a. "Reduction in access time to car park facilities"
b. "Deactivated Exit from car park in B"
c. "Polyclinic internal route changes and consolidation of access points in C"

Scenario 3

The aim of the third scenario is to further reduce the number of vehicles in Via Santa Sofia and to facilitate more efficient access to the various POIs located along the route. To this end, intervention (*d*) has been proposed, which involves extending the shuttle service to improve the connection between the POIs and the "Santa Sofia" park-and-ride.

Currently, a bus line named A-MS is operating, connecting the car park "Santa Sofia" to the metro station "Milo" with a frequency of 5 min, but only during peak hours. In the microsimulation model, an extension of the service to every 5 min was assumed for the whole morning. The expected effect of this measure is a 10% reduction in vehicle flows in Via Santa Sofia, thus contributing to the improvement of accessibility.

In brief, the changes proposed in this scenario are as follows:

a. "Reduction in access time to car park facilities"
b. "Deactivated Exit from car park in B"
c. "Polyclinic internal route changes and consolidation of access points in C"
d. "Increasing the frequency of the A-MS line"

The results of the three scenarios are compared with the current state of affair (i.e. Scenario SoA) and summarized in Table 2.

Analysis of the different scenarios highlights a significant improvement in terms of queue reduction: the first intervention resulted in an improvement of around 70%, the second reached approximately 92%, and the third showed an improvement of about 86%. Travel times also decreased, although this benefit was particularly evident only in the first scenario, with a reduction of 61%.

Table 2. Scenario comparison, LOS, Travel time and Queue Length

Path	LOS S. SoA	LOS S. 1	LOS S. 2	LOS S 3
A-B	F	B	A	A
A-C	F	B	B	B
A-D	F	B	B	B
A-E	F	B	C	B
A-F	F	D		
A-G	F	D	D	C
A-H (BRT1 lane)	F	A	B	B
A-H (inner lane)	F	D	C	B
C-A	F	E		
C-H (outer lane)	F	C		
H (outer lane)-C	F	D	F	F
H (outer lane)-D	F	E	F	D
H (outer lane)-E	F	D	F	D
H (outer lane)-F	F	E		
H (inner lane)-A	D	D	F	E
H (inner lane)-G	F	E	E	E
F – H			B	A

Path	Travel time S. SoA	Travel time S. 1	Travel time S. 2	Travel time S. 3
A (from start of street) - H (inner lane)	7,36 min	2,96 min	2,80 min	2,72 min
A (from start of street) - H (outer lane)	2,70 min	2,87 min	3,41 min	3,06 min

Section	Length of queue S. SoA	Length of queue S. 1	Length of queue S. 2	Length of queue S. 3
1	790 m	429 m	25.93 m	13.95 m
2	524 m	0 m	86.13 m	14.77 m
3	330 m	55 m	33.93 m	41.78 m

5 Conclusions and Future Research

This study proposed and tested a comprehensive methodological approach to support the design and evaluation of targeted interventions aimed at improving traffic conditions and accessibility in complex urban environments. By integrating microsimulation modelling, demand analysis through advanced surveys and sensor data, and the evaluation of alternative intervention scenarios, the methodology allows for a detailed understanding of current dynamics and the potential impacts of low-impact solutions.

The proposed interventions for the analysed case study in the urban area of Catania have been configured as short-term solutions, as they do not require major infrastructural changes. However, to ensure the success of these strategies, a thorough revision of the signage is essential, aimed at directing users towards the Santa Sofia parking lot. In this context, the installation of variable message panels is advisable, as it provides precise and real-time information on parking occupancy. The idea is to allow direct access to the hospital campus only for users with reduced disabilities, while others are guided to the Santa Sofia parking lot, from which the campus can be reached via a shuttle bus service.

These results confirmed that the long access times to the parking lots represent one of the main causes of queues. In particular, the second and third scenarios proposed a complete reorganization of the internal flows within the hospital campus and parking areas, encouraging the use of the park-and-ride facility. Although these measures have been a limited impact on simulations, they significantly improve campus accessibility, especially under conditions of parking saturation. This situation, often not perceived by users waiting to enter, can lead to improper behaviours such as irregular parking along the roadway, which in turn hinders the regular flow of traffic.

The creation of a small-scale digital twin enabled the replication of daily operating conditions, offering a flexible and transferable tool for decision-making. Beyond the specific case of Catania, the proposed methodology is highly replicable and adaptable to a wide range of urban contexts. Thanks to its modular structure and the use of widely available tools, such as microsimulation platforms and sensor-based data collection, it can be applied in different cities to support evidence-based planning and the efficient allocation of resources. Future research will combine macro and micro perspectives, based on macroscopic fundamental diagram theory and urban traffic microcirculation theory, and study an innovative macro traffic control strategy and micro traffic organization method. The evaluation will be conducted through VISSIM dynamic traffic simulation. In this regard, the micro traffic organization method based on the concept of microcirculation can effectively utilize road resources for diversion, significantly improving the service level of intersections and roads in the analysed area.

Acknowledgements. The work of Vincenza Torrisi related to the model conceptualization and development is funded by the European Union (NextGenerationEU), through the MUR-PNRR project SAMOTHRACE (ECS00000022).

References

1. Louro, A., Marques da Costa, N., Marques da Costa, E.: From livable communities to livable metropolis: Challenges for urban mobility in Lisbon Metropolitan Area (Portugal). Int. J. Environ. Res. Public Health **18**(7), 3525 (2021)
2. Okraszewska, R., Romanowska, A., Wołek, M., Oskarbski, J., Birr, K., Jamroz, K.: Integration of a multilevel transport system model into sustainable urban mobility planning. Sustainability **10**(2), 479 (2018)
3. Passenger cars in the EU. (n.d.). https://ec.europa.eu/eurostat/statistics-explained/index.php?title=Passenger_cars_in_the_EU. Accessed 4 April 2025

4. Chatziioannou, I., Alvarez-Icaza, L., Bakogiannis, E., Kyriakidis, C., Chias-Becerril, L.: A structural analysis for the categorization of the negative externalities of transport and the hierarchical organization of sustainable mobility's strategies. Sustainability **12**(15), 6011 (2020)
5. Indicatori del parco veicolare. (n.d.). https://www.istat.it/comunicato-stampa/indicatori-del-parco-veicolare-anno-2023/. Accessed 4 April 2025
6. Flanagan, E., Malmqvist, E., Gustafsson, S., Oudin, A.: Estimated public health benefits of a low-emission zone in Malmö, Sweden. Environ. Res. **214**, 114124 (2022)
7. Margaryan, S.: Low emission zones and population health. J. Health Econ. **76**, 102402 (2021). https://doi.org/10.1016/j.jhealeco.2020.102402
8. Rapporto sulla mobilità degli italiani – ISFORT. (n.d.). https://www.isfort.it/2024/11/16/presentazione-del-21-rapporto-sulla-mobilita-degli-italiani/. Accessed 4 April 2025
9. Capodici, A.E., et al.: Designing microtransit services in suburban areas: a case study in Palermo, Italy. Res. Transp. Bus. Manag. **56**, 101191 (2024)
10. Torrisi, V., Leonardi, P., Barbagallo, A., Ignaccolo, M.: An evaluation of the key features for designing a sustainable demand responsive transport service (DRTS) in urban and suburban contexts. In: AIP Conference Proceedings, vol. 3269, no. 1 (2025). https://pubs.aip.org/aip/acp/article-abstract/3269/1/090014/3332225
11. Torrisi, V., Cocuzza, E., Ignaccolo, M.: Simulation model to assess freight flow effects in the urban–port road interface: a practical use-case for the commercial port in Catania (Italy). Transp. Res. Procedia **83**, 236–243 (2025)
12. Wang, Z., et al.: Mobility digital twin: concept, architecture, case study, and future challenges. IEEE Internet Things J. **9**(18), 17452–17467 (2022)
13. Kušić, K., Schumann, R., Ivanjko, E.: A digital twin in transportation: real-time synergy of traffic data streams and simulation for virtualizing motorway dynamics. Adv. Eng. Inform. **55**, 101858 (2023)
14. Yeon, H., Eom, T., Jang, K., Yeo, J.: DTUMOS, digital twin for large-scale urban mobility operating system. Sci. Rep. **13**(1), 5154 (2023)
15. Grasso, C., Leonardi, L., Mertens, J.S., Torrisi, V.: Real-time communication and digital twin modelling towards smart mobility in the SAMOTHRACE project. In: 2024 IEEE International Symposium on Measurements & Networking (M&N), pp. 1–6. IEEE (2024)
16. Pala, A., et al.: Digital twin for mobility: simulation integrated approach for demand matrices calibration with empirical data (2024)
17. Torrisi, V., Rossetti, S., Barbagallo, A., Leonardi, P., Ignaccolo, M.: A digital twin simulation framework to assess the impact of street experiments: transforming urban mobility in Acireale (Italy). In: Gervasi, O., et al. (eds.) Computational Science and Its Applications – ICCSA 2024 Workshops: Hanoi, Vietnam, July 1–4, 2024, Proceedings, Part IX, pp. 197–210. Springer, Cham (2024). https://doi.org/10.1007/978-3-031-65329-2_13
18. Panwai, S., Dia, H.: Comparative evaluation of microscopic car-following behavior. IEEE Trans. Intell. Transp. Syst. **6**(3), 314–325 (2005)
19. Park, B., Qi, H.: Development and evaluation of a procedure for the calibration of simulation models. Transp. Res. Rec. J. Transp. Res. Board **1934**(1), 208–217 (2005). https://doi.org/10.1177/0361198105193400122
20. Geistefeldt, J., et al.: Assessment of level of service on freeways by microscopic traffic simulation. Transp. Res. Rec. J. Transp. Res. Board **2461**(1), 41–49 (2014). https://doi.org/10.3141/2461-06
21. Kabit, M.R., Chiew, W.Y., Chai, A., Tirau, L.S., Bujang, Z.: Evaluating the effects of signal control applications on roundabout's LOS performance using VISSIM microsimulation model. Int. J. Integr. Eng. **15**(6), 13–22 (2023)

22. Ziemska-Osuch, M., Osuch, D.: Modeling the assessment of intersections with traffic lights and the significance level of the number of pedestrians in microsimulation models based on the PTV Vissim tool. Sustainability **14**(14), 8945 (2022)
23. Caruso, A., Galluccio, L., Grasso, C., Ignaccolo, M., Inturri, G., Leonardi, P.: Advancing urban traffic monitoring in smart cities: a field experiment with UAV-based system for transport planning and intelligent traffic management

Smart and Happy Cities: Towards a Definition and a Methodology for Evaluating the Emotional Perception of Happiness

Chiara Pinna[1], Alessia Torlini[1], Alenka Poplin[2] , and Chiara Garau[1](✉)

[1] Department of Civil and Environmental Engineering and Architecture (DICAAR), University of Cagliari, Via Marengo 2, 09123 Cagliari, Italy
cgarau@unica.it

[2] Department of Community and Regional Planning, College of Design, Ames, IA, USA

Abstract. This research examines the concept of the human-scale city, developing a technique applicable to neighbourhoods to enhance their sustainability, liveability, walkability, well-being, and the happiness perceived by residents. This study aims to show the importance of an interdisciplinary approach by addressing the methodological gap prevalent in traditional literature that underscores the division between the examination of urban infrastructures, typically within the engineering domain, and the analysis of social dynamics, a focus in a sociology domain. This separation has historically limited the comprehension of the complex processes that influence cities and the experiences of their residents. The methodology adopted for assessing proximity and urban happiness combines qualitative approaches with quantitative studies, including the establishment of indices and indicators directly associated with neighbourhood liveability. This work facilitated the integration of empirical data with the subjective perceptions experienced by users of urban places regarding proximity, safety, comfort, well-being, and pleasure experienced at urban spaces. The application of this approach examined in the San Benedetto neighbourhood of Cagliari (Italy) highlighted the importance of the emotional dimension in evaluating the design effectiveness of an urban environment, aiding in the conceptualisation of an ideal "Happy City" model. This study demonstrates the model's applicability in many urban contexts, emphasising that the realisation of a "A Smart, and Happy City" requires a comprehensive and coordinated spatial approach.

Keywords: Happy City · Smart City · Healthy City · Accessibility · Walkability · Emotions · Proximity · Urban Happiness · Measuring Happiness · Pedestrianisation · Urban Planning · Cagliari

---

This paper is the result of the joint work of the authors. 'Abstract', 'A New Index for Evaluating the "Emotional Perception of the Degree of Happiness" and 'Results' were written jointly by the authors. CP and CG wrote 'A Methodological Approach for Evaluating and Quantifying the Urban Happiness'. AT and CG wrote the 'Introduction'. CG wrote 'A Smart and Happy City: An Effort in Defining it'. And CG and AP wrote 'Discussion and Conclusions'. CG coordinated and supervised the paper.

© The Author(s), under exclusive license to Springer Nature Switzerland AG 2026
O. Gervasi et al. (Eds.): ICCSA 2025, LNCS 15898, pp. 141–159, 2026.
https://doi.org/10.1007/978-3-031-97657-5_9

1 Introduction

The expansion of population and enhanced connectivity among cities connected in networks, together with the evolution of these cities alongside technological and digitalisation processes, has significantly influenced the notion of smartness, impacting both urban and human development [1–3].

It has exacerbated issues such as congestion, environmental pollution, food scarcity and energy crises, as well as presenting challenges for urban governance related to development planning, definitions of more pedestrian areas, more city operations, and urban management processes [4, 5]. However, if these issues have intensified, numerous experiments and studies designed to mitigate them have emerged, employing not only information and communication technologies (ICTs) to transform urban infrastructures, public and private services, and governmental operations, but also by articulating diverse aspects of the quality of human-scale of urban smart life that are associated with sustainability, circularity, and proximity, as well as health, safety, culture, social cohesion, and participation [6].

A further issue identified in the scientific literature is considering in a broaden way the notion of smartness, which has been consistently criticised for adhering to economic rationale and commercial interests rather than advocating beneficial measures for the community [7–12]. This emphasises the lack of a connection between the smart paradigm and social well-being, defined not only as the quality of life of inhabitants but also as happiness in living in a certain place [13, 14]. From these premises, there is a need for examining smartness via a renewed human perspective, linking the notion of the city on a human scale with a framework focused on the evaluation of happiness.

On the one hand, numerous recommendations have been developed to guide urban policy towards the human-scale revitalising of cities. Over time, several theorists have contributed to the development of the concept of the human-scale city – such as Ildefonso Cerdà, Jane Jacobs, Jan Gehl, Christopher Alexander, Léon Krier, Jeff Speck, Salvador Rueda and Carlos Moreno – emphasising the importance of prioritising human and environmental well-being in urban planning to enhance quality of life.

On the other hand, an evaluation of the urban happiness is more difficult to locate in the literature. One of the first documents that recognises the first indications on the regulation of the concept of happiness as the main factor for promoting sustainable development and achieving the Millennium Development Goals [15] is the UN General Assembly [16]. In 2011, it recognised the need for "a more inclusive, equitable, and balanced approach to economic growth that promotes sustainable development, poverty eradication, happiness and well-being of all peoples" [16, p. 1]. The subsequent year, after the inaugural UN High Level Meeting, the report titled Wellbeing and Happiness: Defining a New Economic Paradigm was released, linking happiness and well-being to effective spatial planning practices [17]. In the most recent United Nations documents [18, 19], the word "happiness" is not expressly used. However, expressions representing notions of happiness, such as "healthy, fulfilling lives", "physical and mental health", "health and quality of life", and "human health and well-being" are included. Utilising the Treccani Dictionary's definition of happiness as "a measure of individual well-being" [20]. It is feasible to assert that human happiness is established as a goal in recent United

Nations texts, particularly in the New Urban Agenda, and is profoundly linked to human health and quality of life.

Numerous fields, including psychology, neuroscience, philosophy, economics, and social policy, have endeavoured to quantify and delineate the concept of happiness throughout the years [21, 22]. However, as Ballas argues [23], even though its potential, the concept has not been thoroughly examined in urban planning and geography, even though there is a growing acknowledgement of the opportunity for social and behavioural scientists to incorporate a spatial dimension by identifying urban characteristics that influence subjective happiness and well-being metrics (p. 47). Allal et al. [24] contend, cities must prioritise satisfying the human being and enhancing his/her quality of life (p. 182) from a developmental standpoint. To achieve this, various challenges must be addressed to ensure that cities offer high quality, healthy, and sustainable living environments (p. 183).

The integration of happiness and proximity principles with the Smart City framework requires a complete evaluation approach. Starting from this point of view, the focus of this document is to examine the emotional dimension, specifically studying how the urban structure of a human-scale approach affects the emotions and emotional well-being of its citizens. The examination of the San Benedetto neighbourhood in Cagliari will facilitate the analysis of how proximity to outstanding amenities and spaces contributes to the formation of an urban environment that enhances happiness, mitigates stress, and cultivates a strong sense of community.

The paper has five sections: after this introduction, Sect. 2 presents the notion of Happy City, whilst Sect. 3 delineates a methodological approach for evaluating and quantifying the urban happiness. Section 4 tests the applicability of a new index for evaluating the emotional perception of the degree of happiness, by considering a quantitative and qualitative analysis (Sect. 5). The findings applied in the case study and future prospectives for the study are addressed in Sects. 7 and 8.

2 A Smart and Happy City: An Effort in Defining It

Planning processes designed for establishing a proximity city fundamentally seeks to enhance the quality of life for its inhabitants [25], by fostering their inclination to engage with places. It is important to delineate the differences underlying the concepts of happiness and quality of life, as well as the methodologies used to examine and measure happiness, defined as life satisfaction and subjective well-being [14, 26]. Consequently, the authors reflect on: what is happiness and what does it signify? The same concept of happiness linked to a geographical reality is difficult to articulate unequivocally. On the one hand, happiness is associated with well-being and quality of life; on the other hand, happiness is an emotional feeling of well-being, and when applied to a physical location, it may be viewed as a place that provides long-lasting (positive) feelings. From this viewpoint, the happy city can be perceived as a place that promotes persistent positive emotions (through a eudaimonic lens, as opposed to short-term happiness rooted in hedonistic concept generation), enhancing the community's awareness of both collective and individual spaces, as well as their sense of belonging to that specific environment.

The dual identity of the quality-of-life concept is evident: it is both interpreted objectively and measurable, but also subjectively assessed in relation to the individual's aspirations and social setting. Consequently, recognising the purely subjective nature of happiness, it is reasonable to explore this aspect by posing direct enquiries to those involved using interviews, questionnaires, or surveys. The literature analysis indicates that a happy city is a healthy urban conglomeration designed on a human scale, where the urban structure is smartly reorganised to promote walkability as a superior choice to various forms of mobility. Consequently, it is increasingly recognised that the temporary or permanent pedestrianisation of streets or entire neighbourhoods, defined as an intervention that restricts vehicle circulation, except for emergency services and specific limitations, enhances urban life quality with beneficial global effects [27]. Moreover, it plays a crucial role in urban regeneration by transforming underutilised areas into vibrant and appealing spaces, thereby positively influencing the local economy. Indeed, an engaging environment motivates citizens to visit and remain, enhancing their opportunities for social interaction and consumption. From this perspective, proximity to services, opportunities, and points of interest is an essential aspect in enhancing quality of life and fostering urban happiness. Moreover, proximity fosters walking or cycling, enhancing not only an active and healthy lifestyle, but also social interactions, incidental encounters, and the formation of neighbourhood relationships, which strengthen the social feeling of community and emotional connections to places. In this context, residents should experience security, comfort, engagement, remembering, and a sense of belonging during their journeys, independent of their destination or purpose [9, 28]. Citizens should feel positive emotions via noise emissions, thermal sensations, and the presence of flora, which together have beneficial impacts on biodiversity and human biological cycles. This type of city, therefore, is defined by the authors as a smart and happy city including not only all the previously mentioned characteristics, but also similar and vital peculiarities such as equity, justice, and inclusion, even if the authors are aware that the combination of all these characteristics cannot consistently guarantee citizens' happiness, but it may contribute to its achievement.

Considering all of these factors, it becomes especially important to examine the empirical relationship between happiness and the quality of one's living environment, in order to identify locally measurable factors that, while not necessarily indicative of happiness, are commonly observed among people who report high levels of happiness:

i) Job opportunities: defined as the availability of financial resources, economic autonomy, and satisfaction in selecting a profession that aligns with the individual's aspirations and passions [29]; (ii) Security [30]; (iii) Civic engagement and social relationships [31]; (iv) Physical and psychological health [27]; (v) Access to and quality of services [32]; (vi) good time: Reconciling professional and personal life minimises stress, strengthens profound connections, and enables dedication to personal interests [27].

These criteria will provide the basis for outlining the methodological approach to the pursuit of happiness, with the aim of addressing the question: "what is the rationale for evaluation, and what methods can be employed for the evaluation of urban happiness? The authors will provide a practical methodology to measure happiness (Sect. 3), identifying the Index "Emotional perception of the degree of happiness" (Sect. 4), followed by the description of the case study of the San Benedetto district in Cagliari on which the method is tested (Sect. 5).

3 A Methodological Approach for Evaluating and Quantifying the Urban Happiness

The methodological approach primarily emphasises the need of envisioning a simultaneously smart and happy city, seeking to address the inquiry: what is the rationale for evaluation, and what methodologies might be used for the assessment of the urban happiness? The current literature presents many methodologies for its evaluation. Richard Layard [33] asserts that measuring happiness requires directly querying people, assuming they are not in a state of absolute poverty.

Other authors attempt to mitigate errors and biases inherent in subjective judgements by establishing quantitative indicators more general [29, 34, 35], or primarily associated with economic situations, security, political engagement [36, 37]. Claudio Marciano highlights Bhutan's initiative to compile a report on the happiness of its citizens using a statistical survey that utilises a range of qualitative and quantitative indicators. The study primarily examines residents' perceptions of the nation and their self-image [38].

Consequently, the authors in this research endeavour to adopt both quantitative and qualitative methodologies to identify and convert locally measurable factors into indices and indicators, which do not necessarily imply happiness but are observed as common parameters among happy people.

The methodology depends on the analytical purpose of assessing urban happiness, ranging from the idea of proximity, which may be measured both qualitatively and quantitatively. The efficacy of an approach that incorporates both quantitative and qualitative analysis is extensively shown in several reputable academic publications [39, 40]. Consequently, the methodology was organised into the following phases: (i) A comprehensive framework encompassing all empirical variables and contributions that affect the relationships between human beings, the environment, and happiness. (ii) A definition of the index "Emotional Perception of the Degree of Happiness," along with its associated indicators and sub-indicators at the neighbourhood level. (iii) A deep investigation of approaches; standardised urban planning tools and software (QGIS, DepthmapX); techniques for selecting and computing quantitative sub-indicators. (iv) Definition of qualitative analysis to support and validate the outcomes of the calculation method for the "Emotional Perception of the Degree of Happiness" index, which may also highlight the needs, desires, and essential concerns identified by users of the case study area. (v) A comparison of the outcomes from the quantitative and qualitative analyses.

4 A New Index for Evaluating the "Emotional Perception of the Degree of Happiness"

The emotional perception of happiness is determined by the emotions elicited by a place regarding security, pleasantness, sociability, manifestations of joy, and stress. To analyse these factors, it is important to delineate and examine the physical components along the pathways and the surrounding areas that provide the framework for conducting the quantitative evaluation. To estimate each parameter, a grading scale of normalised scores was established to evaluate the appropriateness of each indication and facilitate the comparison and integration of the data. Table 1 shows the indicators ("Security", "Pleasantness", "Sociability", "Manifestations of joy" and "Stress") and sub-indicators that help define the "Emotional perception of the degree of happiness".

The index is expressed in formula 1:

$$Ieph = \frac{(Ia + Ib + Ic + Id + Ie)}{5} \quad (1)$$

The index "Emotional perception of the degree of happiness" (I) is given by the average of the indicators "Security" (Ia), "Pleasantness" (Ib), "Sociability" (Ic), "Manifestations of joy"(Id) and "Stress" (Ie).

(a) *"Security"* is evaluated by spontaneous observation, allowing for the attribution of a particular level of felt safety, which may be determined by analysing the seven sub-indicators outlined in Table 1 and described as follows: (i) the "visibility of buildings" reflects the degree to which a place is observable from neighbouring structures, so enabling the assessment of its spontaneous surveillance, considering also the *"type and height of such buildings"*.

The pedestrian *"Level of Service"* sub-indicator quantifies the frequency of pedestrian presence in places, determined by the number of people there.

The "presence of signs of degradation" is determined by averaging the condition of the elements present (Sce) in relation to their functioning and the overall degradation condition (Scd) of the site, which includes the presence of rubbish, graffiti, or evidence of drug use. One other important sub-indicators for assessing felt safety is the *"proportion of functioning light points"* to the total number installed.

The adult attitude of holding children's hands implicitly conveys a feeling of trust in allowing them freedom of movement within neighbourhood pathways and areas.

(b) "Pleasantness" is assessed based on the memorability a space evokes in the user, which includes the presence of distinguishable and aesthetically pleasing, organic, and coherent elements. This is quantified as the average of: the presence of distinctive elements, gradients, human-scale elements. Speck [27] observes that cities such as Rome may initially seem entirely unwelcoming to pedestrians and without of standard features aligned with soft mobility. Nonetheless, these cities are regarded as some of the finest cities for walking, not due to pedestrian comfort, but rather because of the visual allure presented by the urban landscape. Gradients signify the enhancement of a spatial quality in a specific direction, facilitating the natural differentiation of our motions' orientation. Human scale is the incorporation of features proportionate to the human body, using combinations and contrasts among structures, furniture, and ornamentation, including trees, flower boxes, and seating.

(c) "Sociability" is assessed by observing citizens' behaviour in communal areas, specifically through direct observation of seniors socialising, adolescents and or children engaging in play, and the presence of young people.

Table 1. Definition of the Index of "Emotional perception of the degree of happiness"

Index	Indicators	Attributes	Sub-Indicators	Calculation Methods
Emotional perception of the degree of happiness	a) Security	Perceived Security	Visibility of buildings [41]	Visible = 1 Partly visible = 0.6 Not visible = 0.1
			Building Type [41]	Building > 9 floors = 1 Building 4–8 floors = 0.8 Building 1–3 floors = 0.6 Single Family Homes = 0.3 Isolated building/total absence of buildings = 0.1
			Presence of functions with extended service hours [41]	Yes = 1 No = 0.1
			Pedestrian Level of Service (LOS) (fruin) [41]	Very busy = 1 Average busy = 0.5 Slightly busy = 0.1
			Signs of degradation [41]	(Condition of the present elements + General condition of degradation)/2 = (Sce + Scd)/2
			Proportion of functioning light points [41]	Light points = Nfunctioning/Ntotal
			Adults' attitude to holding children's hands	Percentage of children held by the hand
	b) Pleasantness	Recognisable, notable, conspicuous, articulated spaces	Presence of distinctive elements [42, 43]	Yes = 1 No = 0.1

(continued)

Table 1. (*continued*)

Index	Indicators	Attributes	Sub-Indicators	Calculation Methods
			Gradients [42, 43]	Yes = 1 No = 0.1
			Human scale [42, 43]	Yes = 1 No = 0.1
	c) Sociability	Socially attractive spaces	Seniors socialising with peers	Number of elderly $\geq 5 = 1$ $5 >$ Seniors $\geq 3 = 0.6$ Seniors $< 3 = 0.1$
			Adolescents and/or children playing	Adolescents and/or children $\geq 5 = 1$ $5 >$ Adolescents and/or children $\geq 3 = 0.6$ Adolescents and/or children $< 3 = 0.1$
			Adolescents and/or children attending spaces	Adolescents and/or children $\geq 8 = 1$ $8 <$ Adolescents and/or children $\geq 3 = 0.6$ Adolescents and/or children $< 3 = 0.1$
	d) Manifestations of joy	Perception of serenity	Serene adults	Number of serene adults/ number of adults
			Serene Adolescents or children	Number of happy adolescents or children/ number of adolescents or children
	e) Stress factors	Perception of discomfort	Waiting time for crossings [44]	$t < 60s = 1$ $t = 60s = 0.5$ $t > 60s = 0.1$

(d) similarly, "Manifestations of joy" are assessed about the notion of serenely seen in adults and youngsters crossing the neighbourhood streets. The evaluations of the sub-indicator estimates were conducted across a complete week, including weekdays, to avoid restricting the studies to a singular time frame.

(e) The literature review identified "Stress factors", especially the time citizens expend navigating urban environments. Consequently, assessing vehicular traffic and the time pedestrians spend at road crossings is acknowledged as crucial for understanding perceptions of discomfort and stress. The waiting time for pedestrian crossings is expressed numerically as a function of the waiting time considered excessive at a pedestrian traffic light (> 60 s) [44, 45].

5 Qualitative Analysis

Quantitative analyses were integrated with qualitative analyses, a procedure acknowledged in the literature as effective [46–51]. Consequently, a questionnaire titled "Degree of Perceived Happiness, Accessibility, and Neighbourhood Seurity" was developed based on a review of the scientific literature [52, 53] and insights from Sect. 2. As a result, the surveys addressing economic well-being and health were omitted, although recognising their significance.

The questionnaire comprises thirty-two questions, organised into 3 sections to facilitate subsequent comparison with quantitative analysis results: 1) accessibility to neighbourhood services and movement; 2) perceived security; 3) comfort, pleasantness, sociability and happiness. The authors provide 9 of the 32 questions that focus mainly on the assessment of happiness:

1) How would you rate the ease of walking to neighbourhood services? (Please provide a rating from 1 to 5; 1 = Difficult; 5 = Easy). Briefly indicate the reason.

    What is your level of comfort with walking alone in the neighbourhood streets? (Please provide a rating from 1 to 5; 1 = Very Unsafe; 5 = Very Safe): _____.

    Specify the reasons (multiple responses are permitted): ☐ Good/poor lighting ☐ Adequate/insufficient signage and condition of pedestrian paths ☐ Presence/absence of spontaneous surveillance (linked to the simultaneous presence of people in an area) ☐ Presence/absence of crime episodes ☐ Well-regulated/chaotic vehicular traffic ☐ Deep/poor knowledge of neighbourhood areas ☐ Other: _____.

3) How would you assess the overall noise level in the neighbourhood streets you frequently visit? (Please provide a rating from 1 to 5; 1 = little noise; 5 = excessive noise): _____.
4) Are you aware of any initiatives or organisations that promote social engagement within the neighbourhood? (many responses may be indicated):

    ☐ Volunteer associations ☐ Children's activities ☐ Senior activities ☐ Artistic and cultural workshops ☐ Sports activities ☐ I do not know ☐ I am aware of those not specified ☐ Specify whether you think there are more activities and/or organisations that facilitate your social engagement in the neighbourhood, which were not mentioned in the previous question: _____.

5) Did you see yourself as actively engaged in the changes that happened in the neighbourhood? (Please provide a rating from 1 to 5; 1 = I experienced exclusion at every phase; 5 = Completely engaged) _____.

    Were you satisfied with the work that impacted the neighborhood's streets? Why?

6) For residents: do you like living in the neighborhood? (Please provide a rating from 1 to 5; 1 = Not much; 5 = A lot) _____ Briefly indicate the reason: _____.
7) For residents: to how much does living in your neighbourhood enhance your happiness? (Evaluate on a scale from 1 to 5; 1 = Little; 5 = Significantly) _____ Briefly indicate the reason: _____.
8) With a view to a future redevelopment of the neighborhood and transportation reorganisation, would you support the pedestrianisation of certain streets? _____ What concerns would you have about this?

☐ Adequate parking availability ☐ Public transportation efficiency ☐ Residential accessibility ☐ Reduced speed ☐ Other: _____.

9) Is there a specific place or street in the neighbourhood that evokes a good or negative emotion in you (joy, positive expectations, anger, discomfort, melancholy, etc.)? Specify the street(s) in close proximity that you contemplate, the feeling it evokes, and the rationale for it. _____.

The subsequent section delineates the case study under examination, followed by a comprehensive presentation of the quantitative and qualitative analyses conducted, demonstrating the integration of both methodologies resulting in a holistic understanding of urban happiness within the neighbourhood chosen as a case study.

6 The Case Study of the San Benedetto Neighbourhood in Cagliari (Italy)

Cagliari is situated in the southern region of Sardinia (Italy), overlooking the Tyrrhenian Sea and covering an area of around 86.05 square kilometres [54]. The population of Cagliari is around 150,679 people [55]. The selected research area for method implementation and validation is San Benedetto, a vibrant neighbourhood situated in the eastern part of Cagliari (Fig. 1).

In 2022, the neighbourhood's resident population was 7,921, representing around 5% of Cagliari's total population, with an average density of 18,929 inhabitants per square kilometre. Consequently, the layout of this neighbourhood provides an optimal basis for debates and studies on walkability, accessibility, social dimensions, and the subjective well-being of residents. It is, in reality, one of the neighbourhoods with the greatest diversity in primary and secondary services, including various shops, educational institutions, a theatre, a tribunal, a market, and public transportation choices, including the metro-tram service. Additionally, a substantial flow of pedestrians is attracted by the commercial services, the historical significance of particular locations, and the presence of two major urban attractions, the Civic Market and the Cagliari Metro Station. These elements are promising factors in the context of a potential partial pedestrianisation of the neighbourhood, an important initiative outlined in the Strategic Master Plan of the Metropolitan City of Cagliari [56].

In this context, future scenarios impacting the San Benedetto neighbourhood may serve as an exemplary pilot model to guide further urban redevelopment initiatives aimed at transforming the whole municipality of Cagliari into a smart and happy city of proximity.

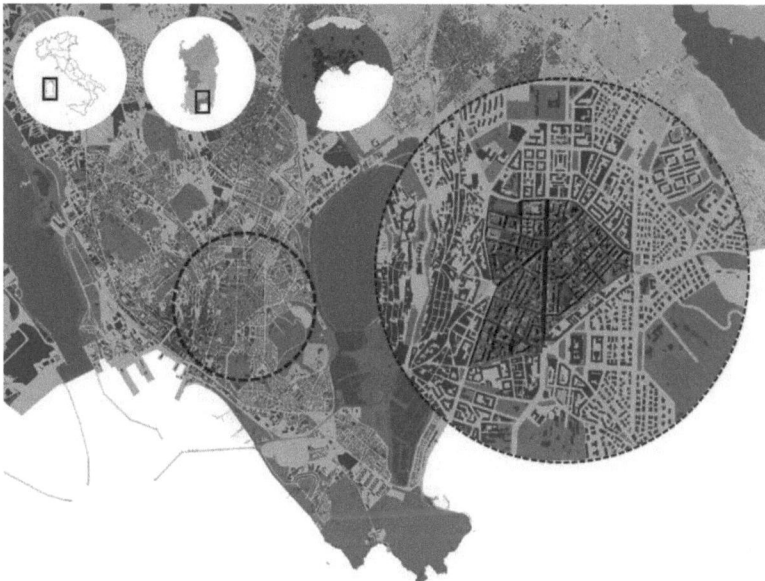

Fig. 1. San Benedetto Neighbourhood in Cagliari, Italy (authors' elaboration)

7 Results

The integration of quantitative and qualitative study enabled to delineate the happiness level inside the San Benedetto neighbourhood. In particular, the quantitative analysis performed using QGIS indicates the following results:

a) Security (Fig. 2): the degree of perceived security changes between "adequate" and "good". The "adults' attitude towards holding children's hands" was the most significant sub-indicator, the assessment of the other sub-indicators is mostly favourable, particularly evident in the closeness of squares and along the main roads.

b) Pleasantness (Fig. 3): Evaluations of the neighbourhood routes show significant variability, with scores spanning from poor to optimal levels; specifically, the streets that evoke the highest memorability are those including notable buildings and identity assets of renowned historical and cultural significance.

c, d) Sociability (Fig. 4.a)/Manifestations of joy (Fig. 4.b): direct observation of users in communal spaces has revealed a heightened inclination among adults, adolescents, and children to congregate harmoniously in proximity to squares and main roads significantly influenced by commercial and food services.

e) Stress Factors (Fig. 4.c): Surveys conducted to assess waiting times at pedestrian crossings revealed that pedestrians are compelled to wait over a minute only on the most congested routes with traffic lights.

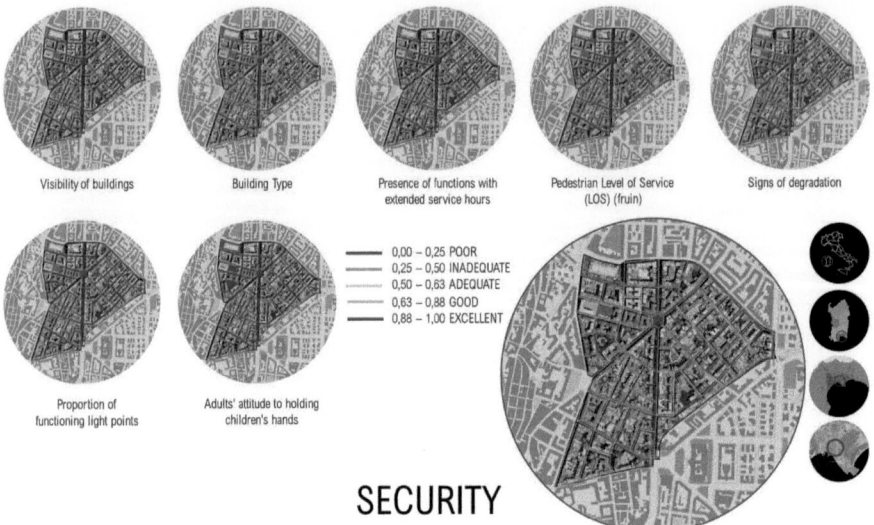

Fig. 2. "Security" indicator and related sub-indicators (authors' elaboration)

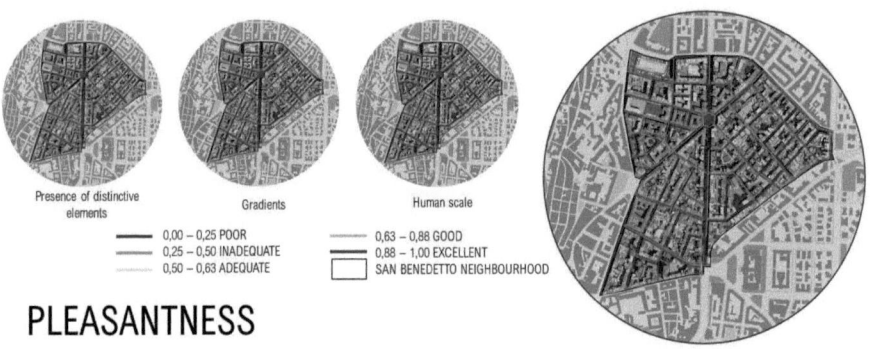

Fig. 3. "Pleasantness" indicator and related sub-indicators (authors' elaboration)

The index of "Emotional perception of the degree of happiness" shows an adequate general evaluation (Fig. 5).

The results derived from the quantitative analysis may be juxtaposed with the responses to the questionnaire titled "Degree of Perceived Happiness, Accessibility, and Security of the Neighbourhood," which was conducted to citizens of the San Benedetto neighbourhood in Cagliari.

The questionnaire, distributed over approximately 30 days, received a total of 117 responses. The authors analysed in this research the most representative. The responding population sample demonstrates diversity in age distribution: 33.3% are aged 31–45 years, 30.8% are 46–60 years, 21.4% are 18–30 years, and only 14.5% are over 60 years. Notably, there is a predominance of women, comprising 76.1% of respondents.

Fig. 4. Indicators "Sociability" (1.), "Manifestations of joy" (2.) and "Stress factors" (3.) Source: Authors' elaboration.

Fig. 5. Index of "Emotional perception of the degree of happiness" (authors' elaboration).

The majority of participants reside in the San Benedetto neighbourhood (57.3%), followed by those who visit for shopping, dining, or utilising community spaces (18.8%), those employed in the area (12%), and individuals who transit through the neighbourhood (9.4%). A mere 2.6% expressed a general attraction for this part of the city.

The poll indicated that accessing the services on foot is extremely simple (scale 5, 52.2% of respondents) and easy (scale 4, 35.7% of respondents).

The predominantly good security level identified in the quantitative research is supported by the respondents' subjective perceptions. Moreover, the adults' firm attitude to guide children by the hand along the analysed routes may be associated with significant automobile traffic, a concern identified as an important stressful factor by the respondents. The overall high security level is further reinforced by the predominance of users identifying as female, a circumstance that may have negatively influenced perceptions.

The survey revealed that, overall, residents felt rather safe (scale 5, 23.1% of respondents) and safe (scale 4, 47% of respondents) while walking alone through the neighbourhood streets. Concurrently, citizens experience significant insecurity, with 2.6% feeling very uncomfortable (scale 1), 6% feeling somewhat uneasy (scale 2), and 25% feeling a bit safe (scale 3).

The unpleasant perception mostly originates from women under 45, who mention chaotic traffic, inadequate illumination and spontaneous surveillance, poor state of pathways, insufficient pedestrian signs, and report occurrences of crime. A female user aged 31 to 45 underscores the absence of police surveillance, which is subsequently represented in a common need.

One interesting result from the survey is that the neighbourhood is rich in activities and organisations, although lacking sufficient recognition. Indeed, the majority of respondents (70.9%) indicate that they are unaware of any activities or associations that facilitate social engagement within the neighbourhood. Only 18.8% are aware of sports activities, 14.5% are conscious of children's activities, 12% of voluntary associations, 6% of artistic and cultural workshops, and 5.1% of activities for the elderly.

An additional aspect revealed by the survey relates to the degree of citizen engagement in the changes impacting different areas of the city throughout the years. The emotions elicited in the interviewees concerning the interventions undertaken thus far in San Benedetto were examined, specifically in response to the question, "Did you perceive yourself as an active participant in the changes that have transpired in the neighbourhood?" 44.4% reported feeling excluded in every phase (scale 1), 26.5% felt excluded (scale 2), 24.8% did not feel excluded but also not included (scale 3), 4.3% felt involved (scale 4), and 0% felt fully involved (scale 5).

Concerning the satisfaction level with the street improvements in the neighbourhood, the most pertinent feedback includes: "I observed an enhancement in convenience (increased space and seating at urban transport stops) as well as improved order on the streets". "I am dissatisfied; they have diminished the availability of parking".

"I observed a deterioration in traffic conditions".

Additionally, it is evident that 60.7% of users support the pedestrianisation of some streets. Support for pedestrianisation does not imply the absence of concerns, which, according to users, primarily pertain to the quantity of parking spaces (57.3%), access to residences (43.6%), the efficacy of public transport (41%), and reduced speed (14.5%).

The analysis of neighbourhood happiness concludes with enquiries about the feelings and sensations elicited by the utilisation of spaces among the statistical population. 65.2% of the sampled residents reported great satisfaction with their neighbourhood (scale 5), 23.2% of them stated satisfaction (scale 4), attributing it to the availability of services, tranquilly, social connections, strategic location, and overall quality of life.

Overall, for the surveyed residents, residing in the San Benedetto neighbourhood significantly enhances their happiness, in a very significant way (for 28.6%, scale 5), in a significant way (for 46%, scale 4), in a non-significant but not even significant way (for 15.9%, scale 3), a little (for 6.3%, scale 2) and finally very little (for 3.2%, scale 1). The final inquiry in the questionnaire pertains to the sentiments and emotions elicited by specific streets or areas in the subjects, depicted on a map categorised

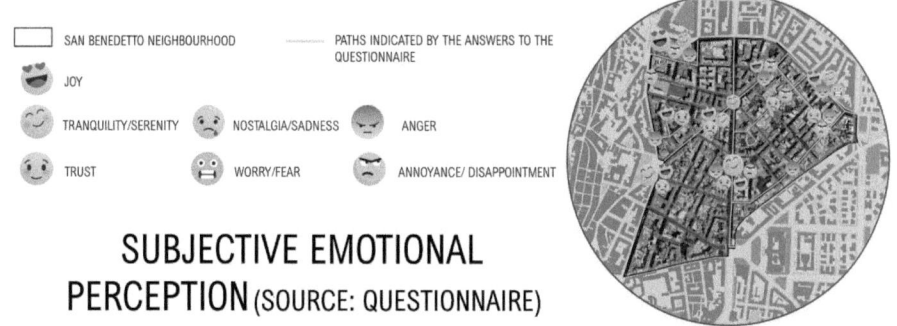

Fig. 6. Subjective emotional perception in response to "Is there a particular area or street in the neighbourhood that evokes a positive or negative feeling in you? Indicate the street(s) in the area you think of the emotion it evokes, and the reason" (authors' elaboration).

as: joy, tranquility /serenity, confidence in the future, nostalgia/sadness, worry/fear, annoyance/disappointment, and anger (Fig. 6).

8 Discussion and Conclusions

This study and the analysis of the scientific literature in urban, sociological, and architectural domains indicate that, regardless of territorial, spatial, economic, and sociocultural disparities, the key components of any sustainable and human-scale urban model must include proximity and walkability, which significantly influence the subjective perceptions of users involved in the qualitative study.

The research underscores a key aspect: the subjective experience of urban environments is as relevant to examine as quantitative assessments. While the overall convergence of the analytical information supports the notion that the physical attributes of an urban environment affect quality of life, the observed gaps indicate that effective urban planning does not naturally ensure a favourable response from residents.

In fact, the questionnaire indicates that negative emotions associated with a location predominantly originate from memories, experiences, and past sensations, thereby reinforcing the notion that spatial perception is shaped by social and cultural influences, including personal experiences, expectations, values, and interpersonal relationships.

Consequently, it is advantageous to enhance urban surveys with methodologies that examine individual and collective perceptions of a particular space in relation to personal and socio-cultural factors, thereby understanding how to change the perception of a place, not only by improving it physically but also by fostering positive experiential relationships with users.

From this viewpoint, a well-designed outdoor game could be an effective analysis tool to transform the subjective perception of a place, both individually and collectively. By engaging the player's senses, the outdoor game may facilitate the creation of emotionally resonant memories, foster the exchange of experiences that enhance a feeling of belonging and identity, and promote a profound understanding of the location, making it safer and more valued.

Urban planning should recognise the significance of both direct and indirect collection of subjective data, as well as the active engagement of citizens in the design of urban environments, to guarantee solutions that address their needs and expectations, while not neglecting elements that may be ignored in a non-participatory design approach.

The qualitative research indicates that people are inclined to accept soft mobility as their primary method of transportation and are receptive to initiatives aimed at pedestrianising certain routes, suggesting a clear favourable disposition towards this significant transition. Nonetheless, the issues that arose illustrate the challenges of meeting people's requirements by altering their habits and facilitating natural adaption to new lifestyles without competing alternatives.

Finally, the analysis conducted in this paper highlighted a strong link between happiness and proximity. For this reason, the authors propose as future research to deepen the analysis of the level of proximity at the neighbourhood level, using the same methodology, but also adding in the same analysis indices that measure accessibility, functionality of spaces and the social perception of citizens. These indices could constitute a "Global Index for Measuring Urban Well-Being" by considering together the proximity, the smartness and the happiness inside an urban environment [57].

Acknowledgements. This study was partially supported within the "e.INS – Ecosystem of Innovation for Next Generation Sardinia" funded by the Italian Ministry of University and Research under the Next-Generation EU Programme (National Recovery and Resilience Plan – PNRR, M4C2, INVESTMENT 1.5 –DD 1056 of 23/06/2022, ECS00000038). In particular, the "Results" was funded by eINS. This study reflects only the authors' views and opinions, and neither the European Union nor the European Commission can be considered responsible for them. This study was also partially supported by the project "RAMÉ RegCITIES: spatial analyses foR co-creAting the future of sMartest and happiEst REGions/CITIES. Comparisons between Cagliari in Italy and Des Moines in the US", founded by the program "Bando 2023 Mobilità Giovani Ricercatori (MGR)". This study was also supported by the MUR through the project "SMART3R-FLITS: SMART Transport for Travellers and Freight Logistics Integration Towards Sustainability" (Project protocol: 2022J38SR9; CUP Code: F53D23005630006), financed with the PRIN 2022 (Research Projects of National Relevance) program. We authorise the MUR to reproduce and distribute reprints for Governmental purposes, notwithstanding any copyright notations thereon. Any opinions, findings, and conclusions, or recommendations expressed in this material are those of the authors and do not necessarily reflect the views of the MUR.

References

1. Yang, R., Zhen, F.: Smart city development models: a cross-cultural regional analysis from theory to practice. Res. Globalization **8**, 100221 (2024)
2. Lim, Y., Edelenbos, J., Gianoli, A.: What is the impact of smart city development? Empirical evidence from a Smart City Impact Index. Urban Gov. **4**(1), 47–55 (2024)
3. Azzari, M., et al.: Smart city governance strategies to better move towards a smart urbanism. In: Gervasi, O., et al. (eds.) ICCSA 2018. LNCS, vol. 10962, pp. 639–653. Springer, Cham (2018). https://doi.org/10.1007/978-3-319-95168-3_43
4. Shami, M.R., Bigdeli Rad, V., Moinifar, M.: Evaluation and measurement of indicators of quality of urban smart living in Tehran city. Sustainable city **5**(4), 177–192 (2023)
5. Garau, C., et al.: Smart governance models to optimise urban planning under uncertainty by decision trees. In: International Conference on Computational Science and Its Applications, pp. 551–564. Springer International Publishing, Cham (2021)
6. Garau, C., Desogus, G., Campisi, T.: A preliminary survey on happy-based urban and mobility strategies: evaluation of european best practices. In: International Conference on Innovation in Urban and Regional Planning, pp. 472–483. Springer Nature Switzerland, Cham (2023)
7. Wiig, A.: IBM's smart city as techno-utopian policy mobility. City **19**(2–3), 258–273 (2015)
8. Caprotti, F.: Future cities: moving from technical to human needs. Palgrave Commun. **4**(1), 1–4 (2018)
9. Chen, C.W.: From smart cities to a happy and sustainable society: urban happiness as a critical pathway toward sustainability transitions. Local Environ. **27**(12), 1536–1545 (2022). https://doi.org/10.1080/13549839.2022.2119379
10. Garau, C., et al.: Governing technology-based urbanism. In: The Routledge Companion to Smart Cities, pp. 157–174. Routledge, New York (2020). https://doi.org/10.4324/9781315178387-12
11. Zhu, H., Shen, L., Ren, Y.: How can smart city shape a happier life? The mechanism for developing a Happiness Driven Smart City. Sustain. Cities Soc. **80**, 103791 (2022)
12. Sobhaninia, S., Samavati, S., Aldrich, D.P.: Designing for happiness, building for resilience: a systematic review of key factors for cities. Int. J. Urban Sustain. Dev. **16**(1), 360–378 (2024)
13. Mirzan, H., Bahreini, A., Moeinaddini, M., Asadi-Shekari, Z., Shah, M.Z., Sultan, Z.: Identify significant indicators for a happy city. Plann. Malaysia (4) (2016)
14. Kourtit, K., Neuts, B., Nijkamp, P., Wahlström, M.H.: Cityphilia and cityphobia: a multiscalar search for city love in Flanders. J. Urban Manage. **13**(3), 319–331 (2024). https://doi.org/10.1016/j.jum.2024.04.004
15. United Nations. UN Documentation: Development. Dag Hammarskjöld Library, United Nations. https://research.un.org/en/docs/dev/2000-2015
16. United Nations. Happiness: towards a holistic approach to development: resolution/adopted by the General Assembly. A/RES/65/309, UN. General Assembly (65th sess.: 2010–2011). https://digitallibrary.un.org/record/715187?v=pdf#record-files-collapse-header
17. United Nations Headquarters: Defining a New Economic Paradigm. The Report of the High-Level Meeting. New York (2012). https://sustainabledevelopment.un.org/content/documents/617BhutanReport_WEB_F.pdf
18. United Nations. Resolution Adopted by the General Assembly on 23 December 2016: 71/256, "New Urban Agenda". United Nations, New York, NY, USA (2017)
19. United Nations: Reporting on the Implementation of the New Urban Agenda. United Nations Human Settlements Programme (UN-Habitat) (2024). https://www.urbanagendaplatform.org/sites/default/files/2024-05/NUA%20Reporting%20Guidlines.pdf
20. Dizionario di Economia e Finanza. Felicità. Treccani (2012)

21. Huang, Y., Li, Y., Clark, W.A.: Family connections and subjective wellbeing in transitional China. J. Happiness Stud. **25**(4), 33 (2024)
22. Gaglione, F., Zucaro, C.G.F., Cottrill, C.: 15-minute neighbourhood accessibility: a comparison between Naples and London. Eur. Transport **85**, 1–16 (2021)
23. Ballas, D.: What makes a 'happy city'? Cities **32**, S39–S50 (2013)
24. Allal, A., Boudjemaa, K., Dehimi, S.: The effect of spatial differences on the quality of urban life a comparative analytical study of three cities in the high plateaux region of Algeria. Geo J. Tourism Geosites **40**(1), 181–190 (2022)
25. Jalongo, G.: La città, l' «Arturbain» e il «Seminaire Robert Auzelle», il trasversale gioco dei saperi – nel progetto e nella promozione della città. *Rivista Internazionale di Cultura Urbanistica*, 06. Università degli Studi di Napoli Federico II (2020)
26. Veenhoven, R.: Qualità della vita e felicità – Non proprio la stessa cosa. Salute e Qualità della Vita **6**, 67–95 (2001)
27. Speck, J.: Walkable City: how downtown can save America, one step at a time. Farrar, Straus and Giroux (2012)
28. Mirzaei, S., Zangiabadi, A.: Studying and complying dimensions, indicators and variables related to a happy city. Int. Rev. Spatial Plann. Sustain. Dev. **9**(2), 94–111 (2021)
29. Better Life Index: OECD Guidelines on researching subjective well-being: Report. https://read.oecd-ilibrary.org/economics/oecd-guidelines-on-measuring-subjective-well-being_9789264191655-en#page1
30. Associazione Nazionale Comuni Italiani. https://www.anci.it/
31. Fabbri, M.: Dalla città autoritaria alla città felice. Agenda17 – Webmagazine del Laboratorio Design of Science (2024)
32. ISTAT: Benessere e sostenibilità (2010). https://www.istat.it/it/benessere-e-sostenibilit%C3%A0
33. Layard, R.: Happiness: Lessons From A New Science. Penguin Press (2005)
34. Happy Planet Index, HPI – Methodological Report. https://happyplanetindex.org/HPI_2024_methodology.pdf
35. World Happiness Report, UN – World Happiness Report (2019). https://s3.amazonaws.com/happiness-report/2019/WHR19.pdf
36. Putnam, R.: La tradizione civica nelle Regioni italiane, Mondadori (1993)
37. Sabatini, F.: Un atlante del Capitale Sociale italiano. Terzo Forum annuale per giovani ricercatori (2005)
38. Marciano, C.: Felicità Civica, verso una definizione operativa. felicitacivica.it (p. 12) (2020). chrome-extension://efaidnbmnnnibpcajpcglclefindmkaj/https://felicitacivica.it/wp-content/uploads/2020/07/Felicit%C3%A0-Civica_-verso-una-definizione-operativa.pdf
39. Garau, C., Annunziata, A., Yamu, C. H., D'Orlando, D., Giuman, M.: Investigating the socio-spatial logic of historic urban areas through space syntax. A comparative analysis of the Roman towns Cosa, Nora, Timgad and Thuburbo Majus. TeMA, J. Land Use, Mobility Environ. (2023)
40. Russo, A., et al.: Accessibility and mobility in the small mountain municipality of zafferana etnea (Sicily): coupling of walkability assessment and space syntax. In: International Conference on Computational Science and Its Applications, pp. 338–352. Springer International Publishing, Cham (2022).
41. Garau, C.: Università degli studi di Cagliari, Facoltà di Ingegneria e Architettura, Corso di Pianificazione Ambientale AA 2021/2022 (2022)
42. Hillier, B., Hanson, J.: The Social Logic of Space. Cambridge University Press (1984)
43. Lynch, K.A.: The Image of the City. The M.I.T. Press, Massachusetts Institute of Technology Cambridge, Massachusetts, and London, England (1960)
44. Automobile Club d'Italia: *Zero barriere*, ACI linee guida attraversamenti pedonali (2011)

45. Codice della strada, Decreto Legislativo 30 aprile 1992, n.285. Bosetti & Gatti
46. Glaser, B.G., Strauss, A.L.: The Discovery of Grounded Theory: Strategies for Qualitative Research. Aldine, New York (1967)
47. Annunziata, A., Garau, C.: Understanding kid-friendly urban space for a more inclusive smart city: The case study of Cagliari (Italy). In: Computational Science and Its Applications–ICCSA 2018: 18th International Conference, Melbourne, VIC, Australia, 2–5 July 2018, Proceedings, Part III 18, pp. 589–605. Springer International Publishing (2018)
48. Garau, C., Annunziata, A., Coni, M.: A methodological framework for assessing practicability of the urban space: the survey on conditions of practicable environments (SCOPE) procedure applied in the case study of Cagliari (Italy). Sustainability **10**(11), 4189 (2018)
49. Garau, C., Annunziata, A.: Smart city governance and children's agency: an assessment of the green infrastructure impact on children's activities in Cagliari (Italy) with the tool "opportunities for children in urban spaces (OCUS)." Sustainability **11**(18), 4848 (2019)
50. Hennink, M., Hutter, I., Bailey, A.: Qualitative Research Methods. Sage (2020)
51. Garau, C., Annunziata, A.: Supporting children's independent activities in smart and playable public places. Sustainability **12**(20), 8352 (2020)
52. De Vos, J., Lättman, K., van der Vlugt, A.L., Welsch, J., Otsuka, N.: Determinants and effects of perceived walkability: a literature review, conceptual model and research agenda. Taylor & Francis (2022)
53. Sallis, J.F., et al.: Evaluating a brief self-report measure of neighborhood environments for physical activity research and surveillance: physical activity neighborhood environment scale (PANES). J. Phys. Act. Health **7**(4), 533–540 (2010). https://doi.org/10.1123/jpah.7.4.533
54. Wikipedia – Estensione di Cagliari, https://it.wikipedia.org/wiki/Cagliari. ultimo accesso 14 Jan 2025
55. Comune di Cagliari – Atlante demografico 2022. https://www.comune.cagliari.it/portale/page/it/atlante_demografico_2022?contentId=DOC145954 (2022), ultimo accesso 14 Jan 2025
56. Città Metropolitana di Cagliari – Piano Strategico, Piano Strategico per lo sviluppo della Città Metropolitana di Cagliari, Regione Sardegna. https://cittametropolitanacagliari.it/portale/page/it/focus_piano_strategico?contentId=FCS9131. Ultimo accesso 14 Jan 2025
57. Torlini, A., Pinna, C., Garau, C.: Smart, close, and happy city: a global index for measuring urban well-being. the case study of the san benedetto neighbourhood, Cagliari (Italy). In: Gervasi, O., Murgante, B., Garau, C., Karaca, Y., Faginas Lago, M.N., Scorza, F., Braga, A. (eds.) 25th International Conference on Computational Science and Its Applications (ICCSA 2025), Springer, Ciam (2025, in press)

GIS-Based Accessibility and Safety Assessment in Small Historic Centres in Inner Areas. Pilot Application in Stigliano and Interoperability with a Digital Twin

Barbara Caselli[1(✉)], Altea Panebianco[1], Silvia La Placa[2], and Rossella Laera[3]

[1] Department of Engineering and Architecture, University of Parma, Parco Area Delle Scienze, 181/A, 43124 Parma, Italy
barbara.caselli@unipr.it
[2] Department of Civil Engineering and Architecture, University of Pavia, Via Ferrata 3, 27100 Pavia, Italy
[3] Department for Humanistic, Scientific and Social Innovation, University of Basilicata, Matera Campus, Via Lanera 20, 75100 Matera, Italy

Abstract. The high vulnerability and exposure to environmental risk of most historic villages in Italian inland areas, together with the poor accessibility, the degradation imposed by abandonment, and the increase in the elderly population, make interventions for the functional rehabilitation or reconversion of the built heritage and related public space complex and controversial. This opens questions also with respect to the evaluation and identification of possible actions to improve territorial and local accessibility emphasizing the need to consider among the priority the redevelopment, transformation and securing of the public space. Within this framework, the article experiments with a possible decision-supporting evaluation process in the minor historic center of Stigliano (MT), the lead municipality of the inner area Montagna Materana and currently the site of an experimental inter-university research project on digital twin implementation. The contribution gives a first reading of information collected through digital survey and GIS-based collaborative data collection techniques and set up a methodology to plan and prioritise interventions aimed at improving accessibility and safety. The methodology is based on a set of indicators for evaluating usability, walkability, and vulnerability. The objective is twofold: on the one hand, to ensure accessibility and safety of the routes that provide access to services and relational nodes within the historic center, with particular attention to daily use and the most fragile users; on the other hand, to make tourist usability more attractive, comfortable and inclusive.

Future developments of the research are aimed at exploring the potential of new digital technologies, like the digital twin, to improve the implemented decision support tool, efficiently informing planning and management processes, as well as improving spatial (not only physical) accessibility and the enhancement of landscape, environmental, cultural, historical and community resources.

Keywords: accessibility · safety · minor historic village · public space · digital twin

1 Accessibility as a Key Issue for Local Development, Heritage Valorisation and Social Resilience

Italian inner areas are characterised by fragile situations, exacerbated by relentless depopulation and the consequent weakening of territorial presidium. Their progressive marginalisation has acceleratedthe loss of services and resources, a trend that began with the concentration of economic and human capital in the main urban and metropolitan centres.

Various cohesion policies at both the European and Italian level have been activated to address the increasing territorial disparities and attempt to reverse the processes of human capital loss, population aging, economic stagnation and cultural heritage deterioration. Many of these policies, including Next Generation EU, the National Recovery and Resilience Plan (PNRR), and the Italian National Strategy for inner areas (SNAI) 2021–2027, focus a significant portion of funding resources on the system of villages and minor historical centres. Hamlets, indeed, remain the historical territorial armoury of rural and mountainous areas, preserving a heritage of exceptional cultural, landscape, architectural and artistic value as well as a fundamental economic and social resource capable of reconciling production, trade, conviviality and a sense of community. Despite their fragility, these areas draw strength from these historic settlements where people, services, and cultural assets (tangible and intangible) are still concentrated [1]. Unfortunately, the effects of marginalisation and human capital erosion also affect the built heritage, which is often in a state of neglect and degradation. Furthermore, the high vulnerability and exposure to environmental risk in inner areas, especially to hydrogeological risk, together with poor accessibility conditions both at the territorial and urban scale, make any hypothesis of functional recovery/reconversion of the built heritage other than 'musealisation' complex.

The valorisation of the built heritage starts primarily by reconsidering the issue of accessibility [2]. Many studies in the literature focus on improving territorial accessibility which is, indeed, crucial for making inner areas more attractive for potential new residents [3]. Some approaches analyse how to enhance accessibility by acting both on mobility supply and local territorial capital, bringing back services, knowledge, and forms of interaction [4], and sometimes investigating the applicability of technological innovations without altering the historical memory of the place [5]. In certain cases, research has explored the specificity of the concept of proximity in low-density contexts, introducing specific indices [6].

All these approaches are certainly relevant but pay less attention to the issue of internal accessibility in small historic centres. In these contexts, the methodologies applied to large or medium-sized non-marginal towns [e.g. 7, 8] can hardly be adapted. Only a few studies use rigorous and quantitative methods for developing local accessibility indices [9, 10] and specific decision-support tools to orient redevelopment, transformation, and securing of public spaces. Ensuring the full usability of public spaces for all social categories and guaranteeing access to an essential set of services, especially in mountain sites, are indeed crucial aspects not only for resident population, considering the high incidence of the elderly [11], but also for fostering more inclusive forms of cultural tourism. Sustainable cultural tourism is indeed one of the pillars for local development of inner areas, as emphasised by several scholars [i.a. 12].

There have been some documented experiences in Italy regarding accessibility and inclusivity within minor historic centres, implemented by public authorities at regional and local levels, as well as by private or nonprofit associations. Some of these initiatives promote the improvement of remote accessibility through virtual reality or digital twins[1] [13, 14]. Unfortunately, awareness of the actual effectiveness of these initiatives in producing physical transformations of public spaces is still limited.

Few existing studies also attempt to integrate local accessibility levels with the crucial issue of built heritage vulnerability to environmental risks, i.e., seismic risk [15] or hydrogeological risk. While there is extensive literature on the rehabilitation and securing of the built heritage, including the use of advanced technologies [i.a. 16], there are few studies focusing on open space (paths, squares, public parks, etc.).

It is notable a GIS-based method to assess accessibility levels in synergy with the built heritage seismic vulnerability developed as a support tool for the reconstruction plan of the small historic centres of Navelli (AQ) affected by the 2009 earthquake in Abruzzo (Italy) [17]. Building on this last study, the present contribution refines the methodological approach to support the planning of interventions aimed at improving accessibility for all and securing public spaces. It considers all potential users of the site, primarily the still-residing population and potential tourists. The framework of this study is the PRIN project GO-IN! [18] aimed at testing the effectiveness of a 3D GIS model, based on digital twin technology, in supporting the planning and management of historic heritage in inner areas, with a specific focus on accessibility. The project is still ongoing, and the case study for experimentation is a portion of the historic centre of Stigliano (Basilicata, Italy), a leader municipality of the Inner Area 'Montagna Materana'.

The methodology applied in the pilot area aims to become a replicable decision-support protocol for contexts with similar characteristics and dynamics. The article presents in Sect. 2.1 the methodological framework for assessing accessibility and safety in open spaces within minor historic centres. Subsequently, Sects. 2.2 and 2.3 introduce the case study and the GIS-based analytical model. Section 3 presents the main results of the application to the pilot case, while Sect. 4 discusses the findings and outlines potential advancements of the research through an enhanced exploitation of digital twin technology tested within the GO-IN! project.

---

[1] Cittadella, città d'arte. https://www.visitcittadella.it/articolo-rassegna/il-patrimonio-storico-accessibile-ai-disabili/ (2020), last accessed last accessed 2025/03/20; Tecnologia CoperniKo nel Monferrato. https://www.coperniko.com/valorizzazione-e-accessibilita-del-patrimonio-culturale-mediante-la-realta-virtuale/ (2022), last accessed last accessed 2025/03/20; Dozza, Città Metropolitana di Bologna. https://www.cittametropolitana.bo.it/portale/Comunicazione/Archivio_news/Dozza_il_borgo_e_i_suoi_itinerari_accessibili_anche_alle_persone_sorde (2022), last accessed 2025/03/20; Piccoli S.M., I centri storici siciliani fanno rete e si aprono al turismo inclusivo, Artribune. Retrieved from: https://www.artribune.com/turismo/2024/07/turismo-inclusivo-sicilia/ (2024) last accessed 2025/03/20.

2 Materials and Methods

2.1 Methodological Framework for Accessibility and Safety Assessment as Decision-Making Support Tool

Improving the heritage usability in small historic centres requires balancing inclusive accessibility and safety. In small historic villages, it is still notably challenging to apply the principles of 'accessibility for all' while ensuring a network of usable spaces for a wide variety of users – not only residents but also potential tourists [19, 20] – while respecting the historical character of the place.

Improving walkability emerges as a crucial operational concept to facilitate mobility [21], especially for people with limited motor abilities. This is particularly important in steep areas, where slopes, stairs, and uneven paving make movement difficult. Ensuring accessibility to key public facilities, outdoor gathering places, and sites of historical and architectural significance could be relevant both for settled communities and for promoting forms of cultural tourism. The various field inspections also revealed the great role played by public spaces in the pilot area (streets and squares in particular) for people gathering and sociality.

With regard to safety – understood as the prevention of potential damage to people and property in public spaces [22] – the vulnerability levels of the built environment, particularly concerning abandonment dynamics, degradation, and geological instability, emerge as key issues to be assessed. Open spaces are also directly affected by the conditions of surrounding buildings and the degree of space usage, which directly correlates with an increase in exposure value [23].

Considering these aspects, the proposed analytical methodology, aimed at identifying intervention priorities in minor historic villages, considers a series of indicators to assess:

1. *Usage Intensity (Ui),* defined as the potential of spaces to enhance human capabilities by supporting autonomy, active mobility, and functional, recreational, and social activities. To calculate the usage intensity indicator, factors such as access to relevant services or functions, spatial configuration (continuous or enclosed), density of in-use buildings facing the public space, the presence of tourism-related routes, social streets and social hotspots [24] – i.e., elements that encourage gathering and serve as meeting points for the local community – are evaluated.
2. *Walkability (Wi)* refers to the quality and practicability of spaces that support walking. This indicator is calculated by assessing factors such as the geometric and structural characteristics of pathways (slope, dimensions, elevation changes, surface type, and maintenance state), architectural barriers (presence of stairs, obstacles, or discontinuities), and potential pedestrian-vehicle interferences even if, evidently, this appears less relevant in small historic centres.
3. *Vulnerability (Vi)* is a key component for determining potential damage, indicating the predisposition of a system to be affected. The vulnerability indicator is calculated by evaluating the presence of structural degradation signs in buildings, cracks or subsidence in pavements, and possible failures in retaining walls.

Open spaces are treated as key urban components and divided into minimum operational units characterised by 'homogeneity' in relation to orography, morphology, use and paving materials. Each minimum unit is analysed through a set of qualitative and quantitative attributes, pertaining to both intrinsic and extrinsic characteristics (related to configurational properties and the features of the surrounding built environment).

By combining these attributes, scores are assigned to assess the factors involved in each indicator evaluation, as illustrated in the following tables (Tables 1, 2 and 3).

Table 1. Factors of the Usage intensity indicator (Ui) – qualitative and quantitative assessment.

Factors	Qualitative and qualitative assessement	
u1 – Access to specialised buildings with relevant public and cultural services	Present/museum, social-cultural or religious facilities;	3
	Present/administrative buildings or other facilities of public interest;	2
	Present/buildings of historical value;	1
	Absent	−1
u2 – Density of abandoned buildings	No abandoned buildings;	2
	Less than 25%;	1
	25%–50%;	−1
	More than 50%	−2
u3 – Social hotsposts (density of recreational, commercial or public street level activities)	More than 50%;	3
	25% – 50%:	2
	Less than 25%;	1
	No street level activities	−1
u4 – Route characteristics	Continuous in both directions;	2
	Continuous with final widening;	1
	Temporarily interrupted;	−1
	Cul-de-sac	−1
u5 – Social streets (paths that spontaneously become contact and meeting points)	Mixed traffic (carriageway-pedestrian) and presence of seating;	3
	Pedestrian traffic (width greater than 1.5 m) and presence of seating;	2
	Roadway and presence of seating;	1
	Absence of seating along the route	−1
u6 – Tourist route	Present;	1
	Absent	−1

Table 2. Factors of the Walkability indicator (Wi) – qualitative and quantitative assessment.

Factors	Qualitative and qualitative assessement	
w1 – Car/pedestrian interference	Pedestrian way;	2
	Roadway with pavement; Mixed roadway-pedestrian traffic and road width greater than or equal to 4.25 m;	1
	Mixed roadway-pedestrian traffic and road width less than 4.25 m;	−1
	Roadway and no pavement	−2
w2 – Pedestrian practicability	Roadway with pavement or pedestrian way larger than or equal to 1.50 m;	2
	Mixed roadway-pedestrian traffic and no pavement;	1
	Roadway with pavement or pedestrian way 0.90 m to 1.50 m wide;	−1
	Roadway with pavement or pedestrian way less than 0.90 m;	−2
	Stairway	−3
w3 – Change in level / longitudinal slope	Longitudinal slope lower than 4%;	2
	Longitudinal slope between 4% and 8%;	1
	Longitudinal slope higher than 8%;	−1
	Stairway	−2
w4 – Discontinuity/obstacles	Absent;	1
	Present	−2
w5 – Paving material	Asphalt;	2
	Brick or stone slabs;	1
	Gravel, dirt road, uneven paving, wasteland or lawn	−2
w6 – Paving maintenance level	Excellent;	2
	Good;	1
	Sufficient;	−1
	Poor	−2

Indicators are computed using the following formulae (Eq. 1–3), and results are then normalized from 0 to 1 based on the minimum and maximum values each indicator can assume (Table 4).

$$Ui = \frac{\sum_{1}^{n} u_n}{n} \qquad (1)$$

Table 3. Factors of the Vulnerability indicator (Vi) – qualitative and quantitative assessment.

Factors	Qualitative and qualitative assessement	
v1 – Density of buildings with signs of structural deterioration	No deteriorated buildings;	1
	Less than 25%;	−1
	25% – 50%;	−2
	More than 50%	−3
v2 – Spatial configuration/degree of space enclosure	Open on four sides;	2
	Open on three sides;	−1
	Open on two sides;	−2
	Open on one side	−3
v3 – Density of buildings with poor roof maintenance	No deteriorated roofs;	1
	Less than 25%;	−1
	25% – 50%;	−2
	More than 50%	−3
v4 – Presence of retaining walls	Absent or present without signs of deterioration;	1
	Present with signs of deterioration	−1
v5 – Downhill slope to the space	Absent;	1
	Present	−1
v6 – Pavement cracking	Absent;	1
	Present	−1

$$Wi = \frac{\sum_1^n w_n}{n} \quad (2)$$

$$Vi = \frac{\sum_1^n v_n}{n} \quad (3)$$

Table 4. Indicators rankings of normalized values.

Ui	Wi	Vi
0.00 – 0.20 very low	0.00 – 0.20 poor	0.00 – 0.20 very low
0.21 – 0.40 low	0.21 – 0.40 modest	0.21 – 0.40 low
0.41 – 0.60 average	0.41 – 0.60 average	0.41 – 0.60 average
0.61 – 0.80 high	0.61 – 0.80 good	0.61 – 0.80 high
0.81 – 1.00 very high	0.81 – 1.00 very good	0.81 – 1.00 very high

Through these indicators and rankings, an *Accessibility Index (AI)* can be determined as the product of Ui and Wi. Additionally, a *Potential Harm Index (HI)* can be obtained by multiplying again Ui by Vi. These are calculated using the following formulae and evaluation matrices (Tables 5 and 6).

Table 5. Accessibility index (AI): formula and evaluation matrix.

Accessibility Index $AI = Ui \times Wi$		Wi			
		good (1)	sufficient (2)	modest (3)	poor (4)
Ui	very high (1)	20	15	10	5
	high (2)	16	12	8	4
	avarage (3)	12	9	6	3
	low (4)	8	6	4	2
	very low (5)	4	3	2	1
Accessibility ranking		Minimal 1-3	Medium 4-9	High 10-20	

Table 6. Potential harm index (HI): formula and evaluation matrix.

Potential harm Index $HI = Ui \times Vi$		Vi				
		very high (5)	high (4)	avarage (3)	low (2)	very low (1)
Ui	very high (5)	25	20	15	10	5
	high (4)	20	16	12	8	4
	avarage (3)	15	12	9	6	3
	low (2)	10	8	6	4	2
	very low (1)	5	4	3	2	1
Potential Damage ranking		Minimal 1-2	Low 3-5	Medium 6-10	High 12-16	Very high 20-25

2.2 Case Study: A Pilot Area in the Historical Village of Stigliano (MT)

The methodological framework is then tested on a pilot area. Stigliano is an Italian municipality located in the Basilicata Region (province of Matera), covering an area of approximately 210 km². It lies within the Lucanian Apennines at an altitude of 909 m above sea level. Stigliano serves as the lead municipality of the Montagna Materana inner area [25], which includes 7 other municipalities[2] considered ultra-peripheral with

---

[2] Accettura, Aliano, Cirigliano, Craco, Gorgoglione, Oliveto Lucano, and San Mauro Forte.

typical demographic decline, coupled with a rapid population aging [26]. Despite being the most populous (about 3,500 inhabitants on December 31, 2023), Stigliano has experienced a significant population loss over the last two decades (−14%). The geographic position, orographic configuration, infrastructure conditions, and distance from major urban centres (80 km from Matera, and 100 km from Potenza) limit access to essential services such as education, healthcare, and social support. Additionally, the area's geological and geomorphological characteristics make it highly susceptible to landslides. The built-up area lies along the slopes of Monte Serra, bordering the fragile *calanchi* landscape, and is surrounded by areas with varying degrees of risk. Recently, the village has been affected by a significant landslide that caused the collapse of a hillside in the northern sector of its urban expansion area.

The pilot area selected for this project contains historically and architecturally significant features and a street network with medium-to-high slope due to orographic configuration. The urban fabric, originally dense and stratified, has progressively thinned over time due to targeted demolitions of degraded buildings. In fact, the area partly falls within the perimeter of a "Transfer Plan" (*Piano di Trasferimento*) established in 1973 following a disastrous hydrogeological event. Since then, much of the built environment has been subject to depopulation and deterioration. Recent geological studies suggest the hydrogeological risk may be lower than previously assessed, opening the possibility of removing the constraint. However, years of neglect have significantly increased the site vulnerability (Fig. 1).

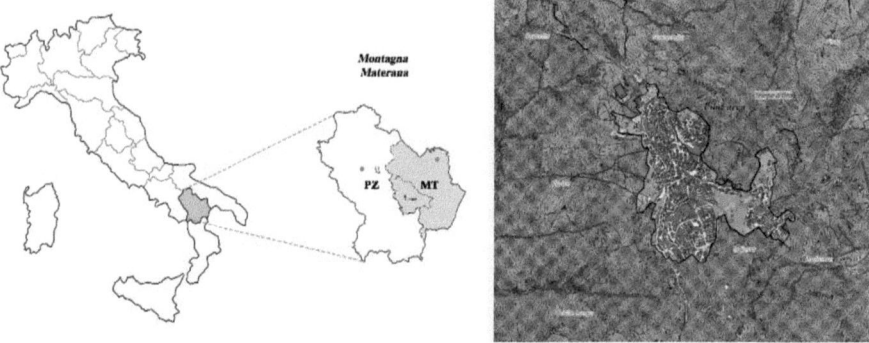

Fig. 1. Territorial framework of the pilot area in Stigliano (MT), Italy (authors' elaboration, based on spatial data from Istat.it and the Basilicata Region Geoportal)

Despite these challenges, the area has not been completely abandoned. Several key landmarks remain near the transfer zone, such as the Church of Santa Maria, the Museum of Rural Civilization, the Farmer's House, and the main market square (Fig. 2).

Fig. 2. The historic village of Stigliano, within the pilot area (authors' photos).

2.3 The GIS-Based Data Model and Data Collection Platform

Data required to assess intensity of use, walkability, and vulnerability of open spaces in the pilot area were analysed using a Spatial Information System (SIS), applying GIS techniques for data-modelling, collection, and management. Firstly, a GIS data model was developed by refining and expanding previous research conducted at the University of Parma [27]. The GIS data model was constructed using a vector-based data structure, enabling an in-depth analysis of the historical built environment, represented by three main semantically organised and correlated feature classes: buildings, fronts and open space. These main feature classes are complemented by housing numbers and cadastral information to help associate each building/space with a specific address, land regime and property (Fig. 3).

Secondly, a data collection protocol was set to populate the feature classes. Along with detailed cataloging and GIS mapping of the built environment elements, this approach involved a structured on-site audit through collaborative data collection. For this purpose, a GIS platform was configured based on the data model, using ArcGIS Pro and ArcGIS Online. Survey forms were set up for each feature class and networked through the ArcGIS Survey123 application. A four-day field survey, conducted by eight trained auditors divided into three teams, enabled systematic data collection through mobile survey forms for each feature class.

All feature classes were then populated according to the data model semantic structure, collecting qualitative and quantitative information aimed at assessing the intensity of use, walkability, and vulnerability of open spaces.

Finally, data management and processing, supported by the correlation of feature classes within the GIS database, produced new information associated with each open space unit. This resulted in the qualitative and quantitative assessment used to assign scores to the factors involved in the computing of U_i, W_i, and V_i indicators (as illustrated in Tables 1, 2 and 3).

3 Results

GIS data processing produced thematic maps showing: the open space intensity of use (Fig. 4), based on activity density and social factors; walkability (Fig. 5), assessing how well spaces support users with different mobility levels; and vulnerability (Fig. 6), highlighting damage and deterioration in both built and open areas and their spatial

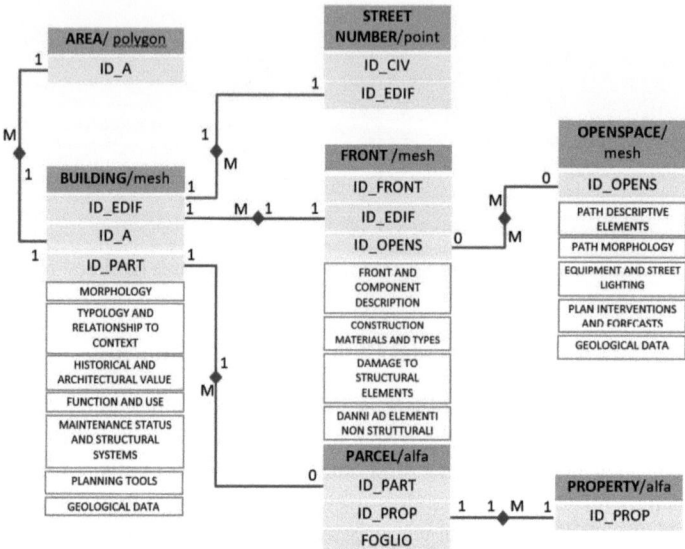

Fig. 3. GIS data model (authors' elaboration)

relationships. Overall, all three representations confirm that the southeastern sector of the built environment, characterized by steeper terrain, presents critical issues. The pathway system in this area is marked by slopes often exceeding 8% and is structured as networks of stairways and steps. This likely contributes to the high percentages of buildings in a state of abandonment and poor maintenance conditions observed in this area. Critical issues are also evident in the northwestern portion of the built environment, between Largo Fieramosca and Villa Marina. The primary concern here is the area's heightened vulnerability, evident from clear signs of instability linked to hydro-geological problems.

The vulnerability affects both accessibility and the presence of social hotspots, even in areas that, despite having favourable walkability characteristics, are not immune to these challenges. The historic core around the Church of Santa Maria, despite low usage intensity due to widespread building abandonment and a lack of social hotspots, shows more favorable walkability conditions.

By combining the results of the accessibility, walkability, and vulnerability indicators, as previously mentioned, the values for the Accessibility Index (Fig. 7) and the Potential Harm Index (Fig. 8) were obtained.

The thematic maps, not only confirm previous findings, but also reveal a network of moderately accessible routes that, with targeted interventions, could improve access to several areas of the historic centre. However, these pathways exhibit relatively high-risk exposure, making it necessary to integrate the data to gain a clear understanding of the nature of the interventions required for both public spaces and the adjacent buildings.

Fig. 4. Map of the usage intensity indicator (Ui). Authors' elaboration

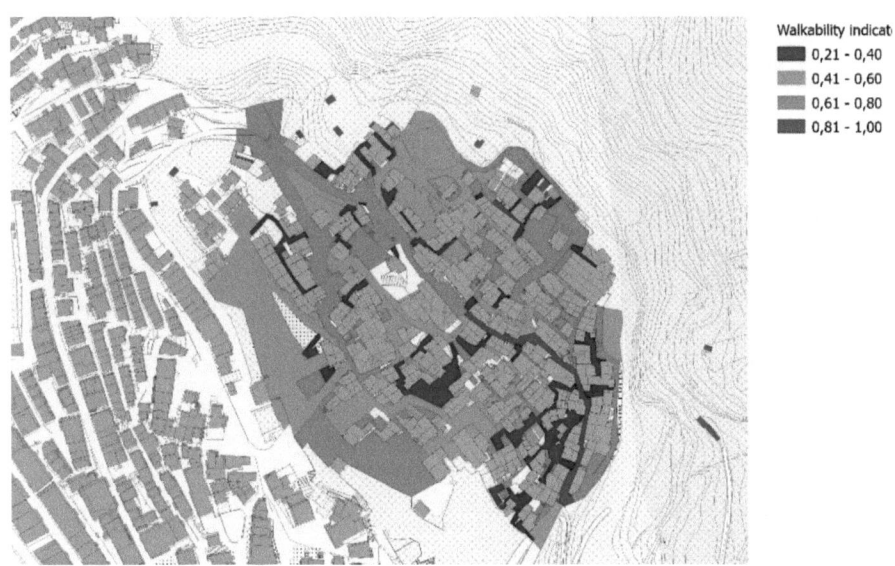

Fig. 5. Map of the walkability indicator (Wi). Authors' elaboration

Fig. 6. Map of the vulnerability indicator (Vi). Authors' elaboration

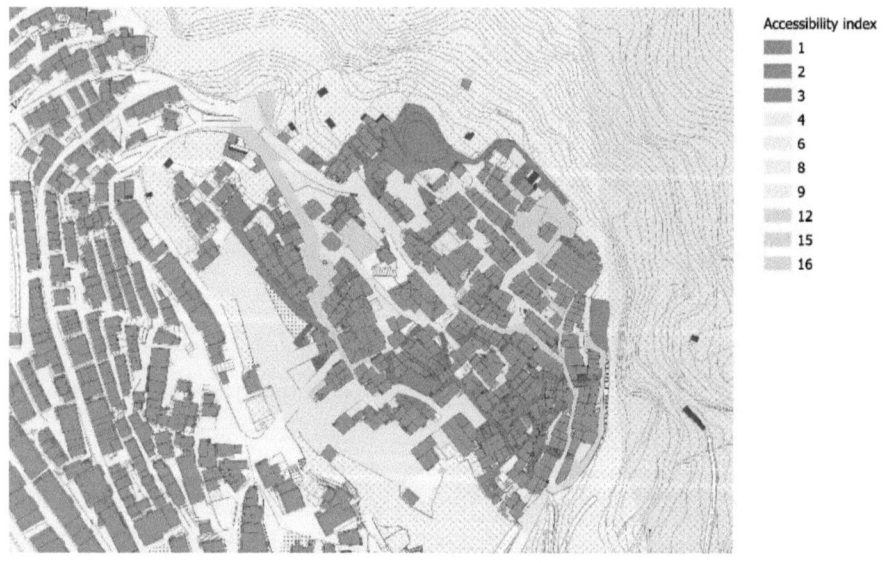

Fig. 7. Map of accessibility index (AI). Authors' elaboration

Fig. 8. Map of the potential harm index (HI). Authors' elaboration

4 Discussion and Conclusions

The article has illustrated the application of a GIS-based quantitative methodology in a pilot area of the village of Stigliano (MT) to facilitate knowledge acquisition aimed at supporting decision-making processes for improving accessibility for all and ensuring the safe usability of the built heritage.

There are still few experiments involving specific analytical methodologies for these historic settlements, which are often marginal but where it is crucial to maintain adequate levels of safety and accessibility. This built environment serves both as the daily living space for the remaining residents and as valuable cultural heritage attractive for potential tourists. The desire to promote the small centres from a tourism perspective further underscores the importance of enhancing the inclusivity and safety of the historic fabric, which is typically the most attractive area for visitors.

The methodology effectively evaluates various quality and safety factors related to pathways and open spaces – primarily public ones – by correlating them with the characteristics of the surrounding built environment. The developed and tested method is rigorous yet accessible, even for technicians working in municipal administration offices. The direct interaction with local authorities within the GO-IN! project has enabled a continuous exchange on the methodological approach.

The results of the analyses provide initial data useful for selecting priority interventions for public space redevelopment, safety enhancement, or simply pathways and open space local improvements. However, to proceed to the operational identification of intervention strategies, the addition of a survey on the potential 'transformability' of spaces could further improve the methodological approach. In fact, defining concrete intervention strategies requires a deeper understanding of space usability and level of 'transformability' based on several key factors, i.e., public/private ownership (which is not always easy to determine in these contexts), previous urban transformations (demolition or redevelopment operations), the need for structural interventions, and the historical-testimonial value of spaces (determining the constraint level). Because this additional information is often hard to obtain, direct involvement of local administration and communities is essential. The ongoing nature of the project provides an opportunity to further explore these aspects.

Experimental validation of the results has in any case confirmed the effectiveness of the method. However, some limitations can be identified. Firstly, the indicators rely on a specific set of attributes whose selection, though grounded in previous research and field validation, remains partially context dependent. Certain variables – such as the presence of social hotspots or building frontage continuity – may carry different weight or significance in other urban settings. Moreover, the pilot area of Stigliano presents a distinct morphological and territorial configuration, with steep orography, hydrogeological risks, and a legacy of targeted demolition. These characteristics may have influenced both the performance of the indicators and the data collection process. The application of the same methodology in other small historic centres with different morphological, demographic, or infrastructural conditions may be essential to assess its robustness and potential broad replicability.

Secondly, the indicators are built on proxies and spatial characteristics, which are useful for objective analysis but may not fully capture the subjective perception of accessibility or safety experienced by users. In this sense, initiating public involvement actions would help to integrate the flow of information.

Finally, the 'cost' of extensive field surveys necessary to update the Spatial Information System (SIS), ensuring adequate knowledge of historic heritage, might not be sustainable from a technical and financial point of view. However, it should be emphasised that the SIS was built according to semantic interoperability with a 3D digital model derived from the innovative integration of topographic and photogrammetric survey. The interoperability allows to easily integrate the two technologies and resulting databases. Completing the prototype will provide an opportunity to better test the potential for automated information acquisition relevant to usability, walkability and vulnerability analyses, directly from the 3D digital model.

It is important to specify that the 3D digital model created and still expandable currently serves only as a foundation for developing a full digital twin of Stigliano. The digital twin technology under development could lead to automated documentation processes, facilitating the scalability to the entire historic centre and its replicability in similar contexts [28] – provided that the necessary financial resources and expertise are available. For instance, based on the results of specific thematic maps related to severe structural damage, targeted surveys could be conducted at regular intervals to update the system accordingly. Alternatively, sensors could be installed in the public space to enable real-time simulations. The data collected by these sensors could then be integrated into the 3D digital model, generating a wide range of information. The potential of this product is certainly significant. However, considering the specific urban context (both in terms of territorial morphology and depopulation conditions), it would be more effective to test the first strategy, before proceeding with the installation of sensors (Fig. 9).

Fig. 9. 3D model of the pilot area in Stigliano – macro-modelling (Image produced by DadaLab, University of Pavia).

As a further future development of the project, the developed prototype will soon be shared with the municipality's technical office to assess its functionality in supporting knowledge-building processes, urban planning and management. Stigliano was chosen as pilot area also because its administrative and technical office is more structured compared to nearby hamlets of the Montagna Materana area. In addition, the project will also provide for capacity-building activities to train technicians in using and querying the 3D digital model integrated with the SIS.

As a further future development, the prototype will also be made accessible through a virtual platform enriched with informational content about local and territorial resources [29], aiming to trigger virtuous processes for local development. Accessibility can drive renewed tourism appeal, drawing on local cultural resources and enhanced by remote access systems based on new technologies and widespread mass communication channels (social media, web, smartphone apps). These tools hold the potential not only to increase tourist appeal by enabling a more inclusive experience of both tangible and intangible cultural resources but also to promote new economic sectors and supply chains. However, for remote accessibility to be truly effective, it should not remain confined to the digital world but foster long-range relational dynamics and encourage online visitors to physically experience the territory.

Therefore, promoting remote accessibility should go hand in hand with a fundamental preventive effort to improve the physical access to cultural heritage and safety in small historic centres. Despite the risk of progressive abandonment, these actions are essential for preserving identity, fostering sustainable development, and reinforcing the role of hamlets as living, resilient places rather than mere relics of the past.

Acknowledgments. This research was granted by PNRR-M4C2- I1.1 – MUR Call for proposals n.104 of 02–02-2022 – PRIN 2022 – ERC sector SH5- Project title: GO-IN! diGital platfOrm for INner areas. Interactive virtual platforms for the enhancement of fragile contexts and their cultural heritage – Project Code 2022THKLFF – CUP Code D53D23015580006 – Funded by the European Union – NextGenerationEU

The project is coordinated by the University of Pavia (PI Prof. Francesca Picchio) with the University of Basilicata (unit leader Prof. Marianna Calia) and the University of Parma (unit leader Prof. Barbara Caselli).

Author Contributions. The authors jointly contributed to the paper. Conceptualisation, B.C. and A.P.; methodology, B.C. and A.P.; software, A.P.; validation, B.C. and A.P.; formal analysis, A.P.; investigation, B.C., A.P., S.L. and R.L.; data curation, A.P., S.L. and R.L.; writing—original draft preparation, B.C.; writing—review and editing, B.C., A.P., S.L. and R.L.; supervision, B.C. All authors have read and agreed to the published version of the manuscript.

Disclosure of Interests. The authors have no competing interests to declare that are relevant to the content of this article.

References

1. Stegmeijer, E., Veldpaus, L.: Research agenda for heritage planning. perspectives for Europe (and beyond). In: Stegmeijer, E., Veldpaus, L. (eds.) A Research Agenda for Heritage Planning: Perspectives from Europe. Edward Elgar Publishing (2021). https://doi.org/10.4337/9781788974639.00030
2. Buratti, N., Ferrari, C. (eds.): La valorizzazione del patrimonio di prossimità tra fragilità e sviluppo locale. FrancoAngeli, Milano (2011)
3. Coni M., Garau C., Maltinti F., Pinna F.: Accessibility improvements and place-based organization in the Island of Sardinia (Italy). In: Gervasi, O., et al.: Computational Science and Its Applications – ICCSA 2020. ICCSA 2020. Lecture Notes in Computer Science, vol 12255. Springer, Cham (2020). https://doi.org/10.1007/978-3-030-58820-5
4. Bacci, E., Cotella, G., Vitale, B.E.: Improving accessibility to reverse marginalisation processes in Valle Arroscia, Italy. In: Vitale, B.E., Cotella, G., Staricco, L. (eds.) Rural Accessibility in European Regions, pp. 101–118. Routledge, New York (2021)
5. Lombardo, L., Colajanni, S., Campisi, T.: Aree interne inclusive, una possibilità per le Madonie. Criteri smart per riprogettare il costruito storico, tra innovazione tecnologica e accessibilità. In: Fatiguso, F., Fiorito, F., De Fino, M., Cantatore, E. (eds.) In Transizione: sfide e opportunità per l'ambiente costruito, pp. 1621–1639. EdicomEdizioni, Monfalcone (2023)
6. Vendemmia, B., Lanza, G.: Redefining marginality on Italian Apennines: an approach to reconsider the notion of basic needs in low density territories. In Region. The J. ERSA **9**(2), 131–148 (2022)
7. Ignaccolo, M., Inturri, G, Giuffrida, N., Le Pira, M., Torrisi, V.: A step towards walkable environments: spatial analysis of pedestrian compatibility in an urban context – European Transport-Trasporti Europei, **76**(6)(2020)
8. Campisi, T., Basbas, S., Tesoriere, G., Trouva, M., Papas, T., Mrak, I.: How to create walking friendly cities. A multi-criteria analysis of the central open market area of Rijeka. Sustainability **12**(22), 9470 (2020). https://doi.org/10.3390/su12229470
9. Pucci, P., Carboni, L., Lanza, G.: Accessibilità di prossimità in un territorio montano. In: Archivio di Studi Urbani e Regionali, vol. 135, pp. 5–26 (2023). https://doi.org/10.3280/ASUR2022-135001

10. Marconcini, S., Treccani, D., Díaz-Vilariño, L., Adami, A.: A data collection framework for managing accessibility and inclusion in urban heritage. ISPRS Ann. Photogramm. Remote Sens. Spatial Inf. Sci. **VIII-M-1–2021**, 101–108 (2021). https://doi.org/10.5194/isprs-annals-VIII-M-1-2021-101-2021
11. Gargiulo, C., Zucaro, F., Gaglione, F.: A set of variables for the elderly accessibility in urban areas. Tema. J. Land Use, Mobility Environ. 53–66 (2018). https://doi.org/10.6092/1970-9870/5738
12. Bizzarri, C., Regenerative tourism: new perspectives for italian inland areaa. In: Trono, A., Kosmas, P., Castronuovo, V. (eds.), Managing Natural and Cultural Heritage for a Durable Tourism, pp. 189–202. SpringerNature (2024). https://doi.org/10.1007/978-3-031-52041-9
13. Longo, D., Boeri, A., Turillazzi, B., Orlandi, S.: Cultural heritage and interoperable open platforms: strategies for knowledge, accessibility, enhancement and networking. In: Sustainable development and planning XI. WIT Transactions on Ecology and the environment; pp. 371–382 (2020) https://doi.org/10.2495/SDP200301
14. Chioni, C., Pezzica, C., Favargiotti, S.: Territorial Digital Twins: a key for increasing the community resilienze of fragile mountain inner territories? Sustain. Dev. **32**(2), 1548–1563 (2024). https://doi.org/10.1002/sd.2688
15. Tira, M., Bonotti, R.: Urban planning and seismic risk: conclusive remarks. Ingegneria sismica **1–2**, 140–143 (2013)
16. Santangelo, A., Melandri, E., Marzani, G., Tondelli, S., Ugolini, A.: Enhancing resilience of cultural heritage in historical areas: a collection of good practices. Sustainability **14**(9), 5171 (2022). https://doi.org/10.3390/su14095171
17. Carra, M., Rossetti, S., Caselli, B.: Public space planning in minor historic centres exposed to seismic risk: lessons learnt from the experience. In :Navelli (AQ), UPLAND – ISSN 2531–9906, 7:1, pp. 25–38 (2023). https://doi.org/10.6092/2531-9906/10031
18. Panebianco, A., Caselli, B.: Piattaforme digitali per le aree interne: il caso studio di Stigliano. In: Cardaci, A., Picchio, F., Versaci, A. (eds.) ReUSO 2024. Documentazione, restauro e rigenerazione sostenibile del patrimonio costruito, pp. 1737–1746. Publica, Alghero (2024)
19. Pires Rosa, M., Landim Tavares, I., Santos Loureiro, N. (eds.) Cultural accessible pedestrian ways. The case of Faro historic centre. J. Tourism Heritage Res. **3**(2), 75–95 (2020)
20. Casacchia, P. (ed.) Accessibilità e inclusività nei centri storici minori. Esperienze e riflessioni per una migliore fruizione del patrimonio materiale e immateriale. RomaTrE-Press, Roma (2023)
21. Valverde-Caballero, L.S., Mendoza-Salazar, L.M., Butron-Revilla, C.L., Suarez-Lopez, E., Aguilar-Ruiz, J.S.: Walkability index for world heritage cities in developing countries. Environ. Plann. B: Urban Anal. City Sci. **52**(1), 76–96 (2025). https://doi.org/10.1177/23998083241250265
22. Tira, M.: Pianificare la città sicura. Roma: Dedalo (1997)
23. Bergantino, A.S., Troiani, G., Bashir, T., Pagliara, F.: How vulnerable are road networks to shocks? An analysis through accessibility indicators. Sustain. Futu. **9**, 100471 (2025). https://doi.org/10.1016/j.sftr.2025.100471
24. Garau, C., Annunziata, A.: Public Open Spaces: connecting people, squares and streets by measuring the usability through the Villanova district in Cagliari, Italy. Transport. Res. Procedia **60**, 314–321 (2022). https://doi.org/10.1016/j.trpro.2021.12.041
25. Agenzia per la Coesione Territoriale Regione Basilicata, Ministero dell'Istruzione, dell'Università e della Ricerca, Ministero delle Infrastrutture e dei Trasporti, Agenzia Nazionale per le Politiche Attive del Lavoro, Ministero delle politiche Agricole Alimentari, Forestali e del Turismo, Ministero della Salute, Comune di Stigliano (Capofila), Strategia Nazionale Aree Interne. Accordo di programma quadro Regione Basilicata "AREA INTERNA – MONTAGNA MATERANA", all. 1. (2017)

26. Faggian, A., Pezzi, G.M., Urso, G.: Valutazione del documento: "Preliminare di Strategia", Area pilota: Montagna materana Basilicata. 2017. Gran Sasso Science Institute
27. Ventura, P., Carra, M., Rossetti, S., Caselli, B., Zazzi. M.: La post-emergenza sismica nei centri storici minori. Il Piano di ricostruzione di Navelli (2011–2019). In: Francini, M., Palermo, A., Viapiana, M. (eds.) Il piano di emergenza nell'uso e nella gestione del territorio – Atti del Convegno Scientifico Società Italiana degli Urbanisti, 22–23 novembre 2019, Rende (Cs), pp. 66–88. Milano: Franco Angeli (2020)
28. Doria, E., La Placa, S., Miceli, A.: Il GIS come strumento di analisi urbana per la gestione del Life Cycle della città. In: 3D BETHLEHEM Gestione e controllo della crescita urbana per lo sviluppo del patrimonio ed il miglioramento della vita nella città di Betlemme, pp. 138–165; Firenze: Edifir Edizioni Firenze s.r.l. (2022)
29. Laera, R., Pedone, R., Micucci, P.: Disseminazione artistica e solidale nel comune di Stigliano (MT). Strategia pilota per rilanciare le Aree Interne della Montagna Materana. Atti del convegno Le Università per le città e i territori. Proposte per l'integrazione tra politiche universitarie e politiche urbane. Working Papers Urb@nit, vol. 15, pp. 290–298 (2023)

UX Mobility 2025: Placing User Experience at the Center of Urban Mobility: Methods and Frameworks (UXM 2025)

*Wiz*RD: A Personalized Wayfinding Platform for Enhanced Urban Navigation

Jacopo Maltagliati[✉], Alberto Leporati, and Daniela Micucci

University of Milano-Bicocca, DISCo, Viale Sarca 336 Building 14, 20126 Milan, Italy
j.maltagliati@campus.unimib.it,
{alberto.leporati,daniela.micucci}@unimib.it

Abstract. Wayfinding platforms help users navigate both indoor and outdoor environments in real-time. Many existing systems primarily optimize either distance or time, neglecting other important factors such as personal comfort, perception of safety, or emotional responses to the environment.

To overcome these limitations, we designed *Wiz*RD, a new wayfinding platform that allows users to express their preferences and obtain routes that optimize them. This is made possible by the fact that *Wiz*RD can automatically acquire and integrate new data sources, also enabling the definition of customized routing algorithms that take into account both data sources and user preferences. In addition, to support decision-making, *Wiz*RD includes a visualization dashboard that facilitates users' understanding of how different environmental factors affect the recommended routes. Finally, the platform supports multimodal navigation by integrating vehicle interchange stations called LUMIs.

A prototype implementation developed for the area around the University of Milano-Bicocca demonstrates the platform's ability to handle multimodal navigation and to address the specific needs of vulnerable people, such as the ones with impaired mobility, women, and children.

Keywords: Routing · Customized Wayfinding · Planning · Interactive Data Visualization

1 Introduction

Navigation in urban areas has become increasingly dependent on wayfinding solutions, which assist users in planning their trips and making more informed mobility decisions by providing directions for navigating indoor and outdoor environments in real time, reducing or eliminating printed maps.

Wayfinding platforms, however, often disregard human factors such as safety, comfort, or emotional response to the environment when calculating routes, optimizing for travel time or distance instead. Although incorporating such factors into routing algorithms is computationally feasible [3], the definition of effective metrics and cost functions that reflect user preferences, producing personalized and inclusive results, remains challenging.

Several routing systems that rely on diverse data sources have been proposed. For instance, Balata et al. [1] proposed a navigation system for people with visual impairment that relies on existing landmarks to insert contextual information in directions given to users. Similarly, SearchPath [6] provides culturally relevant itineraries by combining known Points of Interest, such as museums and exhibitions, user preferences, and multimedia content. Both approaches succeed in producing personalized and contextually relevant routes. However, they have limited adaptability to changes in the environment or the application's requirements due to their use of static datasets. Integrating support for frequently updated datasets is essential, as highlighted by Taghipour et al. [7], who compared several models for travel time prediction. Their study showed a significant increase in the predictive capabilities of all models when presented with data from diverse, contextually relevant sources.

The importance of integrating dynamic datasets, such as public transport timetables, is shown by the study conducted by the authors of the FAVOUR algorithm [4]. FAVOUR calculates the route based on the current situation (e.g., traffic and weather) and the user's preferences, which are continuously updated while using the service. Multimodal transportation solutions, however, present their challenges: Bast et al. [2] discuss the efficiency of route planning algorithms in large transportation networks, particularly highlighting the complexities associated with multimodal route planning.

Many existing systems still cannot provide customized routing solutions or dynamically integrate environmental data. In response to those limitations, we present *Wiz*RD, a flexible and modular wayfinding platform designed to integrate multiple, diverse data sources that offers users extensive customization options. Unlike conventional routers that attempt to minimize travel time or distance, *Wiz*RD optimizes the calculated route according to user preferences while considering environmental factors expressed in the dataset and supports:

- the integration of heterogeneous data, including road network information, pre-calculated metrics, and real-time data from external providers;
- customizable cost functions that can be used to provide routes that respect users' preferences regarding safety, accessibility, or infrastructure quality;
- a data visualization system that helps users understand how the combination of the dataset and different preferences influence routing decisions;
- the combination of different transportation modes (e.g., walking, cycling, and shared vehicle services), properly following road regulations (e.g., bikes cannot travel on footways);
- the use of shared vehicle services via exchange points called LUMIs (Last-Mile User Mobility Interchanges).

Moreover, *Wiz*RD is particularly attentive to the needs of vulnerable groups, including individuals with mobility impairments, women, and children, by enabling the avoidance of barriers and the prioritization of safer or more comfortable paths.

We developed a prototype application for accessible wayfinding in the area surrounding the University of Milano-Bicocca, highlighting the capabilities of

*Wiz*RD. This real-world implementation demonstrates the platform's ability to compute personalized and context-aware routes based on user-defined preferences dynamically and to integrate new data sources, such as walkability [5] metrics, through dedicated procedures.

The rest of the paper is organized as follows: Sect. 2 provides an overview of *Wiz*RD and introduces its functionalities; Sect. 3 describes its architecture; Sect. 4 discusses the use case we developed; and Sect. 5 presents the conclusions and future research directions.

2 The *Wiz*RD Platform

This section provides an overview of the capabilities offered by the platform. Two main categories of users have been identified: *end users* and *knowledge integrators*. *End users* can interact with the system in two ways: they can request a route from one point to another, potentially using vehicles available at LUMIs, or they can view specific properties of the network, either in its entirety or limited to a specific subset, such as cycling paths. *Knowledge integrators*, on the other hand, are responsible for extending the system's functionalities by enriching the database with additional metrics that characterize road segments (such as walkability indexes).

2.1 Routing Support

The *Wiz*RD platform integrates multiple data sources to supplement each segment with diverse metrics, providing a more detailed road network representation. For example, a specific segment might have associated a walkability score of 10 (out of 100) from one source and a greenness score of 1 (out of 10) from another. The platform relies on a database to store and process heterogeneous data, using it to calculate routes optimized for a combination of metrics that differ from traditional distance- or time-based criteria. With this system, the *Wiz*RD platform can adapt to user preferences: for example, users may prioritize routes with lower pollution levels, paths characterized by greater walkability, or routes optimized for accessibility in cases of limited mobility.

*Wiz*RD also supports multimodal navigation, letting users combine walking and sustainable vehicles, such as bikes, e-bikes, and e-scooters. The platform also has built-in support for exchange points (LUMIs), where users may rent a vehicle or return it. When users select a shared vehicle, the system directs users to the nearest LUMI and then to the LUMI nearest to their destination. This only applies if a rental route takes less than just walking, in which case the system defaults to the latter. Ultimately, the router enforces regulatory constraints: for example, if a portion of the route (e.g., a crossing) requires the user to dismount from their bike, the system suggests a modal switch to ensure compliance with traffic regulations.

Figure 1 illustrates a multimodal route where users rent an e-scooter to travel from Building U9 to Building U6 of the Bicocca University campus. Another

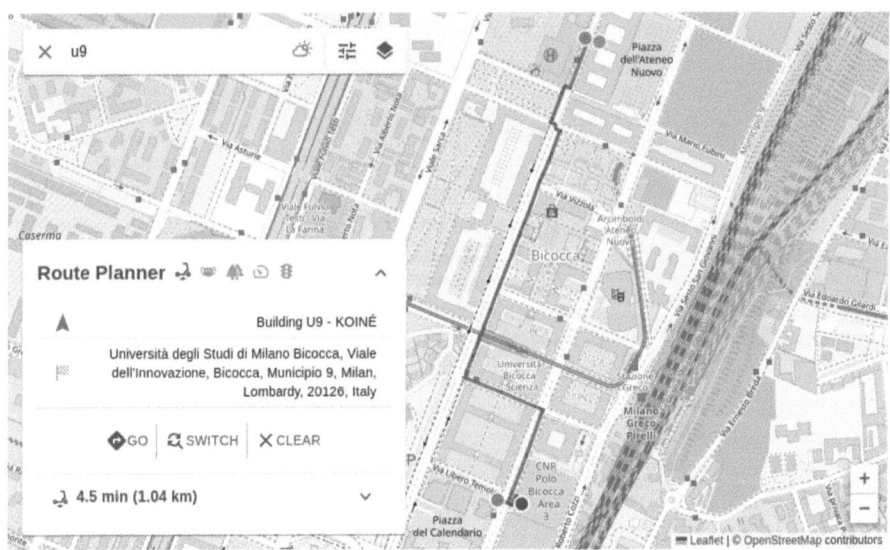

Fig. 1. Example of a multimodal route proposed to a user who wishes to rent an e-scooter to travel between university buildings, as presented by our prototype application.

example is shown in Fig. 2, where the system suggests a mode transition to comply with traffic regulations. In this scenario, we asked the router to provide a route to Building U14, traveling by e-bike. The system directs the user to the nearest cycleway (highlighted in orange), which terminates abruptly. At this point, the system instructs the user to dismount and walk along a connecting path (highlighted in blue) before resuming cycling on a service road. This example shows how the router adheres to legal constraints while respecting users' preferences.

2.2 Visualization Support

The *Wiz*RD platform provides a data visualization component that creates and displays *views* that represent selected attributes of specific portions of the road network. Views are overlaid on the interactive map, giving users a visual interpretation of the data stored in the platform's database, and are characterized by three key aspects:

1. They support **filtering** based on predefined criteria. Through filters, users can select specific subsets of the network, such as roads, footways, cycleways, or greenways, and analyze specific features: for example, a user may isolate pedestrian paths to examine walkability-related metrics.
2. They give a visual **representation of data sources**, which may include various attributes such as air quality, traffic conditions, infrastructure quality,

Fig. 2. Example of a multimodal route considering road network constraints; the highlighted pink area indicates the section pictured on the right. (Color figure online)

safety, accessibility, and walkability. Data can be displayed as individual metrics or synthesized through computational *functions* that combine multiple parameters to produce an aggregate value for each segment. These functions (see Fig. 3) enable users to personalize their navigation experience by creating specific criteria for route computation.

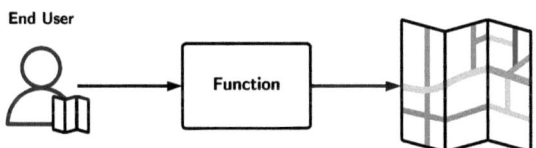

Fig. 3. Functions compute data for real-time visualization.

3. They can be **colored** according to specific attributes, giving a visual representation of variations in the dataset. Users can apply a uniform color to highlight specific segments (e.g., walkways or cycleways) or use a gradient scale to visualize differences in a selected metric (e.g., traffic colored by badness). Advanced customization options, including opacity and line width, can also be adjusted according to presented data. For instance, the default visualization strategy for air quality data uses wide, semi-transparent lines to simulate low granularity. An example of different visualization strategies is shown in Fig. 4.

In summary, *Wiz*RD's visualization component enables interactive data exploration and analysis, helping users gain deeper insights into the spatial distribution of critical infrastructure features.

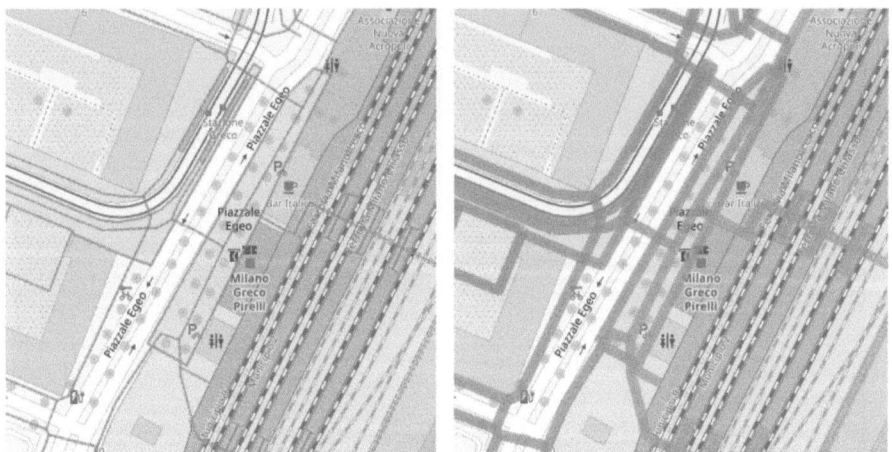

Fig. 4. Example of a preset view showing footways in coral (left) and a custom view visualizing air quality data in footways (right).

2.3 Knowledge Base Augmentation Support

The *Wiz*RD platform integrates various data sources, which contain values associated with specific segments of the road network. Each value corresponds to a distinct metric: pollution levels, traffic density, accessibility, or green space. Adding a new source associates more data to road segments and makes the network more capable of representing different aspects of the road infrastructure. When computing routes, these values provide weights for each road segment: by combining them and adjusting their relative importance, users can prioritize factors like safety, environmental impact, or accessibility and personalize their routes.

Knowledge integrators can also define ***procedures*** (see Fig. 5) to automatically perform complex operations on the dataset during the data preparation stage, ensuring that the results are readily available for later use.

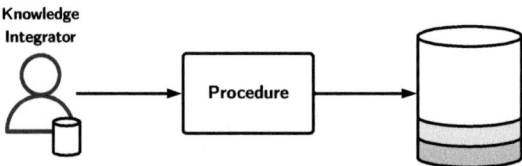

Fig. 5. Procedures handle data computation during the preparation stage and cache the results for future use.

3 *Wiz*RD Platform: Architecture

*Wiz*RD follows a traditional client-server architecture as depicted in Fig. 6. The *Data Provisioning* component is responsible for ingesting the map and related data, including data sources and processing procedures. The *Data Access* component manages data storage and ensures availability, while the *Data Consumption* component handles user interaction with the platform.

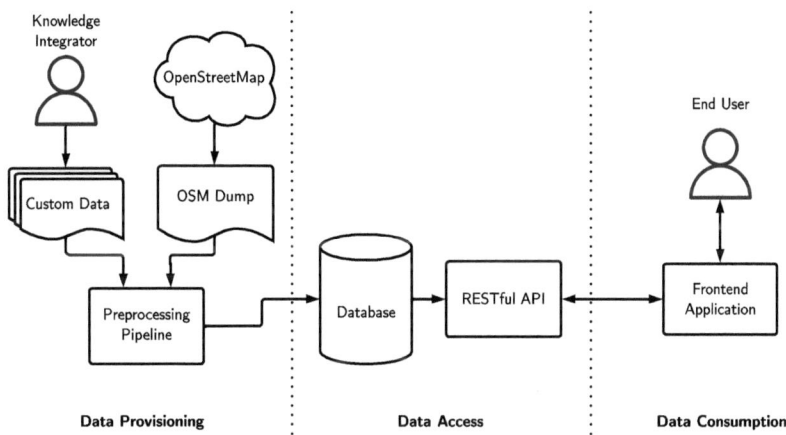

Fig. 6. Overview of *Wiz*RD's architecture.

3.1 Data Provisioning

*Wiz*RD uses the OpenStreetMap (OSM) dataset as a base layer for road network data and street classification. OSM has been chosen due to its comprehensive coverage and open data model.

The preprocessing pipeline is essential for obtaining raw data from OSM and transforming it into a format suitable for backend processing. The pipeline automates the conversion process through a set of scripts, ensuring that the system operates with up-to-date and accurate data. The pipeline consists of three main steps, as illustrated in Fig. 7.

- **Map Retrieval**: The first step retrieves OSM data for a specified area, storing it in a dump file. This process relies on osmconvert[1] to extract data within a defined bounding box.
- **Graph Building**: The second step transforms the OSM data into a graph structure that can be used for routing. The script ensures that the graph is optimized for routing. Indeed, the script: *i)* preserves road classifications (e.g., primary roads, bike lanes) and surface types (e.g., asphalt, gravel) to assign appropriate weights for routing; *ii)* identifies and handles one-way

---

[1] https://wiki.openstreetmap.org/wiki/Osmconvert

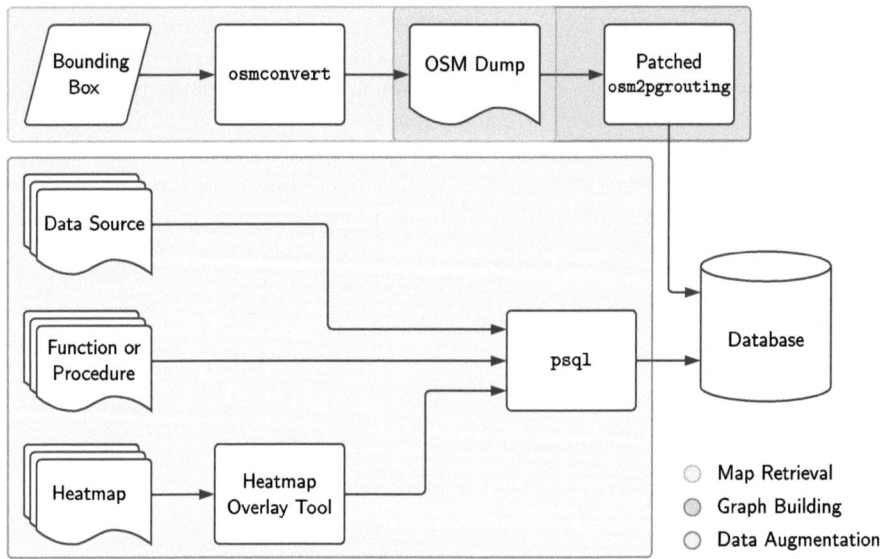

Fig. 7. Overview of *Wiz*RD's preprocessing pipeline.

roads, greenways, and pedestrian crossings, ensuring that the graph accurately reflects real-world conditions; *iii)* removes isolated graph components (e.g., non-walkable areas) that do not contribute to valid routes. The script uses a modified version of `osm2pgrouting`[2].
- **Data Augmentation**: The final step integrates data from external sources such as Points of Interest (POIs), traffic data, pollution, and Walkability Indexes (WIs) into the database. At this point, data from loosely coupled sources (i.e., heatmaps encoded as single-channel images) can be overlaid onto the graph. Different layers of the same data point can be stored concurrently in *profile* mode. This mode can be helpful in simulating real-world scenarios, such as traffic during different times of the day or pollution levels in different seasons. This step also loads user-defined functions (for online calculations) and procedures (for offline calculations) in the database.

3.2 Data Access

The backend uses the PostgreSQL database to store the road network and the data sources. In particular, the backend uses the PostGIS extension[3], which supports geospatial data types and operations. Table 1 presents a summary of the contents of the database.

---

[2] https://github.com/pgRouting/osm2pgrouting.
[3] https://postgis.net.

Table 1. Summary of tables used in the database.

Table	Description
`ways`	Data from the OSM dataset, including vertex pairs $\langle V_s, V_t \rangle$
`data`	Additional data that is not strictly required for building the network
`pois`	Data related to Points of Interest (POIs)
`modes`	Descriptions of supported modes of transportation, including their maximum speeds and the cost of rental
`ddesc`	Description of the columns in the `data` table
`fdesc`	Description of user-provided functions

To summarize the main datasets currently integrated into the platform, Table 2 provides an overview of their types, sources, and purposes.

Table 2. Data sources integrated into the *Wiz*RD platform.

Dataset	Source	Description
Road Network	OpenStreetMap[a]	Topology of the road network and accessory data including qualitative information such as street names, pavement surface type, and road classification, and quantitative information such as length
Points of Interest	Manually Generated	Points of Interest, including their names, coordinates, types, and accessory information
Walkability Indexes	Survey[b]	Quantitative indices that express the desirability of a route for pedestrians, such as infrastructure quality, accessibility, and safety
Traffic Data	TomTom Traffic[c]	Information regarding vehicular traffic such as its density, speed, and average travel time
Air Quality	Breezometer[d]	Mean European Air Quality Index (EAQI) value for each segment

[a] The dataset is gathered from OpenStreetMap (https://www.openstreetmap.org) using `osmconvert`
[b] The dataset was sourced from a survey conducted by the Department of Sociology and Social Research, University of Milano-Bicocca
[c] The dataset was sourced from TomTom (https://www.tomtom.com/products/traffic-stats/) on 22 September 2023
[d] The dataset was sourced from Breezometer (https://www.breezometer.com/air-quality-index/) on 22 September 2023

For route computation, the backend makes use of pgRouting[4], a PostgreSQL extension that supports several routing algorithms, including Dijkstra's, A*, and K-Shortest Paths (KSP). pgRouting requires a preprocessing step to build a graph representing the road network, on which routes are calculated by minimizing the route's cost.

User-defined cost functions can be supplied to the algorithm to optimize routing for specific scenarios and preferences. For example, a cost function that combines the type of vehicle, traffic conditions, and user preferences regarding air pollution can be used along with Dijkstra's algorithm to provide a personalized route. Users can pick their preferred algorithm from a list, select the desired cost function, and adjust related parameters. Additionally, multimodal routes can be requested, integrating LUMIs for users wanting to rent a vehicle.

The routing system's modular architecture offers a great degree of flexibility and allows knowledge integrators to tailor the platform for various use cases. Examples of target applications include personalizable navigation systems for end users and systems capable of estimating likely routes under various scenarios, such as the presence of green areas, commercial zones, traffic conditions, and the characteristics of different user groups.

Functions and procedures are written in the PostgreSQL dialect and are directly stored in the database during the Data Augmentation step. Recall that functions are used to perform real-time computations, such as calculating the cost of segments or generating data for visualization. In contrast, knowledge integrators typically define procedures and use them for offline computations during the data augmentation phase, as they allow for the pre-calculation and caching of the results of complex computations.

Finally, the backend exposes several RESTful API endpoints (some of them listed in Table 3) that facilitate communication with the frontend. These APIs support various operations, such as retrieving views, POIs, and calculating routes. Some endpoints are tailored explicitly for routing through LUMI stations.

3.3 Data Consumption

*Wiz*RD follows a client-server architecture, where the client is a frontend application responsible for user interaction and graphical representation of the data stored and processed by the backend server; communication between the two is handled via a RESTful API. Geospatial data is represented in GeoJSON[5] format, making it suitable for visualization with map rendering libraries such as Leaflet.js[6].

The frontend is a React-based Single-Page Application (SPA) running in a Node.js environment. It utilizes React-MUI[7] to draw UI elements. The following components provide user interaction:

---

[4] https://pgrouting.org.
[5] https://geojson.org/.
[6] https://leafletjs.com.
[7] https://mui.com.

Table 3. Summary of endpoints that are available through the API.

Endpoint	Method	Description
/desc/data	GET	Returns a specific Data Description
/desc/func	GET	Returns a specific Function Description
/mode	GET	Returns a specific transportation mode
/mode/all	GET	Returns all available transportation modes
/poi/all	GET	Returns all POIs of a given type
/poi/nearest	GET	Returns the POI of a given type closest to a set of coordinates
/point/nearest	GET	Returns the closest point to a set of coordinates
/route	POST	Calculates a Route
/route/lumi	POST	Calculates a Route that passes through LUMIs
/view	GET	Returns a view, given a filter and a data source

- **Map Component**: Built with Leaflet.js, this interactive map allows users to zoom, pan, and place markers for route planning. It integrates the OpenStreetMap Tile Server[8] for map tiles and the Nominatim API[9] for geocoding. Users can switch between different map themes (e.g., light or dark) and overlay geospatial data layers, such as traffic conditions or pollution levels, using Leaflet layers (see Fig. 8).

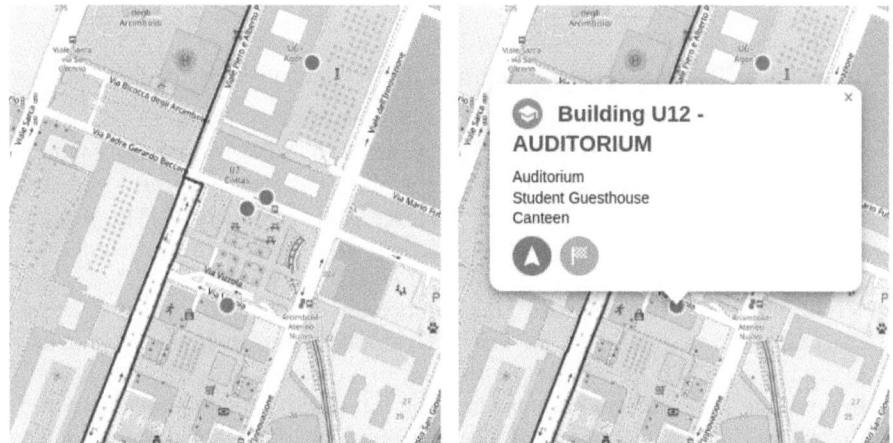

Fig. 8. A map showing cycleways, in blue, and campus buildings as red dots (left). The popup shown on the right gives information about the selected building. (Color figure online)

---

[8] https://wiki.openstreetmap.org/wiki/OpenStreetMap_Carto.
[9] https://nominatim.org.

– **Routing Options Component**: This module enables users to configure route preferences, including the selection of transportation modes (e.g., walking, biking, or driving) and additional constraints such as avoiding specific road types. Developed with React.js and Material-UI, it provides an intuitive interface for customizing routing parameters (see Fig. 9).

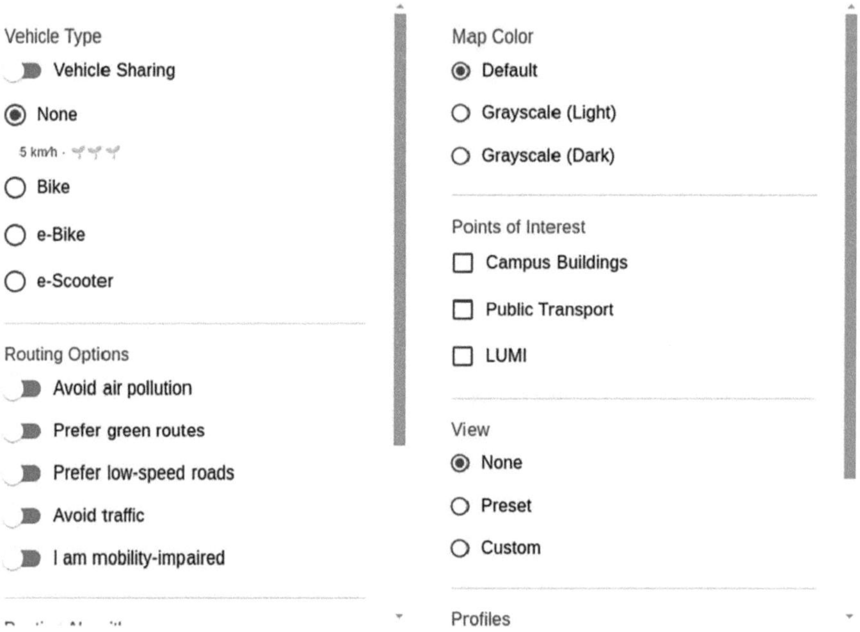

Fig. 9. The Routing Options panel (left) and the Visualization panel (right).

– **Route Planner Component**: This component allows users to calculate routes while displaying real-time updates on travel time, distance, and step-by-step directions. It dynamically retrieves routing data from the backend and renders the calculated route on the map with distinct markers and paths (see Fig. 10).
– **Visualization Component**: This component displays additional layers on the map that may be used for interactive operations, such as checking how many bikes are left at a LUMI or routing to a campus building. As shown in Fig. 11, the same system can also be used for static displays that allow users to explore datasets such as road network topology, traffic, or pollution levels. It also complements the routing system by providing a clear understanding of the influence of various factors on route selection based on user preferences and urban conditions. The visualization system has been built with React-MUI and Leaflet.js and is highly customizable, enabling users to tailor the displayed information to their specific needs. Figure 9 shows the Visualization panel, which can be used to turn layers on or off and change their appearance.

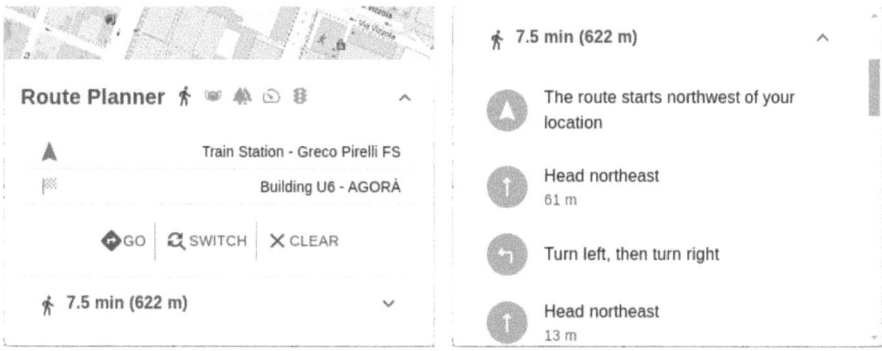

Fig. 10. The Route Planner (left) and the uncollapsed Directions section (right).

Fig. 11. Example of a data visualization overlay showing traffic data on the road network.

4 Use Case: Supporting Interactive Wayfinding for the MUSA Project

To validate our platform's feasibility and aid development, we created an application that caters to the needs of the MUSA project[10]. The prototype demonstrates the capabilities of the *Wiz*RD platform and aims at providing multimodal travel solutions for university students. As such, the application focuses on the area surrounding the main campus of the University of Milano-Bicocca, located in the Bicocca neighborhood of Milan.

---

[10] https://musascarl.it/.

4.1 The MUSA Project

This study was developed within the framework of the "Multi-layered Urban Sustainability Action (MUSA) – Spoke 1 – Urban Regeneration – Cities of the Future" project, funded by NextGenerationEU[11].

The MUSA framework involves a consortium of universities, research organizations, and companies under the leadership of the University of Milano-Bicocca. It aims to create a more sustainable, resilient, digital urban ecosystem by leveraging advanced research and public-private collaboration. In particular, Spoke 1 focuses on urban regeneration, seen from many different points of view. Among the objectives of Spoke 1 is the development of innovative strategies, practical methodologies, and intelligent tools for safe and sustainable intermodal mobility, supporting active mobility, and sustainable urban planning.

MUSA Spoke 1's research activities related to sustainable mobility focus on the university districts of Città Studi, Bicocca, and MIND in Milan and aim to develop innovative solutions for urban sustainability, including:

- Digitalization and green transition, to improve energy efficiency and reduce the environmental impact of cities.
- Sustainable mobility and intelligent infrastructure, focusing on low-impact transport and intelligent mobility.
- Urban regeneration and social inclusion to improve the quality of life in urban areas.

4.2 Usage Example

This section provides an example of how the MUSA Wayfinding application could be employed effectively for navigation on the Bicocca University campus.

Step 1 – Search: Students new to the campus must reach Building U7 for their class. Arriving at the campus by subway without a personal vehicle, they open the application and use the search bar to find the "Bicocca M5" subway station. The application returns several results, including the desired station. They select it, and a marker with a popup appears on the map. They tap the *Set as Starting Point* button from the popup, adding the metro station to the Route Planner.

Since they have a general idea of the location of building U7, they navigate to the Visualization panel and enable markers for all university buildings. They then tap on the marker closest to their estimated location of Building U7. When the popup appears, they set it as their destination using the appropriate button, adding the building to the Route Planner.

---

[11] https://musascarl.it/en/musa-urban-en/.

Step 2 – Route Preferences: Not feeling like walking, the students open the Routing Options menu and select the e-scooter rental option. Additionally, as they have asthma, they enable the *Avoid Pollution* preference to minimize exposure to pollutants that could trigger their condition. After closing the Routing Options menu, they observe that the icons in the Route Planner have updated: an e-scooter icon has appeared, and the face mask icon is now highlighted, indicating that their preferences have been applied.

Step 3 – Calculating the Route: The students tap the *Go!* button to initiate route calculation. The application then computes the most suitable course based on their preferences and proposes it to the students by visualizing it on the map. If the students are unsatisfied, they can modify one or more routing options to explore alternative paths.

5 Conclusions and Future Work

We presented *Wiz*RD, a wayfinding platform that integrates personalization and situational awareness, enabling users to define preferences and contextual needs through an intuitive interface. *Wiz*RD integrates diverse data sources and allows application administrators to enrich and customize the navigation graph. It also offers a visualization dashboard that helps users understand how personal preferences and environmental factors influence route selection.

An application developed within the MUSA project was designed to implement and validate the principles underlying *Wiz*RD, focusing on the area surrounding the University of Milano-Bicocca.

As future research avenues, integrating new data sources – including real-time data, such as traffic conditions or local event information – could improve the ability of *Wiz*RD to adapt to changing conditions dynamically and enhance the platform's ability to address increasingly diverse user needs. Moreover, the adoption of artificial intelligence and machine learning techniques could support more sophisticated route customization, enabling the platform to learn from user behavior and continuously refine its recommendations. However, while these technologies offer significant potential for personalization, they also introduce critical challenges related to bias, user privacy, and transparency. Thus, their integration should be handled with caution and with a clear understanding of these implications.

Collaboration with local authorities and mobility service providers could strengthen multimodal navigation (by having more and different vehicles available in LUMIs), improve data accuracy, and facilitate the platform's integration into broader urban mobility and sustainability initiatives. Ultimately, we believe that *Wiz*RD is also a valid tool for urban planners and policy-makers thanks to its powerful data processing and visualization systems. With the right combination of these components, the platform can assist in visualizing and identifying specific mobility patterns. As such, *Wiz*RD could be used to develop policies that promote safer, more inclusive, and more sustainable urban mobility practices.

Acknowledgement. This work has been developed within the MUSA – Multilayered Urban Sustainability Action – project, funded by the European Union – NextGenerationEU, under the National Recovery and Resilience Plan (NRRP) Mission 4 Component 2 Investment Line 1.5: Strengthening of research structures and creation of R&D "innovation ecosystems", set up of "territorial leaders in R&D".

References

1. Balata, J., Mikovec, Z., Slavik, P.: Landmark-enhanced route itineraries for navigation of blind pedestrians in urban environment. J. Multimodal User Interfaces **12**(3), 181–198 (2018). https://doi.org/10.1007/s12193-018-0263-5
2. Bast, H., et al.: Route planning in transportation networks (2015). https://arxiv.org/abs/1504.05140
3. Bolten, N., Mukherjee, S., Sipeeva, V., Tanweer, A., Caspi, A.: A pedestrian-centered data approach for equitable access to urban infrastructure environments. IBM J. Res. Dev. **61**(6), 10–1 (2017). https://doi.org/10.1147/JRD.2017.2736279
4. Campigotto, P., Rudloff, C., Leodolter, M., Bauer, D.: Personalized and situation-aware multimodal route recommendations: the FAVOUR algorithm. IEEE Trans. Intell. Transp. Syst. **18**(1), 92–102 (2017). https://doi.org/10.1109/TITS.2016.2565643
5. Cardoso, M., Milias, V., Harteveld, M.: Developing a city-specific walkability index through a participatory approach. AGILE: GIScience Ser. **5**, 2 (2024). https://doi.org/10.5194/agile-giss-5-2-2024. https://agile-giss.copernicus.org/articles/5/2/2024/
6. Palazzo, Y., Calegari, S., Avogadro, P., Dominoni, M.: The navigation of multi-itineraries for the cultural heritage context. In: Gervasi, O., et al. (eds.) ICCSA 2020. LNCS, vol. 12253, pp. 544–552. Springer, Cham (2020). https://doi.org/10.1007/978-3-030-58814-4_40
7. Taghipour, H., Parsa, A.B., Mohammadian, A.K.: A dynamic approach to predict travel time in real time using data-driven techniques and comprehensive data sources. Transp. Eng. **2**, 100025 (2020). https://doi.org/10.1016/j.treng.2020.100025

Development of a Walkability Index in Support of Urban Planning Decision-Making

Gerardo Carpentieri[✉] [iD], Carmen Guida[iD], and Andrés David Maglione[iD]

University of Naples Federico II, Napoli, Italy
gerardo.carpentieri@unina.it

Abstract. By 2030, cities will be home for more than 60% of the global population. In the drive for sustainability, the challenges facing urban planning will be particularly important. In this regard, walking emerges as a powerful tool. Walkable environments offer social, economic, and environmental benefits, but pedestrian mobility is often overlooked in urban infrastructure investments. Differently than the classical conception of "accessibility", "walkability" adds new emphasis on spatial quality and the capacity of the environment to encourage pedestrian mobility. Walkability is defined both as the degree to which open spaces encourage walking and, within suitable distances, the presence of accessible destinations. This article proposes a methodology integrating indirect audit and GIS-based for comprehensive assessment of walkability at the neighbourhood level. The results yield a gravitational accessibility measure enriched by a composite index, highlighting deficiencies in the open space system and guiding urban-planning interventions.

Keywords: First Keyword · Second Keyword · Third Keyword

1 Introduction

The escalating trend of urbanisation, with UN (United Nations) projections indicating that over 60% of the global population will reside in urban areas by 2030, presents significant challenges for sustainable urban development and public health [1]. Enhancing walking accessibility—or walkability—is increasingly recognised as a critical strategy to address these challenges. Walkable environments are linked to a multitude of social, economic, and environmental benefits [2], including improved public health through reduced chronic diseases [3, 4], lower air pollution [5], increased property values [6], enhanced social interaction and cohesion [7, 8], and various psychological benefits [9]. However, despite these clear advantages, investment in urban infrastructure often fails to adequately prioritise pedestrian mobility [10].

Historically, urban design since the advent of the automobile has predominantly favoured car-oriented layouts, with a strong emphasis on road and parking infrastructure. Consequently, retrofitting cities to be more pedestrian-friendly is not only costly but also confronts ingrained societal attitudes. The substantial long-term benefits of pedestrian-friendly policies are often underappreciated and overlooked in decision-making processes. This oversight is compounded by a general lack of comprehensive data on pedestrian movements, preferences, and needs, hindering policymakers' ability to justify and prioritise investments in appropriate infrastructure. Furthermore, urban planning practices frequently lack standardised methodologies capable of holistically accounting for the physical, social, and environmental variables influencing walkability, which are applicable for both ex-ante and ex-post evaluations.

The current state of the art in measuring pedestrian mobility largely focuses on quantitative metrics related to the distribution and accessibility of spaces, services, and movement activities, typically expressed in terms of impediments such as journey time, cost, and distance [12, 13]. While these methods provide valuable data on network efficiency and spatial reach, they possess a significant limitation: a tendency to overlook the crucial qualitative aspects of the urban environment that actively encourage or discourage walking. Factors such as the perceived attractiveness, safety, and comfort of routes, as well as the nuanced effects of individual constraints and preferences, are often inadequately captured [13–16]. Thus, conventional accessibility measures fall short of providing a comprehensive understanding of walkability, representing a distinct gap in the current literature and practical tools.

To address this identified gap and advance beyond existing methodologies, our research introduces a novel framework for assessing the quality of the urban walking environment. This framework employs a hybrid quantitative-qualitative methodology, which innovatively combines established accessibility measures (e.g., proximity to essential services) with a detailed qualitative and quantitative assessment of key features within the open-space network. Our focus on open spaces—defined in urban planning as unbuilt, publicly accessible areas like parks, squares, sidewalks, and greenways—is deliberate. These spaces are integral to pedestrian mobility and offer the highest potential for positive transformation. Safe, accessible, and well-designed open spaces are crucial for a successful pedestrian network, offering pleasant environments that encourage walking as a primary mode of transport and improving connectivity between different urban zones, thereby making walking a more attractive option and reducing reliance on motor vehicles [17].

This comprehensive approach aims to overcome the limitations of previous methods by providing a more holistic measure of walkability. The findings are expected to have significant implications for urban planning, offering practical solutions and robust data to support policymakers in identifying priority areas for intervention and in championing investment in pedestrian-centric urban futures.

2 Literature Review

"Walkability" can be seen as a measure of the extent to which an environment contributes to the promotion of walking as the main form of transport [18]. This concept transcends the classic definition of pedestrian "accessibility" as the distribution of opportunities in space, and takes into consideration factors that shape the relationships between individuals and urban space [14] Many studies, however, apply the terms of accessibility and walkability interchangeably [19, 20]. Recently, [21] systematically reviewed the proliferation of the two terms in pedestrian research, revealing that they have typically been used as near synonyms, particularly in relation to road design.

Within the scientific debate, accessibility is often applied as an operational concept expressing the degree of connection of an area with respect to the surrounding environment, i.e. transport linkages between land uses [22]. Accessibility can also be defined as the potential for interaction with a specific place within urban space, thus as the measurement of impediments to movement [11]. The literature provides further definitions of accessibility based on the economic theory of random utility, which states that individuals are rational agents that behave to maximize their expected benefit or utility [23, 24]. According to such approaches, utility-based accessibility measures the ease of reaching destinations of value to the individual, considering their specific needs and preferences.

However, for pedestrians, these definitions may be limiting. According to Hess [25], for example, accessibility in regard to walking could incorporate the idea of reaching multiple destinations within comfortable times, such as between five and twenty minutes. The concept of the "15-min city" emphasizes the importance of having essential services within comfortable walking distance. Moreno et al. [26] propose that destinations can be classified in terms of the six fundamental social functions of living, working, caring, provisioning, and recreation. The purpose of travel, however, can vary depending on socioeconomic factors. Weng et al. (2019) [27] assessed the relative importance of services in categories such as education, healthcare, municipal administration, finance, telecommunications, commercial services and services for the elderly. The importance of these was evaluated through a questionnaire that asked respondents to specify the frequency of their visits to the services within a month. The results showed that distinct categories of the population visited services of different natures; for example, markets were more frequently visited by the elderly than schools.

Table 1 summarises six studies that, as in Weng et al. [27], propose methodologies for measurement of pedestrian accessibility to essential services at the neighbourhood level. Each study examines a different city, examining the proximity of essential services referenced by the planning documents for the different municipalities. Plan Melbourne 2017–2050 [28], for example, proposes that pedestrian accessibility to essential services can create healthier and more liveable communities, and that accessibility must be considered in relation to combinations of land uses, housing types and quality public transportation. Plan Melbourne introduces the concept of the "20-min neighbourhood" in three pilot projects: Croydon South, Strathmore, and Sunshine West, where 20 min is the desired limit for arrival to or return from a service, on foot. Examining the six studies for the different cities, we are able to identify seven service categories to which access is seen as essential for the activities of neighbourhood residents.

Both the academic and non-academic literature (scientific and grey literature) tend to define pedestrian accessibility quantitatively, as the sum of services and opportunities reachable on foot from a starting point, typically a person's residence. However, focusing solely on residence as the starting point for accessibility measures can be restrictive [29].

The levels of pedestrian mobility, however, does not depend solely on the distribution of activities and their distances from the individuals' residence [14]. Pedestrians will make their choices differently, varying their destinations and routes based on personal and environmental factors [30]. In recent years, therefore, there has been a trend

Table 1. Municipalities and proximity services.

		Edinburgh	Barcelona	Alghero	Krakow	Melbourne	Gothenburg
Mobility	Bus Stop	*	*		*	*	*
	Train Stop		*		*	*	
	Parking Spot	*					
	Bike Stop						*
Education	Nursery			*	*	*	*
	Preschool	*	*	*	*	*	
	Primary School	*	*	*	*	*	
	Secondary School	*	*	*		*	
	University			*			
	Library	*		*	*	*	
Food retail	Market	*		*	*	*	*
	Supermarket	*		*	*	*	*
	Restaurant	*		*	*	*	
	Bar	*			*	*	
Retail	Shop	*		*	*		*
Health	Assistance			*		*	*
	Clinic			*			
	Pharmacy					*	*
	Hospital			*			
Leisure	Cinema	*		*			*
	Theatre	*		*			
	Museum			*			
	Sport facility				*	*	*
	Gym				*		*
Urban space	Green area	*		*	*	*	*
	Square	*		*		*	*
	Playground	*			*		*
		[50]	[47]	[14]	[48]	[28]	[49]

towards including perceptive and social factors in measurement of "walkability", advancing a more multidimensional concept [15], in particular including consideration of the environmental character of open spaces in the development of measures of pedestrian accessibility [15, 31].

Researchers have explored different spatial factors related to walkability. Cervero & Kockelman (1997) [32] found that higher building density, mixed land use, and well-designed urban landscapes can reduce car dependence and promote choices for mobility via public transportation, cycling and walking. The authors summarise the determining factors along dimensions of "Density, Diversity, and Design (3D)". Additional dimensions, including proximity to public transportation and destination accessibility, have been incorporated over time and the list of spatial factors associated with walkability has grown considerably. Ewing & Handy (2009) [33] classify the characteristics of the urban environment that encourage walking into five categories: imaginability, enclosure, human scale, transparency, and complexity. The London Planning Advisory Committee (2004) introduced the "5C" approach, emphasizing that pedestrian-friendly places should be "connected, convenient, comfortable, convivial, and conspicuous". Moura et al. (2017) [34] subsequently expanded this, arguing that citizens must be involved in shaping the walkable street environment, and therefore that planning must consider "coexistence and engagement".

The conceptualization of open space as a network of potential movement can assist planners in encouraging walking choices. Surfaces can be classified as exclusively pedestrian (e.g. pedestrian-only streets), mixed (parallel flows of pedestrian and vehicles), and crossing (signalled or non-signalled). Design should limit conflicts between cars and pedestrians through the separation of surfaces [35] and should provide plausible "desired lines" for pedestrian movement, including appropriate crossings.

In line with Blečić et al. (2020) [36], we survey the literature considering four factors in the conception of walkability in urban spaces: (1) efficiency and comfort; (2) safety; (3) pleasantness; and (4) attractiveness. Within each of these, we attempt to group the variables with the greatest influence on that factor of walkability. Our proposal is that design in consideration of these factors and variables can improve the potential of the built environment, allowing more effective use of opportunities. The factors are not mutually exclusive, but rather complement each other and contribute to a comprehensive evaluation of walkability. Table 1 summarizes found in literature and linked with the four factors of walkability.

Beginning from theoretical definitions, researchers have developed techniques for the assessment of walkability. These can be classified into two main operational categories: assessment at the macro level (city, city sector), and at the street or neighbourhood level.

The studies at macroscale apply factors such as connectivity, density and variety of uses into consideration in the measure of pedestrian accessibility [46]. A popular tool in this category is the Walk Score (2023) [47], which uses an algorithm to assign points to areas based on distance from services, population density and other metrics. The Walkability Index [48] considers building density, multifunctionality and connectivity (measured by calculating the frequency of road junctions in each area), as well as the net areas of commercial activities. The operability of macroscale studies is supported by GIS (Geographical Information System) software such as ArcGIS, GRASS or QGIS, which simplify data collection and processing. QGIS in particular is an easy-to-use

Table 2. Factors and ensamples of variables influencing walkability.

Factors	Description	Examples of Variables	References
Efficiency and Comfort	Convenience and ease of walking and no presence of difficulties and constraints. Includes physical features that affect pedestrian movement and the use of open space	Cost; Distance; Time; Route continuity; Protection; Lighting; Floor maintenance; Transit signals	[37–39]
Safety	Exposure of pedestrians to traffic-related risks (including conflict factors and interference or protection) and the sense of personal security understood as uncertainty transmitted by the urban environment	Traffic volume; Maximum speed; Street parking; Crossing geometry; Flow separation; Acoustic and Light signals; Crime rate; Lighting; Cleanliness level	[40, 41]
Pleasantness	"Vibrant" and "beautiful" atmosphere that features an urban design which encourages the pedestrian to spend time in that space	Space atmosphere; Aesthetics; Architectural and Urban design quality; Surface texture; Building permeability; Urban texture	[34, 42, 43]
Attractiveness	Presence, opportunities and services accessible on foot	Number; Density; Measure and Diversity of space uses; Hours of operation; Number of opportunities; Frequency of service	[14, 44, 45]

open-source platform, operable on a full range of functions using algorithms loaded as code or plugins.

Studies at the neighbourhood or street level, instead, typically assess the quality of paths, directing attention to the physical and perceptual characteristics of the built environment, such as sidewalk width, qualities of pavement, permeability of open spaces, but also the sense of security [49]. This type of evaluation can be carried out using surveys, interviews and questionnaires, and through direct audits by expert observers, analysing subjective factors related to walkability. The better-known direct audit methods include SPACES (Systematic Pedestrian and Cycling Environmental Scan), the PBIC Checklist (Pedestrian and Bicycle Information Center) and PEDS (Pedestrian Environment Data Scan). In place of visual checks at street level, the audit of the built environment can also be conducted by tools such as Google Street View [40, 41]. Differently than direct audit or interviews, some methodologies assess walkability though GPS-linked data provided by the mobile phones of pedestrians, or gathered using machine learning [51–53].

From this literature review, we can see that the concept of walkability has evolved over time, in particular taking on multidimensional and multiscale aspects for a fuller, more wholistic vision of the relationships between pedestrians and urban space, and applying mixed tools of data gathering in assessment.

3 Methodology

Open spaces, in the context of urban planning, refer to areas that are not built upon and are typically accessible to the public, such as sidewalks, squares, parks and green spaces. Walkability is then understood as the degree to which the system of open spaces, and presence of destinations useful in daily life, encourages and supports walking as the mobility mode. The main objective of methodology presented in this paper is the creation of a walkability index at a neighbourhood scale, that can be implemented to support urban planning decision processes.

Figure 1 shows the methodology workflow, which consists of five phases. First, the open space system is identified and conceptualized as a network. Next, data on the system's components, as well as origins and destinations, are collected. Then, each component of the system is assigned a grade based on four factors, collectively forming the Walkability Index (W_i), thereby evaluating the quality of the open spaces. This W_i is then incorporated into the Total Walkability Score (TWS), an accessibility assessment that also accounts for the time needed to reach destinations. Finally, the Total Walkability Score helps identify the areas with the most critical issues, and guides the implementation of interventions.

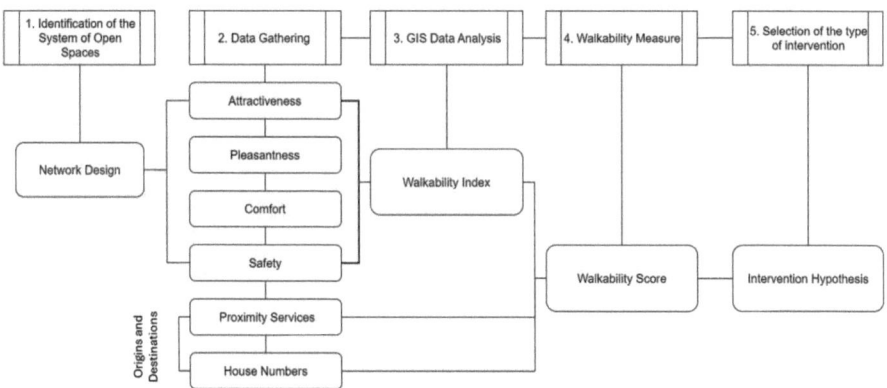

Fig. 1. Methodology workflow

The proposed measure takes the name of Total Walkability Score (TWS), representing the degree of proximity of a destination from an origin, following a walking path within open space that is attractive, pleasant, comfortable and safe. The component terms are defined as follows:

1. Origin – a pedestrian residence;
2. Destination – the service areas grouped under the seven categories indicated in Table 1 of the preceding literature review;

3. Path – the route between origin and destination with least restrictions, conceptualized in terms of the types of surfaces travelled by pedestrians through the relative open spaces;
4. Attractiveness, comfort, pleasantness and safety – the factors listed in Table 2 of the preceding literature review, represented by the selection of independent and observable variables explaining the relative factor.

$$TWS_n = \sum K_m * \delta_m \quad (1) \qquad TWS_n \in \{0,1\}$$

$$\begin{cases} \begin{cases} \delta_m = 1 \rightarrow p_n \in \Omega_m \\ \delta_m = 0 \nrightarrow p_n \in \Omega_m \end{cases} & \begin{array}{l} p_n = \text{n-th origin} \\ \Omega_m = \text{Service area of typology of the m-th service} \\ t_{mn} = \text{Time from n to m} \\ W_i = \text{Walkability index of the i-th component} \\ v: 5 \text{ km/h} \\ l_i = \text{I-th segment length} \end{array} \\ \begin{cases} p_n \in \Omega_m \rightarrow t_{mn} \\ \leq 15 min \\ t_{mn} = \sum (W_i * v) * l_i \end{cases} \end{cases} \quad (1)$$

The TWS represents the sum of the weights K_m of each service category that can be accessed in a maximum time of 15 min, considered as the maximum time that each pedestrian is willing to walk. δ_m represents is a Kronecker delta, which assumes the value 1 when the destination is reachable within the selected threshold and 0 if not. Equation 1 is used to calculate the TWS of the segment n though the weighted sum of the values of each variable.

The Walkability Index (W_i) is integrated within the measurement in the calculation of the time needed to reach the proximity service. This measure is multiplied by the average pedestrian speed that is assumed equal to 5 km/h according with previous literature [43, 44] and by the length of each stretch travelled, which varies from section to section. The W_i measures the suitability of the pedestrian paths inside the open spaces. It can be analytically computed using Eq. 2, so that it represents the weighted sum of four indices (Safety Index (Is), Attractiveness Index (Ia), Comfort and Efficiency Index (Ic) and Pleasantness Index (Ip)) that represent factors not directly measurable, but which are explained by 14 qualitative and quantitative variables. The K represents the weight of each factor.

$$W_i = K_s \cdot Is_i + K_c \cdot Ic_i + K_a \cdot Ia_i + K_p \cdot Ip_i$$
$$K_s + K_c + K_a + K_p = 1 \qquad (2)$$
$$W_i \in \{0, 1\}$$

4 Conclusions

Walkability is a concept that extends beyond mere accessibility, considering not just the proximity of destinations but also the crucial quality of pedestrian paths and the overall user experience. While accessibility is traditionally defined as the potential for interaction within urban space, focusing on quantifiable factors like time, cost, and distance [54], walkability delves deeper. It considers the spatial quality of the environment and how it actively encourages or discourages pedestrian mobility [46].

A review of the literature reveals that accessibility and walkability are often conflated, leading to knowledge gaps in urban planning practices. Many studies prioritize quantitative accessibility metrics without sufficiently incorporating the qualitative aspects vital to walkability, such as perceived safety, comfort, and aesthetic appeal. This narrow focus can result in planning strategies that, while providing accessible environments, fail to create genuinely walkable ones, thereby discouraging pedestrian activity even when destinations are nearby. For instance, a neighbourhood may feature well-distributed amenities, but poor sidewalk conditions or unsafe street crossings can significantly deter walking.

Our study addresses this critical gap by proposing a novel hybrid methodology that integrates both quantitative and qualitative approaches to assess walkability comprehensively. This methodology builds upon existing literature but significantly extends it by focusing on a holistic evaluation of urban features that influence people's willingness to walk. Unlike previous models that primarily consider impediments such as time, cost, and distance, our approach also meticulously assesses the qualitative dimensions of the walking experience.

The methodology utilizes two interconnected components: a Walkability Index (Wi) to evaluate the quality of individual pedestrian paths and a Total Walkability Score (TWS) to account for the broader network structure and service locations. Specifically, the Walkability Index (Wi) evaluates the quality of pedestrian paths within the open space network by considering four key factors: safety, comfort, attractiveness, and pleasantness. Each factor is further broken down into measurable variables, with weights assigned based on a targeted survey of pedestrian preferences. The Total Walkability Score (TWS) then combines the Wi with data on network structure and the location of origins (e.g., residences) and destinations (e.g., proximity services). It reflects pedestrian accessibility to services while critically considering the quality of the walking experience required to reach them. The TWS is calculated by identifying services reachable within a 15-min walk along suitable paths, factoring in the service type's weight derived from another user survey.

This GIS-based methodology is designed to provide effective support for decision-making in policy and planning, offering a comprehensive assessment of the multifaceted concept of walkability. It moves beyond traditional accessibility measures by systematically integrating the quality of pedestrian paths with service proximity, utilizing both objective open-source data and resident preference data collected via questionnaires. Combining the results of Wi and TWS with population density data can guide decision-makers towards prioritising interventions in areas with the most significant need for improvement. To further substantiate its practical application and demonstrate its added value, future developments of this study will involve a rigorous comparison of our proposed indicators (Wi and TWS) with established walkability and accessibility measures. This comparative analysis will ideally be tested across diverse urban case studies, aiming to validate the enhanced insights and practical benefits our comprehensive framework offers to urban planners and policymakers.

References

1. Vardoulakis, S., Kinney, P.: Grand challenges in sustainable cities and health. Front. Sustain. Cities (2019). https://doi.org/10.3389/frsc.2019.00007
2. Litman, T.A.: Economic value of walkability. J. Transp. Res. Board **1828**(1), 3–11 (2003). https://doi.org/10.3141/1828-01
3. Paulo dos Anjos Souza Barbosa, J., et al.: Walkability, overweight, and obesity in adults: a systematic review of observational studies. Int. J. Environ. Res. Public Health **16**(17), 3135 (2019). https://doi.org/10.3390/ijerph16173135
4. Wali, B., Frank, L.D., Chapman, J., Fox, E.H.: Role of walkability, bike infrastructure, and greenspace in combatting chronic diseases: a heterogeneous ecological analysis in the United States. Sustain. Cities Soc. **113**, 105550 (2024). https://doi.org/10.1016/j.scs.2024.105550
5. Keall, M.D., Shaw, C., Chapman, R., Howden-Chapman, P.: Reductions in carbon dioxide emissions from an intervention to promote cycling and walking: a case study from New Zealand. Transp. Res. Part D: Transp. Environ. **65**, 687–696 (2018). https://doi.org/10.1016/j.trd.2018.10.004
6. Kim, E.J., Kim, H.: Neighborhood walkability and housing prices: a correlation study. Sustainability **12**(2), 593 (2020). https://doi.org/10.3390/su12020593
7. Baobeid, A., Koç, M., Al-Ghamdi, S.G.: Walkability and its relationships with health, sustainability, and livability: elements of physical environment and evaluation frameworks. Front. Built Environ. (2021). https://doi.org/10.3389/fbuil.2021.721218
8. Sonta, A., Jiang, X.: Rethinking walkability: exploring the relationship between urban form and neighborhood social cohesion. Sustain. Cities Soc. **99**, 104903 (2023). https://doi.org/10.1016/j.scs.2023.104903
9. Johansson, M., Hartig, T., Staats, H.: Psychological benefits of walking: moderation by company and outdoor environment. Appl. Psychol. Health Well Being **3**(3), 261–280 (2011). https://doi.org/10.1111/j.1758-0854.2011.01051.x
10. Yang, L., van Dam, K.H., Majumdar, A., Anvari, B., Ochieng, W.Y., Zhang, L.: Integrated design of transport infrastructure and public spaces considering human behavior: a review of state-of-the-art methods and tools. Front. Architect. Res. **8**(4), 429–453 (2019). https://doi.org/10.1016/j.foar.2019.08.003
11. Hansen, W.G.: How accessibility shapes land use. J. Am. Inst. Plann. **25**(2), 73–76 (1959). https://doi.org/10.1080/01944365908978307
12. Soria-Lara, J.A., Valenzuela-Montes, L.M., Pinho, P.: Using 'mobility environments" in practice: lessons from a metropolitan transit corridor in Spain. J. Environ. Planning Policy Manage. **17**(5), 553–572 (2015). https://doi.org/10.1080/1523908X.2014.991779
13. Lo, R.H.: Walkability: what is it? J. Urbanism: Int. Res. Placemaking Urban Sustain. **2**(2), 145–166 (2009). https://doi.org/10.1080/17549170903092867
14. Blečić, I., Cecchini, A., Fancello, G., Talu, V., Trunfio, G.A.: Walkability and urban capabilities: evaluation and planning decision support. Territorio (2015). https://doi.org/10.14609/Ti_1_15_4e
15. Forsyth, A.: What is a walkable place? The walkability debate in urban design. Urban Des. Int. **20**(4), 274–292 (2015). https://doi.org/10.1057/udi.2015.22
16. Carpentieri, G., et al.: Perceptions of safety for women in urban areas: a spatial regression analysis in the City of Naples. In: Gervasi, O., Murgante, B., Garau, C., Taniar, D., Maria, A., Rocha, A.C., Noelia, M., Lago, F. (eds.) Computational Science and Its Applications – ICCSA 2024 Workshops: Hanoi, Vietnam, July 1–4, 2024, Proceedings, Part IX, pp. 35–48. Springer Nature Switzerland, Cham (2024). https://doi.org/10.1007/978-3-031-65329-2_3
17. Guida, C., Carpentieri, G.: Quality of life in the urban environment and primary health services for the elderly during the Covid-19 pandemic: an application to the city of Milan (Italy). Cities **110**, 103038 (2021). https://doi.org/10.1016/j.cities.2020.103038

18. Southworth, M.: Designing the walkable City. J. Urban Plann. Dev. **131**(4), 246–257 (2005). https://doi.org/10.1061/(ASCE)0733-9488(2005)131:4(246)
19. Van Kamp, I., Leidelmeijer, K., Marsman, G., De Hollander, A.: Urban environmental quality and human well-being. Landsc. Urban Plan. **65**(1–2), 5–18 (2003). https://doi.org/10.1016/s0169-2046(02)00232-3
20. Eckert, N.H., Padilha, J.C.: Terminologies and definitions for urban planning. In: Filho, W.L., Azul, A.M., Brandli, L., Özuyar, P.G., Wall, T. (eds.) Industry, Innovation and Infrastructure, pp. 1–10. Springer International Publishing, Cham (2019). https://doi.org/10.1007/978-3-319-71059-4_80-2
21. Abusaada, H., Elshater, A.: Decoding near synonyms in pedestrianization research: a numerical analysis and summative approach. Urban Sci. **8**(2), 45 (2024). https://doi.org/10.3390/urbansci8020045
22. Guida, C., Caglioni, M.: Urban accessibility: the paradox, the paradigms and the measures. A scientific review. TeMA – J. Land Use, Mobility Environ. **2**, 149–168 (2020). https://doi.org/10.6092/1970-9870/6743
23. Nassir, N., Hickman, M., Malekzadeh, A., Irannezhad, E.: A utility-based travel impedance measure for public transit network accessibility. Transport. Res. Part a Policy Pract. **88**, 26–39 (2016). https://doi.org/10.1016/j.tra.2016.03.007
24. Guzman, L.A., Cantillo-Garcia, V.A., Oviedo, D., Arellana, J.: How much is accessibility worth? Utility-based accessibility to evaluate transport policies. J. Transp. Geogr. **112**, 103683 (2023). https://doi.org/10.1016/j.jtrangeo.2023.103683
25. Hess, D.B.: Walking to the bus: perceived versus actual walking distance to bus stops for older adults. Transportation **39**(2), 247–266 (2012). https://doi.org/10.1007/s11116-011-9341-1
26. Moreno, C., Allam, Z., Chabaud, D., Gall, C., Pratlong, F.: Introducing the "15-minute city": sustainability, resilience and place identity in future post-pandemic cities. Smart Cities **4**(1), 93–111 (2021). https://doi.org/10.3390/smartcities4010006
27. Weng, M., et al.: The 15-minute walkable neighborhoods: measurement, social inequalities and implications for building healthy communities in urban China. J. Transp. Health **13**, 259–273 (2019). https://doi.org/10.1016/j.jth.2019.05.005
28. State Government of Victoria: Plan Melbourne 2017–2050 (2017). https://www.planning.vic.gov.au/guides-and-resources/strategies-and-initiatives/plan-melbourne/the-plan
29. Saelens, B.E., Sallis, J.F., Frank, L.D.: Environmental correlates of walking and cycling: findings from the transportation, urban design, and planning literatures. Ann. Behav. Med. **25**(2), 80–91 (2003). https://doi.org/10.1207/S15324796ABM2502_03
30. Fonseca, F., et al.: Built environment attributes and their influence on walkability. Int. J. Sustain. Transp. **16**(7), 660–679 (2022). https://doi.org/10.1080/15568318.2021.1914793
31. Papa, E., Carpentieri, G., Guida, C.: Measuring walking accessibility to public transport for the elderly: the case of Naples. TeMA – J. Land Use, Mobility Environ. 105–116 (2018). https://doi.org/10.6092/1970-9870/5766
32. Cervero, R., Kockelman, K.: Travel demand and the 3Ds: density, diversity, and design. Transp. Res. Part D: Transp. Environ. **2**(3), 199–219 (1997). https://doi.org/10.1016/S1361-9209(97)00009-6
33. Ewing, R., Handy, S.: Measuring the unmeasurable: Urban design qualities related to walkability. J. Urban Des. **14**(1), 65–84 (2009). https://doi.org/10.1080/13574800802451155
34. Moura, F., Cambra, P., Gonçalves, A.B.: Measuring walkability for distinct pedestrian groups with a participatory assessment method: a case study in Lisbon. Landsc. Urban Plan. **157**, 282–296 (2017). https://doi.org/10.1016/J.LANDURBPLAN.2016.07.002
35. Baghdadi, N., Mallet, C., Zribi, M.: Network Analysis and Routing with QGIS-(2018). http://www.portailsig.org/content/grass-gis-geometries-topologies-et-consequences-pratiques

36. Blečić, I., Congiu, T., Fancello, G., Trunfio, G.A.: Planning and design support tools for walkability: a guide for Urban analysts. Sustainability **12**(11), 4405 (2020). https://doi.org/10.3390/su12114405
37. Arellana, J., Saltarín, M., Larrañaga, A.M., Alvarez, V., Henao, C.A.: Urban walkability considering pedestrians' perceptions of the built environment: a 10-year re-view and a case study in a medium-sized city in Latin America. Transp. Rev. **40**(2), 183–203 (2020). https://doi.org/10.1080/01441647.2019.1703842
38. Ortega, E., Martín, B., López-Lambas, M.E., Soria-Lara, J.A.: Evaluating the impact of urban design scenarios on walking accessibility: the case of the Madrid 'Centro' district. Sustain. Cities Soc. **74**, 103156 (2021). https://doi.org/10.1016/j.scs.2021.103156
39. Rahman, A.: A GIS-based, microscale walkability assessment integrating the local topography. J. Transp. Geogr. **103**, 103405 (2022). https://doi.org/10.1016/j.jtrangeo.2022.103405
40. Global Designing Cities Initiative: Global Street Design Guide. ISBN: 9781610917018 (2016). https://globaldesigningcities.org/publication/global-street-design-guide/utilities-and-infrastructure/lighting-and-technology/lighting-design-guidance/
41. Montella, A., Chiaradonna, S., De Saint Mihiel, A.C., Lovegrove, G., Nunziante, P., Riccardi, M.R.: Sustainable complete streets design criteria and case study in Naples, Italy. Sustainability **14**(20), 13142 (2022). https://doi.org/10.3390/su142013142car
42. D'Orso, G., Migliore, M.: A GIS-based method for evaluating the walkability of a pedestrian environment and prioritised investments. J. Transp. Geogr. **82**, 102555 (2020). https://doi.org/10.1016/j.jtrangeo.2019.102555
43. Ignaccolo, M., Inturri, G., Giuffrida, N., Le Pira, M., Torrisi, V., Calabrò, G.: A step towards walkable environments: spatial analysis of pedestrian compatibility in an urban context. Trasporti Europei 76, Paper N° 6 (2020).
44. Gorrini, A.: GIS and Space Syntax Applications for Environmental Psychology: The case of walkability for children in Bologna (2021). https://doi.org/10.13140/RG.2.2.36348.67207
45. Stefanidis, R.-M., Bartzokas-Tsiompras, A.: Where to improve pedestrian streetscapes: prioritizing and mapping street-level walkability interventions in Cape Town's city centre. Urbani Izziv **33**(2), 115–126 (2022). https://doi.org/10.5379/urbani-izziv-en-2022-33-02-05
46. Telega, A., Telega, I., Bieda, A.: Measuring walkability with GIS—methods overview and new approach proposal. Sustainability **13**(4), 1–17 (2021). https://doi.org/10.3390/su13041883
47. Walk Score (2023). https://www.walkscore.com/
48. Leslie, E., Coffee, N., Frank, L., Owen, N., Bauman, A., Hugo, G.: Walkability of local communities: using geographic information systems to objectively assess relevant environmental attributes. Health Place **13**(1), 111–122 (2007). https://doi.org/10.1016/j.healthplace.2005.11.001
49. Muhs, C.D., Clifton, K.J.: Do characteristics of walkable environments support bicycling? Toward a definition of bicycle-supported development. J. Transport Land Use **9**(2), 147–188 (2016). https://doi.org/10.5198/jtlu.2015.727
50. Ki, D., Chen, Z., Lee, S., Lieu, S.: A novel walkability index using google street view and deep learning. Sustain. Cities Soc. **99**, 104896 (2023). https://doi.org/10.1016/j.scs.2023.104896
51. Yin, L., Wang, Z.: Measuring visual enclosure for street walkability: using machine learning algorithms and Google Street View imagery. Appl. Geogr. **76**, 147–153 (2016). https://doi.org/10.1016/j.apgeog.2016.09.024
52. Di Ruocco, I.: Mobilising equity. Emerging evidence for integrating vulnerable communities. TeMA - J. Land Use, Mobil. Environ. **18**(1), 95–112 (2025). https://doi.org/10.6093/1970-9870/10872

53. D'Amico, A.: Urban spaces and pedestrian mobility: the role of urban design for enhancing walkability. TeMA - J. Land Use, Mobil. Environ. **16**(3), 639–644 (2023). https://doi.org/10.6093/1970-9870/10327
54. Tekolla, A.W., Tarekegn, A.G., Tulu, G.S.: Measuring the walkability of areas around Addis Ababa LRT stations by integrating Analytic Hierarchal Process (AHP) and GIS. TeMA - J. Land Use, Mobil. Environ. **17**(3), 423–438 (2024). https://doi.org/10.6093/1970-9870/11025

Virtual Reality and Augmented reality and applications (VRA 2025)

Real-Time Rigging and Secondary Motion for Sketch-Based 3D Characters

Chau Thi Ma and Tam Minh Le(✉)

Faculty of Information Technology, VNU University of Engineering and Technology, Hanoi, Vietnam
`letam166204@gmail.com`

Abstract. Sketch-based modeling systems simplify the creation of 3D characters, but animating them remains a challenging task due to the complexity of rigging and secondary motion control. Traditional animation workflows require extensive manual effort to define skeletal structures and dynamic motion, making the process time-consuming and technically demanding. This creates a gap between creative expression and technical challenges. To address the problem, we propose an interactive framework that combines real-time skeletonization with secondary motion generation using a mass-spring system. Our system includes three key functions: (i) the user sketches a character, (ii) the system automatically generates a rigged skeleton, and (iii) the system applies dynamic animations without the need for manual keyframing. The system combines the best aspects of two methods: the simplicity and accessibility of sketch-based modeling, and the expressive, physics-driven secondary motion provided by the mass-spring system. Beginner animators can create expressive, physics-driven animations effortlessly without tedious adjustments.

Keywords: Sketch-based modeling · Mass-spring system · Real-time animation

1 Introduction

Computer graphics (CG) play a fundamental role in various industries, including video games, virtual and augmented reality (VR/AR), scientific visualization, material simulation, and education [18]. In the gaming industry, animations enhance player immersion and bring characters to life. VR and AR applications rely on dynamic 3D content to create interactive experiences, while material simulations use physics-based animations to study real-world behavior in engineering and scientific fields. As CG continues to expand into new domains, the demand for accessible and efficient 3D modeling and animation tools has grown significantly.

However, creating 3D animations remains a challenging and labor-intensive process that requires expertise in multiple disciplines. 3D modeling, the first step in animation, involves constructing detailed objects and characters, often requiring years of practice with tools like Blender[1] 3ds Max[2] and Maya[3] To simplify this process, sketch-based modeling systems such as Teddy [12], MonsterMash [8], and FiberMesh [20] have been developed. These systems allow users to generate plausible 3D models from 2D sketches, significantly lowering the barrier to entry for beginners.

While sketch-based modeling helps create static 3D models, rigging—the process of defining an internal skeleton and binding it to a mesh—remains a major hurdle. Rigging requires technical proficiency and manual adjustments to ensure proper articulation for animation. To address this, automatic skeletonization systems such as RealSkel [16] and RigMesh [5] have been introduced, reducing the need for manual rigging and streamlining the animation workflow.

Even with rigged models, animation is still complex, especially when incorporating secondary motion effects like swaying hair, bouncing cloth, or dynamic character movement. Various physics-based animation techniques have been developed to assist animators, including Fast Mass-spring Systems [15], spring bone dynamics in tools like Cartoon Animator 5[4] These techniques automate secondary motion, enhancing realism without requiring frame-by-frame keyframing.

As seen in this workflow, animation is a multi-step process that includes modeling, rigging, and animation, not to mention additional elements like texturing and lighting [9]. Even though many tools exist, beginner animators may still struggle to integrate all these processes seamlessly. The steep learning curve and technical complexity can hinder creativity and slow down production. To bridge this gap, we introduce a sketch-based 3D modeling system with real-time skeletonization and built-in spring bone dynamics. Our system leverages the real-time skeletonization technique RealSkel [16] by integrating the Fast Mass-spring system [15]. This allows for automatic rigging while introducing real-time dynamic, bouncy effects, eliminating the need for manual setup. Our method is heavily inspired by Fast Mass-spring Systems [15] but differs in two key aspects. While their study focuses on physically accurate motion, our framework emphasizes secondary motion to enhance expressiveness, with less focus on achieving perfect realism. Secondly, whereas existing approaches treat mass-spring systems as mesh-based physics simulations for cloth and hair, we simplify the process by using spring bones for object animation. This makes our system more intuitive and accessible for novice users in animation.

2 Background and Notation

2.1 Related Works

Sketch-Based Modeling. The pioneering sketch-based system, Teddy [12], significantly simplifies shape modeling by allowing users to create 3D forms with

---

[1] Blender2023: https://www.blender.org.
[2] Max2023: https://www.autodesk.com/products/3ds-max.
[3] Maya2023: https://www.autodesk.com/products/maya.
[4] Cartoon Animator 5: https://www.reallusion.com/cartoon-animator/.

just a few strokes. Over time, numerous follow-up works [8,14,20,25,26] have expanded on this approach, enabling the creation of more complex shapes and making sketch-based modeling more comprehensive. These systems offer a fun and intuitive experience for novice users, making 3D modeling more accessible. However, their simplicity can be a drawback for professionals who require precise control over model accuracy.

Rigging and Skeletonization. In modern character animation pipelines, a rig consists of a skeleton, a cycle-free graph where nodes represent joints and edges represent bones. Skin weights define how the model's surface deforms in response to skeletal movement [5]. Because of the complexity of the manual process, automatic skeletonization and rigging techniques have been extensively researched. Given a static character mesh and a generic skeleton, Pinocchio [3] adapts the skeleton to the character and attaches it to the surface, allowing skeletal motion data to animate the character. RigMesh [6] extends this concept by creating a rig for each sketched part in real-time, and update the rig as parts are merged or cut. More recent approaches have leveraged deep learning for automation. RigNet [29] introduces a neural network that predicts a skeleton that matches the animator expectations in joint placement and topology. For single-image rigging, Object Wake-up [30] reconstructs 3D objects and generates skeletons from 2D images using deep implicit functions. Specifically for sketch-based modeling, RealSkel [16] provides a real-time skeletonization technique. Despite these advancements, automatic skeletonization and rigging alone is not sufficient for high-quality animation. Proper rigging still requires refinement, such as adjusting joint positions, fine-tuning skin weights, and incorporating inverse kinematics (IK).

Mass-Spring System. Mass-spring systems have long been used in both scientific computing and physics-based animation to simulate movement and deformation [4]. These systems represent objects as networks of interconnected masses and springs, enabling realistic simulations of elasticity, bending, and other physical behaviors. Early models for cloth simulation [7,22] demonstrated how simple physics-based structures could produce visually convincing motion. They have also been applied to approximate the deformation of volumetric solids [27] and linear elements such as hair [23,24]. Spring bone dynamics, as seen in tools like Cartoon Animator 5[5] and VRM[6] provide simplified secondary motion effects, making them valuable for game development and AR/VR applications. Researchers have also improved these methods for greater stability and efficiency, with the Fast Mass-Spring method [15] introducing a more efficient solver for real-time deformable object simulation.

After reviewing related works, we find that RealSkel [16] and the Fast Mass-Spring method [15] align well with our research objectives. These methods fulfill key requirements, including real-time skeletonization to quickly generate an ani-

---

[5] Cartoon Animator 5: https://www.reallusion.com/cartoon-animator/spring-animation.html.

[6] Vrm Springbone: https://vrm.dev/en/univrm/springbone/univrm_secondary/.

matable skeleton from sketches, and efficient mass-spring simulations for responsive motion. Therefore, in the following sections, we examine the fundamental concepts behind these two influential works. A clear understanding of their methodologies is essential for implementing our system and effectively integrating their strengths.

2.2 Real-Time Skeletonization for Sketch-Based Modeling

The method consists of three main steps: local sub-skeleton extraction, sub-skeleton connection, and global skeleton refinement. First, the local skeleton is extracted from the processed polygon stroke, forming a subpart along with the corresponding sub-mesh. Next, individual sub-skeletons are connected based on their intersections and the sequential order in which the subparts were created. Finally, a global refinement process allows users to adjust the skeleton structure with coarse-to-fine control, ensuring an optimized and animation-ready hierarchy.

2.3 Fast Simulation of Mass-Spring Systems

The fast mass-spring system technique provides an efficient way to solve mass-spring systems governed by Hooke's Law through a rapid implicit method [15]. Instead of directly solving the system's equations, this technique reformulates the problem as an optimization task. Based on Newton's second law, we derive:

$$\mathbf{p}_{n+1} = \mathbf{p}_n + h\mathbf{v}_{n+1} \tag{1}$$

$$\mathbf{v}_{n+1} = \mathbf{v}_n + h\mathbf{M}^{-1}\mathbf{f}(\mathbf{p}_{n+1}) \tag{2}$$

Using the position update equation from implicit Euler integration, we can express velocity in terms of discrete differences.

Backward Difference Approximation. The velocity at time step n is given by:

$$h\mathbf{v}_n = \mathbf{p}_n - \mathbf{p}_{n-1} \tag{3}$$

Forward Difference Approximation. Similarly, the velocity at the next time step $n+1$ can be written as:

$$h\mathbf{v}_{n+1} = \mathbf{p}_{n+1} - \mathbf{p}_n \tag{4}$$

To eliminate velocity from the implicit Euler update, we multiply Eq. (2) by h and substitute Eqs. (3) and (4). To simplify notation, define $\mathbf{x} := \mathbf{p}_{n+1}$ and $\mathbf{y} := 2\mathbf{p}_n - \mathbf{p}_{n-1}$. Multiplying both sides of this equation by the mass matrix $\mathbf{M}$, we obtain a more compact form:

$$\mathbf{M}(\mathbf{x} - \mathbf{y}) = h^2 \mathbf{f}(\mathbf{x}) \tag{5}$$

Reformulating the Energy Potential. As stated in the paper by [15], the main idea of their technique is to reformulate the energy potential E in a way that will allow us to employ a block coordinate descent method. In a mass-spring system, the elastic potential energy represents the energy stored in a deformed spring. According to Hooke's Law, the potential energy function is given by:

$$E(\mathbf{p}_i, \mathbf{p}_j) = \frac{1}{2}k(\|\mathbf{p}_i - \mathbf{p}_j\| - r_{ij})^2 \quad (6)$$

Because of the $\|\mathbf{p}_i - \mathbf{p}_j\|$ term, calculating E is a non-linear problem. The presence of this square root function means that the energy function is not a simple quadratic function. An interesting discovery has been made to simplify and accelerate the optimization algorithm. Specifically, for each spring, the nonlinear energy function can be reformulated as a smaller, independent optimization problem. This means, we need to find the vector of length that is as close as possible to the current spring vector.

$$(\|\mathbf{p}_i - \mathbf{p}_j\| - r_{ij})^2 = \min_{\mathbf{d}_{ij} \in \mathbb{R}^3, \|\mathbf{d}\| = r_{ij}} \|(\mathbf{p}_i - \mathbf{p}_j) - \mathbf{d}_{ij}\|^2$$

Since $\mathbf{f}(\mathbf{x})$ represents the force, and force is the negative gradient of potential energy [10], we have:

$$\mathbf{f}(\mathbf{x}) = -\nabla E(\mathbf{x}) \quad (7)$$

Substituting this into Eq. (5) gives:

$$\mathbf{M}(\mathbf{x} - \mathbf{y}) = -h^2 \nabla E(\mathbf{x}) \quad (8)$$

This matches the critical point condition of the function:

$$g(\mathbf{x}) = \frac{1}{2}(\mathbf{x} - \mathbf{y})^T \mathbf{M}(\mathbf{x} - \mathbf{y}) + h^2 E(\mathbf{x}) \quad (9)$$

since setting $\nabla g(\mathbf{x}) = 0$ results in:

$$\mathbf{M}(\mathbf{x} - \mathbf{y}) + h^2 \nabla E(\mathbf{x}) = 0 \quad (10)$$

Thus, the solutions to Eq. (5) correspond to the critical points of the function given in (9). This leads to an optimization formulation $min_\mathbf{x} g(\mathbf{x})$. This formulation, known as variational implicit Euler [19], allows solving the motion equations using optimization techniques instead of direct integration. This approach avoids numerical instability and large time-step restrictions that often arise in explicit integration methods [2].

From the method described in the paper [15], we know that the potential energy of the system can be written as:

$$E(\mathbf{x}) = \min_{\mathbf{d} \in U} \left(\frac{1}{2} \mathbf{x}^T \mathbf{L} \mathbf{x} - \mathbf{x}^T \mathbf{J} \mathbf{d} + \mathbf{x}^T \mathbf{f}_{\text{ext}} \right) \quad (11)$$

where $U = \{(\mathbf{d}_1, \ldots, \mathbf{d}_s) \in \mathbb{R}^{2s} \mid \|\mathbf{d}_i\| = r_i\}$ represents the set of rest-length spring directions.

Now, substituting Eq. (11) into (9), we obtain:

$$\begin{aligned} g(\mathbf{x}) &= \frac{1}{2}(\mathbf{x} - \mathbf{y})^T \mathbf{M}(\mathbf{x} - \mathbf{y}) + h^2 \min_{\mathbf{d} \in U} \left(\frac{1}{2} \mathbf{x}^T \mathbf{L}\, \mathbf{x} - \mathbf{x}^T \mathbf{J} \mathbf{d} + \mathbf{x}^T \mathbf{f}_{\text{ext}} \right) \\ &= \min_{\mathbf{x} \in \mathbb{R}^{3m}, \mathbf{d} \in U} \left[\frac{1}{2} \mathbf{x}^T \mathbf{M}\, \mathbf{x} - \mathbf{x}^T \mathbf{M}\, \mathbf{y} + \frac{1}{2} \mathbf{y}^T \mathbf{M}\, \mathbf{y} + h^2 \left(\frac{1}{2} \mathbf{x}^T \mathbf{L}\, \mathbf{x} - \mathbf{x}^T \mathbf{J} \mathbf{d} + \mathbf{x}^T \mathbf{f}_{\text{ext}} \right) \right] \end{aligned}$$
(12)

Since we are minimizing with respect to $\mathbf{x}$, the constant term $\mathbf{y}^T \mathbf{M}\, \mathbf{y}$ can be ignored. Also, for simplification we introduce $\mathbf{b}$ as $\mathbf{b} = h^2 \mathbf{f}_{ext} - \mathbf{M}\mathbf{y}$. We obtain the following:

$$g(\mathbf{x}) = \min_{\mathbf{x} \in \mathbb{R}^{3m}, \mathbf{d} \in U} \left(\frac{1}{2} \mathbf{x}^T (\mathbf{M} + h^2 \mathbf{L}) \mathbf{x} - h^2 \mathbf{x}^T \mathbf{J} \mathbf{d} + \mathbf{x}^T \mathbf{b} \right) \tag{13}$$

Thus, Eq. (13) represents the final optimization problem, where the minimizer x^* provides the exact solution to the implicit Euler timestep.

3 Method

3.1 System Overview

Figure 1 highlights the key differences between the original RealSkel [16] system (left) and our proposed approach (right). Both frameworks follow a similar initial workflow: beginning with a hand-drawn 2D silhouette, performing automatic skeleton extraction, and optionally allowing users to add subparts.

In RealSkel, once the skeleton is generated and the shape undergoes skinning, users can directly interact with joints to produce real-time rigid animations. By contrast, our approach extends this workflow by integrating a Mass-Spring System for Skeletons after the skinning stage. This addition introduces secondary motion effects, allowing for real-time dynamic animation. In comparison, the original system applies strictly rigid transformations, lacking the dynamic movement achieved in our method.

We divide our system into three procedures:

1. **Automatic Skeleton Extraction:** The system first applies constrained Delaunay triangulation [21] to process the input stroke. Here, we define the user's hand-drawn input as the silhouette of the model. The spine of the polygon, which also serves as the model's skeleton, is then automatically determined using the method described by [1].
2. **3D Shape Generation & Skinning:** A 3D shape is then generated from the 2D silhouette using the approach outlined in [12]. Initially, at this stage, we elevate the vertices of the spine by an amount proportional to their distance from the polygon. The user, however, can adjust the model's inflation by modifying the thickness parameter afterward. The system constructs a polygonal mesh that wraps around the spine and polygon, ensuring that sections

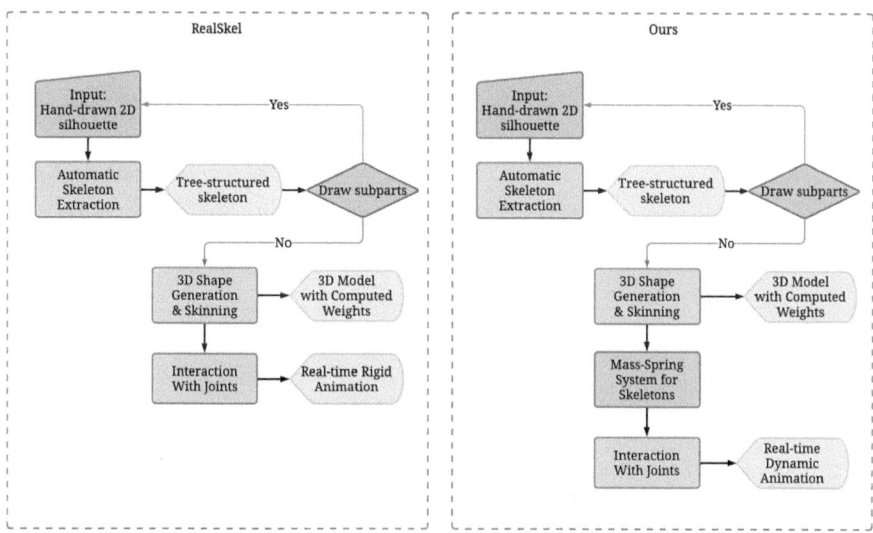

Fig. 1. Comparison of RealSkel and Our Approach. The original RealSkel system (left) directly applies rigid animation after skeleton extraction and skinning. Our approach (right) introduces a Mass-Spring System for Skeletons (highlighted in pink), adding secondary motion effects for real-time dynamic animation. (Color figure online)

form oval shapes and calculate. Skinning weights are then automatically computed using Bounded Biharmonic Weights (BBW) [13], preparing the model for skinning transformation via Linear Blend Skinning (LBS).

3. **Mass-spring System for Skeletons** To implement a mass-spring system for skeletal dynamics, we adapt the method proposed by [15], originally designed for cloth simulation, to a hierarchical skeletal structure. Unlike cloth, which is typically modeled as a network graph with interconnected nodes, a skeleton is inherently tree-structured, where each joint has a single parent and potentially multiple children. We treat each joint as a mass node and each bone as a spring to simulate skeletal dynamics. Although there are three types of springs: structural, bend and shear [11], in this study, we have not yet implemented shear and bend springs, which also play a crucial role in simulating more flexible deformations. Instead, we focus solely on structural springs to maintain bone length while introducing secondary motion effects.

The user can then draw additional subparts to expand the model, triggering a new cycle of skeletonization, meshing, and skinning.

3.2 Functions

In this section, we present the system's functionality from the user's perspective (see Fig. 2).

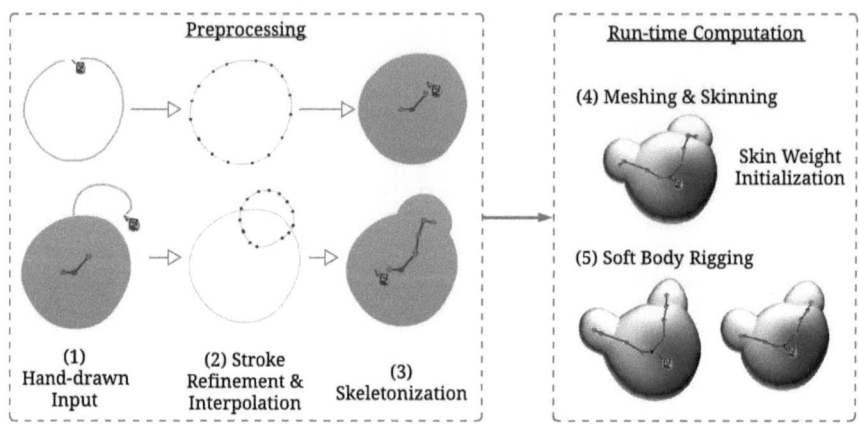

Fig. 2. Overview of the sketch-based soft body rigging system. (1) The user provides a hand-drawn input to define the contour of the shape. (2) Stroke refinement and interpolation are performed to generate a cleaner representation. (3) A skeleton is extracted from the refined strokes to define the deformation structure. The first row illustrates the process when drawing a single part of the 3D model, while the second row shows the process of merging multiple sub-parts to create a larger model. (4) A meshing and skinning process assigns weights to the structure, generating a simulation mesh. (5) The system applies soft body rigging using a mass-spring system to enable physics-driven deformation. The final animation utilizes a combination of LBS for primary deformation and a Spring Bone system for secondary dynamic motion.

First, the user begins by providing a hand-drawn sketch, which serves as the initial input for the modeling process. The system then refines and interpolates the strokes to generate a smooth and consistent shape. Next, a skeleton is extracted from the refined strokes, defining the structural framework of the model. Once the skeleton is established, the user can press 'D' to initiate the meshing and skinning stage. The system automatically computes weight initialization based on the mesh structure. Soft-body rigging is applied using a mass-spring system, enabling the model to exhibit dynamic deformations. The user can then select individual joints in the skeleton to manipulate, causing the entire structure to move dynamically as if connected by springs. Notably, when the user grabs a joint, it is considered fixed within the mass-spring system and is fully controlled by user movement for ease of use and convenience.

3.3 Implementation

Thanks to the work by [15], computing the mass-spring system state at each time step is simplified into a straightforward iterative process based on a local-global approach:

- **Step 1 (Local Update)**: Given the current positions **p**, determine d_{ij} for each spring.

- **Step 2 (Global Update):** Using all computed vectors d_{ij}, update $\mathbf{x}$ by minimizing the quadratic energy function described in Eq. (13).
- **Step 3 (Convergence Check):** If the solution has not yet converged, return to Step 1. If the maximum number of iterations is exceeded, terminate the algorithm.

We implemented our method using $C++$ and the *Qt* framework[7] *CMake*[8] is also required for build configuration and project management. The linear system was solved using the *Eigen* library[9].

The source code for the original RealSkel system is publicly available at: https://github.com/jingma-git/RealSkel.

Our implementation is available at: https://github.com/maple1606/Sketch-to-Model

Building Matrices. Before solving for the new positions of nodes, we construct three key matrices $\mathbf{L}$, $\mathbf{J}$ and $\mathbf{M}$ described in the original paper [15]. The process is detailed in Algorithm 1.

Algorithm 1. Construction of $\mathbf{L}$, $\mathbf{J}$, and $\mathbf{M}$

Require: Spring system with n points and s springs.
1: Initialize empty sparse matrices $\mathbf{L}$, $\mathbf{J}$, and $\mathbf{M}$.
2: $h^2 \leftarrow$ time step squared.
3: **for each** spring k connecting nodes (i,j) **do**
4:     **for each** coordinate $d \in \{x,y,z\}$ **do**
5:         $l_{3i+d,3i+d} \mathrel{+}= k_k$, $l_{3j+d,3j+d} \mathrel{+}= k_k$
6:         $l_{3i+d,3j+d} \mathrel{-}= k_k$, $l_{3j+d,3i+d} \mathrel{-}= k_k$
7:     **end for**
8: **end for**
9: **for each** spring k connecting nodes (i,j) **do**
10:     **for each** coordinate $d \in \{x,y,z\}$ **do**
11:         $j_{3i+d,3k+d} \mathrel{+}= k_k$, $j_{3j+d,3k+d} \mathrel{-}= k_k$
12:     **end for**
13: **end for**
14: **for each** node i **do**
15:     **for each** coordinate $d \in \{x,y,z\}$ **do**
16:         $m_{3i+d,3i+d} \leftarrow m_i$
17:     **end for**
18: **end for**
19: Precompute $\mathbf{A} = \mathbf{M} + h^2\mathbf{L}$ and factorize for solving.

---

[7] Qt2023: https://www.qt.io/.
[8] CMake2025: https://cmake.org/.
[9] eigenweb: https://eigen.tuxfamily.org.

Local Update. The local update relies on local information for each spring. Specifically, it computes the spring direction vectors for each spring in the system, ensuring that they maintain their rest length constraint. Algorithm 2 details the local update step.

Algorithm 2. Local Update for Mass-spring System

Require: Current positions $\mathbf{p}$, rest lengths r_{ij} of springs
Ensure: Updated spring direction vectors $\mathbf{d}_{ij}$
1: $j \leftarrow 0$
2: **for** each spring $(i, j) \in$ system's spring list **do**
3:      Compute displacement vector: $\mathbf{p}_{12} \leftarrow \mathbf{p}_i - \mathbf{p}_j$
4:      Normalize the displacement: $\hat{\mathbf{p}}_{12} \leftarrow \frac{\mathbf{p}_{12}}{\|\mathbf{p}_{12}\|}$
5:      Compute updated spring direction: $\mathbf{d}_{ij} \leftarrow r_{ij} \cdot \hat{\mathbf{p}}_{12}$
6:      Store $\mathbf{d}_{ij}$ in spring direction list
7:      $j \leftarrow j + 1$
8: **end for**

Global Update. The global update, on the other hand, involves all springs simultaneously. In this step, we solve for $\mathbf{x}$ while keeping $\mathbf{d}$ fixed. We start from the quadratic minimization problem described in Eq. (13). To find the optimal $\mathbf{x}$, we take the gradient with respect to $\mathbf{x}$ and set it to zero:

$$\frac{\partial}{\partial \mathbf{x}} \left(\frac{1}{2} \mathbf{x}^T (\mathbf{M} + h^2 \mathbf{L}) \mathbf{x} - h^2 \mathbf{x}^T \mathbf{J} \mathbf{d} + \mathbf{x}^T \mathbf{b} \right) = 0 \quad (14)$$

Since $\mathbf{L}$ is symmetric and positive semi-definite, the system matrix $\mathbf{M} + h^2 \mathbf{L}$ is symmetric positive definite, this simplifies to:

$$(\mathbf{M} + h^2 \mathbf{L}) \mathbf{x} - h^2 \mathbf{J} \mathbf{d} + \mathbf{b} = 0 \quad (15)$$

Rearranging, we obtain:

$$(\mathbf{M} + h^2 \mathbf{L}) \mathbf{x} = h^2 \mathbf{J} \mathbf{d} - \mathbf{b}. \quad (16)$$

This is a convex quadratic system where $\mathbf{M}$ represents the mass matrix, $h^2 \mathbf{L}$ accounts for stiffness from the implicit Euler integration, $h^2 \mathbf{J} \mathbf{d}$ encodes local deformation constraints, and $\mathbf{b}$ contains external forces and previous state dependencies.

Since the system matrix $\mathbf{M} + h^2 \mathbf{L}$ is symmetric positive definite, this guarantees the existence of a unique solution, which we solve efficiently using Cholesky factorization. By precomputing this factorization (since the system matrix remains constant when mass, timestep, and connectivity do not change), we significantly speed up the computation in each iteration. Algorithm 3 details the global update step.

Algorithm 3. Global Update Step

Require: Precomputed matrices $\mathbf{M}, \mathbf{L}, \mathbf{J}$ and external forces $\mathbf{f}_{\text{ext}}$.
1: Compute the right-hand side:
$$\mathbf{b} = h^2 \mathbf{f}_{\text{ext}} - \mathbf{M}\mathbf{y}.$$
2: Compute $\mathbf{x}$:
$$\mathbf{x} = (\mathbf{M} + h^2 \mathbf{L})^{-1}(h^2 \mathbf{J}\mathbf{d} - \mathbf{b}).$$
3: Update the system state with $\mathbf{x}$.

Convergence Check. For ease of implementation, our simulation assumes convergence after a fixed number of iterations (e.g., 100). However, more advanced stopping criteria could be employed to adaptively determine convergence based on error thresholds or energy minimization.

Algorithm 4. Mass-Spring Solver with Fixed Iterations

Require: Maximum iterations n
1: Store previous state: $\mathbf{p}_{n-1} \leftarrow \mathbf{p}_n$
2: **for** $i = 1$ to n **do**
3:     **Local Step:** Update spring directions $\mathbf{d}_{ij}$ by normalizing displacement vectors
4:     **Global Step:** Solve for $\mathbf{x}$ using the precomputed Cholesky factorization
5: **end for**
---

4 Results and Discussion

4.1 Experimental Setup

For performance evaluation, all experiments were conducted on an AMD Ryzen 7 7840H processor with Radeon 780M Graphics. To ensure consistency, auto-parallelization was disabled, and all computations were performed on a single thread. Following the sub-stepping strategy [17], we set the time step to $h = 1/60$ s, corresponding to a 60 FPS simulation rate. As for external forces, we only consider gravitational acceleration $g = 9.8 \, \text{m/s}^2$ [10] and user-applied forces, which arise from direct interactions such as pulling, pushing, or manipulating the system.

As for user interaction, the object responds to physics forces only when the user moves a joint with the mouse, allowing for precise control over movement. However, a limitation of this approach is that forces are not applied continuously, meaning the object lacks ongoing secondary motion unless actively manipulated. As a result, animation techniques like follow-through, slow-in, slow-out [28] may appear less pronounced.

4.2 Dynamic Motion Effects

Figure 3 illustrates the dynamic deformation response of our method under different external forces. The leftmost objects represent the initial state before any deformation is applied. The green dot marks the central joint, which, when moved, causes the entire object to follow its position, exhibiting dynamic effects.

When subjected to stretching forces (moving the mouse in one direction), the skeleton expands, causing the structure to elongate. Conversely, applying compression forces (moving the mouse in the opposite direction) causes the skeleton to contract. The stress distribution, visualized in red, highlights regions experiencing higher deformation. In contrast, without incorporating a mass-spring system into the bones, the object remains rigid and unchanged regardless of how the central joint is moved.

However, a significant limitation of our method stems from the automatic BBW computation within the framework by [16]. The weight distribution is uneven, as evidenced by the red stress area being concentrated in a specific region rather than being evenly spread across the entire model. Moreover, users cannot manually adjust the weights or change the structure of the skeleton, which further restricts control over the deformation behavior. As a result, moving a blue joint does not propagate its influence effectively to other joints, reducing the clarity of localized deformations. While re-implementing BBW could enhance

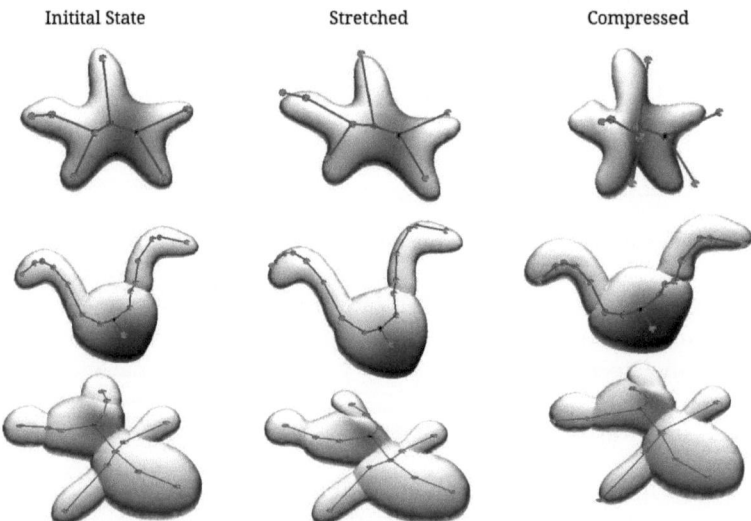

Fig. 3. Dynamic deformation effects under different external forces. The leftmost column represents the initial state before deformation. The stretched column shows the effect of applying external forces that elongate the structure, while the compressed column illustrates the deformation when forces are applied in the opposite direction. The internal skeleton (red lines) adapts dynamically, and the stress distribution (highlighted in red) indicates regions experiencing high deformation. (Color figure online)

weight distribution and deformation accuracy, this is beyond the scope of our study. This limitation remains a key challenge in our approach.

Another limitation is that while we successfully introduce secondary animation, the resulting motion is not as bouncy as observed in well-known frameworks such as Cartoon Animator 5[10] and VRM[11] This can be attributed to the absence of shear and bending springs in our implementation, as discussed in Sect. 3.1.

4.3 Effects of Stiffness Parameter

Stiffness determines how resistant a spring is to deformation, controlling how quickly it returns to its original shape after being stretched or compressed. The unit of stiffness is Newtons per meter (N/m) [10], meaning a higher stiffness value results in less deformation under the same force, leading to more rigid motion [4]. Therefore, adjusting the stiffness parameter is key to getting the best dynamic effects for each character. Since no pre-computation is needed, users can tweak stiffness in real time to find the most natural movement. As shown in Table 1, choosing the right stiffness is important. Because our system adds spring effects to bones for simple object animation (not for cloth or hair), lower stiffness values generally work better.

Table 1. Effects of different stiffness levels on dynamic motion.

Stiffness Level (N/m)	Effect
Too Low (<5)	Unstable, vibrating, or numerical errors in calculation
Low (5–10)	Fast but may overshoot, slight jittering
Medium (10–100)	Balanced, elastic, natural-looking motion
High (>100)	Slow, bouncy motion is barely noticeable

4.4 Complexity

The local update function, as described in Sect. 3.3, iterates over all springs in the system and updates their directions. The complexity for this step is therefore $\mathcal{O}(n)$.

The global update function, as described in Sect. 3.3, involves solving a linear system. Since we use Cholesky decomposition, the factorization of the $n \times n$ system matrix requires $\mathcal{O}(n^3)$ operations. Once factorized, solving for x using forward and backward substitution takes $\mathcal{O}(n^2)$ time. The overall complexity of the global update step is therefore $\mathcal{O}(n^3)$. Although this complexity may seem large, our system remains computationally feasible as it is applied to skeletal

---

[10] Cartoon Animator 5: https://www.reallusion.com/cartoon-animator/spring-animation.html.
[11] VRM Springbone: https://vrm.dev/en/univrm/springbone/univrm_secondary/.

structures rather than dense meshes. In typical cases, the number of joints does not exceed $n = 1000$, leading to $n^3 = 1000^3 = 1,000,000,000$. Empirical tests show that for typical character skeletons ($n \leq 30$), the update process completes within milliseconds, ensuring smooth interactive performance. Thus, the computational cost is acceptable within our application domain.

5 Conclusion

In this work, we introduced a sketch-based 3D modeling system that integrates real-time skeletonization with mass-spring dynamics, enabling users to easily create soft-body effects for 3D characters. By leveraging the RealSkel [16] framework for automatic skeleton extraction and mass-spring physics [15] for skeletal dynamics, our system allows for the generation of dynamic secondary motion without the need for complex rigging or extensive animation expertise.

While the system successfully bridges sketch-based modeling and dynamic animation, there are several avenues for future work. One important direction is to refine the weight distribution process to achieve smoother and more consistent deformations across the model. Another key area is enabling continuous secondary motion without requiring user input, allowing the model to exhibit persistent dynamic effects. Additionally, expanding the system to include bend and shear springs would further enhance the flexibility and realism of the character's movements. To ensure that the system remains efficient and scalable, future work will also focus on improving computational performance, particularly for more complex models or detailed animations.

By addressing these challenges, we aim to enhance the system's capabilities, making it a more powerful and user-friendly tool, not only for animators but also for educational purposes in simulating materials.

References

1. Aichholzer, O., Aurenhammer, F.: Straight skeletons for general polygonal figures in the plane. In: Cai, J.-Y., Wong, C.K. (eds.) COCOON 1996. LNCS, vol. 1090, pp. 117–126. Springer, Heidelberg (1996). https://doi.org/10.1007/3-540-61332-3_144
2. Baraff, D., Witkin, A.: Large steps in cloth simulation. In: Proceedings of the 25th Annual Conference on Computer Graphics and Interactive Techniques, SIGGRAPH 1998, pp. 43–54. Association for Computing Machinery, New York (1998). https://doi.org/10.1145/280814.280821
3. Baran, I., Popović, J.: Pinocchio: automatic skeleton generation for 3D models. ACM Trans. Graph. (TOG) **26**(3), 33 (2007)
4. Bargteil, A.W., Shinar, T.: An introduction to physics-based animation. In: ACM SIGGRAPH 2019 Courses. SIGGRAPH 2019. Association for Computing Machinery, New York (2019). https://doi.org/10.1145/3305366.3328050
5. Borosán, P., Jin, M., DeCarlo, D., Gingold, Y., Nealen, A.: Rigmesh: automatic rigging for part-based shape modeling and deformation. ACM Trans. Graph. **31**(6), 1–9 (2012). https://doi.org/10.1145/2366145.2366217

6. Borosán, P., Auzinger, T., Wimmer, M.: Rigmesh: automatic rigging for articulated characters. Comput. Graph. Forum **31**(2pt3), 381–390 (2012)
7. Bridson, R., Fedkiw, R., Anderson, J.: Robust treatment of collisions, contact and friction for cloth animation. ACM Trans. Graph. **21**(3), 594–603 (2002). https://doi.org/10.1145/566654.566623
8. Dvoroznak, M., Sykora, D., Curless, B., Curtis, C.J., Sorkine-Hornung, O., Salesin, D.H.: Monster mash: a single-view approach to casual 3D modeling and animation, pp. 1–12. New York, NY, USA (2020)
9. Foley, J.D., van Dam, A., Feiner, S.K., Hughes, J.F.: Computer Graphics: Principles and Practice, 2nd edn. Addison-Wesley Longman Publishing Co., Inc, USA (1990)
10. Halliday, D., Resnick, R., Walker, J.: Fundamentals of Physics. Halliday & Resnick Fundamentals of Physics. John Wiley & Sons Canada, Limited (2010)
11. Hsiao, S.W., Chen, R.Q.: A method of drawing cloth patterns with fabric behavior. In: Proceedings of the 5th WSEAS International Conference on Applied Computer Science, ACOS 2006, pp. 635–640. World Scientific and Engineering Academy and Society (WSEAS), Stevens Point, Wisconsin, USA (2006)
12. Igarashi, T., Matsuoka, S., Tanaka, H.: Teddy: A Sketching Interface for 3D Freeform Design, 1st edn. Association for Computing Machinery, New York (1999)
13. Jacobson, A., Baran, I., Popović, J., Sorkine, O.: Bounded biharmonic weights for real-time deformation. ACM Trans. Graph. **30**(4) (2011). https://doi.org/10.1145/2010324.1964973
14. Karpenko, O.A., Hughes, J.F.: Smoothsketch: 3D free-form shapes from complex sketches. ACM Trans. Graph. **25**(3), 589–598 (2006)
15. Liu, T., Bargteil, A.W., O'Brien, J.F., Kavan, L.: Fast simulation of mass-spring systems. ACM Trans. Graph. **32**(6) (2013). https://doi.org/10.1145/2508363.2508406
16. Ma, X., Xie, S., Takayama, K.: Realskel: real-time skeletonization for sketch-based modeling. Comput. Graph. Forum **40**(7), 123–133 (2021)
17. Macklin, M., et al.: Small steps in physics simulation. In: Proceedings of the 18th Annual ACM SIGGRAPH/Eurographics Symposium on Computer Animation. SCA 2019. Association for Computing Machinery, New York (2019). https://doi.org/10.1145/3309486.3340247
18. Marschner, S., Shirley, P.: Fundamentals of Computer Graphics, 4th edn. A. K. Peters Ltd, USA (2016)
19. Martin, S., Thomaszewski, B., Grinspun, E., Gross, M.: Example-based elastic materials. ACM Trans. Graph. **30**(4) (2011). https://doi.org/10.1145/2010324.1964967
20. Nealen, A., Igarashi, T., Sorkine, O., Alexa, M.: Fibermesh: designing freeform surfaces with 3D curves. ACM Trans. Graph. **26**(3), 41-es (2007). https://doi.org/10.1145/1276377.1276429
21. Paul Chew, L.: Constrained delaunay triangulations. Algorithmica **4**(1–4), 97–108 (1989). https://doi.org/10.1007/BF01553881
22. Provot, X.: Deformation constraints in a mass-spring model to describe rigid cloth behaviour. In: Proceedings of Graphics Interface 1995, GI 1995, pp. 147–154. Canadian Human-Computer Communications Society, Toronto, Ontario, Canada (1995)
23. Rosenblum, R.E., Carlson, W.E., Tripp, E., III.: Simulating the structure and dynamics of human hair: modelling, rendering and animation. J. Vis. Comput. Animat. **2**(4), 141–148 (1991)
24. Selle, A., Lentine, M., Fedkiw, R.: A mass spring model for hair simulation. ACM Trans. Graph. **27**(3), 1–11 (2008). https://doi.org/10.1145/1360612.1360663

25. Sugihara, M., De Groot, E., Wyvill, B., Schmidt, R.: A sketch-based method to control deformation in a skeletal implicit surface modeler. In: Proceedings of the Fifth Eurographics Conference on Sketch-Based Interfaces and Modeling, SBM 2008, pp. 65–72. Eurographics Association, Goslar, DEU (2008)
26. Tai, C.L., Zhang, H., Fong, J.: Prototype modeling from sketched silhouettes based on convolution surfaces. Comput. Graph. Forum **23**, 71–84 (2004). https://doi.org/10.1111/j.1467-8659.2004.00006.x
27. Teschner, M., Heidelberger, B., Müller, M., Gross, M.: A versatile and robust model for geometrically complex deformable solids, pp. 312–319 (2004). https://doi.org/10.1109/CGI.2004.1309227
28. Thomas, F., Johnston, O.: Disney Animation: The Illusion of Life. Abbeville Press, New York (1981)
29. Xu, Z., Zhou, Y., Kalogerakis, E., Landreth, C., Singh, K.: Rignet: neural rigging for articulated characters. In: ACM Transactions on Graphics (TOG), vol. 39, p. 67. ACM (2020)
30. Yang, J., et al.: Object wake-up: 3D object rigging from a single image (2021). https://arxiv.org/abs/2108.02708

Digital Heritage to Improve Accessibility and Break Down Architectural Barriers

Damiano Perri[1]([✉]), Sara Martinelli[1], Osvaldo Gervasi[1], David Berti[2], and Gilberto Zinourov Roncalli di Montorio[2]

[1] Department of Mathematics and Computer Science, University of Perugia, Perugia, Italy
{damiano.perri,osvaldo.gervasi}@unipg.it
[2] ART S.p.A., Passignano sul Trasimeno, Perugia, Italy
{david.berti,gilberto.zinourov}@artgroup-spa.com

Abstract. This work aims to create a navigable virtual environment of the Bufalini Castle through virtual reality viewers, allowing the elimination of physical barriers and ensuring full accessibility to cultural sites. The majestic building, built during the 15th century, has an architectural conformation that is not easily accessible to people with mobility disabilities. The structure's design, featuring narrow passages, multiple staircases, and a lack of elevators, currently restricts exploration for visitors using wheelchairs or facing other mobility challenges. The creation of the 3D scenario mainly uses virtual reality technologies. However, to ensure a good level of realism, photogrammetry involves capturing extensive photographic datasets of the castle, which are then processed to create geometrically accurate and texturally rich meshes, capturing a high level of graphic detail and realism essential for an engaging user experience.

Keywords: Virtual Reality · Metaverse · Digital Twin · Cultural Heritage

1 Introduction

The Bufalini Castle is located in the small town of San Giustino, in the province of Perugia, in the Upper Tiber Valley. It is one of the very few historic stately homes that has remained intact, in fact, inside it is still possible to find most of the decorations and furnishings dating back to the period between the 16th and 20th centuries. The Castle also boasts a fantastic surrounding park, consisting of an 'Italian-style' garden with lemon groves, fountains and a labyrinth. Taking into account the Castle's conformation, the fact that it is a historical asset whose structure is difficult to modify, and the fact that it is of great cultural interest, it was chosen as a use case to improve accessibility through modern Virtual Reality technologies.

Virtual Reality (VR) allows the creation of simulated environments through the use of a computer or other devices like smartphones, tablets and headsets.

This is an immersive technology, i.e. one that can interactively involve the user projected into any 3D location, and through the use of special devices the user can interact with the environment. These devices can be standard input devices such as a keyboard and mouse, or multimodal devices such as a wired glove and/or an omnidirectional treadmill. Thus, users interact with virtual 3D objects in real time in an intuitive and natural way, perceiving them as real and coming to understand, analyse and communicate. It allows for first-person adventures and experiences, breaking down geographical barriers and simulating any setting. It stems from the idea of replicating reality as accurately as possible visually, audibly, tactilely and even olfactively, in order to perform actions in virtual space that are difficult or impossible to emulate in the real world, overcoming physical, economic and security limitations.

This approach becomes even more crucial, happening in this time of fast-paced evolution of all digital ecosystems around us, where the interaction with information acquires new layers and stratifications of complexity, which dictates the necessity for adopting technologies which grant always more immersive and accessible user experiences. Immersivity which should safeguards both searching for information and infering, retrieving or discovering information in a specific informative or spatial context, where clues can be structured to grant sensemaking and proper content understandability [1].

Virtual reality succeeds in creating virtual environments and experiences using a combination of hardware (e.g. wearable visors, tracking systems, graphics processing) and software (i.e. web-based or local applications).

The strength of this technology lies in the fact that it makes the virtual environment feel similar to the real world. Hence, the subject goes from being an observer of an action to becoming its protagonist, able to see, hear, manipulate objects that do not exist, travel through spaces without a place in the company of people who are elsewhere. This active process of interaction with the virtual world produces the sense of presence, i.e. the feeling of being in the virtual environment [2].

The use of virtual reality has many advantages, for example it offers the opportunity to experience various situations without the need to physically create them, reducing costs and risks [3].

2 Related Works

The evolution of architecture has always been conditioned by technological innovation; indeed, it is digital technology that progressively brings buildings and places to life. This has led to the design of buildings with a multi-sensory approach, i.e. involving other senses besides sight, particularly in museums. The difficulty arises when trying to reconstruct the 3D model of historical and archaeological objects and monuments in their current condition. Methodologies that generate precise geometry and a very high level of realism are required. Currently, there are tools that allow sophisticated processing such as laser scanning of the landscape, automatic orientation and measurement operations, and the generation of digital orthoimages [4].

Virtual environments created from images have the exact same characteristics as 3D models created with modelling software, so it will be possible to manipulate, navigate and enrich them with important information and data of a different nature, such as text and audio, useful for better describing the object under examination [5]. Photogrammetry is a technique that reconstructs 3D models from a set of photographs taken on purpose [6]. The results have a very high quality that could hardly be achieved by manually recreating objects and textures. The difficulty of this technique concerns the large number of vertices and faces that are created, so the limitation is the computational power of the machine used to process the images [7].

Today, the use of GPUs has greatly increased the level of available computational power, allowing the creation of very complex models in a short time. GPUs are extremely important for AI [8,9]; they are used for training large language models, but they are also needed for generating 3D scenarios and running computer graphics applications such as video and serious games [10,11]. Each image is divided into many adjacent polygons to form faces, the number of which depends on the degree of realism and quality of the result [12]. This technique is very useful in cases where manual modelling of polygonal details is complex and the result unsatisfactory, photogrammetry allows a very high level of realism by exploiting artificial intelligence techniques for the realisation of the most complex parts.

The photographs to be used as a dataset of images to realise the model must be of a sufficiently large number to cover all the angles of the object, and there must be a certain level of overlap to ensure a homogeneous mesh without holes. The ideal overlap percentage is around 70 per cent. The degree of confidence in the final result depends mainly on the photographer's ability to set the right parameters according to environment, light and subject. It is crucial to make sure that the entire photo set has the same focal length and lighting.

The drone used is a DJI MINI 3. This is a compact and ultra-light camera drone with a foldable design and a weight of less than 249g. It allows 4K HDR video and has an extended battery life that can provide a maximum flight time of up to 38 min. The camera used for shooting is equipped with a 1/1.3-inch CMOS sensor, the focal length is 6.7 mm, the aperture is fixed at f/1.7, exposure time is 1/320 with ISO 100, color space sRGB. The resolution of the camera is 4000×2250 pixels (9.0 MegaPixels).

Figure 1 shows the steps in the reconstruction of the castle. The work was divided into four stages: the first stage was the inspection and analysis of the building with the support of the castle staff, the second stage involves taking photographs with the drone with the preset shooting parameters, the third stage involves reconstruction by photogrammetry using the open source software OpenDroneMap[1], and finally the fourth stage involves obtaining the 3D model and its optimisation using Blender[2].

---

[1] https://opendronemap.org/.
[2] https://www.blender.org/.

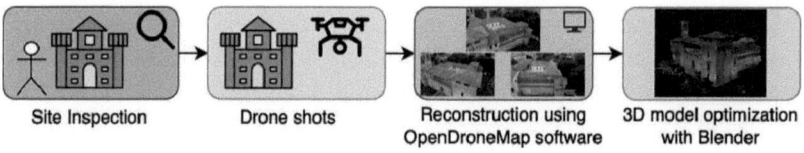

Fig. 1. Phases in the photogrammetric reconstruction of a castle: from survey to 3D model.

The amount of photography required is proportional to the size of the object [5]. In addition to photogrammetry, LiDAR technologies are often used. This is a sensor that fires a pulse of infrared light at an object and is able to detect the distance by calculating the time it takes for it to bounce back to the sensor [13]. In recent years, LiDAR has developed in the field of 3D scanning for smartphones. Now present in the latest IOS devices, it provides a longer-range capture than is possible with Face ID [14]. By analysing the time and power of the laser pulse bounce, LiDAR devices can generate dense point clouds that accurately capture the details of scanned objects. This allows LiDAR to capture 3D space in real time, thus benefiting time and resolution. The calculations required to create the 3D models generated by scanning real-world scenarios can also be done in the cloud; in fact, there are services that researchers can use to leverage computational power for a fee, such as Matterport[3] [15–18].

Virtual reality applications can then be integrated within complex environments in order to implement metaverses, i.e. multi-user interactive scenarios that can allow the creation of immersive experiences, also from a social point of view [19]. The metaverse applied to tourism can, in fact, be understood as an environment where tourists can first experience the place to be visited, building expectations while breaking down physical and temporal barriers [20].

3 Discussion

After having undertaken a complex study of the best technologies in use today for the realisation of Digital Twin, especially in the architectural field, taking into account the characteristics of each one and the various difficulties of the subject to be reproduced, the methods of project development were defined. Given the size of the subject to be represented, manual reproduction is difficult, so it is appropriate to make use of the technique of photogrammetry. This technique, thanks to the use of Artificial Intelligence algorithms, makes it possible to achieve very high performance results in a short time, with a high level of detail and photorealism.

First of all, a survey was made of both the exterior and interior of the castle. The exterior was recorded in the form of photographic and videographic documentation using a professional drone. Figure 2 shows a detail of the castle, seen

---

[3] https://matterport.com/.

from the outside, taken by the drone. Figure 3 shows the castle and the drone mapping the exterior surface.

Fig. 2. Aerial view of the castle taken by drone

By analysing the interior of the castle, the three main rooms were identified, which were then the subject of the computer graphics reconstruction procedure.

- **Il Salone**, *The Hall*: is located on the ground floor, therefore relatively easily accessible to all, but worth reproducing virtually given its beauty and size. This room also serves to demonstrate the power of this technology in large and detailed environments.
- **La camera degli Dei pagani o di Giove**, *The chamber of the pagan Gods or Jupiter,*: we find it going up the first ramp of the staircase, therefore inaccessible to those with motor disabilities, as it is impossible to install equipment such as lifts or platforms. This is one of the rooms open to the public, which would therefore generate inequality between people.
- **La Camera di Apollo**, *The Chamber of Apollo*: going up to the top floor of the donjon, exactly above the previously mentioned room, we find this room, which has been open to the public for a few months, but is absolutely inaccessible for those with mobility difficulties, given the three flights of stairs that have to be tackled to reach it.

Fig. 3. Exterior view of the castle with detail on the drone being mapped

3.1 Reconstruction of the Interior

To create the virtual environment of the interiors, it was necessary to take 360-degree photographic scans of fixed rotation points. The software used was Matterport. Therefore, as a first step, the room was scanned to take a series of surveys in order to cover the entire surface, maintaining a maximum distance of about three steps between scans. The device to be used for scanning had to be equipped with the LiDAR sensor, which can calculate distances and depths by exploiting the bounce time of light on objects. For greater accuracy it was necessary to keep the scanning device, which in my case was the cell phone, as still as possible. To do this, a tripod was used, which allowed for rotation while maintaining the same starting point and height.

Thirteen consecutive scans were required for the reconstruction of the living room, as it is the largest and most complex room.

The living room scan was the one for which the most time was spent. A total of thirteen consecutive scans were made, following a line that started from one of the room's entry points and then continued by circling around the large dining table and back to the starting point.

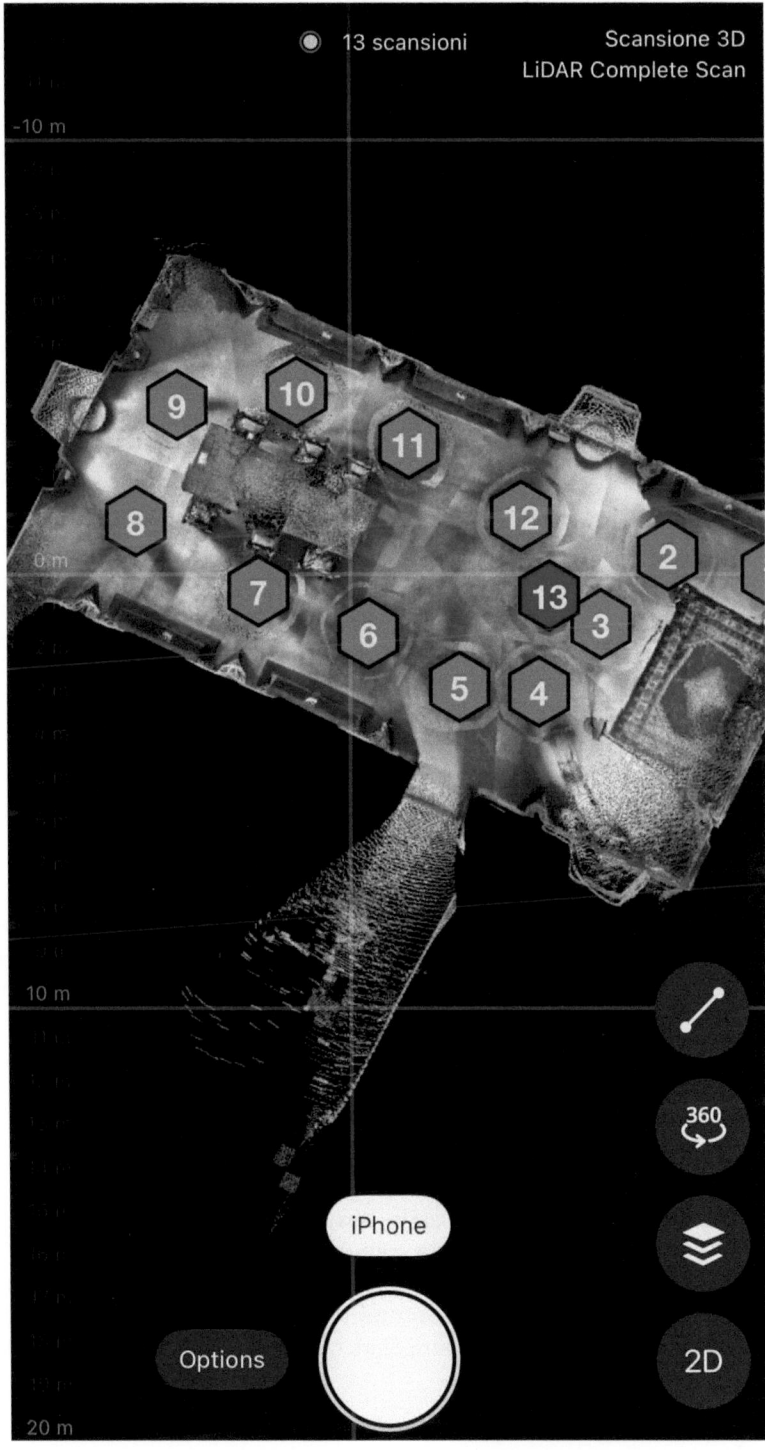

Fig. 4. Scans made in the hall of Bufalini Castle

The Pagan Gods Room Scan, on the other hand, took less time because it is a smaller room, so the number of frames to be captured and modeled was greatly reduced.

Figure 4 shows the result of the scans in the hall of Bufalini Castle. The environment is faithfully reproduced, with all the details and decorations present in the room and the user can move around the room, observing the environment from different angles and heights.

Fig. 5. Result of the scans in the hall of Bufalini Castle

Once the scanning process was completed, all previously processed work could be found in the application, with the option of uploading to the Cloud, for matching with the bespoke account and processing the work to create the virtual environment. The upload phase does not have a well-defined time, because it varies depending on the number of scans and details that the program needs to reproduce. The time required for the processing of the scans is about 24 h, after which the virtual environment is ready for use.

3.2 Reconstruction of the External Environment of the Castle

The external environment of the castle was reconstructed using a drone. The drone was equipped with a camera capable of taking high-resolution photographs, which were then processed by a software that created a 3D model of the castle. The drone was flown around the castle, taking photographs from different angles and heights, to ensure that the entire surface was covered. The photographs were then processed by the software, which created a 3D model of the castle. Figure 6 shows the drone used to capture the photographs of the castle. The 3D model was then imported into a virtual reality environment, where it could be explored by users. The virtual reality environment allowed users to explore the exterior of the castle, as if they were actually there.

Fig. 6. Drone used to capture photographs of the castle

Figure 7 shows the 3D model of the castle, which was created using the photographs taken by the drone.

Fig. 7. The castel reconstructed in 3D

4 Conclusions

After a detailed study and testing of the best technologies currently available for the virtual reproduction of complex environments, the most suitable methodologies were defined to fulfill our goal, i.e. to break down physical barriers and ensure accessibility to cultural heritage even for people with walking difficulties or financial difficulties that prevent them from making long journeys and physically demanding trips. In this regard, thanks to the use of a combination of technologies such as virtual reality and photogrammetry, using devices such as smartphones equipped with the LiDAR sensor and drones, it was possible to recreate the environments in an extremely faithful and detailed manner. The cultural asset that was chosen as the subject of representation was the Bufalini Castle, a building of extreme beauty and a place of excellence from a cultural point of view for the area of San Giustino, a small town in the center of Italy.

The work was divided into two main parts, the first concerning the development of the interior and then that of the exterior of the building, which presented different characteristics and difficulties of execution. For the interior, three of the castle's rooms, significant for their beauty and accessibility, were reproduced. The technology used, through the LiDAR sensor, made it possible to recreate extremely realistic environments that guarantee an immersive visit to the areas, which would otherwise be inaccessible. With regard to the exterior, on the other hand, a 3D model of the building was reconstructed through the use of drone scans, which make it possible to faithfully reproduce large subjects that would be difficult to reproduce manually. The work carried out is therefore very important to ensure that the level of accessibility of the cultural asset is raised, as well as a great opportunity for the dissemination of culture, mitigating inequalities between people.

A possible future development could be the addition of virtual tours in all areas of the Castle inaccessible to the disabled. For example, an interactive totem could be placed at the base of each staircase. The combination of physical and virtual tours would create a mixed environment, which would still safeguard the interest in physically visiting the Castle, while allowing everyone to visit it in its entirety. It would also allow the Authority to visit those rooms that are not yet open to the public for security reasons or architectural problems, greatly reducing the costs of making them safe and physically accessible. To make the experience extremely immersive, the museum could equip itself with devices such as visors and set up interactive guided tours. This could bring in a younger public, who are fascinated by technology and in a spirit of gamified entertainment can learn cultural notions and become passionate about environments they would not otherwise have considered. This is therefore a very useful starting point for possible future projects that will benefit citizens.

Acknowledgments. We would like to thank the staff of Bufalini Castle for their crucial support and for allowing us access for photographic footage and drone scanning of the exterior. We would like to thank the Davide Piampiano committee (https://www.comitatodavidepiampiano.com/) for providing some of the hardware needed for the work. With this research, we are carrying forward Davide Piampiano's vision for sustainable and digitised tourism.

References

1. White, R.W., Shah, C.: Panmodal information interaction. Commun. ACM **68**(4), 33–36 (2025). https://doi.org/10.1145/3701534. ISSN: 0001-0782
2. Zhang, Z., Wang, C., Weng, D., Liu, Y., Wang, Y.: Symmetrical reality: toward a unified framework for physical and virtual reality. In: 2019 IEEE Conference on Virtual Reality and 3D User Interfaces (VR), pp. 1275–1276 (2019). https://doi.org/10.1109/VR.2019.8797970
3. Liu, Y., Sun, Q., Tang, Y., Li, Y., Jiang, W., Wu, J.: Virtual reality system for industrial training. In: 2020 International Conference on Virtual Reality and Visualization (ICVRV), pp. 338–339 (2020). https://doi.org/10.1109/ICVRV51359.2020.00091
4. Poullis, C., You, S., Neumann, U.: Rapid creation of large-scale photorealistic virtual environments. In: 2008 IEEE Virtual Reality Conference, pp. 153–160 (2008). https://doi.org/10.1109/VR.2008.4480767
5. Gervasi, O., Perri, D., Simonetti, M., Tasso, S.: Strategies for the digitalization of cultural heritage. In: Gervasi, O., Murgante, B., Misra, S., Rocha, A.M.A.C., Garau, C. (eds.) Computational Science and Its Applications – ICCSA 2022 Workshops, pp. 486–502. Springer, Cham (2022). ISBN: 978-3-031-10592-0

6. Sindayihebura, A., et al.: Monitoring land degradation using drone photogrammetry for the Mugoboka (Eastern Bujumbura, Burundi) case study. In: IGARSS 2024 - 2024 IEEE International Geoscience and Remote Sensing Symposium, pp. 1607–1609 (2024). https://doi.org/10.1109/IGARSS53475.2024.10641664
7. Daniel, M.X.S., Appadurai, N.K., Suan, W.B.: Enhancing realism and creativity in video/filmmaking utilising photogrammetry assets in CGI environments. In: 2023 IEEE 21st Student Conference on Research and Development (SCOReD), pp. 369–378 (2023). https://doi.org/10.1109/SCOReD60679.2023.10563856
8. Tamilarasi, T., Muthulakshmi, P.: Machine vision algorithm for detection and maturity prediction of Brinjal. Smart Agric. Technol. **7**, 100402 (2024). https://doi.org/10.1016/j.atech.2024.100402. ISSN: 2772-3755
9. Vella, F., Cefal, R.M., Costantini, A., Gervasi, O., Tanci, C.: GPU computing in EGI environment using a cloud approach. In: 2011 International Conference on Computational Science and Its Applications, pp. 150–155 (2011). https://doi.org/10.1109/ICCSA.2011.61
10. Perri, D., Fortunelli, M., Simonetti, M., Magni, R., Carloni, J., Gervasi, O.: Rapid prototyping of virtual reality cognitive exercises in a tele-rehabilitation context. Electronics **10**(4), 1–16 (2021). https://doi.org/10.3390/electronics10040457
11. Perri, D., Simonetti, M., Gervasi, O.: Deploying serious games for cognitive rehabilitation. Computers **11**(7) (2022). https://doi.org/10.3390/computers11070103. https://www.scopus.com/inward/record.uri?eid=2-s2.0-85133209387&doi=10.3390%2fcomputers11070103&partnerID=40&md5=5c8b784acf53e7c9573a05e80e9480bc
12. Santucci, F., Frenguelli, F., De Angelis, A., Cuccaro, I., Perri, D., Simonetti, M.: An immersive open source environment using godot. In: Gervasi, O., et al. (eds.) ICCSA 2020. LNCS, vol. 12255, pp. 784–798. Springer, Cham (2020). https://doi.org/10.1007/978-3-030-58820-5_56
13. Guan, W., You, S., Neumann, U.: Recognition-driven 3D navigation in large-scale virtual environments. In: 2011 IEEE Virtual Reality Conference, pp. 71–74 (2011). https://doi.org/10.1109/VR.2011.5759439
14. Lease, B.A., Chiam, D.H., Lim, K.H., Phang, J.T.S.: Development of 3D scanned environment in virtual reality. In: 2023 International Conference on Digital Applications, Transformation & Economy (ICDATE), pp. 1–4 (2023). https://doi.org/10.1109/ICDATE58146.2023.10248625
15. Perri, D., Simonetti, M., Gervasi, O.: Synthetic data generation to speed-up the object recognition pipeline. Electronics **11**(1) (2022). https://doi.org/10.3390/electronics11010002
16. Cuijie, Y., Biyan, L.: Research on optimization strategies for GPU cluster cloud rendering virtual simulation resources. In: 2024 14th International Conference on Information Technology in Medicine and Education (ITME), pp. 392–395 (2024). https://doi.org/10.1109/ITME63426.2024.00084
17. Perri, D., Simonetti, M., Lombardi, A., Faginas-Lago, N., Gervasi, O.: A new method for binary classification of proteins with machine learning. In: Gervasi, O., et al. (eds.) ICCSA 2021. LNCS, vol. 12958, pp. 388–397. Springer, Cham (2021). https://doi.org/10.1007/978-3-030-87016-4_29
18. Montella, R., et al.: Enabling the CUDA unified memory model in edge, cloud and HPC offloaded GPU kernels. In: 2022 22nd IEEE International Symposium on Cluster, Cloud and Internet Computing (CCGrid), pp. 834–841 (2022). https://doi.org/10.1109/CCGrid54584.2022.00099

19. Perey, C.: Interoperability is a fundamental requirement for the open metaverse. In: 2024 IEEE International Symposium on Emerging Metaverse (ISEMV), pp. 21–24 (2024). https://doi.org/10.1109/ISEMV63338.2024.00019
20. Perri, D., Di Blasi, S.R., Forlani, F., Gervasi, O.: Exploring the metaverse: opportunities for tourism and territorial development. In: Lecture Notes in Computer Science (including subseries Lecture Notes in Artificial Intelligence and Lecture Notes in Bioinformatics). LNCS, vol. 14825, pp. 141–153 (2024). https://doi.org/10.1007/978-3-031-65343-8_9

Hierarchical Sort-Based Parallel Interest-Matching Algorithm for Distributed Simulations

Ma Thị Châu[1] and Lê Thái Thịnh[2]

[1] HMI Lab, University of Engineering and Technology, Vietnam National University Hanoi, Hanoi, Vietnam
chaumt@vnu.edu.com
[2] University of Engineering and Technology, Vietnam National University Hanoi, Hanoi, Vietnam
23025091@vnu.edu.com

Abstract. Distributed virtual environments (DVEs) form the foundation for many real-time applications, such as online multiplayer games, virtual reality simulations, and collaborative systems. In these environments, a continuous flow of dynamic updates occurs, making it crucial to filter and deliver only the relevant information to each participant. This process, known as interest matching, ensures that each entity receives only the data it needs, thereby reducing bandwidth usage. Traditional methods do not fully exploit the parallel capabilities of modern multiprocessor hardware. The Hierarchical Sort-Based Parallel Interest Matching algorithm improves this process by organizing update and subscription regions into a hierarchical data structure and leveraging parallel processing. This paper identifies and addresses specific algorithmic shortcomings in the original HSP-IM, integrates the enhanced approach within the Unity engine, and conducts experimental benchmark comparisons to establish a foundation for developing simulation applications—particularly distributed VR/AR systems. Our findings demonstrate that advanced interest-matching techniques can be effectively implemented on widely used simulation platforms.

Keywords: Distributed virtual environment · Interest matching · Parallel computation

1 Introduction

DVEs are increasingly utilized across various applications, from online multiplayer games to immersive virtual reality experiences. These virtual reality applications require efficient data exchange mechanisms to facilitate real-time interaction among numerous entities. For example, in applications such as virtual museums or classrooms using VR, users expect a smooth experience while navigating complex virtual worlds populated by hundreds or thousands of objects and other participants. Typically, a publish-subscribe framework is employed in these systems, where updates are broadcast and selectively delivered based on the interests of recipients. However, without effective filtering, such systems can become inundated with irrelevant messages, leading to increased network bandwidth consumption as the simulation scale expands.

Early approaches were predominantly designed for sequential processing, which meant they couldn't fully exploit the parallelism offered by modern multicore processors. Recent advancements like HSP-SIM tackle this issue by organizing both update and subscription regions into hierarchical data structures, which minimizes redundant comparisons and leverages concurrency for enhanced performance. Furthermore, instead of recalculating all overlapping regions in every update cycle—even when only a few entities have changed—HSP-DIM employs incremental matching to reprocess only the modified regions, substantially reducing unnecessary computations. From now on, HSP-IM will refer to the core hierarchical sort-based parallel interest matching method, which can be implemented in either its static (HSP-SIM) or dynamic (HSP-DIM) variant.

Although evaluations in controlled environments have demonstrated the scalability and efficiency of the HSP-IM algorithm, its implementation in practical settings introduces additional challenges. In this paper, we extend existing HSP-IM techniques by addressing algorithmic shortcomings and adapting the method into the widely used Unity simulation engine on standard hardware. The primary contributions of this article are as follows:

- **Algorithmic enhancement**: Specific issues in the original HSP-IM algorithm have been identified and resolved, thereby enhancing its overall accuracy. Additionally, a redundant step has been eliminated to improve performance.
- **Unity Integration**: The refined algorithm is adapted for Unity's Job System, demonstrating that advanced interest-matching techniques can be effectively implemented on widely used simulation platforms.
- **Empirical Validation**: Benchmark comparisons were performed against the original HSP-DIM results, and an additional experiment was conducted to compare and analyze the overall performance of HSP-DIM and HSP-SIM. The results indicate that its performance under real-world conditions is very promising.

2 Related Work

Interest matching has long posed a critical challenge in distributed virtual environments, directly affecting the efficiency of data distribution among numerous entities. Most existing interest management approaches fall into four categories: aura-based, grid-based, hybrid-based, and visibility-based schemes [1]. Visibility-based techniques incorporate occlusion and detailed geometry for very precise filtering, but their high ray-casting overhead and geometric complexity place them outside the scope of this work. Aura-based methods determine relevance by modeling the exact area of influence of each entity. Brute-force interest matching in aura-based yields O(m × n) complexity and becomes costly as entities increase. Sort-based [3] further improves aura-based scalability by sorting updates and subscription lists along each axis, reducing pairwise scan. Grid-based [2] schemes partition space into fixed-size cells, restricting potential overlap check operation to nearby buckets - this trades some precision for faster membership/neighborhood lookups. Finally, hybrid methods combine the advantages of these two paradigms to balance precision and computational cost. However, all of which struggled with scalability, often became impractical in modern large-scale simulations.

To overcome these limitations, researchers began exploring parallel solutions that leveraged multi-core processors. For instance, Liu and Theodoropoulos [4] presented a parallel approach based on grid decomposition, while Marzolla et al. [5] introduced a parallel version of the sort-based method that achieved better scalability by distributing the workload among multiple threads. These parallel methods marked a step forward in handling the expanding complexity of interest matching.

A further advancement is the hierarchical sort-based parallel interest matching technique, referred to as HSP-SIM [6], which organizes subscription regions into a full binary-dimensional tree to minimize redundant comparisons via hierarchical partitioning and distribute the matching process across multiple processing cores. Empirical evaluations demonstrated significant improvements over earlier parallel solutions, particularly with very large numbers of entities. More recently, HSP-DIM has emerged as a dynamic enhancement to this model; instead of recalculating all overlaps in every update cycle, HSP-DIM [7] updates only the parts of the data structure that change, making it highly effective in scenarios where updates are frequent yet involve only a fraction of the total entities. Together, HSP-SIM and HSP-DIM represent important progress in efficiently managing data distribution for large-scale simulation environments.

3 Methodology

3.1 Problem Definition

In distributed virtual environments, each participant or entity is associated with spatial regions that govern data communication. An **update region** defines the area over which an entity broadcasts its state changes, while a **subscription region** represents the area for which a participant is interested in receiving updates. Both regions are typically modeled as axis-aligned bounding boxes (AABBs) in dimensional space, which simplify the representation of spatial extents. Each region is characterized by its lower and upper bounds along each spatial dimension. Consequently, two regions are considered to overlap if they share a common sub-interval across all dimensions. Interest matching is the process of identifying which subscription regions intersect with update regions.

3.2 Algorithm Framework

Data Structures. A core component of this method is the Binary Dimensional Tree (BDT) data structure. The BDT is a full binary tree that recursively partitions each dimensional space into smaller subregions. Given a domain $[0, L)$, it is divided into two equal segments at each hierarchical level. At level i, every node, denoted as *IMNode*, represents a subinterval of length $L/2^i$. Each node not only identifies a specific spatial segment but also serves as a container that organizes range data into distinct categories. In particular, each node contains:

- **lowerList:** stores ranges with their lower bound falling within the node
- **upperList:** stores ranges with their upper bound located within the node
- **coverList:** stores ranges that completely span the node's interval
- **insideList:** available in leaf nodes, holds ranges whose both lower and upper bounds lie entirely within the node

These containers are essential for efficiently determining overlapping regions. They enable the algorithm to localize search to those ranges most likely to intersect, thereby reducing unnecessary comparisons by offering these following properties.

Property 1. *if range R belongs to the upperList of $IMNode_{i,j}$, then R either belongs to the lowerList of $IMNode_{i,j-1}$ or R belongs to the lowerList of $IMNode_{i,j-2}$ and the coverList of $IMNode_{i,j-1}$.*

Property 2. *If range R belongs to coverList of $IMNode_{i,j}$, then it also belongs to lowerList of $IMNode_{i,j-1}$.*

In the context of interest matching, let $R_1 = [L_1, U_1)$ and $R_2 = [L_2, U_2)$ be two ranges. These ranges overlap if and only if the lower bound of one must be less than the upper bound of the other, and vice versa:

$$L_1 < U_2 \quad \text{and} \quad L_2 < U_1.$$

This fundamental condition, combined with Property 1 and Property 2, leads to the following theorems:

Theorem 1. *Given that ub is the lower bound of the range U matching with $IMNode_{i,j}$ that it reside in, every range in $upperList_{i,j}$ that is greater than ub and all range in $coverList_{i,j}$ overlaps with U.*

Theorem 2. *Given that ub is the upper bound of the range U matching with $IMNode_{i,j}$ that it reside in, every range in $lowerList_{i,j}$ that is less than ub overlaps with U.*

Theorem 3. *Given that ub is the lower bound of the range U matching with $IMNode_{i,j}$ that it cross, every range in $lowerList_{i,j}$ overlaps with U.*

Theorem 4. *Given that range U matching with $IMNode_{i,j}$ that it cover, every range in $insideList_{i,j}$ overlaps with U.*

Algorithm Workflow. The proposed algorithm follows a structured workflow comprising three primary steps (Algorithm 1). First, the MappingRangeToTree procedure embeds both update and subscription regions into a BDP tree, ensuring that the regions within each node are maintained in sorted order. This structure exploits the hierarchical relationships between nodes to enable efficient management and comparison of regions. Secondly, the dynamic approach includes a RecalculatingOverlapResult step—absent in the static method—that preserves the overlaps for unchanged regions, thereby minimizing redundant computations during the matching process. Finally, the MatchingTreeToTree step computes the overlaps between update and subscription regions in parallel. Unlike the static approach, which process all overlaps, the dynamic method compares only the modified regions. In practice, the matching-update procedure is invoked periodically rather than on every frame, since interest matching is computationally expensive, yet it need to be frequent enough to ensure the DVE's view up-to-date to every user.

Algorithm 1. Matching Update

MatchingUpdate()
1: MAPPINGRANGETOTREE()
2: RECALCULATEOVERLAPRESULT()
3: MATCHINGTREETOTREE()

Mapping Ranges to BDT. To embed a range into the tree, the HSP-DIM algorithm first determines the appropriate level based on the range's size. It then locates the *IMNodes* with which the range intersects and inserts the range into the corresponding containers. Specifically, if the range's size is smaller than the unit length at the leaf level h, then it is inserted at leaf node. Otherwise, it is inserted at level l where

$$\frac{L}{2^{l+1}} \leq \text{size}(R_i) < \frac{L}{2^l},$$

with $\text{size}(R_i) < L$ and $l > 0$. Next, the algorithm computes the indices $lrid$ and $urid$ for the lower and upper bounds LR_i and UR_i, respectively, as follows:

$$lrid = \left\lfloor \frac{LR_i \times 2^l}{L} \right\rfloor, \quad urid = \left\lfloor \frac{UR_i \times 2^l}{L} \right\rfloor.$$

If $urid = lrid$ and $l = h$, then both bounds lie within the same leaf node and the range is added to the *insideList* container. Otherwise, since the range's size is less than twice the unit length at level l, it can intersect at most two nodes; thus, the range is added to the *lowerList* of *IMNode$_{l,lrid}$* and the *upperList* of *IMNode$_{l,urid}$*. Additionally, if $urid - lrid = 2$, it is also added to *IMNode$_{l,lrid+1}$*'s *coverList*. Finally, the algorithm independently sorts the *insideList*, *lowerList*, and *upperList* in non-decreasing order based on their boundary values, this can be performed concurrently. Once this mapping process is complete, all range information is embedded in the BDP tree, which can then be used to perform efficient interest matching between update regions and subscription regions.

Matching Sorted List Ranges to a BDT Tree. This section provide a detailed explanation of the algorithm for matching a sorted list of ranges to a BDT tree, as described in Algorithm 2. The algorithm's main loop iterates through each element ub in the sorted list of bounds, and comparing it with each leaf node of the tree that it fall into, from left most ($lrid$) to right most ($urid$). If ub falls within the current node $IMNode_{h,i}$, we apply either Theorem 1 or Theorem 2, depending on whether ub represents upper or lower bound (line 10–17). Additionally, the bound lower of R is added into an auxiliary container and remove from when meet its upper bound, $newInList$, which keeps track of ranges that span multiple nodes. In case ub not falls within the current node, in other word it is crossing multiple node, the algorithm then applies Theorems 3 and 4 for each item in $newInList$ (lines 23–26). Given the hierarchical structure of BDT, where a bound intersect with current leaf nodes, it also overlaps with its ancestor nodes. Due to this, a bubble up loop (Line 9, 23, 27) ensure matching included for all levels.

Additionally, the *SortMatch* method employs a variant of the sort-based matching approach to identify intersections between the current bound (ub) and the inside ranges that complement Algorithm 2. Two red-black trees are used as containers for ub and the inside ranges, as they need to be maintained in sorted order while supporting frequent insertions and deletions.

Matching Between Tree Parallel. To match two BDT trees, one approach is to iterate over all sorted ranges from the first tree and compare them with the second tree. However, to fully exploit multiprocessor capabilities, the hierarchical dimensional partitioning of the BDT tree is leveraged to distribute matching workloads in parallel. For each $IMNode_{i,j}$ node, two lists are retrieved: *crossNodeRange* and *insideRange*. *CrossNodeRange* is formed by concatenating $lowerList_{i,j}$ with the corresponding bound from $upperList_{i,j+1}$ and $upperList_{i,j+2}$ which refer to the same range stored in the $lowerList_{i,j}$. Meanwhile, *insideRange* corresponds to $insideList_{i,j}$. Both containers remain sorted because the lists within each node are pre-sorted, and ranges in subsequent nodes are always larger than those in the current node. Once these lists are prepared, a sorted list matching to tree procedure (Algorithm 2) is applied to compare each sorted list with their counterpart trees, thereby efficiently identifying all overlaps concurrently. The key difference between dynamic matching (Algorithm 3) and static matching (Algorithm 4) lies in how input are extracted from each tree. In the dynamic approach, only the modified parts of one tree are compared to the other tree, and vice versa. By contrast, the static approach compares both trees in their entirety within a single pass.

3.3 Algorithm Enhancement

This article has introduced corrections and eliminated redundant steps in the original algorithm. Notably, the proposed method in the original paper did not incorporate Theorem 4 as a rule in Algorithm Matching (Algorithm 2). Without Theorem 4, the algorithm could miss overlaps between ranges that span multiple

Algorithm 2. Matching sorted list ranges in with BDT

Matching(sortList, BDT)
1: $overlapSet \leftarrow \emptyset$ ▷ set of all ranges in sortedList that overlap
2: $upset, subset \leftarrow \emptyset$ ▷ two red-black trees store bounds
3: $sub_{i,j}, slb_{i,j}, sib_{i,j}$: an iterator of upperList, lowerList, insideList
4: $ub \leftarrow$ sortedList.begin()
5: $right \leftarrow$ maximun ID of the leaf node intersecting sortedList
6: $left, i \leftarrow$ minimun ID of the leaf node intersecting sortedList
7: **while** $ub \neq$ sortedList.end() & $i \neq right$ **do**
8:     **if** ub fall into $IMNode_{h,i}$ **then**
9:         **for** $l \leftarrow h, k \leftarrow i$ to 0 by $l \leftarrow l-1, k \leftarrow k \div 2$ **do**
10:             **if** ub is lower bound **then**
11:                 $R.overlapSet+ = upperList_{l,k}.Where(upper \leq ub)$ ▷ Theorem 1
12:                 $R.overlapSet+ = coverList_{l,k}$ ▷ Theorem 1
13:                 **if** $(l = h)$ **then** newInList.insert(R)
14:             **else if** ub is upper bound **then**
15:                 $R.overlapSet+ = lowerList_{l,k}.Where(lower > ub)$ ▷ Theorem 2
16:                 **if** $(l = h)$ **then** newInList.remove(R)
17:             **end if**
18:         **end for**
19:         SORTMATCH($ub, sib_i, upset, subset$)
20:         $ub \leftarrow ub.next$
21:     **else if then**
22:         **for** $R \in$ newInList **do**
23:             **for** $l \leftarrow h, k \leftarrow i$ to 0 by $l \leftarrow l-1, k \leftarrow k/2$ **do**
24:                 $R.overlapSet+ = lowerList_{l,k}$ ▷ Theorem 3
25:                 **if** $(l = h$ & R cover $IMNode_{h,k})$ **then**
26:                     $R.overlapSet+ = insideList_{l,k}$ ▷ Theorem 4
27:                 **if** $(k \bmod 2 = 1)$ **then** $k \leftarrow k \div 2$ **else breaks;**
28:             **end for**
29:         **end for**
30:         $i \leftarrow i + 1$
31:     **end if**
32: **end while**

nodes and the inside ranges within those nodes—an issue arising when ranges vary in size and reside at different tree levels.

A further enhancement addresses performance by removing the "Merge Overlap Result" step from the original paper and shifting its workload to a lookup operation. In the original design, merging final results—by intersecting overlaps across all dimensions—was output-sensitive hence computationally expensive. Offloading this process to a hash-based lookup container now provides constant-time access for each participant in the DVE.

Algorithm 3. Dynamic matching between BDT parallel

MatchingTreeToTree()
1: **for all** $IMNode_{l,k} \in UpdateBDT$ **in parallel do**
2:     **if** $(l = h)$ **then** MATCHING$([Modified]insideRanges_{l,k}, SubcribtionBDT)$
3:     $crossNodeRanges \leftarrow lowerRanges_{l,k}$
4:     **for** $b \in upperRange_{l,k+1} \cup upperRange_{l,k+2}$ **do**
5:         **if** $Range(b) \in lowerRange_{l,k}$ **then**
6:             $crossNodeRanges.PushBack(b)$
7:         **end if**
8:     **end for**
9:     MATCHING$([Modified]crossNodeRanges_{l,k}, SubcribtionBDT)$
10: **end for**
11: **for all** $IMNode_{l,k} \in SubcribtionBDT$ **in parallel do**
12:     **if** $(l = h)$ **then** MATCHING$([Modified]insideRanges_{l,k}, UpdateBDT)$
13:     $crossNodeRanges \leftarrow lowerRanges_{l,k}$
14:     **for** $b \in upperRange_{l,k+1} \cup upperRange_{l,k+2}$ **do**
15:         **if** $Range(b) \in lowerRange_{l,k}$ **then**
16:             $crossNodeRanges.PushBack(b)$
17:         **end if**
18:     **end for**
19:     MATCHING$([Modified]crossNodeRanges_{l,k}, UpdateBDT)$
20: **end for**

4 Experimental Setup and Analysis

4.1 Implementation Details

This section describes the implementation of the refined HSP-IM algorithms, developed in Unity (version 6000.1.16f) using C#. The algorithms were integrated using Unity's Job System to manage parallel processing and were tuned for optimal performance. The development environment consisted of a standard computer equipped with an Intel Core i7 processor supporting 11 logical cores and 16 GB of RAM, running a 64-bit version of Windows 10. Each data point represents the mean of 50 independent repetitions.

4.2 Benchmark Testing Environment

To evaluate the algorithm's performance, a benchmarking framework similar to that described in [7] is employed. The benchmark involves update and subscription ranges of equal size, randomly distributed within a multi-dimensional space, and the matching algorithm determines all intersections among them. The number of ranges, N, determines the dataset size, comprises $n = N/2$ subscription regions and $m = N/2$ update regions. The overlap ratio, α, represents the proportion of the total area occupied by the regions in the space as a measure of spatial density. Additionally, the modify ratio, f, represents the fraction of ranges that change with each update. This experiment compares our empirical implementation with the original results.

Algorithm 4. Static matching between BDT parallel

MatchingTreeToTree()
1: **for all** $IMNode_{l,k} \in UpdateBDT$ **in parallel do**
2:    **if** $(l = h)$ **then** MATCHING($insideRanges_{l,k}, SubcribtionBDT$)
3:    $crossNodeRanges \leftarrow lowerRanges_{l,k}$
4:    **for** $b \in upperRange_{l,k+1} \cup upperRange_{l,k+2}$ **do**
5:      **if** $Range(b) \in lowerRange_{l,k}$ **then**
6:         $crossNodeRanges.PushBack(b)$
7:      **end if**
8:    **end for**
9:    MATCHING($crossNodeRanges_{l,k}, SubcribtionBDT$)
10: **end for**

Benchmark Result Validation. In order to compare benchmark results related to the scalability of the algorithm, we measuring execution time required to find intersections as the number of ranges N increased while keeping α constant with $f = 1$. As shown in the table, our measured execution times were approximately 15 times higher than the original authors' results, yet the overall performance trend remained consistent. Notably, our implementation utilized 8 threads compared to the authors' 64 threads, which accounts for a threefold speedup in their experiments. However, even after considering thread count, there remains about a five-fold discrepancy in absolute execution times. This additional difference is likely due to the overhead introduced by hardware architecture and algorithm implementation. Nevertheless, the observed scalability trend clearly demonstrates that the algorithm remains linear manner for large scale data (Table 1).

Table 1. Performance Comparison with the Original HSP-DIM matching

Number of ranges (N)	Original HSP-DIM matching execution time (ms)	Our HSP-DIM matching execution time (ms)
10^2	-	0.26
2×10^2	-	0.33
10^3	-	1.1
2×10^3	-	1.9
10^4	0.6	5.4
2×10^4	0.9	12.2
10^5	4	59
2×10^5	7	120
10^6	40	-
2×10^6	80	-

Overall Stepwise Performance Evaluation. Because HSP-IM comprises multiple sequential steps, evaluating the total runtime is crucial to determining its feasibility. In the experiments described below, each step is measured for different strategies includes *Static* and *Dynamic*, denoted *Dynamic f*, where f represents the fraction of modified ranges (e.g., *Dynamic 0.1*).

First, the mapping step is evaluated (Fig. 1). Overall, it exhibits an almost linear increase in runtime. The *Dynamic 0.1* configuration is only slightly faster than the *Static*, whereas *Dynamic 1* performs significantly worse. This is because the dynamic approach uses binary insertion, which has a worst-case complexity of n^2, and requires binary deletion as well, while the *Static* method performs a bulk sort on all ranges at once. We use C#'s built-in sorting method, which is an introspective sort (introsort) that generally defaults to heapsort for large inputs, providing $O(n\log n)$ complexity. Moreover, even though binary insertion and deletion are quadratic, these operations are partitioned and parallelized, meaning that each sort operates on a smaller data subset concurrently, making the process appear nearly linear. In fact, the *Static* can even achieve slightly sub-linear performance.

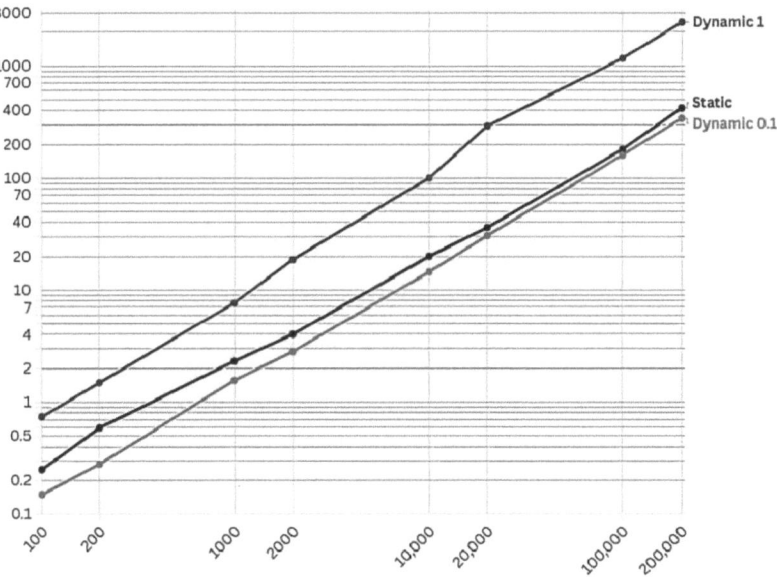

Fig. 1. Mapping execution time

Next, unlike the synthesis benchmark, the matching step only measures the time needed to identify overlaps, this evaluation also accounts for the output-sensitive nature of the recording result step (Fig. 2). Overall, the matching process tends to scale more rapidly as the dataset grows. With an increasing number of ranges, more overlaps occur, causing the performance curve to shift from linear to worst-case quadratic scenario. *Dynamic 1* is slower than *Static*, and nearly doubles at large data, because *Dynamic 1* is matching redundantly the modified ranges, which are all the ranges, twice. Meanwhile, *Dynamic 0.1* is the most efficient, highlighting the benefit of calculating only the parts that change.

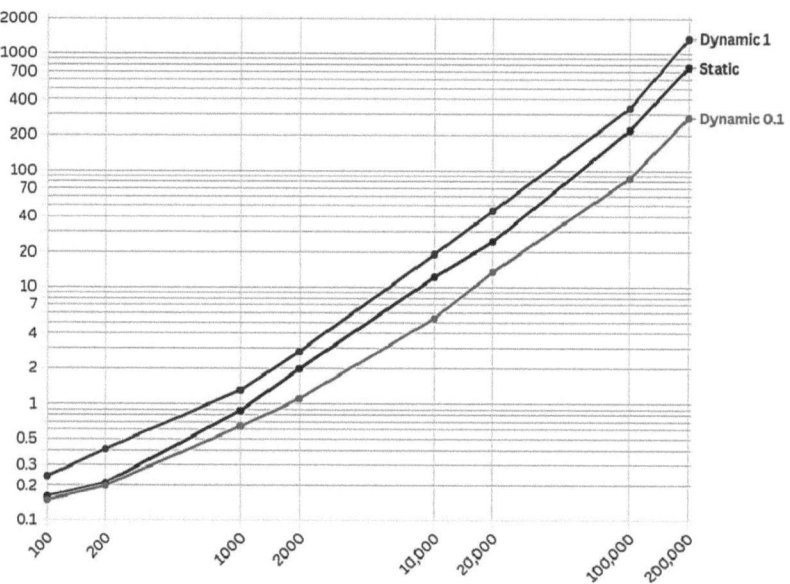

Fig. 2. Matching execution time

Finally, the recalculation of overlap results is examined. Being output-sensitive, it shows a steep slope on a log-log chart (Fig. 3). Regardless of the modification ratio, the workload remains nearly the same. This step involves iterating over the overlap results and removing the entries if they involve modified entities. Its performance suffers for two reasons. First, iterating through a hashset container is inherently costly, also within the Unity Job System design, it must be converted into an array to be iterated which is also computationally expensive. Secondly, Job's max allocation is limited to 2GB. Meanwhile, memory must be preallocated and cannot be resized within a Parallel Job, which forces the hashset to accommodate the maximum possible overlaps. As a result, processing stalls at 10,000 ranges due to the quadratic growth in memory usage. Once that limit is reached, the performance behavior changes; after that point, discrepancies arise only due to the process of recalculating on the actual overlap results. The Static also requires small amount of time to clear old results, which can be considered as "recalculation time".

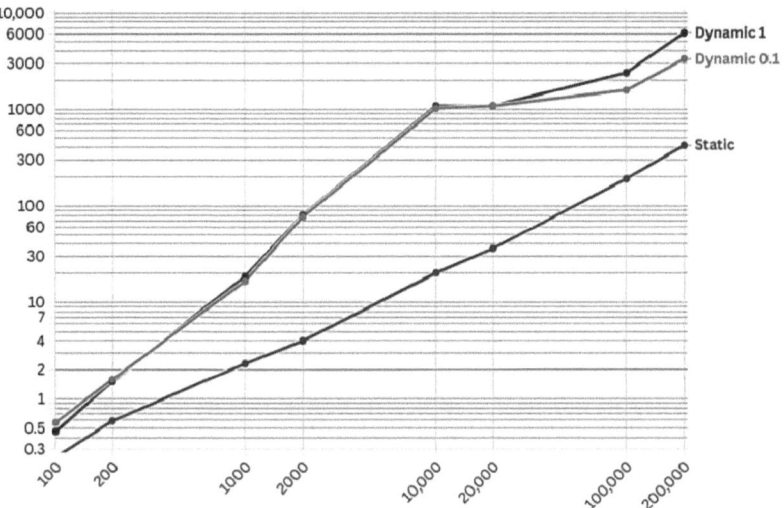

Fig. 3. Recalculate overlap result execution time

4.3 Discussion

In general, the static approach generally outperforms its dynamic counterpart. Although the dynamic method reduces the input size to only the modified data, it introduces an additional output-sensitive step to retain previous results, which undermines its overall efficiency. The mapping process, which operates independently of matching, can be adapted based on the modification ratio: for instance, when the modification ratio exceeds 0.15, the dynamic mapping strategy is recommended, and otherwise the static mapping approach is preferable. Additionally, the current implementation introduces extra steps—data flattening and unflattening, due to data oriented design of the Job System—to convert reference-based, nested data into a blittable, flat structure, and back. These conversions account for up to 25% of the total runtime.

In practice, a threshold of 30 FPS (approximately 33 ms per frame) is typically considered acceptable for real-time simulations. Empirical data suggests that handling up to 2000 ranges is practical to meet this frame budget, as processing 1,000 and 2,000 ranges takes about 6.0 ms and 13.4 ms respectively. Taking into account that some of the available time must be reserved for other tasks, such as other simulation logic and physics.

5 Conclusion

This work refines the original HSP-IM algorithm with minor corrections and optimizations, successfully integrating both HSP-DIM and HSP-SIM into Unity's Job System on standard hardware. The findings indicate that a static matching approach, combined with an adaptive mapping strategy, yields the most practical performance. Although the reproduced experimental results do not fully match the original due to differences in implementation and hardware architecture, HSP-IM remains consistent with baseline expectations and performs acceptably up to 2,000 ranges in a shared virtual environment. This demonstrates its feasibility for distributed simulation applications like VR, AR developed with widely used engine like Unity, where thousands of users might participate simultaneously. Future efforts will focus on further optimizing algorithmic steps tied to the Job System, designing data structures that integrate more efficiently to reduce overhead, and conduct more diverse scenarios, such as multiple varying range sizes, practical movement patterns.

References

1. Liu, E.S., Theodoropoulos, G.K.: Interest management for distributed virtual environments: a survey. ACM Comput. Surv. **46**(4), Article 51, 42 p (2014). http://dx.doi.org/10.1145/2535417
2. Tan, G., Zhang, Y., Ayani, R.: A hybrid approach to data distribution management. In: Proceedings of 4th IEEE International Workshop on Distributed Simulation and Real-Time Applications (DS-RT), San Francisco, CA, USA, 24–26 August 2000, pp. 55–61 (2000). https://doi.org/10.1109/DISRTA.2000.874064
3. Raczy, C., Tan, G., Yu, J.: A sort-based DDM matching algorithm for HLA. ACM Trans. Model. Comput. Simul. **15**(1), 14–38 (2005). https://doi.org/10.1145/1044322.1044324
4. Liu, E.S., Theodoropoulos, G.: A fast parallel matching algorithm for continuous interest management. In: Proceedings of the 2010 Winter Simulation Conference (WSC), Baltimore, MD, USA, 5–8 December 2010, pp. 1490–1500 (2010). https://doi.org/10.1109/WSC.2010.5679043
5. Marzolla, M., D'Angelo, G., Mandrioli, M.: A parallel data distribution management algorithm. In: Proceedings of 17th IEEE/ACM International Symposium on Distributed Simulation and Real Time Applications (DS-RT), Delft, Netherlands, 30 October–1 November 2013, pp. 145–152 (2013). https://doi.org/10.1109/DS-RT.2013.23
6. Tang, W., Yao, Y., Zhu, F., Chen, B., Cai, W.: A parallel hierarchical sort-based interest matching algorithm. In: Proceedings of the 2021 ACM SIGSIM Conference on Principles of Advanced Discrete Simulation (SIGSIM-PADS 2021), pp. 1–12. ACM, New York (2021). https://doi.org/10.1145/3437959.3459259
7. Tang, W., Yao, Y., Ou, L., Chen, K.: Hierarchical sort-based parallel algorithm for dynamic interest matching. J. Parallel Distrib. Comput. **188**, 104867 (2024). https://doi.org/10.1016/j.jpdc.2024.104867

Fast Agent-Based Solution to Evaluate the Matching of Public Transport Offer vs Citizen Mobility Demand

Marco Fanfani, Alberto Giovannoni, Luciano Alessandro Ipsaro Palesi, Ammarah Irum, and Paolo Nesi[✉]

Department of Information Engineering, Distributed Systems and Internet Technology Lab (DISIT), University of Florence, Via Santa Marta, 3, 50139 Florence, Italy
paolo.nesi@unfi.it
https://www.disit.org/, https://www.snap4city.org

Abstract. Public transportation is fundamental to support the mobility demand of citizens and drive the development of sustainable and green mobility in smart city scenarios. However, planning an efficient public transport system is a challenging task since it requires on the one hand to deploy a widespread, fast, and reliable system able to fully respond to the mobility demand. On the other hand, financial sustainability must be guaranteed by avoiding excessive and unfruitful expenses that could in the long run hamper the whole transportation system. Therefore, to find such a balance, there is the need for tools able to analyze and evaluate the match between the transportation offer and the mobility demand to allow city officers and decision makers to plan optimal services. To respond to this necessity, in this paper we propose an agent-based solution, that, differently from available software, is easily configurable, requires minimal input, and is able to carry out simulation in a timely manner yet providing useful and accurate insights. Moreover, the proposed solution can be easily adopted for what-if analysis frameworks, thus realizing an extremely valuable tool for smart city transportation planning.

Keywords: Public transport offer vs demand · Simulation · Agent-based · Smart mobility

1 Introduction

Due to an ever-increasing urban population, public administrations must face novel and complex challenges spanning several domains to guarantee citizens a high quality of life. Among them, public mobility is one of the significant issues and it is critically significant to minimize the gap between the Transport, Public or Private, which is the offer and the mobility demand while maintaining optimal operational cost at transit provider's end [1]. Moreover, United Nation, UN, Sustainable Development Goals, SDGs, related to sustainable cities and communities indicate that nearly half of the global urban population lack feasible and equitable access to public transport [2]. Thus, to calibrate the public transport offer, transportation agencies make significant assessments for planning their offer through specific simulations aiming at optimizing resources such as time and cost.

In the context of smart cities, the availability of diverse static, historic and real-time data, obtained from multiple sources such as transportation data, mobile cellular data, sensors data, vehicular and persons mobility data [3], can enable the development of new solutions fundamental in shaping the future of urban transportation infrastructure and helping the policy makers to make data-driven decisions. The data-driven insights play a pivotal role in evaluating the efficacy of demand-responsive transportation frameworks by laying a fact-based foundation for decision-making processes, thus ensuring an optimal, cost-effective and socially viable design of public transport infrastructure. To reinforce smart mobility in an urban setting Smart City Digital Twins (SCDTs) platforms [4] are fundamental decision support systems for suggesting and assessing the effects of infrastructure and service changes through simulated analysis and automatic optimization before introducing such changes in the real environment [5], the what-if analysis. Thus, in transportation offer modeling, the need to have a flexible, user-friendly and fast simulation tool capable to address the challenges of complex scenarios is evident.

Over the years, Agent Based Modeling, ABM, has emerged as a leading technique to simulate complexity in diverse social systems, including mobility [6]. ABMs, by representing individual agents as autonomous entities interacting with each other and the environment, have been extensively employed at micro-simulation scale accounting for details such as pedestrians' and drivers' behaviors [7]. Agents act as autonomous entities in the simulated environment where they are capable to achieve their specific objectives [8]. Such autonomous behavior of agents makes ABMs particularly appropriate for the representation of agents in transportation offer vs citizen mobility demand. However, despite the effectiveness of various simulation software, building transportation demand modelling simulation scenarios is a complex and time-consuming process that requires high technical experience or compromises [9]. Thus, a few ABM systems have been proposed to address the complexity of transportation systems. *SimMobility* is a multi-scale, comprehensive agent-based simulation platform that integrates demand modeling and urban mobility analysis to support decision-making in transport planning [10]. However, *SimMobility* significantly demands computational resources making large-scale or long-term simulations particularly difficult. *AnyLogic* is a multimethod, agent-based simulation platform that integrates system dynamics modelling, enabling complex system analysis and data-driven decision-making across numerous domains, including transportation and logistics [11], while the high licensing cost limits accessibility for smaller organizations and academic institutions. Additionally, large-scale agent-based simulations require relevant computational resources, which can affect performance in highly complex scenarios. *NetLogo* provides multi-agent modelling environment focused on adaptive interactions and decentralized decision-making across various scientific domains [12]. *NetLogo* has been designed for models of moderate size and becomes inefficient as the number of agents increases significantly and programming knowledge is required to configure agents. *GIS and Agent-based Modelling Architecture, GAMA,* is an agent-based platform that couples heterogeneous data and modeling paradigms to simulate transportation scenarios [13]. It requires high computational resources, especially for large-scale scenarios. *Simulation of Urban Mobility, SUMO,* is multimodal, open-source traffic simulation software that is capable to address demand modelling alongside other transport related issues [14]. SUMO has some computational limits when dealing with huge scenarios (in terms of number of agents, since each person is also an agent) since it requires careful setups, and it is time-consuming to run. *Multi-Agent Transport Simulation, MATSim,* and *TRANSIMS* have been designed to provide information on traffic impacts to transportation advisors [15, 16]. However, together with *SimMobility, MATSim* and *TRANSIMS* simulators focus on specific problems (e.g., traffic assignment generation) making them more purpose-oriented, less interactive and flexible than other simulators [17]. For instance, *MATSim* is an activity-based, large-scale multi-agent transport simulator which is not ideal solution for multi-day simulation as it takes long time to reach an equilibrium state with longer period of simulation due to the increase in the number of possible activities per agent to be tested [18]. Additionally, *MATSim* representation of public transport is limited, it is less detailed than specialized systems and may be approximate in handling schedules and vehicle capacities. The *Advanced Interactive Microscopic Simulator for Urban and Non-Urban Networks, Aimsun,* can be deployed to analyze exigency handling for various transportation problems by traffic engineers and policy makers. Multiple tools are provided within the software from simulating dedicated bus journeys to analyzing large-scale regions using microscopic, mesoscopic and hybrid simulation methods [19]. *PTV Vissim* for micro area modelling [20], is one of the comprehensive tools to perform simulations for public transport, urban planning, traffic engineering, etc. However, it requires expensive subscriptions and considerable effort in simulation setup.

It's worth noticing that most of the above-mentioned ABM tools demand settings on detailed parameters including road networks, vehicle routes, speed, and flows, traffic light signal configurations, pedestrian behaviors and activities, at any aggregation level [21]. The management of single agent for each pedestrian creates a significant barrier to users limiting their capacity to configure transport scenarios rapidly and effectively and can be a hindrance for those who need flexible and quick access to results, such as policy makers, or urban planners [22]. Moreover, they can be computationally expensive having to model any minimal interaction between the numerous agents and the environment, thus limiting their applicability in huge scenarios and for what-if analysis, that usually requires to instantiate multiple scenarios to assess the impact of possible changes. Finally, requiring complex configurations, is very difficult to set up those tools without human intervention, preventing their exploitation in automatic optimization solutions as the one described in [5].

A different approach was proposed by *DORAM* in [23], where a statistical model was defined to analyze public transport offer against demand achieving fast-computability and producing Key Performance Indicators, KPIs, about the number of pick-ups and drop-offs at each bus stop. This method required as input the total daily number of pick-ups and drop-offs that are distributed among the transportation stops by taking into account the probabilities of each stop to be a start, end, or transit and exploiting some weights (calibrated on the basis of actual measures gathered by PT service providers) to model the commuting probability. However, this method was not able to provide relevant KPIs like the unmet demand or the mean travel time and requires some calibration data not easy to obtain, limiting its applicability.

In Table 1, a summary of the comparative analysis for the discussed microsimulation software is reported considering their functionality, focusing on critical parameters such

Table 1. Comparison of simulators for PT offer vs mobility demand analysis: (✓) indicates that the solution satisfies the requirement, (×) non satisfied. (~) partial fulfillment, and (?) not clear accessible information to be assessed.

Simulator	Open source	Multi-modality	Scale on huge scenario	Fast computation	Easy & fast setup	Produce KPIs
SimMobility	✓	~	×	×	✓	✓
AnyLogic	×	✓	×	×	✓	✓
NetLogo	✓	✓	×	×	×	✓
GAMA	✓	✓	×	×	✓	✓
SUMO	✓	✓	×	×	×	✓
MATSim	✓	~	~	×		✓
TRANSIMS	✓	~	×	×	✓	✓
Aimsun	×	✓	?	?	✓	✓
PTV Vissim	×	✓	✓	?	×	✓
DORAM	✓	×	✓	✓	×	~
Proposed in this paper	✓	✓	✓	✓	✓	✓

as open-source availability, multimodality (i.e., the possibility to model different means of transportation like buses, tram, train, etc.), scalability on huge scenarios, computational efficiency, ease of setup, and the ability to provide KPIs to the decision makers. The findings indicate that free accessibility is a dominant characteristic among most simulators, with significant exceptions that include *AnyLogic*, *Aimsun*, and *PTV Vissim*. Multimodality is widely supported as well as sufficiently relevant KPI production. However, a few solutions seem to be usable on huge scenarios and long timespans. Additionally, computational efficiency remains a challenge for most simulators and the possibility to have easy and fast setups is rarely offered, since often manual customization (which sometimes requires programming skills) is required to create an error-free road network, setting-up several elements, such as vehicle trajectories, OD (origin destination) matrices, activity plans for citizens' mobility, traffic signal temporization, etc.

For these reasons, in this paper, we propose a novel open-source agent-based approach to address the problem of the transportation offer and demand matching by satisfying significant requirements into the system while focusing on strongly reducing computational costs. Thanks to multithreading architecture and a reasoned simplification of the ABM paradigm, the proposed solution is able to carry out simulations with strongly reduced execution time, without requiring complex setups, and it is capable of scaling on huge scenarios including whole cities spanning on multiple days providing sensible KPIs to assess the quality of the transportation offer with respect to the actual demand of mobility. Such improvements allow the system to be effectively exploited in a what-if analysis framework and eventually be enforced into a digital twin platform for public transport optimization. This work has been carried out in the context of the Spoke 9 of the Italian National Center for Sustainable Mobility (CN MOST) [24], and the CN MOST flagship OPTIFaaS and scalability project SASUAM. The proposed solution has been developed in the Snap4City framework [25, 26], https://www.snap4city.org.

The paper is organized as follows. In Sect. 2, after presenting a series of functional requirements defined to guide the method development, the solution is described. In Sect. 3, a case study is reported to show the effectiveness of the proposed approach illustrating its applications in a what-if analysis. Finally, in Sect. 4 conclusions are drawn.

2 The Proposed Solution

As stated in the previous section, in this paper we propose a novel agent-based simulator, developed exploiting the Snap4City open-source framework [27. 28], to analyze the urban transport and identify possible deficiencies in terms of under or over provisioned services with respect to the citizen mobility demand.

To guide the design of this novel solution the following functional requirements have been identified:

R1. **Selection of the working area**: the system must allow the user to define the area of interest in which the simulation has to work, from city hamlets to whole metropolitan areas.

R2. **Selection of the working timespan**: the system must allow the user to define the timespan on which the simulation runs, from a few hours to days.

R3. **Offer specification format compatibility**: to set the transportation service input the system must be able to accept at least the GTFS format [29] to specify PT services routes, lines/rides, bus stops, timetables, etc. (**R3.a**). Optionally, other standards should be supported, e.g., NeTEx [30] (**R3.b**). Additional information on transportation vehicles' capacity should be supported (**R3.c**).

R4. **Multimodal solutions**: the simulator must be able to consider urban travel solutions including different transportation modalities, like for example buses, trams, and trains, and optionally also the sharing offer.

R5. **Mobility demand specification format**: to know the citizen mobility demand in the form of Origin-Destination Matrix (ODMs) commonly used representation formats must be supported, as for example the Matrix Market Exchange Format, MTX, [31] (**R5.a**). Additionally, geographical data formats like Shapefiles or GeoJSON, WKT, or standard as the MGRS [32], must be supported to define the shapes of the zones used in the ODMs (**R5.b**). In substance, ODM can refer to administrative shapes or regular grids at different scales.

R6. **Modal and Multimodal routing**: to produce trajectories for the city users in the simulation according to the ODMs, a routing service must be exploited (**R6.a**). This additionally requires information about the city road graph. Such routing must be performed in reasonable times to allow a fast simulation (**R6.b**).

R7. **Computational scalability**: the simulation must be able to run efficiently and with acceptable execution time, even for large areas, large timespan, the huge number of vehicles and pedestrians considered.

R8. **Track vehicle status**: the simulator must allow the operator to evaluate position and occupancy of each transport vehicle/service every time instant of the simulation.

R9. **Track stop status**: the system must allow the operator to count the number of people waiting at stops, getting in/out, and also their waiting time, and the number of people on each vehicle at each time instant of the simulation.

R10. **Key Performance Indicator (KPI) production**: once a simulation is completed, the system must produce a series of indicators to measure the performance of the transportation offer with respect to the specified demand. Such indicators could include mean travel time, meat waiting time at stops, crowed stops, vehicle occupancy, people or areas not served, number of served city users at each stop over time, number of people getting off, etc.

The proposed solution is able to satisfy all the above requirements as discussed in the following sections and demonstrated in Sect. 3.

2.1 Architectural Overview and Data Flow

Before performing the simulation, a setup of a few parameters is needed, such as to specify: the area of interest, the timespan, and the offer and demand inputs. This allows to define the context of simulation scenario. Wide areas (**R1**) can be specified by using the minimum and maximum latitude and longitude coordinates (bounding box) of the area under study. Datetime is used to set the simulation timespan, which may insist on several days (**R2**). To input the transportation offer, the GTFS files are supported (**R3.a**) and vehicle capacity can be specified (**R3.c**). Multimodal solutions are considered, allowing people to travel using buses, trams, and urban trains (**R4**). Before starting the simulation, the GTFS files (i.e., *agency.txt*, *calendar_dates.txt*, *routes.txt*, *shapes.txt*, *stop_times.txt*, *stops.txt*, *trips.txt*) are automatically analyzed and the data is reorganized as a compact representation into a single JSON where a structure for each single vehicle is defined. Such a structure includes the vehicle IDs (route ID, line name and ID, shape ID), day of operation, and the stop list, that is an array in which each stop is described with an ID, latitude and longitude coordinates, and time. This compact structure simplifies filtering to extract the vehicles that have to be considered in the simulation (having at least two stops in the simulation area and operating in the considered time window) and the agent construction during the simulation.

Demand ODMs can be loaded by using different file formats, including MTX (**R5.a**). At this moment our system supports MGRS areas to describe origins and destinations (**R5.b**). Note that additional geographic formats can be included in the future with minor effort, Snap4City already supports them as models. As for the offer, also the demand is filtered according to the simulation area and the used time span.

To obtain routes (**R6**), the GraphHopper router [33] is exploited providing as input the city road graph extracted from OpenStreetMap [34], and the GTFS files. This enables the possibility of obtaining multimodal travel paths by exploiting both walking and multimodal services. Note that, since ODM are provided according to specific geographic zones, it is possible to approximate the starting and ending positions of people's travels with the centroid of the zones, instead of randomly selecting a different starting/ending point for each person. Such approximation simplifies the computing of people's routing since multiple people's routes can be obtained with a single request and has a limited impact on the evaluation of the transportation when the zones used are sufficiently small. Moreover, to provide a fast computation of the trajectories we devised a scalable system able to distribute the routing requests on multiple GraphHopper instances to balance the load and speed-up the computation. Additionally, a caching system based on a relational database has been realized to store previously computed routes to be quickly retrieved when executing new simulations on the same scenario with only partial changes in the demand. Thanks to multithreading programming and other measures described in the following, the proposed solution achieves fast execution times even on huge scenarios (**R7**) encompassing wide areas, simulating several days, and considering thousands of vehicles and passengers. Moreover, to reduce memory consumption both the transportation vehicles and the ODM data are dynamically loaded in the simulator: a vehicle is kept in the simulation only for the time required to complete its route, similarly pedestrians are generated into the simulation at their starting stop and removed once reaching their destination.

2.2 Agent Modelling

In the proposed simulator all transportation vehicles (buses, trams, and trains) are modelled as independent agents able to actively interact with the environment. This allows us to track the vehicle status, responding to R8, and indirectly track the stop/station status, fulfilling **R9**. Differently, pedestrians are modelled as passive elements that can be viewed as packages that appear at the stops and wait to take some transportation means to move over the city. Such a solution lightens the computational burden without estimating the status/position of each person at each time instant of the simulation. Indeed, pedestrians are following their precomputed routes. For this reason, we make people appear at the stops, with a delay with respect to their starting time related to the walking distance they have to cover between their origin and the transportation stop/station (this also allows them to estimate their intermediate positions if needed). Note also that the number of people that usually have to be included into a realistic large-scale simulation is much greater than the number of vehicles (usually hundreds of thousands of passengers are served by a few thousand transportation vehicles). Avoiding modeling pedestrians as agents is extremely advantageous to reduce computational times and required hardware resources.

During the simulation each vehicle follows its route according to the GTFS and stops at specific times in all the simulation areas in which one of their stops/stations falls (as for pedestrian starting/ending position, transportation stops are also mapped on the ODM areas). During the simulation, each vehicle collects the pedestrians waiting at the stops considering its max and actual occupancy, i.e., when the vehicle is full, additional people are not allowed to get on board. Then, the vehicle continues its path following the timings specified in the GTFS and changing dynamically its real time occupancy. In other simulators, e.g., SUMO, the movements of the vehicles are computed on the basis of all the variables considered in the simulation, thus increasing dramatically the computational times. Such behavior produces route timings that are very close to those reported in the GTFS, that is indeed created taking into account the real travel times. The proposed solution avoids this complexity to obtain a relevant speed up in the computation of the simulation. It could be observed that this choice would limit the applicability of our simulator when considering particular days on which private vehicles running on the streets cause unusual traffic jams and consequent delays on the transportation routes (part for the cases in which reserved paths/lanes are dedicated to public transportation). However, these events can be also modelled by computing beforehand the level of traffic congestion, using for example [35], and then altering the travel times of the transportation routes according to the estimated reduced speed.

Every time a vehicle reaches a stop, some passengers may get off, in this case, the occupancy counter is decreased leaving space to get new passengers on board. When the person's trip includes a final transportation route, her/his travel ends, with an ending time augmented by the walking time required to reach her/his destination. On the other hand, if multiple (even multimodal) transportation routes are required, the pedestrian is moved to the next stop taking time, where she/he appears at a later time to take into account the walking time. Examples of modelled trips are shown in Fig. 1.

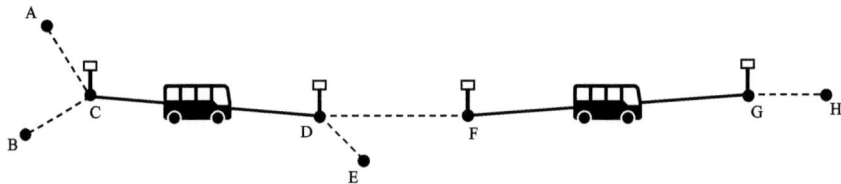

Fig. 1. Example of trips modeled in the proposed simulator. Suppose A and B are starting position for the travels of two persons, Alice and Bob. Both will reach the first stop in C and will catch the bus taking them to D. Then, Alice walks to E, ending her journey. Differently, Bob will walk to E, take the second bus, reach G and then walk to his destination in H. In our simulator movement done by foot are handled considering the required walking times. For example, if Alice starts from A at 9:00 and walking from A to C requires 7 min, she will appear at the first stop in C at 9:07. Similarly, if Bob drop-off in D at 9:30, he disappears and reappears in F at 9:42, considering a walking time of 12 min between D and F. Same considerations apply on the other paths done by foot (e.g., D–E and G–H).

The simulation runs for N time instants $T = \{t_0, t_1, \ldots, t_{N-1}\}$ and all vehicles are updated every $\Delta_V = t_i - t_{i-1}$ by checking their status and executing the pick-ups and drop-offs for those vehicles that at t_i have a scheduled stop in the GTFS. New pedestrians are added every $\Delta_P \gg \Delta_V$, according to the ODM data, and following the procedure described above. If a pedestrian enters the simulation at time t_j it will appear at the first stop indicated by the routing at a time $\hat{t}_j = t_j + \delta_w$, where δ_w is the walking time spent from the origin to the stop. δ_w, that could also be zero, is computed by the GraphHopper according to an average walking speed that can be set by the operator.

2.3 KPI Computation

Once the simulation is completed, the system produces in output a series of KPIs that can be used to summarize the performance of the transport system with respect to the citizen mobility demand (fulfilling **R10**). In our solution, we consider the following KPIs.

Unmet Demand: Total number of people that were not able to get on the transportation vehicle since its maximum capacity was reached. This highlights the main deficiencies of the transportation system and can be used to identify the most critical lines that are under provision.

Mean Travel Time (*MTT*) Ratio: By taking as *expected mean travel time* (MTT_e) the average travel time estimated by the routing algorithm for each person, and the *actual mean travel time* (MTT_a) as the average time measured after the simulation, we define the $MTT = MTT_a/MTT_e \in [1, \infty)$. Whether $MTT = 1$, the transportation works as expected, demonstrating its sufficiency in satisfying all people's demands. Otherwise, if values greater than 1 are achieved, this indicates some deficiencies, since increased MTT_a are due to the impossibility to take the expected transportation vehicle due to overcrowding.

Vehicle Occupancy Reports the number of passengers on the transportation vehicles. It can be represented as an average percentage with respect to the total vehicle capacity, or can be specified for single transportation lines, producing histograms to show how the number of passengers varies along a route or at different times.

Number of Pick-Ups and Drop-Offs: This KPI indicates the number of people getting on and off the transportation vehicles at given stops. This can give insights into the most used stops and provide also the **level of crowding** at given stops, which is useful to identify critical spots since crowded areas can be problematic for both security and sanitary reasons.

Average Waiting Time: This is the mean time spent by the pedestrian at the stop waiting for a non-fully occupied transportation vehicle that can take them to their destination. High waiting times indicate an insufficient transportation vehicle frequency.

Average Walking Time: This indicator counts the average time spent on foot by the pedestrians. If the transportation system is sufficiently widespread around the city such times should be low. Otherwise, there are probably underserved areas that force people to walk longer to reach the transportation stops. It is also possible to provide the number of pedestrians walking longer than a given threshold and potentially highlight the specific problematic areas. Note that at this moment this indicator can be directly computed from the router output. However, in the future pedestrians could be improved with a propensity to walk that could rise the longer they wait for the transportation vehicle.

In the next section an experimental case of study is presented to show the effectiveness of the proposed method.

3 Experimental Case Study

To show the effectiveness of the proposed method, we report in this section a case study carried out on the city of Florence, Italy. We consider an area wider than the Florence municipality, including also suburban areas like Sesto Fiorentino, Scandicci, and Bagno a Ripoli. In Fig. 2 a map of the area is shown. This area has been split into 4624 MGSR zones (i.e., a 64×64 grid), each cell with a dimension of 200×200 m.

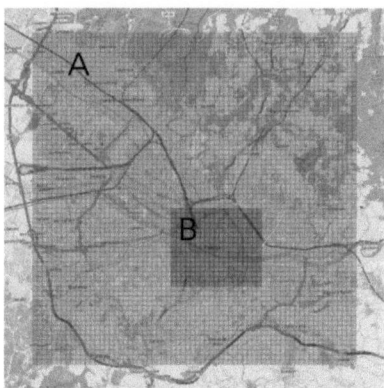

Fig. 2. Map of the area used for the case study (shown in EPSG:32632 for better viewing). The 4624 MGRS cells, with dimension of 200 × 200 meters, used to partition the area are showed over the map. In red the inner area A and in blue the outer area B used to generate the ODMs for the different time slots.

The simulation has been run on a timespan of five working days, from the 00:00 of November 11th, 2024 (Monday) to the 23:59 of November 15th, 2024 (Friday). Offer has been modeled according to GTFS data provided by the PT service providers, i.e. Autolinee Toscane (buses), Gest (trams), and Trenitalia (trains). A total of 8570 vehicles per day has been considered (7254 buses, 882 trams, and 434 trains).

Since we do not have access to real data to specify the citizen demand, we created simulated ODMs: considering **150000** passenger per day, we distributed the starting travel times of the pedestrians following to the traffic curve reported in [35] where a strong rise of trips is registered between after 07:00 with a peak at 09:00 in the morning. Then the number of trips slightly reduces and stays rather constat between 10:00 and 16:00, reaching a second peak at 17:00, followed by a progressive drop from 18:00 to 23:00. A histogram illustrating the number of passengers starting their journey in each hour is shown in Fig. 3. We use this temporal distribution for all five working days.

Differently, origins and destinations have been randomly selected, with independent samples for each day, using different origin-destination probabilities for zones in the outer (A) or inner (B) areas, as shown in Fig. 2. The inner area (B) includes the central part of Florence where most of the offices and attractions are located. Differently the outer area (A) includes the outskirts of the city with many residential districts. Therefore, we modelled ODMs such that between 05:00 to 10:00 we have a probability $P_{Orig}^{OUT} = 0.8$ to select one the outer areas as origin, and $P_{Dest}^{OUT} = 0.2$ to select those areas as destination. Complementarily, for the cells in the inner area we set probability of $P_{Orig}^{IN} = 0.2$ and $P_{Dest}^{IN} = 0.8$, respectively to select one of those cells as origin or destination. Then in the successive time slot, from 11:00 to 16:00, the probabilities have been changed as $P_{Orig}^{OUT} = 0.6$, $P_{Dest}^{OUT} = 0.4$, $P_{Orig}^{IN} = 0.4$ and $P_{Dest}^{IN} = 0.6$. Finally in the evening from 17:00 to 23:00, we set $P_{Orig}^{OUT} = 0.2$, $P_{Dest}^{OUT} = 0.8$, $P_{Orig}^{IN} = 0.8$ and $P_{Dest}^{IN} = 0.2$. Such probabilities have been defined to broadly model the people's flow that in the morning and during the afternoon tend to move from the outer area to the city center to go to work, and in the evening perform the opposite trip to go back home. We are aware that this kind of data generation is a simplification of the transportation demand patterns in a city, thus producing ODMs that could not fully agree with real people's movements along the day. However, with these tests we want to demonstrate the capabilities of the proposed solution and not perform an actual analysis of the transport services in Florence, thus such an approximation is sufficient for the scope of this work.

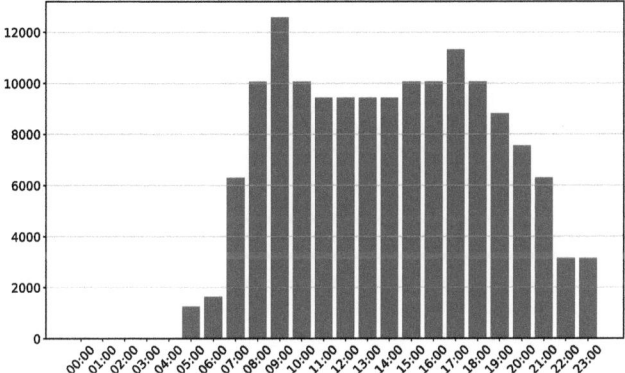

Fig. 3. Temporal distribution of starting time of people's trip used in the case study to generate ODMs.

The simulation has been executed on a workstation equipped with a CPU with 4 cores at 2.30 GHz and 24 GB RAM. In addition, four instances of the GraphHopper router have been exploited on different virtual machines, each with 29 cores at 2.30 GHz and 64 GB RAM, using a RAM-drive configuration. Queries toward GraphHopper instances have been performed using REST APIs over HTTP from the machine running the simulator. Query results were also saved on a relational database realizing the cache system described in Sect. 2.1. Note that two kinds of tests have been performed to assess the impact of the caching systems: in the first test, the database cache was empty and progressively filled. Then we repeated the test using the preloaded cache to observe the achievable speed-up. In Table 2 the computational times required to preprocess the GTFS and execute one day of simulation have been reported for the two tests. As can be seen, GTFS preprocessing requires around 30 min, of which most of the time is used to compute the compact JSON representation described in Sect. 2.1. Note that the JSON construction from the GTFS data is carried out only when a new GTFS is released, usually once every two or three months. Filtering the relevant vehicles from the processed GTFS and the pedestrians from the ODMs is instead a very fast operation, in the order of a few seconds. Once the preprocessing is performed, one day of simulation is typically completed in 2765 s, if the routing cache is empty and the GraphHopper services must be queried to obtain the routings. Differently, when the cache is available, simulation times are strongly reduced to 271 s on average, with a speed-up of 10 times. This can be extremely useful when the operator needs to repeat the simulation with minimal changes, as usually happens when carrying out what-if analysis looking for an improvement by changing the transportation offer with the same mobility demand.

Table 2. Computational times.

Step	Times (s)
GTFS conversion	1802
GTFS and ODM filtering	10
Simulation of 1 day (empty cache)	2765
Simulation of 1 day (using cache)	271

After completing the simulation, KPIs described in Sect. 2.3 are computed and made accessible for the operator. Hereafter some examples have been reported.

Table 3. Measured values for the following KPIs: unmet demand, MTT ratio, average waiting time, and average walking time (with in bracket the number of travelers having to walk for more than 20 min).

Day	Unmet Demand	MTT Ratio	Average Waiting Time (s)	Average Walking Time (s)
Monday	34885	1.217	472	362 (24428)
Tuesday	34813	1.217	475	363 (24301)
Wednesday	35077	1.223	477	361 (24133)
Thursday	34693	1.216	478	362 (24468)
Friday	34584	1.207	481	361 (24229)

In Table 3, the unmet demand, MTT ratio, average waiting time, and average walking time (with in bracket the number of travelers having to walk for more than 20 min) have been included. As expected, very few differences are appreciable among the days since the transportation vehicles schedule is stable for the working days and the demand can be produced by ODM or generated with the same random procedure. In assessing an actual transportation offer, such numbers would highlight that more than 23% of the demand is unable to reach the destination and among those able to arrive at the destination an average of 20% increased travel time is measured. Waiting times at the stops are in order of 8 min (for those that are able to get on the vehicles) while on average 6 min' walk are required to complete a trip (with only 16% of people forced to walk for more than 20 min).

To show the pick-ups and drop-offs, Figure 4 reports the histograms illustrating the number of people boarding and descending from buses at two representative bus stops. The first one (plots in Fig. 4, a, c, e, g, and i) is a stop in the inner area (San Marco square), while the second (see Fig. 4, b, d, f, h, and j) is a stop located in the outer area (Via Baracca, il Barco). As can be observed, at the inner area stop, most of the drop-offs are concentrated in the first hours of the days and decrease during the afternoon and evening. Conversely, at the outer area bus stop drop-offs are concentrated in the late hours. This

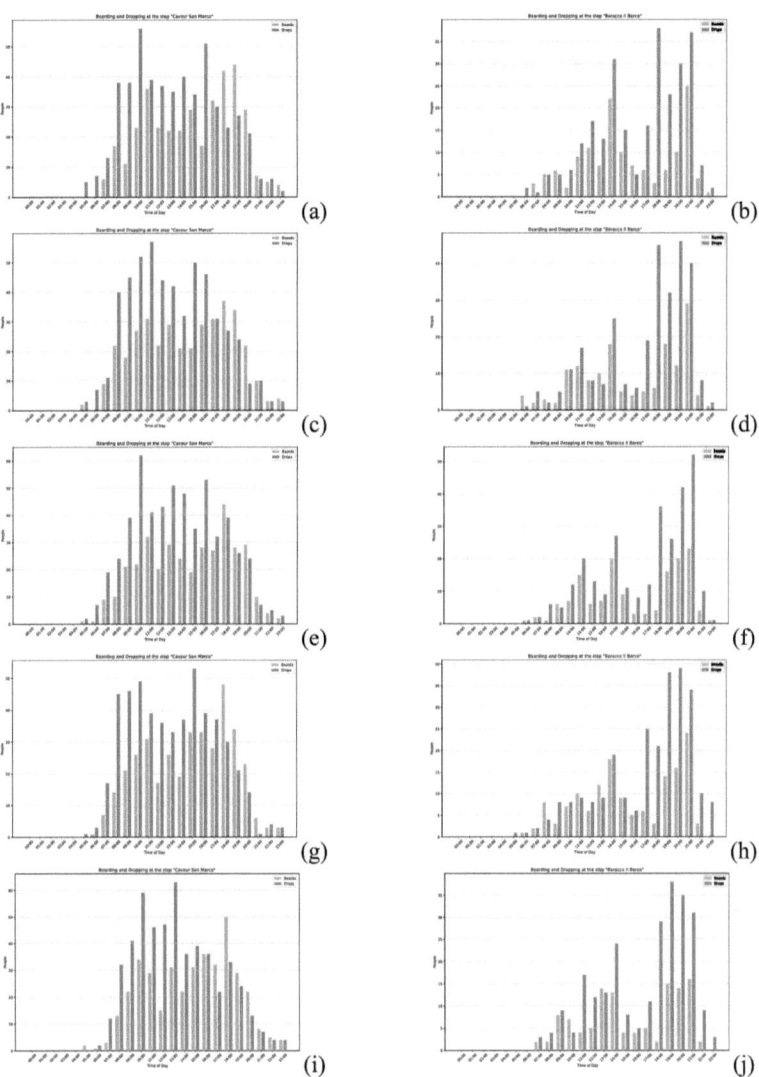

Fig. 4. Pick-ups (green) and drop-off (red) for two different stops. In the first column a stop in the inner area, in the right column a stop in the outer area. From top to bottom the different days of the week (from Monday to Friday).

behavior is aligned with the demand generated where the inner area is the most probable destination during the morning, while the outer area is a probable destination during the evening. Pick-ups for the inner area stop following a specular behavior concentrating in the second part of the days. Differently in the outer stop, pick-ups are not particularly concentrated in the morning. Indeed, the inner stop is a bus terminal for some of the lines stopping by, thus it is used both for trips going into the inner area and for those in the opposite direction. Differently, the outer stop is a transit stop from which the buses pass then move further away toward external city areas, thus it is mostly used to travel from the inner to the outer areas in the evening. As illustrated in Fig. 5, it is also possible to show aggregated pick-ups and drop-offs for a given stop, thus obtaining the crowding level at the stop, and providing details on the contribution of the single lines (for example, in Figure 5, four bus lines stop at the same location).

Finally, the bus occupancy level can be analyzed. Figure 6 presents the occupancy level of the bus line/ride sketched on the map (see Fig. 6a) in two moments of the day: a morning trip, from 09:26 to 10:40 (see Fig. 6b), and an evening trip, from 19:25 to 20:32 (see Fig. 6c). Observing the distribution over time, in which each bin corresponds to the people on-board at each stop (stops in outer areas are represented in blue, in the inner areas in red), it is possible to note that in the morning trip the bus progressively fills up by picking up people in outer areas, then starts to drop-offs passengers when reaching the inner areas. Conversely, an opposite behavior can be observed in the evening ride with passengers boarding at stops in the inner area and dropping off the bus in outer areas. Such results further align with the demand specified in input, therefore confirming the capability of the proposed solution to produce correct estimates on the transportation usage.

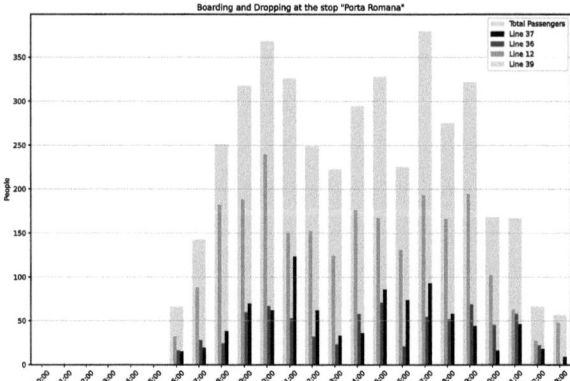

Fig. 5. Aggregated pick-ups and drop-offs at a bus stop with details on single lines.

3.1 What-if Analysis

To further show the effectiveness of our solution, hereafter an example of what-if analysis is presented. After running the simulation, we noticed that at a few stops, at specific time slots presented a huge number of people waiting for a bus and not being able to board since the passing vehicles were full. For example, on Monday at 17:39 the simulator listed 655 people waiting at Porta Romana bus stop to board bus 12 (on the ride running from 17:19 to 17:47).

We tried to add new rides on the same line to observe how these changes would impact the transportation service. First, we added a new ride operating in the same time window from 17:19 to 17:47. This in practice doubled the number of possible passengers

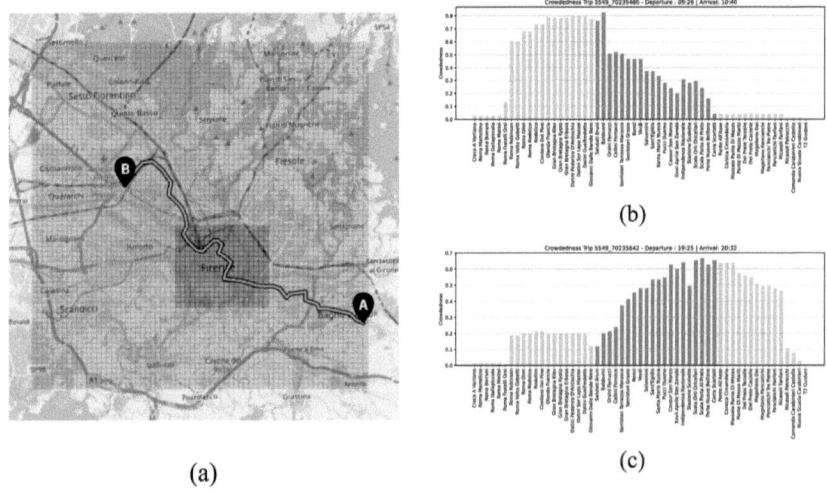

Fig. 6. Occupancy level for two rides on the same line. In (a) the bus line that travels from A to B has been reported over the map. In (b) the occupancy level for the morning ride (traveling from 09:26 to 10:40). In (c) the occupancy level for the evening route, from 19:25 to 20:32. Blue histogram bins indicate stops in the outer area, while reb bins are related to stops in in inner area.

Table 4. What-If experiments. New rides have been added in the simulation to observe the impact of the changes in reducing the number of people waiting at the inspected stop.

Experiment	Number of added rides	Added ride operating times	People waiting at the stop
Original	0		655
What-If #1	1	17:19–17:47	579
What-If #2	2	17:02–17:47	503
What-If #3	3	16:46–17:47	426
What-If #4	4	16:29–17:47	357

for the critical ride and produced a reduction in the number of people waiting passing from 655 to 579. Then we tried to introduce additional rides in previous windows. Results are shown in Table 4. As can be seen, by progressively adding new buses running on the same line the people waiting to be served progressively reduced passing from 655 to 579 with an additional ride, to 503 with two new rides, to 426 with three, to 357 adding four new rides. Note that a reduction of approximately 75 people for each new ride is observed, equal to the capacity set for the buses. This confirms that our solution is able to adapt properly to the input changes and can be effectively used to carry out what-if analysis in a very short time (since, as described above, by avoiding recomputing the routing the simulations terminate in less than 5 min). The solution resulted in being much faster than SUMO simulator in both setup and execution.

4 Conclusions

In this paper we have presented a novel solution to assess the match between transportation offer and city users mobility demand using agent-based simulations. Different from available state-of-the-art solutions, our method fulfills all the defined requirements, needs minimal input (i.e. GTFS and ODM describing respectively the offer and the demand, plus the city road graph), avoiding the need for any manual setup, and is able to provide quick full-day simulations that can run in a few minutes for huge area. Once the simulation is completed, a series of KPIs is produced to evaluate unmet demand, mean travel times, average waiting and walking times, number of pick-ups and drop-offs at specific stops, and the level of occupancy of any ride while traveling.

As shown in the experimental section, the proposed solution produces results that permit the actual simulation and react correctly to changes in the offer and demand. In addition, the solution has been capable of identifying the critical conditions, thus confirming its validity. Moreover, it can be easily used to perform what-if analysis to assess the impact of possible changes in the transportation service. Finally, since no manual input is required to configure a simulation and fast computation times are achieved, our solution can be effectively enforced into an automatic optimization framework exploiting for example reinforced learning to produce the most relevant solutions for solving transportation deficiencies strongly reducing the human effort, thus helping decision-makers in planning activities. The solution resulted in being much faster than SUMO simulator in both setup and execution.

Acknowledgements. This study has been carried out in the context of the Spoke 9 of the Italian National Center for Sustainable Mobility (CN MOST), and the CN MOST flagship project OPTIFaaS and scalability project SASUAM.

References

1. Kaeoruean, K., Phithakkitnukoon, S., Demissie, M.G., Kattan, L., Ratti, C.: Analysis of demand–supply gaps in public transit systems based on census and GTFS data: a case study of Calgary, Canada. Public Transp. **12**, 483–516 (2020)
2. SDG indicators (no date) United Nations. https://unstats.un.org/sdgs/report/2020/goal-11/. Accessed: 12 Feb 2025
3. Bellini, P., Bilotta, S., Collini, E., Fanfani, M., Nesi, P.: Data sources and models for integrated mobility and transport solutions. Sensors **24**(2), 441 (2024)
4. Adreani, L., Bellini, P., Fanfani, M., Nesi, P., Pantaleo, G.: Smart city digital twin framework for real-time multi-data integration and wide public distribution. IEEE Access **12**, 76277–76303 (2024). https://doi.org/10.1109/ACCESS.2024.3406795
5. Bellini, P., Collini, E., Fanfani, M., Palesi, L.A.I., Nesi, P.: Smart city digital twin platform architecture for mobility and transport decision support systems. In: 2024 IEEE International Conference on Big Data (BigData), pp. 5486–5495. IEEE (2024)
6. Shaharuddin, R.A., Misro, M.Y.: Traffic simulation using agent based modelling. In: AIP Conference Proceedings, vol. 2423, No. 1. AIP Publishing (202)
7. Bernhardt, K.:. Agent-based modeling in transportation. In: Artificial Intelligence in Transportation, 72 (2007)

8. Nguyen, J., Powers, S.T., Urquhart, N., Farrenkopf, T., Guckert, M.: An overview of agent-based traffic simulators. Transport. Res. Interdisc. Perspect. **12**, 100486 (2021)
9. Azfar, T., Weidner, J., Raheem, A., Ke, R., Cheu, R.L.: Efficient procedure of building university campus models for digital twin simulation. IEEE J. Radio Freq. Identif. **6**, 769–773 (2022)
10. Adnan, M., Pereira, F.C., Lima Azevedo, C.M., et al.: SimMobility: a multiscale integrated agent-based simulation platform. In: Transportation Research board 95th annual meeting, pp. 10–14. Washington, United States (2016)
11. Grigoryev, I.: AnyLogic in three days: Modeling and simulation textbook. The AnyLogic Company (2018)
12. Wilensky, U., Rand, W.: Modeling Natural, Social, and Engineered Complex Systems with NetLogo. The MIT Press (2015)
13. Taillandier, P., Gaudou, B., Grignard, A., et al.: Building, composing and experimenting complex spatial models with the GAMA platform. GeoInformatica **23**, 299–322 (2019). https://doi.org/10.1007/s10707-018-00339-6
14. Behrisch, M., Bieker, L., Erdmann, J., Krajzewicz, D.: SUMO–simulation of urban mobility: an overview. In: Proceedings of SIMUL 2011, The Third International Conference on Advances in System Simulation. ThinkMind (2011)
15. Horni, A., Nagel, K., Axhausen, K.W.: Introducing matsim. In: Horni, A., Nagel, K., Axhausen, K.W. (eds.) The multi-agent transport simulation MATSim, pp. 3–8. Ubiquity Press (2016). https://doi.org/10.5334/baw.1
16. Smith, L., Beckman, R., Baggerly, K.:TRANSIMS: Transportation analysis and simulation system. Los Alamos (1995)
17. Codeca, L., Erdmann, J., Cahill, V., Haerri, J.: Saga: An activity-based multi-modal mobility scenariogenerator for sumo. In: SUMO Conference Proceedings, vol. 1, pp. 39–58 (2020)
18. Ordóñez Medina, S.A.: Multi-day activity models: an extension of the Multi-Agent Transport Simulation (MATSim). Arbeitsberichte Verkehrs-Und Raumplanung, 1211 (2016)
19. Aimsun. (n.d.). Technical Notes Archives. Retrieved 14 Feb 2025. https://www.aimsun.com/category/technical-notes/
20. Ullah, M.R., Khattak, K.S., Khan, Z.H., Khan, M.A., Minallah, N., Khan, A.N.: Vehicular traffic simulation software: a systematic comparative analysis. Pakistan J. Eng. Technol. **4**(1), 66–78 (2021)
21. Ejercito, P.M., Nebrija, K.G.E., Feria, R.P., Lara-Figueroa, L.L.: Traffic simulation software review. In: 2017 8th International Conference on Information, Intelligence, Systems & Applications (IISA), pp. 1–4. IEEE (2017)
22. Li, S., Azfar, T., Ke, R.: Chatsumo: Large language model for automating traffic scenario generation in simulation of urban mobility. IEEE Trans. Intell. Veh. (2024)
23. Arman, A., Badii, C., Bellini, P., Bilotta, S., Nesi, P., Paolucci, M.: Analyzing demand with respect to offer of mobility. Appl. Sci. **12**(18), 8982 (2022)
24. Alberti, F., et al.: Mobile mapping to support an integrated transport-territory modelling approach. Int. Arch. Photogramm. Remote. Sens. Spat. Inf. Sci. **48**, 1–7 (2023)
25. Bellini, P., Bilotta, S., Collini, E., Fanfani, M., Nesi, P.: Mobility and transport data for city digital twin modeling and exploitation. In: 2023 IEEE International Smart Cities Conference (ISC2), pp. 1–7. IEEE (2023)
26. Adreani, L., Bellini, P., Fanfani, M., Nesi, P., Pantaleo, G.: Design and develop of a smart city digital twin with 3d representation and user interface for what-if analysis. In: Gervasi, O., et al. (eds.) Computational Science and Its Applications – ICCSA 2023 Workshops: Athens, Greece, July 3–6, 2023, Proceedings, Part VIII, pp. 531–548. Springer Nature Switzerland, Cham (2023). https://doi.org/10.1007/978-3-031-37126-4_34

27. Bellini, P., Bilotta, S., Palesi, A.L.I., Nesi, P., Pantaleo, G.: Vehicular traffic flow reconstruction analysis to mitigate scenarios with large city changes. IEEE Access **10**, 131061–131075 (2022). https://doi.org/10.1109/ACCESS.2022.3229183
28. Fanfani, M., Palesi, L.A.I., Nesi, P.: Microservices' libraries enabling server-side business logic visual programming for digital twins. SoftwareX **27**, 101805 (2024). https://doi.org/10.1016/j.softx.2024.101805
29. General Transit Feed Specification. https://gtfs.org/. Accessed on 26th Feb 2025
30. Network Timetable Exchange. https://transmodel-cen.eu/index.php/netex/. Accessed on 26 Feb 2025)
31. Matrix Market Exchange Format. https://math.nist.gov/MatrixMarket/. Accessed 26 Feb 2025
32. Military Grid Reference System. https://mgrs-data.org/. Accessed 26 Feb2025
33. GraphHopper: Directions API Route Planning. https://www.graphhopper.com/. Accessed 26 Feb 2025
34. OpenStreetMap. https://www.openstreetmap.org/. Accessed on 26 Feb 2025
35. Bilotta, S., Nesi, P.: Traffic flow reconstruction by solving indeterminacy on traffic distribution at junctions. Futur. Gener. Comput. Syst. **114**, 649–660 (2021)

A Strategy Utilizing an LLM and Augmented Reality for Handling the Missing Data: A Case Study Using Unity, Vuforia and ChatGPT

Enio Vicente de Limas[1], Rita de Fátima Rodrigues Guimarães[2], Bianchi Serique Meiguins[3], Leonardo Chaves Dutra da Rocha[4], Diego Roberto Colombo Dias[5], and Marcelo de Paiva Guimarães[6(✉)]

[1] Centro Universitário Campo Limpo Paulista (Unifaccamp), Campo Limpo Paulista, SP, Brazil
[2] Instituto Federal de São Paulo (IFSP), Jundiaí, SP, Brazil
[3] Federal University of Pará (UFPA), Belém, PA, Brazil
bianchi@ufpa.br
[4] Universidade Federal de São João del-Rei (UFSJ), São João del-Rei, MG, Brazil
lcrocha@ufsj.edu.brr
[5] Federal University of Espirito do Santo (UFES), Vitório, ES, Brazil
diego.dias@ufes.br
[6] Federal University of São Paulo (Unifesp), Osasco, SP, Brazil
marcelo.paiva@unifesp.br

Abstract. The presence of missing data in databases is common, which can make difficult or even prevent their analysis. Therefore, it is necessary to address them, for example, by filling in values or removing records or columns. This paper aims to present a strategy to facilitate the handling of missing data. To achieve this goal, the strategy uses an LLM (Large Language Models) for generating code and conducting data analysis, and 3D visualizations with Augmented Reality to understand the data missing. This strategy has been implemented in a case study, where users can visually explore, measure, and handle the data missing. The results indicate that the strategy can facilitate the analysis and handling of missing data; however, an increase in the complexity of visualizations and handling of data missing was observed as the scale of the datasets increased.

Keywords: Missing data · Visualization · Augmented reality · LLM · ChatGPT

1 Introduction

Data analysis is a crucial part of many fields, from science to business. However, a common challenge faced is the presence of missing data, which can compromise the quality and reliability of the conclusion obtained [9]. Missing data refers to information that should have been provided but, for some reason, was not. This can occur due to intentional human factors (e.g., not knowing how to respond, refusing to respond, and neglect) or unintentional factors (e.g., distraction, technical problems, and forgetfulness) [4,19]. Regardless of the cause, missing data can introduce biases and reduce the statistical power of the analyses.

Selecting the appropriate imputation method to fill in missing data is a challenge, as each method has its own assumptions and limitations. Simple methods, such as mean or median imputation, may be insufficient to capture the variability of the data. On the other hand, more complex methods, such as multiple imputation or machine learning-based algorithms, require greater computational power and a deep understanding of the data context. There are many factors involved in each method of handling missing data that need to be understood before selecting one of them. Otherwise, new problems may arise, such as overfitting when utilizing interpolation over hardly dispersed information [16].

Understanding missing data in a database presents a challenge that requires analysis to identify patterns and underlying causes of the missing data. The absence can be classified as random (MCAR), where the lack of data is not related to other values, or non-random (MAR or MNAR), where the absence is associated with other observed values or the missing values themselves [7,9].

Visualization is a promising tool for identifying patterns and underlying causes of missing data. By representing data graphically, it is possible to identify trends, anomalies, and gaps that might not be apparent in raw data. Through various graphical representations, such as heat maps, missing value matrices, and bar charts, one can understand where and how missing data occurs. For example, heat maps can depict concentrations of missing values across different features and instances, revealing if data absence is random or clustered. Bar charts can compare the frequency of missing data across different categories, indicating if certain groups are more prone to missing data. 3D charts can be useful for understanding missing values because they provide an enhanced visual representation of data patterns and anomalies. By mapping missing data onto the third axis, such as color intensity or size of data points, 3D charts can effectively highlight the distribution and clustering of missing values within the dataset. This enhanced visualization capacity enables a better grasp of the spatial distribution of missing data and helps identify any potential patterns or trends associated with their absence, facilitating the choice of imputation method to be used.

The capability of Large Language Models (LLMs) to extract statistical information about patterns and characteristics of missing data further enhances their potential as valuable tools for extracting information from databases. Additionally, LLMs can assist in generating imputation strategies or recommending appropriate methods for handling missing data based on statistical principles and machine learning algorithms. Moreover, LLMs can generate initial programming code, automate tasks, and improve productivity [10,22,25].

This paper aims to present a strategy to handle data missing; and, a case study illustrating our strategy. This strategy consists of a cycle with two subcycles: (1) Data Analysis and (2) Data Treatment. An LLM is utilized to support the generation of source code for the 3D charts, extract information from the database, and develop methods for handling missing data. Additionally, Augmented reality (AR) is used to enhance understanding of missing data through 3D charts overlaid on the real world and to assist in selecting the appropriate methods to apply. The cycle is restarted and executed until the user is satisfied with the handling of the missing data.

The remainder of this paper is organized as follows. Section 2 discusses prior work related to this research. Section 3 describes the strategy. Section 4 shows a case study involving our strategy. Finally, Sect. 5 presents our conclusions.

2 Related Work

Visualization is a powerful tool for analyzing and sharing information. Humans process visual data rapidly, and visualization enables them to interpret it from various perspectives. This leads to a deeper understanding of problems and the identification of trends [6].

Costa et al. [24] developed an AR application that uses markers for creating, manipulating, and interacting with visualizations. However, they encountered difficulties in selecting virtual objects and filtering information. To address these issues, they suggested implementing menus to assist with these tasks. Miranda et al. [13] proposed a mobile AR application for data visualization. They used markers to interact with the visualizations. They also noted limitations in interacting with the visualization content, such as the restricted number of markers that can be recognized simultaneously and challenges in selection methods.

Padwal et al. [15] also explore the use of AR for data visualization. They created a prototype application that demonstrates various visualization techniques using AR. Tong et al. [23] investigated the interaction with printed data visualizations in AR. The participants of their study considered the interactions using AR intuitive and engaging, despite some physical limitations and properties of paper as a medium. Chandra, Jamiy, and Reza [17] evaluate various conventional visualization techniques and their application in creating visualizations with AR. They also explore the potential of integrating big data techniques with AR. They argue that most applications are still in the early stages, due to limitations such as hardware constraints, usability issues, and integration challenges. They emphasize that enhancing the user experience is the main benefit of visualizations with augmented reality.

Sjöbergh and Tanaka [21] explore the use of data visualization to handle missing data within real big data projects. They emphasize the importance of understanding the nature of missing data before selecting a treatment method. Furthermore, they highlight that while certain visualizations are suitable for specific types of missing data, others may not be as effective. Hence, a diverse range of visualization methods is essential for comprehensively addressing the nuances of missing data.

Addressing missing data is of critical importance in the field of machine learning, as it directly affects model performance and accuracy. Effectively managing missing data is essential to ensure the quality, reliability, and validity of insights derived from the data.

The machine learning field has extensively studied the impact of missing data and methods to handle it [2,3,11]. Proper processing of missing data is crucial to ensure the quality, reliability, and accuracy of the insights derived from the data. The strategy proposed in this paper uses an LLM for code generation and data analysis, combined with 3D visualizations using AR to better understand the characteristics of missing data. This approach facilitates the selection of appropriate methods for handling missing data while maintaining flexibility to incorporate additional visualizations and techniques as needed.

3 Strategy

Our strategy aims to provide resources for exploratory data analysis and thus facilitate the selection of a method to handle missing data. To achieve this, it seeks to identify, locate, and measure the missing data. Additionally, it aims to facilitate the selection of methods for handling other data anomalies, such as outliers and data inconsistencies.

The objective of the Data Analysis sub-cycle is to provide visualizations through 3D charts to identify, assess, locate, and manage anomalies in a specific dataset. To achieve this, it uses AR technology. One of the strengths of visualization with AR is the wide visual space available for presenting information [13]. The sub-cycle is initiated when an AR marker is detected. Each marker corresponds to a query previously constructed in the dataset. Subsequently, the information resulting from the query is presented as 3D charts overlaid on the real environment. The displayed information includes, for example, the total amount of data, the total amount of missing data, and the percentage of missing data relative to the total amount of data. This allows for precise measurement and location of missing data. The process of creating new charts can be assisted by a LLM.

The Data Treatment sub-cycle aims to manipulate the data through the selection of methods for handling missing data (e.g., record elimination, mean values, and regression [1,5,9,12,18,20]) in an AR menu. An intermediate task of this sub-cycle involves analyzing the characteristics of each column from the database to choose the method that will be applied. Each method is designed for specific missing data characteristics (e.g., type and amount of missing data). Panda and Adhikari [16] discuss the techniques that are frequently used (e.g., missing data ignoring, missing data imputation, missing data model) to handle missing data and, in addition, propose the use of correlation between attributes. Specific analysis should be performed before choosing the method because it potentially impacts the analyses and treatment results [14]. If the available methods are not sufficient, an LLM can be used to support the creation of the method source code. Using an LLM tool can significantly enhance analyst productivity. One key advantage is its ability to provide quick information and answers related to missing data and coding. Instead of manually searching forums or documents, analysts can ask the LLM tool questions and receive real-time responses. This not only saves time but also allows analysts to focus on higher value-added tasks, thereby increasing the overall efficiency of the missing data handling treatment.

Figure 1 depicts an overview of the strategy, which consists of the following steps:

- Step 1: the first sub-cycle, Data Analysis, begins when the device's camera detects an AR marker. Then, a query to the dataset is performed, and a 3D chart is added to the environment. This allows the initial analysis of the data (for example, the amount of missing data per column);
- Step 2: the user can follow two paths:
  - Step 2.1: create and analyze a new 3D chart assisted by an LLM; associates the new chart with a new marker; (The visualization is not satisfactory) and return to Step 1; or
  - Step 2.2: initialize the Data Treatment sub-cycle, and go to Step 3 (The visualization provided a satisfactory understanding);
- Step 3: using the AR menu from the Data Treatment sub-cycle, the user selects one of the available methods for handling the missing data in the dataset
- Step 4: the user can follow two paths:
  - Step 4.1: apply a method for handling missing data, and go to Step 1 (There is an appropriate method in the menu to be used); finish or
  - Step 4.2: generate the code for data missing assisted by a LLM; add the new method to the AR menu, (There is not an appropriate method in the menu to be used); and go to Step 4;

The sub-cycles are executed until the conditions for data visualization and/or handling of missing data are satisfied. Therefore, the strategy aims to improve the efficiency of data visualization and handling of missing data, using available technologies.

4 Case Study

An application was developed to illustrate the implementation of the strategy, called MDT-AR (Missing Data Treatment with the help of Augmented Reality). It was created using Unity and Vuforia. Unity is a game engine equipped with a complete set of integrated tools based on Microsoft C# for developing 2D and 3D games. Vuforia is a SDK (software development kit) for mobile devices that enables the creation of AR applications. It detects and tracks physical objects from real-world camera images, then overlays virtual elements such as graphics, animations, videos, and texts. This creates a fusion between the real world and virtual elements through the device's camera. The C# programming language enables interactions with these virtual objects.

MDT-AR consists of two modules, one for each sub-cycle (Data analysis and Data treatment). The following sub-sections detail each of the modules.

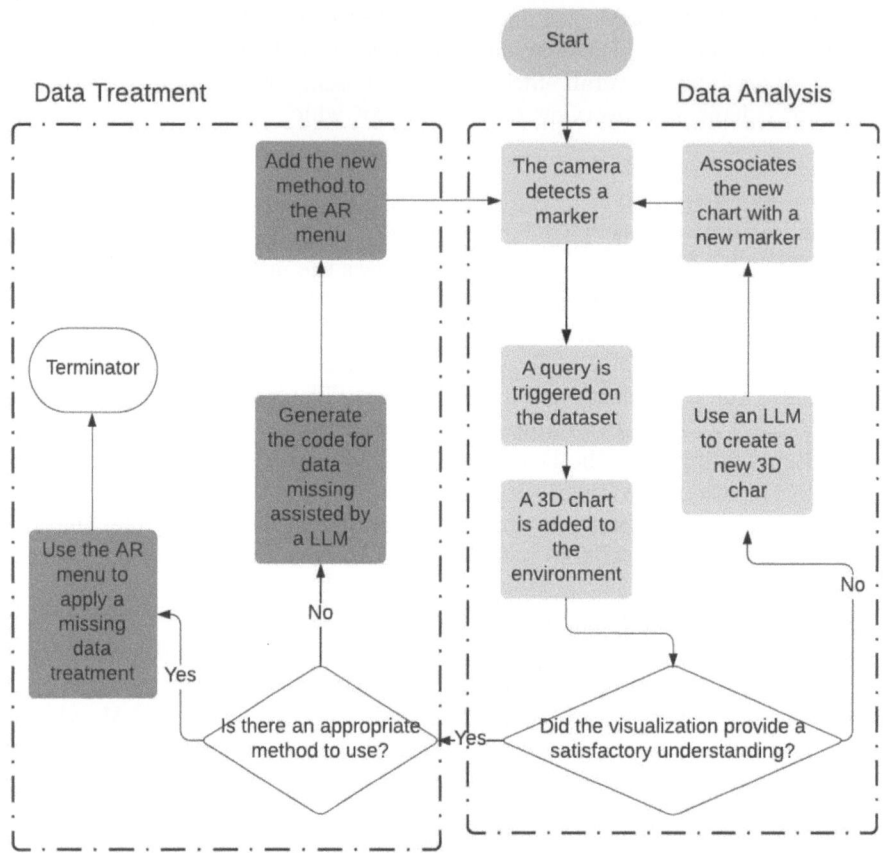

Fig. 1. Strategy overview

4.1 Data Analysis Module

The main objective of this module is to present 3D charts to enable the identification, assessment, location, and measurement of missing data and other anomalies in a specific dataset. When an AR marker is detected, a predefined SQL query is triggered in the database. Then, a 3D chart displays the query results. The graph can show, for example, the total amount of data, the quantity of missing data, and the percentage of missing data. To perform different queries, you need to change the marker or create new ones.

Figure 2 depicts an example of a chart generated showing missing data from a database. In this example, the *Description* column (green) has 917 instances, of which 105 are null data, representing 11.45% of the total data in that column. The *Desc_Title* column (black) has 917 instances, of which 207 are missing data, representing 21.92% of the total data in this column. The *Desc_Title_Formatted* column (blue) has 917 instances, of which 207 are missing data, representing

21.92% of the total data in this column. When the marker is rotated, the quality of the visualizations is improved according to the desired orientation.

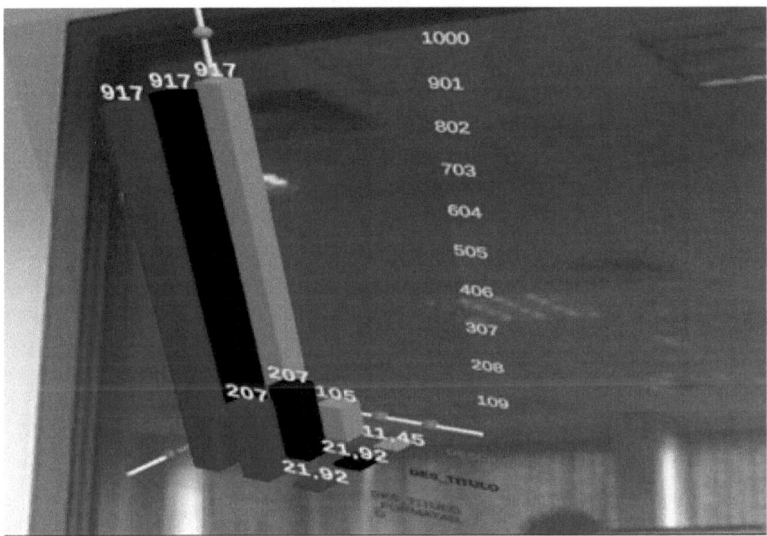

Fig. 2. 3D visual analysis of missing data

If the visualization has provided a satisfactory understanding of the data, you can then start the process of processing the missing data. Otherwise, you can visualize the data using another previously constructed chart or by requesting the LLM tool's assistance in creating a new chart. This new 3D chart will be linked to a new marker, and this sub-cycle will restart.

In this case study, ChatGPT 3.5 was used as an LLM to assist the MDT-AR. We used a data file in .csv format with 1000 records and 8 columns, 6 of which are categorical and 2 of which are numerical. Figure 3 illustrates the missing data highlighted in red.

Name	Gender	Start Date	Last Login Time	Salary	Bonus %	Senior Management	Team
Douglas	Male	8/6/1993	12:42 PM	97308	6945	true	Marketing
Thomas	Male	3/31/1996	6:53 AM	61933	4.17	true	
Maria	Female	4/23/1993	11:17 AM	130590	11858	false	Finance
Jerry	Male	3/4/2005	1:00 PM	138705	9.34	true	Finance
Larry	Male	1/24/1998	4:47 PM	101004	1389	true	Client Services
Dennis	Male	4/18/1987	1:35 AM	115163	10125	false	Legal
Ruby	Female	8/17/1987	4:20 PM	65476	10012	true	Product
	Female	7/20/2015	10:43 AM	45906	11598		Finance
Angela	Female	11/22/2005	6:29 AM	95570	18523	true	Engineering
Frances	Female	8/8/2002	6:51 AM	139852	7524	true	Business Development
Louise	Female	8/12/1980	9:01 AM	63241	15132	true	

Fig. 3. Case study data source (Color figure online)

The interaction with the LLM to solve tasks is done through a *prompt*, which makes the model behave according to the context [8]. Various interactions with the *prompt* improve the accuracy and relevance of the answers, making the model more effective in generating relevant information [26]. In the case study, there were 12 interactions to analyze and apply the method of treating missing data.

In the initial interactions via the ChatGPT *prompt*, a code was requested to display the statistical description using the following text: "Generate information about statistics on the numerical data from a .csv file.". Listing 1.1 shows the result, which contains source code that executed returns the main statistical information of the data (count, mean, standard deviation, min, 25th percentile, median, 75th percentile, and max) and transposes it for easier viewing. The *generate_statistics_from_file* function has been sufficiently created, which receives a file path as input, reads the data into a DataFrame and returns a DataFrame with statistical summaries for the numerical columns. An example of how to use it was also created. The generated code could run without any modifications.

```
def generate_statistics_from_file(file_path):
    # Read the data from the file into a DataFrame
    df = pd.read_csv(file_path)
    # Select only numerical columns
    numerical_df = df.select_dtypes(include=['number'])
    # Generate basic statistical summary
    statistical_summary = numerical_df.describe().transpose()
    # Add median
    statistical_summary['median'] = numerical_df.median()
    # Add variance
    statistical_summary['variance'] = numerical_df.var()
    # Add standard deviation
    statistical_summary['std_dev'] = numerical_df.std()
    return statistical_summary

# Example usage
file_path = 'path_to_your_file.csv'
statistics = generate_statistics_from_file(file_path)
print(statistics)
```

Listing 1.1. Using ChatGPT to generate source code to retrieve statistics from a data source.

We also asked the following *prompt*: "Create a script using 3D bar charts in C# for Unity to visualize the total missing data for each column and the percentage of missing data.". Listing 1.2 shows the result, it creates 3D bars to visualize the missing data for each column and the percentage of missing data. The *VisualizeMissingData* method was created to calculate the total missing data and the percentage of missing data for each column, and to draw bars accordingly. The *DrawBar* method draws a bar at the specified position, with the given height and color. The code needed adjustments for the desired dataset.

```
using System.Collections.Generic;
using UnityEngine;

public class MissingDataVisualization: MonoBehaviour
{
    ...
    private void VisualizeMissingData()
    {
        int numRows = data.GetLength(0);
        int numCols = data.GetLength(1);
        ...
        float percentage = (float)missingCount / numRows * 100f;
        // Draw bar for total missing data
        DrawBar(startX + j * barWidth, 0f, missingCount, Color.blue);
        // Draw bar for percentage of missing data
        DrawBar(startX + j * barWidth, 1f, percentage, Color.red);
    }

    private void DrawBar(float x, float z, float height, Color color)
    {
        GameObject bar = new GameObject("Bar");
        bar.transform.parent = transform;
        LineRenderer lineRenderer = bar.AddComponent<LineRenderer>();
        ...
    }
}
```

Listing 1.2. 3D chart to visualize missing data

While ChatGPT 3.5 can provide a useful starting point for 3D charts in Unity, they have significant limitations. Creating high-quality 3D graphics typically requires specialized knowledge and iterative adjustments. Moreover, ChatGPT 3.5 is not directly integrated with Unity. Therefore, the code generated cannot directly interact with the Unity environment or debugger in real-time. ChatGPT 3.5 can be used as an assisting tool but not as a comprehensive solution for generating code for 3D charts in Unity.

4.2 Data Treatment Module

Besides understanding the characteristics of missing data during the analysis stage, knowing its type is essential to apply the correct treatment method. In this manner, you can choose one of the available methods from the virtual menu from the case study: average, mode, or regression. It is also possible to find missing data values from a box plot.

If the user is satisfied with the applied data treatment, they can conclude the sub-cycle or request the application of another method. ChatGPT 3.5 can assist in creating new methods if needed. When the virtual menu is accessed again, a new method becomes available, prompting a restart of the sub-cycle. Figure 4 depicts the virtual menu with the available treatment methods. This boxplot displays the quantity of records(*regs*), showing the number of outliers above the upper whisker (*Outliers_GT*) and the number of outliers below the lower whisker (Outliers_LT).

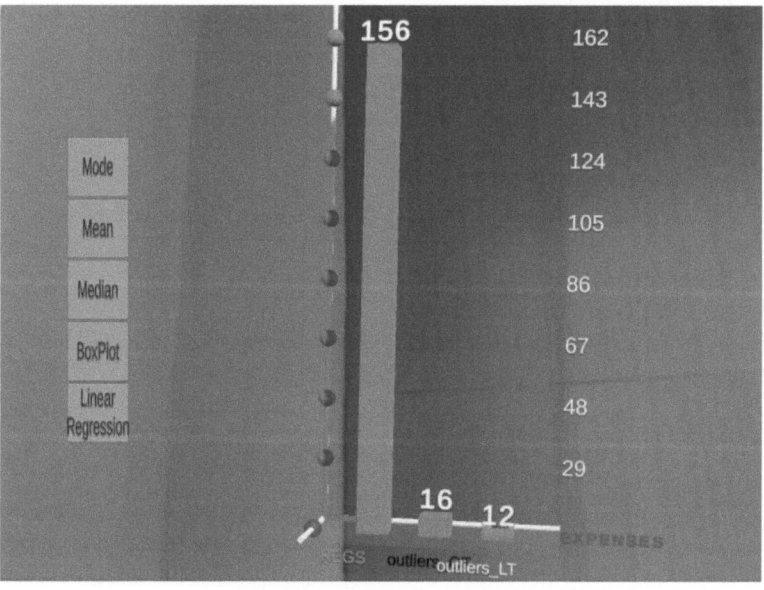

Fig. 4. Methods for data treatment

In cases where the available methods do not meet the requirements, ChatGPT 3.5 can be utilized to assist in creating a customized treatment method. We request the following task via the *prompt*: "Create a C# for unity to replace the categorical columns with missing data using mode imputation". Listing 1.3 shows the result, it creates a script to replace the data. The *ImputeMode* method is responsible for replacing the data. This code needed adjustments for the desired dataset.

```csharp
public class ModeImputation : MonoBehaviour
{
    void Start()
    {
        ...
        ImputeMode(data);
        ...
    }
    void ImputeMode(List<Dictionary<string, object>> data)
    {
        // Get all columns
        ...
        foreach (var column in columns)
        {
            // Filter out rows with missing values in the current column
            ...
                // Calculate the mode (most frequent value)
                var mode = values
                    .GroupBy(v => v)
                    .OrderByDescending(g => g.Count())
                    .First()
                    .Key;
                // Impute missing values with the mode
                foreach (var row in data.Where(row => row[column] ==null))
                {
                    row[column] = mode;
                }
        }
    }
}
```

Listing 1.3. Method to replace the categorical data

The use of ChatGPT 3.5 in the case study accelerated the data analysis and treatment by providing statistical calculations and generating code. However, the generated code always required adjustments before it could be effectively used. In total, 12 interactions were conducted via prompts. In the end, the missing data was successfully treated. The fields highlighted in green in Fig. 5 illustrate the treatment of missing data that was carried out.

Figure 6 depicts the 3D chart after the missing data treatment has been applied. It shows the total amount of data in each column, the total amount of missing data, and the percentage of missing data. Both the total amount and percentage of missing data are zero, indicating successful data processing. This step completes the strategy cycle in the MDT-AR.

Name	Gender	Start Date	Last Login Time	Salary	Bonus %	Senior Management	Team
Douglas	Male	8/6/1993	12:42 PM	97308	6945.0	True	Marketing
Thomas	Male	3/31/1996	6:53 AM	61933	4.17	True	Client Services
Maria	Female	4/23/1993	11:17 AM	130590	11858.0	False	Finance
Jerry	Male	3/4/2005	1:00 PM	138705	9.34	True	Finance
Larry	Male	1/24/1998	4:47 PM	101004	1389.0	True	Client Services
Dennis	Male	4/18/1987	1:35 AM	115163	10125.0	False	Legal
Ruby	Female	8/17/1987	4:20 PM	65476	10012.0	True	Product
Marilyn	Female	7/20/2015	10:43 AM	45906	11598.0	True	Finance
Angela	Female	11/22/2005	6:29 AM	95570	18523.0	True	Engineering
Frances	Female	8/8/2002	6:51 AM	139852	7524.0	True	Business Development
Louise	Female	8/12/1980	9:01 AM	63241	15132.0	True	Client Services

Fig. 5. Dataset after treatment of missing data (Color figure online)

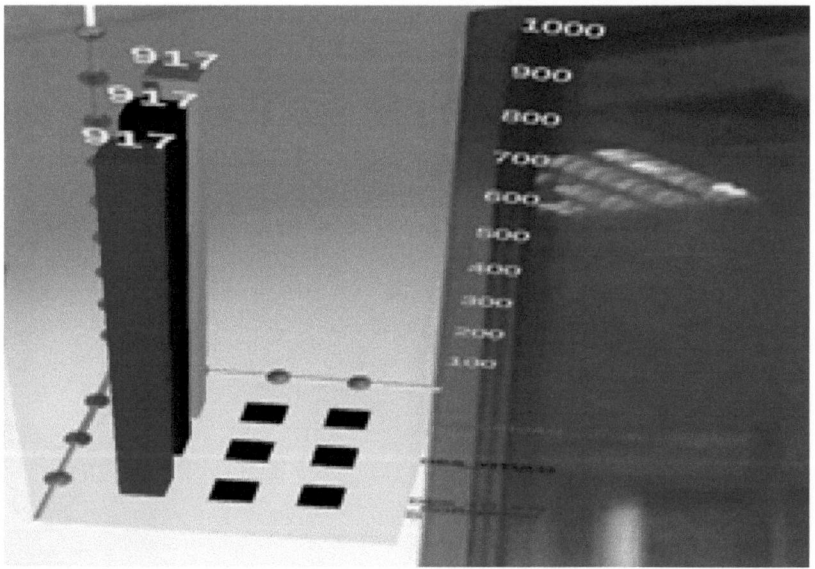

Fig. 6. Post-treatment data

The case study MDT-AR still faces some limitations, such as performance degradation in visualizations as the data volume increases, the absence of comparison features between different methods, the lack of precise graphics control, and it requires technical knowledge in both data analysis and software development. However, it remains a promising tool due to its potential to facilitate the identification of missing data patterns, enhance user engagement with attractive visualizations, and provide interactivity—allowing users to manipulate, rotate, and explore models from various angles and perspectives. Furthermore, it can be extended and modified to incorporate new data visualization and treatment methods. Although ChatGPT's code generation integration with Unity exists, the current version of MDT-AR does not utilize this feature, primarily due to the need for code modifications to meet specific visualization requirements. Instead, the code generated by ChatGPT is received via an HTTP response, parsed in

Unity, and the source code is extracted. Currently, the MDT-AR user must be a developer with proficiency in AR application development, expertise in dataset manipulation, experience interacting with LLMs, and knowledge of handling missing data.

5 Conclusion

In this paper, we present a strategy developed to address missing data in a dataset. The strategy includes two sub-cycles: the Data Analysis sub-cycle, and the Data Treatment sub-cycle, both utilizing augmented reality. Additionally, the strategy incorporates the use of an LLM as a support tool, assisting in data analysis and processing.

To demonstrate the implementation of our strategy, we developed an application called MDT-AR, designed to analyze and process the missing data in a database. This application was built using the Unity game engine, Vuforia, and the LLM ChatGPT 3.5.

The AR features for handling missing data provide users with an intuitive and immersive visualization experience, enabling a detailed understanding of the data. This technology offers a wide variety of ways to visualize the data, which motivates research. It allows users to manipulate, rotate, and explore models from various angles and perspectives, seamlessly integrating virtual objects with the real world.

While LLMs like ChatGPT 3.5 can serve as valuable tools for offering general guidance and code examples, they have notable limitations in assisting with the analysis and handling of missing data. Effective data analysis and handling typically necessitate a combination of expert knowledge, access to real data, utilization of advanced statistical techniques, and a deep understanding of the data context, all of which may be beyond the current capabilities of LLMs.

Future work involves adding new analytical tools, such as additional chart types, and implementing new methods for handling missing data. Additionally, we plan to conduct tests with larger data volumes and perform user evaluations to further refine and enhance the application.

Acknowledgment. The authors acknowledge partial funding from the Coordination for the Improvement of Higher Education Personnel - Brazil (CAPES) - Funding Code 001, the National Council for Scientific and Technological Development (CNPq), and the Research Support Foundation of the State of Minas Gerais (FAPEMIG). We also thank the Research and Innovation Support Foundation of Espírito Santo (FAPES) for the resources provided through the PROAPEM project (368/2022 - P: 2022-NGKM5) and the PDPG project (129/2021 - P: 2021-GL60J), which were fundamental to the completion of this work.

References

1. Alabadla, M., et al.: Systematic review of using machine learning in imputing missing values. IEEE Access **10**, 44483–44502 (2022). https://doi.org/10.1109/ACCESS.2022.3160841
2. Cenitta, D., Arjunan, R.V.: Missing data imputation using machine learning algorithm for supervised learning. In: 2021 International Conference on Computer Communication and Informatics (ICCCI), pp. 1–5 (2021). https://doi.org/10.1109/ICCCI50826.2021.9402558
3. Emmanuel, T., Maupong, T., Mpoeleng, D., Semong, T., Mphago, B., Tabona, O.: A survey on missing data in machine learning. J. Big Data **8**(1), 140 (2021). https://doi.org/10.1186/s40537-021-00516-9
4. Enders, C.K.: Missing data: an update on the state of the art. Psychol. Methods (2023). https://doi.org/10.1037/met0000563
5. Faizin, R.N., Riasetiawan, M., Ashari, A.: A review of missing sensor data imputation methods. In: 2019 5th International Conference on Science and Technology (ICST), vol. 1, pp. 1–6 (2019). https://doi.org/10.1109/ICST47872.2019.9166287
6. Hirve, S.A., Ch, P.R.: Improving big data analytics with interactive augmented reality. Int. J. Inf. Syst. Modeling Des. (IJISMD) **13**(7), 1–11 (2022). https://ideas.repec.org/a/igg/jismd0/v13y2022i7p1-11.html
7. Little, R., Rubin, D.: Statistical analysis with missing data. Wiley Series in Probability and Mathematical Statistics. Probability and Mathematical Statistics. Wiley (2002). http://books.google.com/books?id=aYPwAAAAMAAJ
8. Liu, P., Yuan, W., Fu, J., Jiang, Z., Hayashi, H., Neubig, G.: Pre-train, prompt, and predict: a systematic survey of prompting methods in natural language processing. ACM Comput. Surv. **55**(9) (2023). https://doi.org/10.1145/3560815
9. Liu, Q., Hauswirth, M.: A provenance meta learning framework for missing data handling methods selection. In: 2020 11th IEEE Annual Ubiquitous Computing, Electronics & Mobile Communication Conference (UEMCON), pp. 0349–0358 (2020). https://doi.org/10.1109/UEMCON51285.2020.9298089
10. Liu, Z., Tang, Y., Luo, X., Zhou, Y., Zhang, L.F.: No need to lift a finger anymore? Assessing the quality of code generation by chatgpt. IEEE Trans. Softw. Eng. 1–35 (2024). https://doi.org/10.1109/TSE.2024.3392499
11. Makaba, T., Dogo, E.: A comparison of strategies for missing values in data on machine learning classification algorithms. In: 2019 International Multidisciplinary Information Technology and Engineering Conference (IMITEC), pp. 1–7 (2019). https://doi.org/10.1109/IMITEC45504.2019.9015889
12. Miao, X., Wu, Y., Chen, L., Gao, Y., Yin, J.: An experimental survey of missing data imputation algorithms. IEEE Trans. Knowl. Data Eng. **35**(7), 6630–6650 (2023). https://doi.org/10.1109/TKDE.2022.3186498
13. Miranda, B.P., Queiroz, V.F., Araújo, T.D.O., Santos, C.G.R., Meiguins, B.S.: A low-cost multi-user augmented reality application for data visualization. Multimedia Tools Appl. **81**(11), 14773–14801 (2022). https://doi.org/10.1007/s11042-021-11141-2
14. Othman, L.B., Yahia, S.B.: A multiple criteria evaluation technique for missing values imputation. In: 2018 12th International Conference on Research Challenges in Information Science (RCIS), pp. 1–12 (2018). https://doi.org/10.1109/RCIS.2018.8406659
15. Padwal, P., Singh, Y., Singh, J., Pansambal, S.: Dvar: data visualization using augmented reality. In: 2021 2nd Global Conference for Advancement in Technology (GCAT), pp. 1–6 (2021). https://doi.org/10.1109/GCAT52182.2021.9587831

16. Panda, B.S., Kumar Adhikari, R.: A method for classification of missing values using data mining techniques. In: 2020 International Conference on Computer Science, Engineering and Applications (ICCSEA), pp. 1–5 (2020). https://doi.org/10.1109/ICCSEA49143.2020.9132935
17. Ramaseri Chandra, A.N., El Jamiy, F., Reza, H.: Augmented reality for big data visualization: a review. In: 2019 International Conference on Computational Science and Computational Intelligence (CSCI), pp. 1269–1274 (2019). https://doi.org/10.1109/CSCI49370.2019.00238
18. Santos, M.S., Pereira, R.C., Costa, A.F., Soares, J.P., Santos, J., Abreu, P.H.: Generating synthetic missing data: a review by missing mechanism. IEEE Access **7**, 11651–11667 (2019). https://doi.org/10.1109/ACCESS.2019.2891360
19. Schafer, J.L., Graham, J.W.: Missing data: our view of the state of the art. Psychol. Methods **7**(2), 147–177 (2002)
20. Sharifyanov, N., Latypova, V.: A method of filling missing values in data using data mining. In: 2023 IX International Conference on Information Technology and Nanotechnology (ITNT), pp. 1–5 (2023). https://doi.org/10.1109/ITNT57377.2023.10139280
21. Sjöbergh, J., Tanaka, Y.: Visualizing missing values. In: 2017 21st International Conference Information Visualisation (IV), pp. 242–249 (2017). https://api.semanticscholar.org/CorpusID:30613266
22. Su, H., Ai, J., Yu, D., Zhang, H.: An evaluation method for large language models' code generation capability. In: 2023 10th International Conference on Dependable Systems and Their Applications (DSA), pp. 831–838 (2023). https://doi.org/10.1109/DSA59317.2023.00118
23. Tong, W., et al.: Exploring interactions with printed data visualizations in augmented reality. IEEE Trans. Visual Comput. Graphics **29**(1), 418–428 (2023). https://doi.org/10.1109/TVCG.2022.3209386
24. Victor Costa, I., Favacho Queiroz, V., Pinto Miranda, B., Abreu de Freitas, A., Gustavo Resque dos Santos, C., Serique Meiguins, B.: A card-based interaction to design visualizations in augmented reality environments. In: 2019 23rd International Conference in Information Visualization, Part II, pp. 52–55 (2019). https://doi.org/10.1109/IV-2.2019.00019
25. Wang, J., Chen, Y.: A review on code generation with LLMs: application and evaluation. In: 2023 IEEE International Conference on Medical Artificial Intelligence (MedAI), pp. 284–289 (2023). https://doi.org/10.1109/MedAI59581.2023.00044
26. White, J., et al.: A prompt pattern catalog to enhance prompt engineering with chatgpt (2023)

Workshop on Advanced and Computational Methods for Earth Science Applications (WACM4ES 2025)

A Bridge Between Soil Science and Photonics: A Novel Framework for Urban Green Space Assessment

Francesca Sanfilippo[1,2](✉) , Lorenza Tuccio[1] , Lucia Cavigli[1] ,
Francesca Rossi[1] , Giorgio Querzoli[2] , Ivan Blecic[2] , Andrea Vacca[3] ,
and Paolo Matteini[1]

[1] CNR-Institute of Applied Physics "Nello Carrara" (IFAC), Via Madonna del Piano, 10, 50019 Sesto Fiorentino (FI), Italy
f.sanfilippo@studenti.unica.it

[2] Department of Civil, EnvironmentalandArchitecturalEngineering(DICAAR), University of Cagliari, Via Marengo, 2 09123 Cagliari, Italy

[3] Department of Chemical and Geological Sciences, University of Cagliari, UniversityCampus, D - 09042 Monserrato, Block, Italy

Abstract. Urban green spaces mitigate key urbanization impacts such as pollution and climate change exacerbation; although optical technologies have predominantly focused on documenting plant stress responses to atmospheric drivers, the critical role of soil quality in mediating vegetation's physiological adaptations - spanning both primary, and secondary metabolism - remains understudied. The work develops an integrated methodology combining portable photonic tools (an NDVI sensor, a Dualex analyzer, and a Raman spectrometer) with soil analysis to assess *Quercus Ilex L.* metabolic status in the urban, periurban and rural areas. Our approach cross-validates optical measurements of physiological changes with soil variable analysis, enabling comprehensive plant health assessment. Preliminary results demonstrate significant soil-plant physiological correlations across both biometric and photonic parameters. The combined analysis enhances data robustness, confirming photonic measurements through soil diagnostics. This dual-method approach addresses a critical research gap in urban ecology by synergizing optical monitoring with edaphic factor analysis. The methodology provides deeper insight into urban ecosystems where plants face complex, unregulated stressors. Key findings include that soil quality significantly influences photonic-derived physiological indicators, optical measurements gain reliability when correlated with soil parameters, and urban vegetation management requires to be integrated soil-plant monitoring. This study provides insights to guide the implementation of photon-based tools in urban green space management. The integrated approach supports evidence-based policies for sustainable urban resilience, optimizing vegetation maintenance through combined optical and soil diagnostics. Our methodology offers a practical framework for monitoring urban tree status under multiple stress factors while maintaining scientific rigor in data collection and interpretation.

Keywords: Urban green spaces · edaphic analysis · photonic tools

© The Author(s), under exclusive license to Springer Nature Switzerland AG 2026
O. Gervasi et al. (Eds.): ICCSA 2025, LNCS 15898, pp. 291–308, 2026.
https://doi.org/10.1007/978-3-031-97657-5_18

1 Introduction

Urban green spaces represent fundamental nature-based solutions for counteracting the negative effects of urbanization but too often, the focus is solely on the effects that urbanization has on the air compartment and assessing the exacerbation that this process causes on the impacts of climate change and atmospheric pollution [1–3]. In previous studies we investigated plant physiological responses to urban environmental stressors using advanced optical technologies. However, the role of soil quality was not sufficiently explored, focusing the experimental study at the leaf level, on the effects of the atmospheric compartment [4–6]. In the present study we propose a methodological approach, innovatively combining traditional biometric measurements with advanced photonic techniques, to capture both structural and functional responses. This dual perspective, integrating soil analysis, enables us to quantify adaptive strategies through correlation patterns, validate optical indicators against morphological changes, and identify threshold responses to environmental stressors. The study was conducted on Quercus ilex L. (QI) specimens in Cagliari, a rapidly expanding Mediterranean coastal city. The Mediterranean basin represents a critical hotspot for studying plant-environmental interactions, particularly for keystone species like QI, that dominate these ecosystems [7, 8]. The study specifically examines how QI manages the Mediterranean "stress triangle" of nutritional limitations, water deficit, and edaphic extremes through integrated morphological and biochemical adjustments. This evergreen sclerophyllous is our focal species, because it shows remarkable adaptability to diverse edaphic conditions, making it an ideal model for studying soil-plant relationships in stress-prone environments [9–16]. Our research is based on a dual assessment approach. On one hand, we conducted vegetation monitoring with portable photonic techniques, employing an NDVI sensor, a Dualex fluorescence analyzer, and a Raman spectrometer. This allowed us to measure photosynthetic efficiency, pigment dynamics, and the production of specific defense compounds. On the other hand, we performed soil profiling, evaluating essential nutrients such as organic carbon, nitrogen, and phosphorus, analyzing structural characteristics like texture and water retention capacity, and measuring potential contaminants including heavy metals and salts, revealing significant interactions. The innovative aspect of our method lies in comparing results obtained from optical techniques with soil analysis. This approach addresses two major limitations in urban plant studies. Optical instruments are often used to evaluate plants without considering the characteristics of the soil in which they grow. Furthermore, urban soils frequently present unique combinations of stress factors that differ from those found in natural environments [17, 18]. By analyzing QI specimens distributed along Cagliari's urbanization gradient, we were able to observe how soil quality influences the species' adaptation strategies [19–21]. Our results provide new insights into the species' plasticity in resource allocation and the reliability of non-invasive optical methods for stress detection. This study contributes to the advancement of urban ecology in several ways. First, it identifies practical reference points for applying optical techniques in human-modified soils, based on experimental findings. Second, it quantifies the physiological effects of urban soil stress factors on plants. Finally, it proposes an innovative method that can be adopted by municipal administrations to complement the monitoring of the status of green spaces. [22–24]. Overall, our integrated approach offers municipal managers practical support for improving urban green space management - for example by optimizing soil amendment practices, selecting more resilient species based on soil characteristics, and implementing early warning systems that combine optical indicators with soil analysis. In line with these insights, it is evident that urban ecology must consider the interconnection between air pollution, soil quality, and plant adaptability to promote sustainable urban environments [25, 26]. Addressing these multifaceted aspects will be essential to enhance the resilience of urban green spaces, particularly in Mediterranean cities facing unique climatic challenges and anthropogenic pressures.

2 Methodology

This research was conducted in two differentiated environments within the metropolitan area of Cagliari: a densely populated central district and a more sparsely developed peripheral zone. The selection of these sites was guided by the strategic positioning of air quality monitoring stations managed by the Regional Environmental Protection Agency (ARPAS), ensuring representative coverage of the city's pollution gradients. The central monitoring station was in Cagliari along Via Cadello, while the peripheral station was situated in the municipality of Monserrato. To establish a baseline for natural background conditions, an additional control site was included 3 km far from the town of Seulo, designated by ARPAS as a "maintenance area" due to its minimal anthropogenic influence and suitability for monitoring long-range atmospheric transport of pollutants [27–31]. Within each zone, 6 individual QI specimens were selected for analysis. This species was chosen for its ecological dominance in Mediterranean urban landscapes and its well-established role as a reliable bioindicator of air quality [32].

The analysis of five-year environmental data (2019–2023) identified late October 2024 as the optimal period for sampling, a choice driven by the need to jointly evaluate: the combined effects of atmospheric pollution and summer climatic stress (characterized by high temperatures, intense solar radiation, and reduced precipitation) on both soil and plant physiology; the acute and chronic responses of QI to these multiple pressures, within a climate change context that cannot be separated from the analysis of Mediterranean urban ecosystems. Field measurements employed three complementary optical techniques to non-destructively assess plant stress responses. The normalized difference vegetation index (NDVI) was acquired using a handheld GreenSeeker sensor (Trimble) to evaluate canopy health at the whole-plant level. Leaf-level physiological status was characterized using a Dualex instrument (Force-A, Orsay, France) that measures chlorophyll fluorescence denoted DxChl, epidermal flavonols and anthocyanins, compounds directly involved in photoprotection and oxidative stress mitigation, reported under the acronyms DxFlav, DxAnth and finally DxNBI, that was used to estimate the nitrogen nutritional status of the plant [33–35]. Molecular composition was further analyzed using a Mini-Raman Power portable spectrometer (Lightnovo) equipped with a 785 nm excitation laser, which detected vibrational modes characteristic of carotenoids (RI1526 in the text refers to the intensity of the 1526 cm^{-1} Raman band that is characteristic of carotenoids) and of polyphenols (RI1626 that is the intensity of the 1626 cm^{-1} band ascribed to phenolic compounds) [36–38]. Our research team developed the measurement protocol, a comprehensive sampling of each tree's southeastern aspect to control solar exposure effects. For the Dualex measurements, twenty leaves per tree were analyzed (totaling 120 leaves per site), while Raman spectroscopy was performed on ten leaves per tree (60 leaves per site). Each specimen also received a single NDVI measurement to maintain consistency in canopy-scale assessment. Complementary biometric analyses included determinations of leaf area and fresh-to-dry weight ratios to evaluate potential morphological adaptations to pollution stress. The measurements were conducted in situ without destructive sampling, except for Raman analysis, conducted indoors within 2 h of leaf harvesting. Regarding soil, all operational phases—from soil sample collection to subsequent laboratory analyses—were conducted in strict compliance with the provisions of the Decreto Ministeriale 13 Settembre 1999 («Metodi ufficiali di analisi chimica del suolo»), issued by the Ministry of Agricultural Policies [39].

Soil sampling was performed at the base of each selected tree at a depth of 50 cm. As each study area included 6 trees, this operation generated 6 individual samples per site. In Cagliari, where trees were distributed across two distinct zones, a specific strategy was adopted to optimize analysis: samples collected beneath 3 trees from the first area were thoroughly mixed to form a single 1 kg composite sample ("Soil A"), while 3 samples from the second area were combined to create "Soil B". This approach pre-served each zone's distinctive characteristics while reducing laboratory analyses. Moreover, it ensured full sample representativeness as required by ministerial regulations. This phase proved critical for guaranteeing the reliability of subsequent laboratory tests. In Monserrato, all trees fell within a homogeneous area. Here, the 6 initial samples were combined into a single 1 kg representative sample ("Soil C"), reflecting the site's natural soil variability. A similar approach was applied in Seulo, where specimens were clustered within 3 m of each other in a uniform pedological context. All subsamples were homogenized to produce "Soil D", maintaining the representativeness of the entire area. This methodology offered dual advantages: it preserved natural soil heterogeneity across zones while optimizing analytical processes without compromising data reliability. Composite sampling notably minimized localized errors, providing robust insights into each site's pedological features. For the preparation and physicochemical characterization of composite samples (A, B, C, D), all analyses followed official protocols [40]. Sample preparation included standardized drying, crushing, and sieving procedures. Granulometric characterization involved both skeleton determination (separation of particles > 2 mm) and fine fraction analysis via pipette sedimentation [41]. Soil reaction (pH) was measured in water using a glass electrode, strictly adhering to the decree's procedural specifications [42]. Beyond these fundamental analyses, all additional physicochemical tests—including organic matter content and cation exchange capacity—were performed using certified, standardized methods in full compliance with ministerial guidelines.

3 Results

Table 1 shows the physicochemical properties of soils A-D, with color-coded values: red (exceeds legal limits, D.Lgs. 152/2006), black (moderate ranges), and green (low ranges), according to the Sardinia Region guidelines [43, 44]. The dataset encompasses chemical properties (pH, carbonates, organic carbon, nitrogen), nutrient availability, water retention parameters, and heavy metal concentrations, providing a comprehensive assessment of edaphic conditions. For each soil parameter, we chose to report only physical and physiological responses that had a moderate to high R correlation value of at least: ± 0.60 [45]. In this way, we focused on an actual adaptation response of QI to that value of the investigated parameter.

Table 1. Comparative analysis of soil characteristics (pH, TCaCO3: Total Calcium Carbonate ACaCO3: Active Calcium Carbonate, SOC: Soil Organic Carbon, TN: Total Nitrogen, C/N ratio: Carbon to Nitrogen ratio, AP: Available Phosphorus, EX Ca: Exchangeable Calcium, EX Mg: Exchangeable Magnesium, EX K: Exchangeable Potassium, EX Na: Exchangeable Sodium, CEC: Cation Exchange Capacity, EC: Electrical Conductivity, FC: Field Capacity, PWP: Permanent Wilting Point, PAW: Plant Available Water, As: Arsenic, Cd: Cadmium, Cr: Chromium, Hg: Mercury, Ni: Nickel, Pb: Lead, Cu: Copper, Zn: Zinc) and QI performance metrics (morphological, photosynthetic and secondary metabolites) across four soil classes (A-D): LA = leaf area, FW = fresh weight, DW = dry weight, LMA = LMA = leaf mass per area, SLA = specific leaf area, DxChl = chlorophyll index, DxFlav = flavonol index, DxAnth = anthocyanin index, DxNBI = nitrogen balance index, NDVI = normalized difference vegetation index, RI1526 = Raman intensity of the 1526 cm^{-1} band, RI1626 = Raman intensity of the 1626 cm^{-1} band).

	Ph	LA	FW	DW	LMA	NDVI
A	7.4	56.53	0.19	1.10	0.02	0.62
B	7.1	68.15	0.23	1.35	0.02	0.56
C	6.8	84.67	0.30	1.78	0.02	0.56
D	7.2	109.13	0.33	1.82	0.02	0.59

	TCaCo3 g/Kg	LA	LMA	SLA	Flav	Anth	RI$_{1526}$	RI$_{1626}$
A	97.5	56.53	0.02	51.61	1.36	0.07	33.48	3.28
B	20	68.15	0.02	51.20	1.48	0.13	34.81	3.01
C	59.6	84.67	0.02	48.03	1.34	0.07	34.56	3.36
D	241	109.13	0.02	60.29	1.27	0.07	37.57	3.61

	ACaCo3 g/Kg	LA	LMA	SLA	Flav	Anth	RI$_{1526}$	RI$_{1626}$

(*continued*)

Table 1. (*continued*)

A	25	56.53	0.02	51.61	1.36	0.07		
B	1.3	68.15	0.02	51.20	1.48	0.13	34.81	3.01
C	13.8	84.67	0.02	48.03	1.34	0.07	34.56	3.36
D	53.8	109.13	0.02	60.29	1.27	0.07	37.57	3.61

	SOC g/Kg	LA	FW	DW	Chl	Flav	RI_{1526}	RI_{1626}
A	13	56.53	0.19	1.10	61.58	1.36	33.48	3.28
B	16.4	68.15	0.23	1.35	45.94	1.48	34.81	3.01
C	29.5	84.67	0.30	1.78	51.25	1.34	34.56	3.36
D	35.3	109.13	0.33	1.82	42.17	1.27	37.57	3.61

	TN g/Kg	LA	FW	DW	Chl	Flav	RI_{1526}	RI_{1626}
A	1.14	56.53	0.19	1.10	61.58	1.36	33.48	3.28
B	1.39	68.15	0.23	1.35	45.94	1.48	34.81	3.01
C	2.34	84.67	0.30	1.78	51.25	1.34	34.56	3.36
D	2.91	109.13	0.33	1.82	42.17	1.27	37.57	3.61

	C/N ratio	LA	FW	DW	NDVI
A	11.4	56.53	0.19	1.10	0.62
B	11.8	68.15	0.23	1.35	0.56
C	12.6	84.67	0.30	1.78	0.56
D	12.1	109.13	0.33	1.82	0.59

	AP mg/Kg	LMA	SLA	NDVI
A	6.5	0.02	51.61	0.62
B	11.8	0.02	51.20	0.56
C	24.8	0.02	48.03	0.56
D	5.48	0.02	60.29	0.59

	EX Ca mg/Kg	Chl	NBI	RI_{1526}
A	342	61.58	45.28	33.48
B	572	45.94	31.11	34.81

(*continued*)

Table 1. (*continued*)

C		376	51.25	38.46	34.56
D		544	42.17	33.13	37.57

	EX Mg mg/Kg	Chl	Anth	NBI
A	50	61.58	0.07	45.28
B	96	45.94	0.13	31.11
C	17	51.25	0.07	38.46
D	69	42.17	0.07	33.13

	EX K mg/Kg	LMA	SLA	Flav	Anth	NDVI	RI_{1626}
A	26	0.02	51.61	1.36	0.07	0.62	3.28
B	73	0.02	51.20	1.48	0.13	0.56	3.01
C	48	0.02	48.03	1.34	0.07	0.56	3.36
D	15	0.02	60.29	1.27	0.07	0.59	3.61

	EX Na mg/Kg	LA	FW	DW	Flav	Anth	RI_{1626}
A	36	56.53	0.19	1.10	1.36	0.07	3.28
B	39	68.15	0.23	1.35	1.48	0.13	3.01
C	32	84.67	0.30	1.78	1.34	0.07	3.36
D	32	109.13	0.33	1.82	1.27	0.07	3.61

	CECmeq/100 g	Chl	NBI	RI_{1526}
A	13.9	61.58	45.28	33.48
B	25.5	45.94	31.11	34.81
C	14.4	51.25	38.46	34.56
D	23.9	42.17	33.13	37.57

	EC dS/m	LA	FW	DW	Flav	Anth	RI_{1626}
A	2.142	56.53	0.19	1.10	1.36	0.07	3.28
B	2.524	68.15	0.23	1.35	1.48	0.13	3.01
C	0.973	84.67	0.30	1.78	1.34	0.07	3.36
D	0.661	109.1	0.33	1.82	1.27	0.07	3.61

(*continued*)

Table 1. (*continued*)

	FC %	LA	FW	DW	LMA	SLA	Chl	RI$_{1526}$	RI$_{1626}$
A	25.1	56.53	0.19	1.10	0.02	51.61	61.58	33.48	3.28
B	26.6	68.15	0.23	1.35	0.02	51.20	45.94	34.81	3.01
C	28	84.67	0.30	1.78	0.02	48.03	51.25	34.56	3.36
D	32.8	109.1	0.33	1.82	0.02	60.29	42.17	37.57	3.61

	PWP %	LA	FW	DW	LMA	SLA	Chl	RI$_{1526}$	RI$_{1626}$
A	13.4	56.53	0.19	1.10	0.02	51.61	61.58	33.48	3.28
B	14.3	68.15	0.23	1.35	0.02	51.20	45.94	34.81	3.01
C	15.1	84.67	0.30	1.78	0.02	48.03	51.25	34.56	3.36
D	18	109.1	0.33	1.82	0.02	60.29	42.17	37.57	3.61

	PAW	LA	FW	DW	LMA	SLA	Chl	RI$_{1526}$	RI$_{1626}$
A	11.7	56.53	0.19	1.10	0.019	51.61	61.58	33.48	3.28
B	12.3	68.15	0.23	1.35	0.020	51.20	45.94	34.81	3.01
C	12.9	84.67	0.30	1.78	0.021	48.03	51.25	34.56	3.36
D	14.8	109.1	0.33	1.82	0.017	60.29	42.17	37.57	3.61

	As mg/kg	LMA	SLA	RI$_{1526}$	RI$_{1626}$
A	3.06	0.019	51.61	33.48	3.28
B	0.001	0.020	51.20	34.81	3.01
C	0.001	0.021	48.03	34.56	3.36
D	8.15	0.017	60.29	37.57	3.61

	Cr mg/kg	LA	FW	LMA	SLA	Chl	Flav	RI$_{1526}$	RI$_{1626}$
A	29.8	56.53	0.19	0.019	51.61	61.58	1.36	33.48	3.28
B	27.6	68.15	0.23	0.020	51.20	45.94	1.48	34.81	3.01
C	27.9	84.67	0.30	0.021	48.03	51.25	1.34	34.56	3.36
D	18	109.1	0.33	0.017	60.29	42.17	1.27	37.57	3.61

	Ni mg/kg	LA	FW	DW	Chl	NBI	NDVI	RI$_{1526}$
A	21.4	56.53	0.19	1.10	61.58	45.28	0.62	33.48
B	11.8	68.15	0.23	1.35	45.94	31.11	0.56	34.81
C	15.5	84.67	0.30	1.78	51.25	38.46	0.56	34.56

(*continued*)

Table 1. (*continued*)

D	10.9	109.1	0.33	1.82	42.17	33.13	0.59	37.57

	Pb mg/kg	LMA	SLA
A	24.3	0.019	51.61
B	7.14	0.020	51.20
C	67.3	0.021	48.03
D	10.1	0.017	60.29

	Cu mg/kg	LMA	SLA
A	22.1	0.019	51.61
B	15.5	0.020	51.20
C	62.8	0.021	48.03
D	9.13	0.017	60.29

	Zn mg/kg	LMA	SLA
A	75.7	0.019	51.61
B	58.6	0.020	51.20
C	160	0.021	48.03
D	32.3	0.017	60.29

Table 2 presents Pearson's correlation matrix quantifying relationships between these edaphic factors and plant response variables across four distinct levels: vegetative metrics (LA, FW, DW), leaf morphological characteristics (LMA, SLA), physiological indicators (chlorophyll content - DxChl, nitrogen balance index - DxNBI, normalized difference vegetation index - NDVI), and secondary metabolites such as flavonoids (DxFlav), anthocyanins (DxAnth), carotenoids (RI1526), polyphenols (RI1626). This two-tiered approach enables the identification of not only the distinctive environmental features of each soil type, but, more importantly, the functional relationships between specific edaphic factors and QI adaptive strategies, as evidenced by the correlation patterns.

4 Discussion

This research examines the interactions between soil properties and QI responses through an integrated analytical approach. In general, pH represents a crucial factor for nutrient availability, with extreme values (pH < < 7 acidic or > > 7 alkaline) limiting absorption [46, 47]. Soil A (pH 7.4) exhibits lower values of LA, FW, and DW, which correlate negatively with pH (R = −0.56 and −0.66). The lower LMA (R = −0.53) may

Table 2. R Pearson's correlation matrix between edaphic parameters and morpho-physiological responses in QI. The analysis examines relationships between soil characteristics (chemical properties, nutrient availability, water retention, heavy metals) and plant traits (growth metrics, leaf morphology, photosynthetic indicators, and secondary metabolites.

	pH	T CaCO$_3$	A CaCO$_3$	SOC	TN	C/N
LA	−0.32	0.75	0.69	0.97	0.98	0.64
FW	−0.56	0.58	0.53	0.99	0.99	0.83
DW	−0.66	0.46	0.42	0.97	0.96	0.89
LMA	−0.53	−0.93	−0.90	−0.46	−0.51	0.19
SLA	0.46	0.91	0.87	0.50	0.55	−0.14
DXChl	0.36	−0.35	−0.25	−0.66	−0.68	−0.48
DXFlav	−0.01	−0.83	−0.86	−0.74	−0.75	−0.37
DXAnth	−0.17	−0.66	−0.74	−0.44	−0.45	−0.15
DXNbi	0.35	−0.08	0.03	−0.41	−0.42	−0.34
NDVI	0.90	0.47	0.54	−0.30	−0.26	−0.72
RI$_{1526}$	−0.06	0.79	0.72	0.81	0.84	0.36
RI$_{1626}$	0.03	0.90	0.91	0.80	0.82	0.37
	A P	EX Ca	EX Mg	EX K	EX Na	CEC
LA	0.00	0.44	−0.06	−0.43	−0.74	0.39
FW	0.29	0.28	−0.28	−0.31	−0.82	0.22
DW	0.40	0.27	−0.31	−0.20	−0.79	0.20
LMA	0.77	−0.45	−0.38	0.72	0.31	−0.48
SLA	−0.74	0.54	0.43	−0.65	−0.29	0.56
DXChl	0.02	−0.88	−0.46	−0.14	0.18	−0.84
DXFlav	0.09	0.27	0.54	0.88	0.93	0.29
DXAnth	0.10	0.59	0.68	0.90	0.81	0.59
DXNbi	0.00	−0.94	−0.62	−0.41	−0.12	−0.91
NDVI	−0.75	−0.38	0.01	−0.74	−0.01	−0.31
RI$_{1526}$	−0.30	0.68	0.29	−0.40	−0.48	0.65
RI$_{1626}$	−0.16	−0.11	−0.40	−0.87	−0.90	−0.13
	EC 25 °C	FC p.F 2.5	PWP p.F 4.2	PAW	As	Cd
LA	−0.88	0.98	0.98	0.99	0.65	N/A
FW	−0.92	0.89	0.89	0.90	0.43	N/A
DW	−0.89	0.83	0.83	0.84	0.31	N/A
LMA	0.43	−0.75	−0.76	−0.74	−0.97	N/A

(*continued*)

Table 2. (*continued*)

	pH	T CaCO$_3$	A CaCO$_3$	SOC	T N	C/N
SLA	−0.44	0.79	0.80	0.79	0.95	N/A
DXChl	0.40	−0.78	−0.78	−0.78	−0.32	N/A
DXFlav	0.90	−0.68	−0.68	−0.68	−0.73	N/A
DXAnth	0.69	−0.35	−0.34	−0.35	−0.58	N/A
DXNbi	0.10	−0.54	−0.54	−0.54	−0.08	N/A
NDVI	0.09	−0.11	−0.10	−0.11	0.57	N/A
RI$_{1526}$	−0.67	0.97	0.98	0.97	0.75	N/A
RI$_{1626}$	−0.91	0.79	0.78	0.79	0.80	N/A
	Cr	Hg	Ni	Pb	Cu	Zn
LA	−0.92	N/A	−0.70	0.00	−0.06	−0.17
FW	−0.76	N/A	−0.64	0.27	0.23	0.12
DW	−0.68	N/A	−0.65	0.35	0.32	0.21
LMA	0.87	N/A	0.37	0.63	0.73	0.80
SLA	−0.91	N/A	−0.47	−0.65	−0.73	−0.80
DXChl	0.76	N/A	0.99	0.33	0.28	0.36
DXFlav	0.61	N/A	−0.03	−0.27	−0.12	−0.04
DXAnth	0.29	N/A	−0.41	−0.37	−0.21	−0.16
DXNbi	0.55	N/A	0.98	0.42	0.32	0.37
NDVI	−0.04	N/A	0.61	−0.35	−0.47	−0.45
RI$_{1526}$	−0.99	N/A	−0.80	−0.37	−0.41	−0.51
RI$_{1626}$	−0.73	N/A	−0.12	0.15	0.00	−0.09

result from micronutrient deficiencies. Even with reduced growth, a slightly alkaline pH corresponds to higher NDVI values (R = 0.90; highest in Soil A: 0.62, Table 1), showing that QI keeps a good vegetative state. The highest chlorophyll concentration is observed in plants grown in these soils, though the correlation remains weak (DxChl, R = 0.36), confirming that pH is not the determining factor. More neutral soils (B: pH 7.1; C: 6.8; D: 7.2) show a better balance between growth and nutrient availability, and here too, given the low correlation, pH does not emerge as the driver of vegetative growth.

The texture influences water retention, aeration, and vegetative growth. Clay soils (A) limit growth (low LA, FW, DW) improve photosynthetic efficiency (high NDVI and DxChl). Loamy–sand soils (D) favor more robust growth (high LA, FW, DW) but with lower photosynthetic efficiency (low NDVI and DxChl). Intermediate textures (B/C) show intermediate vegetative performance.

TCaCO3 and ACaCO3 greatly affect nutrient availability, influencing both growth and secondary metabolism. TCa CO3 correlates positively with LA (R = 0.75), polyphenols (RI1626, R = 0.90), carotenoids (RI1526, R = 0.79), and specific leaf area (SLA,

R = 0.91), but negatively with LMA (R = −0.93), flavonoids (DxFlav, R = −0.83), and anthocyanins (DxAnth, R = −0.66). ACa CO3 shows similar effects: positive on LA (R = 0.69), RI1626 (R = 0.91), RI1526 (R = 0.72), and SLA (R = 0.87), negative on LMA (R = −0.90), DxFlav (R = −0.86), and DxAnth (R = −0.74), indicating changes due to environmental stresses like nutrient deficiency.

SOC is a key factor for fertility and growth, with strong positive correlations with LA (R = 0.97), FW (R = 0.99), DW (R = 0.97), RI1526 (R = 0.81), and RI1626 (R = 0.80).

Minor negative effects on DxChl (R = −0.66) and DxFlav (R = −0.74) are observed. Soil D (the richest in carbon) shows the best plant growth, while soil A (the poorest) shows the worst growth.

TN is essential for both vegetative development and protein synthesis, as shown by its strong positive correlations with LA, FW, and DW (R > 0.96).

A high correlation is also found with RI1526 (R = 0.84) and RI1626 (R = 0.82), indicating a positive action on carotenoids and polyphenols synthesis. However, an excess of TN (>2.2 g/kg), such as that observed in soil D, inhibits chlorophyll, as shown by the negative correlation with DxChl (R = −0.68), probably due to a balance between chlorophyll synthesis and other nitrogen compounds; there is also a decrease in flavonoid synthesis and DxFlav (R = −0.75), which negatively affects some aspects of secondary metabolism.

The C/N Ratio is an indicator of soil quality and nutrient availability, as it affects organic matter decomposition and nitrogen mineralization, with positive correlations with LA (R = 0.64), FW (R = 0.83), and DW (R = 0.89), but negative with NDVI (R = −0.72). This suggests that a high ratio can favor vegetative growth due to better organic carbon availability but limits photosynthetic efficiency due to lower nitrogen availability, confirming its role as a primary growth driver.

AP increases leaf density (LMA, R = 0.77) but moderately, likely due to phosphorus's role in protein and cell membrane synthesis. High phosphorus levels reduce leaf expansion (SLA, R = −0.74) and NDVI (R = −0.75), indicating a trade-off between structural growth and photosynthetic efficiency.

Exchangeable calcium (EX-Ca) correlates positively with carotenoids (RI1526, R = 0.68), but negatively with chlorophyll (DxChl, R = −0.88), likely due to nutritional imbalances or inhibitory effects. The correlation is also negative with nitrogen balance index (DxNBI, R = −0.94), which could be explained with a negative interaction between calcium and nitrogen that limits nitrogen absorption or use by QI. Magnesium (EX–Mg) shows a negative correlation with chlorophyll (DxChl, R = −0.46), despite the role of this element in chlorophyll synthesis, which can be ascribed to nutritional imbalance or interaction with other nutrients. This nutrient stimulates anthocyanins (DxAnth, R = 0.68) and, to a lesser extent, flavonoids, essential pigments for stress defense. Magnesium also shows a negative correlation with DxNBI, due to a negative interaction between magnesium and nitrogen that limits nitrogen absorption.

Potassium (EX K) boosts flavonoids (R = 0.88), anthocyanins (R = 0.90), and LMA (R = 0.71), helping leaf density and defense pigments, but oddly lowers polyphenols (RI1626, R = −0.90), perhaps due to complex nutrient interactions. Concerning NDVI

($R = -0.74$) and SLA ($R = -0.64$), potassium shows an inhibitory effect on photosynthetic efficiency and leaf expansion. Sodium (EX Na) increases DxFlav ($R = 0.88$) and DxAnth ($R = 0.90$) as a stress response but damages growth (negative FW, DW, LA) and inhibits polyphenol production ($R = -0.90$).

CEC enhances carotenoid production (RI1526, $R = 0.65$) but strongly reduces the nitrogen balance index (DxNBI, $R = -0.92$), possibly due to competition between exchangeable cations and nitrogen uptake by the plant. The correlation is also negative with DxChl ($R = -0.84$), due to nutritional imbalances or highlighting complex interactions between exchangeable cations and chlorophyll synthesis.

EC: seems to reduce growth (negative LA, FW, DW) and polyphenols (RI1626, $R = -0.90$) but stimulates DxFlav ($R = 0.90$) and DxAnth ($R = 0.69$) as defense, a trend particularly observed in soils A and B.

FC, PWP, PAW show strong positive correlations with LA, FW, DW, SLA, RI1526, and RI1626 ($R > 0.78$), but negative with LMA, DxChl, and DxFlav, suggesting that greater water availability favors growth at the expense of some defense mechanisms like flavonoids, which are likely deemed unnecessary for combatting water stress.

Heavy metals (As, Cr, Ni, Pb, Cu, Zn) are present at low concentrations, with limited impact on growth but notable adaptive responses in plant metabolism. At very low concentrations, As increases SLA, indicating a peculiar adaptation to moderate abiotic stress. The reduction in leaf thickness (LMA, $R = -0.97$) can be explained as follows: at sub-toxic concentrations, As can activate adaptive responses similar to hormesis, where mild stress temporarily stimulates growth, leading QI to invest in leaf expansion (↑ area, ↓ thickness) to maximize photosynthesis, increase transpiration to reduce the toxic substance, compensating for metabolic stress. An increase in carotenoid and polyphenol concentrations is noted as a response to stress associated with leaf thickening.

At low doses, Cr stimulates LMA and DxChl ($R = 0.87$ and 0.76, respectively), though it does not activate carotenoid and polyphenol synthesis, likely because the stress level is too mild to trigger such responses. However, a "light" defense pathway is activated with an increase in flavonoids as a precaution, without full oxidative alarm, supporting the fact that defense mechanisms are active and functional.

Ni displays a typical pattern of metals with dual nutrient/toxicity roles; it shows a positive correlation with DxChl ($R = 0.99$), where QI prioritizes photosynthetic activity (also improving DxNBI and NDVI) over leaf expansion, sacrificing structural growth (LA, FW, DW show negative correlations). At very low concentrations, nickel does not produce enough reactive oxygen species (ROS) to trigger the synthesis of carotenoids, which normally act as antioxidants.

Pb, Cu, and Zn appear to induce thicker leaves (positive LMA) to limit oxidative damage, amplifying its sclerophyllous nature, but reducing SLA, with Zn being the most marked ($R = -0.80$). This reduction can occur because growth in area is sacrificed in favor of robustness. Additionally, Pb, Cu, and Zn alter water absorption, leading to more compact leaves (↑ LMA) but less cell expansion (↓ SLA).

QI reacts differently to soil traits, adapting based on environmental conditions. Leaf growth and biomass (LA, FW, DW) are primarily influenced by organic carbon and nitrogen availability, which act as true engines of vegetative development. A soil rich in organic matter with a good carbon-nitrogen balance (optimal C/N ratio) favors broader leaves and greater biomass. Conversely, alkaline pH and high salinity limit growth, though not necessarily compromising plant vitality, as evidenced by high NDVI values in alkaline soils. Regarding photosynthetic efficiency, parameters like chlorophyll, NDVI, and nitrogen balance are particularly affected by water availability and calcium carbonate presence, which e.g. can improve leaf reflectance (and thus NDVI readings) even under reduced growth conditions. However, excess phosphorus or calcium may inhibit photosynthesis, likely due to nutritional imbalances altering chloroplast functionality. Secondary metabolites (flavonoids, anthocyanins, carotenoids, total polyphenols) respond to more specific stresses. Soils rich in calcium carbonate promote the production of polyphenols and carotenoids. In contrast, high levels of potassium and sodium increase flavonoids and anthocyanins, reflecting a defensive reaction to ionic stress. Heavy metals like lead, copper, and zinc result in thicker (high LMA) and more compact leaves, reducing leaf expansion (SLA) to limit toxic uptake. In contrast, nickel and arsenic at low doses show dual effects: the former favors chlorophyll but inhibits carotenoids, while the latter triggers a hormetic response, temporarily increasing SLA and antioxidant metabolites.

Ultimately, QI demonstrates great adaptive plasticity: in fertile soils, it prioritizes growth, while in harsher conditions (poor, calcareous, or contaminated soils), it invests in structural and metabolic defenses. This flexibility explains its success in Mediterranean ecosystems, where it faces multiple environmental stressors.

5 Conclusions

The collected data demonstrates that QI modulates its physiology in distinct ways depending on soil characteristics, with clearly distinguishable responses at both structural and biochemical levels. Soil properties—particularly organic carbon content (SOC), nitrogen (TN), calcium carbonate, and water availability—directly influence leaf architecture. Nutrient-rich soils promote greater leaf expansion (LA) and biomass accumulation (FW, DW), whereas calcium carbonate-rich soils induce thinner leaves (low LMA, high SLA), likely as an adaptation to optimize photosynthetic efficiency under potential nutrient stress. Simultaneously, optical analyses reveal that these same edaphic conditions also affect physiological parameters. Soils with high SOC and TN, while stimulating growth, appear to reduce photosynthetic efficiency per unit area, as indicated by lower chlorophyll (DxChl) levels and increased carotenoids (RI1526), which may serve as supplementary protection against light stress. Conversely, calcareous soils, while reducing the synthesis of certain secondary metabolites like flavonoids (DxFlav), enhance other polyphenols (RI1626), suggesting a targeted defensive response against specific abiotic stressors. A particularly interesting aspect is the role of water availability (PAW), which emerges as the primary driver of foliar growth while having a limited impact on stress-related metabolites. This indicates that while water primarily influences vegetative development, other soil factors trigger more refined physiological mechanisms, detectable through optical measurements.

While it is well known that soil conditions affect plant status, the novelty of this work lies elsewhere: the consistency and complementarity between edaphic and photonic data is a key finding, which also reveals the limitations of photonic instruments. Optical analyses in fact record only the physiological state of plants, without digging deeper into the reasons behind the observed responses; edaphic analyses, on the other hand, inform us about the causes underlying the behavior recorded by optical instruments. Considering this, an integrated approach is recommended. Through this methodological integration it is possible to obtain a complete understanding of plant responses, especially in complex and variable environments such as urban ones. This study also allows us to verify how the responses recorded by optical instruments correspond to morphological variations in leaves. This correlation demonstrates for the first time how such modifications can be effectively monitored through innovative optical approaches. This validates the reliability of optical techniques in detecting real physiological states, free from artifacts, while also highlighting their user-friendly application. Their simplicity of use—requiring minimal training and no destructive sampling—positions them as a promising tool for rapid, scalable plant health monitoring. In summary, QI exhibits a sophisticated response capacity: it prioritizes structural adaptations (leaf growth, thickness) when soil resources (water, nutrients) are limited while activating biochemical responses (synthesis of pigments and antioxidants) in the presence of specific stressors such as high pH or metal accumulation. This duality not only fully justifies the optical observations but also suggests that integrating photonic sensors with edaphic analyses could offer an innovative approach to studying plant adaptation in complex environmental conditions. The next stages of the research will focus on more in-depth statistical analyses aimed at evaluating to what extent soil characteristics influence the data acquired through advanced photonic instrumentation. However, while soil represents one of the factors potentially modulating the physiological responses of QI, we hypothesize that its influence should be interpreted conditionally, within the broader environmental context. This cautious approach appears particularly relevant when comparing data from different locations, where multiple confounding factors may coexist. Therefore, the next phase will systematically extend the investigation to other environmental compartments. This integrated approach will allow for a comprehensive understanding of the influence exerted by each compartment on the species' physiological responses under the three different environmental conditions (urban, suburban, and rural). In this way, it will be possible to achieve a more robust validation of the results obtained through photonic techniques, whose data—as already observed for the soil—are supported by consistent and well-justified evidence.

References

1. Tucci, F., Giampaoletti, M., Nava, F., Tulelli, V.: Verso la neutralità climatica di architetture e città green (2023)
2. Nieuwenhuijsen, M.J.: New urban models for more sustainable, liveable and healthier cities post covid19; reducing air pollution, noise and heat island effects and increasing green space and physical activity. Environment International. 157, p. Article 10685 (2021)
3. Brears, R.C.: Nature-Based Solutions to 21st Century Challenges, 1st ed., Routledge (2020)
4. Ramos-González, O.M.: The green areas of san juan, puerto rico. Ecology and Society **19**(3) (2014)
5. Li, F., et al.: Spatio-temporal patterns of the use of urban green spaces and external factors contributing to their use in central beijing. Int. J. Environ. Res. Public Health **14**(3), 237 (2017)

6. Badiu, D.L., et al.: Is urban green space per capita a valuable target to achieve cities' sustainability goals? romania as a case study. Ecol. Ind. **70**, 53–66 (2016)
7. Liyaqat, I., et al.: Xylogenesis responses to a mediterranean climate in holm oak (quercus ilex l.). Forests **15**(8), 1386 (2024)
8. Giorgi, F.: Climate change hot-spots. Geophysical Research Letters **33**(8) (2006)
9. Agnelli, A., et al.: Holm oak (quercus ilex l.) rhizosphere affects limestone-derived soil under a multi-centennial forest. Plant and Soil **400**(1–2), 297–314 (2015)
10. Barquero, J., et al.: Biogeochemical prospecting of metallic critical raw materials: soil to plant transfer in sw ciudad real province, spain. Environ. Sci. Pollut. Res. **31**(20), 29536–29548 (2024)
11. Bogdziewicz, M., Fernández-Martínez, M., Espelta, J., Ogaya, R., Peñuelas, J.: Is forest fecundity resistant to drought? results from an 18-yr rainfall-reduction experiment. New Phytol. **227**(4), 1073–1080 (2020)
12. Cubera, E., Moreno, G.: Effect of single quercus ilex trees upon spatial and seasonal changes in soil water content in dehesas of central western Spain. Annals of Forest Science **64**(3), 355–364 (2007)
13. Díez-Hermano, S., et al.: Rhizosphere mycobiome diversity in four declining mediterranean tree species. Frontiers in Forests and Global Change **6** (2023)
14. Hoff, C., Rambal, S.: An examination of the interaction between climate, soil and leaf area index in a quercus ilex ecosystem. Ann. For. Sci. **60**(2), 153–161 (2003)
15. Limousin, J., Rambal, S., Ourcival, J., Rocheteau, A., Joffre, R., Rodríguez-Cortina, R.: Long-term transpiration change with rainfall decline in a mediter- ranean quercus ilex forest. Glob. Change Biol. **15**(9), 2163–2175 (2009)
16. Souad, E., Amraoui, M.: Effect of soil properties on growth of quercus ilex l. in humid and cold mountains of morocco. Appl. Environ. Soil Sci. **2020**, 1–9 (2020)
17. Прокофьева, Т. В., et al.: Inclusion of soils and soil-like bodies of urban territories into the russian soil classification system. Eurasian Soil Science **47**(10), 1276–1287 (2014)
18. Liu, L., et al.: Impact of urbanization on soil microbial diversity and composition in the megacity of shanghai. Land Degradation & Development **33**(2), 282–293 (2021)
19. Rolo, V., Moreno, G.: Shrub species affect distinctively the functioning of scattered quercus ilex trees in mediterranean open woodlands. For. Ecol. Manage. **261**(11), 1750–1759 (2011)
20. García-Fayos, P., Monleón, V.J., Espigares, T., Ibarra, J.M.N., Bochet, E.: Increasing aridity threatens the sexual regeneration of quercus ilex(holm oak) in mediterranean ecosystems. PLoS ONE **15**(10), e0239755 (2020)
21. Pardos, M., Calama, R.: Adaptive strategies of seedlings of four mediterra- nean co-occurring tree species in response to light and moderate drought: a nursery approach. Forests **13**(2), 154 (2022)
22. Roman, L.A., Scatena, F.N.: Street tree survival in New York City: comparing species, site conditions, and planting programs. Urban Forestry & Urban Greening **10**(2), 99–106 (2011)
23. Li, T., Meng, L., Herman, U., Lu, Z., Crittenden, J.: A survey of soil enzyme activities along major roads in Beijing: the implications for traffic corridor green space management. Int. J. Environ. Res. Public Health **12**(10), 12475–12488 (2015)
24. Sonti, N.F., Pregitzer, C.C., Hallett, R.A.: Native tree seedling growth and physiology responds to variable soil conditions of urban natural areas. Restor. Ecol. **30**, e13653 (2022)
25. Hopkins, L.P., January-Bevers, D.J., Caton, E.K., Campos, L.A.: A simple tree planting framework to improve climate, air pollution, health, and urban heat in vulnerable locations using non-traditional partners. Plants, People, Planet **3**(2), 166–182 (2021)
26. Bankole, A.O., et al.: Air quality assessment of ubeji community near petroleum-related activities. Open Journal of Air Pollution **13**(02), 57–71 (2024)

27. Falcioni, R., et al.: Classification and Prediction by Pigment Content in Lettuce (Lactuca sativa L.) Varieties Using Machine Learning and ATR-FTIR Spectroscopy. Plants **11**(24), 3413 (2022)
28. Alfani, A., Baldantoni, D., Maisto, G., Bartoli, G., Virzo De Santo, A.: Temporal and spatial variation in C, N, S and trace element contents in the leaves of Quer- cus ilex within the urban area of Naples. Environ. Pollut. **109**, 119–129 (2000)
29. Alfani, A., Maisto, G., Prati, M.V., Baldantoni, D.: Leaves of Quercus Ilex L. as bio-monitors of PAHs in the air of Naples (Italy). Atmos. Environ. **35**, 3553–3559 (2001)
30. Maisto, G., Alfani, A., Baldantoni, D., De Marco, A., Virzo De Santo, A.: Trace me-tals in the soil and in Q. ilex L. leaves at anthropic and remote sites of the Campania Region of Italy. Geoderma **122**, 269–279 (2004)
31. De Nicola, F., Maisto, G., Prati, M.V., Alfani, A.: Temporal variations in PAH con-centrations in Quercus ilex L. (holm oak) leaves in an urban area. Chemosphere **61**, 432–440 (2005)
32. De Nicola, F., Maisto, G., Prati, M.V., Alfani, A.: Leaf accumulation of trace elements and polycyclic aromatic hydrocarbons (PAHs) in Quercus ilex L. Environmental Pollution **153**, 376–383 (2008)
33. Cerovic, Z.G., Masdoumier, G., Ghozlen, N.B., Latouche, G.: A new optical leaf-clip meter for simultaneous non-destructive assessment of leaf chlorophyll and epidermal flavonoids. Physiol. Plant. **146**, 251–260 (2012)
34. Agati, G., et al.: Nondestructive optical sensing of flavonols and chlorophyll in white head cab-bage (Brassica oleracea L. var. capitata subvar. alba) grown under different nitrogen regimens. J. Agricult. Food Chem. **13**, 85–94 (2016)
35. Lo Piccolo, E., et al.: Multiple Consequences Induced by Epidermally-Located Anthocyanins in Young, Mature and Senescent Leaves of Prunus. Frontiers in Plant Science **9**, 917 (2018)
36. Akpolat, H., et al.: High-throughput phenotyping approach for screening major carotenoids of tomato by handheld Raman spectroscopy using chemo- metric Methods. Sensors **20**(13), 3723 (2020)
37. Traksele, L., Snitka, V.: Surface-enhanced Raman spectroscopy for the characterization of Vaccinium myrtillus L. bilberries of the Baltic-Nordic regions. European Food Res. Technol. **248**, 427–435 (2022)
38. Matteini, P., Distefano, C., de Angelis, M., Agati, G.: Assessment of nitrate levels in greenhouse-grown spinaches by Raman spectroscopy: A tool for sustainable agriculture and food security. J. Agricult. Food Res. **21** (2025)
39. Ministry of Agricultural Policies: Ministerial Decree of 13/09/1999. Approval of the "Of-ficial Methods of Chemical Analysis of Soil". In: Gazzetta Ufficiale, Suppl. Ordin. n° 248, pp.21/10/1999
40. Colombo, C., Miano, T.: Metodi di analisi chimica del suolo. 1a ed. Collana di Agronomia, vol. 12. FrancoAngeli, Milano (2023)
41. Indorante, S.J., Follmer, L.R., Hammer, R.D., Koenig, P.G.: Particle-size analysis by a modified pipette procedure. Soil Sci. Soc. Am. J. **54**, 560–563 (1990)
42. Conyers, M.K., Davey, B.G.: Observations on some routine methods for soil pH determination. Soil Sci. **145**, 29–36 (1988)
43. Repubblica Italiana, Parlamento: Decreto Legislativo 3 aprile 2006, n. 152 (2006). Norme in materia ambientale. Gazzetta Ufficiale n. 88 del 14 aprile 2006, Suppl. Ordinario n. 96, Roma
44. Agris, Regione Autonoma della Sardegna, Settore Suolo, Territorio e Ambiente (2016). Linee Guida all'Interpretazione delle Analisi del Suolo. Agenzia Regionale per la Ricerca Scientifica e l'Innovazione in Agricoltura, Cagliari
45. Schober, P., Boer, C., Schwarte, L.A.: Correlation coefficients: appropriate use and interpre-tation. Anesth. Analg. **126**(5), 1763–1768 (2018)
46. George, P., et al.: Divergent national-scale trends of microbial and animal biodiversity revealed across diverse temperate soil ecosystems. Nat. Commun. **10**(1), 1107 (2019)

47. Feng, X., Sun, X., Li, S., Zhang, J., Hu, N.: Relationship study among soils physicochemical properties and bacterial communities in Urban Green Space and promotion of its composition and Network Analysis. Agron. J. **113**, 515–526 (2021)

A Multiparametric Investigation of an Earthquake by a Jupyter Notebook: The Case Study of the Amatrice-Norcia Italian Seismic Sequence 2016-2017

Dedalo Marchetti[1](✉), Daniele Bailo[1], Jan Michalek[2], Rossana Paciello[1], Giuseppe Falcone[1], and Alessandro Piscini[1]

[1] Istituto Nazionale di Geofisica e Vulcanologia (INGV), 00143 Rome, Italy
dedalo.marchetti@ingv.it
[2] University of Bergen, Bergen, Norway

Abstract. We present a Virtual Research Environment (VRE), developed in the form of a Jupyter Notebook, devoted to a multidisciplinary and multiparametric analysis of an earthquake. In particular, the VRE retrieves and analyses lithospheric, atmospheric and ionospheric parameters from various sources. Among them, we selected the Open Data of the European Plate Observing System (EPOS) for the earthquake catalogue, integrated with the atmospheric climatological archive MERRA-2 provided by NASA, and the satellite magnetic data of the Swarm mission produced by ESA. The open-source code and friendly environment of Jupyter Notebook allow future users to personalise the research parameters (e.g., investigated time, area of interest) and apply the same VRE to other earthquakes. The VRE is designed for the 2016 seismic sequence that affected Central Italy, characterised by the $Mw = 6.0$ earthquake near Accumoli and Amatrice on August 24, 2016, and the $Mw = 6.5$ earthquake near Norcia on October 30, 2016. The Jupyter Notebook performs: 1) seismological investigations such as the calculus of cumulated Benioff strain and released energy weighted for the distance of the target event; 2) extraction of typical atmospheric values and identification of possible anomalies and 3) searching for small oscillations of magnetic field not likely related to geomagnetic activity. Finally, a graphical comparison of all the investigations is provided to search for possible interactions among the different geo-layers. In the context of studying the preparation phase of the 2016–2017 Italian Seismic Sequence, we provide a tool for exploiting and integrating multiparametric EPOS data with other datasets.

Keywords: Jupyter Notebook · lithosphere · atmosphere · ionosphere · pre-earthquake signals

1 Introduction

Here, we introduce the European Plate Observing System (EPOS), the Jupyter notebook, and the Italian Amatrice-Norcia 2016–2017 seismic sequence, as well as multiparametric studies of the preparation phase of the earthquake, investigating possible lithosphere-atmosphere-ionospheric anomalies.

1.1 EPOS and Jupyter Notebooks

The European Plate Observing System (EPOS ERIC) was conceived in 1997 as a European Research Infrastructure Consortium (ERIC) [1] in order to provide a research infrastructure in Solid Earth Sciences at the pan-European level. EPOS is in continuous evolution and already hit several milestones: in 2015, it started the implementation phase; in 2018, EPOS-ERIC was established; in 2020, it started the Pilot Operational Phase, and it became completely operational in 2023. One of the most important tools provided by EPOS is the Data Portal (https://www.epos-eu.org/dataportal), which is a multiparametric platform collecting datasets from multiple sources [2].

The Data Portal is populated by several services managed by Thematic Core Services (TCS) communities. The data are linked and not copied to EPOS after homogenisation and quality check through metadata harmonisation to facilitate the development of multidisciplinary studies and also the final user that can access from a common interface. Ten TCS communities representing specific disciplines are present nowadays in EPOS Data Portal: Seismology [3], Near-Fault Observatories [4], GNSS Data and Products [5], Volcano Observations [6], Satellite Data [7], Geomagnetic Observations [8], Anthropogenic Hazards [9], Geological Information and Modelling [10], Multi-Scale Laboratories [11], and Tsunami [12].

The integration of more than 300 interoperable multidisciplinary services in the EPOS central hub system is based on a microservice-based architecture [13]. EPOS Data Portal is distributed under a GPL license as open-source software (https://epos-eu.github.io/epos-open-source/) and complies with the FAIR Principles [14], encouraging interdisciplinary cooperation and technological development in Earth sciences and beyond. Considering the intrinsic multidisciplinary and multiparametric nature of the research on the preparation phase of the earthquakes in the view of Lithosphere Atmosphere and Ionosphere Coupling [15], the EPOS infrastructure can provide crucial support to implement and improve these analyses.

We used a Jupyter Notebook to implement and share our Virtual Research Environment (VRE). Jupyter Notebook was developed a few years ago to provide an easy way to share code among different researchers and communities, being executable, including results and explanations [16]. Jupyter Notebook generally uses a Python kernel, but also others are available and integrable. For example, we first developed the VRE in Matlab code, and a version in Python is under development.

1.2 Italian Amatrice-Norcia 2016–2017 Seismic Sequence

On 24 August 2016 at 1:33 Universal Time (UT), an earthquake of moment magnitude $Mw = 6.0$ hit Central Italy close to the towns of Accumoli and Amatrice. Furthermore, a very long seismic sequence started, and a larger event occurred after more than two months, on 30 October 2016, close to the town of Norcia. The location of the seismic sequence was in the Central Apennine chain, which is mainly characterized by an extensional tectonic setting. The mainshock was the largest magnitude event in Italy in the previous thirty-five years, following the Irpinia earthquake in 1980 [17].

Several studies have been done in order to study the preparation phase of the Italian seismic sequence 2016–2017. Piscini et al. [18] investigated three atmospheric parameters: skin temperature, total column water vapour and total column ozone. They were retrieved from the European Center for Medium-range Weather Forecast (ECMWF) from different datasets: ERA-Interim, a climatological archive and an operational Integrated Forecasting System (IFS). The climatological archive data provided historical trends starting from 1979 with Worldwide coverage, while the operational one delivered updated data every three hours. The authors identified a sequence of atmospheric anomalies that started with water vapour and skin temperature followed in a few days by an increase of Ozone in Central Italy preceding about 40 days the start of the seismic sequence. Marchetti et al. [19] analysed the ionospheric magnetic field, identifying interesting anomalous tracks about 3.5 days before the two larger shocks in Central Italy (Amatrice and Norcia events). Fidani et al. [20] installed several electromagnetic ground observatories in Central Italy, and they identified possible anomalous electrical and magnetic field signals on the ground possibly related to the 2016 seismic sequence. The analysis of the variations of the permanent GNSS positions provided useful indications to understand possible anomalous tectonic movements before the earthquake, as reported by Panza et al. [21]. Finally, a chain of lithospheric, atmospheric and ionospheric anomalies was proposed by Marchetti et al. [22], suggesting that they could be induced by the accumulation of stress in preparation for the 2016 seismic sequence of central Italy.

1.3 The Possible Lithosphere Atmosphere Ionosphere Coupling Before the Earthquake Occurrence

The possible Lithosphere Atmosphere Ionosphere Coupling (LAIC) before the earthquake occurrence was proposed about 30 years ago [23]. It aims to explain several phenomena recorded before the earthquake occurrence, especially the electromagnetic signals. Several authors recorded anomalous geomagnetic field signals or electromagnetic variations of the bottom layer of the ionosphere in preparation for earthquakes in the USA, Indonesia, Japan and other countries [24–26]. However, recording an anomaly before an earthquake does not necessarily imply a causal-effect relationship. It's necessary to provide some more pieces of evidence and a theory that may explain how the accumulation of stress in a fault with an impending earthquake can generate anomalies. The topic is so controversial that there is still no definitive conclusion [27]. Nevertheless, understanding that some phenomena would be linked to the preparation phase of an earthquake does not mean that we are able to predict such an earthquake. So, the present research is devoted to finding signals possibly related to the preparation phase of earthquakes but not to predict them directly. In principle, this could seem a contradiction, but it can be considered a step necessary but not sufficient for the prediction of an earthquake. As an example, a sign of the accumulation of stress on a fault could underline the activity and even nucleation of an earthquake but not provide information about the incoming time, so not finally, a prediction which requires defining at least position, time, magnitude, percentage of confidence to be scientific reliable [28].

Several theories have been proposed to explain the detected phenomena before the earthquakes and, more in general, the possible LAIC. A milestone theory is the one called "dilatancy" proposed by Scholz [29] in the early seventies. He proposed that the preparation phase of an earthquake is composed of different phases, and their duration is proportional (in logarithm scale) to the magnitude of the incoming event. The latter hypothesis was also empirically identified in different types of pre-earthquake signals by Japanese seismologist Rikitake [30]. Recently, such a relationship between the anticipation time and magnitude of the incoming earthquake was confirmed even for magnetic anomalies detected by the satellite constellation Swarm [31, 32]. The different stages of preparation for an earthquake can be identified by noticing variations of seismological parameters (e.g., the ratio Vp/Vs of the primary over the secondary speed of seismic waves), followed by underground fluid movements and reduction of electrical resistivity of the crust. The underground fluid movements could transport trace gases on Earth's surface as radon [33]. The radon introduced in the atmosphere decays, and the alpha-radiative particles can ionise atmospheric molecules, producing alterations in atmospheric and even ionospheric electric fields. In addition, the accumulation of charges in the atmosphere may induce a chain of phenomena, such as the hydration of aggregation molecules, increase of aerosol, drop of relative humidity and emission of outgoing longwave radiation [34, 35]. Other theories proposed a more direct mechanism for the generation of electromagnetic anomalies, such as the one by Molchan and Hayakawa [36], based on the separation of charges at fault level due to stress increase. An innovative theory was proposed by Freund [37, 38]. He proposed that the stress increase can break some peroxy-links of the minerals in the rocks at the fault level, releasing positive charges called p-holes. The p-holes could accumulate on the Earth's surface and induce electrical anomalies in the atmosphere and ionosphere as modelled (analytically and numerically) by Kuo et al. [39]. They showed that electron density anomalies could propagate up to about 2000 km altitude from the accumulation of electrical charges on Earth's surface. However, other authors argued some mistakes [40] in the simulation regarding the electrical conductivity of the atmosphere. A response from the original authors was provided, showing that the results in the ionosphere can also be confirmed with the suggested correction [41]. Nonetheless, the contrast underlines a difficult conclusion on the topic. A recent Special Issue on this topic is available as Open Source in [42].

2 Data

The Virtual Research Environment (VRE) was developed in the form of a Jupyter Notebook. The general idea is shown in Fig. 1. The VRE collects data from different sources, elaborates the data, and, whenever possible, integrates them together. A list of the data and analysed parameters is reported in Table 1 and a specific description of them is provided in the following subsections.

Table 1. List of the analysed datasets and parameters.

Geo-layer	Dataset	Parameters	Type of analysis
Lithosphere	EMSC-CSEM (by EPOS)	Earthquake catalogue	• Time series of number of events • Cumulative Benioff stress • ES (Energy weighted for distance)
	SGO-EPND (by EPOS)	GNSS Weekly Positions Time series	• Time series of variations along transects • Maps of rate of positions drift
Atmosphere	MERRA-2 (by NASA)	Surface Air Temperature	• Historical time series (1980–2024) characterization compared with the year of the earthquake
		SO_2	
		Dimethyl Sulphide	
		Aerosol Optical Thickness	
		CO	
		Surface Latent Heat Flux	
		Relative Humidity	
Ionosphere	Swarm satellites (by ESA)	East component of the magnetic field measurement	• Selection of data above epicentral area and track detrending to analyses residuals

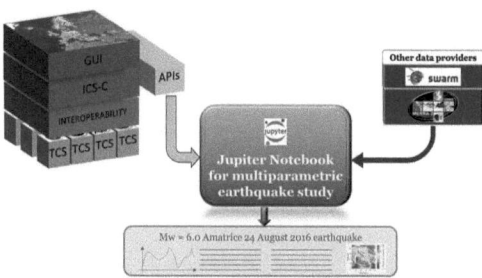

Fig. 1. Sketch of the VRE. The core of the VRE is the Jupiter Notebook. It retrieves most data (e.g., the earthquake catalogue) from the EPOS platform via APIs and integrates it with other external data sources, such as Swarm satellite geomagnetic data. It provides an output report with information on the Italian Seismic sequence 2016, graphs, and analyses of the retrieved data.

2.1 Datasets for Lithosphere Atmosphere and Ionosphere

In order to investigate the lithosphere, the earthquake catalogue and the GNSS positions were selected. For the earthquake catalogue, we selected the EPOS "Parameters of modern earthquakes (1998-present) - FDSN event" provided by Thematic Core Service (TCS) Seismology of EPOS Data Portal [3]. This earthquake catalogue ingests several data providers contributing to the European Mediterranean Seismological Centre (EMSC-CSEM). INGV (Italian National Institute of Geophysics and Volcanology) is the data provider for the Italian territory (i.e., the area of this study). Consequently, the earthquake catalogue analysed in this case study was originally created by INGV, and it's also available in the ISIDE repository [43]. However, the advantage of downloading from EPOS infrastructure is that the same research environment can be easily applied to any other earthquake in Europe and the Mediterranean area.

The area of research is the Dobrovolsky's circle defined by its radius "R_{Dob}":

$$R_{Dob}[km] = 10^{(0.43 \times M)} \quad (1)$$

where "M" is the earthquake's magnitude (preferably moment magnitude). This area was proposed by Dobrovolsky [44] as the one where we can expect to record signs of the seismic event preparation. The earthquake catalogue was downloaded in a larger area (a square with a side length of 2 times $R_{Dob} + 10°$ for latitude and longitude, as visible in Fig. 2. Nevertheless, the following analyses will select only the events inside Dobrovolsky's circular area.

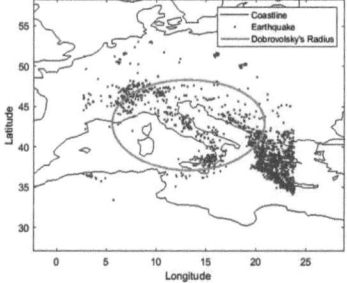

Fig. 2. Maps of the downloaded seismic events from the EPOS earthquake catalogue in the 8 months before the start of the Amatrice-Norcia Italian seismic sequence 2016–2017.

With regards to the Global Navigation Satellite System (GNSS) network, this VRE automatically makes two calls to the EPOS Data Platform: the first one is to retrieve the list of the stations in the area of interest, while the second one is to download the time series of GNSS positions. The data are provided by the TCS-GNSS of EPOS [5]. The area of interest of GNSS data analysis was reduced with respect to the full Dobrovoslky's area, as we expect the tectonic deformations closer to the incoming seismic event and not in other tectonic systems. Consequently, the square inscribed into Dobrovolsky's circle was the research area for GNSS data. The map of the available GNSS stations is shown in Fig. 3.

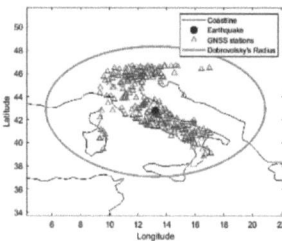

Fig. 3. Map of the GNSS stations available in the EPOS network within the research area (square inscribed in Dobrovolsky's circle).

The weekly time series were retrieved for the selected GNSS stations, and further selection was made for the specific investigation. In fact, the analysis has been conducted on each couple of stations whose direction is along a transect of the fault of the target earthquake (in this case, Amatrice/Norcia) or using all the stations at a certain time and calculating the rate of variation of the three components (North-East-Up) from one measurement to the next one.

The geo-layer of the atmosphere was investigated using the data from the climatological archive Modern-Era Retrospective analysis for Research and Applications version 2 (MERRA-2) provided by NASA [45]. It contains an estimation of several physical and chemical atmospheric parameters from 1980 to the present on a regular grid in space and time. The resolution is 0.5° latitude, 0.625° longitude and 1 hour in time. It is updated monthly, and it ingests data from ground, airborne, and satellite sources. Then, it fits over a physical/empirical atmospheric model. Data are open with a free account in the EarthData portal. Here, we retrieved seven parameters: Surface Air Temperature, Sulphur Dioxide (SO_2), Dimethyl Sulphide (DMS), Aerosol Optical Thickness (AOT), Carbon Monoxide (CO), Surface Latent Heat Flux (SLHF) and Relative Humidity (RH).

The ionosphere was studied by analysing the European Space Agency (ESA) magnetic data recorded by the three-identical satellite mission Swarm. It's the state-of-the-art monitoring of the Earth's magnetic field from space. It's been in orbit since November 2013 [46]. ESA provides the data openly by dissemination server (swarm-diss.eo.esa.int) by https browser or ftp with EarthObservation ESA free credentials. The data are organised in daily files, which contain all orbits with a resolution of 1 Hz (Low Rate) that we selected for this work (50 Hz is also available).

3 Methods and Results

The above dataset has been analysed by a general workflow illustrated in Fig. 4 and described in the following lines. The description is divided in:

3.1. Lithosphere – investigation of the earthquake catalogue
3.2. Lithosphere – investigation of the GNSS position data
3.3. Atmosphere – investigation of the climatological data
3.4. Ionosphere – investigation of the satellite magnetic data
3.5. Summary view

Fig. 4. Workflow of the developed VRE to study the lithosphere, atmosphere and ionosphere with a multiparametric and multidisciplinary study.

3.1 Lithosphere – Earthquake Catalogue Investigation

The earthquake catalogue was first filtered for several constraints: minimum earthquake magnitude, maximum hypocentral depth and distance from the target earthquake epicentre. The selection of these constraints applied to the seismic catalogue is based on seismological settings. In particular, the minimum magnitude is the "Completeness magnitude" (Mc) of the earthquake catalogue, i.e., the minimum magnitude that is surely detected. Events of lower magnitude can be present in the catalogue (for example, shallow earthquakes close to a seismic station), but not all earthquakes of that magnitude [47]. The maximum distance is set to Dobrovolsky's radius. The maximum depth was fixed at 50 km, according to previous studies [32].

Using the selected events, the Benioff cumulative strain was computed according to the original formulation [48]. Firstly, for each (i-th) seismic event, the earthquake energy "E_i" was estimated using its magnitude "M" by Gutenberg-Richter law:

$$E_i[J] = 10^{(1.5 \times M + 4.8)} \qquad (2)$$

Then, the cumulative Benioff Strain $S(t)$ was estimated as the sum of the square root of the energy of the i-th seismic events up to time t:

$$S(t) = \sum_{i \leq t} \sqrt{E_i} \qquad (3)$$

The VRE then provides two graphs with the cumulative number of events and the Cumulative Benioff Strain in the selected period, like the ones reported in Fig. 5.

In addition to Benioff cumulative strain, the second parameter, "E_S", related to the seismicity, was estimated. Prof. Katsumi Hattori introduced this parameter to understand if the area surrounding a monitoring station (e.g., magnetic observatory) was seismic active or not [49, 50]. It was calculated using the distance of the seismic event from the monitoring station. Here, the distance "r" is computed from the target earthquake. The E_S is then calculated daily (i.e., summing all i-events that occurred on the same day):

$$E_S = \sum_i \frac{E_i}{r^2} \qquad (4)$$

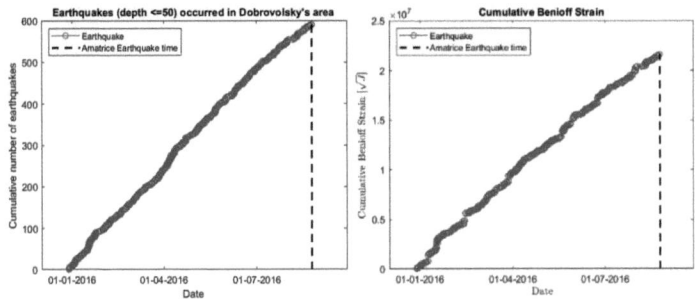

Fig. 5. The cumulative number of earthquakes (left panel) and cumulative Benioff strain (right panel) occurred in the eight months before the start of the Amatrice-Norcia Italian seismic sequence 2016–2017

The result is shown as a time series of daily values of E_S as well as a cumulative trend as reported in Fig. 6.

3.2 Lithosphere – GNSS Data Investigation

GNSS data investigation was explored using two different approaches: a time series of a couple of stations along the transects of the seismic fault or mapping the rate of position variations.

The transect is the perpendicular direction with respect to the fault. We focused on the analysis of variations of GNSS positions along the transect, considering the interesting results obtained by Panza et al. [21]. However, here, we are developing a new method without necessarily reconstructing or replicating their results. One important difference is that in [21], the authors used several GNSS stations aligned along the transect, while here, we used only two stations whose direction is along a transect of the main fault of the target event.

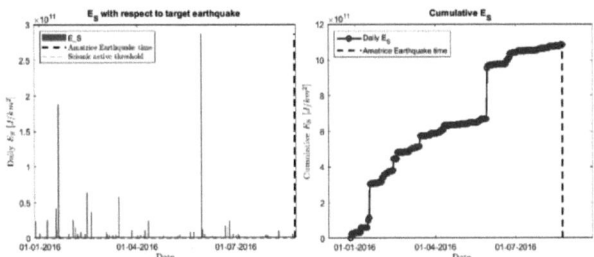

Fig. 6. Daily (left panel) and cumulative trend (right panel) of the ES parameter (earthquake energy weighted for squared distance from the target earthquake).

The first step was to divide the GNSS stations that were on the footwall by the ones on the hanging wall of the main fault. We achieved this by calculating the angle of the GNSS station with respect to the target earthquakes and then considering this angle with respect to the Strike of the fault (one of the input parameters of the VRE). A graphical map shows the stations after this division with two different colours, as reported in Fig. 7 (left panel). We would underline that such a division on the footwall and hanging wall regards only the direction of the main fault but not the real extension of the fault. Consequently, a GNSS station marked on the hanging wall (footwall) could be on another fault system but not on the target event's footwall (hanging wall).

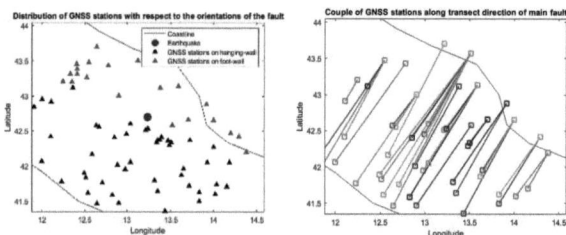

Fig. 7. Maps of the GNSS stations. Left panel: GNSS stations are divided into the ones that are on the footwall and on the hanging wall of the main fault of the target event. Right panel: Couple of GNSS stations along the transects of the main target fault.

To search all the couple GNSS stations on the transects, each one on the hanging wall was selected, and the angle with respect to the GNSS stations on the footwall was calculated. If such an angle was perpendicular to the strike of the main target fault, the couple of stations were selected as belonging to one transect. All the detected couples of stations along a transect of the main fault are reported in the right panel of Fig. 7.

Then, for each couple of GNSS stations, the two time series of the three positions displacements (North, East, Up) were selected, and after resampling the second stations on the same time step of the first one, the differential position was calculated:

$$\begin{vmatrix} \Delta N(t_i) \\ \Delta E(t_i) \\ \Delta U(t_i) \end{vmatrix} = \begin{vmatrix} North_{station1}(t_i) - North_{station2}(t_i) \\ East_{station1}(t_i) - East_{station2}(t_i) \\ Up_{station1}(t_i) - Up_{station2}(t_i) \end{vmatrix} \quad (5)$$

The results visible in Fig. 8 were plotted firstly in a two-dimensional graph with a vertical axis, the differential displacement for each component, and the horizontal time. Secondly, a three-dimensional graph was realised, calculating the transect's distance to the target earthquake's epicentre.

A second approach to investigate the GNSS data was carried out producing maps of variation of the recorded positions in Central Italy. We firstly homogenised the data in a tensor with dimensions of time, station and the three recorded positions. The space was first filled with available data. The values were interpolated with the previous and following measurements for the time steps without measurements at one station. If one or both were not available, the value was not used. Then, the differences of the two consecutive timesteps for each GNSS were computed and divided for the time intercurred from among the two steps, i.e., estimating the variation rate of the measured positions at all available stations. With all the available data, a map was then interpolated for each timestep (weekly). An example is provided in Fig. 9.

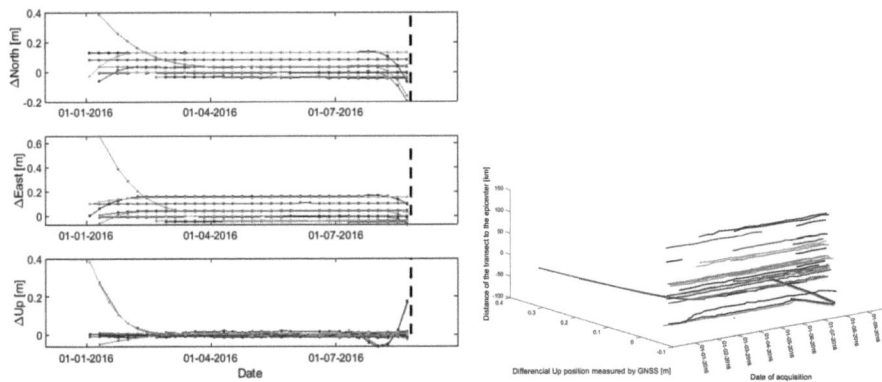

Fig. 8. Time series of differential displacements of couple of stations along the transects of the main fault.

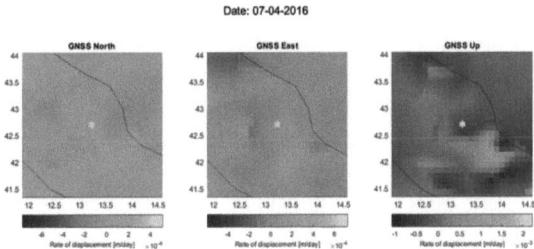

Fig. 9. Rate of variation of the positions measured by GNSS stations in Central Italy.

3.3 Atmosphere – Investigation of the Climatological Data

For the investigation of the atmospheric climatological data, we applied an approach similar to the Climatological Analysis for seismic PRecursor Identification (CAPRI) algorithm developed by Piscini et al. [18]. A similar algorithm that is the one inserted in this VRE is called "MErra-2 ANalysis to search Seismic precursors" (MEANS) [51]. The MEANS analysis steps for each atmospheric parameter "P" are the following:

1. Calculus of spatial average of P;
2. Calculus of mean value of P for each year;
3. Calculus of multi-year trend of parameter P from 1980 to present with corresponding plot and linear fit;
4. The slope of the linear fit is removed in order to take into account possible global warming (i.e., a multi-year trend) not related to the earthquake;
5. Each year is then checked for possible outlier values, and eventually, the year with an outlier is removed. For example, SO_2 could be high during a volcanic eruption, compromising the average;
6. Calculus of mean and standard deviation "std" of P for each specific day (e.g., mean(P) and std(P) of 1 Jan., mean(P) and std(P) of 2 Jan. And so on);

7. Comparison of the value of the earthquake with the average ones and if the specific day is greater (or lower for humidity) of mean plus two standard deviations is computed as an anomalous day;
8. The cumulative plot of the anomalies as a function of time is carried out.

3.4 Ionosphere – Investigation of the Satellite Magnetic Data

The magnetic data were investigated using an approach similar to the one of the MAgnetic Swarm anomaly detection by Spline analysis (MASS) algorithms, successfully applied to specific earthquakes (e.g., Nepal 2015 [52]; Indonesia 2018 [53]) and statistical worldwide correlation with M5.5 + earthquakes [31, 32].

In order to extract eventual anomalous magnetic signals in ionosphere, the algorithm applies the following steps to ESA Swarm data:

1. Select the satellite tracks that crossed the research area (Dobrovolsky's circle) during the investigated time, preserving the full tracks within -50° and + 50° geomagnetic latitude.
2. Estimate the first derivative, "FD", by calculating the first differences (sample-by-sample) divided for the time between the two samples.
3. Fitting a smoothing spline to the FD and subtracting it from FD. This produces the track residual, as shown for ten random tracks in Fig. 10.
4. Using a moving window of 3° latitude, search for possible anomalies, i.e., windows with root mean square larger than "threshold" multiplied by the root mean square of the whole track. In this example, the threshold was set to 4.0, but the user can run the VRE by selecting another threshold.
5. Calculating and plotting the cumulative trend of anomalies as a function of the time.

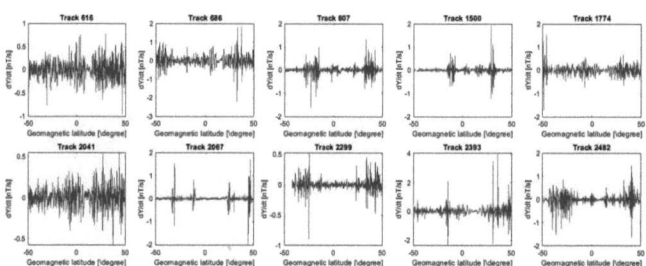

Fig. 10. Examples of ten tracks residuals of the East component of the magnetic field.

3.5 Summary View

Finally, the VRE provides a summary of the analyses in the form of a common view reported in Fig. 11. Here, the calculated time series of lithospheric, atmospheric and ionospheric data are reported together with a common horizontal time axis. The target earthquake time is marked by a vertical black dashed line. This picture allows the researcher to identify possible common trends (e.g., an increase of anomalies) that may suggest an interaction between the geo-layers, i.e. a coupling, as identified in previous studies [53, 54].

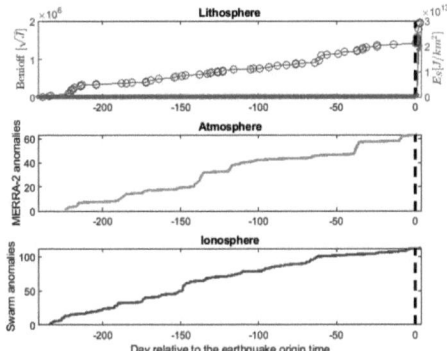

Fig. 11. Summary view of the multidisciplinary and multiparametric investigation of the preparation of the Italian seismic sequence Amatrice-Norcia by visualising time series of lithospheric atmospheric and ionospheric data.

4 Discussion and Future Perspectives

From the lithosphere investigation, it was interesting to note the cumulative trend of E_S parameter presented in Fig. 6. In fact, two timeframes of higher seismic activity during the 8 months preceding the start (on 24 August 2016) of the Italian Amatrice-Norcia 2016–2017 seismic sequence within the Dobrovolskys's area:

1. About 225 days before the start of the seismic sequence
2. About 60 days before the start of the seismic sequence

However, the E_S parameter shows a very much higher value for the second event. This is due to the closeness to the target event. It was an earthquake of magnitude Mw = 4.4 that occurred on the North side of Bolsena Lake in Central Italy on 30 May 2016 (see Fig. 12). This seismic event was about 104 km from the 24 August 2016 Amatrice earthquake and 95 km away from the 30 October 2016 Norcia earthquake. Nevertheless, the involved faults are very far and not directly connected.

From the analysis of GNSS positions recorded in Central Italy in the 8 months before the seismic sequence, it was possible to identify an interesting trend in the North time series (see Fig. 8). However, from the detailed plot considering the distance of each transect from the epicentre, the interesting profile is far from the epicentre, so it's probably not connected with the preparation for the earthquake. Still, some of the maps of the rate of variation of GNSS positions present interesting patterns, as the one reported in Fig. 9. It's worth noting that at this time, other anomalies were recorded and reported: here, the atmospheric trend shows an increase that followed such days (see green trend in Fig. 11 at about day -140) and Barberio et al. [55] detected an increase in heavy metals

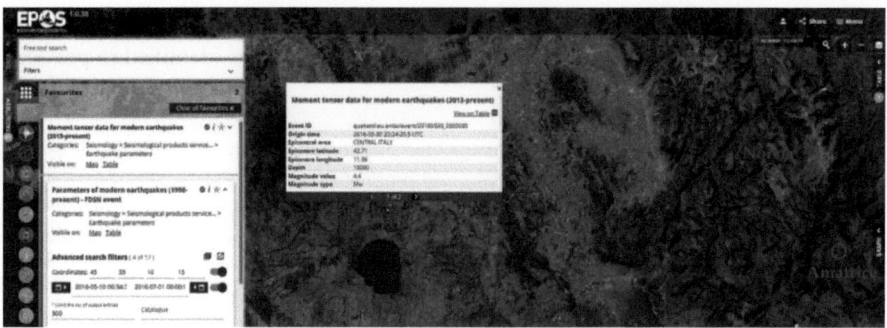

Fig. 12. Localization of the Mw = 4.4 earthquake occurred on 30 May 2016. Positions of the towns of Amatrice and Norcia are marked.

in water wells close to Sulmona town in April 2016. However, our main object of this present work is to present a flexible environment, and we leave the scientific discussions to other works, for example [22].

Finally, the Jupyter Notebook allows the user to easily integrate new data and features to expand the present research framework. Furthermore, the analysis of another earthquake is very easy as most of the part of the Notebook automatically downloads the necessary data, calculate the region of interest automatically, and replots all the output according to the new input parameters. Regarding the region of the World that can be analysed, some limitations are provided if a dataset is focused only on a specific region (for example, local earthquake catalogue). However, some ongoing work on the EPOS platform is devoted to a wider integration with other open-source similar platforms that can overpass even such limitations. In conclusion, the developed VRE provides a tool that any researcher can use to verify the obtained results independently and to reuse, modify the parameters, or analyse other case studies (earthquakes, volcanic eruptions, or other natural or anthropogenic hazards). Such an open approach can also help the advancement of understanding of the preparation phase of the earthquake, facilitating cooperation and exchanges among several researchers of the World, hopefully improving the knowledge.

Software Repository. The VRE described in this paper is available at: https://github.com/dedalomarchetti/VRE_Amatrice (https://doi.org/10.5281/zenodo.15365530).

Acknowledgments. We acknowledge the EPOS-MUR initiative and International Team 23–583 "Investigation of the Lithosphere Atmosphere Ionosphere Coupling (LAIC) Mechanism before the Natural Hazards" led by Dedalo Marchetti and Essam Ghamry. We acknowledge Saioa Arquero Campuzano, Antonella Peresan, Francisco Javier Pavón-Carrasco, Zhang Yiqun, Angelo De Santis, Gianfranco Cianchini, Zhu Kaiguang, Loredana Perrone and Maurizio Soldani for useful discussions and help in developing some of the codes that inspired the present work.

Disclosure of Interests. The authors have no competing interests to declare that are relevant to the content of this article.

References

1. Cocco, M., et al.: The EPOS Research Infrastructure: a federated approach to integrate solid Earth science data and services. Annals of Geophysics **65**, DM208 (2022). https://doi.org/10.4401/ag-8756
2. Bailo, D., et al.: The EPOS multi-disciplinary Data Portal for integrated access to solid Earth science datasets. Sci Data. **10**, 784 (2023). https://doi.org/10.1038/s41597-023-02697-9
3. Haslinger, F., et al.: Coordinated and Interoperable Seismological Data and Product Services in Europe: the EPOS Thematic Core Service for Seismology. Annals of Geophysics **65**, DM213 (2022). https://doi.org/10.4401/ag-8767
4. Chiaraluce, L., et al.: The Near Fault Observatory community in Europe: a new resource for faulting and hazard studies. Annals of Geophysics **65**, DM316 (2022). https://doi.org/10.4401/ag-8778
5. Fernandes, R., et al.: A new European service to share GNSS Data and Products. Annals of Geophysics **65**, DM317 (2022). https://doi.org/10.4401/ag-8776
6. Puglisi, G., et al.: The integrated multidisciplinary European volcano infrastructure: from the conception to the implementation. Annals of Geophysics **65**, DM320 (2022). https://doi.org/10.4401/ag-8794
7. Manunta, M.: The satellite component of the EPOS infrastructure: Thematic Core Service Satellite Data. Geophysical Research Abstracts **21**, EGU2019–16052 (2019)
8. Reay, S., et al.: Updates and future plans at the World Data Centre for Geomagnetism, Edinburgh. IAGA-IASPEI Joint Scientific Assembly 2021, Virtual (2021)
9. Orlecka-Sikora, B., et al.: An open data infrastructure for the study of anthropogenic hazards linked to georesource exploitation. Sci Data. **7**, 89 (2020). https://doi.org/10.1038/s41597-020-0429-3
10. Urvois, M., et al.: Integrating geological data in Europe to foster multidisciplinary research. Annals of Geophysics **65**, DM319 (2022). https://doi.org/10.4401/ag-8817
11. Wessels, R., et al.: Transnational Access to Research Facilities: an EPOS service to promote multi-domain Solid Earth Sciences in Europe. Annals of Geophysics **65**, DM214 (2022). https://doi.org/10.4401/ag-8768
12. Babeyko, A., et al.: Towards the new Thematic Core Service Tsunami within the EPOS Research Infrastructure. Annals of Geophysics **65**, DM215 (2022). https://doi.org/10.4401/ag-8762
13. Bailo, D., et al.: Integrated access to multidisciplinary data through semantically interoperable services in a metadata-driven platform for solid earth science. In: Garoufallou, E., Vlachidis, A. (eds.) Metadata and Semantic Research, pp. 235–247. Springer Nature Switzerland, Cham (2023)
14. Wilkinson, M.D., et al.: The FAIR Guiding Principles for scientific data management and stewardship. Sci Data. **3**, 160018 (2016). https://doi.org/10.1038/sdata.2016.18
15. Ouzounov, D., Pulinets, S., Hattori, K., Taylor, P.: Pre-earthquake processes: a multidisciplinary approach to earthquake prediction studies. American geophysical union, Washington Hoboken (2018)
16. Thomas, K., et al.: Jupyter Development Team: Jupyter Notebooks – a publishing format for reproducible computational workflows. In: Positioning and Power in Academic Publishing: Players, Agents and Agendas. IOS Press (2016). https://doi.org/10.3233/978-1-61499-649-1-87
17. Bernard, P., Zollo, A.: The Irpinia (Italy) 1980 earthquake: detailed analysis of a complex normal faulting. J. Geophy. Res. Solid Earth. **94**, 1631–1647 (1989). https://doi.org/10.1029/JB094iB02p01631

18. Piscini, A., De Santis, A., Marchetti, D., Cianchini, G.: A Multi-parametric Climatological Approach to Study the 2016 Amatrice-Norcia (Central Italy) Earthquake Preparatory Phase. Pure Appl. Geophys. **174**, 3673–3688 (2017). https://doi.org/10.1007/s00024-017-1597-8
19. Marchetti, D., et al.: Magnetic field and electron density anomalies from swarm satellites preceding the major earthquakes of the 2016–2017 Amatrice-Norcia (Central Italy) Seismic Sequence. Pure Appl. Geophys. **177**, 305–319 (2020). https://doi.org/10.1007/s00024-019-02138-y
20. Fidani, C., Orsini, M., Iezzi, G., Vicentini, N., Stoppa, F.: Electric and Magnetic Recordings by Chieti CIEN Station During the Intense 2016–2017 Seismic Swarms in Central Italy. Front. Earth Sci. **8**, 536332 (2020). https://doi.org/10.3389/feart.2020.536332
21. Panza, G.F., Peresan, A., Sansò, F., Crespi, M., Mazzoni, A., Nascetti, A.: How geodesy can contribute to the understanding and prediction of earthquakes. Rend. Fis. Acc. Lincei. **29**, 81–93 (2018). https://doi.org/10.1007/s12210-017-0626-y
22. Marchetti, D., et al.: Pre-earthquake chain processes detected from ground to satellite altitude in preparation of the 2016–2017 seismic sequence in Central Italy. Remote Sensing of Environment. **229**, 93–99 (2019). https://doi.org/10.1016/j.rse.2019.04.033
23. Molchanov, O., et al.: Lithosphere-atmosphere-ionosphere coupling as governing mechanism for preseismic short-term events in atmosphere and ionosphere. Nat. Hazards Earth Syst. Sci. **4**, 757–767 (2004). https://doi.org/10.5194/nhess-4-757-2004
24. Fraser-Smith, A.C., et al.: Low-frequency magnetic field measurements near the epicenter of the Ms 7.1 Loma Prieta Earthquake. Geophys. Res. Lett. **17**, 1465–1468 (1990). https://doi.org/10.1029/GL017i009p01465
25. Hayakawa, M., Itoh, T., Hattori, K., Yumoto, K.: ULF electromagnetic precursors for an earthquake at Biak, Indonesia on February 17, 1996. Geophys. Res. Lett. **27**, 1531–1534 (2000). https://doi.org/10.1029/1999GL005432
26. Hattori, K., Serita, A., Yoshino, C., Hayakawa, M., Isezaki, N.: Singular spectral analysis and principal component analysis for signal discrimination of ULF geomagnetic data associated with 2000 Izu Island Earthquake Swarm. Physics and Chemistry of the Earth, Parts A/B/C. **31**, 281–291 (2006). https://doi.org/10.1016/j.pce.2006.02.034
27. Geller, R.J.: Earthquake prediction: a critical review. Geophys. J. Int. **131**, 425–450 (1997). https://doi.org/10.1111/j.1365-246X.1997.tb06588.x
28. Kanamori, H.: 72 - Earthquake Prediction: An Overview. In: Lee, W.H.K., Kanamori, H., Jennings, P.C., Kisslinger, C. (eds.) International Geophysics, pp. 1205–1216. Academic Press (2003). https://doi.org/10.1016/S0074-6142(03)80186-9
29. Scholz, C.H., Sykes, L.R., Aggarwal, Y.P.: Earthquake prediction: a physical basis. Science **181**, 803–810 (1973). https://doi.org/10.1126/science.181.4102.803
30. Rikitake, T.: Earthquake precursors in Japan: Precursor time and detectability. Tectonophysics **136**, 265–282 (1987). https://doi.org/10.1016/0040-1951(87)90029-1
31. De Santis, A., et al.: Precursory worldwide signatures of earthquake occurrences on Swarm satellite data. Sci. Rep. **9**, 20287 (2019). https://doi.org/10.1038/s41598-019-56599-1
32. Marchetti, D., et al.: Worldwide statistical correlation of eight years of swarm satellite data with M5.5+ earthquakes: new hints about the preseismic phenomena from space. Remote Sensing. **14**, 2649 (2022). https://doi.org/10.3390/rs14112649
33. Etiope, G., Martinelli, G.: Migration of carrier and trace gases in the geosphere: an overview. Phys. Earth Planet. Inter. **129**, 185–204 (2002). https://doi.org/10.1016/S0031-9201(01)00292-8
34. Pulinets, S., Ouzounov, D.: Lithosphere–Atmosphere–Ionosphere Coupling (LAIC) model – An unified concept for earthquake precursors validation. J. Asian Earth Sci. **41**, 371–382 (2011). https://doi.org/10.1016/j.jseaes.2010.03.005

35. Pulinets, S., Ouzounov, D., Karelin, A., Boyarchuk, K.: Earthquake Precursors in the Atmosphere and Ionosphere: New Concepts. Springer Netherlands, Dordrecht (2022). https://doi.org/10.1007/978-94-024-2172-9
36. Molchanov, O.A., Hayakawa, M.: Generation of ULF electromagnetic emissions by microfracturing. Geophys. Res. Lett. **22**, 3091–3094 (1995). https://doi.org/10.1029/95GL00781
37. Freund, F.: Pre-earthquake signals: Underlying physical processes. J. Asian Earth Sci. **41**, 383–400 (2011). https://doi.org/10.1016/j.jseaes.2010.03.009
38. Freund, F., Ouillon, G., Scoville, J., Sornette, D.: Earthquake precursors in the light of peroxy defects theory: Critical review of systematic observations. Eur. Phys. J. Spec. Top. **230**, 7–46 (2021). https://doi.org/10.1140/epjst/e2020-000243-x
39. Kuo, C.L., Lee, L.C., Huba, J.D.: An improved coupling model for the lithosphere-atmosphere-ionosphere system. J. Geophys. Res. Space Physics **119**, 3189–3205 (2014). https://doi.org/10.1002/2013JA019392
40. Prokhorov, B.E., Zolotov, O.V.: Comment on "An improved coupling model for the lithosphere-atmosphere-ionosphere system" by Kuo et al. [2014]: COMMENTS ON "AN IMPROVED COUPLING..." J. Geophys. Res. Space Physics. **122**, 4865–4868 (2017). https://doi.org/10.1002/2016JA023441
41. Kuo, C.-L., Lee, L.-C.: Reply to comment by B. E. Prokhorov and O. V. Zolotov on "An improved coupling model for the lithosphere-atmosphere-ionosphere system": Reply to Comment. J. Geophys. Res. Space Physics. **122**, 4869–4874 (2017). https://doi.org/10.1002/2016JA023579
42. Marchetti, D., Yuan, Y., Zhu, K.: Editorial of Special Issue "Remote Sensing Observations to Improve Knowledge of Lithosphere–Atmosphere–Ionosphere Coupling during the Preparatory Phase of Earthquakes." Remote Sensing. 16, (2024). https://doi.org/10.3390/rs16061064
43. ISIDe Working Group: Italian Seismological Instrumental and Parametric Database (ISIDe). (2007). https://doi.org/10.13127/ISIDE
44. Dobrovolsky, I.P., Zubkov, S.I., Miachkin, V.I.: Estimation of the size of earthquake preparation zones. PAGEOPH. **117**, 1025–1044 (1979). https://doi.org/10.1007/BF00876083
45. Gelaro, R., et al.: The modern-era retrospective analysis for research and applications, version 2 (MERRA-2). J. Climate **30**, 5419–5454 (2017). https://doi.org/10.1175/JCLI-D-16-0758.1
46. Friis-Christensen, E., Lühr, H., Hulot, G.: Swarm: a constellation to study the Earth's magnetic field. Earth Planet Sp. **58**, 351–358 (2006). https://doi.org/10.1186/BF03351933
47. Woessner, J., Wiemer, S.: Assessing the quality of earthquake catalogues: estimating the magnitude of completeness and its uncertainty. Bull. Seismol. Soc. Am. **95**, 684–698 (2005). https://doi.org/10.1785/0120040007
48. Benioff, H.: Global strain accumulation and release as revealed by great earthquakes. GSA Bulletin. **62**, 331–338 (1951). https://doi.org/10.1130/0016-7606(1951)62[331:GSAARA]2.0.CO;2
49. Hattori, K., Han, P., Yoshino, C., Febriani, F., Yamaguchi, H., Chen, C.-H.: Investigation of ULF seismo-magnetic phenomena in Kanto, Japan during 2000–2010: case studies and statistical studies. Surv. Geophys. **34**, 293–316 (2013). https://doi.org/10.1007/s10712-012-9215-x
50. Han, P., et al.: Statistical analysis of ULF seismomagnetic phenomena at Kakioka, Japan, during 2001–2010: ULF SEISMO-MAGNETIC PHENOMENA AT KAKIOKA. J. Geophys. Res. Space Physics **119**, 4998–5011 (2014). https://doi.org/10.1002/2014JA019789
51. Piscini, A., Marchetti, D., De Santis, A.: Multi-parametric climatological analysis associated with global significant volcanic eruptions during 2002–2017. Pure Appl. Geophys. **176**, 3629–3647 (2019). https://doi.org/10.1007/s00024-019-02147-x

52. De Santis, A., Balasis, G., Pavón-Carrasco, F.J., Cianchini, G., Mandea, M.: Potential earthquake precursory pattern from space: The 2015 Nepal event as seen by magnetic Swarm satellites. Earth Planet. Sci. Lett. **461**, 119–126 (2017). https://doi.org/10.1016/j.epsl.2016.12.037
53. Marchetti, D., et al.: Possible lithosphere-atmosphere-ionosphere coupling effects prior to the 2018 Mw = 7.5 Indonesia earthquake from seismic, atmospheric and ionospheric data. J. Asian Earth Sci. **188**, 104097 (2020). https://doi.org/10.1016/j.jseaes.2019.104097
54. Marchetti, D.: Observation of the preparation phase associated with Mw = 7.2 Haiti earthquake on 14 August 2021 from a geophysical data point of view. Geosciences. **14**, (2024). https://doi.org/10.3390/geosciences14040096
55. Barberio, M.D., Barbieri, M., Billi, A., Doglioni, C., Petitta, M.: Hydrogeochemical changes before and during the 2016 Amatrice-Norcia seismic sequence (central Italy). Sci. Rep. **7**, 11735 (2017). https://doi.org/10.1038/s41598-017-11990-8

Mapping of the Multi-risk Analysis for the Cultural Heritage of Sardinia from the Pre-Nuragic and Nuragic Periods: Initial Results of the RETURN Project

Enrica Vecchi(✉) ⓘ, Marco Cigagna, Donatella Rita Fiorino ⓘ, Battista Grosso ⓘ, Elisa Pilia ⓘ, Francesco Pinna ⓘ, and Giuseppina Vacca ⓘ

Department of Civil and Environmental Engineering and Architecture (DICAAR), University of Cagliari, 09123 Cagliari, Italy
enrica.vecchi@unica.it

Abstract. Sardinia's cultural heritage features unique prehistoric structures from the pre-Nuragic and Nuragic periods (5th–6th centuries BC). These include Nuraghi, giants' tombs, sanctuaries, Domus de Janas, dolmens, menhirs, and megalithic circles. Given their complexity and the increasing threat from climate change, a comprehensive database and spatial mapping system are vital for their preservation. This study presents initial findings from Project RETURN (multi-Risk sciEnce for resilienT commUnities undeR a changiNg climate), which focuses on systematic risk analysis for Sardinia's cultural heritage. A unified database was created using public inventories, standardizing data and assigning simplified attributes based on monument dimensions (e.g., tall, subterranean). GIS tools enabled precise georeferencing, material characterization (via lithological maps), and automatic exclusion of sediment categories based on proximity and area size. Each structure was assigned vulnerability levels (Very Low to Very High) based on geometry and construction material, in relation to four hazard types: hydraulic, hydrogeological, seismic, and wildfire. Hazard data from regional sources were normalized and matched to monument locations. This allowed for the generation of both individual and multi-risk maps using a consistent five-level classification system. The resulting spatial analyses provide valuable insights into the exposure and resilience of heritage sites across Sardinia. These findings support informed decision-making for conservation efforts, with risk visualizations available at both site and regional scales.

Keywords: Multi-risk · cultural heritage · GIS · mapping

1 Introduction

Sardinia's cultural heritage is marked by unique structures that date back to the pre-Nuragic (5th to 3rd millennium BC) and Nuragic (18th to 6th centuries BC) periods, spanning the Neolithic to the Early Iron Age [1–3]. Indeed, this era saw the arising of various structures of significant historical and archaeological value. Notable ancient megalithic edifices characteristic of the island include Nuraghi, giant's tombs, sanctuaries, Domus de Janas, caves, shelters, menhirs, dolmens, and megalithic circles. Given the uniqueness, complexity, and diversity of these constructions, creating a comprehensive and updated database along with detailed mapping of each site is essential for monitoring and preserving this heritage. This task is especially critical in light of the complex territorial context, where environmental phenomena are exacerbated by climate change. In this regard, Geographic Information Systems (GIS) serve as crucial tools, allowing for the integration of data from various sources, accurate site georeferencing, and the combination of specific attributes, in addition to enabling a wide range of spatial analyses to derive further insights [4–8].

Although there is an increasing amount of research on the vulnerability of cultural heritage to environmental hazards, most existing studies tend to focus on structures from the medieval to modern periods. These studies often assess risks at broader geographic scales, such as urban areas or landscape units [9, 10]. In contrast, prehistoric monuments, particularly those in Sardinia, represent complex and context-specific subjects that require further in-depth investigation. Notably, there is currently no comprehensive official database that includes the island's prehistoric structures, which differ significantly in both architecture and environmental context from those found in other regions of Italy [11]. Furthermore, Sardinia faces unique hazard challenges, such as uneven seismic activity, specific hydrogeological risks, and an increasing frequency of wildfires, all of which complicate heritage management efforts [12–14].

This study presents the initial findings from Project RETURN (multi-Risk sciEnce for resilienT commUnities undeR a changiNg climate), which focuses on the systematic mapping of multi-risk analyses concerning Sardinian cultural heritage from the Nuragic and pre-Nuragic periods. In particular, the GIS environment supported all phases of the analysis, starting from the finalization of the database. Official maps concerning hydraulic, hydrogeological (referred to as "landslides"), and wildfires hazards were used, whereas a uniform value was applied for seismic hazard across the region. The vulnerability of structures based on their dimensions and geometry was assessed and is reported in this paper for the sake of completeness, even though a full explanation is beyond the scope of this paper. A detailed spatial analysis was conducted to determine construction materials based on a proximity principle applied to the official regional lithologic map. Finally, by properly defining the database, automated GIS and Python-based procedures were employed to associate vulnerabilities and hazard values with each considered monument, allowing for the retrieval of respective risk and multi-risk values [15–17]. As a primary result, the multi-risk analysis adopted a maximum approach, providing insights into possible critical situations related to specific monuments or municipality that would require more careful management.

The novel contribution of this research lies in its monument-specific approach, which integrates hazard exposure, structural characteristics, and inferred construction materials into a unified, replicable GIS-based framework. This enables the generation of risk maps at both micro (individual monument) and macro (regional) scales—offering a valuable decision-support tool for cultural heritage management, maintenance, and adaptation planning. By addressing data gaps and developing site-specific assessments in a region lacking centralized records, this work sets a foundation for proactive heritage risk governance in Sardinia and offers a scalable methodology for other contexts.

2 Materials

2.1 Database and Building Typologies

The primary objective of this study was to create a unified database of the cultural heritage sites in the Sardinia region, specifically those from the pre-Nuragic period (5th to 3rd millennium BC) and the Nuragic period (18th to 6th centuries BC). In particular, the final database was designed for GIS use and formatted as a vector dataset in shapefile format. To achieve this, two publicly available inventories were utilized. The first was obtained from "SardegnArcheologica," an initiative focused on cataloging and georeferencing Sardinia's archaeological sites, with a particular emphasis on Nuraghi [18]. This open-access database is available for both online browsing and downloading and includes a significant number of monuments, such as Nuraghi and Giants' tombs, reflecting the extensive distribution of these structures across Sardinia. The second data source, "Nurnet – La rete dei Nuraghi," stems from a participatory initiative aimed at documenting and promoting Sardinia's Nuragic and pre-Nuragic cultural heritage [19]. This inventory is accessible through a dedicated Geoportal, a web-based platform that allows interactive access to data. Therefore, expert and non-expert users—such as citizens, tourists, associations, and institutions—can visualize and browse site information and also directly contribute by adding or updating data, including textual descriptions and photographs. Because of this, the data in this inventory is continually updated and undergoes a reviewing phase by experts in the field, which should be taken into account when using it.

For this study, we focused on different building typologies covered by both databases. To avoid duplication, we first extracted the chosen typologies from the SardegnArcheologica inventory and used the Nurnet database to complete the categories that were not present in the first source, as shown in Table 1.

After downloading the two datasets in shapefile format, we first selected the chosen building typologies from the data sources, ensuring a common format was applied and essential information was simplified. The combination of these two data sources resulted in a total of 7,335 monuments located throughout Sardinia. Figure 1a displays the Sardinian map with the completed regional database, while the pie chart in Fig. 1b illustrates the percentage of coverage of the various types of structures.

Table 1. Building typologies retrieved from the two regional public inventories of archaeological monuments.

SardegnArcheologica	Nurnet
Nuraghi	Domus de Janas
Giants' tombs	Menhir
Springs	Dolmen
Sacred wells	Caves and shelters
Sanctuaries	Megalithic circles

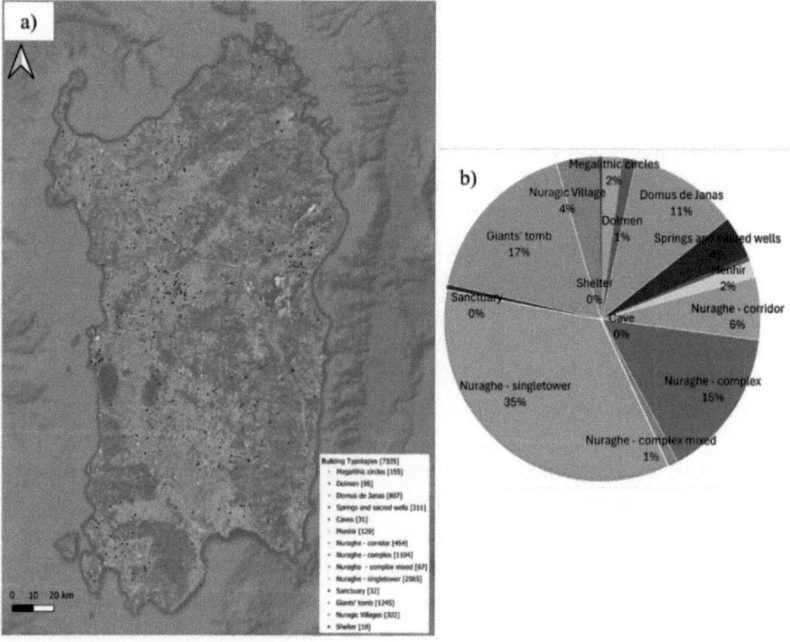

Fig. 1. Completed regional database with the building typologies (a); pie chart showing typology percentages (b).

In parallel, the building typologies were characterized with specific attributes based on their geometry and dimensions, considering the overall proportions of each type of structure (tall, equidimensional, small, subterranean, wide). For the sake of simplicity, a numerical ID was assigned to each typology, as listed in Table 2, which also provides information regarding historical periods.

2.2 Materials Analysis

In addition to the dimensional characteristics of each structure, we focused on the construction materials, which are crucial for assessing the monuments' vulnerability to

Table 2. Classification of the selected building typologies in terms of geometry and historical period.

ID	Building Typology	Geometry	Period
5.1	Nuraghe – corridor	Equidimensional (B)	1700–1350 B.C., Middle Bronze Age
5.2	Nuraghe – singletower	Equidimensional (B)	1500–1350 B.C
5.3	Nuraghe - complex	Equidimensional (B)	
5.4	Giants' tomb	Wide (E)	Bronze Age
5.5	Sacred weels	Subterranean (D)	Bronze Age, early Iron Age
5.6	Domus de Janas	Subterranean (D)	1800–1600 B.C., Middle Neolithic
5.7	Cave	Subterranean (D)	From 5th to the end of the 3rd millennium B.C
5.8	Shelter	Small (C)	From 5th to the end of the 3rd millennium B.C
5.9	Menhir	Tall (A)	From Neolithic to Copper Age
5.10	Dolmen	Tall (A)	From Neolithic to Copper Age
5.11	Megalithic circles	Tall (A)	Middle Neolithic
5.12	Sanctuary	Wide (E)	
5.13	Nuragic Village	Wide (E)	1350 B.C. – 950 B.C

various hazards. However, this information is not available for most of the mapped sites, with only a few significant ones from cultural and touristic perspectives providing material details. Consequently, some simplifying assumptions were necessary during this step of the analysis. Given the complexity of the territory and the significant topographical variations - even among nearby areas - it seemed unlikely that non-local materials would be used for construction. Therefore, we deduced the construction materials from the in-situ lithology. This assumption is also supported by real cases that confirm the use of local materials for constructions, especially considering the weight of the megalithic blocks. Notable examples include the famous Su Nuraxi of Barumini, Santu Antine, and Losa, which suggest that transporting massive stones over long distances would be impractical, leading to a preference for locally abundant stones.

Despite the supporting reasons for using lithological maps, this approach has some limitations. Indeed, while these maps can provide general geological information, they may not accurately reflect localized material selections. In certain cases, short-range transportation of materials might have been practical or necessary due to specific properties or symbolic significance. Furthermore, some changes that occurred after deposition could lead to discrepancies between the original materials and the current lithological context. Future steps will aim to validate this analysis through field surveys, archaeological reports, or the integration of other data sources to enhance reliability.

The construction materials for each monument was determined though a spatial analysis conducted using QGIS software, based on the official regional lithological map shown in Fig. 2 [20]. For clarity, the map's legend in Fig. 2 presents the classifications with associated alphanumeric labels corresponding to the different lithologies; additional information can be obtained by consulting the original data source.

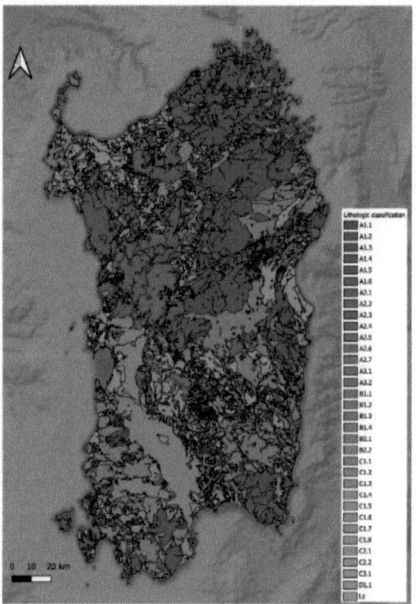

Fig. 2. Lithologic map of Sardinia [20].

The official classification of lithologic materials includes 34 detailed categories, covering a variety of rock types as well as other classifications such as lakes and anthropogenic artifacts. Based on the aforementioned assumptions, it was necessary to exclude categories that do not represent viable construction materials, specifically sedimentary rocks, lakes, and anthropogenic artifacts.

After sampling the lithologic map at the locations of the monuments and assigning the corresponding classes to each, a procedure using GIS and Python was implemented to address cases related to the excluded classes. For monuments located within polygons associated with the excluded categories, the algorithm searches the neighboring polygons to identify the most probable lithology based on a detailed proximity principle. In particular, the analysis focused on the following parameters:

- dist_b: Shortest distance between the monument and the polygon's boundary
- area: Area of the polygon
- dist_c: Distance between the monument and the polygon's centroid

For each neighboring polygon i, different weights were assigned as follows:

$$w_{i,dist\_b} = \frac{1}{dist\_b_i} \quad (1)$$

$$w_{i,area} = \frac{area_i}{\sum_i^n area_i} \quad (2)$$

$$w_{i,dist\_c} = \frac{1}{dist\_c_i} \quad (3)$$

where n represents the total number of neighboring polygons.

The final score was calculated as:

$$S_i = w_{i,dist\_b}^{\alpha} \cdot w_{i,area}^{\beta} \cdot w_{i,dist\_c}^{\gamma} \quad (4)$$

In Eq. (4), α and β were set equal to 1, while γ was assigned a value of 2. The distances from the polygon's boundary and the area of the polygon were considered linearly, ensuring that polygons closer to the monument were preferred and larger polygons had a proportional impact without dominating the score. The distance from the polygon's centroid was given a quadratic weight, making it the most significant factor, and prioritizing it over the other two factors. Indeed, given the complexity and irregular shapes of the lithology polygons, a closer centroid suggests that the majority of the polygon is distributed near or around the monument. This weighting methodology helps to filter out polygons with misleading thin extensions or elongated parts that might otherwise appear relevant due to proximity based on boundary distance. Such polygons reaching close to the monument, having a small boundary distance, could falsely suggest a strong relevance. Moreover, the resulting ranking is more robust since the score decreases more sharply as the centroid distance increases compared to the other parameters (α and β). This ensures that only polygons with most of their mass near the monument remain highly ranked. By using this metric of proximity, we achieved a better understanding of the polygon's actual location and we were able to identify the most likely construction material, corresponding to the lithology with the highest score.

Next, the appropriate valid lithologic class was assigned to each monument, grouping them into macro-categories as shown in Table 3 to simplify the analysis. This clustering not only simplifies the classification process but also supports the underlying hypothesis of the spatial analysis used to derive the construction materials, as it averages the initial detailed categories.

Table 3. Grouped materials categories.

Official lithologic class	New class
A1.1, A1.2, A1.3, A1.4, A1.5, A1.6	Granites
A2.1, A2.2, A2.4	Trachytes auctorum
A2.3, A.2.5, A.2.6, A2.7	Alkaline vulcalites (basalts)
B1.1, B1.2, B1.3, B1.4, B2.1	Metamorphites
B2.2, C2.1, C2.2	Carbonates

The spatial analysis results for defining the construction material are illustrated in Fig. 3a. Figure 3b presents a pie chart that shows the percentage distribution of each material classification.

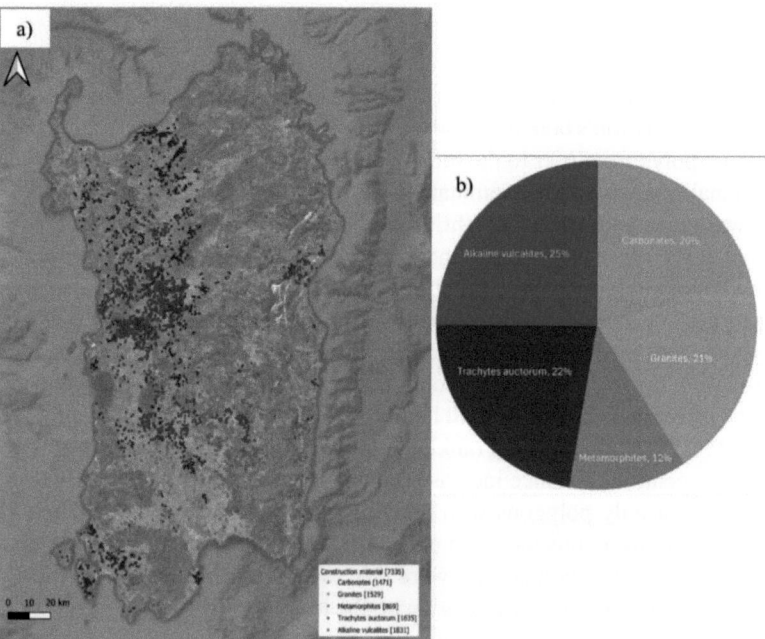

Fig. 3. Completed regional database with the construction materials (a); pie chart depicting materials percentages (b).

3 Methods

3.1 Vulnerability Analysis

Based on the previously established classifications regarding geometry and construction materials, two types of vulnerability were defined, which vary depending on the related hazard i (Hydraulic - h, Landslides - l, Wildfire - w, Seismic - s). These vulnerabilities are defined as follows:

- $V_{geom,i}$: Vulnerability related to geometry
- $V_{mat,i}$: Vulnerability related to construction material

To achieve this, specific matrices were developed to assess the level of vulnerability based on both geometric and material characteristics. In particular, each was classified into 5 levels: Very Low (VL), Low (L), Medium (M), High (H), and Very High (VH), corresponding to numerical values ranging from 1 (VL) to 5 (VH). An example of the vulnerability matrix related to hydraulic hazard is presented in Table 4, while the complete set of matrixes can be found in the Appendix. It is important to note that the detailed considerations leading to the construction of the vulnerability matrices are beyond the scope of this paper, which focuses instead on spatial analysis and mapping.

Table 4. Example of vulnerability matrix related to hydraulic hazard.

Building ID	$V_{geom,h}$	Material	$V_{mat,h}$
5.1	2	Granites	1
5.2	2	Trachytes auctorum	1
5.3	2	Alkaline vulcalites	2
5.4	3	Metamorphites	3
5.5	4	Carbonates	4
5.6	4		
5.7	4		
5.8	3		
5.9	2		
5.10	2		
5.11	2		
5.12	3		

In this phase, proper codification of the database was essential to automatically associate each monument with its related vulnerabilities, depending on the building type and construction material used. As a result, the database was completed with eight additional fields, representing two types of vulnerability for four considered hazards: $V_{geom,h}$; $V_{mat,h}$; $V_{geom,l}$; $V_{mat,l}$; $V_{geom,w}$; $V_{mat,w}$; $V_{geom,s}$; $V_{mat,s}$.

3.2 Hazards

The hazard analysis was based on the official maps sourced from the PAI (Piano Stralcio per l'Assetto Idrogeologico) and the Geoportal of the Sardinia region [21–23]. Specifically, maps for the hydraulic and hydrogeological ("landslides") hazards were retrieved from the first source, while the second was used to download the wildfire map, given its specificity for the Sardinia region, which particularly suffers from this issue [24, 25]. Conversely, since Sardinia is known to be particularly stable from a seismic point of view [26–28], no seismic hazard map was employed, and a fixed hazard value was applied instead, which will be further discussed. For more detailed information, please consult the official maps and their classifications.

As a preliminary step, the official hazard maps were resampled on the monuments' positions, generating additional fields that contained the corresponding official hazard classes. Subsequently, the official categories were simplified, providing a numeric and unified classification divided into five classes with equivalent meanings. The adopted approach is detailed in Table 5, which outlines the official hazard classes alongside their corresponding values for our analysis. Notably, for the wildfire hazard, the two classifications are equivalent since the official maps already employed a numeric classification. Here, the lower class is absent, denoting the region's inherent fire exposure. As mentioned earlier, a constant value of $H_s = 1$ was assigned to the seismic hazard to indicate the low seismicity in Sardinia while preventing a total underestimation of the issue (without using class 0).

Table 5. Adopted classification on the hazard classes, starting from the official categories.

Hydraulic h		Landslides l		Wildfires w		Seismic s
official	new	official	new	official	new	Constant value
Hi0	0	Hg0	0	/	/	$H_s = 1$
Hi1	1	Hg1	1	1	1	
Hi2	2	Hg2	2	2	2	
Hi3	3	Hg3	3	3	3	
Hi4	4	Hg4	4	4	4	
No value	0	No value	0	/	/	

Following this step, four new fields were associated to each monument: H_h; H_l; H_w; H_s.

4 Results

Having completed the monuments' database with the associated classes of vulnerabilities and hazards enabled the assessment of the related risks. In general, the risk can be calculated as follows [29, 30]:

$$R = V \cdot H \qquad (5)$$

where V is the vulnerability and H is the associated hazard value.

The following paragraphs detail the workflow applied to create regional risk maps, focusing on both individual risk levels and multi-risk combinations, always adhering to the mentioned five-levels classification system.

4.1 Risk Analysis

For each hazard i (hydraulic, landslides, wildfires, and seismic) we calculated the associated risk value R_i as:

$$R_i = H_i \cdot V_{geom,i} \cdot V_{mat,i} \qquad (6)$$

Subsequently, normalization was applied to adjust the final values to the five-level scale, considering the minimum and maximum possible risk values $R_{i,min}$ and $R_{i,max}$:

$$R_{i,min} = 0 \qquad (7)$$

$$R_{i,max} = H_{i,max} \cdot V_{geom,i,max} \cdot V_{mat,i,max} = 4 \cdot 5 \cdot 5 = 100 \qquad (8)$$

At this point, each risk value was reclassified according to the criteria outlined in Table 6, which divides values from 1 to 100 into 5 distinct risk classes.

Table 6. Risk classification according to the 5-level scale.

0-20	20-40	40-60	60-80	80-100
1	2	3	4	5
VL	L	M	H	VH

For each risk, we produced a comprehensive map reporting risk values associated with each considered monument (Figs. 4 and 5).

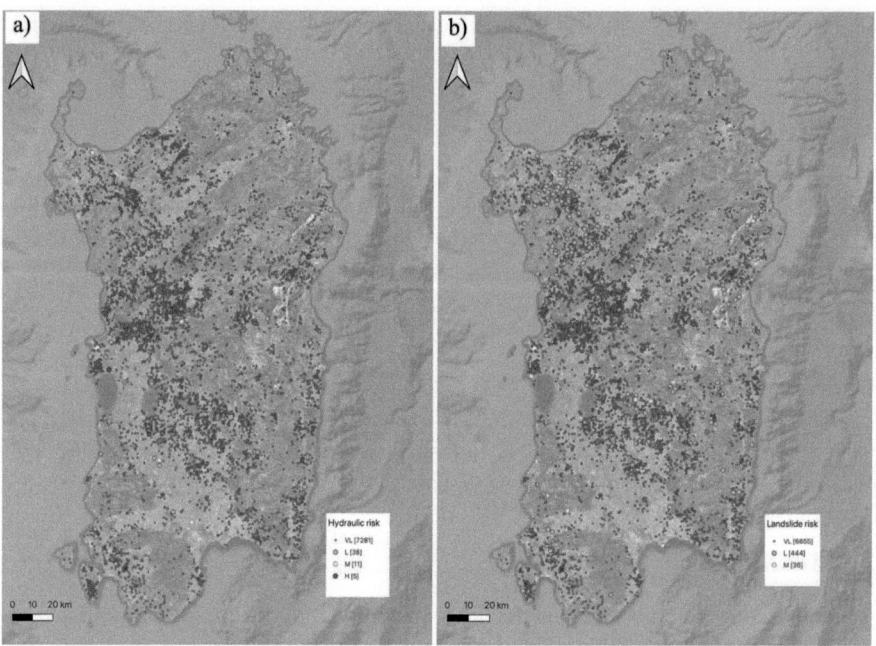

Fig. 4. Risk maps for hydraulic (a) and landslides risks (b).

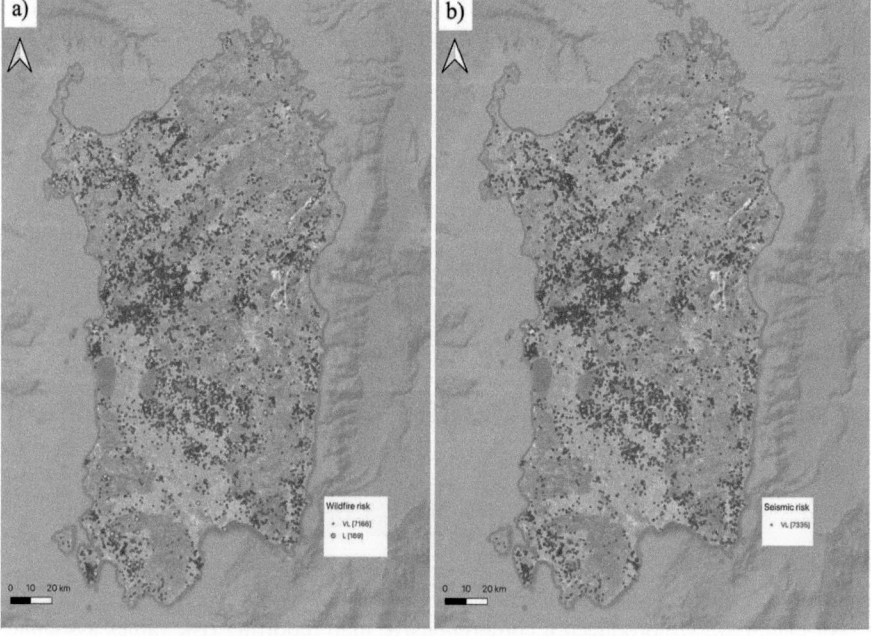

Fig. 5. Risk maps for wildfires (a) and seismic risks (b).

4.2 Multi-Risk Analysis

Monuments

For each monument we had the previously computed risk values, R_i, associated with each individual hazard. We then assigned the multi-risk value to each monument by taking the maximum of the individual risk values:

$$MR_{monument} = \max(R_h, R_l, R_w, R_s) \qquad (9)$$

Therefore, the obtained MR values were already aligned to the 5-level scale classification described in Table 6. The selected approach adopts a conservative estimation that describes the worst-case scenario while also assuming no interaction between the considered hazards. Figure 6 displays the multi-risk map for all the selected monuments (a) along with a pie chart illustrating the percentage of each risk class. This map shows the prevalence of low-risk classes, particularly focusing on those that belong to the very low category. These values, despite some high hazard levels across the region, especially concerning the wildfire risk, were expected due to the low associated vulnerabilities related to strong rock or subterranean structures.

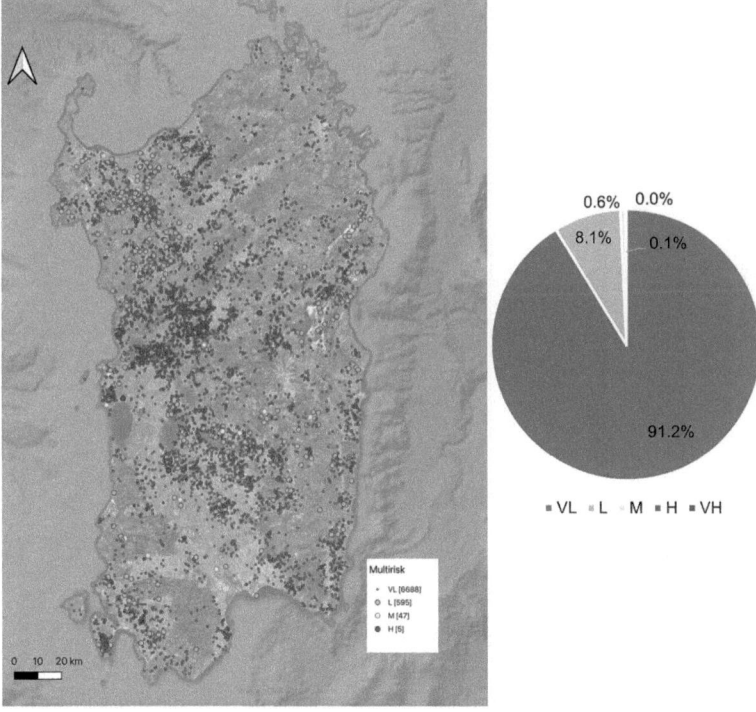

Fig. 6. Multi-risk map of the selected monuments (a); pie chart of classes' percentages (b).

Municipalities

For each municipality, we considered the number n of related monuments, and we assigned the corresponding multi-risk value as follows:

$$MR_{municipality} = \max(MR_{monuments}) \tag{10}$$

This conservative approach aims at highlighting critical situations in municipalities where at least one element is in a critical condition, thereby suggesting the need for greater caution in managing these areas. Figure 7 presents the multi-risk map at the municipality level (a) and a pie chart showing the percentage of each class.

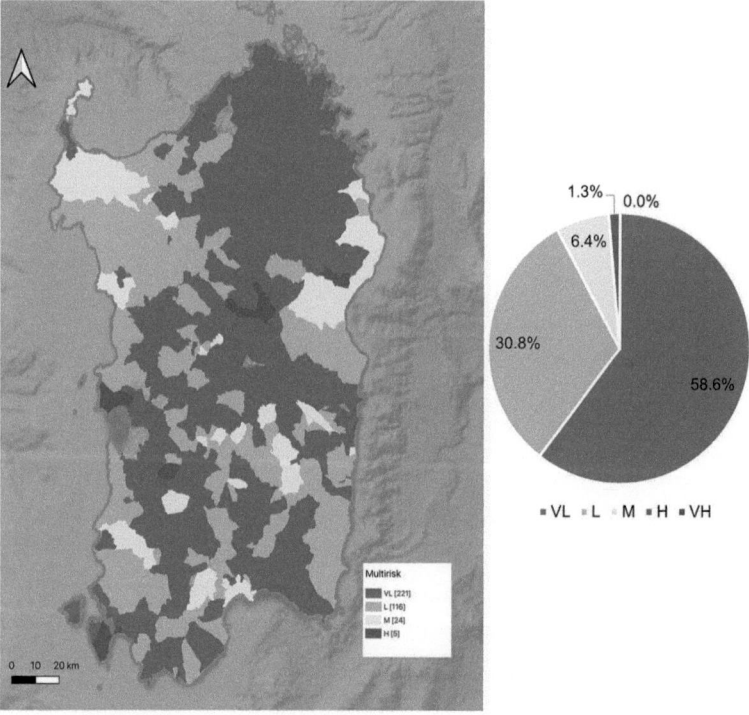

Fig. 7. Multi-risk map of Sardinia's municipalities (a); pie chart of classes' percentages (b).

5 Discussion and Conclusions

This paper aims to establish the foundation for a comprehensive database that documents cultural heritage sites from the pre-Nuragic and Nuragic periods in Sardinia. The first outcome highlights the wide number and dense distribution of these unique constructions, with over 7,000 features spread across the region. The distribution and characterization of these sites are increasingly significant for both researchers and the general public, as they hold considerable historical and archaeological value for the region. In this context, effective management and preservation are crucial to promote accessibility and enhance the understanding of Sardinia's rich archaeological heritage, thereby fostering greater public engagement with the island's cultural landscape. This detailed database was utilized to conduct automated spatial analyses and procedures to assess the exposure of these monuments to various risks, including hydraulic, hydrogeological, wildfire, and seismic threats.

The reported risk analysis describes a stable situation for most of the considered monuments in Sardinia. Specifically, the percentages for the very low (VL) risk class range from 93% for landslides to 100% for seismic risks. In particular, the high percentage relating to seismic risk was completely expected, given the typical stability of the Sardinia region. This scenario is also reflected by the multi-risk analysis, besides applying a conservative approach by assigning the maximum single risks as multi-risk value. In this analysis, the 91% of the monuments fall into the very low class, while 8% are classified as low. The more critical classes (high and very high) show percentages close to zero.

The multi-risk analysis was also conducted at the municipality level, in order to highlight possible critical situations that may require more careful management, potentially leading to increased administrative costs. This computation, which also follows a conservative approach by assigning the highest risk among the local monuments to the entire municipality area, describes a slightly more critical situation compared to the analysis at the monument level. Due to the previous results, none of the municipalities falls into the very high risk category, while 1.3% and 6.4% belong are classified as high and medium risk, respectively. This kind of computation mainly resulted in a shift from the very low to the low risk class, with approximately 59% in the very low class and 31% in the low class.

The maximum risk approach selects the highest individual risk among multiple hazards to represent overall risk. This method simplifies decision-making by focusing on the most severe potential impact and can be used in certain multi-hazard assessments. For example, the study by Martín-Raya et al. (2024) employs a quasi-maximum approach, analyzing each hazard separately and identifying areas where multiple hazards overlap [31]. However, since their study examines the entire La Palma region, it addresses a different challenge than our analysis, which focuses on the monument level. Kappes et al. (2012) discuss the practical applications of various multi-risk analyses, particularly in disaster risk management, urban planning, and emergency response [32]. They highlight that all existing methods have limitations, indicating that the maximization method might be useful in some cases but could oversimplify complex interactions and dependencies among hazards.

In this context, the primary objective of our multi-risk assessment is to provide a valuable tool for the initial planning of structure management and preservation. The proposed assessment prioritizes the most severe risks, thereby enhancing resilience against the most damaging potential events. The results can be effectively visualized at the monument level using colour scales based on the final risk value. Alternatively, they can be aggregated at a macro-aerial scale to quickly understanding the risk levels across the Sardinia region. This study's insights establish a foundation for developing monitoring parameters for cultural heritage. Additionally, further research will focus on implementing more advanced multi-risk analyses that account for interactions and potential cumulative effects.

Funding. This research was funded by PNRR - PE3 - RETURN - multi-Risk sciEnce for resilienT commUnities undeR a changiNg climate (CODICE MUR PE0000005).

Appendix

See Tables 7, 8 and 9.

Table 7. Vulnerability matrix for the landslides hazard.

Building ID	$V_{geom,l}$	Material	$V_{mat,l}$
5.1	2	Granites	2
5.2	2	Trachytes auctorum	2
5.3	2	Alkaline vulcalites	3
5.7	3		
5.8	2		
5.9	4		
5.10	4		
5.11	4		
5.12	2		

Table 8. Vulnerability matrix for the wildfires hazard.

Building ID	$V_{geom,l}$	Material	$V_{mat,l}$
5.1	2	Granites	1
5.2	2	Trachytes auctorum	2
5.3	2	Alkaline vulcalites	1
5.4	2	Metamorphites	2
5.5	1	Carbonates	3
5.6	1		
5.7	1		
5.8	2		
5.9	3		
5.10	3		
5.11	3		
5.12	2		

Table 9. Vulnerability matrix for the seismic hazard.

Building ID	$V_{geom,s}$	Material	$V_{mat,s}$
5.1	2	Granites	2
5.2	2	Trachytes auctorum	1
5.3	2	Alkaline vulcalites	3
5.4	2	Metamorphites	3
5.5	3	Carbonates	4
5.6	3		
5.7	3		
5.8	2		
5.9	4		
5.10	4		
5.11	4		
5.12	2		

References

1. UNESCO World Heritage Centre. Art and Architecture in the Prehistory of Sardinia. The domus de janas. https://whc.unesco.org/en/tentativelists/6523/. Last accessed 01 March 2025
2. Schirru, D., Perra, M., Holt, E., Lai, L.: A reassessment of the relative chronology of the Sardinian Middle Bronze Age: Results from the excavations of Nuraghe Sa Conca 'e sa Cresia, Siddi, Sardinia (2023)
3. Cicilloni, R., Cabras, M., Porcedda, F., Cámara Serrano, J.A.: Protohistoric landscapes in Sardinia (Italy): Territorial control and exploitation of natural resources in the Middle and Late Bronze Ages. Cuadernos de Prehistoria y Arqueología **31**, 19–38 (2021)
4. Longley, P.A., Goodchild, M.F., Maguire, D.J., Rhind, D.W.: Geographic information science and systems. John Wiley & Sons, Hoboken (2015)
5. O'sullivan, D., Unwin, D.: Geographic information analysis. John Wiley & Sons, Hoboken (2002)
6. Rocheford, M.K.: GIS for Science: Applying Mapping and Spatial Analytics. Photogramm. Eng. Remote. Sens. **87**(2), 75–76 (2021)
7. Vecchi, E., Tavasci, L., Giorgini, E., Gandolfi, S.: A priori estimation of radar satellite interferometry's sensitivity for landslide monitoring in the Italian Emilia-Romagna region. Remote Sensing **16**(14), 2562 (2024)
8. De Montis, et al.: Integration of Geomatic, Geophysical and Chemical Data in a GIS Environment for Monitoring Contaminated Soils. In: International Conference on Computational Science and Its Applications, pp. 351–368. Springer Nature Switzerland, Cham (2024)
9. Bosco, C., Spano, D., Bacciu, V., Marras, S., Sirca, C.: Wildfire risk mapping and climate adaptation strategies in Mediterranean heritage areas. Sustainability **4**(10), 5987 (2022). https://doi.org/10.3390/su14105987
10. Bellomaria, G., Molfino, M.T., Fiorelli, M.: ArCo: The Italian cultural heritage knowledge graph. ArXiv (2019). https://arxiv.org/abs/1905.02840
11. UNIFI-IBAM-CNR. Risk maps for archaeological sites in southern Italy (2020)

12. Murgante, B., Borruso, G.: Geospatial technologies and climate change. Springer, Cham (2013)
13. Di Stefano, A., et al.: Wildfire risk in cultural landscapes: A case from central Italy. J. Cult. Herit. **48**, 141–151 (2021)
14. Cigna, F., et al.: The use of satellite data for risk assessment in cultural heritage. Remote Sensing **10**(8), 1226 (2018)
15. Olteanu, I., Crenganiş, L.M., Diac, M., Precul, A.M.: Sustainable approach of a multi-hazard risk assessment using GIS customized for Ungheni areal situated in the metropolitan area of Iasi. Sustainability **16**(11), 4485 (2024). https://doi.org/10.3390/su16114485
16. Bhunia, G.S., Shit, P.K.: Geospatial technology for multi-hazard risk assessment. In: Shit, P.K., Pourghasemi, H.R., Bhunia, G.S., Das, P., Narsimha, A. (eds.) Geospatial Technology for Environmental Hazards. Advances in Geographic Information Science. Springer, Cham (2022). https://doi.org/10.1007/978-3-030-75197-5_1
17. Shah, F.H., Ali, A., Iqbal, M.M.: A review on hazard risk assessment using remote sensing and GIS. Journal Central Asian Scientific Press **5**, 252–261 (2020)
18. SardegnArcheologica. "About.", https://www.sardegnarcheologica.it/text/1000/en. Last accessed 01 March 2025
19. Nurnet Geoportal. Nurnet Geoportal, n.d., https://nurnet.crs4.it/nurnetgeo/. Last accessed 01 March 2025
20. Regione Autonoma della Sardegna. Sardegna GeoNetwork, https://webgis2.regione.sardegna.it/geonetwork/srv/eng/catalog.search#/metadata/R_SARDEG:7a2ce3e7-2686-4c10-8df9-3a3c0ad013f2. Last accessed 01 March 2025
21. Regione Autonoma della Sardegna. Piano Stralcio di Bacino per l'Assetto Idrogeologico (PAI). 2006, https://autoritadibacino.regione.sardegna.it/pianificazione/piano-stralcio-di-bacino-per-lassetto-idrogeologico-pai/. Last accessed 01 March 2025
22. Regione Autonoma della Sardegna. Sardegna GeoNetwork, https://www.sardegnageoportale.it/webgis2/sardegnamappe/?map=pai. Last accessed 01 March 2025
23. Regione Autonoma della Sardegna, Direzione Generale della Protezione Civile. Carta del Pericolo Incendio Boschivo e di Interfaccia 2017. 2017, https://webgis2.regione.sardegna.it/geonetwork/srv/api/records/R_SARDEG:b3eff8cf-9cfc-497b-8423-3fc5a0749b51. Last accessed 01 March 2025
24. Salis, M., et al.: Analyzing seasonal patterns of wildfire exposure factors in Sardinia. Italy. Environmental Monitoring and Assessment **187**, 1–20 (2015)
25. Cardil, A., Salis, M., Spano, D., Delogu, G., Molina Terren, D.: Large wildland fires and extreme temperatures in Sardinia (Italy). iForest-Biogeosciences and Forestry **7**(3), 162 (2014)
26. Meletti, C., Camassi, R., Castelli, V.: A reappraisal of the seismicity of Sardinia. Italy. Seismological Society of America **92**(2A), 1148–1158 (2021)
27. Gorshkov, A., et al.: On the seismic potential of the Corsica-Sardinia block. Rendiconti Lincei. Scienze Fisiche e Naturali **32**, 715–728 (2021)
28. Anselmi, M., et al.: Microseismic assessment and fault characterization at the Sulcis (South-Western Sardinia) field laboratory. Int. J. Greenhouse Gas Control **95**, 102974 (2020)
29. Intergovernmental Panel on Climate Change (IPCC). Climate Change 2014: Impacts, Adaptation, and Vulnerability (Fifth Assessment Report, AR5). Cambridge University Press (2014). https://www.ipcc.ch/report/ar5/
30. Crichton, D.: The risk triangle. In: Ingleton, J. (ed.) Natural disaster management, pp. 102–103. Tudor Rose, London (1999)
31. Martín-Raya, N., Díaz-Pacheco, J., López-Díez, A.: Multi-hazard risk assessment analysis in La Palma: an approach for risk mitigation. Geoenvironmental Disasters **11**(1), 33 (2024)
32. Kappes, M.S., Keiler, M., von Elverfeldt, K., et al.: Challenges of analyzing multi-hazard risk: a review. Nat. Hazards **64**, 1925–1958 (2012). https://doi.org/10.1007/s11069-012-0294-2

PHD Showcase Papers

Effects of Different Attention Mechanisms Applied on 3D Models in Video Classification

Mohammad Rasras[1](✉), Iuliana Marin[2], Șerban Radu[3], and Irina Mocanu[3]

[1] Doctoral School of Automatic Control and Computers, National University of Science and Technology POLITEHNICA Bucharest, Splaiul Independenței 313, 060042 Bucharest, Romania
mohammad.rasras@stud.fils.upb.ro

[2] Faculty of Engineering in Foreign Languages, National University of Science and Technology POLITEHNICA Bucharest, Splaiul Independenței 313, 060042 Bucharest, Romania
iuliana.marin@upb.ro

[3] Faculty of Automatic Control and Computers, National University of Science and Technology POLITEHNICA Bucharest, Splaiul Independenței 313, 060042 Bucharest, Romania
{serban.radu,irina.mocanu}@upb.ro

Abstract. Human action recognition has become an important research focus in computer vision due to the wide range of applications where it is used. 3D Resnet-based CNN models, particularly MC3, R3D, and R(2 + 1)D, have different convolutional filters to extract spatiotemporal features. This paper investigates the impact of reducing the captured knowledge from temporal data, while increasing the resolution of the frames. To establish this experiment, we created similar designs to the three originals, but with a dropout layer added before the final classifier. Secondly, we then developed ten new versions for each one of these three designs. The variants include special attention blocks within their architecture, such as convolutional block attention module (CBAM), temporal convolution networks (TCN), in addition to multi-headed and channel attention mechanisms. The purpose behind that is to observe the extent of the influence each of these blocks has on performance for the restricted-temporal models. The results of testing all the models on UCF101 have shown accuracy of 88.98% for the variant with multiheaded attention added to the modified R(2 + 1)D. This paper concludes the significance of missing temporal features in the performance of the newly created increased resolution models. The variants had different behavior on class-level accuracy, despite the similarity of their enhancements to the overall performance.

Keywords: Self Attention · Video Classification · Human Action Recognition · Channel Attention

1 Introduction

One of the most significant areas in the computer vision discipline is human action recognition (HAR), which depends on data gathered by sensors, such as cameras [1]. This field has been involved in various domains, for instance in video surveillance

[2, 3], healthcare assistance [4], sports analytics [5], and entertainment [6]. Moreover, deep learning algorithms, including Convolutional (CNN) and Recurrent (RNN) Neural Networks, have played a role in the development of the computer vision field in the last decade [7]. For instance, image classification has benefited not only from the birth of large datasets, such as ImageNet [8], but also from the deeper designs of 2D CNNs, including VGG-16 [9], AlexNet [10], Inception [11], ResNet [12], and DenseNet [13]. Those new models have shown capabilities in extracting spatial features from images and, consequently, a remarkable improvement in performance.

Motivated by the success of 2D architectures on still images, researchers started to investigate the ability to apply these frameworks on video classification tasks. However, the results were lower compared to when applied on still images. The performance gap between image and video classifiers is due to the nature of videos, which are simply sequences of frames that associate motion with them. As a result, this made scientists think of other techniques to overcome the weaker accuracy obtained on clips.

Prior to the advent of Transformer models, deep learning vision-based human action recognition relied on three major approaches, namely two-streams 2D CNN, RNN, and 3D CNN-based models. As its name indicates, the first technique consists of two branches. One is used to extract spatial features from RGB images, while the second operates on the temporal information obtained from optical flow data [14, 15]. RNNs, on the other hand, have a built-in memory that allows handling sequences of data, but struggled due to the vanishing grading descend, which was better managed in its gated Long-Short Term Memory (LSTM) variant. Generally, RNNs and their variants are not well-suited for extracting spatial features, and hence, they were embodied within models that combine them with 2D CNN frameworks to overcome this issue [16–18].

Expanding deep 2D classification models, such as Inception and Resnet [17, 19], into 3D ones was the main interest of researchers [20]. The output of these extended designs demonstrated the ability to extract both spatial and temporal information. In addition, the performance of these 3-dimensional setups can compete and even outperform, in some cases [21–23], both RNN and two-stream 2D CNN-based state-of-art methods. Moreover, the ease of implementation and the direct employment of 3D CNNs on RGB videos without the extra need to extract the optical flow for motion, contributed to making these architectures the most dominant approaches [24].

In this paper, we considered the three R3D, MC3, and R(2 + 1)D frameworks [25], as we first created three identical to the original architecture to be trained on UCF101 [26], except a dropout layer was added before the final network, which then served as backbones used for developing ten distinct variants. Each of these variants is distinguished by a specific attention unit. We setup our experiment to first assess the impact of reduced temporal and increased spatial features on these backbones' performance, and then we studied the improvement that occurred in each variant.

The paper is organized as: Chapter 2 outlines related work regarding HAR 3D CNN models, followed by Chapter 3, that describes the experimental setup comprising data preprocessing, training, and model configurations. Analysis and discussions obtained from the results of our experiment are presented in Chapter 4. The last chapter is related to conclusions and future work.

2 Related Work

State-of-the-art research evolves around different methods, such as two-streams, RNN, and transformers, in addition to 3D-based models covered in this section.

One of the earliest HAR 3D CNN-based designs was done by [19], their named C3D novel model has eight convolutional layers with a common kernel size of 3 on all dimensions. The outcome of this work proved competitive capability of capturing spatiotemporal data compared to current state-of-the-art models. Afterwards, some researchers, such as [27], transferred the concept of extending current powerful deep 2D image classifiers, particularly DenseNet, into 3D setups. The results demonstrated higher accuracy on benchmark datasets compared to other HAR models.

The success of expanding deep 2D frameworks into 3D kernelled ones continued, as how authors in [28] performed on Inception as a backbone model. Because of the high accuracy achieved on RGB input, authors also considered utilizing it in a two-stream setup that employs the optical flow in it. Inflating 2D models into 3D ones is usually accompanied by a large amount of data. This makes the training of these frameworks computationally expensive. Therefore, researchers responded to this issue by representing the 3D kernelled networks differently, i.e. splitting them into a combination of temporal and spatial parts. This technique prevailed in many 3D-based configurations. One of the state arts works that resembles this concept was carried out by authors in [25], who built a mixed setup of the 3D and 2D CNNs based on the original 2D ResNet. The first two layers employ the 3D CNNs, whereas the rest use the 2D ones.

The concept of factorizing the 3D network showed not only an improvement in efficiency, but also an increase of overall performance compared to standard 3D Resnet. Thus, other mainstream research continued to apply this mechanism. Another design proposed in the paper [29] decomposes the three-dimensional convolutions in the model into sequentially separate 2D and 1D to capture spatial and motion, respectively. Adoption of this mechanism yielded an increase in accuracy and a drop in a number of parameters compared to the original three-dimensional one. Impressed by their outcomes, the authors replicated the model as part of a two-stream configuration.

In another way of focusing on separating spatial and temporal extraction methods, authors in [30] introduced a novel model that uses two paths-mechanism for handling this compound data. The slow path in this model operated on high-resolution frames, while the fast one handled the temporal dynamics. The contrast in this configuration demonstrated high performance in video classification tasks.

Authors in [31] built a two-stream 3D model. As 3D architecture can capture both spatial and temporal data, the authors implemented a second 3D stream that operates on optical flow. This second added path was used in training to influence the first RGB stream by transferring knowledge, which is a setup also known as the teacher-student framework. In this case, the teacher stream works on optical flow, representing motion, and then distills its learned extracted capabilities on temporal dynamics to the student path that handles the RGB input. Other state-of-the-art methods, such as in [32], addressed the utilization of 3D models by introducing a block that groups similar temporal features and consequently reduces the number of computations. Designers of this work stated a 33–53% reduction in computation cost, while maintaining the same or higher performance. Another 2D backbone was expanded to a 3D video classifier, as [33] did on VGG-16.

The authors of this work combined the strength of image classification achieved by the VGG-16 network with the LSTM capability for handling sequences. The designed model of this work is suitable to run in a real-time setup.

In this paper, we adopt the three models proposed by [25], namely the R(2 + 1)D, R3D, and MC3, as we mentioned previously. The main reason for our choice, rather than their high performance, is that although these three frameworks share the same 18 layers of depth and are based on the ResNet 2D framework, they differ in the way they implement their convolutional filters which we will address in the coming sections.

3 Experimental Setup

We started our experiment by implementing different mechanisms compared to the models proposed by [25]. As we initially applied a functionality that checks the number of frames in a clip not to exceed a limit of 48. If the video contains fewer than that, all of them will be extracted, otherwise, a uniform subsampling is applied to extract exactly the maximum allowed number. The purpose of this configuration is that videos in UCF101 vary in length, and we wanted to have consistent temporal content out of them, in other words, we intentionally reduced the temporal knowledge in longer videos.

In the first part of the experiment, we modified the original MC3, R3D, and R(2 + 1)D [25] to create backbones for each, by adding a dropout layer, with a value of 0.4, for each one of them before the fully connected layer (fc), to increase the generalization of models. From now on in this article, we refer to those backbones as M-MC3, M-R3D, and M-R(2 + 1)D, based on which we later propose ten variants that include different attention mechanisms.

The UCF dataset contains 101 actions, distributed in five categories related to the actions that occur either with objects, including musical instruments, or with another individual, in addition to sports. Figure 1 demonstrates some extracted frames for random actions.

Apply eye makeup, lipstick, and yo-yo are actions in the human-object category, examples of body-motions are handstand pushups, handstand walking, and walking with dog. The human-human interaction includes class labels, such as head massage, band marching, and haircut. Playing musical instruments has activities, like playing cello, daf, and dhol. The sport's category contains actions like parallel bars, long jump, and cliff diving. The dataset's clips have 25 frames per second and a resolution of 320 x 240. The total number of videos is 13,320, with an average of 7.21 s in length.

3.1 Data Preprocessing

After the videos were preprocessed initially to have a maximum of 48 frames, as described previously, they are passed afterwards to the data augmentation pipeline. Here, another functionality ensures the clip is at least 32 frames long. If they are shorter, the last frame is then repeated to pad the sequence until it reaches that minimum value. A temporal subsampling technique then operates to select 16 consecutive frames with random starting points, to create temporal variability that enhances the model's training process of learning.

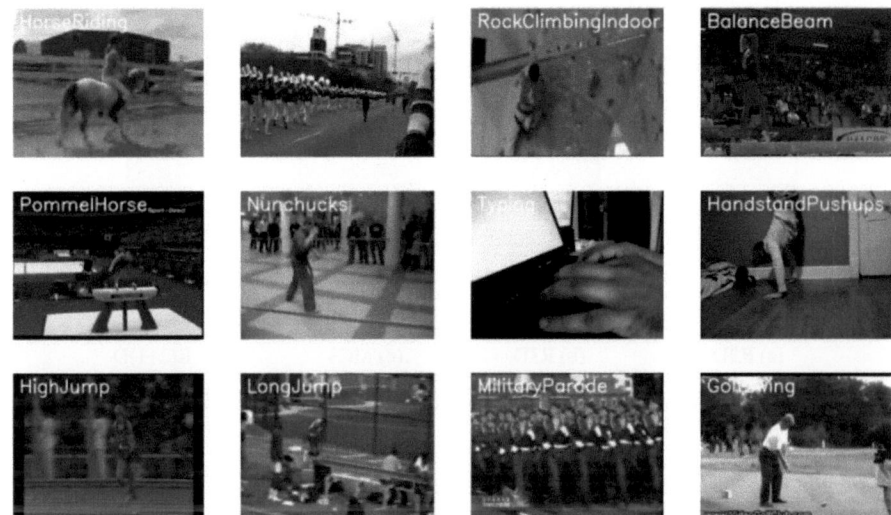

Fig. 1. Samples of extracted frames extracted from twelve actions of UCF101 dataset.

Spatial transformation is built differently compared to the original setup, as it first resizes each frame to 256 x 256 pixels, and then crops it at the center to have a resolution of 224 x 224, where the author's work in [25] had 112 x 112 instead. Additionally, color jittering and horizontal flipping were then applied. Similarly, the same methodology of temporal augmentation was implemented in the testing split, except that the temporal subsampling generates three clips for each video processed, all with different random starting points to enhance evaluation results by averaging the three values.

There are two main differences between our data preprocessing approaches and the original work, which are related to the temporal and spatial features passing to the model. Our goal, by this contrast, is to study the impact of the reduced temporal and the increased spatial features on the overall model's performance. We used UCF101 as a benchmark dataset for our tests and split 1 was adopted for the training and evaluation.

3.2 Models' Configuration

Based on the original MC3, R3D, and R(2 + 1)D models, which share the same number of layers, and were pretrained on the Kinetics-400 [34] dataset, we started our experiments by finetuning on UCF101 the new M-MC3, M-R3D, and M-R(2 + 1)D models that differ from originals by only adding the dropout layer before fc, as mentioned above. Figure 2 demonstrates the architecture of the original frameworks.

The ten new variants that we proposed based on the modified backbones contain attention blocks, namely temporal attention [33] that aids in improving the temporal feature representation by focusing on relevant information within the sequence of frames. Squeeze and excitation mechanism (SE) [35] that focuses on certain channels used in determining features by effectively enhancing most important feature maps, while ignoring irrelevant ones. The Convolutional Block Attention Module (CBAM) [36], which is

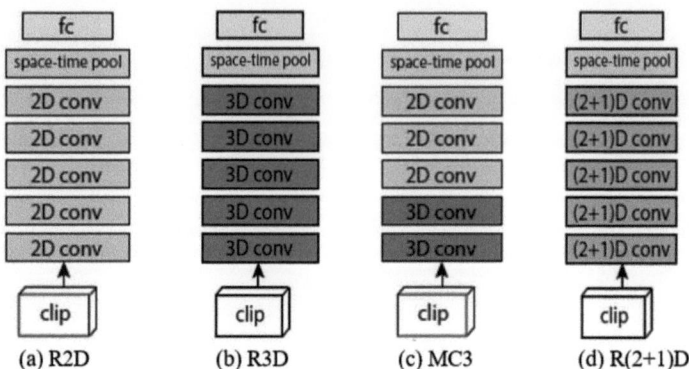

Fig. 2. The architectures of (a) 2D ResNet; (b) R3D; (c) MC3; and (d) R(2 + 1)D models [18].

a type that utilizes both channel and spatial types of attention, by allowing the network to refine features in both channel and spatial dimensions. Temporal Convolutional Network (TCN) [37], which is powered with a single temporal dimension 1D CNN, helps in modelling long dependencies, due to large receptive fields they have. Figure 3 illustrates the ten created variants.

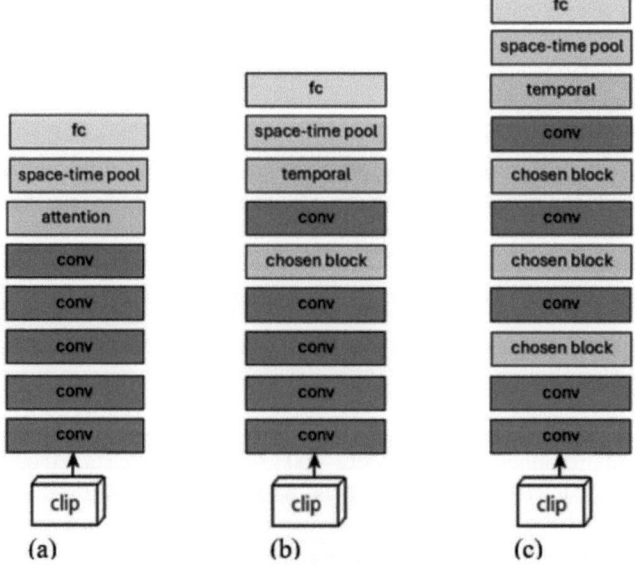

Fig. 3. The ten proposed architectures all incorporating a dropout layer before the fully connected (fc) layer. (a) Variants where the attention block is either spatial or temporal. (b) Variants incorporating specific attention mechanisms, including SE, temporal, a combination of SE and multi-head attention, TCN, and CBAM, applied after layer 3. (c) Variants where the same attention mechanisms (excluding the spatial attention from (a)) are applied after layers 1, 2, and 3.

The ten new variations, that all contain the defined dropout layer before the fc one, are named after the block of attention, and their placement, as follows:

- FC-Spatial: adds multi-headed attention on spatial features before final pooling layer.
- FC-Temporal: employs multi-headed temporal attention before the final pooling layer.
- 3-SE: is a variant of FC-Temporal with an SE block after layer 3.
- 3-Temporal: is another variant of FC-Temporal, but it differs in adding a Temporal multi-headed attention layer before and after layer 3.
- 3-Both: employs Temporal multi-headed and SE units after layer 3, while following the same strategy in keeping the final temporal block before the final pooling.
- 3-CBAM: keeps the final temporal layer but implements CBAM after layer 3.
- 3-TCN: is a model like the previous one, except that it adopts the TCN layer instead.
- All-SE: keeps the final temporal layer and adds SE units after layers 1, 2, 3.
- All-Temporal: is the same as All-SE, but instead of SE blocks, it applies on the same placements, multi-headed attention that operates on temporal features.
- All-Together: is based on All-SE and All-Temporal, but uses both SE and multiheaded temporal attentions, instead of separate ones on same locations within the framework.

3.3 Training

In our training process, we employed the Stochastic Gradient Descent (SGD) optimizer with a momentum of 0.9. The learning rate was initially set to 0.001 and a scheduler that drops it by 0.1 factor every 15 epoch was also added. We also considered a weight decay with a value of 0.0005 to enhance the regularization while training the models. Moreover, we applied an early stopping mechanism to avoid overfitting, which also aided in minimizing the training time.

4 Analysis and Discussion

We performed our experiments on the ten variants described in Sect. 3.3. Tables 1, 2 and 3 demonstrate the models, and the epoch at which they stopped training when early stopping was activated, params represent the number of learnable parameters expressed in millions, along with top-1 and top-5 accuracies. Additionally, the tables include the number of classes that show an increase on their original (M-MC3, M-R3D, and M-R(2 + 1)D) accuracy, represented by the no. Inc., in the sixth column.

The highest increase and lowest decrease columns are related to the class that experienced the greatest accuracy increase and decrease among the 101 actions when tested by the corresponding variant. The table's final column (least class/acc) is the measure of the lowest accuracy achieved and its associated class label.

Table 1 shows that all variants created based on the M-MC3 have trained in a smaller number of iterations compared to the M-MC3 model, this implies that despite an increased number of parameters on the variants, they could train faster than the backbone. The top 1 accuracy ranged between 81.2 and 86.1% for the M-MC3 and All-Together models, respectively.

Among the variants that employed different blocks after layer 3 within its architecture, the 3-CBAM achieved the highest top 1 accuracy, followed by 3-TCN, where 3-SE

Table 1. M-MC3 variants analysis.

Variants	Epoch	Params	top-1	top-5	No. Inc	Highest increase	Lowest increase	Least class/acc
M-MC3	28	11.54	81.21	95.88	N/A	N/A	N/A	HighJump/18.92
FC-Spatial	26	12.59	83.82	96.43	51	Basketball/34.28	BreastStroke/−25.00	HighJump/29.73
FC-Temporal	25	12.59	83.4	96.46	49	PommelHorse/34.28	BreastStroke/−35.71	HighJump/24.32
3-SE	22	12.65	83.8	96.67	50	WalkingWithDog/41.67	BreastStroke/−28.57	PizzaTossing/30.30
3-Temporal	24	12.85	84.69	97.33	51	WalkingWithDog/44.45	BreastStroke/−28.57	HighJump/40.54
3-Both	24	12.92	84.54	96.51	54	HighJump/32.43	Archery/−21.95	Nunchucks/34.29
3-CBAM	23	12.60	85.62	96.67	61	MoppingFloor/29.41	HammerThrow/−22.22	CricketBowling/41.67
3-TCN	21	12.79	85.01	96.67	50	PommelHorse/48.57	PlayingSitar/−22.73	HandstandWalking/35.29
All-SE	22	12.68	83.85	96.03	55	HighJump/32.43	Kayaking/−19.44	PizzaTossing/30.30
All-Temporal	25	12.94	86.1	96.64	63	HighJump/35.13	Haircut/−27.27	PizzaTossing/33.33
All-Together	22	13.02	84.88	96.59	54	Basketball/37.14	HandstandPushups/−35.71	HandstandWalking/38.24

had the lowest. Additionally, 3-Temporal recorded the highest top 5 accuracy among all variants, where 3-CBAM and 3-TCN share the same value with 96.67%.

Regarding the tests performed on M-MC3 and its based modifications, we found that all the variants have roughly increased half of the dataset classes' accuracies, for instance, the All-Temporal and 3-CBAM incremented the accuracy of 63, and 61 classes, respectively. Table 1 also indicates that the 3-TCN model has the greatest impact on class "PommelHorse", making it have the highest increase in accuracy.

Both "BreastStroke", and "HandstandPushups" were among all the 101 actions that were negatively affected by FC-Temporal and All-Together models, as they dropped 35.71% from their value on the original M-MC3 backbone.

The last column in Table 1 shows the lowest class accuracy for each variant, here the M-MC3 had the lowest accuracy, 18.92%, associated with "HighJump", the class remained the most misclassified in FC-Spatial, FC-Temporal, 3-temporal vases, despite an increase on its performance compared to the one recorded by the backbone. The 3-CBAM setup recorded the lowest accuracy associated with the "CricketBowling" class, with a value of 41.67%.

Table 2 illustrates that M-R(2 + 1)D based designs are all trained relatively within the same range of epochs. The minimum top 1 accuracy was obtained by the base model M-R(2 + 1)D, and the highest was reached by the 3-Temporal variant as 85.14 and 88.98%, respectively, the latter also recorded the first place among all designs for the highest top 5 value as well.

Table 2, also shows the number of classes that had an increase in accuracy, among all variants, All-Temporal has influenced 44 actions to have an increment on the accuracy compared to backbone, although the variant distinguished "BreastStroke" class by making it the most to gain performance, in addition to making this value the highest increase to an action among the 11 testing models, with an increase of 57.15% to its original accuracy recorded by M-R(2 + 1)D.

Generally, the "BreastStroke" class was positively affected by M-R(2 + 1)D-base models. On the other hand, the action "Shotput" and "HandstandPushups" reduced their

Table 2. M-R(2 + 1)D variants analysis.

Variants	Epoch	Params	top-1	top-5	No. Inc	Highest increase	Lowest decrease	Least class/acc
M-R(2 + 1)D	24	31.35	85.14	96.96	N/A	N/A	N/A	PizzaTossing/27.27
FC-Spatial	26	32.40	87.84	97.7	49	BreastStroke/57.15	RockClimbingIndoor/−19.51	PizzaTossing/42.42
FC-Temporal	26	32.40	88.82	97.81	51	BreastStroke/50.00	Shotput/−21.74	Hammering/45.45
3-SE	25	32.46	87.02	97.75	45	BreastStroke/50.00	PullUps/−21.43	BrushingTeeth/36.11
3-Temporal	26	32.66	88.98	97.86	51	JavelinThrow/35.48	FrontCrawl/−16.21	Nunchucks/51.43
3-Both	22	32.73	87.63	97.65	51	BreastStroke/50.00	PommelHorse/−22.86	PizzaTossing/39.39
3-CBAM	22	32.41	88.55	97.57	53	WalkingWithDog/33.34	HandstandPushups/−28.57	PizzaTossing/42.42
3-TCN	22	32.60	88.21	97.38	52	PizzaTossing/42.43	SalsaSpin/−18.61	Nunchucks/40.00
All-SE	23	32.49	86.52	97.52	51	BreastStroke/39.29	Shotput/−32.61	Hammering/27.27
All-Temporal	25	32.75	87.89	97.62	44	BreastStroke/57.15	Shotput/−36.96	BrushingTeeth/44.44
All-Together	23	32.83	88.9	97.54	53	HighJump/43.24	BenchPress/−22.92	Nunchucks/48.57

accuracies the most among all actions in the UCF101 dataset by testing All-Temporal and 3 CBAM.

The minimum class accuracy, according to Table 2, was of 27.27% for both "PizzaTossing" and "Hammering" activities, that were achieved by the original M-R(2 + 1)D and its base variant All-SE one, respectively. In addition, all the values of the lowest accuracies on classes were below 50%, except the "Nunchucks" one, which was obtained by testing the 3-Temporal setup.

The last ten variants in this part of our experiment are related to M-R3D and its variants. Like Tables 1, 2 and 3 illustrates the behavior of each of these models.

Based on the results from Table 3, the M-R3D based variant finished training in a range of 22–26 epochs. The values of the top-1 accuracy were between 79.99% and 84.44% for the original backbone and 3-SE models, respectively. For the variants with different blocks after layer 3, 3-SE achieved the highest top-1 accuracy with a score of 84.88%, followed by the 3-CBAM with 83.48%, while 3-TCN had the lowest value among them, with 82.16%. Nevertheless, All-Temporal had the greatest top-5 accuracy among the ten variants.

Table 3 also has shown that models 3-CBAM and All-Temporal enhanced performance in 60 classes. The 3-SE model has increased the accuracy to the highest value with 46.94% on the "TennisSwing" activity, followed by 44.90% for the same class tested by 3-CBAM and All-Temporal variants. The "BreastStroke" class has reduced its accuracy the most in the All-Temporal model's testing. The most frequently misclassified class is "PizzaTossing", that recorded the highest accuracy when testing the 3-Temporal and 3-CBAM variants, despite its original 9.09% value by M-R3D.

When studying these three tables, we noticed that the highest top-1 accuracy in each table was achieved by variants with implementations, for instance, 3-Temporal based on both M-MC3 and M-R(2 + 1)D recorded the highest value, whereas the case was for 3-SE based on backbone M-R3D. According to the three tables, the 3-CBAM variant, despite its backbone model, has influenced the greatest number of classes to improve their performance. The most increase to a class label among the tests on M-MC3 was for "PommelHorse", with an increment of 48.57%, which was achieved by the model

Table 3. M-R3D variants analysis.

Variants	Epoch	Params	top-1	top-5	No. Inc	Highest increase	Lowest decrease	Least class/acc
M-R3D	26	33.21	79.99	95.08	N/A	N/A	N/A	PizzaTossing/9.09
FC-Spatial	25	34.26	84.06	95.66	56	TennisSwing/38.78	Shotput/−23.91	PizzaTossing/21.21
FC-Temporal	26	34.53	82.32	95.77	52	BrushingTeeth/41.67	TaiChi/−21.43	PizzaTossing/30.30
3-SE	24	34.33	84.88	96.46	57	TennisSwing/46.94	BreastStroke/−25.00	PizzaTossing/15.15
3-Temporal	26	34.53	82.32	95.77	52	BrushingTeeth/41.67	TaiChi/−21.43	PizzaTossing/30.30
3-Both	24	34.59	82.63	95.59	51	MoppingFloor/32.36	BreastStroke/−21.43	PizzaTossing/21.21
3-CBAM	22	34.27	83.48	96.27	60	TennisSwing/44.90	BreastStroke/−35.72	PizzaTossing/30.30
3-TCN	23	34.46	82.16	95.88	48	BrushingTeeth/36.12	HandstandWalking/−29.41	PizzaTossing/12.12
All-SE	27	34.35	84.06	96.48	57	JavelinThrow/35.49	HandstandPushups/−21.43	HandstandWalking/26.47
All-Temporal	25	34.61	84.11	96.67	60	TennisSwing/44.90	BreastStroke/−46.43	BreastStroke/21.43
All-Together	23	34.70	83.45	95.93	57	TennisSwing/38.78	HandstandWalking/−20.59	PizzaTossing/18.18

3-TCN. Differently, the case was for both variants, FC-Spatial and All-Temporal, based on M-R(2 + 1)D for the "BreastStroke" action.

The last backbone, M-R3D, also had a different variant that added the highest increase on performance to an activity, represented in 3-SE when detecting the "TennisSwing" action. The most frequent class that dropped its performance was "BreastStroke" for M-MC3, "Shotput" in both M-R(2 + 1)D, and M-R3D based variants.

Among all the testing designs, only the based on M-R(2 + 1)D, variant 3-Temporal, had the highest minimum accuracy recorded with a 51.43% detected on "Nunchucks". This case was the only exception among the 33 tests to pass a value of 50% accuracy, as the rest of the models failed to reach.

We further widened our tests to include the worst accurate classes for the original M-MC3, M-R3D, and M-R(2 + 1)D models and then studied the effect of such variation made in the variants on these actions. Tables 4, 5 and 6 list the five actions that were the most misclassified and the value of their accuracies per variant.

Table 4. Accuracy improvement associated with variants on original M-MC3 most five misclassified actions

Least accurate classes	M-MC3	FC-Spatial	FC-Temporal	3-SE	3-Temporal	3-Both	3-CBAM	3-TCN	All-SE	All-Temporal	All-Together
BrushingTeeth	36.11	52.78	50	55.56	61.11	44.44	52.78	47.22	44.44	47.22	50
WalkingWithDog	33.33	52.78	58.33	75	77.78	63.89	52.78	75	52.78	63.89	66.67
HandstandWalking	26.47	52.94	50	50	44.12	38.24	50	35.29	47.06	35.29	38.24
PizzaTossing	24.24	33.33	30.3	30.3	48.48	45.45	45.45	60.61	30.3	33.33	54.55
HighJump	19.92	29.73	24.32	37.84	40.54	51.35	45.95	45.95	51.35	54.05	43.24

In Table 4, the activity "BrushingTeeth" had the most increase in accuracy by the 3–Temporal model, with added 25% extra value to its original value achieved by M-MC3. The same variant among all ten, was also the most booster for the "WalkingWithDog" action, which was originally at 33.33 to become 77.78%.

The original accuracy of 26.47% for class "HandstandWalking" was doubled in the FC-Spatial test case, followed by a value of 50% in both FC-Temporal and 3-SE. In the case of the "PizzaTossing" class, only the 3-TCN model managed to increase its accuracy above 50% with a value of 60.61%.

For the lowest accurate class in the M-MC3 original test," HighJump", the variant All-Temporal achieved the greatest improvement by adding an extra 34.13% accuracy score to it.

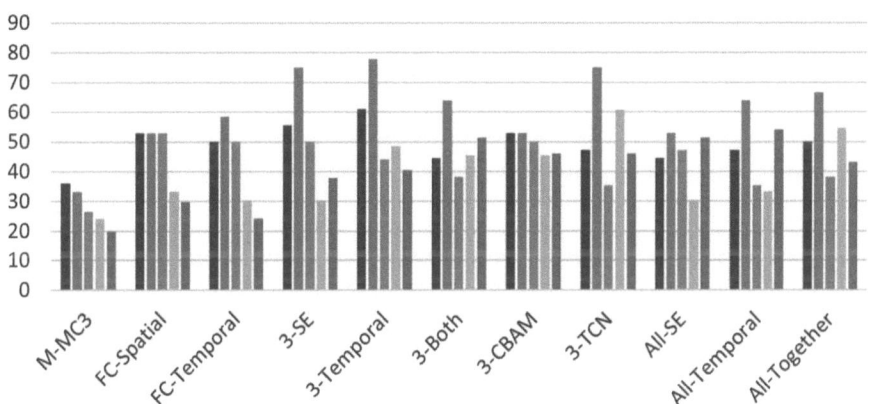

Fig. 4. Accuracies of the most five misclassified actions of M-MC3 per its variants.

Figure 4 visualizes the most five misclassified actions tested by M-MC3 and how their accuracies improve over the 10 variants. In Table 5, the case of the five most misclassified actions for M-R(2 + 1)D shows three common actions as the ones from M-MC3, namely, "BrushingTeeth", "WalkingWithDog", and "PizzaTossing" despite their order.

Table 5. Accuracy improvement associated with variants on original M-R(2 + 1)D most five misclassified actions

Least accurate classes	M-R(2+1)D	FC-Spatial	FC-Temporal	3-SE	3-Temporal	3-Both	3-CBAM	3-TCN	All-SE	All-Temporal	All-Together
WalkingWithDog	47.22	80.56	83.33	72.22	80.56	80.56	80.56	80.56	77.78	80.56	77.78
BrushingTeeth	44.44	47.22	50	36.11	61.11	61.11	58.33	55.56	47.22	44.44	52.78
HighJump	37.84	51.35	59.46	54.05	67.57	54.05	51.35	62.16	64.86	67.57	81.08
BreastStroke	35.71	92.86	85.71	85.71	60.71	85.71	57.14	64.29	75	92.86	67.86
PizzaTossing	27.27	42.42	57.58	45.45	54.55	39.39	42.42	69.7	30.3	57.58	63.64

Table 5 indicates a total increase of 36% was added to the original 47.22% accuracy by the test on variant FC-temporal. Moreover, all variants pushed the accuracy to more than 77% on this activity. The case is different for "BrushingTeeth" which had an accuracy of 44.44% on the base model, as the 3-Spatial model dropped this value by 8.33%, but both the 3-Temporal and 3-Both succeeded in increasing it to become 61.11%.

The third class in this list was "HighJump", with an original test accuracy of 37.84%, which was more than doubled in the All-Together model. The action by the name "Breast-Stroke" had the highest increment to its original performance by models FC-Spatial and All-temporal in which an accuracy of 92.86% was achieved by both.

In the case of the "PizzaTossing" action, its accuracy has shifted from its original value of 27.27% to become 69.7% when tested on the 3-TCN variant.

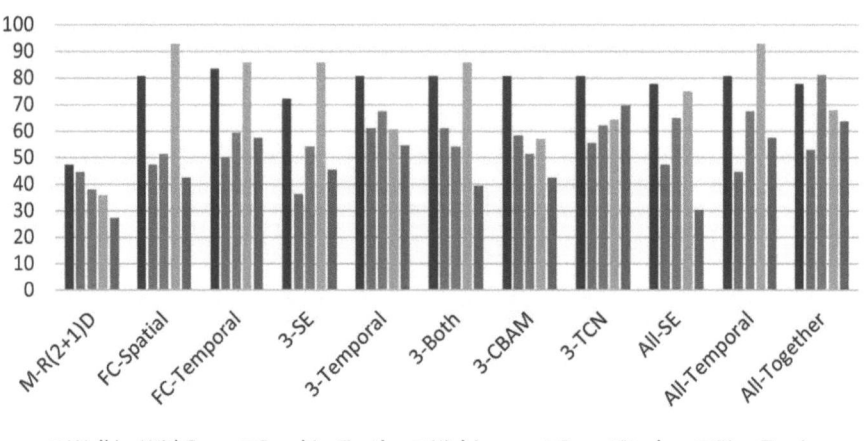

Fig. 5. Accuracies of the most five misclassified actions of M-R(2 + 1)D per its variants.

Figure 5 draws these five actions and their corresponding accuracies across the M-R(2 + 1)D variants. Table 6 details the performance across M-R3D variants for the classes "Nunchucks", Hammering, "JavelinThrow", "BrushingTeeth", and "PizzaTossing".

Table 6. Accuracy improvement associated with variants on original M-R3D most five misclassified actions

Least accurate classes	M-R3D	FC-Spatial	FC-Temporal	3-SE	3-Temporal	3-Both	3-CBAM	3-TCN	All-SE	All-Temporal	All-Together
Nunchucks	40	51.43	57.14	42.86	57.14	25.71	34.29	42.86	37.14	42.86	42.86
Hammering	39.39	63.64	48.48	57.85	48.48	63.64	48.48	39.39	45.45	40.48	48.48
JavelinThrow	35.48	61.29	64.52	70.97	64.52	51.61	74.19	61.29	70.97	70.97	74.19
BrushingTeeth	19.44	55.56	61.11	44.44	61.11	50	52.78	55.56	50	47.22	36.11
PizzaTossing	9.09	21.21	30.3	15.15	30.3	21.21	30.3	12.12	27.27	33.33	18.18

The results shown in Table 6 indicate that the first class had a maximum increase of 17.14% by 3-Temporal. However, the "Hammering" class was nearly doubled in accuracy in the FC-Spatial setup. The "JavelinThrow" action had the highest increase to its original accuracy by the 3-CBAM model recorded 74.19% compared to the original 35.48%. Model All-Together, as Table 6 shows, was the least class that improved among the five considered ones, "BrushingTeeth", but the two models of 3-Temporal and FC-Temporal were beneficial to this action by enhancing its original value from 19.44%

to become slightly above 61%. The most misclassified class in the M-R3D test was "PizzaTossing", with an accuracy of only 9.09%, which was never increased to more than 33.33% by the All-Temporal variant.

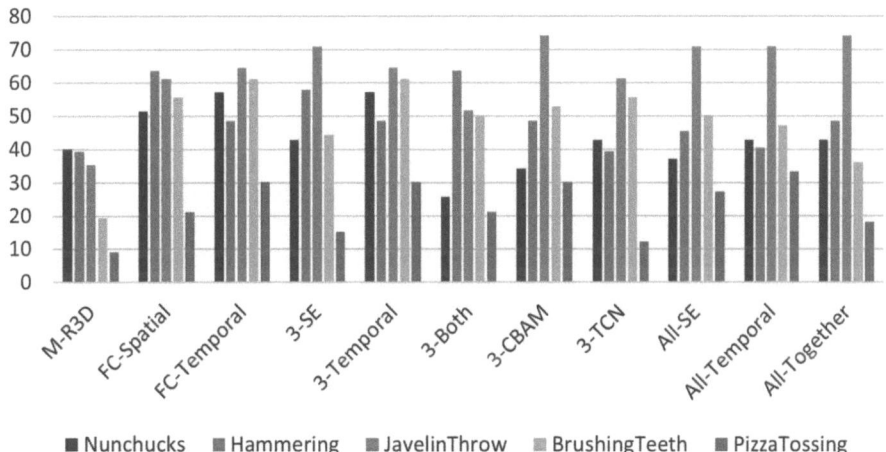

Fig. 6. Accuracies of the most five misclassified actions of M-R3D per its variants.

Figure 6 visualizes the least accurate five actions of M-R3D variants. Tables 4, 5 and 6 show that there are common actions among the three backbones having the lowest accuracies, i.e. "PizzaTossing", and "BrushingTeeth". Generally, the lowest accurate activities in M-MC3, M-R(2 + 1)D, and M-R3D were improved by their variants. Some of these low-performance actions were positively affected by special attention types implemented in a corresponding variant, as the case of "BreastStroke" in M-R(2 + 1)D, and its variant FC-Spatial that improved the original accuracy by the backbone from 35.71 to 92.86%. We also observed that three variants only had a slight to moderate enhancement, i.e. "PizzaTossing".

Our work in this paper was carried out for the purpose of indicating the importance of temporal information that should be passed on to a 3D CNN based model. For this purpose, we referred to the models MC3, R3D, and R(2 + 1)D, which are similar-in architectures state-of-the-art models, but different in their method of extracting the spatial and temporal features due to how their filters are presented in their CNN, for example, if we look at the filters in layer 3 in each of these three models, we see that R3D uses (3, 3, 3), and (1, 3, 3) in MC3, and both of (1, 3, 3) and (3, 1, 1) in the case of R(2 + 1)D.

In our experiments, we initially set up a mechanism that allowed a strict extent of motion to be gathered from videos, which we believed would hinder the model's learning capabilities. We then increased the spatial features in our data augmentation to observe if this step could compensate for the loss of temporal data. Our findings indicated that enhanced appearance could not substitute for that loss in temporal dynamics.

According to the three original models in the paper [25], which stated only R(2 + 1)D to be tested on UCF101 and having an accuracy of 96.8%, where our corresponding M-R(2 + 1)D scored an accuracy of 85.14% on the same dataset. Several factors contributed to this performance gap. Firstly, our testing procedure only sampled three random clips per video, which provided insufficient temporal coverage. Secondly, we did not include spatial augmentations in the test transformation, as in training augmentation. Additionally, the randomness in the starting points of the sampled clips further introduced variance, potentially missing critical temporal activity segments. Moreover, our training mechanism halted the process based on early stopping, as indicated in Tables 1, 2 and 3, compared to the longer training epochs of the original work. Lastly, the added dropout layer before the fc one might hinder optimal learning, despite its advantage in generalizing the model.

In the second part of our experiment, we developed 10 new variants for each backbone model. Each of them employs a different attention mechanism block in one or more locations within the CNN layers in the backbones. Our motivation behind that was, first, to study both the effect and the extent of improvement that such attention block would bring to the temporal-restricted models we earlier created, and second, the actions that this added attention could strongly influence. Our results show that these blocks behave similarly for all base models. As for instance, what a temporal attention block on a variant based on R3D enhanced, was not the same case as in the MC3 setup.

In comparison to the related research, paper [38] proposed an R(2 + 1)D model that adopted a resolution of 112 x 112, in addition to a mechanism to drop frames during training, along a temporal decay of 0.999, and achieved an accuracy of 78.7% on UCF101. Another approach [39] was based on the ResNet-154 transformer model, containing 10 frames, that did lead to an accuracy of 76.64% when testing on UCF101. Utilizing 3D CNN in HAR was also proposed by [40], authors of this work have tested their model on different datasets such as UCF50 and UCF101, on which they scored a value of 79.9% accuracy on the latter dataset. They also stated that the class "HorseRiding" was the most misclassified one. On the other hand, among all our tests, the best performance was related to the variant 3-Temporal of M-R(2 + 1)D model, which achieved an accuracy of 88.98%. "Nunchuks" action was the most misclassified activity related to this model, with a value of 51.43% accuracy.

5 Conclusions

In this paper, we carried out a comparative analysis among three 3D CNN Resnet-based architectures, namely the MC3, R(2 + 1)D, and R3D models, by following a mechanism that restricts the knowledge gathered from motion in video frames; we also increased the resolution of the frames to be double compared to how the training was set on the three original models. We created similar designs that differ in adding a dropout layer for better generalization and trained them on the UCF101 dataset. At another phase of the experiment, we referred to our three modified models named M-MC3, M-R(2 + 1)D, and M-R3D as backbones. Our results indicated an overall drop in modes performance compared to the original work and the backbones showed accuracies of 81.21%, 85.14%, and 79.99 for M-MC3, M-R(2 + 1)D, and M-R3D, respectively. This implied the importance of the temporal features in all the 3D CNN models despite their used filters. In addition to that, another observation we noted was that the enhanced resolution in frames could not compensate for the effect of missing skipped frames.

Based on our modified models, we then developed 10 variants for each, that are similar to the backbone, except that they employ different blocks that utilize attention mechanisms to operate on temporal data, and channel levels. Testing a total of 30 models has shown an increase of up to 4% to the backbones' accuracies. Furthermore, as these variants are relatively close in their overall effect on the models' performance, they differ in their behavior, i.e. their class accuracy levels.

In our future work, we would like to study these added units on different architectures rather than 3D-based models. For instance, on video Transformer, two-streams models will be used, so that we can analytically compare their results with 3D CNNs.

Disclosure of Interests. The authors have no competing interests to declare that are relevant to the content of this article.

References

1. Hu, D., Wang, M., Li, S.: Multi-classifier information fusion for human activity recognition in healthcare facilities. Frontiers of Engineering Management, pp. 1–18 (2025)
2. Khan, H., Yuan, X., Qingge, L., Roy, K.: Violence detection from industrial surveillance videos using deep learning. IEEE Access **13**, 15363–15375 (2025)
3. Elmamoon, M.E.A., Mustapha, A.A.: A comparative study of deep learning models for human activity recognition. Cloud Computing and Data Science, pp. 79–93 (2025)
4. Thakur, D., Dangi, D., Lalwani, P.: A novel hybrid deep learning approach with GWO–WOA optimization technique for human activity recognition. Biomed. Signal Process. Control **99**, 1–11 (2025)
5. Abdellatef, E., Al-Makhlasawy, R.M., Shalaby, W.A.: Detection of human activities using multi-layer convolutional neural network. Sci. Rep. **15**, 1–25 (2025)
6. Hasan, M., Athrey, K.S., Khalid, A., Xie, D., Younessian, E., Braskich, T.: Applications of Computer Vision in Entertainment and Media Industry, pp. 205–238. Computer Vision, Chapman and Hall/CRC (2024)
7. Dutta, S.J., Boongoen, T., Zwiggelaar, R.: Human activity recognition: a review of deep learning-based methods. IET Comput. Vision **19**(1), 1–27 (2025)
8. Deng, J., et al.: ImageNet: a large-scale hierarchical image database. In: IEEE Conference on Computer Vision and Pattern Recognition, pp. 248–255. IEEE (2009)
9. Simonyan, K., Zisserman, A.: Very Deep Convolutional Networks for Large-Scale Image Recognition. arXiv preprint arXiv:1409.1556 (2014)
10. Krizhevsky, A., Sutskever, I., Hinton, G. E.: ImageNet classification with deep convolutional neural networks. Advances in Neural Information Processing Systems **25** (2012)
11. Szegedy, C., et al.: Going deeper with convolutions. In: Proceedings of the IEEE Conference on Computer Vision and Pattern Recognition, pp. 1–9 (2015)
12. He, K., Zhang, X., Ren, S., Sun, J.: Deep residual learning for image recognition. In: Proceedings of the IEEE Conference on Computer Vision and Pattern Recognition, pp. 770–778 (2016)
13. Huang, G., Liu, Z., Van Der Maaten, L., Weinberger, K. Q.: Densely connected convolutional networks. In: Proceedings of the IEEE Conference on Computer Vision and Pattern Recognition, pp. 4700–4708 (2017)

14. Simonyan, K., Zisserman, A.: Two-stream convolutional networks for action recognition in videos. Adv. Neural. Inf. Process. Syst. **27**, 1–9 (2014)
15. SravyaPranati, B., Suma, D., ManjuLatha, C., Putheti, S.: Large-Scale Video Classification with Convolutional Neural Networks. In: Senjyu, T., Mahalle, P.N., Perumal, T., Joshi, A. (eds.) ICTIS 2020. SIST, vol. 196, pp. 689–695. Springer, Singapore (2021). https://doi.org/10.1007/978-981-15-7062-9_69
16. Du, W., Wang, Y., Qiao, Y.: Rpan: An end-to-end recurrent pose-attention network for action recognition in videos. In: Proceedings of the IEEE International Conference on Computer Vision, pp. 3725–3734 (2017)
17. Sun, L., et al.: Lattice long short-term memory for human action recognition. In: Proceedings of the IEEE International Conference on Computer Vision, pp. 2147–2156 (2017)
18. Joudaki, M., Imani, M., Arabnia, H.R.: A new efficient hybrid technique for human action recognition using 2D Conv-RBM and LSTM with optimized frame selection. Technologies **13**, 1–28 (2025)
19. Tran, D., Bourdev, L., Fergus, R., Torresani, L., Paluri, M.: Learning Spatiotemporal Features with 3D Convolutional Networks. In: Proceedings of the IEEE International Conference on Computer Vision, pp. 4489–4497. IEEE, Santiago, Chile (2015)
20. Zhang, H., Zhang, L., Qi, X., Li, H., Torr, P.H., Koniusz, P.: Few-Shot Action Recognition with Permutation-Invariant Attention. In: Vedaldi, A., Bischof, H., Brox, T., Frahm, J.M. (eds.) Computer Vision – ECCV 2020. Lecture Notes in Computer Science, vol. 12350, pp. 525–542. Springer, Cham. (2020)
21. Sun, L., Jia, K., Yeung, D.-Y., Shi, B. E.: Human action recognition using factorized spatio-temporal convolutional networks. In: Proceedings of the IEEE International Conference on Computer Vision (ICCV), pp. 4597–4605. IEEE, Santiago, Chile (2015)
22. Wang, X., Gao, L., Song, J., Shen, H.: Beyond Frame-Level CNN: Saliency-Aware 3-D CNN with LSTM for Video Action Recognition. IEEE Signal Process. Lett. **24**(4), 510–514 (2016)
23. Qiu, Z., Yao, T., Mei, T.: Learning spatio-temporal representation with pseudo-3D residual networks. In: Proceedings of the IEEE International Conference on Computer Vision, pp. 5533–5541 (2017)
24. Sun, Z., et al.: Human action recognition from various data modalities: a review. In: IEEE Transactions on Pattern Analysis and Machine Intelligence **45**(3), pp. 3200–3225 (2023)
25. Tran, D., et al.: A Closer look at spatiotemporal convolutions for action recognition. In: Proceedings of the IEEE Conference on Computer Vision and Pattern Recognition (CVPR), pp. 6450–6459. IEEE, Salt Lake City, UT, USA (2018)
26. Soomro, K., Zamir, A. R., Shah, M.: UCF101: A Dataset of 101 Human Actions Classes from Videos in the Wild. arXiv preprint arXiv:1212.0402 (2012)
27. Diba, A., et al.: Temporal 3D ConvNets: New Architecture and Transfer Learning for Video Classification. arXiv preprint arXiv:1711.08200 (2017)
28. Carreira, J., Zisserman, A.: Quo Vadis, Action Recognition? A New Model and the Kinetics Dataset. In: Proceedings of the IEEE Conference on Computer Vision and Pattern Recognition, pp. 6299–6308 (2017)
29. Vaswani, A., et al.: Attention is All You Need. Advances in Neural Information Processing Systems **30** (2017)
30. Feichtenhofer, C., Fan, H., Malik, J., He, K.: Slowfast Networks for Video Recognition. In: Proceedings of the IEEE/CVF International Conference on Computer Vision, pp. 6202–6211 (2019)
31. Stroud, J., Ross, D., Sun, C., Deng, J., Sukthankar, R.: D3D: Distilled 3D Networks for Video Action Recognition. In: Proceedings of the IEEE/CVF Winter Conference on Applications of Computer Vision, pp. 625–634 (2020)

32. Fayyaz, M., et al.: 3D CNNs with Adaptive Temporal Feature Resolutions. In: Proceedings of the IEEE/CVF Conference on Computer Vision and Pattern Recognition, pp. 4731–4740 (2021)
33. Athira, K.A., Udayan, J.D.: Temporal fusion of time-distributed VGG-16 and LSTM for precise action recognition in video sequences. Procedia Computer Science **233**, 892–901 (2024)
34. Kay, W., et al.: The Kinetics Human Action Video Dataset. arXiv preprint arXiv:1705.06950 (2017)
35. Hu, J., Shen, L., Sun, G.: Squeeze-and-Excitation Networks. In: Proceedings of the IEEE Conference on Computer Vision and Pattern Recognition, pp. 7132–7141 (2018)
36. Woo, S., Park, J., Lee, J. Y., Kweon, I. S.: CBAM: Convolutional Block Attention Module. In: Proceedings of the European Conference on Computer Vision (ECCV), pp. 3–19 (2018)
37. Bai, S., Kolter, J. Z., Koltun, V.: An Empirical Evaluation of Generic Convolutional and Recurrent Networks for Sequence Modeling. arXiv preprint arXiv:1803.01271 (2018)
38. Pan, T., et al.: VideoMoCo: Contrastive Video Representation Learning with Temporally Adversarial Examples. In: Proceedings of the IEEE/CVF Conference on Computer Vision and Pattern Recognition, pp. 11205–11214 (2021)
39. Nguyen, H. P., Ribeiro, B.: Video Action Recognition Collaborative Learning with Dynamics via PSO-ConvNet Transformer. Scientific Reports, pp. 1–18 (2023)
40. Vrskova, R., Hudec, R., Kamencay, P., Sykora, P.: Human Activity Classification using the 3DCNN Architecture. Applied Sciences, pp. 1–17 (2022)

The Real-Time IoT Data Security

Evelyne Hakizimana[(✉)] and Gennady Dik[(✉)]

Saint Petersburg State University, Saint Petersburg, Russia
hakkizimana@gmail.com

Abstract. Our main area of study is IoT security, including its effects and ways to mitigate them in real time. This study focuses on Distributed Denial-of-Service (DDoS) assaults, which pose a serious risk to Internet of Things networks because of the growing number of unprotected devices. We examine the characteristics of DDoS attacks, examine the strategies to detect it, especially in the African setting, and suggest a detection methodology based on algorithms from Adaptive Resonance Theory (ART) and Long Short-Term Memory (LSTM). The detection performance is evaluated using metrics such as F1-score, precision, and recall. By offering an efficient DDoS detection framework, the study helps to improve real-time IoT data security.

Keywords: Distributed Denial-of-Service (DDoS) · Real-time Detection · Long Short-Term Memory (LSTM) · Adaptive Resonance Theory (ART) · Machine Learning · Cybersecurity · Network Security · Africa

1 Introduction

The Internet of Things' (IoT) explosive growth has transformed the way devices interact, opening the door for automation and intelligent services from tech firms [1]. But this increase in connectivity has brought about serious cybersecurity issues. The most serious of these threats to IoT ecosystems are Distributed Denial-of-Service (DDoS) attacks [2], which can disrupt services and result in major operational and financial harm [3].

A DDoS assault comprises several infected devices, frequently deployed globally, flooding a target system with excessive traffic [4]. The attack's purpose is to deplete the target's resources—such as bandwidth, CPU, memory, or application capacity—thereby denying service to legitimate users [5]. In contrast to conventional DoS assaults, which come from a single source, DDoS attacks use botnets made up of thousands or millions of compromised devices, which makes detection and mitigation difficult [6].

DDoS attacks can be categorized mainly into three types: volumetric attacks, protocol attacks, and application layer attacks [7]. Volumetric attacks aim to create enormous volumes of traffic in order to overload the target's network bandwidth. DNS amplification attacks, ICMP floods, and UDP floods are a few examples [8]. These assaults have the ability to overload network infrastructure with traffic quantities that surpass hundreds of gigabits per second. Protocol attacks use server or firewall resources by taking advantage of flaws in network protocols. Ping of Death attacks, which transmit distorted packets to bring down systems, and SYN floods, which take advantage of the TCP three-way handshake, are frequent instances [9]. Application layer attacks the layer 7 of Open Systems Interconnection by making ostensibly valid requests to web servers or APIs, resulting in resource exhaustion, whereas protocol attacks frequently use connection status tables or CPU cycles [6]. Attacks using HTTP floods are one example. These attacks are stealthy and difficult to detect because they mimic normal user behaviour [11].

The relevance of DDoS attacks to the Internet of Things (IoT) is critical, as IoT devices often suffer from weak security configurations, default credentials, and continuous connectivity, making them prime candidates for recruitment into botnets that perpetrate these attacks [12]. These hacked devices increase the scope and severity of DDoS attacks, endangering the reliability of connected services and infrastructures as the IoT ecosystem grows quickly—it is predicted that there will be over 26.1 million devices in 2023 [13].

Understanding and preventing DDoS assaults in IoT contexts is crucial for preserving data security and service availability, especially in light of the quick growth of IoT devices and their integration into vital infrastructures [14].

2 Related Work

It is recognised that since the primary focus of this research is IoT security, more generic cybersecurity techniques might provide insightful information and possible IoT environment application [2]. For example, methods that have been thoroughly researched in traditional cybersecurity domains, such as anomaly detection and network behaviour analysis, could be modified to improve IoT security frameworks. Many strategies have been put forth and put into practice to stop and lessen DDoS attacks, especially in places like Africa where cybersecurity infrastructure may lag behind the fast growth of IoT use [3].

2.1 Hardware and Software Mitigation Tools

Businesses in South Africa are increasingly using a mix of strong firewalls, traffic scrubbing services, and DDoS mitigation devices. Together, these tools provide a layered defence strategy by detecting and filtering malicious traffic in real-time [4]. For instance, to eliminate attacks before they affect networks, SEACOM's DDoS Protect solution uses sophisticated detection algorithms and autonomous response capabilities [8]. It makes it difficult to detect attacks in real time and requires significant computing power.

2.2 Machine Learning-Based Detection

Machine learning methods have been investigated by researchers to differentiate between attack and legitimate communications [6]. Methods like K-Nearest Neighbors (KNN), Naive Bayes, and Logistic Regression have been used to identify network traffic irregularities that could be signs of DDoS attacks. These techniques use traffic characteristics such as protocol type, source IP, and packet size to categorize traffic with low false positive rates and high accuracy [10].

2.3 Cloud and Network-Level Defences

To absorb and mitigate large-scale volumetric attacks, network behavior analysis and cloud-based traffic scrubbing have been used [9]. In order to preserve service availability, these systems examine incoming packets and remove malicious ones before they enter the company network. Although SDN itself creates new vulnerabilities that need to be mitigated, its integration has also been suggested as a way to more effectively respond to attacks and dynamically manage network resources [14].

Together, these approaches highlight a trend toward combining traditional security tools with intelligent, adaptive algorithms to address the evolving nature of DDoS threats in IoT environments [4].

3 Methodology

This study proposes a hybrid detection framework leveraging Long Short-Term Memory (LSTM) and Adaptive Resonance Theory (ART) algorithms to identify DDoS attacks in IoT network traffic.

3.1 LSTM Algorithm

LSTM, a specialized recurrent neural network, is well-suited for sequential data analysis and time-series prediction because it can remember long-term dependencies. Because of this, it works well for analysing network traffic patterns over time and spotting irregularities that could be signs of DDoS attacks. By using temporal features that it has learned, LSTM is able to differentiate between malicious and legitimate traffic.

3.2 ART Algorithm

ART is a neural network model developed for stable pattern recognition and classification. It makes it possible for the system to adjust to new patterns without losing track of previously learnt knowledge. Because of its stability-plasticity balance, ART can adapt to changing attack environments where new DDoS variations are always appearing.

3.3 Detection Process

In order to reliably and real time detection of DDoS attacks in IoT environments, the detection workflow comprises a number of essential steps: The discovery process begins with the continuous collection of network traffic data from IoT devices and their associated gateways. This raw data undergoes preprocessing steps (data is validated) including noise reduction, normalization, and feature encoding to ensure compatibility with the sequential nature of the LSTM model. After preprocessing, the data is segmented into time series and passed through an LSTM network. Preliminary classification is performed by learning the temporal dependencies and patterns associated with different types of network behaviour, including both harmless and malicious activities. The output of the LSTM is a set of probability distributions over all attack categories obtained through the model's SoftMax activation function. These probability vectors are then fed into an Adaptive Resonance Theory (ART) clustering module, which groups similar results and can dynamically identify new or evolving attack patterns without retraining. The ART module increases the detection granularity by adaptively improving ambiguous or uncertain LSTM predictions, especially for unknown attack signatures. Finally, the decision module interprets the combined results of the LSTM and ART stages and determines whether the incoming network traffic represents harmless activity or one of various predefined attack types, such as DDoS, DoS, Mirai, reconnaissance, etc. This hybrid approach ensures both high detection accuracy and the ability to operate in real time, which is critical to ensuring the security of the rapidly evolving IoT ecosystem.

3.4 Evaluation Metrics

To evaluate the applied hybrid detection system, it is planned to use Evaluation Metrics, which are quantitative measures of analysis of the accuracy, performance and reliability of machine learning models.

F1-score, the harmonic mean of precision and recall, balances these two metrics to provide a comprehensive measure of the model's effectiveness, which is particularly important in imbalanced datasets common in data security. Precision measures the proportion of correctly identified attack instances among all instances classified as attacks, reflecting the system's accuracy in minimizing false positives. Recall denotes the proportion of actual attacks that were correctly detected, highlighting the system's ability to minimize false negatives.

This flowchart in Fig. 1 visualizes the sequential steps from raw IoT network data acquisition through preprocessing, model training, classification, and final evaluation to enable real-time DDoS detection.

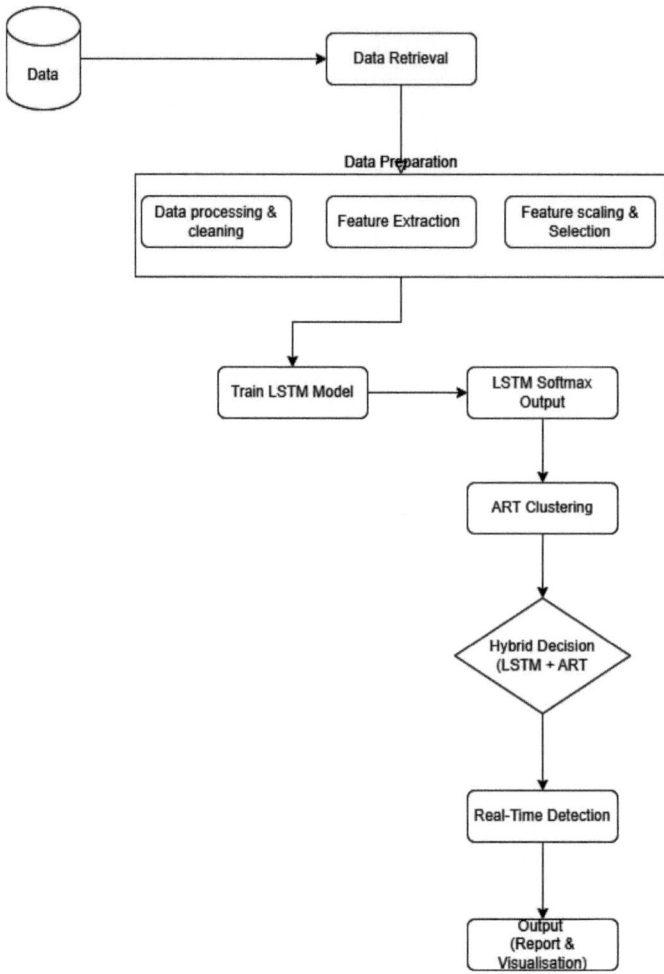

Fig. 1. Model flow chart

4 Practical Implementation

This section examines the experimental findings from our IoT network traffic dataset and presents the real-world application of the suggested hybrid LSTM-ART detection system. The assessment centres on the LSTM model's classification accuracy as well as the specific classification metrics that are obtained from F1-score, precision, and recall.

4.1 Accuracy of LSTM Model

The model's accuracy steadily increases with training, reaching a peak of over 98%. This high accuracy shows that the LSTM network is capable of learning temporal relationships in network traffic data and differentiating between DDoS attack and normal patterns (Fig. 2).

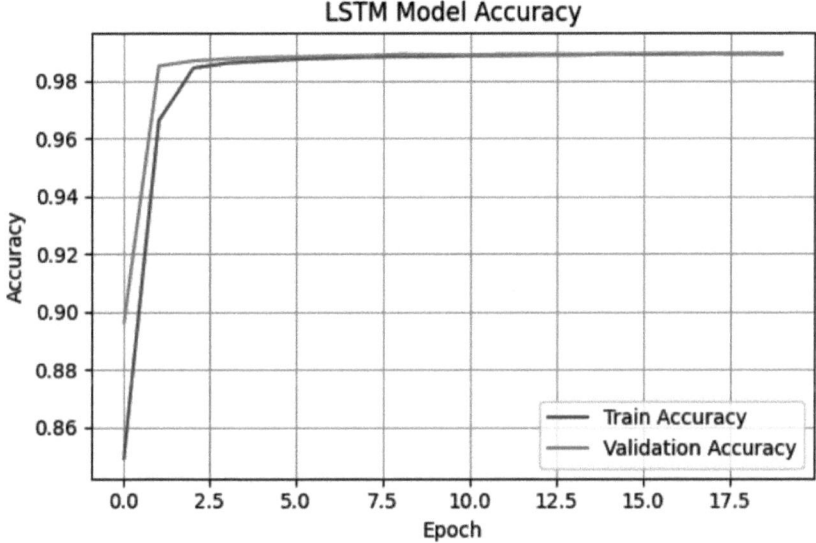

Fig. 2. LSTM model accuracy

The constant convergence of the accuracy measure demonstrates the model's ability to generalize effectively to unknown data, which is critical for real-time detection in dynamic IoT contexts. The LSTM's power to record sequential patterns enables it to detect tiny anomalies indicative of DDoS attacks (Fig. 3).

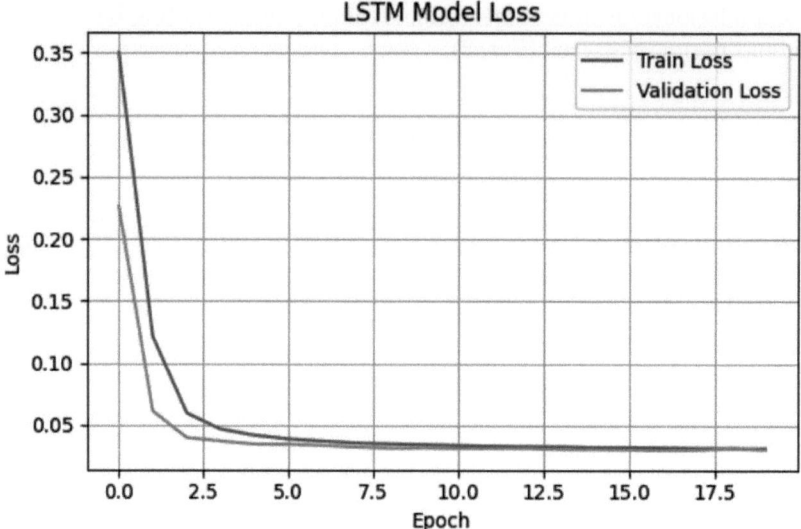

Fig. 3. Model loss convergence

4.2 Classification Report and Metrics

```
◆ LSTM Classification Report:
                      precision    recall  f1-score   support

    Backdoor_Malware       0.00      0.00      0.00        15
       BenignTraffic       0.81      0.93      0.86      4895
      BrowserHijacking     0.00      0.00      0.00        28
      CommandInjection     1.00      0.10      0.17        21
                DDoS       1.00      1.00      1.00    152705
         DNS_Spoofing      0.56      0.33      0.41       807
  DictionaryBruteForce     1.00      0.11      0.19        65
                 DoS       1.00      1.00      1.00     36296
      MITM-ArpSpoofing     0.78      0.67      0.72      1404
                Mirai      1.00      1.00      1.00     11847
                Recon      0.68      0.65      0.66      1427
         SqlInjection      0.00      0.00      0.00        24
      Uploading_Attack     0.00      0.00      0.00         5
     VulnerabilityScan     0.81      0.92      0.86       162
                 XSS       0.00      0.00      0.00        14

            accuracy                           0.99    209715
           macro avg       0.57      0.45      0.46    209715
        weighted avg       0.99      0.99      0.99    209715
```

Fig. 4. Classification report and metrics

Our LSTM model provides exceptional accuracy in threat identification with flawless precision, recall, and F1 score (1.0) in DDoS categorization (Fig. 4).

4.3 Precision Recall

F1 score, and support are the metrics used in the classification report to assess the model. Recall quantifies the detection of every positive instance, whereas precision shows the accuracy of positive predictions. The F1 score is perfect for unbalanced data since it balances the two values. Support determines how many instances of each class there are in reality. When combined, these indicators offer a comprehensive picture of how well the hybrid model can identify various IoT threat types (Fig. 5).

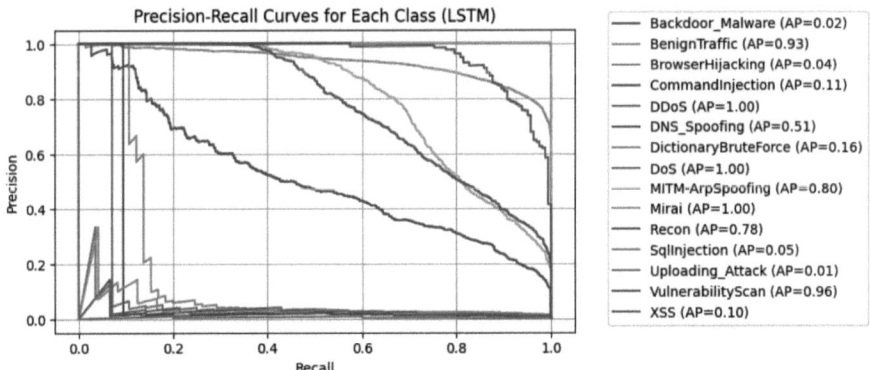

Fig. 5. Precision recall per attacks

4.4 ART Clusters on LSTM SoftMax Outputs

Adaptive Resonance Theory (ART) performs real-time clustering of the probabilistic results generated by the SoftMax layer of the LSTM. By grouping similar SoftMax distributions, ART can dynamically refine classifications and identify new or evolving attack patterns without retraining. This real-time clustering significantly improves the adaptability and responsiveness of attack detection models in rapidly changing IoT environments (Fig. 6).

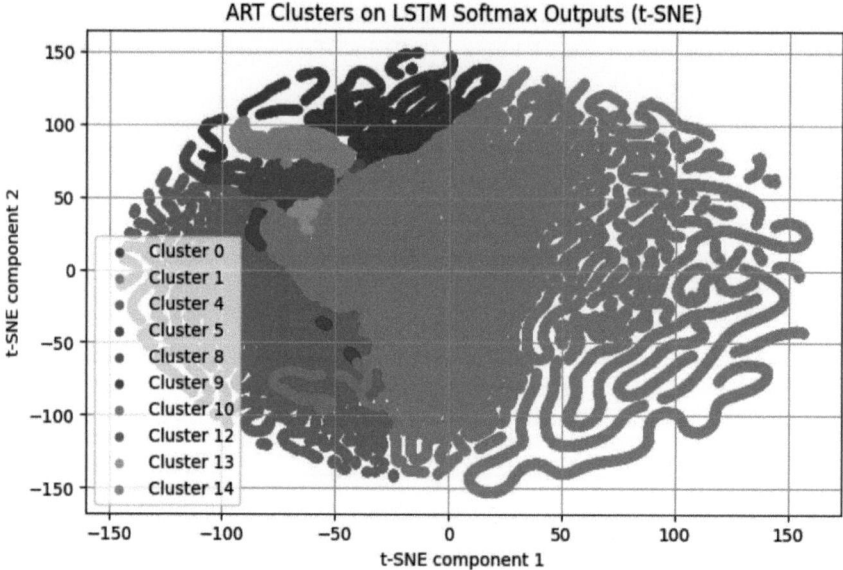

Fig. 6. ART Clustering

4.5 Number of Samples per ART Cluster

The sample distribution among ART (Adaptive Resonance Theory) clusters is depicted in this graph, which shows a notable imbalance. With more than 120,000 samples, Cluster 0 is the largest, whereas the remaining clusters (1, 4, 5, 8, 9, 10, 12, 13, 14) each have fewer than 20,000 samples. The absence of Cluster IDs (2, 3, 6, 7, 11) suggests that there was not enough similarity between the data to generate these groups. The stark difference implies that whereas smaller clusters reflect more specialized subgroups, Cluster 0 represents a dominant pattern in the data. This trend is common in ART algorithms, which frequently generate multiple specialist classifications in addition to a single major "catch-all" category. The results show ART's propensity to focus on broad patterns before identifying minor distinctions, which could be due to either intrinsic data characteristics or the algorithm's parameter sensitivity. Finding significant trends while maintaining significant outliers may be facilitated by this kind of clustering (Fig. 7).

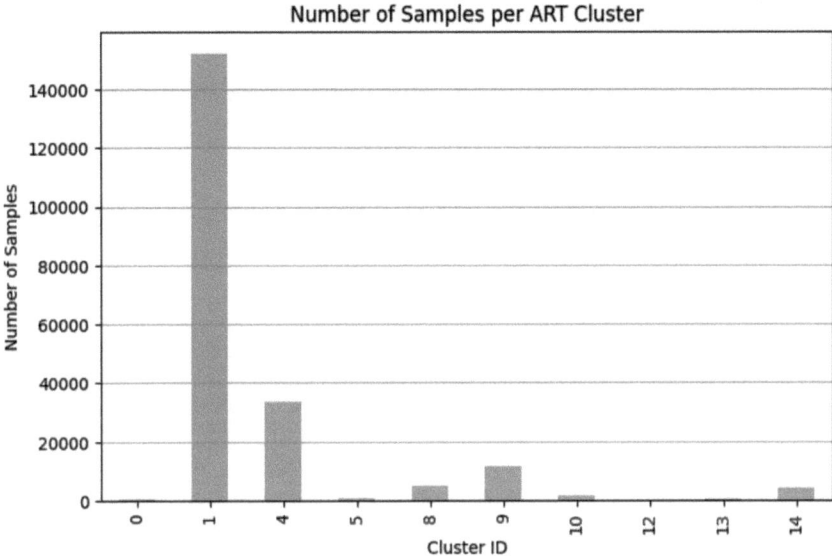

Fig. 7. Number of samples per ART Cluster

5 Conclusion

In this study, the efficacy of combining ART and LSTM algorithms for real-time DDoS attack detection in IoT environments is demonstrated. The hybrid approach uses ART's adaptive classification and LSTM's temporal pattern recognition to achieve a detection accuracy of about 98%. Evaluation using precision, recall, and F1-score metrics confirms the model's balanced performance in correctly identifying attack traffic while minimizing false alarms. These results highlight the potential of advanced machine learning techniques to improve IoT data security against increasingly complex DDoS threats, and future work may concentrate on expanding its applicability across various IoT platforms and integrating this detection system with automated mitigation strategies. Overall, by offering a strong, real-time security solution specifically designed to address the particular difficulties presented by DDoS attacks, our research helps to increase the resilience of IoT infrastructures. In conclusion, it should be noted that the practical implementation serves as an example of the possibility of combining various machine learning algorithms to ensure the security of network traffic.

References

1. Gaur, V.: Security issues in IoT-based environments. Int. Res. J. Eng. Technol. **9001**. www.irjet.net
2. Aldowah, H., Ul Rehman, S., Umar, I.: Security in internet of things: issues, challenges and solutions. In: Saeed, F., Gazem, N., Mohammed, F., Busalim, A. (eds.) IRICT 2018. AISC, vol. 843, pp. 396–405. Springer, Cham (2019). https://doi.org/10.1007/978-3-319-99007-1_38
3. Lata, M., Kumar, V.: Challenges to IoT security: industry perspective. https://www.researchgate.net/publication/373048780
4. Ain, N.U., Sardaraz, M., Tahir, M., Abo Elsoud, M.W., Alourani, A.: Securing IoT networks against DDoS attacks: a hybrid deep learning approach. Sensors **25**(5) (2025). https://doi.org/10.3390/s25051346
5. Zhang, J., Yang, G., Lu, L., Huang, M., Che, M.: A novel visualization method for detecting DDoS network attacks (2010)
6. Bashaiwth, A., Binsalleeh, H., AsSadhan, B.: An explanation of the LSTM model used for DDoS attacks classification. Appl. Sci. (Switz.) **13**(15) (2023). https://doi.org/10.3390/app13158820
7. DDOS BACKGROUND
8. HBK-DDoS-Attack-Handbook-for-Enterprise-May-2021
9. Neto, E.C.P., Dadkhah, S., Ghorbani, A.A.: Collaborative DDoS detection in distributed multi-tenant IoT using federated learning. In: 2022 19th Annual International Conference on Privacy, Security and Trust (PST). IEEE (2022). https://doi.org/10.1109/PST55820.2022.9851984
10. Babjan, S., Yadav, N., Mamatha, G., Sekhar, P.: A new CNN and LSTM algorithm based human activity recognition. https://doi.org/10.48047/nq.2022.20.9.nq44865
11. Sundareswaran, V.: Study of cybersecurity in data breaching. In: Int. J. Adv. Eng. Res. Dev. **5**(03) (2018). https://www.researchgate.net/publication/325300571
12. El-Sofany, H., El-Seoud, S.A., Karam, O.H., Bouallegue, B.: Using machine learning algorithms to enhance IoT system security. Sci. Rep. **14**(1) (2024). https://doi.org/10.1038/s41598-024-62861-y
13. Suvra, D.K.: An efficient real time DDoS detection model using machine learning algorithms (2025). http://arxiv.org/abs/2501.14311
14. Gnana Priya, G., Shriram, S.H., Jeeva, S., Sakthi Priya, G., Balasubadra, K.: Detection of distributed denial of service (DDoS) attack using logistic regression and K nearest neighbor algorithms. Int. J. Intell. Syst. Appl. Eng. http://www.mathtype.com

Short Papers

Short Papers

Machine Learning Models for Intelligent Test Case Selection

Yousof Darwish, Mohammed Al-Refai(✉), and Ahmed Alzubi

Computer Science Department, Faculty of Computer and Information Technology,
Jordan University of Science and Technology, P.O. Box 3030, Irbid 22110, Jordan
mnalrefai@just.edu.jo

Abstract. Regression testing is running test cases after every code change, ensuring that there are no intended breaks in the changes. This study explores the application of machine learning for intelligent test case selection, aiming to reduce testing effort while maintaining test effectiveness. Using a dataset of test case features extracted from commits within the Apache Commons Collections project, we investigated the performance of four classification models: Logistic Regression, Random Forest, Support Vector Classifier (SVC), and Gradient Boosting. Test case selection labels were generated using Ekstazi, a regression test selection technique, to indicate whether a test case would be selected or not. The models were trained and evaluated using a group-based split strategy based on commit hashes to ensure realistic performance estimates that match what is expected in production. Evaluation metrics included accuracy, precision, recall, F1 score, AUC-ROC, and Regression Test Selection (RTS) metrics like safety violation, precision violation, and test suite reduction. The results indicate that Gradient Boosting achieved a favorable balance between test suite reduction and risk mitigation, offering a promising approach for automated test case selection within the context of regression testing. This work highlights the potential of machine learning to replicate and potentially outperform established techniques such as Ekstazi to optimize software testing processes and improve overall development efficiency.

Keywords: Regression test selection · Java software systems · Ekstazi · Static and dynamic analysis · Machine learning

1 Introduction

Regression testing refers to the process of executing test cases following each code modification to verify that no unintentional bugs or failures have been introduced, the number of test cases is generally high, and running them all on each change is costly. Therefore, regression test selection (RTS) optimize regression tests by selection test cases that got affected by code change. Big numbers of research are being dedicated to reduce the cost of regression testing using the approach of RTS [1,2]. To address this challenge, regression test selection

(RTS) tools where developed to reduce the effort of selecting all test cases, and choose the affected test cases only, Among these tools, Ekstazi [3] has shown exceptional results by reducing the number of test cases while ensuring that the selected test cases still effectively evaluate the changes where done. However, these traditional RTS approaches and tools may not always work well in the complex and dynamic nature of the modern systems. In recent years, machine learning has proven itself as an amazing tool for optimizing software testing process. By using historical data, machine learning models can learn patterns and predict the relevance of test cases based on the code changes, offering more flexible approaches to test selection. While the use of machine learning is not new, there still limited research on it's practical application and comparison with established RTS techniques like Ekstazi. This study shows the potential of applying machine learning to the intelligent test case selection within the domain of regression testing. Specifically, we investigate four widely used classification models (Logistic Regression, Random Forest, Support Vector Classifier (SVC), and Gradient Boosting) to demonstrate their effectiveness in the RTS problem. We use a dataset of test case features derived from commits in the apache commons collections project, and evaluate the models using different metrics, including accuracy, precision, recall, and domain-specific metrics like safety violation and test suite reduction.

2 Related Work

A good number of studies have explored techniques to improve software testing, particularly in the domains of regression testing, automation, and the application of machine learning and deep learning techniques. Below, we summarize relevant works that inform and contextualize our approach.

Larsson and Höstklint (2021) – Dynamic Test Case Selection using Machine Learning

In their master's thesis, Larsson and Höstklint [4] propose a machine learning-based model for dynamic test case selection within regression testing. The primary goal is to reduce the number of test cases executed after any code change, without significantly impacting fault detection. They build a supervised learning model using features such as test execution history, code coverage data, and file modification history. Their approach shows that machine learning model can be used to select subsets of test cases and achieve comparable effectiveness to running the full tests, with considerable time savings. This work contributes a practical application of ML to regression testing and demonstrate the importance of feature engineering in learning-based test selection.

Yoo and Harman (2012) – Regression Testing: A Survey

Yoo and Harman [5] provide a comprehensive survey on regression testing techniques, covering three main areas: test case minimization, test case selection, and test case prioritization. They evaluate both static and dynamic analysis techniques and provide classification of existing methods. One of the key contributions is the comparative analysis of strategies in terms of effectiveness, efficiency, and applicability in different contexts. This work does not propose a new method but rather shows the state-of-the-art up to that point, making it a strong reference for anyone researching regression testing optimization.

Zhao, Dua, and Singh (2019) – DeepTest: Testing Autonomous Systems

Zhao et al. [6] present *DeepTest*, a testing for deep neural networks (DNNs) used in autonomous driving systems. The authors recognize that traditional software testing methods fall short when applied to data-driven AI systems. DeepTest generates a made yet realistic driving scenarios by applying transformations (e.g., lighting changes, weather conditions) to input images. These transformations expose corner cases where the deep neural networks gives faulty results (e.g., incorrect steering decisions). This work contributes to the growing area of testing AI-based software and demonstrates how traditional coverage metrics can be extended to neural networks.

Qiu, Zhang, and Khurshid (2019) – Deep Reinforcement Learning for Software Testing

Qiu et al. [7] introduce deep reinforcement learning (DRL) for automated test case generation. Their key is modeling test generation as a reinforcement learning problem, where an agent interacts with the software under test and learns to explode all paths that are likely to expose bugs. The agent receives rewards for uncovering new program behaviors or causing failures, pushing it to intelligently prioritize areas of the code that are more error-prone. Their experimental results show that this method can outperform random testing and traditional methods in terms of coverage and fault detection. This work bridges the gap between AI planning techniques and software test automation.

3 Methodology

3.1 Data Collection and Feature Extraction

To demonstrate the effectiveness of machine learning models in test case selection, we built a dataset from a real-world open-source Java project, namely Apache Commons Collections, a widely-used library that offers reusable data structures for Java. The dataset was constructed by using the historical commits from the oldest SHA 15ad7824 to the newest SHA 6975b056 and extracting both static and dynamic characteristics of test classes across 122 revisions.

Repository and Version History. The Apache Commons Collections repository was cloned from its official Git source, extracting a list of commits was stored. Each commit represents a state of the system, Each commit was included only after verifying that the project built successfully without any errors, The commit selection was designed to ensure coverage across both minor and significant codebase changes, which is important for evaluating the impact on test selection.

Regression Test Selection with Ekstazi. We used Ekstazi, a well-established regression test selection tool for Java, which does a dependency analysis to reduce the set of tests to be rerun after code modifications. Ekstazi was programmatically integrated into the Maven build system by injecting it's profile plugin configuration into the pom.xml file. This integration enabled automatic test selection for each commit using the following steps:

1. The project was cleaned using `mvn clean` to ensure no residual artifacts that affects test selection.
2. Ekstazi was executed via `mvn ekstazi:ekstazi -Pekstazip`, which identifies the minimal set of tests impacted by the changes.
3. The selected test classes were pulled from `.ekstazi` directory within the same project.

This process was repeated for each consecutive pair of commits, simulating realistic regression testing scenarios in a continuous integration pipeline.

Feature Extraction. For each test class located under the standard Maven test directory (`src/test/java`), a set of features was extracted to be used later in the classification. These features aim to capture both static characteristics of the test class and contextual information based on changes in the codebase (Table 1).

Table 1. Extracted features and their descriptions

Feature	Description
`commit_hash`	Git commit identifier corresponding to the version of the project
`test_class`	Fully qualified name of the test class
`ekstazi_selected`	Binary target variable: 1 if the test was selected by Ekstazi, 0 otherwise
`test_class_length`	Total number of lines in the test class, used as a proxy for complexity
`num_test_methods`	Number of methods identified as test cases, either by `@Test` annotation or naming convention
`name_similar_to_changed`	Count of changed source classes whose names partially match the test class name
`unix_time`	Commit timestamp in Unix epoch format, indicating project evolution over time

The static analysis of test classes was performed using the `javalang` parser, which supports syntactic extraction of class and method-level constructs. Changes between code versions were identified using the `git diff` command, filtering only Java source files. The file paths were normalized into class-like representations to enable meaningful similarity comparisons between production and test code artifacts.

The resulting dataset was stored in a structured CSV file and served as the primary input for model training and evaluation in the upcoming stages.

3.2 Data Preprocessing

To prepare the dataset for model training and ensure its suitability for machine learning algorithms, we performed the following data preprocessing steps:

Encoding Categorical Features. Categorical features, such as *commit_hash* and *test_class*, were encoded into numerical representations using Label Encoding. This technique assigns a unique integer to each distinct category within a feature. Label Encoding was chosen for its simplicity and effectiveness in representing categorical data without introducing unnecessary dimensionality [8], as the order of categories is not relevant for our classification task. This transformation allows machine learning models to effectively process and interpret categorical information.

Scaling Numerical Features. Numerical features, including *test_class_length*, *num_test_methods*, *name_similar_to_changed*, and *unix_time*, were scaled using StandardScaler [9]. This technique standardizes numerical features by subtracting the mean and dividing by the standard deviation, resulting in features with zero mean and unit variance. Scaling is important to prevent features with larger ranges from dominating the model training process and ensures that all features contribute equally to the learning process, regardless of their original scales. This step enhances the performance and stability of machine learning models, particularly those sensitive to feature scaling, such as distance-based algorithms and gradient-based optimization methods.

Addressing Class Imbalance. The dataset exhibited a significant class imbalance, with a majority of test cases not selected by Ekstazi. To mitigate the potential bias introduced by this imbalance, we employed the Synthetic Minority Over-sampling Technique (SMOTE) [10]. SMOTE generates synthetic samples of the minority class (Ekstazi-selected test cases) by interpolating between existing minority class data points. This technique effectively balances the class distribution, preventing the model from being overly biased towards the majority class. We used SMOTE with its default parameters to create a balanced dataset, ensuring that both classes are adequately represented during model training and improving the model's ability to generalize to unseen data. These preprocessing steps are essential to enhance the quality and suitability of the dataset for machine learning. Encoding categorical features allows models to handle categorical data effectively. Scaling numerical features ensures that all features contribute equally to the learning process and prevents features with larger ranges from dominating. Addressing class imbalance using SMOTE mitigates potential bias towards the majority class and improves the model's ability to generalize to unseen data. By carefully preprocessing the data, we aim to improve the performance, stability, and robustness of the machine learning models used for intelligent test case selection.

3.3 Feature Engineering

To potentially enhance the predictive power of the machine learning models, we performed feature engineering by creating new features from the existing ones. This process involved two main approaches:

Interaction Features. We engineered interaction features by multiplying pairs of existing features that were hypothesized to have a combined effect on Ekstazi's selection behavior. Specifically, we created the following interaction features:

- *interaction_1*: This feature represents the interaction between *test class length* and *num test methods*, capturing the potential influence of both the length of the test class and the number of test methods within it on test case selection.
- *interaction_2*: This feature represents the interaction between *name similar to changed* and *unix time*, aiming to capture the potential impact of the similarity between test names and changed code, combined with the temporal aspect of the commit.

These interaction features were included to allow models to learn more complex relationships between features that might not be captured by individual features alone.

Polynomial Features. To further explore non-linear relationships within the data, we utilized PolynomialFeatures to generate polynomial features of degree 2 from the numerical features (*test class length, num test methods, name similar to changed*, and *unix time*). This process creates new features by raising the original features to powers up to the specified degree, introducing quadratic terms and potentially capturing curvature in the relationships between features and the target variable.

Feature Selection. After generating the interaction and polynomial features, we performed feature selection to retain only the most relevant features for model training. This was done by calculating the absolute correlation between each feature and the target variable (Ekstazi selection) and removing features with a correlation below a threshold of 0.05. This step aimed to reduce the dimensionality of the dataset, potentially improving model training efficiency and preventing overfitting by excluding features with minimal predictive power.

3.4 Model Selection and Training

For the task of test case selection, we investigated four widely used classification models: Logistic Regression [11], Random Forest [12], Support Vector Classifier (SVC) [13], and Gradient Boosting [14].

Model Selection. The selection of these models was based on their established performance in various classification tasks and their suitability for handling binary classification problems like test case selection. Each model offers a different approach to learning patterns from data, allowing us to explore a diverse range of algorithms and compare their effectiveness for our specific task.

Hyperparameter Tuning. To optimize the performance of each model, we performed hyperparameter tuning using GridSearchCV. This technique involves defining a grid of hyperparameter values for each model and systematically evaluating the model's performance using different combinations of these values. We used 5-fold cross-validation to ensure robust performance estimates during the tuning process. The F1-score was chosen as the evaluation metric for hyperparameter optimization, as it provides a good balance between precision and recall, which are crucial for test case selection.

Group-Based Splitting. To ensure realistic and unbiased performance estimates, we employed a group-based splitting strategy using GroupShuffleSplit. This technique ensures that data points belonging to the same commit (group) are either entirely in the training set or the testing set, preventing data leakage and maintaining the independence of test cases across different commits. This approach is a must for evaluating the models' ability to generalize to unseen commits, as it simulates the real-world scenario of applying the model to new code changes. The data was split into 80% for training and 20% for testing, and the training set was further divided into 75% for training and 25% for validation, maintaining the group-based splitting strategy throughout the process.

4 Results

This section presents the performance results of the four machine learning models evaluated for test case selection with machine learning: Logistic Regression, Random Forest, Support Vector Classifier (SVC), and Gradient Boosting. Each model was trained on the engineered and preprocessed dataset described in the previous sections, with evaluation conducted on a held-out test set using group-based splitting to ensure no data leakage across commits. Performance was assessed using standard classification metrics: accuracy, precision, recall, F1-score, and Area Under the Receiver Operating Characteristic Curve (AUC-ROC). Additionally, Regression Test Selection (RTS) evaluation metrics, including safety violation, precision violation, and test suite reduction, were calculated to further assess the practical effectiveness of the models in reducing test suite sizes while maintaining safety.

4.1 Logistic Regression

The Logistic Regression model achieved an accuracy of 66.67%, with a high recall of 99.82% and a corresponding F1-score of 0.7980. However, the precision was relatively low at 66.47%, indicating a tendency to over-predict the positive class (Ekstazi-selected tests). The AUC-ROC score was 0.4621, suggesting limited ability to discriminate between classes across different thresholds. The classification report showed poor performance in identifying unselected test cases (class 0), with a recall of only 2%.

4.2 Random Forest

The Random Forest classifier attained an accuracy of 61.87%. Notably, it achieved a much higher precision of 83.06%, though this came at the cost of a lower recall of 53.01% compared to Logistic Regression. The F1-score was 0.6472, and the AUC-ROC improved significantly to 0.6688, indicating a better balance between sensitivity and specificity. Unlike Logistic Regression, the model showed greater ability to identify non-selected tests (class 0), achieving a recall of 79% in that category.

4.3 Support Vector Classifier (SVC)

The SVC model produced results similar to Logistic Regression, with an accuracy of 66.67%, precision of 66.43%, and a recall of 100%. This yielded the highest F1-score among all models at 0.7983. However, similar to Logistic Regression, SVC struggled to identify unselected tests, resulting in a recall of only 2% for class 0. AUC-ROC was not available due to the lack of probability scores in the default SVC configuration.

4.4 Gradient Boosting

Gradient Boosting achieved an accuracy of 62.34%, with a precision of 73.82% and a recall of 66.49%. Its F1-score was 0.6996, indicating solid performance across both classes. The AUC-ROC score was 0.6394, slightly lower than Random Forest but still indicative of reasonable classification capability. Gradient Boosting showed a more balanced treatment of both classes, with a 54% recall for class 0 and 66% for class 1.

4.5 Comparative Analysis

A summary of the results is shown in Table 2. While Logistic Regression and SVC achieved the highest recall and F1-scores, they suffered from poor ability to detect unselected tests, as reflected in their low AUC-ROC scores. Random Forest and Gradient Boosting, although slightly less accurate in terms of F1-score, offered more balanced performance and stronger discrimination ability, especially in identifying both positive and negative test cases. These findings highlight the trade-off between aggressive positive class prediction and balanced generalization.

Table 3 presents the RTS evaluation metrics for each model. Random Forest achieved the highest test suite reduction with relatively low safety violation [15], making it the best choice in terms of minimizing test suite size while maintaining a high level of safety. SVC and Logistic Regression had lower test suite reductions and higher safety violations. Gradient Boosting, while offering balanced performance, did not outperform Random Forest in terms of test suite reduction and experienced higher precision violations [15].

Table 2. Classification performance comparison of models

Model	Accuracy	Precision	Recall	F1-score	AUC-ROC
Logistic Regression	0.667	0.665	**0.998**	0.798	0.462
Random Forest	0.619	**0.831**	0.530	0.647	**0.669**
Support Vector Classifier	0.667	0.664	1.000	0.798	N/A
Gradient Boosting	0.623	0.738	0.665	0.700	0.639

Table 3. RTS evaluation metrics comparison of models

Model	Safety Violation	Precision Violation	Test Suite Reduction
Logistic Regression	0.3349	0.0012	0.0094
Random Forest	0.0976	0.4240	**0.5789**
Support Vector Classifier	0.3357	0.0000	0.0070
Gradient Boosting	0.1908	0.2712	0.4058

5 Conclusion

The evaluation of four machine learning models for intelligent test case selection—Logistic Regression, Random Forest, Support Vector Classifier (SVC), and Gradient Boosting—reveals distinct trade-offs in terms of performance, safety, and precision violations, as well as test suite reduction.

Logistic Regression and SVC both exhibited high safety violations, indicating that they are selecting a significant number of tests that Ekstazi did not deem necessary. While both models showed very low precision violations, their test suite reductions were minimal, suggesting that they are rather conservative in their approach. This behavior might be beneficial in situations where minimizing the risk of missing critical tests is a priority, but it results in lower efficiency in terms of reducing the test suite size.

On the other hand, Random Forest achieved the highest test suite reduction but at the cost of a high precision violation. This implies that Random Forest aggressively reduces the test suite, potentially missing important tests that Ekstazi considers essential. This trade-off could be risky, particularly in scenarios where missing critical functionality could lead to significant issues.

Gradient Boosting struck a balance between the extremes. It provided a reasonable test suite reduction while maintaining moderate safety and precision violations. This suggests that Gradient Boosting is neither too aggressive nor too conservative, making it a well-rounded choice for test case selection.

In conclusion, Gradient Boosting appears to be the best overall choice for intelligent test case selection in this specific scenario. It offers a balanced approach that reduces the test suite without significantly compromising the accuracy of test case selection. However, the selection of the optimal model depends on several factors, including:

Risk Tolerance: If the project has a very low tolerance for missing critical bugs, models like Logistic Regression or SVC, with their low precision violations, might be more suitable, despite their limited test suite reduction.

Computational Resources: If reducing execution time is a priority and some risk of missing tests is acceptable, Random Forest could be a viable choice due to its high test suite reduction.

Context: Ultimately, the "best" model is context-dependent. The trade-offs between safety, precision, and test suite reduction should be carefully weighed against the specific needs and priorities of the project. Therefore, it's essential to consider the risk appetite and project objectives before making a final decision.

References

1. Harrold, M.J., et al.: Regression test selection for Java software. In: OOPSLA, pp. 312–326 (2001)
2. Orso, A., Shi, N., Harrold, M.J.: Scaling regression testing to large software systems. In: FSE, pp. 241–251 (2004)
3. Gligoric, M., Eloussi, L., Marinov, D.: Practical regression test selection with dynamic file dependencies. In: ISSTA, pp. 211–222 (2015)
4. Larsson, J., and Höstklint, N.: Dynamic test case selection using machine learning. Master's thesis, Linnaeus University (2021)
5. Yoo, S., Harman, M.: Regression testing minimization, selection and prioritization: a survey. Softw. Test. Verificat. Reliabil. **22**(2), 67–120 (2012)
6. Zhao, Y., Dua, D., and Singh, S.: DeepTest: automated testing of deep-neural-network-driven autonomous cars. In: Proceedings of the 40th International Conference on Software Engineering (2019)

7. Qiu, X., Zhang, L., Khurshid, S.: A deep reinforcement learning framework for software testing. In: Proceedings of the 41st International Conference on Software Engineering (ICSE), pp. 347–358 (2019)
8. Pedregosa, F., et al.: Scikit-learn: machine learning in python. J. Mach. Learn. Res. **12**, 2825–2830 (2011)
9. Scikit-learn: Preprocessing data—StandardScaler. https://scikit-learn.org/stable/modules/generated/sklearn.preprocessing.StandardScaler.html
10. Chawla, N.V., Bowyer, K.W., Hall, L.O., Kegelmeyer, W.P.: SMOTE: synthetic minority over-sampling technique. J. Artif. Intell. Res. **16**, 321–357 (2002)
11. Scikit-learn: Logistic Regression. https://scikit-learn.org/stable/modules/generated/sklearn.linear$\_$i$model.LogisticRegression.html
12. Scikit-learn: Random Forest Classifier. https://scikit-learn.org/stable/modules/generated/sklearn.ensemble.RandomForestClassifier.html
13. Scikit-learn: Support Vector Classification. https://scikit-learn.org/stable/modules/generated/sklearn.svm.SVC.html
14. Scikit-learn: Gradient Boosting Classifier. https://scikit-learn.org/stable/modules/generated/sklearn.ensemble.GradientBoostingClassifier.html
15. Sirin, E., and Gotlieb, A.: Ekstazi: cost-effective and accurate regression testing in the large. In: Proceedings of the 25th International Symposium on Software Testing and Analysis, pp. 347–357 (2016)

Continuous Sky View Factor Calculations Using a Parallel GPU Workflow

Max van der Waal(✉) [iD] and Daniela Maiullari [iD]

Delft University of Technology, 2628 BL Delft, The Netherlands
m.vanderwaal@tudelft.nl

Abstract. The Sky View Factor (SVF) is a key parameter in urban climate modelling, which quantifies the fraction of the visible sky from a given point and allows for the estimation of incident solar radiation, thermal comfort, and urban heat distribution. High resolution in SVF computation is essential for microclimatic studies in the canopy layer, where detailed representations of urban environments are crucial for understanding variations in heat exposure. Traditional SVF calculation methods often rely on sequential processing of shadow projections, however, these methods are computationally intensive and time-consuming, particularly for urban climate analyses at high resolution.

These computational challenges are further magnified when incorporating complex components such as vegetation, where tree crowns exhibit intricate geometries, partial transparency, and permit sky visibility from beneath the canopy. These properties require detailed modeling to account for light penetration and obstruction. This significantly increases the computational cost of Sky View Factor calculations and extends runtime to hours or even days, depending on scale and resolution.

This study introduces a novel GPU-accelerated ray tracing approach for SVF calculation, designed to address the computational limitations of traditional methods for large-scale analyses. By utilizing NVIDIA GPUs and the CUDA programming framework, the method applies parallel computing to perform ray tracing across the full range of azimuth and altitude angles. It estimates SVFs by systematically weighting blocked rays based on their spatial contributions to the hemisphere.

The accuracy of the developed method is validated through two complementary approaches. First, modelled SVF values are compared against theoretical expectations derived from idealized geometric environments. Additionally, a test case on a neighbourhood in Rotterdam is conducted to compare the results of the developed method against those obtained using an established SVF estimation technique using a serial approach. In addition to accuracy, computational efficiency is evaluated by comparing processing times across different study area extents with those of a CPU-based implementation. The proposed GPU workflow achieves a 99% reduction in processing time compared to traditional shadow casting methods performed on a CPU, while maintaining similarly high resolution and accuracy.

Keywords: Sky View Factor · PyCUDA · GPU computing · Ray Tracing · Urban Climate Modelling · Urban Form

1 Introduction

Urban form strongly influences urban climate at the micro and local scale [1, 2], by impacting thermal and aerodynamic processes, contributing to the trapping of solar energy and anthropogenic heat, increasing thermal storage, and reducing wind speed and evaporative cooling [3]. These mechanisms explain why air and surface temperatures are higher in cities than in rural areas, a phenomenon known as the Urban Heat Island (UHI) effect.

In observational and modelling climate studies, a conspicuous number of morphological attributes and descriptors have been used to better understand these multiple relationships with energy and heat exchanges. Among these, vertical openness is a form attribute that conveys the degree of the urban fabric's openness to the sky and determines the amount of incoming shortwave radiation as well as the amount of long-wave radiation returned to the sky [4].

The main parameter that describes vertical openness is the Sky View Factor (SVF), defined as the proportion of sky that is visible at a given location. In quantitative terms, SVF captures the three-dimensional structure of the built environment as a two-dimensional metric [5], expressed as a unitless value between 0 (completely obstructed sky) and 1 (fully unobstructed sky). This parameter effectively quantifies how urban morphology modifies incoming radiation fluxes, directly influencing thermal conditions experienced in cities.

In urban climate studies, spatially explicit representations of SVF values across an entire urban area are critical to modelling urban microclimate and to better understand the distribution of heat exposure. These continuous SVFs are calculated for each pixel within the study region, creating a continuous map of values. Unlike discrete point measurements, these maps reveal patterns of sky view obstruction throughout the modeled environment. By capturing this spatial continuity, researchers can identify patterns and relationships between urban form, climate, and sky view obstruction that would not be apparent from isolated point measurements. This comprehensive spatial perspective helps urban planners and designers make informed decisions about urban compositions, street orientation, and public space design to optimize thermal comfort and mitigate urban heat island effects.

However, the generation of continuous SVF datasets at large scales proves to be computationally expensive and remains a critical challenge in urban climatology. Calculating the SVF for a single location is computationally demanding, as it involves aggregating shadow determinations across a range of azimuth and altitude angles to evaluate sky visibility. This demand increases substantially when the process is scaled to every pixel in a study area to generate continuous SVF maps [6]. High-resolution SVF calculations often require hours of processing time due to the large number of computations involved. This issue limits the integration of SVF-driven analyses into iterative urban design workflows and constrains the spatial extent of heat island studies to localized areas rather than city-wide or regional scales [7].

This study addresses the challenge of reducing the processing time of continuous SVF estimations by proposing a novel GPU-accelerated ray tracing approach. The paper begins with a concise review of existing SVF estimation techniques, outlining their respective benefits and limitations. It then describes the implementation of the proposed GPU-based workflow, along with 3 methods to assess its computational performance. The outcomes of these evaluations are used to demonstrate the method's accuracy and efficiency, followed by a discussion of its practical implications and potential applications.

1.1 Methods for Estimating SVFs

Over the past decades, efforts to quantify the visible sky from urban surfaces have led to a wide array of methods. Traditional techniques such as shadow-casting and ray tracing have laid the groundwork for computational SVF estimation, while newer approaches, such as synthetic fisheye algorithms, offer alternative perspectives that leverage advances in rendering and image-based analysis.

Following the shadow casting method, the SVF is estimated by simulating the obstruction of virtual light sources distributed across a hemispherical dome [8, 9]. Using high-resolution digital elevation models (DEMs), this method projects light rays from predefined azimuth and altitude angles to determine sky visibility. CPU-based implementations are computationally intensive, as they require iterating through thousands of light positions and calculating shadows for each DEM cell. Processing a 1 km2 urban area at 1-m resolution can take hours on standard CPUs, limiting scalability for city-wide analyses. Despite these constraints, shadow casting remains valued for its geometric accuracy and compatibility with coarse-resolution DEMs.

Ray tracing methods estimate SVFs by tracing a multitude of imaginary rays from ground points to the sky dome and calculating the fraction of unobstructed rays. This method, exemplified by tools like HORAYZON [10], processes high-resolution results by iteratively checking intersections between rays and elevations of 3D features. While highly accurate, CPU-based applications struggle with memory management for large datasets, often resorting to terrain simplification or subsampling to reduce computational load [10]. Despite these challenges, ray tracing on CPU achieves sub-0.05 RMSE in validation against fisheye photography [11], making it one of the most reliable methods for estimating continuous SVFs.

Since the introduction of platforms such as Google Street View, the amount of data and access to street-level imagery has grown exponentially. Synthetic fisheye methods generate SVF estimates by creating (artificial) hemispherical views using fisheye photographs, 3D urban models, or satellite data [12]. This approach automates the production of fisheye-like images at arbitrary spatial resolutions (e.g., 5-m grids) and computes SVF through equiangular projection, which corrects distortions inherent in traditional fisheye photography. A key advantage is its reliance on widely available geospatial datasets, eliminating the need for fieldwork. Validation studies comparing synthetic results to ground-truth street view imagery show strong correlations (e.g., $R2 > 0.85$) [13], though vegetation occlusion remains a persistent limitation.

1.2 Study Objective: Parallel Computing Using CUDA

This study aims to develop an approach and related workflow for GPU-accelerated continuous SVF estimation. Parallel computing using GPU acceleration has revolutionized data-intensive fields by leveraging massively parallel architectures to process large datasets faster than traditional CPU-based methods. This approach is particularly interesting for raster data processing and geospatial analyses, where operations on grid-based geospatial arrays benefit from the GPU's ability to execute data-parallel tasks through SIMD/SIMT (single instruction, multiple data/thread) architectures.

CUDA and PyCUDA showed great potential for accelerating raster data processing through data parallelism. CUDA (Compute Unified Device Architecture) is NVIDIA's parallel computing platform that enables developers to harness GPU acceleration for general-purpose processing. PyCUDA allows direct GPU programming within Python environments. This combination enables parallel computations that significantly outperform CPU-based approaches.

To minimize the shared memory contention, data partitioning is applied to match the data to the GPU block sizes. As the capability of GPUs to do conditional logic is limited due to thread divergence, a hybrid CPU-GPU workflow is needed, where logic-heavy tasks should be performed by the CPU, whereas the matrix operations should be offloaded to the GPU for faster processing.

2 Methodology

2.1 Workflow Development

The workflow is structured into four distinct phases, each designed to streamline the process and enhance scalability across large spatial domains.

The first phase involves reading and initializing input parameters. This method relies on ray tracing to assess urban form and vegetation using a set of 2D raster-based elevation models in GeoTIFF format, which are widely available for most locations globally. By utilizing raster elevation data rather than full 3D models, the approach increases both accessibility and computational efficiency.

The workflow is centered on three key elevation datasets:

- Digital Surface Model (DSM): The topographic surface height, including buildings and other anthropogenic structures.
- Canopy Digital Surface Model (CDSM): The height of the vegetation canopy relative to ground level.
- Trunk Digital Surface Model (TDSM): The base height of the vegetation canopy. A point cloud was used to approximate this data. Cloud points resembling vegetation were isolated, clustered, and the 5th percentile of height values within each cluster was selected to represent the canopy base.

Processing parameters such as trace radius and angular interval are defined to balance precision and performance. The trace radius determines the maximum search distance for obstructions, with higher values improving accuracy at the cost of computational time. Similarly, smaller angular intervals produce finer angular resolution but increase processing time. For this study, the maximum trace radius is set to 400 pixels, with an angular interval of 5 degrees.

In the second phase, the CUDA kernel configuration is established. The block size is set to match the GPU thread block structure, and the grid size is calculated accordingly to enable efficient data partitioning. The input data is then transferred from the CPU to the GPU, and GPU memory is allocated for the output arrays.

In the third phase, the core ray tracing routine is performed within the GPU kernel. For this, two nested loops were used: the outer loop iterates over altitude angles, and the inner loop over azimuth angles. These angles are used as directions for the rays to be traced. For each altitude angle, a corresponding weight is computed to represent its contribution to the hemispherical SVF.

Altitude weights are computed using the following expression:

$$A_{weighted} = \cos(\alpha) \cdot \Delta\alpha \cdot \left[\cos\left(\alpha - \frac{2\Delta}{\alpha}\right) - \cos\left(\alpha + \frac{\Delta\alpha}{2}\right)\right] \quad (1)$$

Here, $\cos(\alpha)$ serves as the altitude weighting, reflecting the influence of radiative flux from different sky regions. The remainder of the expression calculates the surface area on the hemisphere associated with a given altitude band and angular interval.

During each iteration of the azimuth loop, rays are traced from each pixel on the DSM, advancing stepwise in the direction defined by the current azimuth and altitude. At each step, the ray's x, y, and z coordinates are updated based on the azimuth, altitude, and current ray length. The ray height is compared against the elevation values from the DSM, CDSM, and TDSM at the corresponding x,y position to determine if any ray obstruction is encountered. If the ray's z-value at that point does not exceed the height of the elevation model, the ray is considered obstructed. If the ray's z-value is higher, it contributes to the SVF based on its computed weight.

In the fourth phase, the SVF at each pixel is calculated as:

$$SVF = \frac{\sum(unobstructed\ ray\ weights)}{\sum(all\ ray\ weights)} \quad (2)$$

When calculated across all pixels, these values yield a continuous SVF map.

This method improves upon traditional SVF estimation techniques by integrating multiple elevation layers and incorporating vertical vegetation structure. The inclusion of the TDSM enables the calculation of SVF beneath tree canopies, thereby capturing visibility at street level—an aspect often overlooked in standard methods that either assess from treetop level or disregard vegetation entirely.

2.2 Assessment Methods

To prove the use of the novel workflow and assess its usability, three additional assessment methods were employed in this study.

Comparison to Theoretical SVF Values

To evaluate the accuracy of the proposed sky view factor (SVF) estimation method, results were systematically compared to theoretical benchmarks derived from idealized geometries. Infinitely long street canyons (height-to-width ratios: 1:2, 1:1, 2:1) and circular basins (height-to-radius ratios: 1:2, 1:1, 2:1) were analyzed, with theoretical SVF values calculated using geometric principles. The circular basin represents a circular urban canyon, where obstructions of uniform height are positioned equidistantly at all angles around the midpoint.

Computed SVF values from the proposed method were compared to theoretical benchmarks, with absolute errors quantified as their numerical differences. This analysis provides a controlled framework to verify accuracy, establishing baseline performance metrics for reliable application in real-world environments. The formulae below are used to calculate the SVF value for the mid-points of infinitely long canyons (Eq. 3) and circular basins (Eq. 4), based on their H: W-ratio.

Infinitely long canyons:

$$SVF_{mid-canyon} = \cos\left(\tan^{-1}(2*H/W)\right) \quad (3)$$

Circular basin:

$$SVF_{mid-basin} = \cos^2(\beta) \quad (4)$$

Comparison Against UMEP in a Real-world Test Case

The second assessment evaluates the proposed GPU-accelerated workflow against the established Urban Multi-scale Environmental Predictor (UMEP) Processing plugin in QGIS [9], using a 1,650 × 1,400-pixel study area (total of 2,310,000 pixels) in Rotterdam's Blijdorp neighborhood. Two SVF calculations were performed with the two methods using the same input data sources, such as elevation data from the AHN[1] and BGT[2]. The absolute error between the two results was calculated.

Computational Time

To evaluate the computational performance of the method across varying input sizes, nine synthetic test environments were created, ranging from 400 × 400 to 2000 × 2000 pixels. Each environment was composed of repeated 200 × 200-pixel tiles featuring a standard geometric pattern: urban canyons with 20 m-high buildings spaced 100 m apart, and 10 m-high trees placed every 10 m along the streets, with a canopy base height of 2.5 m. For each extent, corresponding DSM, CDSM, and TDSM layers were generated to ensure full algorithmic load.

A continuous SVF was estimated using both the proposed method and the UMEP Processing Plugin for QGIS, a widely used CPU-based tool for SVF calculation. For each raster extent, processing times were recorded, and computational performance was evaluated by calculating the average number of pixels processed per second for each extent. This metric provides a comparative measure of efficiency across different spatial resolutions.

---

[1] Actueel Hoogtebestand Nederland.
[2] Basisregistratie Grootschalige Topografie.

3 Results

3.1 Comparison to Theoretical SVF Values

The comparison between the SVF generated for generic canyons with the developed and theoretical methods shows absolute errors ranging from 0.000 to 0.003. The script is run with an angular interval of 5.0 degrees and a maximum trace radius of 400 pixels. These minor deviations are likely due to the angular interval settings. Reducing the interval size would improve the accuracy of the obstruction height determination, leading to more precise SVF values (Table 1).

Table 1. Validation of SVF-calculation based on theoretical SVF-values for different test cases.

	Theoretical SVF	Calculated SVF	Absolute Error
Canyon H:W 1:2	0.8944	0.896	0.003
Canyon H:W 1:1	0.4472	0.766	0.001
Canyon H:W 2:1	0.2425	0.244	0.001
Basin H:R 1:2	0.8000	0.800	0.000
Basin H:R 1:1	0.5000	0.500	0.000
Basin H:R 2:1	0.2000	0.201	0.001

3.2 Test Case – Rotterdam Blijdorp

The SVF values calculated for a sample urban area using the developed workflow show strong agreement with those from UMEP, with a mean difference of − 0.0012 and a mean absolute error below 1%. The spatial discrepancy pattern shows a slight SVF underestimation at building roofs and overestimation in densely obstructed areas. This corresponds to anisotropic errors observed in shadow-casting algorithms when resolving complex vertical structures. The minor deviations fall within empirical tolerances established for urban radiative exchange modelshttps://centaur.reading.ac.uk/85498/1/1-s2.0-S2212095519300604-main.pdf [14], suggesting the method's reliability for urban climate studies (Fig. 1).

3.3 Processing Time

When comparing computing time across the geometrically generated test setups with varying spatial extents, the developed workflow significantly outperforms the CPU-based alternative. While the UMEP Processing Plugin's shadow-casting algorithm exhibited exponential time complexity (68.2 s at 400 × 400 vs. 6,000 s at 2000 × 2000), the GPU implementation maintained near-linear scaling (4.6 to 44.3 s), a 135 times speedup at the largest tested extent. At 2000 × 2000 resolution (4 million pixels), the GPU's 44.3-s runtime translates to an effective throughput of 90,293 pixels/second compared

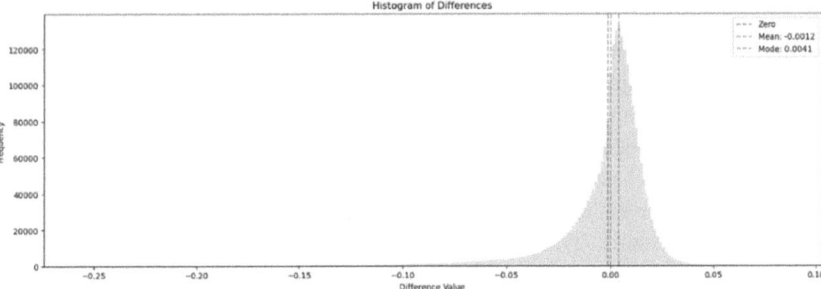

Fig. 1. Differences in SVF values between the CPU-based and proposed SVF estimation method.

to UMEP's 666 pixels/second. For urban climate modeling workflows requiring continuous SVF mapping across city-scale domains (>10 km2), the method eliminates computational bottlenecks inherent to CPU-bound radiative transfer models, enabling simulations previously constrained by hardware limitations (Fig. 2).

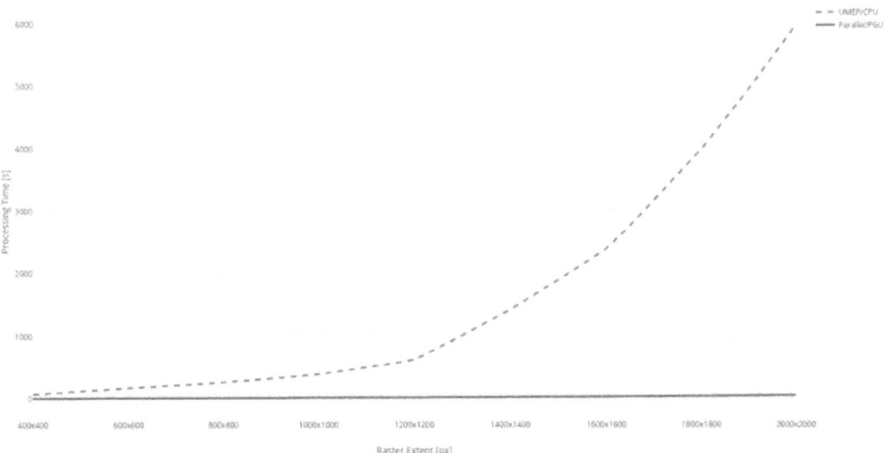

Fig. 2. Processing times of the UMEP Processing plugin for QGIS versus the proposed GPU-accelerated method.

3.4 Workflow Development and Discussions

The accelerated computing capacity enabled by GPU implementation allows for more sophisticated calculations that differentiate between vegetation and building obstructions. This distinction permits more accurate modeling of street-level thermal conditions, particularly in areas with significant tree canopy coverage. The ability to calculate SVF values at the street level underneath tree canopies better represents the actual thermal experience of street users.

The computational efficiency gained through GPU acceleration permits the processing of high-resolution input data (up to resolutions as small as 0.25 m), which was previously impractical. This advancement is significant because the accuracy of SVF calculations is heavily dependent on the resolution of the underlying elevation data. By processing higher resolution data, GPU-accelerated methods produce more accurate representations of the urban environment, capturing nuanced variations in its surroundings that significantly influence radiation exchanges.

Furthermore, GPU acceleration enables the implementation of ray tracing-based algorithms, which have shown greater efficiency improvements compared to shadow casting-based algorithms. The ability to process larger geographic areas with high-resolution data addresses a fundamental limitation in previous approaches, where SVF applications were often restricted to small urban areas due to computational constraints, facilitating comprehensive urban-scale analyses that were previously unfeasible.

The enhanced computational efficiency of GPU-accelerated SVF calculations fundamentally alters how these climate parameters can be incorporated into urban design and planning workflows. Traditionally, SVF calculations are primarily utilized as post-design assessment tools rather than active design instruments. The extended calculation times meant that SVF analysis was typically performed after design decisions had been finalized, serving as a validation mechanism rather than informing the design process itself. With this workflow, thermal comfort assessments can now be completed within minutes. Further acceleration and parallelization of related processes could enable near-instant thermal comfort simulations, offering the ability to evaluate design options in real time and integrate microclimate performance directly into iterative design decision-making.

Despite the significant advancements in SVF calculation methodologies, several methodological considerations warrant attention. The accuracy of SVF calculations remains dependent on the quality and resolution of input data and processing settings. The resolution and accuracy of the SVFs are dependent on the angular resolution and search radius of the rays. While GPU acceleration enables the processing of higher resolution data, the acquisition of detailed urban geometry information, particularly for vegetation structures, presents an ongoing challenge. Additionally, the GPU memory has practical limitations in handling extremely large raster datasets. Most consumer-grade GPUs are equipped with 8 to 24 GB of VRAM, placing an upper bound on the maximum raster extent that can be processed in a single pass. For high-resolution inputs (e.g., 0.25 m), this generally allows for computation of areas up to km^2. Beyond that, memory overflow or allocation failures may occur, requiring raster tiling.

4 Conclusion

This study demonstrates the reliability and advantages of GPU-accelerated SVF estimation through validation against theoretical models and established computational methods. The proposed workflow achieves high computational efficiency while maintaining the accuracy required for urban climate modeling applications.

The GPU-based method exhibited strong agreement with theoretical SVF values across fictional urban geometries, showing absolute errors ≤ 0.003 when compared to Oke's radiation-based models for infinite canyons and circular basins [5]. The validation against UMEP's shadow-casting algorithm in a real-world urban context (Blijdorp,

Rotterdam) further demonstrated a mean absolute error < 1% across 2.31 million spatial units. Spatial error patterns aligned with known anisotropic limitations of raster-based SVF estimation, particularly in complex geometries where roof edges and dense vegetation introduce micro-scale uncertainties [9].

The computational performance analysis revealed substantial efficiency improvements with the GPU-accelerated implementation. The GPU processed 4 million pixels in just 44.3 s, while the UMEP required 6,764 s for the same task at 2000 × 2000 resolution, representing a 135-fold increase in processing speed. The parallelized workflow demonstrates near-linear time complexity, which provides a fundamental advantage over the exponential scaling observed in traditional CPU-based methods. This computational efficiency enables city-scale SVF mapping on standard consumer hardware. The proposed method achieves processing rates of 90,293 pixels per second compared to merely 666 pixels per second with serial CPU processing.

These findings suggest that GPU acceleration effectively removes computational bottlenecks in continuous SVF estimation. This is particularly the case for high-resolution urban climate models requiring frequent radiative exchange updates. The method's validation across theoretical and empirical test cases supports its integration into operational urban planning workflows, where rapid SVF mapping could enhance heat mitigation strategies and microclimate simulations. Future research directions should investigate optimal angular sampling intervals for specific application contexts and extend the parallelization framework to multi-GPU architectures for metropolitan-scale deployments.

Code availability. The source code developed and used in this study is openly available at https://github.com/Maxvdwaal/svf_GPU. The repository includes all scripts necessary to reproduce the main analyses and figures presented in the paper, along with documentation and usage instructions. The code was released under the MIT License, encouraging reuse and adaptation for related research purposes.

Acknowledgements. This work was carried out as part of the "Improving public health through urban greening: A Health Impact Assessment of greening strategies on urban heat stress and heat-related mortality" project, funded by the Resilient Delta Initiative. A portion of the spatial datasets used in this study was kindly provided by the Municipality of Rotterdam. Their contributions are gratefully acknowledged.

Disclosure of Interests. The authors have no competing interests to declare that are relevant to the content of this article.

References

1. Stewart, I.D., Oke, T.R.: Local climate zones for urban temperature studies. Bull. Am. Meteor. Soc. **93**(12), 1879–1900 (2012). https://doi.org/10.1175/bams-d-11-00019.1
2. Middel, A., Häb, K., Brazel, A.J., Martin, C.A., Guhathakurta, S.: Impact of urban form and design on mid-afternoon microclimate in Phoenix Local Climate Zones. Landscape And Urban Planning **122**, 16–28 (2013). https://doi.org/10.1016/j.landurbplan.2013.11.004

3. Middel, A., Lukasczyk, J., Maciejewski, R., Demuzere, M., Roth, M.: Sky View Factor footprints for urban climate modeling. Urban Climate **25**, 120–134 (2018). https://doi.org/10.1016/j.uclim.2018.05.004
4. Maiullari, D.: Urban Form Influence on Microclimate and Building Cooling Demand: An Analytical Framework and Its Application on the Rotterdam Case [Dissertation (TU Delft), Delft University of Technology]. A+BE | Architecture and the Built Environment (2023)
5. Oke, T.R.: Canyon geometry and the nocturnal urban heat island: Comparison of scale model and field observations. J. Climatol. **1**(3), 237–254 (1981). https://doi.org/10.1002/joc.3370010304
6. Li, X., Wang, G.: GPU Accelerated Parallel Computing for Estimating Continuous Sky View Factor Map. Research Square (Research Square) (2021). https://doi.org/10.21203/rs.3.rs-279602/v1
7. Muñoz, D., Beckers, B., Besuievsky, G., Patow, G.: A technique for massive sky view factor calculations in large cities. Int. J. Remote Sens. **39**(12), 4040–4058 (2018). https://doi.org/10.1080/01431161.2018.1452071
8. Ratti, C., Richens, P.: Urban Texture Analysis with Image Processing Techniques. In: Springer eBooks, pp. 49–64 (1999). https://doi.org/10.1007/978-1-4615-5047-1_4
9. Lindberg, F., Grimmond, C.S.B.: The influence of vegetation and building morphology on shadow patterns and mean radiant temperatures in urban areas: model development and evaluation. Theoretical And Applied Climatology **105**(3–4), 311–323 (2011). https://doi.org/10.1007/s00704-010-0382-8
10. Steger, C.R., Steger, B., Schär, C.: HORAYZON v1.2: an efficient and flexible ray-tracing algorithm to compute horizon and sky view factor. Geoscientific Model Development **15**(17), 6817–6840 (2022). https://doi.org/10.5194/gmd-15-6817-2022
11. Bernard, J., Bocher, E., Petit, G., Palominos, S.: Sky view factor calculation in urban context: computational performance and accuracy analysis of two open and free GIS tools. Climate **6**(3), 60 (2018). https://doi.org/10.3390/cli6030060
12. Middel, A., Lukasczyk, J., Maciejewski, R.: Sky view factors from synthetic fisheye photos for thermal comfort routing—a case study in phoenix, Arizona. Urban Planning **2**(1), 19–30 (2017). https://doi.org/10.17645/up.v2i1.855
13. Gong, F., Zeng, Z., Zhang, F., Li, X., Ng, E., Norford, L.K.: Mapping sky, tree, and building view factors of street canyons in a high-density urban environment. Building And Environment **134**, 155–167 (2018). https://doi.org/10.1016/j.buildenv.2018.02.042
14. Dirksen, M., Ronda, R., Theeuwes, N., Pagani, G.: Sky view factor calculations and their application in urban heat island studies. Urban Climate **30**, 100498 (2019). https://doi.org/10.1016/j.uclim.2019.100498

Building the Transition to Clean Energy in Small and Rural Communities: Lessons from the LIFE LOCAL GoGREEN Project

Luigi Santopietro[1](✉) , Monica Salvia[1] , Filomena Pietrapertosa[1] ,
Benjamin Hueber[2] , Michael Strobel[2] , Uli Jakob[2] , Cveta Dimitrova[3],
and Roman Kekec[4]

[1] National Research Council of Italy – Institute of Methodologies for Environmental Analysis (CNR-IMAA), Tito, Italy
`luigi.santopietro@cnr.it`
[2] Dr. Jakob Energy Research GmbH and Co. KG (JER), Weinstadt, Germany
[3] Aberon OOD, Sofia, Bulgaria
[4] Local Energy Agency Spodnje Podravje Prešernova, Ptuj, Slovenia

Abstract. Contributing to the ambitious European goal of becoming the first carbon-neutral continent by 2050 requires coordinated efforts across all levels of governance. However, small and rural communities often struggle to keep pace and are disadvantaged by a number of factors including limited access to financial resources, technical expertise, and the use of planning tools such as decision support systems (DSTs), datasets, and geographic information systems (GIS).

This study presents findings from the LIFE22-CET LOCAL GoGREEN project (2024–2026), which supports six small municipalities located in Bulgaria, Croatia, Slovenia, Italy, Germany, and Spain in their clean energy transition. A common methodological framework was co-designed and shared with the municipalities to guide the development of local case study profiles through structured Self-Assessment Reports (SARs).

The SARs provided valuable insights into local energy and climate planning, enabling the identification of key challenges and opportunities. The final comparative analysis revealed a generally fragmented planning framework, a widespread absence of long-term strategic vision, and limited multi-level cooperation. Moreover, the adoption of DSTs, GIS, and structured data analysis in local planning remains minimal.

Despite focusing on a limited number of cases, the study offers relevant considerations for policy-makers and stakeholders aiming to support the energy transition in rural and small communities across Europe in a more inclusive and effective way.

Keywords: Clean energy transition · LIFE LOCAL GoGREEN · Small municipalities · Local energy planning · Key indicators · SECAP

1 Introduction

Europe aims to become the first carbon-neutral continent by 2050. This ambitious objective is at the heart of the European Green Deal, a comprehensive strategy designed to transform the EU's economy into a sustainable and climate-resilient model. To stay on track, the EU has set interim greenhouse gas (GHG) reduction targets of −40% by 2030 and −90% by 2040, relative to 1990 levels [1].

Meeting these unprecedented challenges will require bold decisions and coordinated action at all levels of governance. In particular, it calls for a radical shift in energy production and consumption, through accelerated deployment of renewable energy, the promotion of energy efficiency measures, and a profound change in consumption patterns.

However, this ambitious roadmap poses significant challenges, especially for small and rural communities, which often face structural and institutional barriers to engaging in the clean energy transition [2]. These communities typically lack the necessary financial resources, technical expertise, and infrastructure [3]. Furthermore, small and rural municipalities are often unfamiliar with the use of decision support tools (DSTs), datasets, and geographic information systems (GIS) in planning processes. All these tools are essential for informed and strategic policy making.

Bridging this gap is essential to ensure that the green transition is both inclusive and effective across Europe [4].

This study aims to contribute to addressing this gap by enhancing the capacity of rural communities to develop and implement policies and strategies that promote sustainability and clean energy. In particular, it presents the results of an analysis carried out within the framework of the European LIFE22-CET LOCAL GoGREEN (LGG) project (https://localgogreen.eu/) on 6 small and rural European municipalities. The LIFE LGG project (2024–2026) supports these communities in their transition to clean energy by providing knowledge, tools, and strategic guidance [5].

This paper focuses on the methodological framework specifically developed within the project to support municipalities in developing their case study profiles based on a common template of a Self-Assessment Report (SAR). It also provides insights into the current situation of small and rural municipalities from a variety of perspectives, highlighting the challenges and opportunities they face in the transition to clean energy.

2 Methodological Framework

To describe the state of play of the pilot cities on energy and climate issues, a common methodological framework was developed to support the pilot municipalities in increasing knowledge and awareness of current and future local energy and waste management systems and related climate and environmental impacts.

This common framework consisted of a Word template developed ad hoc on the basis of the LGG objectives, shared with the partners and refined according to their input. Once finalized, this template was distributed to the 6 pilot municipalities, together with detailed instructions on how to fill it in. It served as the basis for completing a Self-Assessment Report (SAR), defining the initial case study profile, which was extremely useful for all subsequent project activities.

As shown in Fig. 1, the SAR template consisted of six main sections, completed by final conclusions, references and optional annexes. First, an introduction describing and justifying the choice of three priority areas on which all the cities' activities will focus throughout the LGG project. These were selected from the following 5 common priority areas individuate within the project as being of strategic importance for the realization of the clean energy transition:

1. Sustainable transportation and e-mobility (TRA)
2. Energy efficiency of buildings (EEB)
3. Expansion of renewable energy generation (RES)
4. Land use planning for increased carbon absorption (LUC)
5. Waste-to-energy (WTE)

Second, a section focused on the multi-level governance system in each country, in order to present the overall context and drivers of policies and strategies at the municipal level. Third, a focus on the pilot municipality, in terms of general description (geography, climate, demographic and socio-economic data) and in terms of commitments made on climate change mitigation and adaptation issues. This section also focused on the management structures in place in the municipality to plan, implement and monitor the strategies and actions, and on the use of data and decision support tools in current planning practices. A fourth section aimed to describe urban planning instruments as well as current and future climate change mitigation (and adaptation) plans, strategies and actions. To provide a more comprehensive overview of the municipality's activities, initiatives and networking with other cities, a list of current and past national and international projects of possible interest to the LGG objectives was also requested. The fifth section aimed to characterise the three selected priority areas in terms of infrastructure, describing both their current state and the planned new infrastructures. A reflection on the most pressing critical issues, but also on the opportunities for the pilot city to implement actions and measures in each of the selected priority areas, concludes the main part of the SAR document.

Once the pilot cities had developed a draft version of their case study profile based on the common SAR, these documents were reviewed internally in order to improve the

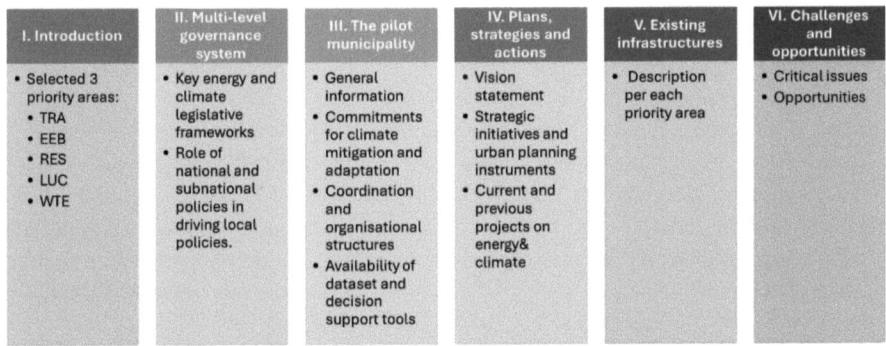

Fig. 1. Structure of the SAR template

quality of the study, but more importantly to assist the cities in completing the missing data and information and to help them with the most complex sections.

Despite this, considerable difficulties were encountered by cities in compiling their case study profiles as will be highlighted in the following section on results.

3 Critical Review of the SARs Contents

The SARs were compiled by each municipality and the level of completeness of the data submitted in each section is shown in Fig. 2. Generally, all sections were fullfilled, although section II and VI did not address all parts completely. The detailed contents of each SAR section will be analysed in the following paragraphs.

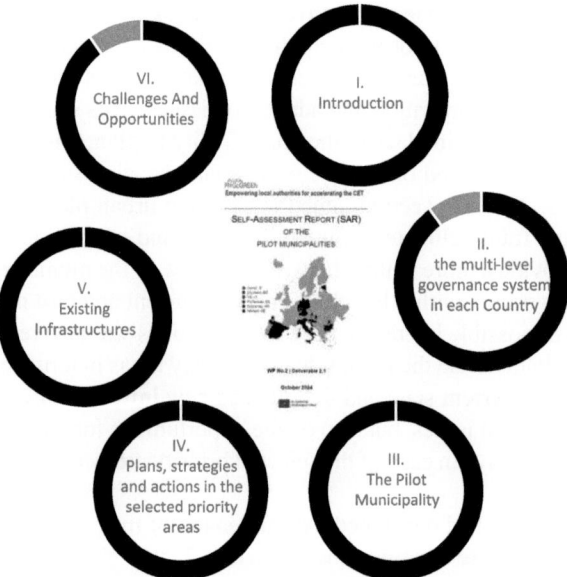

Fig. 2. Completeness of SAR sections

I. *Section 1: Introduction*

In Fig. 3 the selection of the 3 (out of 5) priority areas is shown by each municipality. Regarding the choice of each pilot, three main results emerged: i) a preponderance of the Transport – TRA, Energy Efficiency of Buildings – EEB and Residential – RES priority areas in the case studies demonstrating or showing a "traditional" approach to the selection of sectors closely related to energy; (ii) a reluctance to plan mitigation actions not strictly related to energy or transport, such as the land use and agriculture sector (only one municipality selected the LUC sector); and (iii) a total lack of interest in the waste-to-energy sector, although energy production from waste is increasing at European level and has reached 6.3% according to EUROSTAT data [6].

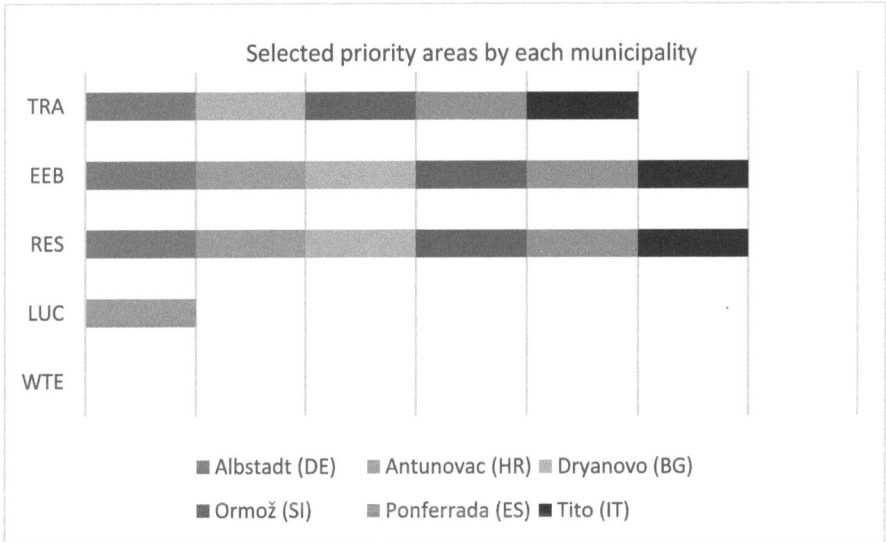

Fig. 3. Selected priority areas by each municipality. The acronyms in the legend are the following: Sustainable transportation and e-mobility (TRA), Energy efficiency of buildings (EEB), Expansion of renewable energy generation (RES), Land use planning for increased carbon absorption (LUC), Waste-to-energy (WTE)

In terms of actions envisaged for aech priority area (Fig. 4) the EEB sector is the first with a total of 30 actions, while TRA and RES sectors have an average of 3 actions declared per municipality. Among the municipalities, Albstadt has the highest overall number of actions planned. However, looking at the status implementation submitted by each municipality, most of the actions are in place and a small number of them could benefit from the support and implementation of the LGG project activities.

II. *Section 2: Multi-Level Governance System*

All municipalities have completed the multi-level governance section; however, its concept is generally lacking/misunderstood. Indeed, all municipalities have only detailed their legislative framework related to each priority area. Only Ormož municipality has specific energy and climate legislation at municipal level, while the other municipalities refer to a broader energy and climate legislation implemented at regional/national level. It is worth noting that, in all cases except for Ormož, national and subnational authorities are key players in driving energy and climate local policies.

III. *Section 3: The Pilot Municipality*

In terms of commitment to mitigation and adaptation, the entire totality of municipalities has made a commitment to mitigation and is fully aligned with the LGG project pillars.

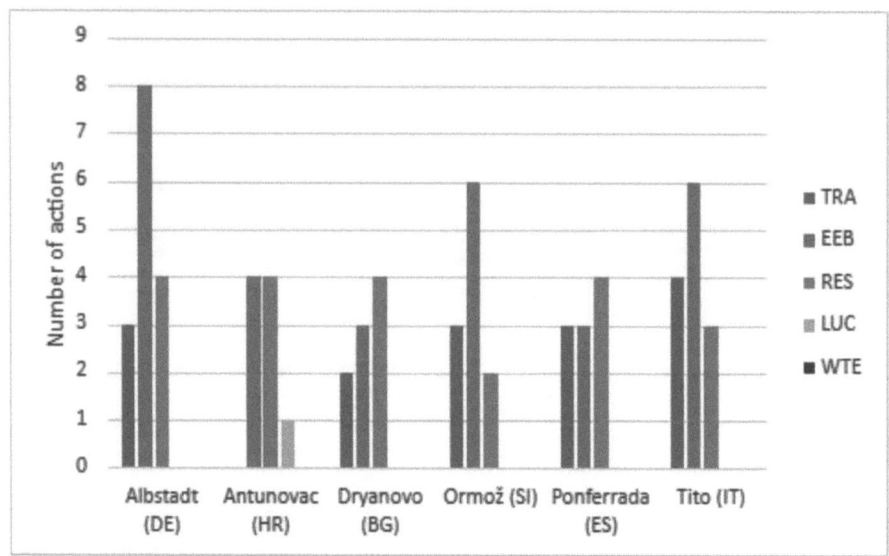

Fig. 4. Number of actions per priority area envisaged. The acronyms in the legend are the following: Sustainable transportation and e-mobility (TRA), Energy efficiency of buildings (EEB), Expansion of renewable energy generation (RES), Land use planning for increased carbon absorption (LUC), Waste-to-energy (WTE)

Specifically, 4 out of 6 municipalities have also declared an adaptation commitment, but for 2 municipalities (Ponferrada and Ormož) this commitment was not linked to a legislative framework but to a voluntary membership of the Global Covenant of Mayors for Climate and Energy initiative.

In terms of coordination and organisational structures, it is important to note that all municipalities have an energy and environmental office, and in some cases (e.g. Albstadt) an urban planning office, including a climate and energy manager, is being set up.

However, when it comes to the use of Decision Support Tools and datasets, only half of the municipalities addressed this aspect in detail. This highlights a general lack of awareness about the value of tools and datasets in supporting a comprehensive design of effective climate actions.

IV. *Section 4: Plans, strategies and actions*

In this section of the SAR, pilot cities were first asked to articulate their vision statement. Of the 6 pilot cities, only 3 have defined a clear vision for the future, among these, Albstadt has a holistic municipal vision (which includes improving the quality of life for citizens), while Ormož and Dryanovo define their vision in the context of developing a plan (the SECAP and the Integrated Development Plan of the Municipality of Dryanovo, respectively). A vision could establish a comprehensive and holistic framework of the impacts and effectiveness of the actions/projects planned. Moreover, it can also be represented by objectives or outcomes that lead to the achievement of the goals expected. This boost for the implementation of the actions is clearly stated in three SARs while the others did not respond either because of a lack of it or because they are aware of it.

In terms of plans and strategies, the 6 pilot cities introduced a total of 18 documents. More detailed information on the current planning situation in the LGG pilot cities is provided in Sect. 3.

V. *Section 5: Existing Infrastructures*

This section described the current state of the infrastructure in each municipality according to the selected priority areas. Existing infrastructure includes, for example, the sustainable transport infrastructure sector, the private/public and commercial building stock (condition, estimated consumption, type of energy sources) or the types of energy efficiency technologies installed, estimated energy savings/revenues.

Obviously, the highest share of actions related to existing infrastructure among municipalities was directed to the EEB sector. However, it is worth noting the detailed description of Albstadt's transport infrastructure, especially for public transport; the Antunovac's current practices on land use planning to increase the green belt area, as well as the established policy to minimize urban/suburban sprawl and the design of additional green zones in urban areas.

VI. *Section 6: Challenges and opportunities*

all municipalities highlighted in this section their drivers and barriers in implementing the actions planned in their priority areas towards the clean energy transition. Most of them provided a direct comparison between challenges and opportunities while Albstadt municipality carried out a SWOT analysis to give an overview of all challenges and opportunities, but also weaknesses and threads. In this perspective, the SWOT analysis can support municipalities in identifying better solutions in designing/improving their actions within the priority areas [7–9].

4 Discussions and Conclusions

The transition to clean energy and carbon neutrality is an ambitious but necessary goal for all European cities. It will help make Europe the world's first carbon-neutral continent, as set out in the EU Green Deal and committed to in the EU Climate Change Law. This strong will of the European Union comes up against strong operational difficulties, especially among small and rural municipalities, for which the lack of dedicated and highly experienced staff, as well as limited economic resources, are common problems. Supporting these municipalities on this challenging transition path is one of the main objectives of the LIFE Local GoGreen project, which recognizes the need to have to base future visions, policies and strategies on solid roots provided by a thorough and holistic knowledge of the local reference system.

The study focuses on the joint efforts made to establish this baseline scenario, on which medium- to long-term transition scenarios are built for each of the six pilot cities. The study reports and critically compares the experience gained in designing, transferring and applying a common methodological framework to enable cities to develop their case study profiles. This framework, based on a Self-Assessment Report (SAR), was shared with the cities in the design phase, transferred to them, completed with section-by-section guidelines, filled in by each city, reviewed internally and then finalized by each city, taking into account the suggested improvements and additional clarifications.

A critical comparison of the six SARs obtained at the end of this process, allowed to highlight the light and dark sides of a comprehensive approach to energy and climate issues in small and rural towns. First, in most cases the planning framework is very fragmented and seems to lack a common long-term vision. Second, the effectiveness of multi-level cooperation still seems to be limited. Third, the use of decision support tools (DST), GIS and data sets in common planning practices is also quite limited.

Although limited to only six municipalities in different European countries, these findings could be of relevant interest to policy planners and decision-makers at all levels of government in assessing the actual state of the art in many municipalities across Europe and in outlining effective support to make their ambitions for a clean energy and carbon neutral pathway a reality.

The next steps of the LIFE Local GoGreen project are aimed at carrying out a GAP analysis to identify the barriers to the implementation of energy transition measures and to provide practical recommendations for the design of policy interventions in each of the priority areas selected by the pilot municipalities.

Acknowledgments. This research was conducted as part of the LOCAL GoGREEN project (01/11/2023- 31/10/2026), which received funding from the European Union Programme for the Environment and Climate Action (LIFE) under grant agreement No. 101120811. We would like to thank the six partner pilot municipalities on which this work is based: Ormož (SI), Dryanovo (BG), Tito (IT), Ponferrada (ES), Antunovac (HR), Albstadt (DE).

Disclosure of Interests. The authors have no competing interests to declare that are relevant to the content of this article.

References

1. Mikropoulos, E., et al.: Examining pathways for a climate neutral Europe by 2050; A model comparison analysis including integrated assessment models and energy system models. Energy **319**, 134809 (2025). https://doi.org/10.1016/j.energy.2025.134809
2. Streimikiene, D., Baležentis, T., Volkov, A., Morkūnas, M., Žičkienė, A., Streimikis, J.: Barriers and drivers of renewable energy penetration in rural areas. Energies **14**(20), 6452 (2021). https://doi.org/10.3390/en14206452
3. Chen, M., Chen, C., Jin, C., Li, B., Zhang, Y., Zhu, P.: Evaluation and obstacle analysis of sustainable development in small towns based on multi-source big data: a case study of 782 top small towns in China. J. Environ. Manage. **366**, 121847 (2024). https://doi.org/10.1016/j.jenvman.2024.121847
4. Salvia, M., Pietrapertosa, F., D'Alonzo, V., Clerici Maestosi, P., Simoes, S.G., Reckien, D.: Key dimensions of cities' engagement in the transition to climate neutrality. J. Environ. Manage. **344**, 118519 (2023). https://doi.org/10.1016/j.jenvman.2023.118519
5. Salvia, M., et al.: Empowering local authorities to accelerate the clean energy transition: the local Gogreen project. In: Sustainable Development and Planning 2024 Conference publication – WIT Transactions on Ecology and the Environment, pp. 847–858 (2024). https://doi.org/10.2495/SDP240701
6. EUROSTAT: Growth in waste recovery in 2022. https://ec.europa.eu/eurostat/web/products-eurostat-news/w/ddn-20241017-1. Last accessed 7 May 2025

7. Terrados, J., Almonacid, G., Hontoria, L.: Regional energy planning through SWOT analysis and strategic planning tools. Renew. Sustain. Energy Rev. **11**, 1275–1287 (2007). https://doi.org/10.1016/j.rser.2005.08.003
8. Georgi, B., et al.: Urban adaptation to climate change in Europe: Challenges and opportunities for cities together with supportive national and European policies (2012)
9. Comino, E., Ferretti, V.: Indicators-based spatial SWOT analysis: Supporting the strategic planning and management of complex territorial systems. Ecol. Indic. **60**, 1104–1117 (2016). https://doi.org/10.1016/j.ecolind.2015.09.003
10. Kern, K., Alber, G., Energy, S., Policy, C.: Governing climate change in cities: modes of urban climate governance in multi-level systems. Compet. Cities Climate Change. **171**, 171–195 (2008)

Air Quality and Climate Planning: Paving the Way for Better Integration

Angela Pilogallo[1,2(✉)], Luigi Santopietro[1], Filomena Pietrapertosa[1,2], and Monica Salvia[1,2]

[1] Institute of Methodologies for Environmental Analysis, National Research Council of Italy, Tito, PZ, Italy
`angela.pilogallo@cnr.it`
[2] National Biodiversity Future Center, Palermo, Italy

Abstract. Scientific literature increasingly recognizes air quality (AQ) and climate change (CC) as two interconnected issues since many of the same sources are responsible for both greenhouse gas (GHG) emissions and air pollutants. This overlap means that integrated strategies could result in relevant synergies covering not only environmental issues but also social, economic and public health-related implications.

This research explores how air-climate integration is approached within a multi-level governance framework, with a focus on identifying the main factors driving upscaling dynamics. To support this, the study emphasizes the importance of knowledge exchange among cities (horizontal upscaling) and engagement with regional governments to both enhance the conditions for replicability (vertical upscaling) and establish binding standards across municipalities (hierarchical upscaling). Targeting resilient, carbon-neutral and healthy cities, the results provide insights into a better understanding of how well-performing climate actions can be multiplied, accelerated and broadened to pursue a more effective air quality and climate integration.

Keywords: Climate plans · Air quality · Healthy cities · Multi-level governance · Upscaling

1 Introduction

Climate change (CC) and air quality (AQ) are two closely related environmental issues and represent key global challenges requiring proactive and collaborative multi-level policies [1].

However, because of the nature and lifetimes of the compounds involved as well as the time horizons set to target goals, they are usually addressed by different policy departments. At the European level, the Directorate-General for Environment (DG-ENV) deals with AQ while the DG CLIMA (Directorate-General for Climate Action) is in charge of addressing climate change and related impacts [2].

On the climate front, sub-national governments have already been acknowledged as key players in taking actions to address major CC-related challenges. However, an increasing number of scholars emphasize that cities are best positioned also to produce environmental co-benefits from climate policies, such as to pursue an improvement of local AQ [3]. Furthermore, with the rise of voluntary initiatives and transnational networks, cities have become innovation boosters able to foster integrated strategies that contribute to the achievement of multiple sustainability goals [4–6].

In order to widen the impact of integrated CC and AQ strategies through the involvement of the upper levels of governance [7], a promising strand of research focuses on upscaling local climate policies [8]. This is defined as the process by which an initiative expands its area of impact and can reach a greater number of people in different places and/or at higher levels over time [9].

It can rely on knowledge exchange among cities (horizontal upscaling), involve several levels of governance (vertical upscaling) or it can be founded on legally binding rules (hierarchical upscaling) [10].

The aim of this work is to contribute to this research strand by focusing on the integration between air quality and climate plans through a multi-level governance system. After assessing the level of AQ-CC integration within climate plans, the paper identifies and investigates different upscaling dynamics by analyzing the case study of the Tuscany region.

The results provide insights about key drivers of upscaling, paving the way for a better understanding of how well-performing urban climate action and its governance can be multiplied, accelerated and broadened [11] coupling environmental benefits with broader societal, strategic, and collaborative goals [12].

The paper is structured as follows: the next section presents the case study, and the methodologies used to assess the integration of air quality into climate plans and to investigate the factors driving upscaling. Section 3 presents the main results and discusses them considering a broad body of scientific literature on the topic of upscaling. Finally, Sect. 4 outlines the key conclusions and highlights potential future developments in the research.

2 Materials and Methods

2.1 Case Study

Tuscany is a region in central Italy, stretching from the Apennine Mountains in the east to the Tyrrhenian Sea in the west and covering about 22,990 square kilometers. It includes 273 municipalities shared among 10 provinces: Arezzo, Florence, Grosseto, Livorno, Lucca, Massa-Carrara, Pisa, Pistoia, Prato, Siena.

On the climate side, Tuscany voluntarily approved a regional mitigation strategy, the "Toscana Carbon Neutral", targeting carbon neutrality by 2050. It is implemented through the adoption of ten-year Action Plans involving two main lines of action: reducing greenhouse gas (GHG) emissions through the development of a more circular economy-oriented model and increasing emission absorption through the enhancement of green areas and achieving a net zero emission balance by 2050. The current 2020–2030 Action Plan is based on 6 pillars: i) Electricity production from geothermal source;

ii) Electricity production from solar source; iii) Increasing energy efficiency interventions in public and private buildings; iv) Promotion of circular economy interventions; v) Forestation interventions; vi) Promoting sustainable mobility (Fig. 1).

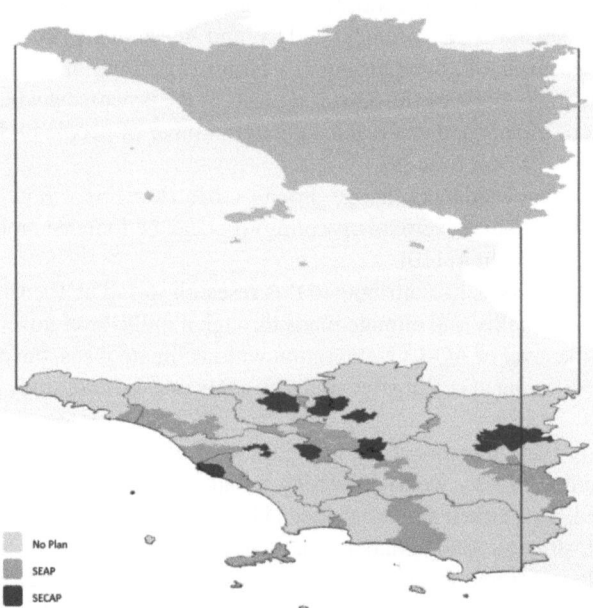

Fig. 1. Overview of climate planning related to the selected case study. At the regional scale Tuscany approved the Toscana Carbon Neutral mitigation plan; at the municipal scale 48 local plans have been approved between SEAP (35) and SECAP (13).

The regional strategy does not foresee any requirement for the municipalities. However, under the umbrella of the Global Covenant of Mayor(GCoM) [13],Tuscanian municipalities have adopted a Sustainable Energy and Climate Action Plan (SECAP) while 33 municipalities approved a Sustainable Energy Action Plan (SEAP).

2.2 The Role of Air Quality in Climate Plans

Sub-national authorities are indeed the most engaged in facing urgent health, social, and environmental challenges [14, 15] with cities in the front line dealing with hotspots of air pollution, noise, heat island effects and other factors detrimental to human health [16]. As cities around the world ramp up efforts to tackle CC, integrating air quality considerations into climate action plans has emerged as both a necessary and strategic move [17]. However, building healthy and sustainable cities requires an assessment of the current degree of integration.

The proposed methodology is based on the following four main criteria:

- Evaluation of the integrated approach [18] pursued during the climate plan's drafting process by a content analysis of the stated objectives;

- The recognition of air pollutants as a co-benefit (or secondary effect) of planned measures to evaluate the degree of coordination between low-carbon development and air quality [19];
- The explicit reference to AQ plans, to both regional and municipal scale to make explicit the synergies potentially deriving from a multi-sectoral approach [20];
- The role assigned to air pollution as an additional risk factor to natural hazards related to CC and exacerbated by extreme events such as heat waves and prolonged droughts [21, 22].

According to the number of criteria fulfilled, to each climate plan was assigned an integration degree ranging from "No integration" (No met criterium) to "Very high" (All criteria fulfilled).

2.3 Investigating Potential Upscaling Dynamics

An upscaling dynamic can be defined as the set of processes that replicate and multiply the most successful strategies [7, 8]. Considering a multi-level governance system, three main types of upscaling are recognized [23].

Horizontal upscaling is based on transfer, replication and knowledge exchange between organizations and authorities that operate at the same level [24]. Typical horizontal upscaling focuses on bilaterally city-to-city interactions as well as through networking arrangements among cities [8], such as trans-municipal networks [23] that cross national borders [25].

Vertical upscaling involves several governance levels, calling for action from supra-municipal authorities to support, perhaps including dedicated funding, the spread of voluntary initiatives [10]. It depends on sub-national and national strategies for broadening climate initiatives and stimulating smaller cities to act. Some examples are the provision of technical support, funding programs or other kinds of incentives.

Hierarchical upscaling entails additional action at the supra-municipal levels of government and is based on legally binding rules exerting their authority to harmonize policies and set standards for all municipalities [7]. As far as climate governance is concerned, these types of actions have found wide use in mitigation [26], for example looking at the EU's mandatory efficiency standards for buildings, not so much in adaptation [27].

Considering the climate planning process across a multi-level governance system [28, 29] and the volunteer approach in leading the development of climate plans at the different sub-national scales [30], the following factors (Table 1) driving the upscaling dynamics were selected in relation to the analyzed case study.

As sub-national climate planning is not mandatory in Italy under the current legislative context, both regional and local climate plans are developed and approved on a voluntary basis. For this reason, any factor guiding hierarchical upscaling could be identified.

Table 1. Driving factors for each upscaling dynamic.

Upscaling dynamic	Driving factors
Horizontal	Membership in climate networks
	Involvement in transnational climate initiatives
	Involvement in transnational project
Vertical	Support from Covenant Territorial Coordinators
	Assistance from Covenant Supporters
Hierarchical	No factors

3 Results and Discussions

The Tuscany region demonstrates a medium level of integration between AQ and climate policies. The region's climate mitigation plan (TCN), in fact, does not explicitly aim to reduce air pollution, even though it lists better air quality as a potential co-benefit of climate actions. Although TCN identifies air pollution as a climate-related risk, it makes no reference to air quality planning efforts.

Looking at the municipal climate plans, the integration landscape is quite varied. Municipalities classified as "No integration" represent 25% of the total number of municipalities with a climate plan. The largest group comprises 23 municipalities (38%) that reach a low degree of integration, while a medium level is observed in 15 municipalities (25%). A high degree of integration is identified in 5 municipalities (8%); the highest degree is achieved by just 3 municipalities (5%). Looking at the municipal climate plans, the integration landscape is quite varied as can be seen in Fig. 2.

Concerning the analysis of factors driving horizontal upscaling, the most widely adopted network among Tuscan municipalities is the Global Covenant of Mayors (GCoM), with 80 out of 273 municipalities (29%) participating. Nevertheless, only 61 of these have proceeded to develop and approve climate plans, resulting in a total of 48 approved plans: 33 SEAPs, 2 Joint SEAPs, and 13 SECAPs. Participation in other international networks is minimal: only three municipalities are part of Eurocities, and Florence is the sole representative in ICLEI. None of the municipalities are affiliated with the Climate Alliance, Energy Cities, or the C40 network. However, Florence, Arezzo, and Prato are members of the Green City Network.

In terms of climate-focused initiatives, only Florence and Prato are involved in the EU Cities Mission. Additionally, 11 other municipalities from their respective provinces (1 from Prato and 10 from Florence) have joined the European Energy Award program. Following the Climate and Environmental Declaration (CED) issued by the Tuscany Region in June 2019, another 9 municipalities, representing roughly 3% of the region, endorsed the declaration within the same year. Regarding the third type of factor, it resulted that 29% of SE(C)APs were drawn up as part of an international EU-funded project.

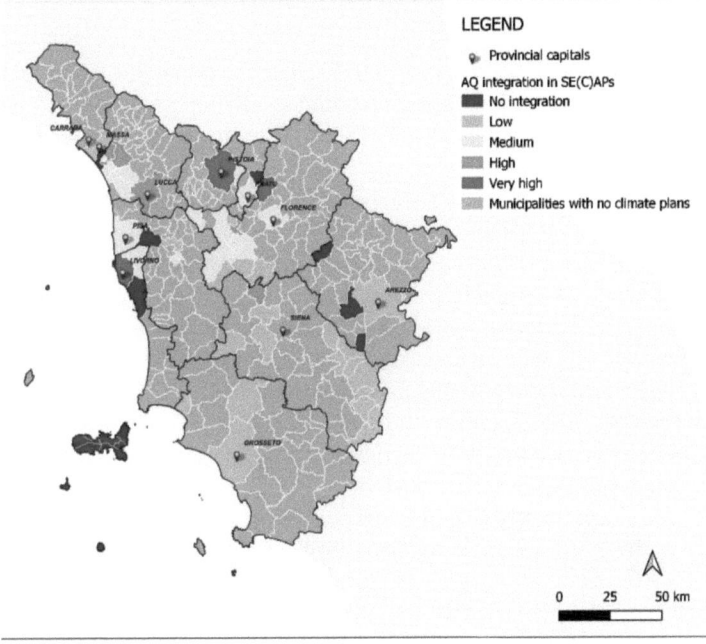

Fig. 2. AQ integration degree assigned to SE(C)APs

Concerning the analysis of factors driving vertical upscaling, 31 municipalities state that their climate plans were approved with the support of a Covenant of Mayors Territorial Coordinator (CTC) under the GCoM framework while 7 plans relied on support from a GCoM Covenant Supporter.

As highlighted by the scientific community, the greatest impact in terms of air quality and climate integration could be reached when the upscaling dynamics interact, creating synergies that imply the involvement of all levels of governance [10]. Horizontal upscaling constitutes a relevant driver of innovation through cross-border knowledge exchange. However, it shows some limits for smaller municipalities because, as highlighted by Kern [9], joining transnational cities networks and institutionalizing climate policy requires certain capacities of the municipal staff. On the other side, vertical upscaling is essential to pursue and support widespread change: without vertical upscaling, good planning practices and initiatives remain little more than "islands of excellence" [10]. Finally, hierarchical upscaling is essential to gather contributions even from cities less engaged in climate challenges, which at least are expected to comply with minimum standards set by regional and national governments [8]. France, for example, has adopted a centralized approach to climate policies with local climate plans required to municipalities [31].

Finally, since the combination of high temperatures, air pollution, and high population density, constitutes a very critical concern in the climate change scenario [32], more efforts are requested to enhance the integration of air quality in adaptation plans.

4 Conclusions

As all levels of governance, from national to local, step up their efforts to address CC, incorporating air quality considerations into climate action plans is increasingly recognized as both essential and strategically beneficial. The connection between air pollution and climate change is in fact not just biophysical; it's also social, economic, and deeply tied to public health and well-being. Clean air goals embedded in climate plans can help the legitimization of efforts to carbon neutrality, improve the quality of life and reduce the incidence of health diseases. Prioritizing cleaner air can also help address environmental justice, as disadvantaged communities often suffer the most from both poor air quality and climate impacts. Incorporating air quality into climate policy planning also boosts economic efficiency, reducing administrative duplication, streamlining implementation, and multiplying returns on investment in mitigation pathways.

The key findings from this research highlight the crucial role of regional and subregional authorities in fostering the integration of air and climate considerations within municipal climate plans. Air quality potential co-benefits, directly experienced by citizens, can be used as an effective lever to boost climate actions and engage local authorities in reinforced pathways towards carbon neutrality.

Acknowledgments. This research was supported by the National Biodiversity Future Centre 2022–2025 (id. Code CN00000033), funded by the Italian National Recovery and Resilience Plan (PNRR Mission 4, Component 2, Investment 1.4).

Disclosure of Interests. The authors have no competing interests to declare that are relevant to the content of this article.

References

1. West, J.J., et al.: Co-benefits of mitigating global greenhouse gas emissions for future air quality and human health. Nat. Clim. Chang. **3**, 885–889 (2013). https://doi.org/10.1038/NCLIMATE2009
2. Maione, M., et al.: Air quality and climate change: designing new win-win policies for Europe. Environ Sci Policy **65**, 48–57 (2016). https://doi.org/10.1016/J.ENVSCI.2016.03.011
3. Puppim de Oliveira, J.A.: Learning how to align climate, environmental and development objectives in cities: lessons from the implementation of climate co-benefits initiatives in urban Asia. J. Cleaner Product. **58**, 7–14 (2013). https://doi.org/10.1016/j.jclepro.2013.08.009
4. Bellinson, R., Chu, E.: Learning pathways and the governance of innovations in urban climate change resilience and adaptation. J. Environ. Planning Policy Manage. **21**, 76–89 (2019). https://doi.org/10.1080/1523908X.2018.1493916
5. Dale, A., et al.: Meeting the climate change challenge: local government climate action in British Columbia, Canada. Climate Policy **20**, 866–880 (2020). https://doi.org/10.1080/14693062.2019.1651244
6. Salvia, M., Pietrapertosa, F., D'Alonzo, V., Clerici Maestosi, P., Simoes, S.G., Reckien, D.: Key dimensions of cities' engagement in the transition to climate neutrality. J. Environ. Manage. **344**, 118519 (2023). https://doi.org/10.1016/J.JENVMAN.2023.118519

7. van Doren, D., Driessen, P.P.J., Runhaar, H., Giezen, M.: Scaling-up low-carbon urban initiatives: towards a better understanding. Urban Stud. **55**, 175–194 (2018). https://doi.org/10.1177/0042098016640456/ASSET/IMAGES/LARGE/10.1177_0042098016640456-FIG1.JPEG
8. Kern, K.: Cities as leaders in EU multilevel climate governance: embedded upscaling of local experiments in Europe. Env Polit. **28**, 125–145 (2019). https://doi.org/10.1080/09644016.2019.1521979
9. Kern, K.: Cities in EU multilevel climate policy: governance capacities, spatial approaches and upscaling of local experiments. In: Handbook on European Union Climate Change Policy and Politics, pp. 1–413. Edward Elgar Publishing Ltd. (2023). https://doi.org/10.4337/9781789906981
10. Fuhr, H., Hickmann, T., Kern, K.: The role of cities in multi-level climate governance: local climate policies and the 1.5 °C target. Curr. Opin. Environ. Sustain. **30**, 1–6 (2018). https://doi.org/10.1016/J.COSUST.2017.10.006
11. Van Der Heijden, J.: Towards a science of scaling for urban climate action and governance. Europ. J. Risk Regul. **14**, 513–525 (2023). https://doi.org/10.1017/ERR.2022.13
12. Oetken, K.J.: Unravelling the why: exploring the increasing recognition and adoption of co-creation in contemporary urban design. Sustain. Commun. **2**, 2477788 (2025). https://doi.org/10.1080/29931282.2025.2477788
13. Local action plans | Covenant of Mayors – Europe, https://eu-mayors.ec.europa.eu/en/action_plan_list#actionPlanListMap, last accessed 2025/01/23
14. Lowe, M., et al.: City planning policies to support health and sustainability: an international comparison of policy indicators for 25 cities. Lancet Glob. Health **10**, e882–e894 (2022). https://doi.org/10.1016/S2214-109X(22)00069-9/ATTACHMENT/39BAD32B-D58E-4D6E-8700-F41915DB6CDC/MMC1.PDF
15. Ren, X.: Breaking the ecological freeze: leading sustainable energy into a higher level of innovation. Sustain. Commun. **1**, 2365217 (2024). https://doi.org/10.1080/29931282.2024.2365217
16. Nieuwenhuijsen, M.J.: New urban models for more sustainable, liveable and healthier cities post covid19; reducing air pollution, noise and heat island effects and increasing green space and physical activity. Environ. Int. **157**, 106850 (2021). https://doi.org/10.1016/J.ENVINT.2021.106850
17. Pilogallo, A., Pietrapertosa, F., Salvia, M.: Are we going towards an effective integration of air quality and climate planning? A comparative analysis for Italian regions. J. Environ. Manage. **368**, 122138 (2024). https://doi.org/10.1016/J.JENVMAN.2024.122138
18. Kleiman, G., et al.: Enhanced integration of health, climate, and air quality management planning at the urban scale. Front. Sustain. Cities **4**, 934672 (2022). https://doi.org/10.3389/FRSC.2022.934672/BIBTEX
19. Liu, T.L., Song, Q.J., Lu, J., Qi, Y.: An integrated approach to evaluating the coupling coordination degree between low-carbon development and air quality in Chinese cities. Adv. Climate Change Res. **12**(5), 710–722 (2021). https://doi.org/10.1016/j.accre.2021.08.001
20. O'Regan, A.C., Nyhan, M.M.: Towards sustainable and net-zero cities: a review of environmental modelling and monitoring tools for optimizing emissions reduction strategies for improved air quality in urban areas. Environ. Res. **231**, 116242 (2023). https://doi.org/10.1016/J.ENVRES.2023.116242
21. Lee, E., Kim, G.: Green space ecosystem services and value evaluation of three-dimensional roads for sustainable cities. Land **12**, 505 (2023). https://doi.org/10.3390/LAND12020505
22. Park, K., Jin, H.G., Baik, J.J.: Do heat waves worsen air quality? A 21-year observational study in Seoul, South Korea. Sci. Total. Environ. **884**, 163798 (2023). https://doi.org/10.1016/J.SCITOTENV.2023.163798

23. Kern, K., Bulkeley, H.: Cities, europeanization and multi-level governance: governing climate change through transnational municipal networks*. JCMS: J. Common Market Stud. **47**(2), 309–332 (2009). https://doi.org/10.1111/j.1468-5965.2009.00806.x
24. Kern, K., Eckersley, P., Haupt, W.: Diffusion and upscaling of municipal climate mitigation and adaptation strategies in Germany. Reg. Environ. Change **23**, 1–12 (2023). https://doi.org/10.1007/S10113-022-02020-Z/FIGURES/2
25. Lambin, E.F., Kim, H., Leape, J., Lee, K.: Scaling up solutions for a sustainability transition. One Earth. **3**, 89–96 (2020). https://doi.org/10.1016/j.oneear.2020.06.010
26. Peeters, M., Athanasiadou, N.: The continued effort sharing approach in EU climate law: binding targets, challenging enforcement? Rev Eur Comp Int Environ Law. **29**, 201–211 (2020). https://doi.org/10.1111/REEL.12356
27. Hall, N., Persson, Å.: Global climate adaptation governance: why is it not legally binding? Europ. J. Int. Relat. **24**(3), 540–566 (2017). https://doi.org/10.1177/1354066117725157
28. Salvia, M., et al.: Climate mitigation in the Mediterranean Europe: an assessment of regional and city-level plans. J. Environ. Manage. **295**, 113146 (2021). https://doi.org/10.1016/J.JENVMAN.2021.113146
29. Pietrapertosa, F., Salvia, M., De Gregorio Hurtado, S., Geneletti, D., D'Alonzo, V., Reckien, D.: Multi-level climate change planning: an analysis of the Italian case. J. Environ. Manage. **289**, 112469 (2021). https://doi.org/10.1016/J.JENVMAN.2021.112469
30. Santopietro, L., Scorza, F., Rossi, A.: Small Municipalities Engaged in Sustainable and Climate Responsive Planning: Evidences from UE-CoM. Lecture Notes in Computer Science (including subseries Lecture Notes in Artificial Intelligence and Lecture Notes in Bioinformatics). 12957 LNCS, 615–620 (2021). https://doi.org/10.1007/978-3-030-87013-3_47/TABLES/3
31. Lesnikowski, A., Biesbroek, R., Ford, J.D., Berrang-Ford, L.: Policy implementation styles and local governments: the case of climate change adaptation. Env Polit. **30**, 753–790 (2021). https://doi.org/10.1080/09644016.2020.1814045
32. Orsetti, E., Tollin, N., Lehmann, M., Valderrama, V.A., Morató, J.: Building resilient cities: climate change and health interlinkages in the planning of public spaces. Int. J. Environ. Res. Public Health **19**(3), 1355 (2022). https://doi.org/10.3390/ijerph19031355

Ensemble Machine Learning Model to Analyse the Correlation Between Environmental Features and Respiratory Admissions in the Emergency Room

Vito Telesca and Maríca Rondinone(✉)

University of Basilicata, 85100 Potenza, Italy
{vito.telesca,marica.rondinone,marica.rondinone}@unibas.it

Abstract. This study proposes an ensemble machine learning model to analyse the association between respiratory Emergency Room (ER) admissions and environmental factors, such as air pollution and weather-climatic conditions. The analysed climatic variables include air temperatures Tmin, Tmax, Taverage, atmospheric pressure P, relative humidity RH, and levels of CO, O_3, PM_{10}, and NO_2. The data were processed as daily averages to ensure consistency and comparability in the analyses. Data on ER, provided by the Policlinico of Bari, cover the period from 2013 to 2023.

The analysis was conducted using ensemble learning techniques, applying three regression models: Random Forest, XGBoost, and Adaboost. The models were trained on a pre-processed database using a 7-day exponential moving average (EMA7) to obtain a more stable time series. Model hyperparameters were optimized through Bayesian optimization. Among the analysed models, XGBoost showed high predictive capacity in test sets. In particular, the R^2 value was 0.772, while the MAE was 0.049 cases/day.

Applying SHAP (SHapley Additive exPlanations) analysis to the XGBoost model allowed us to identify the most important variables influencing hospital admissions and their related patterns. The most relevant features, ranked by importance, were: low values of average air temperature and atmospheric pressure, and high values of CO. The SHAP method, and in particular the use of Bee Swarm plots, were used to globally interpret the results obtained by the model and allowed us to reach the above results. Furthermore, in order to determine for the most important features the values that cause an increase in admission to the emergency room for respiratory diseases, a local analysis was carried out by applying the LIME model which allowed us to say that the greater onset of respiratory diseases is associated with average temperatures lower than 12.28 °C, atmospheric pressure values lower than or equal to 1006.81 hPa and CO concentrations greater than 0.84 mg/m^3.

Keywords: Respiratory Diseases · Random Forest · XGBoost · AdaBoost · Global and Local Interpretability

1 Introduction

Respiratory diseases are a cause of mortality globally and are related to climatic and environmental factors such as air quality, temperature and air pollutants [1, 2]. Scientific studies have shown that fine particulate matter (PM2.5, PM10), nitrogen dioxide (NO2) and sulphur dioxide (SO2) are responsible for the onset of respiratory diseases, especially in areas of high industrialisation and vehicular traffic [3, 4]. Exposure to these pollutants causes impairment of lung function [5, 6], while climatic variables such as intense cold and humidity favour viral infections and allergic reactions [7].

To analyze these dynamics, the study uses ensemble machine learning techniques (Random Forest, XGBoost, AdaBoost) [8] and interprets the results through global and local interpretability methods (SHAP and LIME graphs), in order to identify significant correlations between environmental data and respiratory health. Specifically, after an initial preprocessing of the data and a preliminary correlation analysis between climatic and environmental factors and the target variable, the Random Forest, XGBoost and AdaBoost models (optimized through Bayesian optimization) were applied, whose performances were compared through cross-validation, analysis of metrics and errors and their distribution.

From the comparison between the three models, XGBoost was found to be the one with the best performance and, consequently, the SHAP model was applied to identify the features that best conveyed the model's predictions. Furthermore, the LIME model was used to determine, for the most significant parameters, the threshold values of the quantities.

2 Study Area

In this study, the city of Bari, the capital of Puglia, is examined. Located in Southern Italy and bathed by the Adriatic Sea, the city with a population of 320,000 inhabitants [9], has a Mediterranean climate with hot and sunny summers and mild and rainy winters [10]. To carry out the analyses discussed in this manuscript, hospital data provided by the Policlinico di Bari, one of the most important hospitals in the city, were used, while environmental and climatic data were obtained from local monitoring cabins.

3 Materials and Methods

3.1 Methodology

The workflow of the applied methodology is illustrated in Fig. 1; the steps are the following:

i) after an initial data collection phase, the data underwent preprocessing to handle missing values and align them temporally;

ii) a correlation analysis was then conducted to identify relationships between climatic variables and hospital admissions. The correlation analysis was conducted by calculating both the Pearson coefficient (r) and the relative p-value: the first allows us to understand how much two variables are correlated with each other and presents values that oscillate between 1 (positively correlated variables), 0 (absence of correlation) and -1 (negative correlation, as one variable increases, the other decreases). The p-value, on the other hand, was used to understand if the correlation obtained was statistically significant, in fact, a p-value lower than a threshold of 0.05 supports the conclusion that the correlation is not random [11]. In the case in question, the p-value was found to be lower than the threshold value and therefore the correlation obtained was considered statistically significant;
iii) the data were then normalized to make them comparable;
iv) an Exponential Moving Average (EMA7) filter was applied to reduce daily variability and identify significant trends in the time series. This method smooths the data and improves the quality of predictions;
v) For predictive analysis, three ensemble learning algorithms [12] were utilized:

- Random Forest
- XGBoost
- AdaBoost

These models were chosen for their capability to manage complex data and identify nonlinear relationships between meteorological variables and hospital admissions. In particular, the Random Forest is an algorithm that is based on the use of decision trees built using subsets of data. The final prediction is obtained from the average of the predictions that are provided by the different trees (in the case of regression analysis) or by majority vote (in the case of classification, in which the class that has emerged most from the analysis carried out by the different decision trees is chosen) [13]. The XGBoost (Extreme Gradient Boosting) model is also based on the use of decision trees that work sequentially. The characteristic of this model lies in the ability of the subsequent trees to correct the errors of the previous trees: in this way the model has a high precision and can also be used for very complex analyses [8]. Finally, the AdaBoost (Adaptive Boosting) model is a model that combines simple models in which the subsequent ones will correct the errors of the previous ones, ensuring that in the end, even when combining the results of all the simple models, those that have made the most accurate predictions will have greater weight, thus obtaining, in fact, an extremely reliable and precise prediction [14]. To improve their predictive performance, the models were optimized through hyperparameter tuning using Bayesian optimization. Additionally, a model validation phase was conducted that included [15]:

- Cross-validation to ensure the robustness of the results.
- Calculation of performance metrics (e.g., R^2, MAE, RMSE).
- Analysis of error distribution to identify potential biases in the models;

vi) to ensure transparency in the results and understand the contribution of meteorological variables to predictions, Feature Importance and Explainable Artificial Intelligence (XAI) techniques were adopted [16]. Specifically:

- SHAP (Shapley Additive Explanations) was used to determine feature importance.
- Global and local interpretability was applied to analyze the model's behavior both on a general scale and for individual case studies.

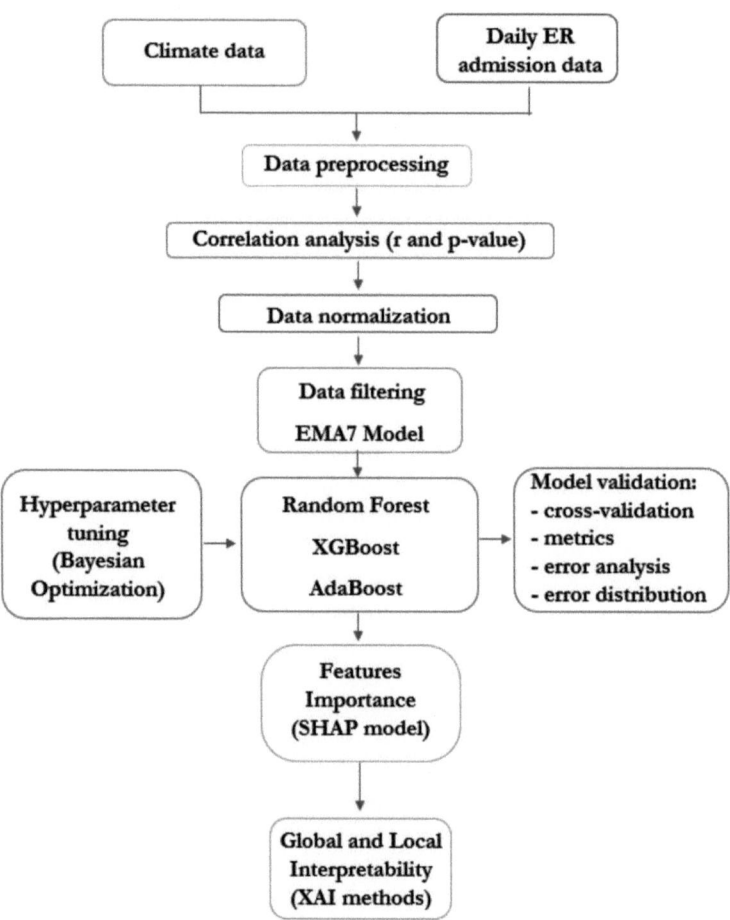

Fig. 1. Methodological framework

The main objective of XAI methodologies is to make artificial intelligence models transparent, thus avoiding the so-called "black-box" processes.

3.2 Meteorological Data

In this study, the data used are of a climatic and environmental nature. In the first case, the average temperature T [°C], the atmospheric pressure P [hPa] and the relative humidity RH [%] were taken into consideration; regarding the environmental parameters, the carbon monoxide CO [mg/m3], the fine particulate matter PM10 [μg/m³], the nitrogen dioxide NO2 [μg/m³] and the ozone O3 [μg/m³] were taken into consideration. The data considered cover a period of ten years, from 2013 to 2023.

To describe the collected data, statistical parameters such as minimum, maximum, mean, standard deviation, median (50th percentile), first, third and fourth quartile (25th, 75th and 90th percentile respectively) were used (Table 1).

Table 1. Statistical description of the data

	T	P	RH	CO	PM10	NO2	O3	RD
min	~0,11	976,60	25,49	0	0	0	0	0
avg	17,83	1011,77	70,29	0,70	22,69	53,02	82,78	5,08
max	36,28	1039,35	99,00	3,00	117,00	157,00	154,00	25,00
std	6,39	8,20	10,50	0,40	11,06	24,55	20,80	3,23
90th	26,67	1022,09	83,51	1,30	36,00	87,00	110,00	9,00
75th	23,47	1017,12	78,00	0,90	28,00	68,00	97,63	7,00
50th	17,28	1012,32	70,76	0,60	21,00	50,00	82,00	4,00
25th	12,36	1006,20	63,23	0,40	15,00	35,00	67,00	3,00

3.3 Emergency Room (ER) Data

The health data used in this study concern patients affected by respiratory diseases and were provided by the Policlinico of Bari, one of the main hospital facilities in Southern Italy. These data include hospitalized for respiratory diseases (RD), diagnoses of asthma and COPD, and other respiratory complications related to adverse environmental conditions. Integrating this information with meteorological data allows for examining possible correlations between air pollution, climatic conditions, and respiratory health in the Bari population.

4 Application to Case Study

4.1 Correlation Analysis

Following the methodological framework, the first step of the analysis involved studying the correlations between the features and the target variable. This was achieved by calculating the Pearson correlation coefficient, r, and the corresponding p-value.

As can be seen (Fig. 2), a negative correlation between RD and temperature ($r = -0.51$) emerges; this suggests that warmer climatic conditions could reduce the risk of RD. A negative correlation is also observed with P ($r = -0.27$), implying that an increase in atmospheric pressure levels could be associated with a decrease of the number of respiratory diseases cases, although the correlation is not very strong. A negative

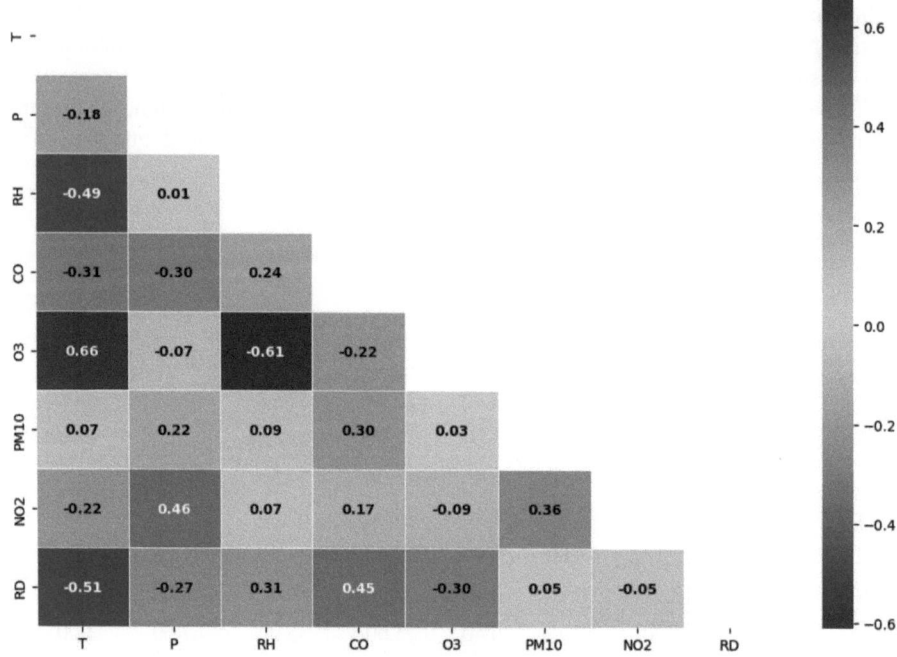

Fig. 2. Correlation matrix

correlation is also found with O_3 (r = −0.30), indicating that an increase in ozone concentration in the air could be associated with a slight reduction in the number of RD cases. Positive correlations are found with RH (r = 0.31), suggesting that an increase in humidity may promote the onset or worsening of respiratory diseases. Finally, a positive correlation is also observed with CO (r = 0.45), suggesting that exposure to these pollutants could significantly increase the risk of developing otitis. Normalization helps to prevent variables with larger numerical values from dominating those with smaller values, ensuring a more balanced assessment of the relationships between variables. Subsequently, to enhance the analysis quality and minimize daily data fluctuations, smoothing was applied using a 7-day Exponential Moving Average (EMA7).

4.2 Machine Learning Models

Once the primary correlations and data were defined, an ensemble model was implemented to enhance the prediction of RD cases, utilizing the combination of multiple predictive algorithms. As mentioned earlier, the models employed were Random Forest, Extreme Gradient Boost, and Adaptive Boost. These three models were fine-tuned using Bayesian optimization, and their performances were then compared (Table 2).

Training a machine learning model with the Random Forest algorithm yielded strong results, with the R^2 coefficient for the test set reaching 0.740. This indicates that the model showed good adaptability and accuracy when predicting a new dataset not seen during training fase. The performance of the model was also validated through the Mean

Table 2. Model performance

Random Forest	XGBoost	AdaBoost post
R2 training (-) = 0.963	R2 training (-) = 0.995	R2 training (-) = 0.999
R^2 test (-) = 0.740	R^2 test (-) = 0.772	R^2 test (-) = 0.789
Mae training (case/day) = 0.02	Mae training (case/day) = 0.007	Mae training (case/day) = 0.001
MAE test (case/day) = 0.053	MAE test (case/day) = 0.049	MAE test (case/day) = 0.045

Absolute Error (MAE), which for the test set was 0.053 cases per day, reflecting a reasonable prediction accuracy. In comparison, the XGBoost model also delivered competitive results, with an R^2 of 0.772 for the test set. The MAE for XGBoost was even lower, at 0.049 cases per day, suggesting a more precise prediction compared to Random Forest. The AdaBoost model achieved the best performance during the training phase, with an R^2 of 0.999 and a MAE of 0.001 cases per day, indicating high accuracy and precision. However, such outstanding results raised concerns about overfitting, potentially making the model less reliable during generalization. In addition to evaluating R^2 and MAE, the error distribution was also examined. Although the XGBoost model showed both overestimation and underestimation (errors within the $\leqslant 20\%$ range), it showed a more favourable error distribution, closely resembling a Gaussian curve (Fig. 3), a key characteristic for enhancing the robustness and generalizability of predictions.

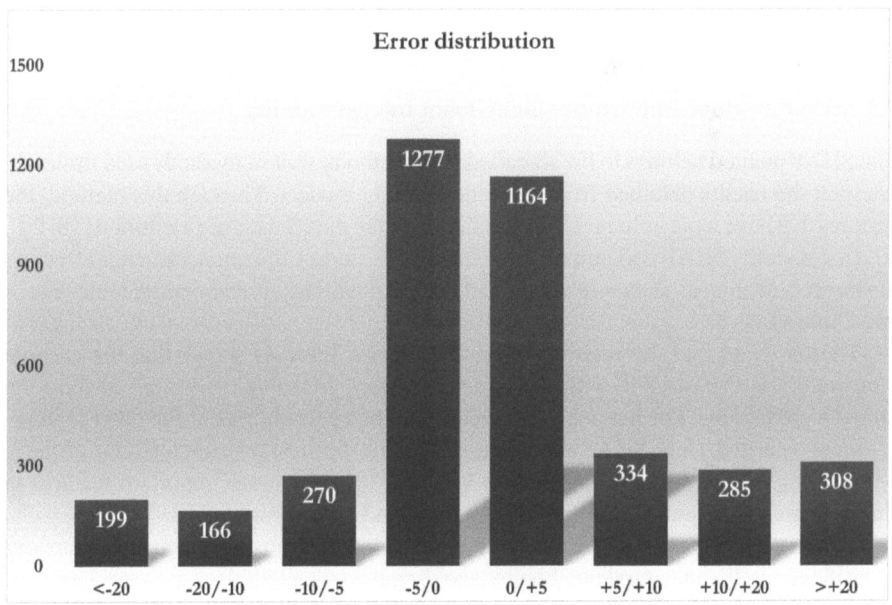

Fig. 3. Error distribution of XGBoost model

The results in Fig. 3 show that the majority of the simulated values (61%) fall within the relatively small error range of ± 5%. Specifically, 31.9% of the simulated values are within the error range of -5% to 0%, while 29.1% fall within the range of 0% to + 5%. This distribution illustrates a strong alignment of the simulation model with the actual values, with a significant percentage of simulated values deviating only slightly from the actual values within the error margin of ± 5%. As you can see, most of the errors fall within the ± 5% range, which allows us to say that the XGBoost model is able to accurately simulate the real values. Furthermore, the robustness of the model was evaluated by applying the k-fold cross-validation procedure, with k = 10 [17] (Table 3).

Table 3. Average Results of Cross Validation

Cross Validation (k-fold = 10)	
R^2 test (-)	0.772
MAE test (case/day)	0.049
MSE test (case/day)^2	0.005
RMSE test (case/day)	0.068

From the results obtained, it can be observed that the model shows good results even on subsets of data unknown to it, allowing us to affirm that it shows a good capacity to generalization. On the basis of this, it is possible to continue the analysis with the application of Features Importance, in order to identify the variables that most influence the model's predictions in terms of access to the emergency room for respiratory diseases.

4.3 SHAP Feature Importance and Global Interpretability

The SHAP method belongs to the so-called XAI methods, that is, methods used to clearly interpret the results obtained from machine learning models. Through this method, the features that have most influenced the prediction of the model used are identified [18–20].

In this study, SHAP was employed to identify the most influential variables affecting the target outcome, as shown in the ranked bar chart and the corresponding table (Fig. 4 and Table 4).

The bar chart and the relative Table (Fig. 4 and Table 4) shows that the average temperature is the variable with the greatest impact, contributing around 38% to the model's predictions. Further analysis reveals that the contributions of the other features are more balanced; since SHAP analysis assumes that the most relevant features are those whose combined contribution reaches at least 70–80%, the other important features in this case are temperature, atmospheric pressure, and carbon monoxide.

The primary objective of XAI techniques is to promote transparency in the behaviour of artificial intelligence models, thereby avoiding the so-called black-box mechanisms.

Global interpretability was further enhanced through the SHAP Bee Swarm plot (Fig. 5), which illustrates both the magnitude and direction of the three most important feature's effects across all predictions.

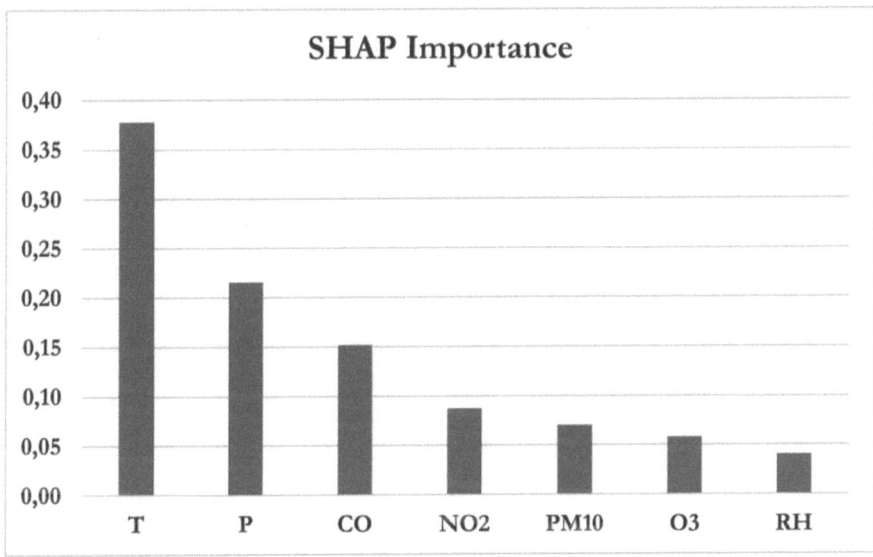

Fig. 4. SHAP feature importance based on SHAP values

Table 4. Percentage contribution of each feature

Feature	% Contribution
T	**0,38**
P	**0,22**
CO	**0,15**
NO2	0,09
PM10	0,07
O3	0,06
RH	0,04

As a visualization tool based on XAI techniques, the Bee Swarm plot provides a comprehensive overview of how input variables influence the model's behaviour on a global scale; the plot clearly shows that the onset of respiratory diseases is generally associated with low values of average temperature and atmospheric pressure, while high levels of carbon monoxide tend to increase the incidence of RDs.

4.4 Local Interpretability

LIME (Local Interpretable Model-agnostic Explanations) is a used technique to enhance the interpretability of complex machine learning models. On the other hand, LIME offers a local approximation of complex models by fitting a surrogate model to a small subset of perturbed data [21]. This simplified local model is interpretable and can be used to

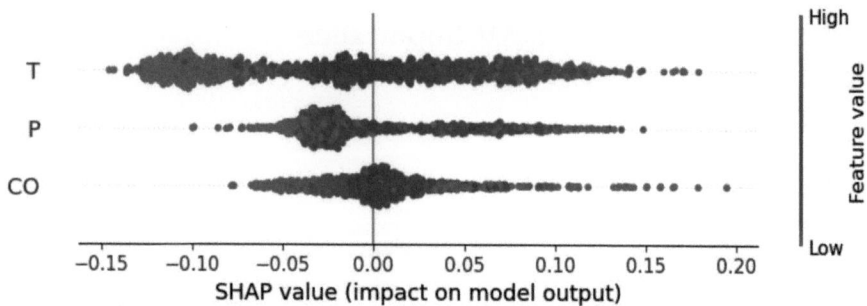

Fig. 5. Bee Swarm plot showing the distribution and impact of T, P and CO

explain how the original model behaves around a specific data point, providing clarity about why a certain prediction was made. In this study, LIME is used to analyse the role of average temperature, atmospheric pressure, and carbon monoxide in the model's predictions. The results obtained are shown in Fig. 6.

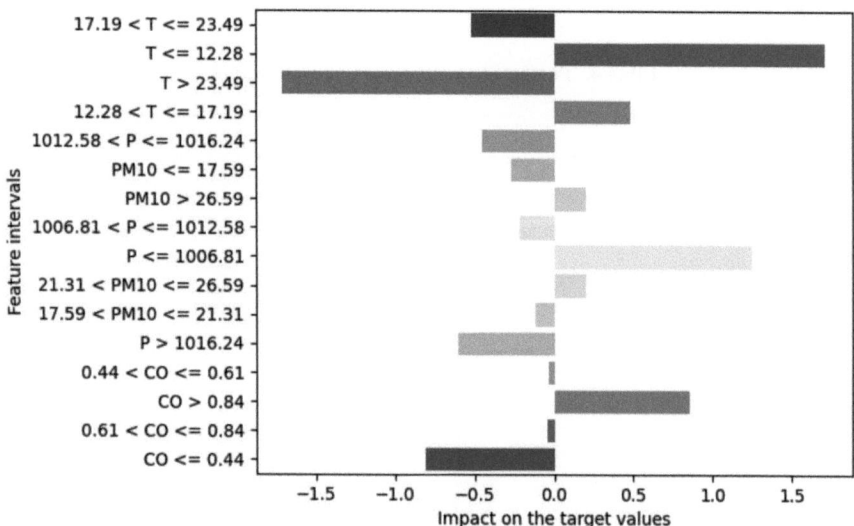

Fig. 6. Significant average temperature, atmospheric pressure and carbon monoxide intervals

The graph in Fig. 6 highlights that temperatures at or below T ≤ 12.28 °C are those most strongly associated with an increased risk of respiratory disease onset. An appreciable influence is also observed within the range 12.28 °C < T ≤ 17.19 °C. On the other hand, for 17.19 °C < T ≤ 23.49 °C and especially for higher temperatures (T > 29.49 °C), the predicted number of RD cases tends to decrease. With regard to atmospheric pressure, values equal to or below P ≤ 1006.81 hPa appear to contribute most significantly to the onset of RD. A transitional effect is noted in the intermediate range 1006.81 < P ≤ 1012.58 hPa. Beyond that, for 1012.58 < P ≤ 1016.24 hPa and

P > 1016.24 hPa, the model forecasts a progressive decline in the number of cases. For carbon monoxide concentrations, the data suggest that lower levels (CO $\leq$ 0.44 mg/m^3) are associated with a reduced number of predicted RD events. Slightly higher values, specifically within the ranges 0.44 < CO $\leq$ 0.61 mg/m^3 and 0.61 < CO $\leq$ 0.84 mg/m^3, show a moderate contribution, whereas the predicted incidence continues to decline for CO levels exceeding 0.84 mg/m^3.

5 Conclusion

This study explored the interaction between meteorological variables and respiratory health in the population of Bari, with the aim of identifying environmental factors that influence the incidence of respiratory diseases (RD). The analysis was conducted using an artificial intelligence approach, which integrated meteorological data from environmental monitoring stations with healthcare information related to emergency department admissions for respiratory diseases. The correlation analysis revealed significant associations between various environmental variables and the frequency of respiratory diseases. The study used an ensemble learning approach that involved the use of the optimized Random Forest, XGBoost and AdaBoost models, whose performance comparison highlighted the XGBoost model as the best performing, since it showed a determination coefficient R^2 equal to 0.772 and a MAE of 0.049 both for the test phase. The subsequent application of the SHAP model with the use of the Bee Swarm Plot allowed for a global interpretation of the results, revealing low temperature and pressure values, and high CO values as the most significant in predicting visits to the ER for respiratory diseases.

The threshold values were then determined through the application of the LIME model which allowed for the local analysis of the results obtained and which showed as threshold values that temperatures $\leq$ 12.28 °C, atmospheric pressures $\leq$ 1006.81 hPa and carbon monoxide concentrations > 0.84 mg/m^3.

In the future, the application of other Machine e Deep Learning algorithms will be developed to obtain higher performances and new global and local interpretability methods to investigate the complex correlations between environmental factors and Emergency Room admissions. In this way it will be possible to link the model results to specific meteorological and environmental predictors, allowing us to know in advance any increases in hospitalizations for cases of respiratory diseases.

A limitation to be taken into consideration concerns the geographical origin of the data. The study is based on the use of environmental and climate data relating to the city of Bari. The health data come from the Policlinico of the same city; however, it is possible that some of the patients examined are not residents of Bari but come from other areas of Puglia, characterized by different climate and environmental conditions from those under study. This discrepancy could cause a bias in the analysis phase since the climate and environmental data used may not reflect the real exposure of the patients. In this regard, in the future, a data selection could be carried out based on the municipality of residence of the patients, in order to obtain an accurate estimate of individual exposure.

Conflicts of Interest.. The authors have no conflicts of interest to declare related to the content of this article.

Ethics Approval and Consent to Participate.. The Emergency Department visit database is fully anonymized according to the privacy code. It is a completely de-identified data set that, as such was not subject to the approval of the ethics committee. No patient contact was made, and patients could not be traced. The data provided not contains any personal information about patients.

References

1. Tran, H.M., Tsai, F.J., Lee, Y.L., Chang, J.H., Chang, L.T., Chang, T.Y., et al.: The impact of air pollution on respiratory diseases in an era of climate change: a review of the current evidence. Sci. Total. Environ. **898**, 166340 (2023). https://doi.org/10.1016/j.scitotenv.2023.166340
2. Salve, H.R., Nawaz, H., Sharma, P., Dey, S., Madan, K., Krishnan, A.: Effectiveness of community and household level Interventions for reducing impact of air pollution on health outcomes - A systematic review. ISEE Conf. Abstract. (2022). https://doi.org/10.1289/isee.2022.P-0949
3. Li, J., et al.: Double trouble: the interaction of PM2.5 and O3 on respiratory hospital admissions. Environ. Pollut.Pollut. **338**, 122665 (2023). https://doi.org/10.1016/j.envpol.2023.122665
4. Mebrahtu, T.F., et al.: The effects of exposure to NO2, PM2.5 and PM10 on health service attendances with respiratory illnesses: a time-series analysis. Environ. Pollut.Pollut. **333**, 122123 (2023). https://doi.org/10.1016/j.envpol.2023.122123
5. Su, J.G., Aslebagh, S., Shahriary, E., Barrett, M., Balmes, J.R.: Impacts from air pollution on respiratory disease outcomes: a meta-analysis. Front. Public Health **12**, 1417450 (2024). https://doi.org/10.3389/fpubh.2024.1417450
6. Zhang, Y., Li, J., Wang, Y., Zhang, L., Li, J., Li, Y., et al.: Association between short-term exposure to air pollution and respiratory diseases among children in China: a systematic review and meta-analysis. Environ. Pollut.Pollut. **268**, 115682 (2021). https://doi.org/10.1016/j.envpol.2020.115682
7. Gasparrini, A., Guo, Y., Hashizume, M., Lavigne, E., Zanobetti, A., Schwartz, J., et al.: Mortality risk attributable to high and low ambient temperature: a multicountry observational study. The Lancet **386**(9991), 369–375 (2015). https://doi.org/10.1016/S0140-6736(15)60585-6
8. Chen, T., Guestrin, C.: *XGBoost: A scalable tree boosting system.* Proceedings of the 22nd ACM SIGKDD International Conference on Knowledge Discovery and Data Mining (KDD'16), pp. 785–794 (2016). https://doi.org/10.1145/2939672.2939785
9. ISTAT - Italian National Institute of Statistics. (in Italian) https://www.istat.it/. Accessed 1 April 2025
10. ISPRA, Italian National Institute for Environmental Protection and Research: https://www.isprambiente.gov.it/it. Accessed 1 April 2025
11. Gogtay, N.J., Thatte, U.M.: Principles of correlation analysis. J. Assoc. Phys. India **65**(3), 78–81 (2017). https://pubmed.ncbi.nlm.nih.gov/28462548/
12. Mienye, I.D., Sun, Y.: A survey of ensemble learning: concepts, algorithms, applications, and prospects. IEEE Access **10**, 99129–99149 (2022). https://doi.org/10.1109/ACCESS.2022.3207287

13. Yang, X., Li, Y., Liu, L., Zang, Z.: Prediction of respiratory diseases based on random forest model. Front. Public Health (2025). https://doi.org/10.3389/fpubh.2025.1537238
14. Gutierrez-Tobal, G.C., Alvarez, D., del Campo, F., Hornero, R.: Utility of AdaBoost to detect sleep apnea-hypopnea syndrome from single-channel airflow. IEEE Trans. Biomed. Eng. **63**(3), 636–646 (2016). https://doi.org/10.1109/TBME.2015.2467188
15. Chicco, D., Warrens, M.J., Jurman, G.: The coefficient of determination R-squared is more informative than SMAPE, MAE, MAPE, MSE and RMSE in regression analysis evaluation. PeerJ Computer Science **7**, e623 (2021). https://doi.org/10.7717/peerj-cs.623
16. Arias-Duart, A., Parés, F., Garcia-Gasulla, D., Giménez-Ábalos, V.: Focus! rating XAI methods and finding biases. In: Proceedings of the 2022 IEEE International Conference on Fuzzy Systems (FUZZ-IEEE), pp. 1–8. https://doi.org/10.1109/FUZZ-IEEE55066.2022.9882821
17. Nti, I.K., Nyarko-Boateng, O., Aning, J.: Performance of machine learning algorithms with different k values in k-fold crossvalidation. Int. J. Inform. Technol. Comput. Sci. **13**(6), 61–71 (2021). https://doi.org/10.5815/ijitcs.2021.06.05
18. Barredo Arrieta, A., Díaz-Rodríguez, N., Del Ser, J., Bennetot, A., Tabik, S., Barbado, A., et al.: Explainable artificial intelligence: a survey. Inform. Fusion **58**, 82–115 (2020). https://doi.org/10.1016/j.inffus.2019.12.012
19. Shaikhina, T., Bhatt, U., Zhang, R., Georgatzis, K., Xiang, A., Weller, A.: Effects of uncertainty on the quality of feature importance explanations. In: AAAI Workshop on Explainable Agency in Artificial Intelligence, AAAI Press (2021). https://umangsbhatt.github.io/reports/AAAI_XAI_QB.pdf
20. Kumar, I.E., Venkatasubramanian, S., Scheidegger, C., Friedler, S.: Problems with Shapley-value-based explanations as feature importance measures. In: Proceedings of the 37th International Conference on Machine Learning, PMLR 119, pp.5491–5500 (2020). https://proceedings.mlr.press/v119/kumar20e.html
21. Salih, A., Raisi-Estabragh, Z., Boscolo Galazzo, I., Radeva, P., Petersen, S. E., Menegaz, G., et al.: A Perspective on Explainable Artificial Intelligence Methods: SHAP and LIME. arXiv preprint arXiv:2305.02012 (2023). https://doi.org/10.48550/arXiv.2305.02012

Author Index

A
Al-Refai, Mohammed 377
Alzubi, Ahmed 377

B
Bailo, Daniele 309
Bella, Francesco 87
Bellia, Sheila 123
Berti, David 229
Blecic, Ivan 291

C
Cappelli, Giuseppe 3, 15, 32, 87
Carpentieri, Gerardo 197
Caselli, Barbara 160
Caushaj, Neritan 87
Cavigli, Lucia 291
Châu, Ma Thị 242
Cigagna, Marco 327
Congiu, Tanja 105

D
D'Apuzzo, Mauro 3, 15, 32, 87
D'Orso, Gabriele 67
da Rocha, Leonardo Chaves Dutra 273
Dario, Esposito 49
Darwish, Yousof 377
de Fátima Rodrigues Guimarães, Rita 273
de Limas, Enio Vicente 273
de Paiva Guimarães, Marcelo 273
di Montorio, Gilberto Zinourov Roncalli 229
Dias, Diego Roberto Colombo 273
Dik, Gennady 364
Dimitrova, Cveta 399

F
Falcone, Giuseppe 309
Fanfani, Marco 255
Federico, Mara 49
Fiorino, Donatella Rita 327

Furioso, Martina 32

G
Gagliardi, Valerio 87
Garau, Chiara 105, 141
Gervasi, Osvaldo 229
Giovannoni, Alberto 255
Grosso, Battista 327
Guida, Carmen 197

H
Hakizimana, Evelyne 364
Hamza, Benacer 49
Hueber, Benjamin 399

I
Ignaccolo, Matteo 67, 123
Inturri, Giuseppe 67
Ipsaro Palesi, Luciano Alessandro 255
Irum, Ammarah 255

J
Jakob, Uli 399

K
Kekec, Roman 399
Khadidja, Khelil Cherfi 49

L
La Placa, Silvia 160
Laera, Rossella 160
Le, Tam Minh 213
Leonardi, Pierfrancesco 123
Leporati, Alberto 181

M
Ma, Chau Thi 213
Maestroni, Davide 87
Maglione, Andrés David 197
Mahabadi, Pooyan Hejazi 87

Maiullari, Daniela 388
Maltagliati, Jacopo 181
Marchetti, Dedalo 309
Marin, Iuliana 347
Martinelli, Sara 229
Matteini, Paolo 291
Meiguins, Bianchi Serique 273
Michalek, Jan 309
Micucci, Daniela 181
Migliore, Marco 67
Misso, Francesco Edoardo 87
Mocanu, Irina 347

N
Nardoianni, Sofia 3, 15, 32, 87
Nesi, Paolo 255
Nicolosi, Vittorio 3, 15, 32

P
Paciello, Rossana 309
Panebianco, Altea 160
Perri, Damiano 229
Pietrapertosa, Filomena 399, 408
Pilia, Elisa 327
Pilogallo, Angela 408
Pinna, Chiara 141
Pinna, Francesco 327
Piscini, Alessandro 309
Plaisant, Alessandro 105
Poplin, Alenka 141

Q
Querzoli, Giorgio 291

R
Radu, Şerban 347
Rasras, Mohammad 347
Rondinone, Maríca 417
Rossi, Francesca 291
Rym, Merzelkad 49

S
Salvia, Monica 399, 408
Sanfilippo, Francesca 291
Santopietro, Luigi 399, 408
Sara, Boudjemaa 49
Strobel, Michael 399
Sturiale, Luisa 67

T
Telesca, Vito 417
Thịnh, Lê Thái 242
Tika, Trigaluh Prastyana 87
Torlini, Alessia 141
Torrisi, Vincenza 67
Tuccio, Lorenza 291

V
Vacca, Andrea 291
Vacca, Giuseppina 327
van der Waal, Max 388
Vecchi, Enrica 327
Vincenza, Torrisi 123

MIX
Papier aus verantwortungsvollen Quellen
Paper from responsible sources
FSC® C105338

If you have any concerns about our products,
you can contact us on
ProductSafety@springernature.com

In case Publisher is established outside the EU,
the EU authorized representative is:
**Springer Nature Customer Service Center GmbH
Europaplatz 3, 69115 Heidelberg, Germany**

Printed by Libri Plureos GmbH
in Hamburg, Germany